R0201226404

05/2020

W9-DAS-807

THE GOLDEN AGE
Wonder Woman
VOLUME TWO

PALM BEACH COUNTY
LIBRARY SYSTEM
3650 Summit Boulevard
West Palm Beach, FL 33406-4198

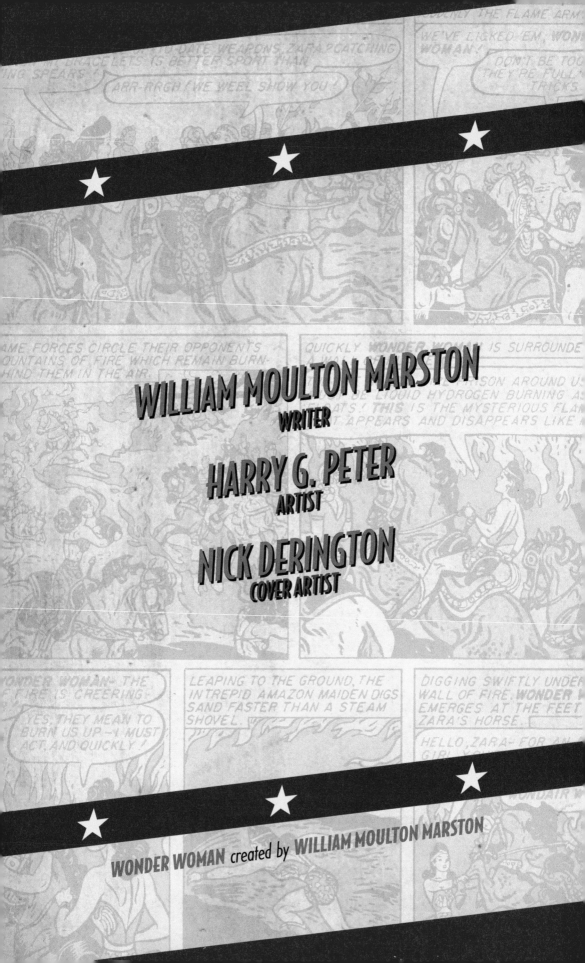

WILLIAM MOULTON MARSTON
WRITER

HARRY G. PETER
ARTIST

NICK DERINGTON
COVER ARTIST

WONDER WOMAN created by WILLIAM MOULTON MARSTON

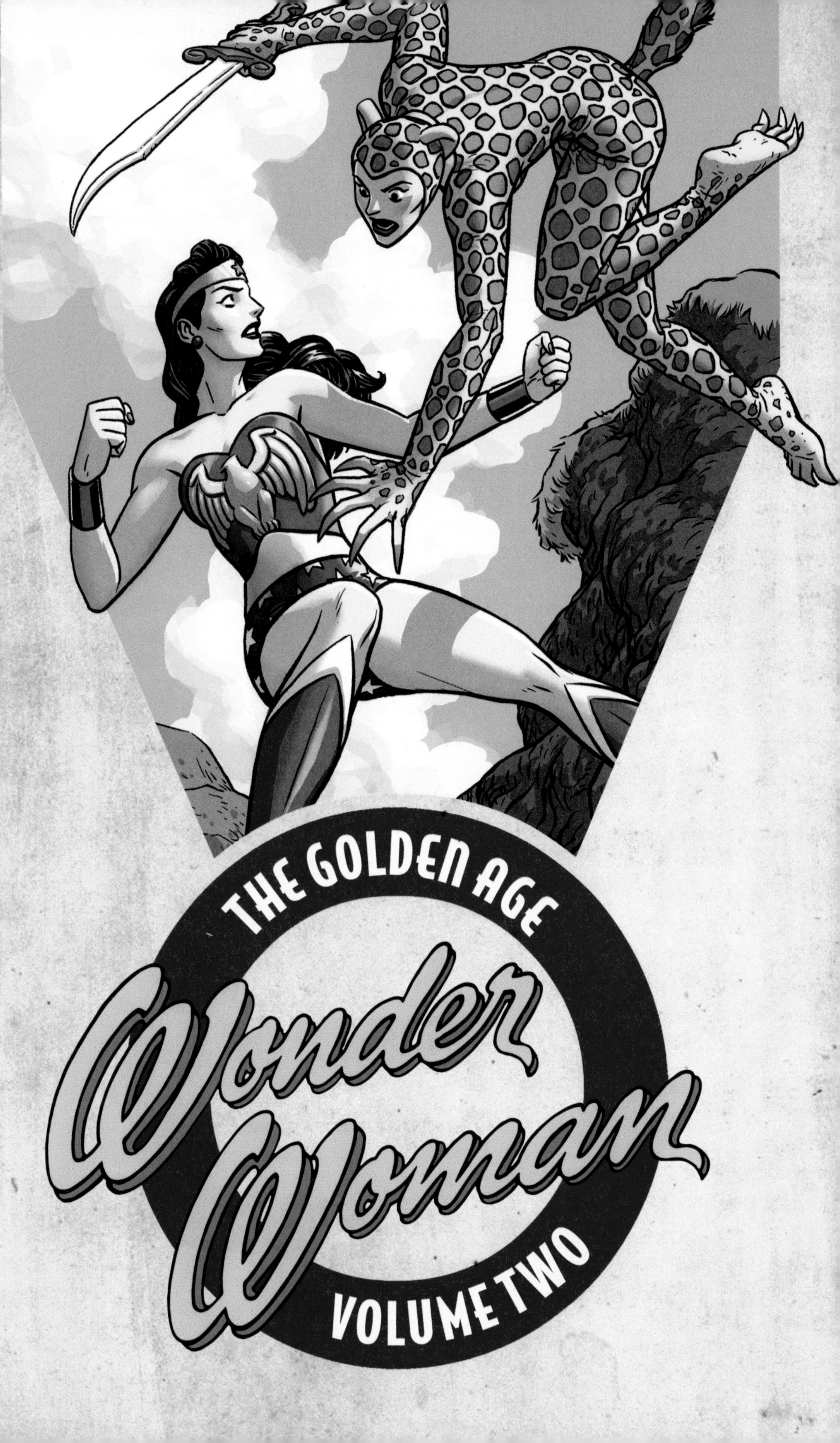

THE GOLDEN AGE

Wonder Woman

VOLUME TWO

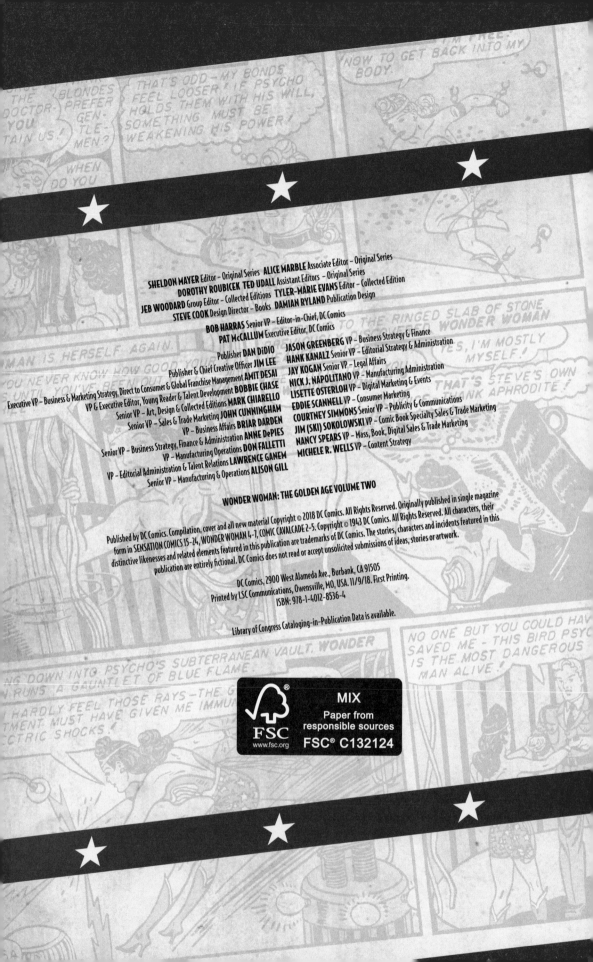

SHELDON MAYER Editor – Original Series ALICE MARBLE Associate Editor – Original Series
DOROTHY ROUBICEK TED UDALL Assistant Editors – Original Series
JEB WOODARD Group Editor – Collected Editions TYLER-MARIE EVANS Editor – Collected Edition
STEVE COOK Design Director – Books DAMIAN RYLAND Publication Design

BOB HARRAS Senior VP – Editor-in-Chief, DC Comics
PAT McCALLUM Executive Editor, DC Comics

Publisher DAN DiDIO   JASON GREENBERG VP – Business Strategy & Finance
Publisher & Chief Creative Officer JIM LEE   HANK KANALZ Senior VP – Editorial Strategy & Administration
VP & Executive Editor, Young Reader & Talent Management AMIT DESAI   JAY KOGAN Senior VP – Legal Affairs
VP & Executive Editor, Young Reader & Talent Development BOBBIE CHASE   NICK J. NAPOLITANO VP – Manufacturing Administration
Senior VP – Art, Design & Collected Editions MARK CHIARELLO   LISETTE OSTERLOH VP – Digital Marketing & Events
Senior VP – Sales & Trade Marketing JOHN CUNNINGHAM   EDDIE SCANNELL VP – Consumer Marketing
VP – Business Affairs BRIAR DARDEN   COURTNEY SIMMONS Senior VP – Publicity & Communications
Senior VP – Business Strategy, Finance & Administration ANNE DePIES   JIM (SKI) SOKOLOWSKI VP – Comic Book Specialty Sales & Trade Marketing
VP – Manufacturing Operations DON FALLETTI   NANCY SPEARS VP – Mass, Book, Digital Sales & Trade Marketing
VP – Editorial Administration & Talent Relations LAWRENCE GANEM   MICHELE R. WELLS VP – Content Strategy
Senior VP – Manufacturing & Operations ALISON GILL

WONDER WOMAN: THE GOLDEN AGE VOLUME TWO

Published by DC Comics. Compilation, cover and all new material Copyright © 2018 DC Comics. All Rights Reserved. Originally published in single magazine form in SENSATION COMICS 15-24, WONDER WOMAN 4-7, COMIC CAVALCADE 2-5. Copyright © 1943 DC Comics. All Rights Reserved. All characters, their distinctive likenesses and related elements featured in this publication are trademarks of DC Comics. The stories, characters and incidents featured in this publication are entirely fictional. DC Comics does not read or accept unsolicited submissions of ideas, stories or artwork.

DC Comics, 2900 West Alameda Ave., Burbank, CA 91505
Printed by LSC Communications, Owensville, MO, USA. 11/9/18. First Printing.
ISBN: 978-1-4012-8536-4

Library of Congress Cataloging-in-Publication Data is available.

MIX
Paper from
responsible sources
FSC® C132124
www.fsc.org

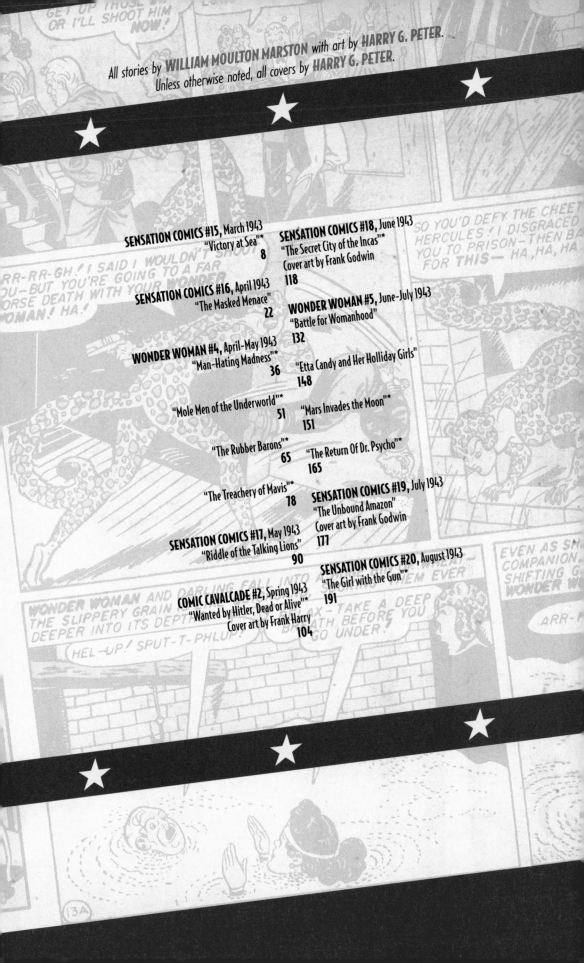

All stories by **WILLIAM MOULTON MARSTON** with art by **HARRY G. PETER.**
Unless otherwise noted, all covers by **HARRY G. PETER.**

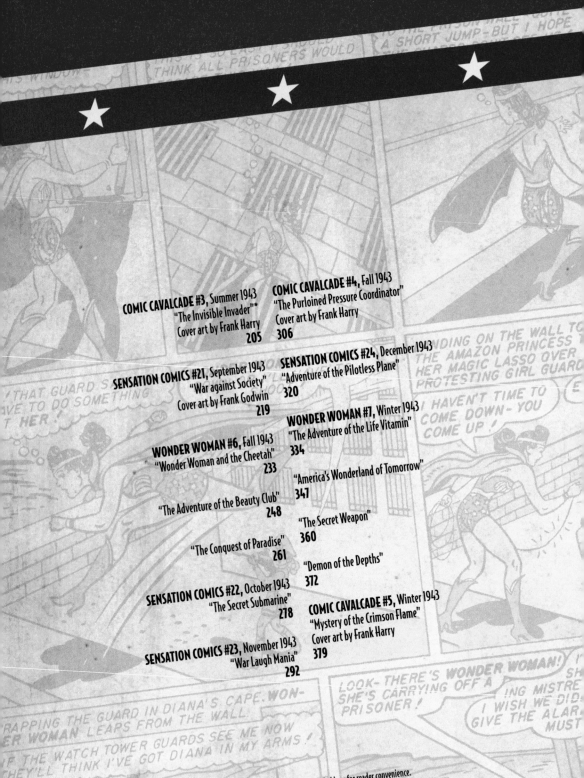

* These stories were originally untitled and are titled here for reader convenience.

DC strives to be as thorough as possible in its effort to determine creators' identities from all available sources.
This process is not perfect, and as a result, some attributions may be incomplete or wrongly assigned.

The comics reprinted in this volume were produced in a time when racism played a larger role in society and popular culture both consciously and unconsciously.
They are mostly unaltered in this collection, with the understanding that they are presented as historical documents.

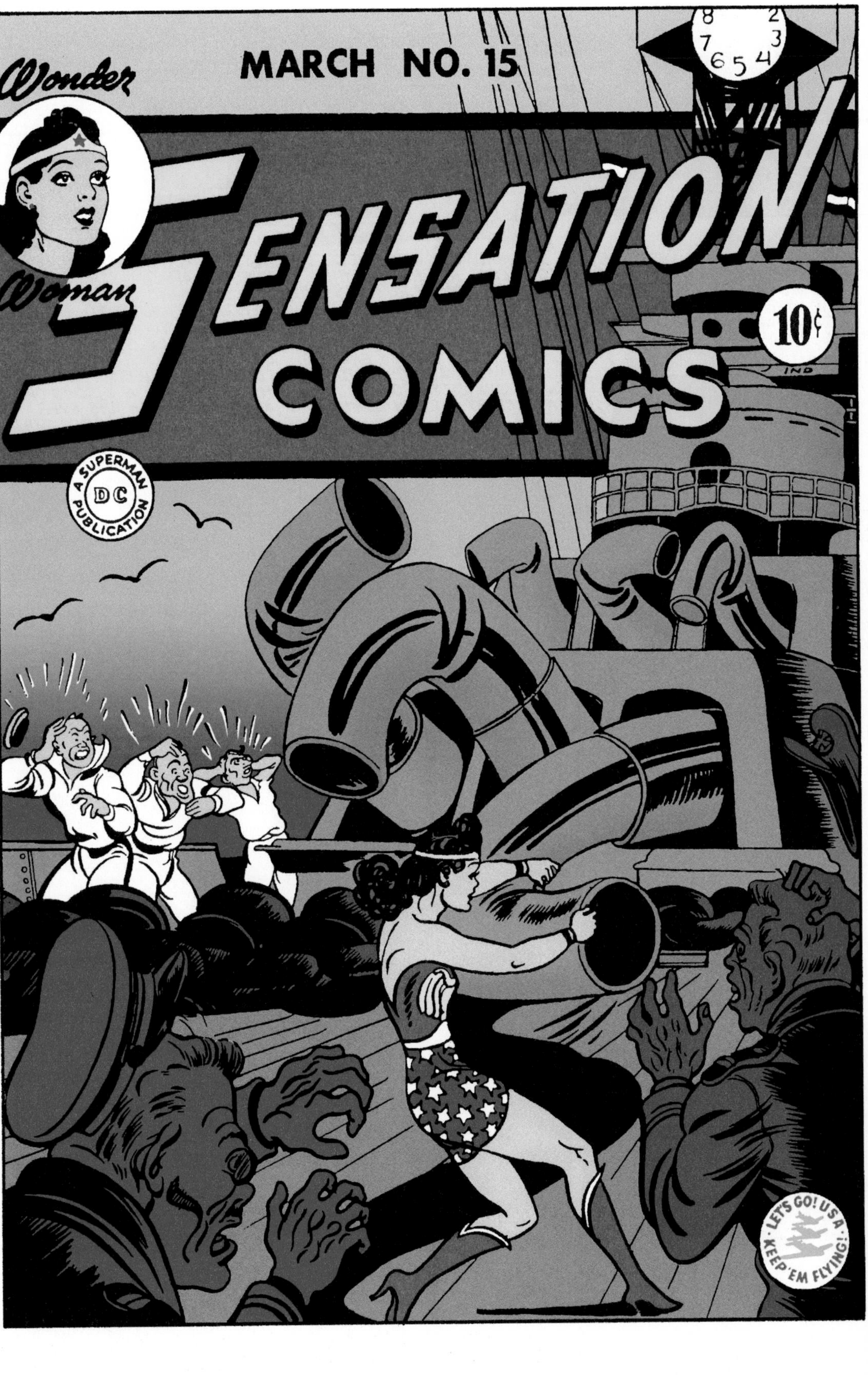
MARCH NO. 15
Wonder Woman
SENSATION COMICS
10¢
IND
A SUPERMAN DC PUBLICATION
LET'S GO! U.S.A. KEEP'EM FLYING!

Wonder Woman

By Charles Moulton

REG. U. S. PAT. OFF.

BEFORE STEVE'S VERY EYES DIANA PRINCE CHANGES TO WONDER WOMAN. CAN SHE CONVINCE HIM, NEVERTHELESS, THAT WHAT HE SAW WAS AN ILLUSION AND STILL MAINTAIN HER DOUBLE IDENTITY?

CONFRONTED WITH THE CLEVEREST LEGAL BRAIN IN AMERICA, WONDER WOMAN PURSUES THIS INSIDIOUS AXIS AGENT FROM PRISON CELL TO OCEAN DEPTHS, PITTING HER AMAZON STRENGTH AGAINST THE MIGHTY ENGINES OF A NAZI BATTLESHIP TO SAVE NEW YORK CITY FROM SURPRISE ATTACK BY GERMAN BOMBS!

BEAUTIFUL AS APHRODITE, WISE AS ATHENA, STRONG AS HERCULES AND SWIFT AS MERCURY, WONDER WOMAN WINGS HER WINNING WAY FROM PARADISE ISLE, SECRET HOME OF THE AMAZONS, WHERE GORGEOUS GIRLS RULE SUPREME, TO THE HEARTS OF MILLIONS OF AMERICANS, FIGHTING EVER FEARLESSLY TO CONQUER EVIL AND CREATE PERMANENT PEACE AND HAPPINESS IN THE WORLD!

DIANA, LINGERING LATE AT HER OFFICE, YIELDS TO A GIRLISH IMPULSE. HOW DIFFERENT I LOOK WEARING THIS CIRCLET—AND WITHOUT MY GLASSES! I CAN'T BLAME STEVE FOR PREFERRING WONDER WOMAN TO DIANA PRINCE!

ISN'T IT SILLY HOW WE GIRLS LOVE TO DRESS UP! IT'S A REAL REST, AFTER A HARD DAY'S WORK, JUST TO PUT ON MY **WONDER WOMAN** CLOTHES!

WHAT'S THAT IN THE DRAWER?

HEARING SOMEONE AT THE DOOR DIANA HASTILY DONS HER GLASSES AND HIDES THE CIRCLET WITH HER HAND.

WHY, DIANA! WHAT'S THE MATTER?

RUN, STEVE—QUICK! THERE'S A BOMB IN MY DESK—

BA-ANG!

SWIFTLY, AS DIANA LEAPS BACKWARD, THE EXPLOSION TEARS OFF HER OUTER GARMENTS, REVEALING THE COSTUME WHICH SHE WEARS UNDERNEATH.

JUMPING JUPITER! THAT BOMB RIPPED MY DIANA DISGUISE TO SHREDS!

STEVE, STAGGERING DAZED TO HIS FEET, SEES NOT DIANA BUT—**WONDER WOMAN!**

GREAT GADZOOKS! D-DIANA—YOU'RE REALLY **WONDER WOMAN!**

I'M CAUGHT THIS TIME! HOW CAN I CONVINCE STEVE I'M NOT MYSELF?

WONDER WOMAN DOES SOME ACROBATIC THINKING.

STEVE, DON'T BE SILLY! THAT EXPLOSION BLEW DIANA OUT THE WINDOW! I'LL JUMP AFTER HER—YOU TAKE THE ELEVATOR!

ALL RIGHT—BUT I DON'T UNDERSTAND—

②

AS STEVE LEAVES THE OFFICE, **WONDER WOMAN** RIPS THE CARPET OFF THE FLOOR.

THIS WILL MAKE A GOOD DUMMY OF DIANA—BUT I'VE GOT TO WORK FAST!

SNATCHING DIANA'S COAT AND HAT FROM THE CLOSET, **WONDER WOMAN** WRAPS THEM AROUND A ROLL OF CARPET.

THIS WILL FOOL STEVE IF HE DOESN'T LOOK TOO CLOSELY AT MY DUMMY DIANA!

I MUST GET DOWN BEFORE STEVE AND LET HIM SEE ME PICK DIANA FROM THE GROUND!

IS DIANA BADLY HURT.?

I CAN'T TELL YET - MUST GET HER TO A HOS-PITAL!

BE CAREFUL OF DI'S ARM—LOOKS BROKEN!

I'LL SET IT MYSELF— DON'T WORRY, STEVE!

THERE'S SOMETHING QUEER ABOUT THIS—I'D SWEAR DIANA CHANGED TO **WONDER WOMAN** BEFORE MY VERY EYES! BUT AFTERWARD **WONDER WOMAN** AND DIANA WERE **BOTH** HERE—OR **WAS** THAT DIANA IN **WON-DER WOMAN'S** ARMS? I WONDER?

③

NEXT MORNING DIANA REPORTS TO COLONEL DARNELL WITH HER RIGHT ARM IN A CAST.

MY DEAR GIRL, YOU OUGHT TO BE IN THE HOSPITAL! YOU CAN'T WORK WITH A BROKEN ARM!

YES, I CAN—I'LL SHOW YOU!

DIANA TAKES DICTATION DIRECT AT THE TYPEWRITER WITH HER LEFT HAND AT 150 WORDS A MINUTE!

EXTRAORDINARY — PRECAUTIONS-MUST-BE-TAKEN-SPIES-PENE-TRATED—HEADQUARTERS-OF-FICE—PLANTING—BOMB---

THIS IS EASY-DICTATE FASTER, IF YOU LIKE, COLONEL!

STEVE, MEANWHILE, TESTS ALL INTELLIGENCE SERVICE EMPLOYEES WITH THE LIE DETECTOR.

NO, SIR, I DIDN'T PLANT THAT BOMB!

YOU'RE TELLING THE TRUTH. OUR STAFF ARE ALL INNOCENT — THANK HEAVEN!

HELLO, STEVE — I'M GLAD *YOU* WEREN'T HURT LAST NIGHT!

DIANA! SO YOUR ARM *WAS* BROKEN! YOU OUGHT NOT TO BE WORKING!

OH, I'M ALL RIGHT! I HEAR YOU'RE GIVING EVERYBODY A LIE DETECTOR TEST — WANT TO TEST *ME?*

HA! HA! I'D LIKE TO PUT THE LIE DETECTOR ON YOU AND SEE WHETHER YOU REALLY *ARE* WONDER WOMAN!

OKAY — I'LL TAKE A LIE DETECTOR TEST.

NO, NO — YOUR BROKEN ARM CONVINCES ME *WONDER WOMAN* MUST HAVE ENTERED JUST AS YOU WERE BLOWN OUT THE WINDOW!

HOPE HE DOESN'T CALL MY BLUFF — HE'S STILL SUSPICIOUS!

BAD NEWS, MAJOR! OUR AGENT R-53 WAS FOUND DEAD — STABBED TO DEATH!

GOOD OLD STAN BRENNAN! THE NAZIS GOT HIM — I WONDER WHAT HE FOUND OUT? BRENNAN PHONED ME YESTERDAY! LISTEN —

STAN BELIEVED A NAZI FLEET WAS ESCORTING AIRPLANE CARRIERS TO BOMB NEW YORK CITY. HE SAID TO HOLD THIS REPORT UNTIL TODAY FOR CONFIRMATION. THERE'LL BE NO CONFIRMATION NOW — BRENNAN'S DEAD!

BY THE GREAT HORN SPOON! THAT'S WHY THEY TRIED TO BOMB *YOU*, DIANA! WITH YOU AND STAN DEAD WE'D HAVE NO WARNING AND NEW YORK MIGHT BE WIPED OUT!

BUT NO — BODY KNEW STAN HAD PHONED ME —

4

SOMEBODY *MUST* HAVE KNOWN! I'LL NOTIFY THE NAVY AND JOIN THE SEARCH FOR THIS GERMAN FLEET — WE'VE GOT TO INTERCEPT IT!

OH STEVE! *DO* BE CAREFUL!

WANNA SHOE-SHINA TODAY?

WHO **COULD** HAVE KNOWN THAT AGENT R-53 CALLED ME? HE USED A PRIVATE LINE—NOBODY WAS IN MY OFFICE—

OKAY, TONY, I'LL HAVE A SHINE.

THIS BOOTBLACK—COULD **HE** HAVE OVERHEARD THAT PHONE CALL YESTERDAY? BY HERA HE **COULD**! HE'D JUST FINISHED SHINING MY SHOES!

TONY, YOU'RE AN AXIS SPY!

NO SPIKKA DA EENGLEESH! TONY NO UNDA-STAND WHATTA YOU SAY—

CUT THAT LINE—YOU'RE NOT TONY! YOU'RE A NAZI MADE UP TO LOOK LIKE HIM—AHH—HH!

UP WITH YOUR HANDS! IF YOU CALL FOR HELP I WILL SHOOT!

HOPING "TONY" WILL TAKE HER TO NAZI SPY HEADQUARTERS, DIANA SUBMITS TO CAPTURE.

SIT QUIET WHILE I PACK THIS BOOTBLACK BOX!

I WILL—DON'T SHOOT!

THERE'S A MESSAGE IN THAT SHOE PASTE COVER—I MUST GET IT!

DIANA'S "BROKEN" ARM PROVES USEFUL.

IT'S GOOD YOU HAVE ONLY ONE HAND TO TIE—SAVES TIME!

I'LL HIDE THIS SHOE-PASTE BOX UNDER MY BANDAGES AND OPEN IT LATER!

I'VE GOT YOU COVERED—WALK ALONG QUIETLY OR I SHOOT!

⑤

LEADING HER TO HIS CAR IN A DESERTED SPOT, THE NAZI PACKS DIANA INTO THE BAGGAGE COMPARTMENT.

I BROUGHT THIS ALONG—YOU WILL NEED IT WHERE YOU'RE GOING—I DON'T THINK!

SOUNDS OMINOUS!

WITH GREAT DIFFICULTY IN HER CRAMPED QUARTERS, DIANA MANAGES TO OPEN THE SHOE-PASTE BOX AND EXTRACT THE PAPER.

THIS MAY BE ONLY A SHOE POLISH AD BUT I HAVE A FEELING IT'S SOMETHING IMPORTANT.

DIANA DECIPHERS A SCRAWLED ADDRESS.

SLICKERY, SMELT AND SLICKERY COUNSELLORS AT LAW 912 TOPLY BLDG.

AT THIS MOMENT THE NAZI AGENT LEAPS FROM THE CAR, SENDING IT INTO DEEP WATER.

SWIFTLY THE CAR PLUNGES INTO THE DEPTHS.

UG-GLUB! WHAT'S THIS, A BURIAL AT SEA? I WANT OUT!

SPLOP! SPLA-ASH CRASH! SWISH

WITH ONE SWEEP OF HER ARMS, DIANA BURSTS HER BONDS AND BREAKS OPEN THE COMPARTMENT.

I'M GLAD THIS TIN BOX IS SO EASY TO BREAK!

USING THE SUNKEN CAR AS AN UNDERWATER DRESSING ROOM, DIANA DONS HER WONDER WOMAN COSTUME

LUCKY I HAD A MIRROR IN MY HAND-BAG- THIS IS HOW MERMAIDS COMB THE FISH OUT OF THEIR HAIR EACH MORNING!

6

THAT ADDRESS ON THE NOTE IN THE SHOE POLISH BOX MUST BE WHERE THE BOOT-BLACK AGENT REPORTS. I'LL PAY THESE LAWYERS A VISIT!

RACING SWIFTLY THROUGH THE CITY WONDER WOMAN ENTERS THE LAW OFFICES OF SLICKERY, SMELT AND SLICKERY.

I WANT TO SEE THE HEAD OF THIS FIRM!

MR. SIMON SLICKERY IS NOT IN-

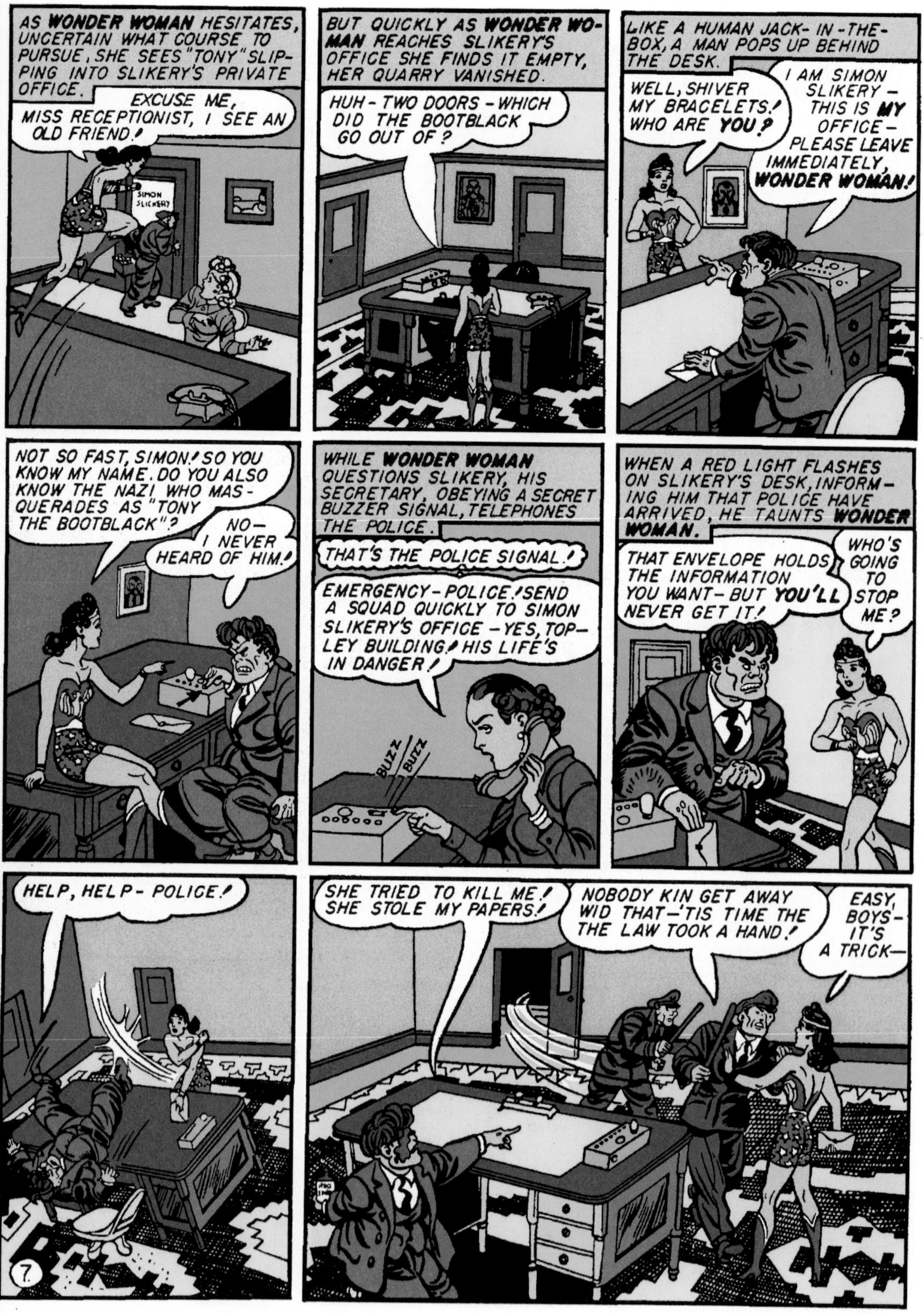
AS WONDER WOMAN HESITATES, UNCERTAIN WHAT COURSE TO PURSUE, SHE SEES "TONY" SLIPPING INTO SLIKERY'S PRIVATE OFFICE.
EXCUSE ME, MISS RECEPTIONIST, I SEE AN OLD FRIEND!
SIMON SLICKERY
BUT QUICKLY AS WONDER WOMAN REACHES SLIKERY'S OFFICE SHE FINDS IT EMPTY, HER QUARRY VANISHED.
HUH - TWO DOORS - WHICH DID THE BOOTBLACK GO OUT OF ?
LIKE A HUMAN JACK-IN-THE-BOX, A MAN POPS UP BEHIND THE DESK.
WELL, SHIVER MY BRACELETS! WHO ARE YOU?
I AM SIMON SLIKERY - THIS IS MY OFFICE - PLEASE LEAVE IMMEDIATELY, WONDER WOMAN!
NOT SO FAST, SIMON! SO YOU KNOW MY NAME. DO YOU ALSO KNOW THE NAZI WHO MASQUERADES AS "TONY THE BOOTBLACK"?
NO - I NEVER HEARD OF HIM!
WHILE WONDER WOMAN QUESTIONS SLIKERY, HIS SECRETARY, OBEYING A SECRET BUZZER SIGNAL, TELEPHONES THE POLICE.
THAT'S THE POLICE SIGNAL!
EMERGENCY - POLICE! SEND A SQUAD QUICKLY TO SIMON SLIKERY'S OFFICE - YES, TOPLEY BUILDING! HIS LIFE'S IN DANGER!
BUZZ BUZZ
WHEN A RED LIGHT FLASHES ON SLIKERY'S DESK, INFORMING HIM THAT POLICE HAVE ARRIVED, HE TAUNTS WONDER WOMAN.
THAT ENVELOPE HOLDS THE INFORMATION YOU WANT - BUT YOU'LL NEVER GET IT!
WHO'S GOING TO STOP ME?
HELP, HELP - POLICE!
7
SHE TRIED TO KILL ME! SHE STOLE MY PAPERS!
NOBODY KIN GET AWAY WID THAT -'TIS TIME THE THE LAW TOOK A HAND!
EASY, BOYS - IT'S A TRICK—

WONDER WOMAN SUBMITS TO ARREST.

I'M **WONDER WOMAN** AND I BELIEVE IN OBEYING THE LAW EVEN THOUGH IT'S USED AGAINST ME BY A CROOK!

SHE IS THE CROOK! SHE'S NOT **WONDER WOMAN** — SHE'S A THIEF!

AT THE POLICE STATION THE SERGEANT TAKES SLIKERY'S WORD.

THIS GIRL IMPERSONATED **WONDER WOMAN** — FIND OUT HER RACKET! I HAVEN'T TIME TO INVESTIGATE — I'M LEAVING ON MY YACHT!

OKAY — WE'LL INTERVIEW HER IN THE "CONFERENCE ROOM!"

WONDER WOMAN GOES INTO "CONFERENCE."

YER WITH TH' PURPLE GANG — ADMIT IT!

YOU KILLED THAT BANK TELLER — CONFESS!

YOU'RE MURDEROUS MAGGIE THE MUG — COME CLEAN!

I WARN YOU BOYS — I'M GETTING SICK OF THIS SILLY GAME!

AT LAST **WONDER WOMAN** CAN RESTRAIN HERSELF NO LONGER.

I GAVE YOU FELLOWS FAIR WARNING — ENOUGH IS ENOUGH!

AWK — UGH THIS DAME'S DYNAMITE!

OU-WOW! SHE'S CRAZY AS A LOON — CALL THE LUNATIC SQUAD!

WONDER WOMAN MAKES A BARGAIN WITH THE SERGEANT.

I'LL SUBMIT TO ANY BONDS YOU LIKE ON TWO CONDITIONS — STOP THIS QUESTION GAME AND GET ME A LAWYER!

OKAY — LET THE BYES TIE YOU UP, NOW, LIKE A GOOD GIRL —

WHILE POLICEMEN STRAP **WONDER WOMAN** IN A STRAIGHT JACKET, SHE MENTAL-RADIOS ETTA CANDY.

ETTA — FIND SIMON SLIKERY'S YACHT AND BOARD IT! I SUSPECT HE'S COMMUNICATING WITH GERMAN BATTLESHIPS — INVESTIGATE!

⑧

ETTA AND HER GIRLS BOARD SLIKERY'S YACHT AT DUSK.

WOO WOO! THIS IS FUN — SH-H-H GIRLS, DON'T GIGGLE!

BUT THE SHREWD SLIKERY, ANTICIPATING A VISIT FROM **WONDER WOMAN'S** FRIENDS, HAS PREPARED A SPECIAL RECEPTION FOR THE GIRLS.

QUIET OR I'LL CHOKE YA!

I OUGHTA HAVE KNOWN THAT ROPE HANGING OVERSIDE FOR US WAS A TRAP!

THE GIRLS ENJOY CHAIN-GANG LIFE.

IN OUR PRISON CELLS WE SIT THINKING ETTA, DEAR, OF YOU AND OF HOW YOU LED US SLAP INTO THIS TRAP— AS OUR FETTERED FEET WE SHAKE TO OLD BEETA LAM WE'RE TRUE BUT THE LAMB WE'RE GOING TO BEAT IS ETTA SAP!

AW GEE, KIDS— HAVE A HEART!

WONDER WOMAN, MEANWHILE, WAITS IMPATIENTLY IN HER CELL.

I HAVE A FEELING THAT THE GIRLS NEED MY HELP—

OH, SERGEANT! WHERE'S THE LAWYER YOU PROMISED TO SEND ME?

TAKE IT EASY, MY GAL— YOU DON'T NEED A LAWYER. I'VE SENT FOR THE BUGHOUSE WAGON!

BUT I'M **NOT** CRAZY—I **AM WONDER WOMAN!** OH—WHAT'S THE USE?

WHEN THE SERGEANT LEAVES HER CELL **WONDER WOMAN** LEAVES IT ALSO.

I HATE TO LEAVE THIS SNUG LITTLE NEST BUT I FEEL THE CALL OF THE GREAT OPEN SPACES.

THEY MUST PUT THESE PRETTY LITTLE BARS HERE FOR ORNAMENT.

9

FROM HER CELL WINDOW **WONDER WOMAN** LEAPS 50 FEET TO AN ELECTRIC WIRE.

LUCKY FOR ME THEY LEFT THIS OLD-FASHIONED OVERHEAD POWER CABLE CROSSING THE PRISON WALL—I CAN ESCAPE THIS WAY WITHOUT HURTING ANY GUARDS.

SPEEDING TO THE WATERFRONT, **WONDER WOMAN** LEARNS THAT SLIKERY'S YACHT HAS JUST LEFT THE HARBOR.

I'LL OVERTAKE THAT SHIP BEFORE SHE'S 10 MILES OUT!

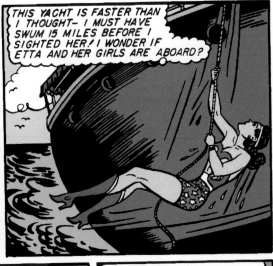

THIS YACHT IS FASTER THAN I THOUGHT— I MUST HAVE SWUM 15 MILES BEFORE I SIGHTED HER! I WONDER IF ETTA AND HER GIRLS ARE ABOARD?

ANOTHER FISH ON MY LINE! I FEARED THAT PRISON MIGHT NOT HOLD YOU, **WONDER WOMAN**, SO I PREPARED A WELCOME FOR YOU!

HOW NICE! BUT YOU SHOULDN'T POINT GUNS AT VISITORS—

I'LL JUST TURN THESE GUN BARRELS SO THEY POINT THE OTHER WAY!

ACH HIMMEL! I AM SHOODING MYSELF!

RAT-TAT RATT-A-

I GREET YOU, MY HOST, AS A GIRL SHOULD GREET THE DEAR FRIEND WHO SENT HER TO PRISON!

STOP! DON'T HIT ME AGAIN OR YOUR GIRL FRIENDS WILL DIE!

IF THAT ANCHOR PLUNGES INTO THE OCEAN, YOUR FRIENDS GO WITH IT. SURRENDER OR THE ANCHOR DROPS!

WHAT FIENDISH CLEVERNESS! I HAVE NO CHOICE— I **MUST** BECOME YOUR PRISONER!

CHAINED TO THE PROW OF THE SHIP LIKE A FIGUREHEAD, **WONDER WOMAN** IS COMPELLED TO SUPPORT THE ANCHOR'S WEIGHT.

IF I DROP THIS ANCHOR THE GIRLS DROWN—APHRODITE HELP ME!

10.

STEVE, MEANWHILE, IS ABOARD A CRUISER SEARCHING FOR THE ENEMY FLEET.

AN AMERICAN YACHT TO STARB'D STANDING OUT TO SEA—THAT'S QUEER!

BETTER INTERCEPT HER, COMMANDER—SHE MAY BE CONTACTING INVASION SHIPS!

WHEN THE YACHT FAILS TO ANSWER RADIO MESSAGES, THE CRUISER DROPS A SHELL ACROSS HER BOW.

THAT'LL STOP HER!

HERE'S A RADIO MESSAGE COMING IN!

GREAT GODFREY! IT'S AN ENEMY CRAFT AND THEY'VE GOT WONDER WOMAN ABOARD, A PRISONER!

THEY SAY WE CAN SEE WONDER WOMAN—WHAT'S THAT MEAN?

THERE SHE IS, COMMANDER—ON THE BOW!

THOSE NASTI RATS—NEVER SAW THE LIKE O' THAT IN MY LIFE! I'LL CAPTURE THAT SHIP IF I HAVE TO CHASE HER TO GERMANY!

BUT THE YACHT IS FAST—FOR HOURS SHE LEADS THE CRUISER A CHASE. THEN, SUDDENLY, GERMAN WARSHIPS APPEAR.

THEY LED US INTO A TRAP!

YES—THIS IS THE GERMAN INVASION FLEET!

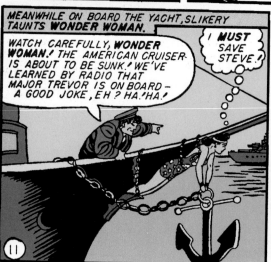

MEANWHILE ON BOARD THE YACHT, SLIKERY TAUNTS WONDER WOMAN.

WATCH CAREFULLY, WONDER WOMAN! THE AMERICAN CRUISER IS ABOUT TO BE SUNK! WE'VE LEARNED BY RADIO THAT MAJOR TREVOR IS ON BOARD—A GOOD JOKE, EH? HA! HA!

I MUST SAVE STEVE!

WONDER WOMAN, PRETENDING THAT HER STRENGTH IS FAILING, LETS THE ANCHOR DOWN.

OH DEAR! I CAN'T HOLD THIS UP ANY LONGER!

EE-K

11

AS THE GIRLS ARE DRAGGED DOWN, **WONDER WOMAN** BREAKS THEIR ANKLE CHAINS.

CLING TO THE ANCHOR CHAIN UNTIL YOU'RE UNDER WATER AND STAY DOWN UNTIL THE SHIP PASSES OVER YOU, THEN SWIM FOR YOUR LIFE!

WHEN THE LAST GIRL IS FREED, **WONDER WOMAN** BREAKS HER OWN CHAINS.

NOW TO SURPRISE SLIKERY AND HIS NASTI CHUM!

EE-EEK!

CLIMBING SWIFTLY TO THE YACHT'S DECK, **WONDER WOMAN** STEALS UP BEHIND SLIKERY AND "TONY."

THERE'S A GOOD JOB FINISHED – I SHOULD RECEIVE AN EXTRA FEE FOR IT!

HO! HO! IT WAS FUN TO WATCH THEM DROWN. LET'S KILL **WONDER WOMAN** QUICKLY BEFORE SHE STARTS TROUBLE!

YOU'RE A LITTLE BEHIND SCHEDULE, "TONY" – TROUBLE HAS ALREADY STARTED. BY THE TIME IT'S FINISHED SLIKERY WON'T BE WORRYING ABOUT AN EXTRA FEE!

AWK-ACH! DER TEUFEL HERSELF!

UNHAND ME, WOMAN!

WONDER WOMAN HERSELF DELIVERS HER PRISONERS TO ETTA AND HER GIRLS.

TAKE THESE "LADY-KILLERS" TO THE CRUISER– I'M OFF TO STOP THE GERMAN FLEET!

WOO! WOO! WE'LL TAKE 'EM– AND HOW!

UG-GLUB! DON'T D-DROWN US!

AS **WONDER WOMAN** SWIMS TO BATTLE, THE GERMAN FLAGSHIP'S BIG GUNS ALMOST REACH THE AMERICAN CRUISER.

DER NEXT SHOT VILL HIT DER AMERICAN PIGS!

⑫

WONDER WOMAN, REACHING THE GERMAN DREADNAUGHT, DIVES FOR THE BATTLESHIP'S PROPELLER.

THIS PROPELLER IS CERTAINLY POWERFUL! BUT I'LL SLOW IT DOWN BY SWIMMING AGAINST IT.

I'VE STOPPED THE PROPELLER! NOW TO HOLD IT STEADY WHILE THE ENGINES TURN THE SHIP OVER.

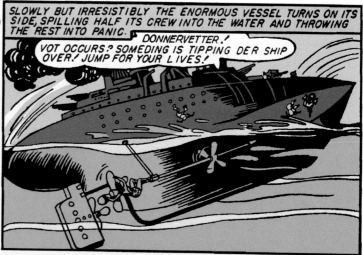

SLOWLY BUT IRRESISTIBLY THE ENORMOUS VESSEL TURNS ON ITS SIDE, SPILLING HALF ITS CREW INTO THE WATER AND THROWING THE REST INTO PANIC.

DONNERVETTER! VOT OCCURS? SOMEDING IS TIPPING DER SHIP OVER! JUMP FOR YOUR LIVES!

DESCRIBING A COMPLETE SOMERSAULT THE DREADNAUGHT TURNS UPSIDE DOWN, THEN RIGHTS ITSELF AGAIN ON THE OTHER SIDE.

VE ARE COMING UP, AGAIN!

DER SHIP'S GONE CRAZY!

WONDER WOMAN, CLIMBING SWIFTLY TO THE BATTLESHIP'S BRIDGE, CONFRONTS THE GERMAN ADMIRAL.

SO IT ISS YOU, VON-DER VOMAN! VE GIF UP— YOU COULD DESTROY EFFERY SHIP! MIT DEMONS VE CANNOT FIGHT!

OKAY - RADIO YOUR FLEET TO SURRENDER!

AMERICAN PRIZE CREWS FROM THE CRUISER ARE PLACED ABOARD THE NAZI BATTLESHIPS, AND FOR THE FIRST TIME IN HISTORY AN ENTIRE ENEMY FLEET IS CAPTURED BY ONE INDIVIDUAL— WONDER WOMAN.

THE STAR-SPANGLED BANNER — OH LONG MAY IT WAVE----

A FEW DAYS LATER DIANA PRINCE - WHOSE "BROKEN" ARM IS HEALING RAPIDLY—ASKS FOR LEAVE FROM THE OFFICE.

COLONEL, MAY I ATTEND THE MASS MEETING TO HONOR WONDER WOMAN?

CERTAINLY, DIANA— THERE'S A HEROINE FOR YOU!

YOU ARE ALL SO NICE TO ME ! - I DON'T KNOW WHAT TO SAY! WHAT I'VE DONE PROVES THIS — THAT NOTHING IS IMPOSSIBLE IF YOU JUST GRIT YOUR TEETH AND TELL YOURSELF I WILL DO IT!

FOLLOW WONDER WOMAN'S ADVENTURES EVERY MONTH IN SENSATION COMICS - THEY'LL THRILL YOU AS NOTHING EVER DID BEFORE!

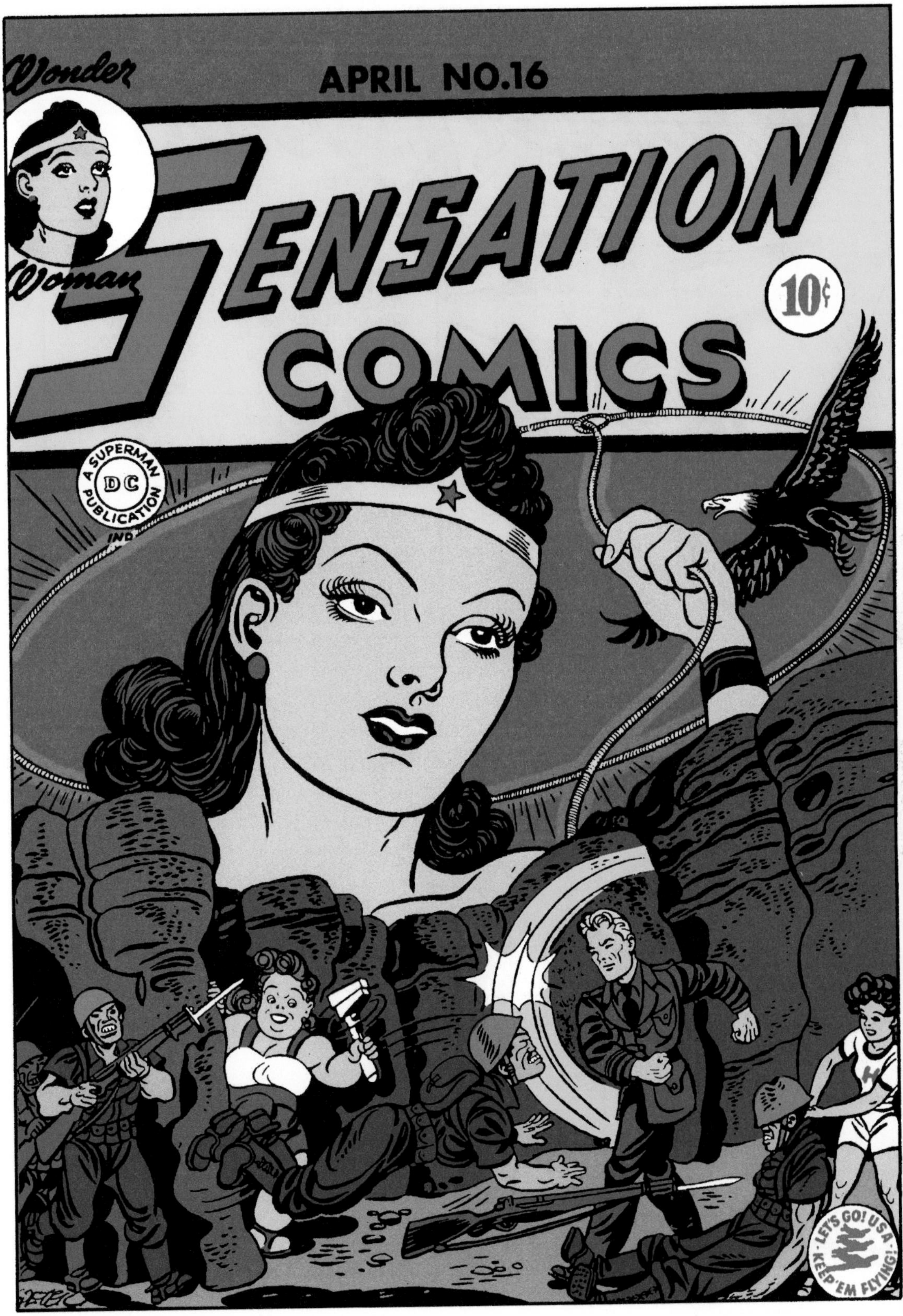
Wonder Woman
APRIL NO.16
SENSATION COMICS
10¢
A SUPERMAN DC PUBLICATION INC
LET'S GO! U.S.A. KEEP 'EM FLYING!

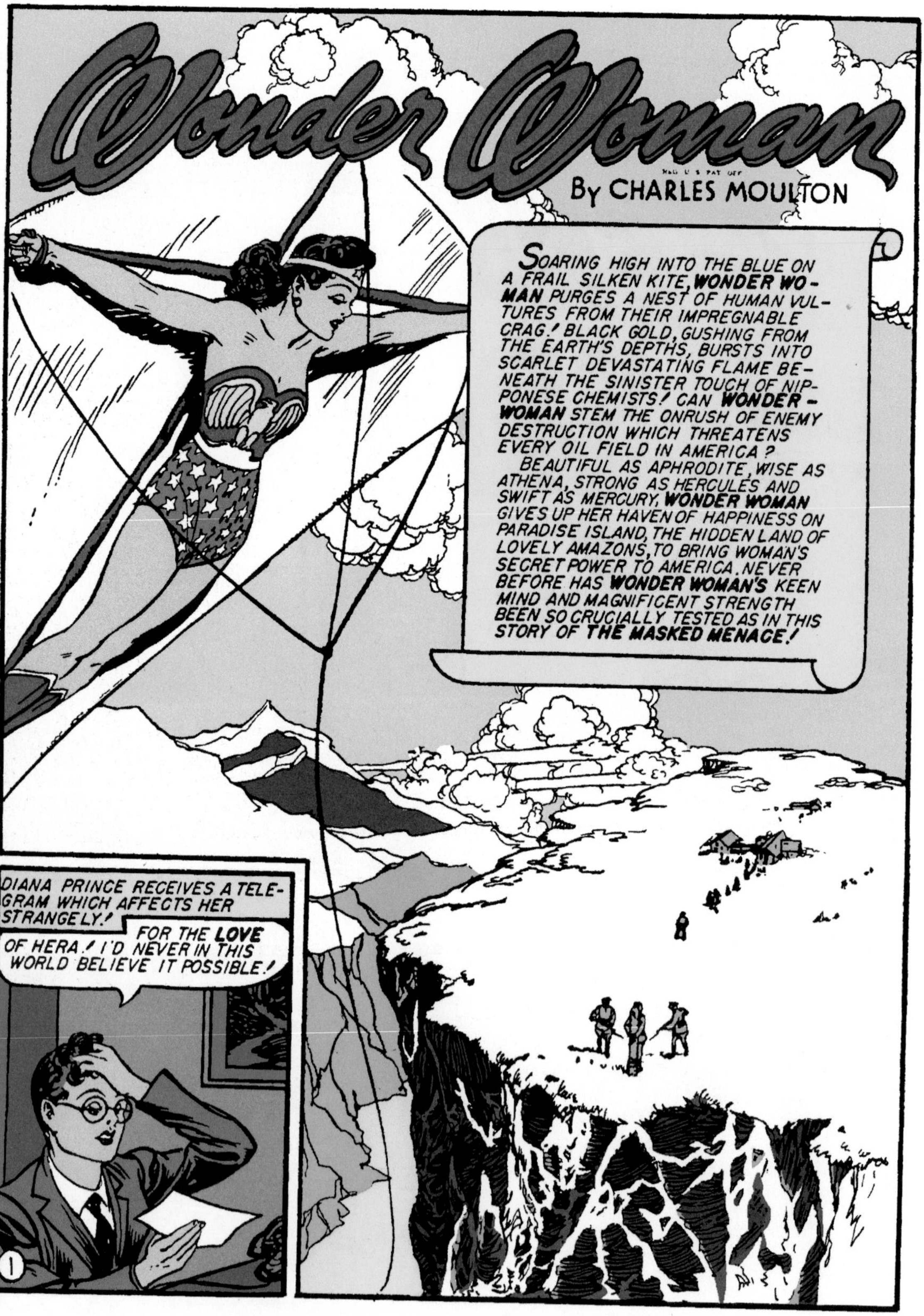

Wonder Woman
REG. U.S. PAT. OFF.
By CHARLES MOULTON
SOARING HIGH INTO THE BLUE ON A FRAIL SILKEN KITE, WONDER WOMAN PURGES A NEST OF HUMAN VULTURES FROM THEIR IMPREGNABLE CRAG! BLACK GOLD, GUSHING FROM THE EARTH'S DEPTHS, BURSTS INTO SCARLET DEVASTATING FLAME BENEATH THE SINISTER TOUCH OF NIPPONESE CHEMISTS! CAN WONDER-WOMAN STEM THE ONRUSH OF ENEMY DESTRUCTION WHICH THREATENS EVERY OIL FIELD IN AMERICA?
BEAUTIFUL AS APHRODITE, WISE AS ATHENA, STRONG AS HERCULES AND SWIFT AS MERCURY, WONDER WOMAN GIVES UP HER HAVEN OF HAPPINESS ON PARADISE ISLAND, THE HIDDEN LAND OF LOVELY AMAZONS, TO BRING WOMAN'S SECRET POWER TO AMERICA. NEVER BEFORE HAS WONDER WOMAN'S KEEN MIND AND MAGNIFICENT STRENGTH BEEN SO CRUCIALLY TESTED AS IN THIS STORY OF THE MASKED MENACE!
DIANA PRINCE RECEIVES A TELEGRAM WHICH AFFECTS HER STRANGELY!
FOR THE LOVE OF HERA! I'D NEVER IN THIS WORLD BELIEVE IT POSSIBLE!
1

STEVE SEEMS EQUALLY AMAZED.

READ THAT!

GREAT CANNABALIS-TIC CATFISH! HOW IN THE NAME OF ROME'S 90 GODS DID THIS EVER HAPPEN?

EVEN THE CONSERVATIVE COLONEL DARNELL IS STARTLED!

CAN YOU BEAT THAT? YOU CERTAINLY MUST GO, DIANA-AND YOU TOO, STEVE- IF YOU CAN MAKE IT!

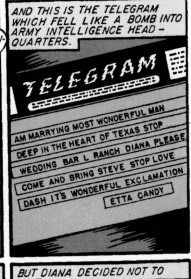

AND THIS IS THE TELEGRAM WHICH FELL LIKE A BOMB INTO ARMY INTELLIGENCE HEAD-QUARTERS.

TELEGRAM

AM MARRYING MOST WONDERFUL MAN DEEP IN THE HEART OF TEXAS STOP WEDDING BAR L RANCH DIANA PLEASE COME AND BRING STEVE STOP LOVE DASH IT'S WONDERFUL EXCLAMATION

ETTA CANDY

IMAGINE ETTA IN LOVE - HA! HA! I'VE GOT TO SEE HER MAN- DO COME, STEVE!

SURE, IF I CAN. I'M GOING TO THE MEXICAN BORDER ANYWAY TO INVESTIGATE JAP SPY ACTIVITY- I'LL MEET YOU AT ETTA'S!

DIANA, TRAVELING BY PLANE, IS GROUNDED AT OKLAHOMA CITY.

SORRY FOLKS, BUT WE'LL HAVE TO WAIT FOR BETTER VISIBILITY. CEILING TO FORT WORTH IS LESS THAN 500 FEET! ROOMS ARE RESERVED AT THE HOTEL.

BUT DIANA DECIDED NOT TO WAIT.

IT'S ONLY A FEW HUNDRED MILES TO THE CANDY RANCH. THINK I'LL RUN THE REST OF THE WAY- I NEED THE EXERCISE!

DIANA CHANGES TO **WONDER WOMAN** AND CARRYING HER SUITCASE, SHE SPEEDS TIRELESSLY ACROSS TEXAS TO THE BAR L RANCH.

I'D BETTER STEP BEHIND THESE COTTONWOOD TREES AND PUT ON MY DIANA CLOTHES AGAIN BEFORE APPEARING AT THE CANDY HOUSE.

BAR-L

②.

DIANA IS CORNERED BY CUPID.

COME OVER TO ZEE TREES! ZARE NO ONE CAN SEE US!

FIFI, MY LOVE, THAT'S AN INSPIRATION!

PFUI, I HOPE THESE LOVE BIRDS DON'T PICK MY TREE FOR COOING!

MON PRINCE! IF YOU LOF ME WHY DO YOU MARRY WIZ ZAT FAT CANDY LOLLYPOP?

MARRY ETTA? HA! HA! I'M ENGAGED TO HER BECAUSE IT SUITS MY PRESENT PURPOSE—WHEN THAT IS ACCOMPLISHED YOU AND I WILL ELOPE!

OH, ZAT IS WONDERFUL! BUT WHAT IS ZIS PURPOSE YOU MUST ACCOMPLISH?

I'LL TELL YOU LATER, WHEN WE'RE MARRIED AND FAR AWAY!

WHAT'S THIS? SOUNDS BAD FOR ETTA!

A TWIG SNAPS UNDER DIANA'S FOOT AND----

SH! ACT UNCONCERNED SHE MAY NOT RECOGNIZE US!

OH! I'VE PUT MY FOOT IN IT THIS TIME!

A FEW MINUTES LATER DIANA ARRIVES AT CANDY HOUSE.

YIP-PEE! HI, DI! BABY, AM I GLAD TO SEE YA!

AND I'M GLAD TO SEE THAT LOVE HASN'T SUBDUED YOUR SPIRITS, ETTA!

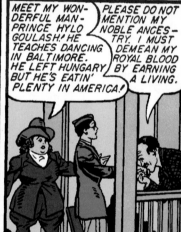

MEET MY WONDERFUL MAN—PRINCE HYLO GOULASH! HE TEACHES DANCING IN BALTIMORE. HE LEFT HUNGARY BUT HE'S EATIN' PLENTY IN AMERICA!

PLEASE DO NOT MENTION MY NOBLE ANCESTRY. I MUST DEMEAN MY ROYAL BLOOD BY EARNING A LIVING.

THIS IS FIFI LA STRANGE, THE FAMOUS DANCER AND MOVIE STAR—SHE'S MY GUEST!

HOW D'YOU DO? HAVEN'T I MET YOU SOMEWHERE BEFORE WITH PRINCE GOULASH?

YOU MUST HAVE SEEN SOMEONE ELSE

NEVAIR!

AS FIFI AND THE PRINCE DISAPPEAR, DIANA TALKS FRANKLY WITH HER FRIEND.

FORGIVE ME, ETTA—BUT ARE YOU SURE THIS PHONY PRINCE REALLY LOVES YOU?

CERTAINLY HE LOVES ME—AND HYLO ISN'T A PHONY!

3.

DIANA'S TALK WITH ETTA IS RUDELY INTERRUPTED.

LISTEN, DI, HYLO'S CRAZY ABOUT ME! HE SAYS I'VE GOT A BETTER FIGURE THAN FIFI!

I HATE TO TELL YOU THIS, BUT— GREAT MINERVA! SOMEONE'S SHOOTING AT ME!

BANG

RUSHING AROUND THE CORNER OF THE HOUSE DIANA FINDS FIFI, A REVOLVER IN HAND.

SO YOU FIRED THAT SHOT!

I FIRE ZEE GUN, OUI! I SHOOT AT SKUNK BUT DO NOT HIT HEEM!

LATER, IN A SECRET CAVE NOT FAR AWAY, A MENACING FIGURE PLOTS THE DESTRUCTION OF TEXAS OIL FIELDS.

POUR THIS NEW JAPANESE CHEMICAL AROUND THE OIL WELL. IT WILL HEAT THE OIL PIPE RED-HOT.

THEN SHE'LL BLOW UP!

YES, THE PIPE WILL EXPLODE AND BLAZING OIL WILL SPOUT HIGH INTO THE AIR. OUR BLACK XO6 WILL HEAT THE PIPE DEEP UNDERGROUND – IT WILL EXPLODE AGAIN IF CAPPED! WE'LL DESTROY THE CANDY GUSHER FIRST!

HARD CANDY, ETTA'S FATHER, RECEIVES ALARMING NEWS FROM A COWBOY.

BOSS, THE OIL WELL BLOWED UP! SHE'S ON FIRE!!

GOL WALLERAT! 'TAINT POSSIBLE THE CANDY GUSHER'S A-BURNIN'! ETTA, PHONE FER HELP-AH'LL GET OVAH THAR PRONTO!

HARD FINDS HIS FIRE FIGHTERS HELPLESS.

GIT YOUR CHEMICALS GOIN'! PREPARE TO CAP THE PIPE! YOU DOGGONE IDJITS—

CHEMICALS WON'T STOP HER! SHE BLEW UNDERGROUND – PIPE CAN'T BE CAPPED!

④

ETTA CALLS FOR HELP ON THE MENTAL RADIO.

CALLING WONDER WOMAN – OUR OIL WELL IS BURNING– MUST BE SABOTAGE! PLEASE HELP –

WONDER WOMAN WILL APPEAR QUICKER THAN ETTA EXPECTS

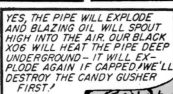

NO USE, **WONDER WOMAN** DOESN'T ANSWER. I'D BETTER TELEPHONE THE FIRE MARSHAL—

WOO! WOO! **WONDER WOMAN** HERSELF! DID YOU COME ON A MAGIC CARPET?

NO—ON MY OWN TWO FEET! COME ON—LET'S GET TO THE BURNING WELL—

WONDER WOMAN AND ETTA QUICKLY JOIN HARD CANDY AT THE BLAZING GUSHER.

I 'PRECIATE YOUR COMIN', MISS **WONDER WOMAN**, BUT THAR HAINT NOTHIN' NOBODY KIN DO! ANY TOOLS WE'D USE WOULD MELT BEFORE WE COULD USE 'EM!

DON'T GIVE UP—LEND ME AN ASBESTOS FIRE-FIGHTER'S SUIT!

CLAD IN ASBESTOS, **WONDER WOMAN** DIGS FASTER THAN A STEAM SHOVEL TO REACH THE BROKEN OIL PIPE.

THIS HEAT IS TERRIFIC—IT'S ROASTING ME THROUGH MY FIREPROOF SUIT!

WONDER WOMAN COOLS OFF BEFORE RETURNING TO HER "IMPOSSIBLE" TASK.

MA'AM, YOU AH TH' BRAVEST FELLAH I EVAH SEE! BUT DON'T TRY TO CAP THAT PIPE—IT'S PLAIN SUICIDE—

NON-SENSE! GET ME ANOTHER FIRE-FIGHTER'S SUIT!

CRAWLING TO THE OIL PIPE, **WONDER WOMAN** CAREFULLY EXAMINES IT.

THIS PIPE IS HEATED DEEP UNDERGROUND—IF I CAP IT, IT'LL EXPLODE AGAIN—I'VE GOT TO PULL IT UP!

DISREGARDING THE SPOUTING VOLCANO OF SEARING FLAME, **WONDER WOMAN** TAKES A FIRM GRIP ON THE HOT OIL PIPE.

I'VE GOT TO PULL THIS PIPE UP QUICKLY BEFORE IT BURNS MY ASBESTOS GLOVES OFF!

EXERTING HER MIGHTY STRENGTH, **WONDER WOMAN** PULLS UP THE LONG BURIED PIPE AMID FRANTIC CHEERS.

THE PIPE HERE IS COOL—THE HEATED SECTION IS COMPLETELY PULLED UP!

YAY-AY **WONDER WOMAN**!

NOW TO STOP THE OIL FLOW!

⑤

TWISTING THE OIL PIPE WITH HER BARE HANDS, **WONDER WOMAN** STOPS THE OIL FLOW FROM UNDERGROUND.

THIS TWIST WILL SEAL THE PIPE QUICKER THAN A CAP.

BREAKING THE PIPE OFF ABOVE THE TWIST, **WONDER WOMAN** HURLS THE STILL BLAZING SECTION A SAFE DISTANCE.

YA-AY **WONDER WOMAN'S** SAVED THE WELL!

WITH THE OIL WELL SAFELY CAPPED, **WONDER WOMAN** INVESTIGATES THE CAUSE OF THE FIRE.

HERE'S SOME EARTH I DUG AWAY FROM AROUND THE WELL- SMELL IT!

SHO' HAS A PECULIAR ODOR!

SOME STRANGE CHEMICAL WAS POURED AROUND YOUR WELL PIPE, HEATING IT AND CAUSING IT TO EXPLODE!

SABOTAGE, EH?

BUT WHO COULD HAVE DONE IT, WON-DER WOMAN?

AS IF IN ANSWER TO ETTA'S QUESTION, STEVE TREVOR ARRIVES.

MR. HARD CANDY, THIS IS MAJOR TREVOR OF THE ARMY INTELLI-GENCE SERVICE!

AH'M HONORED, MAJOR!

I'VE TRACED ENEMY AGENTS TO THIS NEIGH-BORHOOD, MR. CANDY! BUT WE'RE NOT YET SURE OF THEIR IDENTITY!

AN ENEMY AGENT MUST BE HERE ON THE CANDY RANCH, STEVE! I SUSPECT WHO IT IS -ER-- DO YOU KNOW FIFI LA STRANGE?

PLEAS' TO MEET ZE MAJOR! YOU AMERI-CAN OFFICAIRES ARE SO HANDSOME!

I HOPE ZAT SOME NICE MANS GIVE FIFI RIDE BACK TO ZE HOUSE—

I'D BE DELIGHTED!

SHE MUST BE THE ENEMY AGENT-SHE TRIED TO SHOOT DIANA, NOW SHE'S VAMPING STEVE! I HOPE HE'S WISE.

NEAR CANDY HOUSE STEVE STOPS THE CAR AT FIFI'S REQUEST.

WAIT HERE! I'VE SOMETHING TO SHOW YOU-I'LL GET IT FROM MY ROOM, IT WON'T TAKE A MINUTE!

OKAY— BUT HURRY!

6.

AS STEVE WAITS FOR FIFI, OMINOUS FIGURES CREEP UP BEHIND HIM.

I WONDER WHAT THAT GIRL'S UP TO UG-UNH—

THE ENEMY AGENTS DRIVE OFF WITH THE UNCONSCIOUS STEVE, NOT NOTICING HIS CAP LYING ON THE GROUND.

AT A WELL-CAMOUFLAGED HANGAR STEVE'S CAPTORS TRANSFER THEIR PRISONER TO A WAITING PLANE.

WHY NOT KILL THIS FELLOW NOW?

NO! HE'S GOT INFORMATION THE CHIEF WANTS! WE MUST FLY HIM TO ROCK TOP!

FLYING HIGH INTO THE MOUNTAINS, STEVE'S CAPTORS PREPARE TO LAND ON "ROCK TOP."

IT'S A DANGEROUS LANDING—OUGHT TO BE SOME WAY OF REACHING ROCK TOP FROM THE GROUND!

CAN'T BE! IF THERE WAS, SOMEBODY'D FIND THE JAPS' CAMP!

STEVE IS WARMLY WELCOMED TO ROCK TOP.

S-SSO GLAD TO S-SSEE YOU, MAJOR! YOU HAVE S-SS-SO MUCH TO TELL US! THE PLANE WILL RETURN, PLEAS-SE TO ITS HIDDEN HANGAR AND AWAIT ORDERS!

WONDER WOMAN, MEANWHILE, RETURNING TO CANDY HOUSE, MEETS FIFI.

WAIT A MINUTE, WHAT'S YOUR HURRY? AND WHY THE ARTILLERY?

OH-ER-FIFI FIND ZIS REVOLVAIRE—MUS' TAKE EET QUEEK TO MAJOR TREVOR-HE WAIT!

(7)

I'LL GO WITH YOU—I'D LIKE TO TALK WITH STEVE MYSELF! BUT WHERE IS HE? THE CAR'S EMPTY!

OH- I DO NOT KNOW—I LEFT HEEM WAITING IN ZE CAR!

STEVE'S CAP ON THE GROUND-LOOKS AS THO' HE'D BEEN KIDNAPPED!

OH-OH! ZAT IS TEHR-RIBLE!

JUST A MOMENT, MY GIRL— IT'S RUDE TO LEAVE A FRIEND RIGHT IN THE MIDDLE OF AN INTERESTING CONVERSATION!

OH PLEASE! LET ME GO!

NOW MY DEAR, YOU'LL TELL ME THE TRUTH. WHO KID-NAPPED STEVE TREVOR?

I-I-OH SOME-SING COM-PELS ME TO SPEAK FRANK-LY— HE WAS TAKEN BY ENEMY AGENTS!

YOU SAY YOU KNOW THE ENEMY AGENT'S HIDE-OUT— YOU WILL LEAD ME THERE IMMEDIATELY!

I-I THINK YOU WILL REGRET IT. BUT I'M COM-PELLED TO OBEY YOU!

AT THIS MOMENT COMES THE HOLLIDAY COLLEGE BAND PRACTICING A HORSEBACK SERENADE FOR ETTA'S WEDDING.

WE'RE RIDING AND WE'RE PLAYING CARES HIDING, WE ARE PRAYING THAT ETTA CANDY'S MAN WILL BE JUST DAN-DEE!

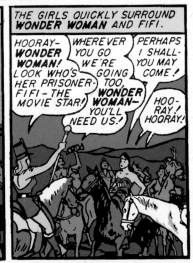

THE GIRLS QUICKLY SURROUND **WONDER WOMAN** AND FIFI.

HOORAY— **WONDER WOMAN!** LOOK WHO'S HER PRISONER— FIFI— THE MOVIE STAR!

WHEREVER YOU GO WE'RE GOING TOO, **WONDER WOMAN**— YOU'LL NEED US!

PERHAPS I SHALL— YOU MAY COME!

HOO-RAY! HOORAY!

NEAR THE SECRET CAVE THE GIRLS DISMOUNT.

THEIR HIDEOUT MAY BE WATCHED—

GO AHEAD— WE'LL TAKE A CHANCE!

TELLING THE GIRLS TO WATCH OUTSIDE, **WONDER WOMAN** AND BRENDA, THEIR LEADER, ENTER THE CAVE.

THE ENEMY AGENTS HAVEN'T ARRIVED YET WITH STEVE.

ZEY MAY NOT COME— EET IS ONLY MY GUESS ZAY BREENG HIM HERE.

FIFI, FREED FROM THE MAGIC LASSO, ESCAPES

I MAY NEED MY MAGIC LASSO IF THERE'S A FIGHT— TIE HER WITH ROPE—

COME HERE YOU LITTLE VIXEN! OH, HECK— SHE GOT AWAY!

MEANWHILE, OUTSIDE THE CAVE THE GIRLS FIND THEMSELVES SURROUNDED.

PUT UP YOUR HANDS! MEN, BIND AND GAG THESE PRISONERS!

WONDER WOMAN, HEARING A CRY OUTSIDE, RUNS TO THE DOOR OF THE CAVE AND FINDS HERSELF IN A CLEVER TRAP.

I AM INFORMED THAT WONDER WOMAN ALWAYS SACRIFICES HERSELF FOR OTHERS — SURRENDER OR YOUR GIRLS DIE!

I HAVE NO CHOICE — I MUST SURRENDER. BUT BIND ME TIGHT IF YOU EXPECT TO KEEP ME CAPTIVE!

I WILL, NEVER FEAR, AND WITH YOUR METAL LASSO. WE KNOW YOU CANNOT BREAK THIS ROPE!

THE PRISONERS ARE LASHED TO PACK MULES AND CARRIED HIGH INTO THE MOUNTAINS.

APPROACHING THE "ROCK TOP" AN OBLIGING GUARD EXPLAINS THE SPY FORTRESS TO WONDER WOMAN.

YOU BOYS LOOK LIKE ITALIANS, DISGUISED AS MEXICANS!

THAT'S RIGHT — THE JAPS BROUGHT US HERE BECAUSE NIPS CAN'T DISGUISE THEMSELVES. THEY STAY UP ON TOP OF THE ROCK — CAN'T REACH IT EXCEPT BY PLANE. THEY FLEW A PRISONER UP THERE TODAY — THEY'LL FLY YOU UP TOMORROW. HA! HA!

IN AN ABANDONED MEXICAN VILLAGE THE GIRLS ARE PLACED IN THE EMPTY JAIL.

IT'S A RELIEF TO GET THESE ROPES OFF!

AREN'T THESE CELLS CUTE — LIKE DOG KENNELS ALL IN A ROW!

⑨

BUT WONDER WOMAN RATES SPECIAL PRECAUTIONS.

AREN'T YOU GOING TO UNTIE MY ARMS?

NO! YOU STAY BOUND! AT YOUR FIRST MOVE TO ESCAPE WE'LL SHOOT YOUR GIRL FRIENDS!

THERE ARE ONLY ITALIANS DISGUISED AS GUARDS IN THE JAIL-- ALL LATINS LOVE MUSIC...HM-M -- I HAVE AN IDEA...

BRENDA-- CAN YOU HEAR ME? ASK THE GUARDS FOR YOUR MUSICAL INSTRUMENTS AND START PLAYING A DANCE TUNE!

I HEAR YOU TALKIN', WONDER WOMAN -- I'LL PASS THE WORD ALONG!

THE MUSIC-LOVING ITALIANS READILY GIVE THE GIRLS THEIR INSTRUMENTS. ALL RIGHT GIRLS, PLAY FUNICULE, FUNICULA-- READY, ONE, TWO, THREE --

SOME THINK THE WORLD IS MADE FOR FUN AND FROLIC-- AND SO DO I, AND SO DO I. SOME THINK IT WRONG TO BE ALL MELANCHOLIC-- AND SO DO I, AND SO DO I-- BUT I-- I LOVE TO SPEND MY TIME IN SINGING SOME JOYOUS SONG --

THE GUARDS CANNOT RESIST THE LURE OF THE GIRLS' MUSIC-- THEY ASK THEIR PRISONERS TO DANCE!

AH, SENORITA! YOUR MUSIC IS DIVINE-- WILL YOU DANCE WITH ME?

WHY CERTAINLY, FERDINAND! I'LL BET YOU CUT A MEAN RUG!

SNAP

⑩

SOON ALL THE GUARDS ARE DANCING.

THE ROSE IN BLOOM IS LIKE PER-FUME DEEP IN THE HEART OF TEXAS!

WHEN THE MUSIC IS LOUDEST **WONDER WOMAN** CRASHES HER CELL DOOR.

NOW A LITTLE ACTION!

CRACK

SMASH

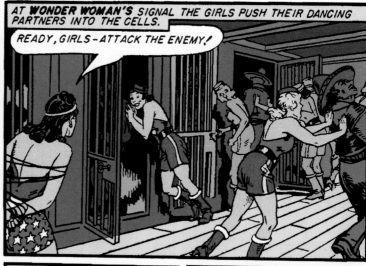

AT **WONDER WOMAN'S** SIGNAL THE GIRLS PUSH THEIR DANCING PARTNERS INTO THE CELLS.

READY, GIRLS - ATTACK THE ENEMY!

UNTIE ME, BRENDA - QUICK! WE MUST CAPTURE THE OUTSIDE GUARDS!

HAVE WE GOT FUN! MEN ARE ALWAYS EASY FOR GIRLS TO CAPTURE!

WONDER WOMAN BURSTS OPEN THE JAIL DOOR. - - - -

CAN'T WAIT TO HUNT UP THE KEYS - THIS JAIL IS NO GOOD ANYWAY!

HOORAY FOR **WONDER WOMAN** AND FUN!

THE GIRLS QUICKLY HERD THE REMAINING GUARDS AND SPIES INTO **WONDER WOMAN'S** LASSO

BACKWARD MARCH TO JAIL, BOYS - WE'VE BEEN KEEPING THE CELLS WARM FOR YOU!

WE C - CAN'T OBEY YOU VERY G-GOOD - BUT WE'RE COMPELLED TO TRY!

THOUGH THEIR GUARDS ARE CAPTURED THE GIRLS CANNOT SCALE THE WEIRD HEIGHT OF ROCK TOP WHERE STEVE IS HELD PRISONER.

EVEN **YOU** CAN'T JUMP HALF A MILE IN THE AIR, **WONDER WOMAN!**

11

THE WIND IS STRONG - HA! AN IDEA. CUT ME TWO SAPLINGS - GET SOME SILK AND THAT REEL OF CONSTRUCTION WIRE FROM THE JAPS' STORE ROOM!

SAY - HAVE YOU GONE NUTS? OKAY - OKAY - WILL DO!

USE THAT CHAIN FOR THE KITE'S TAIL AND ATTACH THE REEL OF WIRE FOR A KITE STRING!

THIS WIND WILL TAKE ME UP ALL-RIGHT—YOU'LL HAVE TO MAN-OEUVRE THE KITE SO IT FLIES OVER THE "INTERNMENT CAMP." READY, GIRLS? LET GO!

HOLD HARD, BRENDA! THAT KITE PULLS LIKE A FREIGHT ENGINE!

UP-UP! SOARS THE KITE—SOON **WONDER WOMAN** IS FLYING DIRECTLY ABOVE HER OBJECTIVE.

HERE COMES SOMETHING, IF YOU DON'T BELIEVE IT GET IN MY WAY!

WONDER WOMAN ARRIVES AT A CRUCIAL MOMENT.

EXCUSE ME, BOYS DO I INTRUDE?

I'LL TELL YOU NOTHING—ER-GULP—**WONDER WOMAN**, MY BEAUTIFUL ANGEL!

THE JAPS RUN LIKE YELLOW CURS FROM **WONDER WOMAN** AND STEVE.

DON'T SHOOT, STEVE—IT'S ALWAYS MORE FUN TO BRING 'EM BACK ALIVE!

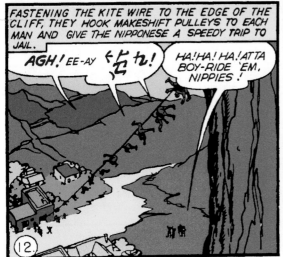

FASTENING THE KITE WIRE TO THE EDGE OF THE CLIFF, THEY HOOK MAKESHIFT PULLEYS TO EACH MAN AND GIVE THE NIPPONESE A SPEEDY TRIP TO JAIL.

AGH! EE-AY

HA! HA! HA! ATTA BOY-RIDE 'EM, NIPPIES!

⑫

WONDER WOMAN AND STEVE FOLLOW THEIR CAPTIVES TO EARTH.

YOU TAKE CHARGE OF THE PRISONERS WHEN WE GET DOWN, STEVE—I MUST HURRY BACK TO CANDY HOUSE TO CATCH THE MASKED MENACE.

OKAY, ANGEL!

RACING BACK TO THE BAR-L, **WONDER WOMAN** MEETS THE MASKED SPY RUNNING AWAY.

WELL TIMED, MY FRIEND! NICE OF YOU TO MEET ME.

UG-AWWK! THIS WOMAN'S A DEMON!

THE MENACE IS UNMASKED.

FOR THE LOVE OF APHRODITE— ETTA'S PHONY PRINCE!

Y-Y-YES—I CONFESS! I'M KARL SCHULTZ— GESTAPO AGENT WORK- ING FOR THE JAPS. I GOT ENGAGED TO ETTA CANDY TO DIRECT OIL WELL SABOTAGE UNSUSPECTED FROM THE CANDY RANCH!

MEANWHILE ETTA HAS BEEN WAITING AT THE CHURCH.

AH RECKON WE'VE WAITED LONG ENOUGH FOR THAT MAVERICK! AH'LL GO GET HIM!

NO, DAD! I WOULDN'T MARRY THAT TWO- TIMING SISSY IF HE WAS THE LAST MAN ON EARTH!

WONDER WOMAN BRINGS BACK THE WANDERING BRIDEGROOM.

ETTA, MEET MR. SCHULTZ, THE EX-MENACE!

SURE I'LL MEET HIM— LIKE THIS!

SOCKO!

WONDER WOMAN MEETS TWO FIFIS.

I'M SEEING DOUBLE— ARE YOU TWINS?

YOU GUESSED IT— OUR REAL NAME'S MALONE. I'M A G-GIRL AND MY SISTER'S THE MOVIE ACTRESS. I IMPERSON- ATED HER TO WATCH SCHULTZ, ALIAS PRINCE GOULASH!

BUT WHY DID YOU SHOOT AT DIANA PRINCE?

I DIDN'T! "GOULASH" SHOT AT DIANA AND I SHOT TO SCARE HIM AWAY. I COULDN'T ARREST HIM UNTIL I PROVED HE WAS AN ENEMY AGENT. YOU BEAT ME TO IT, WONDER WOMAN!

I'M GLAD THAT'S OVER— I'M SICK OF SISSY CLOTHES AND SIMPERING SAPS! ME FOR CANDY AND A GOOD HORSE—I'LL TAKE A LONG RIDE WITH DIANA!

ATTA GIRL, ETTA! I'LL GO GET DIANA FOR YOU!

13.

ETTA'S A GAME GIRL—DIANA MUSTN'T KEEP HER WAITING! AS FOR YOU, YOUNG LADY, LET FIFI BE A LESSON TO YOU. NEVER ACCUSE ANYBODY OF BEING A CROOK UNTIL YOU'VE GOT THE STRAIGHT OF IT YOURSELF!

FOLLOW WONDER WOMAN'S UNIQUE ADVENTURES EVERY MONTH IN SENSATION COMICS.

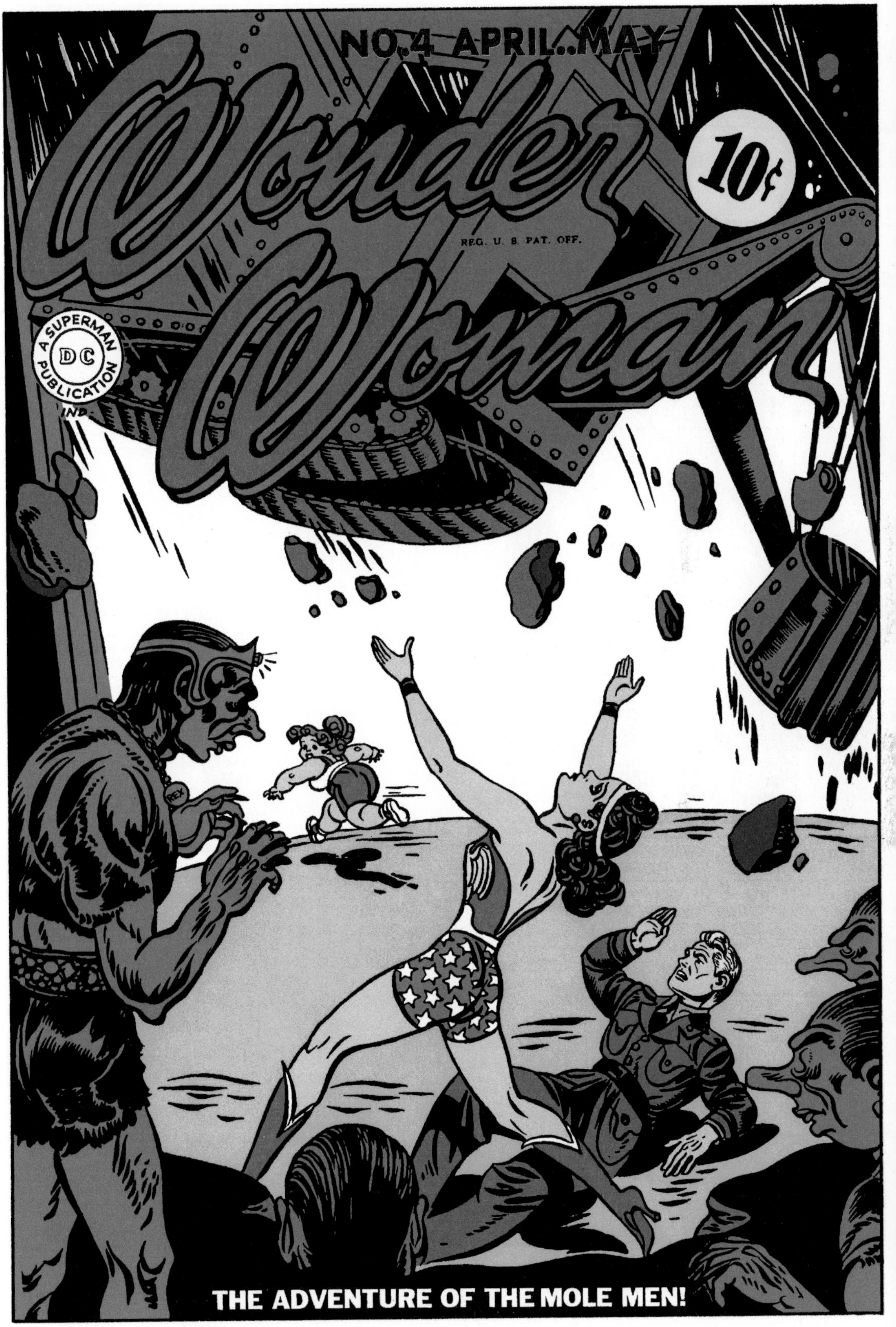
NO.4 APRIL..MAY
Wonder Woman
10¢
REG. U. S. PAT. OFF.
A SUPERMAN DC PUBLICATION INC.
REX
THE ADVENTURE OF THE MOLE MEN!

Wonder Woman

By CHARLES MOULTON

ON FLASHING WINGS OF ETERNAL LIGHT COMES APHRODITE, GODDESS OF LOVE AND BEAUTY, TO TEST THE NEOPHYTE WHOM **WONDER WOMAN** HAS PLEDGED TO HER SERVICE! THREE MIGHTY LABORS OF LOVE MUST THIS FAIR CANDIDATE PERFORM, MORE DANGEROUS AND THRILLING BY FAR THAN THE TWELVE LABORS OF HERCULES. CAN SHE PERFORM SUCCESSFULLY THE PART **WONDER WOMAN** ASSIGNS HER IN SAVING THE WOMEN OF AMERICA FROM STRANGE MAN-HATING MADNESS, DEVISED FOR THEIR DESTRUCTION BY THE CRUEL CUNNING OF HUMANITY'S SUBTLEST ENEMIES?

AGAINST A SWIFTLY SHIFTING BACK DROP OF COLOSSAL WORLD EVENTS, THE MIGHTY AMAZON PRINCESS BATTLES HER ALLURING WAY TO GLORY, WRESTLING WITH TANKS, OUTGUESSING THE BRILLIANT INTRIGUE OF JAPANESE GENERALS AND TESTING APHRODITE'S COURAGEOUS INITIATE IN THE SEETHING CRUCIBLE OF THRILLS AND PERILS UNPARALLELED IN THE ANNALS OF HUMAN EXPERIENCE!

BEAUTIFUL AS APHRODITE, WISE AS ATHENA, STRONG AS HERCULES AND SWIFT AS MERCURY, **WONDER WOMAN** BRINGS TO EMBATTLED AMERICA THAT SECRET POWER OF WOMAN WHICH ALONE CAN DEFEAT EVIL AND CREATE IN ITS STEAD PEACE, HAPPINESS AND THE JOY OF LIVING!

COLONEL DARNELL BRINGS NURSE DIANA A PRETTY PATIENT.

THIS IS MAE WU, OF PEI WHAI, CHINA—SHE HAS RAISED THOUSANDS OF DOLLARS FOR CHINESE RELIEF!

I'VE HEARD MISS WU SPEAK—SHE IS WONDERFUL!

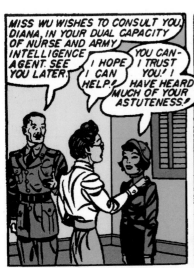

MISS WU WISHES TO CONSULT YOU, DIANA, IN YOUR DUAL CAPACITY OF NURSE AND ARMY INTELLIGENCE AGENT. SEE YOU LATER.

I HOPE I CAN HELP!

YOU CAN-- I TRUST YOU! I HAVE HEARD MUCH OF YOUR ASTUTENESS!

YOU HAVE SEEN SCARS WHERE JAPANESE WHO TAKE MY NATIVE VILLAGE BEAT ME?

YES-- THEY'RE TERRIBLE! YOU SHOWED YOUR BACK TO US NURSES AT THE LECTURE YOU GAVE!

YES-- I HAVE SHOWN AMERICANS ALL OVER COUNTRY HOW JAPS TREAT CHINESE WOMEN-- AMERICA NOW WILL DESTROY JAPAN!

YES, MY DEAR, YOUR JOB IS DONE. AMERICA IS ROUSED-- YOUR SCARS HAVE SERVED THEIR PURPOSE!

YES-- MY WORK HERE IS FINISH. PLEASE TELL ME-- COULD UGLY WHIP SCARS BE REMOVED?

QUITE EASILY, I SHOULD THINK! BUT YOU OUGHT TO CONSULT A DOCTOR-- I'M ONLY A NURSE!

I HAVE CONSULT SURGEON-- HE SAY YES, SIMPLE OPERATION. THEN I GET LETTER-- IT FRIGHTEN ME!

WHY, THIS SAYS-- OH! ER-- IT'S CHINESE, YOU TRANSLATE IT!

AMAZON GIRLS LEARN ALL LANGUAGES-- I ALMOST GAVE MYSELF AWAY!

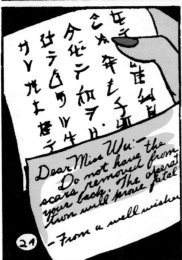

Dear Miss Wu: Do not have the scars removed from your back! The operation will prove fatal --From a well wisher

㉑

HM! CHINESE CHARACTERS DRAWN WITH A PEN-- THE CHINESE USE A BRUSH! LOOKS LIKE AN ENEMY THREAT!

YOU THINK, THEN, THAT SCAR OPERATION ITSELF COULD NOT BE DANGEROUS?

I CAN'T SEE HOW! BUT CONSULT DR. STRONG, HE'S A SKIN SPECIALIST. HERE'S HIS ADDRESS. WHEN YOU GET STRONG'S OPINION COME BACK AND SEE ME.

THANK YOU SO MUCH! I OBEY YOU NOW!

AFTER WORK THAT DAY----

I FEEL UNEASY ABOUT THAT CHINESE GIRL – THINK I'LL CALL AT DR. STRONG'S AND SEE WHAT HE SAYS ABOUT HER!

GREAT SHADES OF PLUTO! IT'S MAE WU –SOMEBODY KNOCKED HER ON THE HEAD JUST AS SHE RANG THE DOCTOR'S DOOR BELL!

B.C. STRONG M.D.

SHE'S DEAD! WHAT A FOOL I WAS TO SEND HER TO A DOCTOR. WHOEVER WROTE THAT THREATENING NOTE ASSUMED SHE WAS GOING TO HAVE HER SCARS REMOVED AND KILLED HER TO PREVENT IT!

WHY WOULD ANYBODY WISH TO STOP THAT POOR CHILD FROM REMOVING WHIP SCARS? THIS COWARD'S ACT MAKES MY BLOOD BOIL – I'LL CATCH THE KILLER OR MY NAME'S NOT WONDER WOMAN!

THERE'S ONE CHANCE IN A THOUSAND I CAN BRING MAE TO LIFE AGAIN! THE BARONESS–ER–MY PRISONER PAULA INVENTED AN ELECTRICAL MACHINE THAT RESTORES LIFE IF APPLIED PROMPTLY. I MUST REACH REFORM ISLAND IN TIME!

HURTLING OVER THE OCEAN AT 2000 MILES AN HOUR IN HER INVISIBLE PLANE, WONDER WOMAN NEARS REFORM ISLAND WHERE PAULA AND HER FORMER SLAVES ARE UNDERGOING TRAINING FOR APHRODITE'S SERVICE.

I HOPE PAULA'S MACHINE IS OKAY!

3

HAIL, PRINCESS- APHRODITE WITH YOU!

AND WITH YOU! QUICK, BRING ME PRISONER PAULA - WE MUST RESTORE A DEAD GIRL'S LIFE!

PAULA IS CALLED FROM PRISONERS' HAND WRESTLING PRACTICE.

JUST A MINUTE, MISTRESS! I —

OBEY INSTANTLY!

FOR DELAY IN OBEDIENCE, MISTRESS, I ASK PUNISHMENT!

GRANTED— YOU SHALL WEAR HEAVIER CHAINS. PAULA, COME QUICKLY.

I BELIEVE THESE GIRLS DISOBEY BECAUSE THEY LIKE TO BE DISCIPLINED!

WONDER WOMAN! OH, HOW HAPPY I AM TO SEE YOU, BELOVED MISTRESS!

AND I TO SEE YOU! OUR GREETINGS MUST WAIT. HERE'S A GIRL WHO'S JUST BEEN KILLED—YOUR ELECTRICAL MACHINE MUST RESTORE HER TO LIFE!

MY MACHINE'S IN PERFECT CONDITION. THEY LET ME WORK IN THE LABORATORY 5 HOURS EACH DAY AND I HAVE REBUILT ALL MY MISUSED INVENTIONS FOR APHRODITE'S SERVICE!

I HAVE A FEELING THIS MACHINE OF YOURS WILL REVIVE THE GIRL—READY, PAULA! SWITCH ON YOUR THIRD ELECTRONIC RAY!

SLOWLY, AS THE WATCHERS WAIT MOTIONLESS, THE DEAD GIRL'S HEART BEGINS TO BEAT, HER CHEST RISES GENTLY, HER PULSES STIR TO RENEWED LIFE!

SHE'S BREATHING!

I FEEL HER PULSE BEAT! PAULA, YOUR MACHINE IS MARVELOUS!

HOURS LATER THE TWO CLEVEREST WOMEN IN THE WORLD LEAVE THEIR PATIENT, HER RECOVERY ASSURED.

A DIFFICULT JOB WELL DONE, PAULA!

THANKS, MISTRESS! BUT IT'LL BE HOURS—PERHAPS DAYS BEFORE HER MEMORY IS RESTORED.

4A

YOU'RE RIGHT, PAULA—THIS CASE WILL TAKE TIME. I'LL SEND A MENTAL MESSAGE TO STEVE TREVOR---

WONDER WOMAN CALLING! I NEED DIANA PRINCE ON A CASE. PLEASE GET HER A WEEK'S LEAVE OF ABSENCE!

I'M **SO** GLAD YOU'RE GOING TO STAY OVERNIGHT! TOMORROW SIX PRISONERS, INCLUDING PAULA, TAKE THEIR TESTS OF PHYSICAL FITNESS FOR APHRODITE'S SERVICE. YOU MUST BE ONE OF OUR JUDGES, PRINCESS!

I'D LOVE TO IF THE QUEEN PERMITS!

AND SO, THE NEXT MORNING, **WONDER WOMAN** TAKES HER PLACE WITH THE QUEEN, HER MOTHER, IN THE PRISON JUDGES' STAND.

HEAR YE, NOBLE AMAZONS AND PRISONERS! OUR QUEEN HIPPOLYTE AND PRINCESS DIANA WILL JUDGE WHETHER APHRODITE'S NEOPHYTES ARE WORTHY!

REMOVE THE NEOPHYTES' CHAINS! THESE SIX CANDIDATES MUST PROVE TO THEIR JUDGES THAT THEY HAVE ATTAINED SUFFICIENT BODILY STRENGTH TO SERVE OUR GODDESS SUCCESSFULLY IN THE MAN-RULED WORLD!

THE FIRST TEST-WEIGHT LIFTING-IS PASSED BY ALL CANDIDATES.

FIRST ON THE RIGHT HAND - THEN THE LEFT. NOW **BOTH** WEIGHTS AT ONCE! GOOD! CARRYING YOUR CHAINS HAS TAUGHT YOU GIRLS TO LIFT HEAVY WEIGHTS!

500 LBS 500 LBS

ONE CANDIDATE FAILS TO LASSO A RUNNING GIRL AT 50 FEET.

HA! HA! MISSED ME!

PHUI! I WONDER IF THIS'LL PUT ME OUT?

IT'S CHAINS AGAIN FOR YOU, WEAK ARM!

I HOPED THEY'D GIVE ME ANOTHER CHANCE!

THE JUDGES ARE RIGHT-FAILING AT SUCH AN EASY TEST OUGHT TO ELIMINATE ANY GIRL!

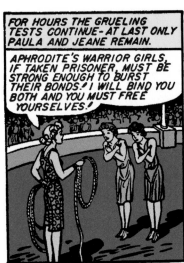

FOR HOURS THE GRUELING TESTS CONTINUE - AT LAST ONLY PAULA AND JEANE REMAIN.

APHRODITE'S WARRIOR GIRLS, IF TAKEN PRISONER, MUST BE STRONG ENOUGH TO BURST THEIR BONDS! I WILL BIND YOU BOTH AND YOU MUST FREE YOURSELVES!

MALA BINDS THE CANDIDATES WITH AMAZON STRENGTH AND SKILL - IN VAIN THEY STRUGGLE FOR FREEDOM.

PULL HARDER, GIRLS - AN AMAZON COULD BREAK THOSE ROPES LIKE PAPER!

HA! HA! ALL "MAN'S-WORLD" GIRLS ARE WEAKLINGS!

HA! HA! THEY'RE HELPLESS!

BUT PAULA, DESPERATELY DE-TERMINED TO WIN, STRAINS FIERCELY AT HER ROPES AND---

I KNEW I COULD DO IT!

HOLA! HOORAH! CHEERS FOR THE STRONG GIRL! HOLA!

SNAP!!

YOU ALONE, PAULA, HAVE PASSED THESE TESTS! YOU WIN BECAUSE YOU HAVE THE WILL-TO-VICTORY. MEN HAVE NOT MADE YOU FEEL INFERIOR-YOU REALIZE THE TRUE STRENGTH OF WOMAN! MY DAUGHTER SHALL PRESENT YOU TO OUR GODDESS!

IN THE TEMPLE OF APHRODITE.

THIS NEOPHYTE, OH, DIVINE GOD-DESS, HAS PROVED HER STRENGTH! SHE PRAYS NOW FOR FURTHER TESTS TO ENTER THY SERVICE!

ART THOU PRE-PARED, NEO-PHYTE, TO RISK THY LIFE FOR LOVE AND BEAU-TY?

OH YES, GODDESS!

TO ENTER MY SERVICE, PAULA, THOU MUST PER-FORM SUCCESSFULLY THREE LABORS OF LOVE - THE FIRST TO SAVE WOMEN OF AMERICA FROM DESTRUCTION BY EVIL FOLLOWERS OF MARS! REMOVE THE NEOPHYTE'S CHAINS!

BUT-BUT HOW CAN I DO THAT?

⑥

OUTSIDE THE TEMPLE MALA MEETS THEM WITH GOOD NEWS!

YOU TWO HAVE PERFORMED A MIRACLE! THAT CHINESE GIRL HAS RECOVERED COMPLETELY-SHE'S WAITING FOR YOU ON REFORM ISLAND!

SCORNING THE AID OF BOATS, THE THREE GIRLS SWIM THE SWIFT CURRENT WITH EASY, POWERFUL STROKES.

I'LL RACE YOU TO REFORM ISLAND, GIRLS!

YOU TWO WILL BEAT ME—BUT NOT BY MUCH! COME ON!

MAE WU TELLS HER STORY.

THIS IS A STRANGE BUSINESS! BY CHANCE I FOUND YOU ON A DOCTOR'S DOORSTEP—PLEASE TELL ALL ABOUT YOURSELF!

WILL DO WONDER WOMAN! WHEN I WAS YOUNG GIRL, I LIVED IN LITTLE CHINESE VILLAGE PEI WHAI UNTIL---

RUN, RUN—THE MONKEY MEN ARE HERE! THE JAPANESE ARE UPON US!

OH! I MUST WARN MY VENERABLE PARENTS—

"THE DWARFS, AS WE CALL THEM, KILLED EVERY MAN IN OUR VILLAGE AND SET OUR HOMES ON FIRE."

"WE GIRLS AND WOMEN WERE ROPED TOGETHER AND DRIVEN BY JAPANESE SOLDIERS TO THEIR CAMP."

MOVE FASTER, LOW-BORN FEMALES!

"CAPTAIN HIDEO, ENEMY INTELLIGENCE OFFICER, QUESTIONED US.

YOU KNOW WHERE CHINESE GENERAL CHANG IS HIDING! TELL ME QUICK OR ELSE—

I KNOW NOTHING OF CHANG—IF I DID, I WOULDN'T TELL YOU!

TIE HER TO A WHIPPING POST WITH THE OTHERS—BUT WAIT! I HAVE AN INSPIRATION! SHE MUST BE WHIPPED CAREFULLY—I'LL DO IT MYSELF!

"HIDEO GAVE ME THE SCARS ON MY BACK. WHEN MY WHIPPING WAS OVER—

I DO KNOW WHERE CHINESE GENERAL CHANG IS HIDING! WHIP ME AGAIN—SEE IF I TELL!

YOUR HONORABLE COURAGE CONQUERS—YOU MAY GO FREE!

"FOR SOME STRANGE REASON HIDEO RELEASED ME! HE EVEN HAD ME ESCORTED TO A CHINESE PORT—

WE GIVE YOU THIS PRISONER—TAKE HER TO YOUR GENERAL!

WILL INDEED DO! LOOK LIKE FUNNY BUSINESS!

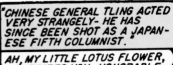

"CHINESE GENERAL TLING ACTED VERY STRANGELY—HE HAS SINCE BEEN SHOT AS A JAPANESE FIFTH COLUMNIST.

AH, MY LITTLE LOTUS FLOWER, I EXPECTED YOU—HONORABLE HIDEO NOTIFIED ME OF YOUR RELEASE!

HOW ODD! THE ENEMY TOLD YOU ABOUT ME!

"AND YET GENERAL TLING DID ME A GREAT FAVOR—"

MAJOR FU, YOU SEEK FOREIGN-EDUCATED WOMEN TO SPEAK FOR CHINESE RELIEF IN AMERICA. HERE IS CHARMING PERSON MISS WU!

MUCH PLEASE TO SEND HER TO AMERICA!

"OH I WAS SO HAPPY! I SPEAK ALL OVER UNITED STATES AND SHOW MARKS OF BEAST ON BACK TO SYMPATHETIC AMERICANS, LIKE GENERAL TLING SUGGEST! I SHOW YOU—

ODD ARRANGEMENT OF MARKS!

I'LL BET THEY MEAN SOMETHING!

4 STRIPES ONE WAY, 3 ANOTHER—COULD MEAN A DATE—4TH MONTH, 3RD DAY—APRIL 3RD! HIDEO MARKED THAT MESSAGE ON MAE'S BACK AND SENT HER TO SHOW IT PUBLICLY SO JAP AGENTS COULD READ IT UNDETECTED!

HOW FIENDISHLY CLEVER! WHEN MISS WU PLANNED TO REMOVE THE MARKS ON HER BACK BY BEAUTY OPERATION, THE JAPS KILLED HER LEST THE CHANGE IN SCARS CONFUSE THEIR PLANS! BUT **WHAT** IS TO HAPPEN APRIL 3RD?

WONDER WOMAN CONSULTS STEVE ON THE MENTAL RADIO.

DO YOU KNOW ANY JAP PLANS FOR ATTACKING AMERICA?

WE'VE HEARD FANTASTIC RUMORS OF A JAPANESE BACILLUS TO BE RELEASED HERE WHICH WILL DRIVE AMERICAN WOMEN INSANE!

EDITOR'S NOTE:
THERE ARE MANY DISEASES KNOWN TO MEDICAL SCIENCE WHICH ATTACK ONE SEX BUT NOT THE OTHER. THE COMMON FORM OF COLOR BLINDNESS, THOUGH INHERITED THROUGH WOMEN, DOES NOT AFFECT FEMALES BUT ONLY MALES. IT IS NOT SURPRISING, THEREFORE, THAT JAPANESE SCIENTISTS COULD FIND A MADNESS GERM WHICH WOULD DRIVE WOMEN CRAZY WHILE LEAVING MEN UNHARMED!

I KNOW NOW THE TERRIBLE JAP PLAN! IT WOULD TURN ALL AMERICAN WOMEN AGAINST THE MEN—CAUSE A CIVIL WAR! TO STOP IT WE MUST GET THE JAP SPY LIST FROM CHINA! IT'S DESPERATELY DANGEROUS—WILL YOU GIRLS GO?

OF COURSE!

LET'S START IMMEDIATELY!

WINGING THEIR WAY FASTER THAN THE WIND IN **WONDER WOMAN'S** AMAZON PLANE, THE THREE BEAUTIFUL MUSKETEERS SWOOP SWIFTLY DOWN NEAR PEI WHAI, CHINA.

I SEE AMERICAN SOLDIERS—WE'LL LAND HERE!

LANDING SILENTLY, UNOBSERVED, THE GIRLS ENTER FIELD HEADQUARTERS OF UNITED STATES MARINES.

AH, GENERAL! WE'RE GLAD TO MEET YOU!

WONDER WOMAN BY ALL THAT'S CRAZY! YOU DO APPEAR AT THE HOTTEST SPOTS—WE'RE ABOUT TO ATTACK!

GENERAL BROWN SHOWS **WONDER WOMAN** THE MILITARY SITUATION.

WE'RE ATTACKING THE VILLAGE OF PEI WHAI AT DAWN—HERE IS OUR APPROACH—

BUT GENERAL—IF YOU SWING BACK AROUND THESE HILLS, YOU WILL TAKE THE JAPS UNAWARE!

THANKS! YOUR KNOWLEDGE OF THE TERRITORY HELPS A LOT! WE ADVANCE AT DAWN—IF **WONDER WOMAN** LEADS WE CANNOT FAIL!

I'LL GO AS A BUCK PRIVATE—BUT **NOT** IN THE REAR RANK!

PAULA, LEARNING THAT GENERAL VON BOP IS VISITING JAPANESE HEADQUARTERS, DECIDES TO TRY DIFFERENT TACTICS.

I KNOW VON BOP—HE THINKS I'M STILL A NAZI SPY. I'LL GO TO HIM DIRECTLY!

VON BOP IS A ✳✳—✕!!—

BE CAREFUL, PAULA!

AS DAWN BREAKS THE MARINES CHARGE STRONGLY FORTIFIED JAPANESE POSITIONS.

AS THE MARINES CLOSE WITH THE ENEMY, FIGHTING HAND-TO-HAND, GENERAL BROWN FALLS WOUNDED.

GO AHEAD, BOYS—REMEMBER PEARL HARBOR!

WONDER WOMAN SWINGS INTO ACTION.

THIS LITTLE GUN OUGHT TO MAKE A HANDY WEAPON - LOOK OUT, NIPPIES, HERE I COME!

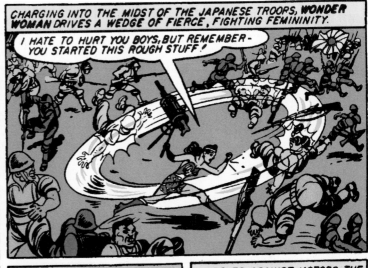

CHARGING INTO THE MIDST OF THE JAPANESE TROOPS, WONDER WOMAN DRIVES A WEDGE OF FIERCE, FIGHTING FEMININITY.

I HATE TO HURT YOU BOYS, BUT REMEMBER - YOU STARTED THIS ROUGH STUFF!

A HUGE JAP TANK LURCHES MENACINGLY FORWARD.

HR-RH! TANK'S GOT US!

LIKE A STREAK OF LIGHT WONDER WOMAN LEAPS STRAIGHT AT THE DEATH-DEALING MONSTER.

OUT OF MY WAY, BOYS - I'VE ALWAYS WANTED TO TACKLE A TANK!

MUSCLES AGAINST MOTORS, THE MIGHTY MECHANICAL JUGGERNAUT MEETS ITS MATCH IN WONDER WOMAN!

ALLEE-OOP! LUCKY THERE ARE NO GUNS IN A TANK'S UNDERSIDE!

AS THE JAP TANK MEN KEEP THEIR TRACTORS TURNING, THEY FORCE THE WAR WAGON INTO A COMPLETE SOMERSAULT AGAINST WONDER WOMAN'S UPWARD THRUST.

OVER SHE GOES!

WOMAN IS. WAR GOD! SHE ISS-S BLACK DRAGON! FLEE - THE DEMONS PURSUE US!

NEAT LITTLE JOB - BUT I MUSTN'T WASTE TIME. I'VE GOT TO CATCH SOME WANDERING JAP INTELLIGENCE OFFICER BEFORE THEY ALL HIGHTAIL!

10

RACING THROUGH THE RECAPTURED VILLAGE **WONDER WOMAN** OVERTAKES A JAPANESE STAFF CAR IN FULL FLIGHT.

I SORT OF FANCY THAT FAT LITTLE FELLOW IN THE MIDDLE - COME, FIDO!

MY NAME NOT FIDO! SS-SOMETHING COMPEL ME TELL TRUTH - I AM SANSU HIDEO, CAPTAIN NIPPONESE INTELLIGENCE!

WELL MET, CAP! YOU'RE THE ONE MAN IN ALL ASIA I WANT MOST ARDENTLY TO INTERVIEW.

LET'S PLAY YOU'RE A JAP BEETLE! TELL ME - WHY DID YOU MARK MAE WU'S BACK WITH A WHIP?

MARKS MEAN FOURTH MONTH, THIRD DAY! INFORM OUR AGENTS WHEN TO RELEASE JAPANESE GNATS ALL OVER AMERICA.

JAP GNATS - WHAT ARE THEY? EXPLAIN!

THEY LITTLE BUGS LIKE FLEAS - CARRY NEW **"WOMANIA"** GERM - MAKE WOMAN BITTEN BY JAP GNATS HATE ALL MEN - ATTACK THEM!

WELL, STEVE WAS RIGHT! SO YOUR AGENTS PLAN TO RELEASE GNATS TO MAKE AMERICAN WOMEN HATE THEIR MEN! GIVE ME YOUR LIST OF AGENTS!

PLEASS-SE - NO HAVE GOT! ONLY LIST INTELLIGENCE HEADQUARTERS, IN CHING FU!

I HAVE A PLAN - YOU SHALL TAKE ME TO CHING FU! BUT FIRST WE'LL RUN BACK TO THE AMERICAN CAMP AND DRESS UP FOR THE TRIP!

PLEASS-SE! LET ME WALK!

MAE WU AND HER CHINESE GIRL FRIENDS CHAIN **WONDER WOMAN** AS HIDEO'S CAPTIVE. BUT THE MAGIC LASSO ON HER WRIST MAKES HIDEO THE REAL PRISONER!

VERY CLEVER - CAPTOR MUST OBEY CAPTIVE!

RIGHT, MARCH, HIDEO, TO CHING FU!

11

PAULA, MEANWHILE, REACHES GENERAL VON BOP'S QUARTERS IN CHING FU.

ACH, HEINRICH! SURELY YOU REMEMBER PAULA VON GUNTHER, GESTAPO 6 KZQ?

BUT YOUR FACE, BARONESS! IT HAS CHANGED!

BAH! NEVER DID I THINK MY FACIAL OPERATION WOULD DECEIVE YOU!

ONE CAN NEVER BE TOO CAREFUL! ONE MOMENT AND I WILL COMPARE THESE PRINTS WITH THE BARONESS'S RECORDS.

IT IS THE BARONESS! BUT WHAT'S THIS—WONDER WOMAN RESCUED PAULA'S CHILD FROM A NAZI PRISON CAMP. ACH HIMMEL! THIS LOOKS SUSPICIOUS—SHE MAY HAVE TURNED AGAINST US!

A THOUSAND PARDONS, DEAR LADY! YOUR CLEVERNESS AT DISGUISE DECEIVED EVEN ME! HOW CAN I SERVE YOU?

I WANT A LIST OF JAPANESE SECRET AGENTS IN AMERICA—THE JAPS KEEP DELAYING. CAN YOU GET IT FOR ME?

VON BOP'S SUSPICIONS BECOME A CERTAINTY— HE PUSHES A SECRET BUTTON IN HIS DESK.

PLEASS-SE-RAISS-SE HANDS!

WHAT'S THIS?

I KNOW YOU WANT THAT LIST FOR WONDER WOMAN, BARONESS! TAKE THE PRISONER TO GENERAL BLATSU FOR "EXAMINATION!"

HIDEO, MEANWHILE, COMPELLED BY THE MAGIC LASSO, TAKES WONDER WOMAN TO GENERAL BLATSU.

THESE CHAINS, GENERAL, DEPRIVE THE PRISONER OF HER MAGIC STRENGTH!

IS-SS TRUE—HAVE HEARD ABOUT WONDER WOMAN! SS-SO NICE TO MEET HER!

12

IS-SS PLEASANT SURPRISE FOR YOU, WONDER WOMAN! YOUR AGENT, YES-SS? SHE'S ABOUT TO BE "EXAMINED." YOU BOTH SS-SEEK OUR LIST OF AMERICAN SECRET AGENTS!

I'VE GOT TO ACT QUICKLY!

BREAKING THE CHAIN THAT BINDS HER TO HIDEO, WONDER WOMAN WHIRLS ON BLATSU.

HERE'S A PLEASANT SURPRISE FOR YOU, GENERAL! YOU'RE COMPELLED TO OBEY ME!

GENERAL BLATSU GIVES WONDER WOMAN THE JAPANESE SPY LIST.

THANK YOU, GENERAL—YOU JAPANESE ARE SO POLITE!

I-I-SS-SOME-THING COMPELS ME!

FORCING HER TWO PRISONERS TO TURN THEIR BACKS, WONDER WOMAN PERFORMS AN ODD ACT.

LUCKY PAULA COVER-ED HER SKIN WITH THAT CHEM-ICAL SHE INVENTED - IT'LL RECORD THIS LIST IN INVISIBLE INK! NO TELLING WHAT MAY HAPPEN —

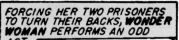

AS WONDER WOMAN TURNS TO SECURE THE PRISONERS, A GUARD SLIPS INTO THE ROOM.

SS-SURRENDER, WONDER WOMAN, OR I SS-SHOOT YOUR FRIEND!

I-I HAVE NO CHOICE- HOW STUPID OF ME!

WE KNOW NOW HOW TO HOLD WONDER WOMAN- KEEP DEATH ALWAYS READY AT THE BARONESS-SS' THROAT! HA! HA! I HAVE AMUS-SING IDEA- TAKE PRISS-SONERS AWAY!

A PLATFORM WITH TWO CAGES IS ERECTED IN THE PUBLIC SQUARE - BY PROCLAMATION JAPANESE RESIDENTS ONLY ARE PERMITTED TO WITNESS THE FORTHCOMING SPECTACLE.

IS SAID AMERICAN WOMEN TO BE EXECUTED!

NO! NO! WONDER WOMAN HERSELF IS TO BE MADE CRAZY!

PAULA IS FIRST SECURED.

DEATH AT YOUR THROAT, BARON-ESS-SS! IF WONDER WOMAN NOT SUBMIT, I SS-STRANGLE YOU!

IF YOU PULL THAT ROPE, FAT FOOL, WON-DER WOMAN'LL THROW YOU OVER THE HIMALAYAS.

BUT WONDER WOMAN WALKS SUBMISSIVELY INTO HER CAGE.

WONDER WOMAN IS-SS HUMAN AFTER ALL! SHE IS PRISS- SONER! MM- A-A-AH!

GENERAL BLATSU ANNOUNCES THE SPECTACLE TO FOLLOW. WE DEMONSTRATE FOR PEOPLE OF JAPAN HOW WOMEN OF AMERICA TOMORROW SHALL BE DRIVEN MAD! JAPANESE GNATS INFECTED WITH BACILLUS "WOMANIA" WILL BE RELEASED IN PRISONERS' CAGES—WATCH CLOSELY THE SO INTERESTING EFFECT OF NOBLE GERMS!

BANZAI!!

BUT AS BLATSU THRUSTS A BOX OF JAP GNATS INTO HER CAGE, **WONDER WOMAN'S** PATIENCE AND HER CHAINS SNAP VIOLENTLY.

GNATS TO YOU, NIPPO! EXCUSE MY PUN—YOU'LL SOON FEEL *PUNISHED!*

AGH-UG-OOP!

THE BOX BREAKS AND A CLOUD OF JAPANESE GNATS SPREADS OVER THE SPECTATORS.

SH-RR-R-IER! OW-WOW-OO! DOWN WITH MEN!

YA-AAH-UMBA! KILL ALL HUSBANDS!

BLATSU, HURLED INTO THE CROWD BY **WONDER WOMAN,** IS ATTACKED WITH SAVAGE FEROCITY BY JAPANESE WOMEN.

GR-RR-RR SNAR-RL! "LORD" BLATSU—"GENERAL" BLATSU—HO HO! MEN ARE NO LONGER OUR MASTERS—*KILL BLATSU!*

AI-EEE! HELP—MERCY!

A JAPANESE GIRL BITTEN BY GNATS AND MAD WITH SUDDEN HATRED OF MEN, SEIZES HIDEO'S THROAT IN A MANIACAL DEATH GRIP.

AGGH! DEATH TO ALL MEN!

TIME TO LEAVE, PAULA! I'LL WRAP YOU IN THIS WIRE MESH TO PROTECT YOU FROM JAP GNATS—THEIR BITES DO NOT INFECT ME BECAUSE I DRANK FROM THE FOUNTAIN OF YOUTH ON PARADISE ISLAND.

CARRYING PAULA, **WONDER WOMAN** RACES TO HER AMAZON PLANE.

WE MUST GET THAT SPY LIST BACK TO AMERICA QUICKLY!

RIGHT! REMEMBER I'M YOUR HUMAN DOCUMENT—DON'T TEAR ME!

REACHING WASHINGTON IN RECORD TIME, **WONDER WOMAN** LEADS THE WAY TO PAULA'S FORMER LABORATORY.

I'VE KEPT YOUR SECRET WORKSHOP, SLAVES AND ALL, THINKING THEY'D BE NEEDED IN APHRODITE'S SERVICE.

YOU THINK OF EVERYTHING, **WONDER WOMAN!**

AFTER TREATING PAULA'S BACK WITH CHEMICALS IT IS PHOTOGRAPHED UNDER INFRARED RAYS.

OKAY, PAULA - THE SPY LIST SHOWS CLEARLY IN **GREEN** PRINT!

THAT'S RIGHT! BUT THE PHOTO WILL BE BLACK AND WHITE.

WITHIN 10 MINUTES **WONDER WOMAN** DELIVERS THE PRINTED SPY LIST TO STEVE.

HERE ARE THE AXIS AGENTS WHO WILL RELEASE JAP GNATS IN EVERY CITY IN AMERICA TOMORROW! YOU'VE GOT TO GET EVERY ONE OF THEM QUICK - I'LL EXPLAIN LATER!

OKAY, ANGEL, WE'LL GET 'EM, DON'T WORRY!

WITH ALL TELEPHONE LINES CLEARED FOR NATIONAL EMERGENCY, ARMY INTELLIGENCE SENDS ITS AGENTS SCURRYING THROUGHOUT THE COUNTRY TO EXTERMINATE THE NIPPONESE PERIL!

SEATTLE - AGENT 4 KX! ARREST SHINSU TODO-

MIAMI? MAX SCHULTZ- ATTABOY! KILL THE GNATS!

OKAY, SAN FRANCISCO- GOT 'EM ALL?

JUST BEFORE DAWN ETTA CANDY BRINGS IN THE LAST ELUSIVE SPY FROM BALTIMORE.

THIS DOUBLE- TWISTED LITTLE PIPSQUEAK TRIED TO GNAT MY GIRLS! I'LL—

HELP! S-SHE KILL ME- GNATS BITE HER!

NONSENSE! IT DOESN'T TAKE GNATS TO MAKE ETTA CANDY WALLOP JAPS!

POW!

WE'VE GOT THEM ALL, ANGEL, THANKS TO YOU AND PAULA!

YOU HAVE SAVED THE WOMEN OF AMERICA! ER- BY THE WAY- I HOPE DIANA'S SAFE?

DIANA'S SAFE AS I AM- I'M EXPECTING HER BACK ANY MINUTE!

DO- DO YOU THINK I PASSED THE FIRST TEST OF APHRODITE?

THAT IS FOR THE GODDESS TO DECIDE! BUT I HAVE NEVER HAD A BRAVER OR MORE LOYAL COMPANION THAN YOU, PAULA- NOR ONE HALF SO CLEVER!

15A

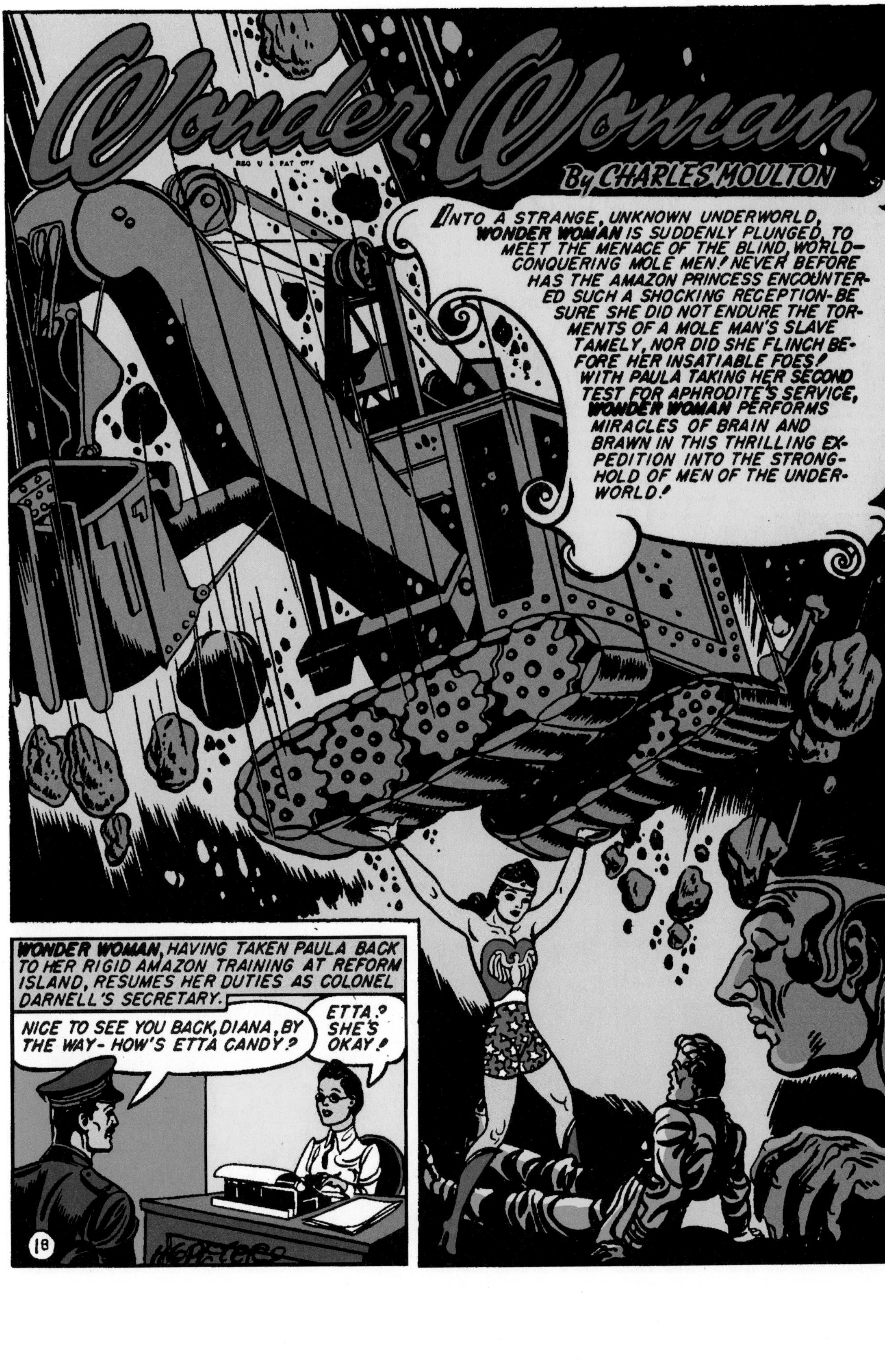
Wonder Woman
REG. U. S. PAT. OFF.
By CHARLES MOULTON
INTO A STRANGE, UNKNOWN UNDERWORLD, WONDER WOMAN IS SUDDENLY PLUNGED, TO MEET THE MENACE OF THE BLIND WORLD-CONQUERING MOLE MEN! NEVER BEFORE HAS THE AMAZON PRINCESS ENCOUNTERED SUCH A SHOCKING RECEPTION-BE SURE SHE DID NOT ENDURE THE TORMENTS OF A MOLE MAN'S SLAVE TAMELY, NOR DID SHE FLINCH BEFORE HER INSATIABLE FOES! WITH PAULA TAKING HER SECOND TEST FOR APHRODITE'S SERVICE, WONDER WOMAN PERFORMS MIRACLES OF BRAIN AND BRAWN IN THIS THRILLING EXPEDITION INTO THE STRONGHOLD OF MEN OF THE UNDERWORLD!
WONDER WOMAN, HAVING TAKEN PAULA BACK TO HER RIGID AMAZON TRAINING AT REFORM ISLAND, RESUMES HER DUTIES AS COLONEL DARNELL'S SECRETARY.
NICE TO SEE YOU BACK, DIANA, BY THE WAY- HOW'S ETTA CANDY?
ETTA? SHE'S OKAY!
18

MY FRIEND MAJOR BLEND WANTS A GIRL'S BAND FOR AN ENTERTAINMENT HIS BOYS ARE GIVING. DO YOU SUPPOSE THE HOLLIDAY COLLEGE GIRLS WILL PLAY?

I'M SURE THEY WILL—I'LL ASK ETTA.

LATER

ETTA SAYS THE HOLLIDAY BAND WILL PLAY IF YOU THINK THEY'RE GOOD ENOUGH—SHE WANTS YOU TO COME OUT AND LISTEN TO A REHEARSAL.

ER-AHEM! I THINK YOU'D BETTER COME WITH ME, DIANA.

THE HOLLIDAY COLLEGE GIRLS STRUT THEIR STUFF FOR COLONEL DARNELL.

FOR HE'S A JOLLY GOOD FEL-LOW!

THE GIRLS KNOW YOU, COLONEL!

TEN PRETTY GIRLS AT THE VILLAGE SCHOOL—AND A BOY LOVED THEM ALL—CUTE AND FAT, SHORT AND TALL—BUT YOU CAN'T MARRY TEN PRETTY GIRLS!

HA! HA! THEY'RE GOOD!

GLORY, GLORY HALLELUJAH! GLORY, GLORY—

THIS BAND IS JUST WHAT WE WANT!

I'LL TELL ETTA—

AS DIANA TALKS TO ETTA CANDY A RUMBLING, TERRIFYING ROAR COMES FROM THE GROUND BENEATH THEIR FEET!

DRIVELLING DRUMSTICKS! WHAT'S THAT NOISE?

I'VE NO IDEA!

2B

THE EARTH TREMBLES AS JETS OF BLACK GAS BURST FORTH FROM UNDERGROUND.

E-EEK! LOOK OUT!

WOO WOO! IT'S AN EARTHQUAKE!

HISS-SS!!
HIS-SS-SS!!
HIS-SS

HOLLIDAY

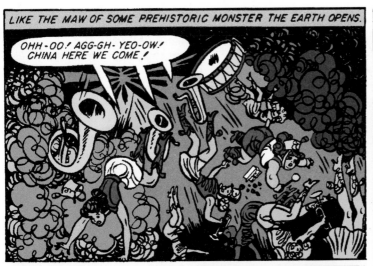

LIKE THE MAW OF SOME PREHISTORIC MONSTER THE EARTH OPENS.

OHH-OO! AGG-GH-YEO-OW! CHINA HERE WE COME!

DIANA, FEELING THE EARTH SLIPPING BENEATH HER FEET, CALLS UPON HER AMAZON POWERS AND LEAPS ABOVE THE FALLING GIRLS.

YE GODS! HERE'S WHERE I NEED MERCURY'S WINGED SANDALS!

DIANA-OH! DIAN-NA!! GREAT HEAVENS-SHE'S LOST!

POOR COLONEL DARNELL-HE THINKS I'M KILLED! I HATE TO WORRY HIM BUT I'VE GOT TO WORK AS WONDER WOMAN AND I CAN'T WASTE TIME.

CHANGING TO WONDER WOMAN AS SHE RUNS, THE AMAZON MAIDEN RACES TOWARD HER INVISIBLE PLANE.

THAT WAS NO EARTHQUAKE! THAT HOLE IN THE EARTH WAS OPENED BY HUMANS- I COULD SEE THEM FAR, FAR BELOW!

I'VE GOT TO INVESTIGATE THE EARTH'S DEPTHS AND I NEED PAULA- SHE HAS GREAT SCIENTIFIC KNOWLEDGE.

MEANWHILE, AT REFORM ISLAND, PAULA IS GREATLY DEPRESSED.

WHY PAULA! NOT WORKING? WHAT'S THE MATTER?

I- I KNOW I FAILED APHRODITE'S FIRST TEST-SHE HASN'T SENT FOR ME SINCE I RETURNED TO TRAINING SCHOOL!

3B

SUPPOSE YOU DID FAIL-THAT'S ALL THE MORE REASON FOR WORKING HARDER! I'M GOING TO PUT YOU THROUGH SOME REAL EXERCISES!

I'LL DO ANYTHING YOU SAY, MISTRESS!

JUST TO LIMBER UP CHIN YOURSELF 50 TIMES! THIS IS THE KIND OF EXERCISE WHERE CHAINS HELP TO STRENGTHEN A GIRL - THEY GIVE YOU MORE WEIGHT TO LIFT.

THEY CERTAINLY DO!

YOU DID VERY WELL, PAULA! YOU COULDN'T HAVE CHINNED YOURSELF EVEN ONCE, A MONTH AGO, WITH THIS 100-POUND WEIGHT ON YOUR FEET! NOW WE'LL SEE HOW HARD YOU CAN HIT AT SINGLE STICK!

EE-OW! A LUSTY BLOW, MY GIRL - GOOD WORK!

I'M NOT AFRAID TO TRUST MY STRENGTH NOW- I KNOW YOU AMAZONS CAN TAKE IT!

PAULA, WITH HER CHAIN BANDS, MUST DEFEND HERSELF AGAINST A DOUBLE SWORD ATTACK.

WELL DEFENDED! HEAVY FETTERS HAVE STRENGTHENED YOUR ARM MUSCLES.

THE QUEEN'S MESSENGER ARRIVES.

APHRODITE SUMMONS PAULA TO THE TEMPLE!

THE GODDESS HAS SEEN YOUR NEW STRENGTH AND SKILL, PAULA-GO QUICKLY!

OH-I WILL! I'M EXCITED AS A SCHOOL GIRL!

IN THE TEMPLE OF APHRODITE.

OH DIVINE GODDESS, I PRESENT THE NEOPHYTE PAULA, AS YOU COMMANDED!

I WAITED TO SUMMON THEE, NEOPHYTE, BECAUSE THY FIRST TEST LEFT SOME DOUBT OF THY WORTHINESS TO TAKE THE SECOND!

I KNEW- SOB-SOB- THAT I HAD FAILED!

THOU MADE MISTAKES- NOT TRUSTING THY NEWFOUND STRENGTH THOU TRIED TRICKERY- DECEPTION. BUT MALA HAS CURED THY FAULT- TODAY AT EXERCISES THOU RELIED UPON THY WOMAN'S POWER AND WON!

4B

OH I AM SO GLAD! NOW MAY I TAKE MY SECOND TEST?

YES! THY SECOND TASK WILL BE TO CAPTURE THE MEN OF THE UNDERWORLD.

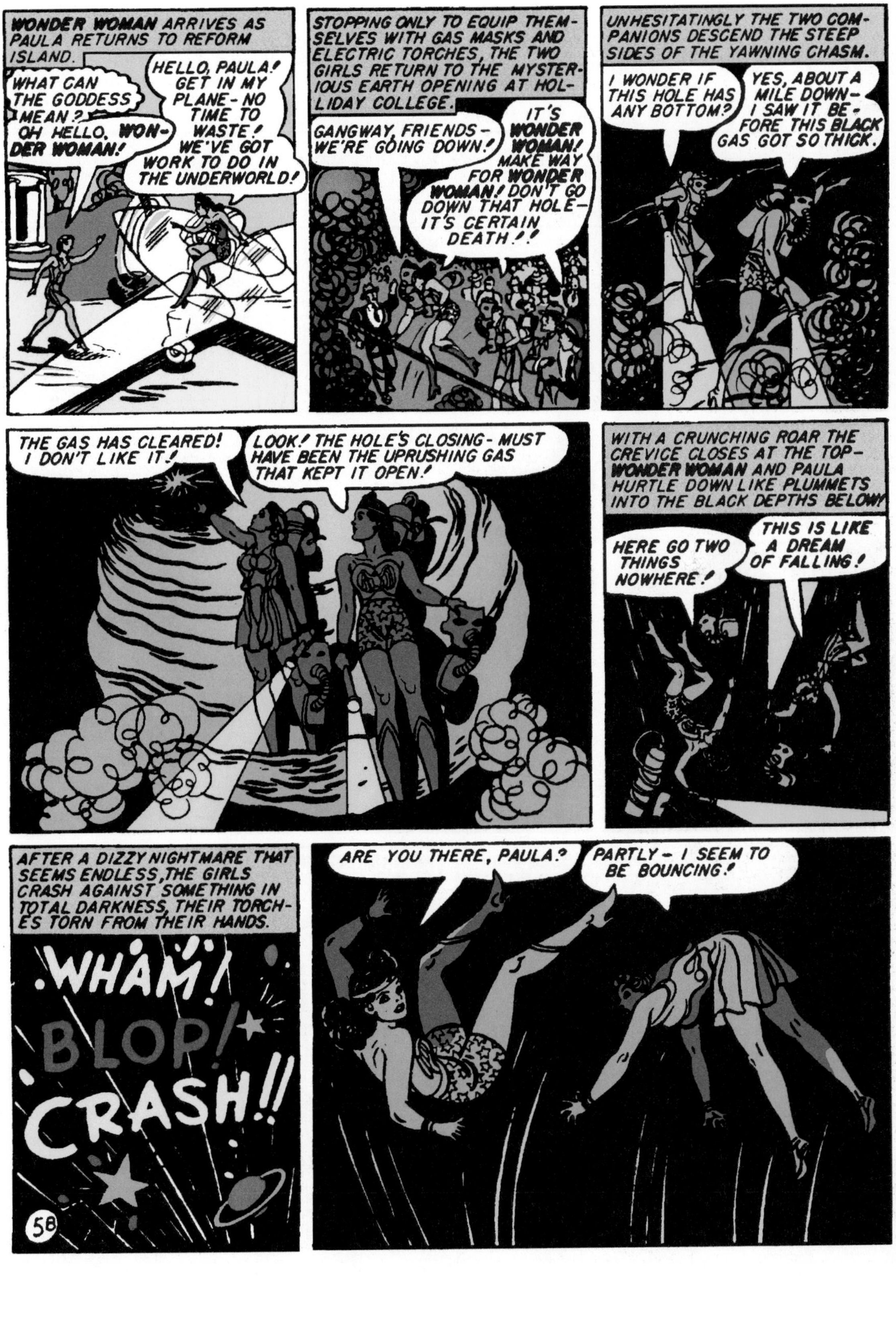
WONDER WOMAN ARRIVES AS PAULA RETURNS TO REFORM ISLAND.
WHAT CAN THE GODDESS MEAN? OH HELLO, WONDER WOMAN!
HELLO, PAULA! GET IN MY PLANE - NO TIME TO WASTE! WE'VE GOT WORK TO DO IN THE UNDERWORLD!
STOPPING ONLY TO EQUIP THEMSELVES WITH GAS MASKS AND ELECTRIC TORCHES, THE TWO GIRLS RETURN TO THE MYSTERIOUS EARTH OPENING AT HOLLIDAY COLLEGE.
GANGWAY, FRIENDS - WE'RE GOING DOWN!
IT'S WONDER WOMAN! MAKE WAY FOR WONDER WOMAN! DON'T GO DOWN THAT HOLE - IT'S CERTAIN DEATH!!
UNHESITATINGLY THE TWO COMPANIONS DESCEND THE STEEP SIDES OF THE YAWNING CHASM.
I WONDER IF THIS HOLE HAS ANY BOTTOM?
YES, ABOUT A MILE DOWN - I SAW IT BEFORE THIS BLACK GAS GOT SO THICK.
THE GAS HAS CLEARED! I DON'T LIKE IT!
LOOK! THE HOLE'S CLOSING - MUST HAVE BEEN THE UPRUSHING GAS THAT KEPT IT OPEN!
WITH A CRUNCHING ROAR THE CREVICE CLOSES AT THE TOP - WONDER WOMAN AND PAULA HURTLE DOWN LIKE PLUMMETS INTO THE BLACK DEPTHS BELOW!
HERE GO TWO THINGS NOWHERE!
THIS IS LIKE A DREAM OF FALLING!
AFTER A DIZZY NIGHTMARE THAT SEEMS ENDLESS, THE GIRLS CRASH AGAINST SOMETHING IN TOTAL DARKNESS, THEIR TORCHES TORN FROM THEIR HANDS.
WHAM!
BLOP!
CRASH!!
58
ARE YOU THERE, PAULA?
PARTLY - I SEEM TO BE BOUNCING!

WE HAVE CAUGHT YOU, GIRLS OF THE UPPER WORLD! LIE STILL AND YOU WON'T BE HURT!

LET'S CAPTURE THEM, **WONDER WOMAN**!

NO—THEY SEEM FRIENDLY, AND IF WE SURRENDER THEY'LL LEAD US TO THE OTHER PRISONERS.

THE LUMINOUS GIRLS WRAP PAULA AND **WONDER WOMAN** TIGHTLY IN SHEETS OF TRANSPARENT RUBBER.

WHERE ARE WE—WHO ARE YOU?

YOU'RE IN THE UNDER-WORLD, RULED BY MOLE MEN! WE ARE THE MOLE MEN'S SLAVES!

WE'RE SORRY FOR YOU—WE WERE CAPTURED FROM THE UPPER WORLD LIKE YOU. THE MOLE MEN ARE BLIND—THEY USE US SLAVES FOR EYES AND OH! THEY ARE CRUEL MASTERS!

BUT HOW CAN **YOU** SEE IN THIS DARKNESS?

IT GROWS LIGHT AS DAY WHEN A GIRL'S EYES GET USED TO IT. MEN'S EYES NEVER BE-COME ADAPTED— THEY GO BLIND QUICKLY LIKE THE MOLE MEN!

THESE METAL POSTS ARE HEAV-ILY CHARGED WITH EARTH STATIC- YOUR RUBBER COVER-ING PROTECTS YOU IF YOU MAKE NO ATTEMPT TO ESCAPE! OUR MASTERS WILL BE HERE PRESENTLY TO DETERMINE YOUR FATE!

I CAN HARDLY WAIT!

BLAKFU, KING OF THE MOLE MEN, FOLLOWS HIS EYES' INTO THE ROOM.

HURRY, STUPID SLAVE- I SAW YOU STUMBLE!

6B

HE SAID HE **SAW** HER STUMBLE YET HIS EYES ARE CLOSED!

THE WOMEN'S BODIES, TREATED WITH PHOTONIC CHEMICALS, GLOW IN THE DARK, AS YOU HAVE SEEN. THEY GENERATE UL-TRAVIOLET RAYS WHICH PENETRATE THE MOLE MEN'S EYELIDS.

I CANNOT **SEE** THESE PRISONERS - THEY'RE NOT PREPARED! WHERE'S CALLA, THE CHIEF SLAVE?

I AM HERE, MASTER! THESE PRISONERS HAVE JUST BEEN CAPTURED — THEY FELL THROUGH THE EARTH DOOR AS IT CLOSED!

NO EXCUSE! REPORT FOR 40 LASHES AT SLAVE CALL! APPLY PHOTONIC FLUID TO THESE CAPTIVES IMMEDIATELY - CHAIN THEM AND BRING THEM BACK TO ME!

YOUR SLAVE OBEYS, MASTER!

PAINT THESE GIRLS WITH PHOTONIC! THE MASTER SAID NOTHING ABOUT CHANGING THEIR COSTUMES - LET THEM KEEP THEIR PRESENT CLOTHES EXCEPT OF COURSE THEIR SHOES!

OG-SLUP! ST-LOP IT!

WILL YOU LET ME WEAR MY BOOTS AND GOLDEN LASSO AFTER I'M PAINTED?

OH NO - I WOULDN'T DARE! THEY'LL BE KEPT BY OUR GUARDS WITH THE OTHER SLAVES' CLOTHES!

THESE SANDALS FEEL AS THOUGH THEY WILL BE HARD TO WEAR!

HA! HA! SISTER, YOU DON'T KNOW WHAT IRON SHOES DO TO A GIRL BUT YOU'LL LEARN!

PAULA, ROUSED TO REBELLION, USES HER NEWLY ACQUIRED AMAZON STRENGTH.

HOLD YOUR ARM STILL - WE CAN'T KEEP THE MASTER WAITING! - UG - UNF!

I'M TIRED OF THIS MASTER "BUSINESS"! I'LL -

78

AN ELECTRIC SHOCK HOLDS PAULA RIGID!

SILLY SLAVE! IF YOU ESCAPE YOUR CHAINS YOU'RE PARALYZED! OUR SANDALS ARE CHARGED WITH EARTH STATIC WHICH PASSES THROUGH OUR FETTERS. IF WE BREAK THEM IT FLOWS THROUGH **US**!

THE MOLE MEN, MEANWHILE, HOLD A COUNCIL OF WAR IN THE KING'S THRONE ROOM.

THE OPENING WE BLEW WITH BLACK GAS TO THE UPPER WORLD MISSED WASHINGTON BY MILES—BAD MISTAKE!

BUT WE CAPTURED NEW EYES!

AS PAULA AND **WONDER WOMAN** ARE LED BEFORE THE KING THEY APPEAR TO THE MOLE MEN LIKE LUMINOUS FIGURES.

I BROUGHT THE NEW GIRLS, YOUR MAJESTY, AS YOU COMMANDED.

LEAVE THEM—I'LL EXAMINE THEM LATER!

BUT TO THE GIRLS THE ENTIRE SCENE IS CLEARLY VISIBLE.

WE MUST CONQUER AMERICA **NOW** AND RULE THE WORLD! FOR CENTURIES WE'VE WAITED FOR UPPER WORLD MEN TO WEAKEN. THE FIRST WORLD WAR SEEMED OUR OPPORTUNITY, BUT IT ENDED TOO QUICKLY—TOO MANY NATIONS SURVIVED!

TODAY 2 BILLION PEOPLE ARE FIGHTING ON EVERY CONTINENT! EVERY NATION IN THE WORLD HAS SEEN CHAOS AND BLOODSHED WITHIN ITS OWN BOUNDARIES, EXCEPT THE UNITED STATES—TAKING OVER THE REST OF THE BATTLE-SCARRED WORLD WILL BE **SIMPLE.**

BUT HOW CAN YOU CONQUER AMERICA?

WHA-AT! A SLAVE GIRL DARES TO SPEAK? I'LL ANSWER—THEN PUNISH! WE'LL UNDERMINE THE AMERICAN CAPITOL, DROP ALL IMPORTANT BUILDINGS TO THE UNDERWORLD, AND CAPTURE GOVERNMENT OFFICIALS. OUR EXCAVATIONS ARE NEARLY COMPLETE!

PUT THESE GIRLS IN THE WORK GANG WITH THE OTHER SLAVES—BUT WAIT! HOLD THIS GIRL FOR PUNISHMENT! CHAIN THE HEAVIEST BALL YOU'VE GOT TO HER NECK BUT MAKE HER KEEP PACE WITH HER COMPANIONS!

8B

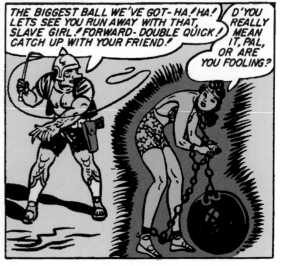

THE BIGGEST BALL WE'VE GOT—HA! HA! LET'S SEE YOU RUN AWAY WITH THAT, SLAVE GIRL! FORWARD—DOUBLE QUICK! CATCH UP WITH YOUR FRIEND!

D'YOU REALLY MEAN IT, PAL, OR ARE YOU FOOLING?

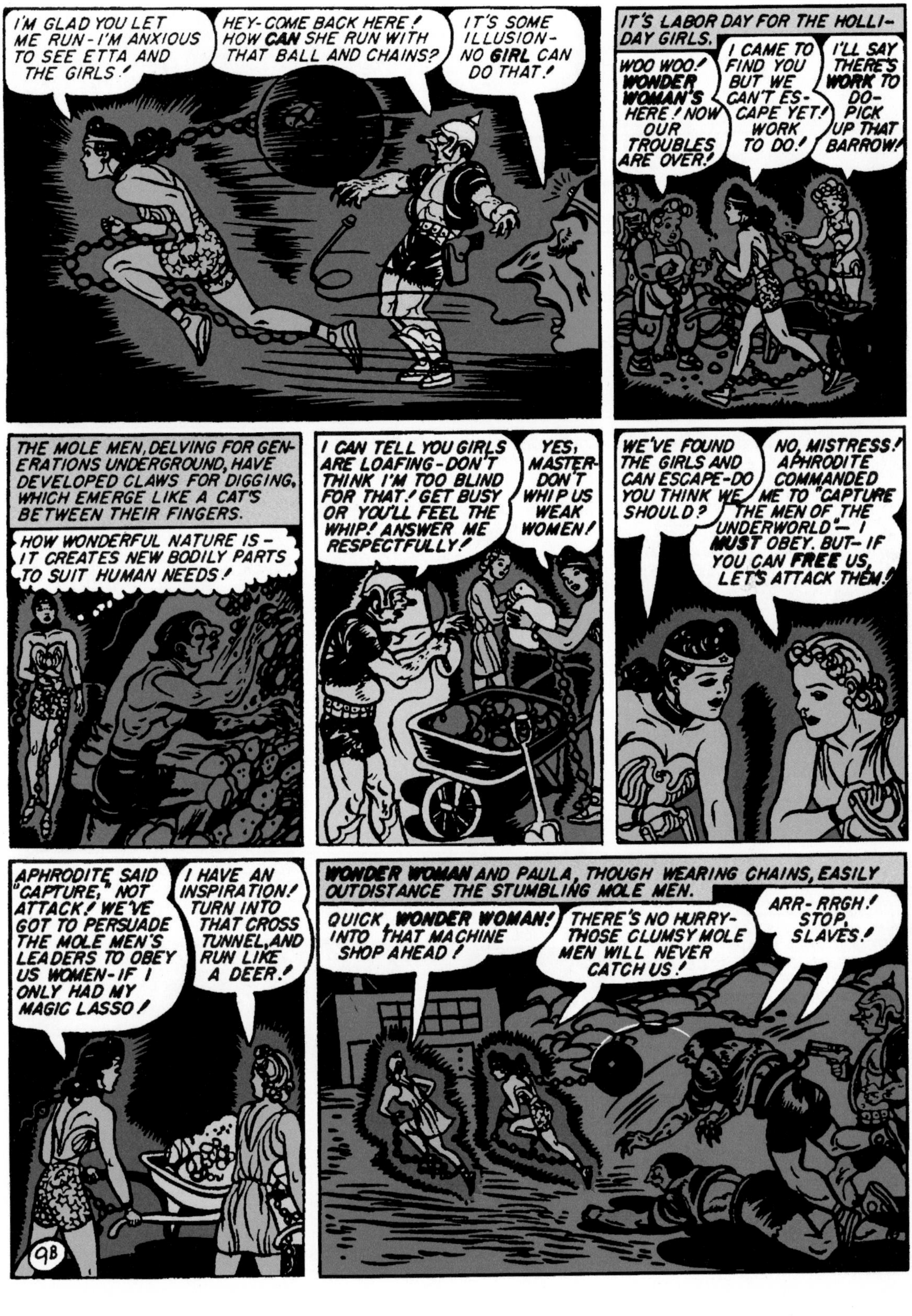
I'M GLAD YOU LET ME RUN - I'M ANXIOUS TO SEE ETTA AND THE GIRLS!
HEY- COME BACK HERE! HOW CAN SHE RUN WITH THAT BALL AND CHAINS?
IT'S SOME ILLUSION- NO GIRL CAN DO THAT!
IT'S LABOR DAY FOR THE HOLLIDAY GIRLS.
WOO WOO! WONDER WOMAN'S HERE! NOW OUR TROUBLES ARE OVER!
I CAME TO FIND YOU BUT WE CAN'T ESCAPE YET! WORK TO DO!
I'LL SAY THERE'S WORK TO DO- PICK UP THAT BARROW!
THE MOLE MEN, DELVING FOR GENERATIONS UNDERGROUND, HAVE DEVELOPED CLAWS FOR DIGGING, WHICH EMERGE LIKE A CAT'S BETWEEN THEIR FINGERS.
HOW WONDERFUL NATURE IS - IT CREATES NEW BODILY PARTS TO SUIT HUMAN NEEDS!
I CAN TELL YOU GIRLS ARE LOAFING - DON'T THINK I'M TOO BLIND FOR THAT! GET BUSY OR YOU'LL FEEL THE WHIP! ANSWER ME RESPECTFULLY!
YES, MASTER- DON'T WHIP US WEAK WOMEN!
WE'VE FOUND THE GIRLS AND CAN ESCAPE - DO YOU THINK WE SHOULD?
NO, MISTRESS! APHRODITE COMMANDED ME TO "CAPTURE THE MEN OF THE UNDERWORLD"- I MUST OBEY. BUT- IF YOU CAN FREE US, LET'S ATTACK THEM!
APHRODITE SAID "CAPTURE," NOT ATTACK! WE'VE GOT TO PERSUADE THE MOLE MEN'S LEADERS TO OBEY US WOMEN - IF I ONLY HAD MY MAGIC LASSO!
I HAVE AN INSPIRATION! TURN INTO THAT CROSS TUNNEL, AND RUN LIKE A DEER!
9B
WONDER WOMAN AND PAULA, THOUGH WEARING CHAINS, EASILY OUTDISTANCE THE STUMBLING MOLE MEN.
QUICK, WONDER WOMAN! INTO THAT MACHINE SHOP AHEAD!
THERE'S NO HURRY- THOSE CLUMSY MOLE MEN WILL NEVER CATCH US!
ARR- RRGH! STOP, SLAVES!

SAFE BEHIND STEEL DOORS, **WONDER WOMAN** PULLS OFF THEIR IRON SANDALS, THEN THEIR CHAINS.

I'LL MAKE LASSOS FOR ALL THE GIRLS AND CHARGE THEM WITH EARTH STATIC FROM THE BATTERIES HERE! WHILE THE ELECTRIC CHARGE LASTS, IT WILL PARALYZE THE MOLE MEN!

PAULA, YOU'RE A GENIUS!

TO PREPARE THE GIRLS FOR THEIR COMING REBELLION, **WONDER WOMAN** CRASHES THROUGH A STONE WALL.

THIS WILL LET ME OUT INTO A BACK PASSAGE WHILE THE MOLE MEN THINK I'M STILL WITH PAULA.

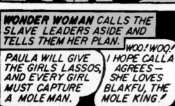

WONDER WOMAN CALLS THE SLAVE LEADERS ASIDE AND TELLS THEM HER PLAN.

PAULA WILL GIVE THE GIRLS LASSOS — AND EVERY GIRL MUST CAPTURE A MOLE MAN.

WOO! WOO! I HOPE CALLA AGREES — SHE LOVES BLAKFU, THE MOLE KING!

THE MOLE MEN WON'T BE HURT. THEY'LL **LOVE** TO BE CAPTURED BY GIRLS! IT WILL BE LOTS MORE FUN FOR THEM THAN FIGHTING AND KILLING PEOPLE!

WELL — LET'S TRY IT. I'M TIRED OF BEING FLOGGED!

BUT **WONDER WOMAN**, STEPPING THROUGH A DOORWAY, FAILS TO NOTICE THE METAL MAT AND —

UGH! I'M CAUGHT — THEIR METAL MAT IS CHARGED WITH STATIC! I'D BETTER HURRY THIS BUSINESS —

HO, GUARDS! COME AND GET ME!

WONDER WOMAN, ONCE MORE IN CHAINS, IS BROUGHT BEFORE THE KING FOR JUDGEMENT.

THE HEAVIEST SHACKLES WON'T SUBDUE THIS SLAVE — SHE MUST DIE! SUMMON THE MOLE LORDS AND ALL CAPTIVE WOMEN — WE'LL TEACH THEM A LESSON!

WHEN THIS GIRL'S CHAINS, ARE REMOVED, SHE MUST DANCE TO SAVE HERSELF FROM ELECTROCUTION! HER SLAVE SANDALS AND THE ELECTRIFIED FLOOR PLATE NEUTRALIZE EACH OTHER IF CONTACTS ARE BRIEF. BUT WHEN SHE STOPS DANCING, SHE WILL DIE!

GIRLS OFTEN SAY THEY CAN DANCE FOREVER - I WONDER HOW THEY'D LIKE TO BE IN MY PLACE AND REALLY *HAVE* TO!

TAKE IT EASY! AND REMEMBER - DON'T TAKE BOTH FEET OFF THE PLATE AT ONCE OR YOUR SANDALS WILL PARALYZE YOU!

PLEASE DON'T DANCE SO HARD - SAVE YOUR WIND! IT'LL TAKE PAULA *HOURS* TO MAKE THOSE LASSOS!

IT *DID* TAKE HOURS - BUT *WONDER WOMAN* DANCED TIRELESSLY ON, TO THE AMAZEMENT OF THE MOLE MEN.

SHE IS WONDERFUL! SHE'S A WITCH - SHE'LL DANCE FOREVER! ENOUGH OF THIS - KILL HER BY TORTURE!

SUDDENLY ETTA CANDY'S BAND BREAKS INTO MELODY.

MARCH ON, MARCH ON, ALL HEARTS RESOLVED - ON LIBERTY OR DEATH!

THAT'S THE SIGNAL! PAULA MUST HAVE SLIPPED THE GIRLS THEIR ELECTRIC LASSOS.

COME ON, KIDS - DANCE!

THE SLAVE GIRLS' DANCING, AS SEEN BY MOLE MEN, IS A FASCINATING SPECTACLE.

WHILE THE UNDERWORLD MEN SIT ENTRANCED, THE SLAVE GIRLS CIRCLE NEARER AND EVER NEARER THEIR INTENDED VICTIMS.

FROM THE LAND OF THE SKY-BLUE WATER, THERE CAME A CAPTIVE MAID!

11B

SUDDENLY, WITH ONE UNITED SHRIEK, THE DANCERS POUNCE ON THEIR PREY - EVERY GIRL LASSOS A MOLEMAN!

AI-EEE-EEK!

I MANAGED TO TEAR THOSE SANDALS OFF BEFORE THEY PARALYZED ME - NOW FOR SOME FUN!

61

THE PARALYZING LASSO CURRENTS SOON TAKE EFFECT, AND THE FIGHT IS WON.

SPORT'S OVER! BUT I'M GLAD TO GET MY BOOTS AND LASSO BACK! TIE UP YOUR MEN, GIRLS, THEN UNLOCK YOUR CHAINS-ELECTRIC SANDALS *FIRST!*

KING BLAKFU, WILL YOU MAKE CALLA YOUR QUEEN, AND RULE THE UNDERWORLD IN PEACE, AS SHE DIRECTS?

I-I'M CRAZY ABOUT CALLA-BUT I WON'T MAKE HER QUEEN!

I HAVE AN IDEA-WELL TRY AN EXPERIMENT!

WITH PRACTICED SURGICAL SKILL **WONDER WOMAN** REMOVES THE DEAD MEMBRANE THAT SEALS BLAKFU'S EYES.

SOON YOU SHALL SEE AGAIN, BLAKFU!

I DON'T *WANT* TO SEE-LET MY EYES ALONE!

TOGETHER PAULA AND **WONDER WOMAN** TREAT BLAKFU'S OPTIC NERVES WITH CHEMICO-ELECTRICAL APPLICATIONS.

CAN YOU SEE ANYTHING?

I CAN SEE LIGHT-ALL COLORS!

HIS VISION IS RESTORED!

FREEING BLAKFU, **WONDER WOMAN** LEADS HIM TO THE NOW LIGHTED THRONE ROOM AND REMOVES HIS EYE BANDAGE.

BLAKFU, BEHOLD YOUR QUEEN!

CALLA-CAN IT BE YOU? I NEVER KNEW THAT SUCH BEAUTY EXISTED, UNTIL THIS MINUTE!

NOW THAT I'VE OPENED YOUR EYES TO THE BEAUTY OF WOMEN, WILL YOU BE GUIDED BY QUEEN CALLA?

I IMPLORE YOU TO RULE ME, BELOVED QUEEN!

THAT'S HARDER THAN BEING YOUR SLAVE-BUT I'LL TRY!

WONDER WOMAN AND PAULA RESTORE SIGHT TO ALL MOLE MEN.

THAT LIGHT'S TOO BRIGHT-IT HURTS MY EYES!

YOU'LL SOON GET USED TO IT-WHEN YOU SEE THE GIRL IN THE NEXT ROOM YOU'LL WANT IT BRIGHTER!

WOO WOO! LOOK **WONDER WOMAN,** I FOUND SOME CANDY!

GIVE ME THAT-IT'S A DYNAMITE STICK! NOW THAT THE MOLE MEN ARE SUBDUED, I'LL SET SOME OF THIS DYNAMITE TO BLAST OUR WAY OUT!

STEVE AND COLONEL DARNELL, MEANWHILE, ARE TRYING FRANTICALLY TO REOPEN THE TUNNEL TO THE UNDERWORLD.

IT'S NO USE—THE POOR GIRLS MUST BE BURIED!

THERE'S JUST A CHANCE THEY FELL THROUGH INTO SOME NATURAL CAVE!

SUDDENLY THE SIDES OF THE EXCAVATION COLLAPSE, BURYING STEVE AND THE COLONEL UNDER TONS OF EARTH.

THEY SHOULDA SHORED THE SIDES!

STEAM SHOVEL'S BURIED TOO—NO HOPE FOR THOSE ARMY GUYS!

BUT AT THIS MOMENT WONDER WOMAN, FAR BELOW, SETS OFF HER DYNAMITE.

ROAR! BOOM!

GREAT JUPITER— LOOK! MEN FALLING—GET LIFE NET QUICK!

COLONEL DARNELL FALLS SAFELY INTO THE RESILIENT RUBBER.

AW, COME ON DOWN, COLONEL! THERE'S MORE COMIN' BEHIND YA!

BEFORE THE GIRLS CAN GET SET AGAIN WITH THE LIFE NET, STEVE TREVOR HURTLES DOWNWARD.

GREAT CAESAR'S GHOST— WONDER WOMAN!

NICE OF YOU TO DROP IN ON ME, STEVE!

13B

BUT BEFORE STEVE CAN MOVE, A STEAM SHOVEL FOLLOWS TREVOR THROUGH THE HOLE ABOVE!

WHEE-EW! THIS IS A MATTER OF SPLIT SECONDS—NOT EVEN TIME TO JUMP!

DROPPING STEVE AT HER FEET, **WONDER WOMAN** CATCHES THE STEAM SHOVEL ON UPSTRETCHED ARMS! THE STRAIN IS TERRIFIC—CAN SHE KEEP THE MASSIVE MACHINE FROM CRUSHING THE MAN SHE LOVES?

I WILL DO IT FOR STEVE!

THE INTREPID AMAZON MAIDEN WINS—SHE HOLDS THAT HUGE WEIGHT IMMOVABLE!

GET OUT FROM UNDER STEVE— I'M BORED WITH THIS ATLAS JOB!

MY ANGEL, YOU'RE WONDERFUL BEYOND WORDS!

WE'LL GIVE THIS STEAM SHOVEL TO THE MOLE MEN. I'M SURE THEY'LL USE IT TO GOOD PURPOSE! HOW CAN WE CLIMB OUT?

WE HAD A MILE OF ROPE LADDER ABOVE, READY FOR EMERGENCIES. THEY'LL LOWER IT SOON!

A STONE KNOCKED THE COLONEL UNCONSCIOUS— I'LL CARRY HIM UP!

IN THE CONFUSION ABOVE GROUND, **WONDER WOMAN** DISAPPEARS. A FEW MINUTES LATER—

DIANA! THE HOLE'S CLOSING—WHERE'S WONDER WOMAN?

SHE AND PAULA JUST DASHED PAST ME FOR PARADISE ISLE—WON'T I DO TO CONSOLE YOU?

AS THE COLONEL RECOVERS CONSCIOUSNESS, DIANA IS HIS FIRST THOUGHT.

DIANA! THANK APHRODITE YOU ARE SAVED!

COLONEL, YOU'RE TALKING MY LANGUAGE!

148

IT'S FUNNY HOW ONE GIRL CAN BE TWO PEOPLE— AND SOME MEN'LL LIKE HER ONE WAY, SOME THE OTHER! BUT WHICHEVER PERSON SHE IS AT THE MOMENT, THE SILLY THING ALWAYS LIKES THE **SAME MAN!**

WONDER WOMAN

By Charles Moulton

LOYAL LAW ENFORCEMENT AGENCIES KEEP CEASELESS VIGIL AGAINST PROWLING PLUNDERERS AND LOOTERS WHO WORK OUTSIDE THE LAW. BUT HOW ABOUT CONSCIENCELESS RASCALS WHO OUTWARDLY PROFESS LOVE FOR THEIR COUNTRY AND ITS LAWS? SCHEMING ROBBER BARONS WHO HIDE BEHIND A FALSE WALL OF DECENCY, AND CALLOUSLY DEFY THE PRINCIPLES OF DEMOCRACY AS THEY TRY TO PLUNDER THE VERY GOVERNMENT ITSELF BY CORNERING THE MARKET ON A PRODUCT ESSENTIAL TO THE SUCCESSFUL PROSECUTION OF THE WAR EFFORT!

IT IS AGAINST SUCH RUTHLESS ROGUES AS THESE THAT **WONDER WOMAN**--AIDED BY THE SCIENTIFIC WIZARDRY OF PAULA, NOW UNDERGOING HER THIRD TREMENDOUS TEST FOR APHRODITE'S SERVICE--PITS HER HAIR-TRIGGER BRAIN AND INCREDIBLE STRENGTH....

DIANA DISCOVERS AN ARMY INTELLIGENCE CLERK READING A CONFIDENTIAL PAPER.

ELVA DOVE! WHAT ARE **YOU** DOING WITH THIS SECRET RUBBER INVESTIGATION REPORT?

WHY-ER-NOTHING! IT MUST HAVE BEEN LEFT ON MY DESK BY MISTAKE!

1C

I DON'T BELIEVE YOU! YOU TOOK THESE PAPERS FROM THE SECRET FILES— I'M GOING TO REPORT YOU TO MAJOR TREVOR!

OH *PLEASE* DON'T DO THAT! I *SWEAR* I'M INNOCENT—

HERE'S A SECRET REPORT THAT MAY PUT FIVE RUBBER MAGNATES IN JAIL AND I CATCH ELVA DOVE, A *FILE CLERK*, READING IT!

ELVA— HMM— THAT HANDSOME BRUNETTE! *SHE* WOULDN'T DO ANYTHING WRONG— THE LIE DETECTOR'LL PROVE IT!

COME, ELVA, YOU'LL HAVE TO TAKE A LIE DETECTOR TEST— COME ALONG, NOW!

I WON'T GO WITH YOU— AGHH— OH, ALL RIGHT— HEAVENS— YOU'RE ALMOST AS STRONG AS A *MAN!*

I'LL ASK YOU QUESTIONS. ANSWER TRUTHFULLY OR YOUR BLOOD PRESSURE CURVE WILL GO UP. ELVA DID YOU TAKE THAT RUBBER REPORT FROM THE SECRET FILES?

NO— *NO!*

WELL I'LL BE JIGGERED— SHE *IS* LYING!

WERE YOU SENT HERE BY SOME RUBBER MANUFACTURER TO SPY ON OUR INVESTIGATION?

OH, NO! CERTAINLY NOT!

ANOTHER LIE— BY THE GREAT HORNED TOAD! THIS GIRL'S *GUILTY!*

WE KNOW NOW THAT YOU ARE SPYING FOR ONE OF THESE MEN UNDER INVESTIGATION. ARE YOU WORKING FOR CORNELIUS QUOD? LARRY HEFTON? SIGMUND SPOIL?

29

NO— NO— NO—

TRUTH— TRUE— OKAY.

ARE YOU THE SECRET AGENT FOR IVAR TORGSON?

NO— *NO!* I DON'T KNOW TORGSON— I *WON'T* TALK— TAKE THIS BAND OFF MY LEG!

SHE LIED ABOUT TORGSON— THAT'S THE LAD SHE'S WORKING FOR!

COLONEL, THIS GIRL READ THE RUBBER REPORT! IF SHE TELLS TORGSON ITS CONTENTS, HE'LL DESTROY HIS SECRET RUBBER EXTRACTION FORMULA, BEFORE WE GET IT!

HOLD THE GIRL INCOMMUNICADO!

OH PLEASE, *LET* ME GO. I WON'T TELL—

I DON'T UNDERSTAND THE SITUATION—PLEASE EXPLAIN!

THE COUNTRY NEEDS RUBBER-*DESPERATELY!* MOST LEADERS IN THE RUBBER INDUSTRY ARE GIVING THEIR MANUFACTURING PLANTS AND PROCESSES FREELY TO THE GOVERNMENT. BUT THE TORGSON CROWD ARE HOLDING OUT!

CAN'T THE GOVERNMENT SEIZE THEIR RUBBER FORMULAS.?

YES—IF WE CAN *FIND* THEM! TORGSON DENIES THAT HE OWNS ANY SECRET PROCESS! IF HE LEARNS THAT WE KNOW HE'S GOT A FORMULA, HE'LL DESTROY IT!

THE FORMULA MUST BE IN HIS SAFE—LET ME RAID TORGSON'S OFFICES!

NO, WAIT! LET *ME* TRY TO LOCATE THE FORMULA FIRST—QUIETLY!

I'LL GIVE YOU UNTIL MIDNIGHT, DIANA—THEN STEVE WILL RAID TORGSON'S HEADQUARTERS.

DIANA MINGLES, UNSUSPECTED, WITH CROWDS OF TORGSON'S GIRLS AT LUNCH HOUR.

I HEAR THERE'S A MEETING OF THE BIG CHIEFS TONIGHT, IN TORGSON'S OFFICE!

YEAH, MUST BE IMPORTANT—QUOD IS HERE FROM CALIFORNIA AND SPOIL'S UP FROM MEXICO!

I'LL INVITE *WONDER WOMAN* TO ATTEND THAT CONFERENCE!

LATER, A BEAUTIFUL FIGURE LEAPS LIGHTLY FROM A NEARBY ROOF TOP, TO THE ROOF OF THE TORGSON BUILDING.

THIS WAY THERE'S LESS CHANCE I'LL BE SEEN BY TORGSON'S GUARDS!

FASTENING HER LASSO TO THE ROOF, **WONDER WOMAN** DESCENDS TO A WINDOW OF TORGSON'S PRIVATE OFFICE.

VERY NICE OF MR. TORGSON TO LEAVE HIS WINDOW SHADE UP A LITTLE, SO I CAN PEEK THROUGH!

3¢

THOUGH THE WINDOW IS SHUT AND LOCKED, **WONDER WOMAN** FINDS NO DIFFICULTY IN OPENING IT.

I HATE TO BREAK THIS WINDOW CATCH, BUT I MUST HEAR WHAT THE TORGSON BOYS ARE SAYING!

SNAP!

WONDER WOMAN IS JUST IN TIME - THE SECRET ASSOCIATES QUICKLY ASSEMBLE.

WE'RE ALL HERE-SKELLY, QUOD, HEFTON, SPOIL AND ME - TO BUSINESS, GENTLEMEN! THE QUESTION! SHALL WE GIVE OUR NEW RUBBER EXTRACTION PROCESS TO THE GOVERNMENT?

SURE, TORGSON WE'D BE CRAZY AS DAFFYDILLS TO GIVE AWAY OUR HARD-EARNED SECRET! IF WE GIVE IT TO THE GOVERNMENT NOW, HOW'LL WE CONTROL THE RUBBER MARKET AFTER THE WAR?

HEAR! HEAR!

ABSO-LUTELY!

I AGREE!

THEN WE ALL AGREE TO HIDE OUR SECRET METHODS! IF THE GOVERNMENT TRIES TO TAKE 'EM, WE'LL DESTROY FORMULAS AND RECORDS. WE-ER-EXCUSE ME-

HELLO, IVAR! IF YOU COULD ONLY SEE ME NOW!

IF TORGSON COULD HAVE SEEN ELVA DOVE AT THAT MOMENT-

YES, DARLING-I'M HAVING A CUTE LITTLE PRISON PARTY WITH A NICE GUARD! LISTEN! G 2 IS WISE- DESTROY ALL RECORDS OF THAT CRYPTO-STEGIA PROCESS- THEY'RE RAIDING TONIGHT!

CRIP-TWO-TEASE-HER HEY! WHA'S 'AT DOUBLE TALK?

WONDER WOMAN, WATCHING AT TORGSON'S WINDOW, SEES THE MEETING BREAK UP.

THEY'RE HURRYING AWAY- I WONDER IF THAT PHONE CALL WARNED TORGSON THAT I'M WATCHING? NOW IT'S UP TO STEVE!

BUT AT THE OFFICE NEXT MORN-ING, STEVE REPORTS FAILURE AND BLAMES DIANA FOR IT.

TORGSON'S SAFE WAS CLEANED OUT- HE'D BURNED ALL HIS PAPERS! IT'S YOUR FAULT, DIANA - HE MUST HAVE CAUGHT YOU SPYING!

THAT'S IMPOSSIBLE! HE-

REGARDLESS OF WHO'S TO BLAME, THIS LEAVES US HELPLESS!

4C

TO EVERYONE'S AMAZEMENT TORGSON HIMSELF WALKS IN!

HEIL, LITTLE HITLERS! I CAME IN CASE YOU WISH TO TORTURE ME! IN NO OTHER MANNER CAN YOU COMPEL ME TO OBEY YOUR ABSURD DEMANDS!

CAN'T COMPEL YOU, EH? WE'LL SEE!

DIANA OBTAINS AUTHORITY TO HANDLE THE CASE HER OWN WAY.

PLEASE LET ME DEAL WITH TORGSON, COLONEL, AND DON'T ASK ME HOW I'M GOING TO DO IT!

WELL-GO AHEAD! BUT BE CAREFUL, DIANA!

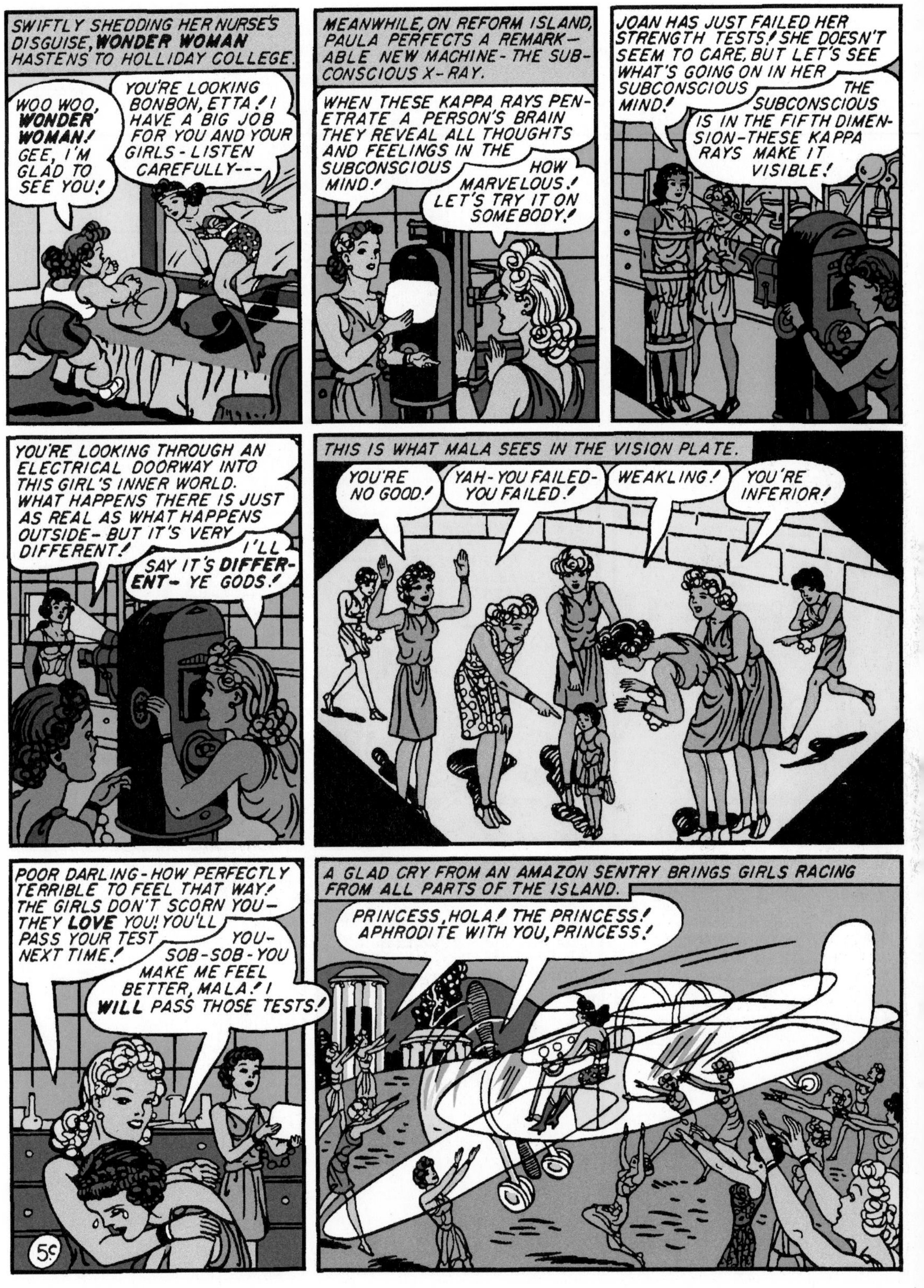
SWIFTLY SHEDDING HER NURSE'S DISGUISE, **WONDER WOMAN** HASTENS TO HOLLIDAY COLLEGE.
WOO WOO, **WONDER WOMAN!** GEE, I'M GLAD TO SEE YOU!
YOU'RE LOOKING BONBON, ETTA! I HAVE A BIG JOB FOR YOU AND YOUR GIRLS - LISTEN CAREFULLY---
MEANWHILE, ON REFORM ISLAND, PAULA PERFECTS A REMARKABLE NEW MACHINE - THE SUBCONSCIOUS X-RAY.
WHEN THESE KAPPA RAYS PENETRATE A PERSON'S BRAIN THEY REVEAL ALL THOUGHTS AND FEELINGS IN THE SUBCONSCIOUS MIND!
HOW MARVELOUS! LET'S TRY IT ON SOMEBODY!
JOAN HAS JUST FAILED HER STRENGTH TESTS! SHE DOESN'T SEEM TO CARE, BUT LET'S SEE WHAT'S GOING ON IN HER SUBCONSCIOUS MIND!
THE SUBCONSCIOUS IS IN THE FIFTH DIMENSION - THESE KAPPA RAYS MAKE IT VISIBLE!
YOU'RE LOOKING THROUGH AN ELECTRICAL DOORWAY INTO THIS GIRL'S INNER WORLD. WHAT HAPPENS THERE IS JUST AS REAL AS WHAT HAPPENS OUTSIDE - BUT IT'S VERY DIFFERENT!
I'LL SAY IT'S **DIFFERENT** - YE GODS!
THIS IS WHAT MALA SEES IN THE VISION PLATE.
YOU'RE NO GOOD!
YAH - YOU FAILED - YOU FAILED!
WEAKLING!
YOU'RE INFERIOR!
POOR DARLING - HOW PERFECTLY TERRIBLE TO FEEL THAT WAY! THE GIRLS DON'T SCORN YOU - THEY **LOVE** YOU! YOU'LL PASS YOUR TEST NEXT TIME!
YOU - SOB - SOB - YOU MAKE ME FEEL BETTER, MALA! I **WILL** PASS THOSE TESTS!
5¢
A GLAD CRY FROM AN AMAZON SENTRY BRINGS GIRLS RACING FROM ALL PARTS OF THE ISLAND.
PRINCESS, HOLA! THE PRINCESS! APHRODITE WITH YOU, PRINCESS!

Panel 1: MY LITTLE PAULA - HOW NICE TO SEE YOU! / YOU HANDLE ME LIKE A CHILD - I THOUGHT I WAS STRONG BUT— / HOLA, PRINCESS! ORDERS FROM APHRODITE— BRING PAULA TO THE TEMPLE!

Panel 2: BEFORE THE GODDESS. / OH GODDESS BEAUTIFUL, I PRESENT THY NEO-PHYTE PAULA FOR JUDGEMENT! / THOU HAST DONE WELL, NEOPHYTE— THY SECOND TEST WAS PASSED WITH GLORY! ART THOU READY FOR THY THIRD TEST? / YES, DIVINE MIS-TRESS!

Panel 3: THY THIRD AND HARDEST LABOR SHALL BE TO CHANGE THE CHARACTER OF MEN AND MAKE THEM SERVE THEIR FELLOW HUMANS. / I - I CAN DO ANYTHING, GODDESS, WITH YOUR HELP AND WONDER WOMAN'S!

Panel 4: WITH PAULA AND HER SUBCON-SCIOUS X-RAY MACHINE, WONDER WOMAN FLIES SWIFTLY BACK TO AMERICA. / CALLING WONDER WOMAN! ELVA DOVE RELEASED FROM PRISON TODAY. WENT TORGSON'S APART-MENT - HASN'T COME OUT! / ELVA'S IN DANGER. I MUST HURRY!

Panel 5: BUT ELVA, MEANWHILE, ENTERS TORGSON'S APARTMENT WITH HAPPY ANTICIPATION. / IVAR! HERE I AM, DARLING - AT LAST! / HUMPH— COME IN!

Panel 6: AREN'T YOU GLAD TO SEE ME, IVAR? AFTER ALL I'VE GONE THROUGH FOR YOU? / FOR ME - HORSERADISH! YOU'RE AFTER DOUGH - SIT DOWN AND I'LL PAY YOU OFF! / 6ᶜ

Panel 7: OH I CAN'T BELIEVE IT - YOU SAID YOU LOVED ME! I WOULDN'T BE YOUR SPY FOR MONEY - I - I LOVE YOU, IVAR— / TAKE YOUR HAND OUTA THAT BAG - YOU'RE NOT PULLING ANY GUN ON ME!

Panel 8: "LOVE"— YOU LITTLE FOOL! IF YOU BELIEVED I'D MARRY YOU, YOU'RE MORE DANGEROUS THAN I THOUGHT! I'M TIRED OF YOU AND YOU KNOW TOO MUCH, SO— / IVAR - OH, IVAR! NOT THAT - DON'T KILL ME!

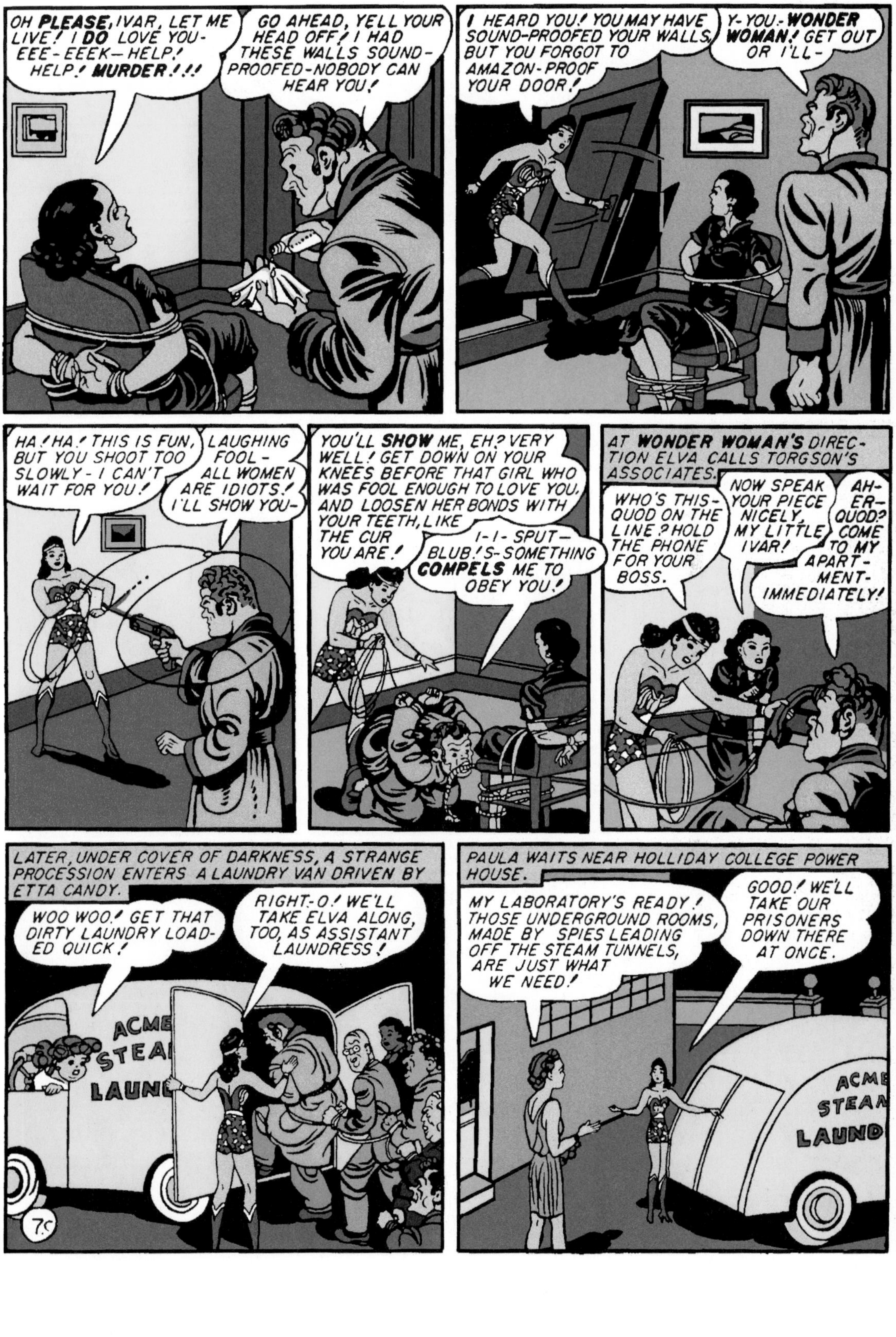

OH PLEASE, IVAR, LET ME LIVE! I DO LOVE YOU-EEE-EEEK—HELP! HELP! MURDER!!!
GO AHEAD, YELL YOUR HEAD OFF! I HAD THESE WALLS SOUND-PROOFED-NOBODY CAN HEAR YOU!
I HEARD YOU! YOU MAY HAVE SOUND-PROOFED YOUR WALLS, BUT YOU FORGOT TO AMAZON-PROOF YOUR DOOR!
Y-YOU-WONDER WOMAN! GET OUT OR I'LL-
HA! HA! THIS IS FUN, BUT YOU SHOOT TOO SLOWLY-I CAN'T WAIT FOR YOU!
LAUGHING FOOL-ALL WOMEN ARE IDIOTS! I'LL SHOW YOU-
YOU'LL SHOW ME, EH? VERY WELL! GET DOWN ON YOUR KNEES BEFORE THAT GIRL WHO WAS FOOL ENOUGH TO LOVE YOU, AND LOOSEN HER BONDS WITH YOUR TEETH, LIKE THE CUR YOU ARE!
I-I-SPUT-BLUB! S-SOMETHING COMPELS ME TO OBEY YOU!
AT WONDER WOMAN'S DIRECTION ELVA CALLS TORGSON'S ASSOCIATES.
WHO'S THIS-QUOD ON THE LINE? HOLD THE PHONE FOR YOUR BOSS.
NOW SPEAK YOUR PIECE NICELY, MY LITTLE IVAR!
AH-ER-QUOD? COME TO MY APARTMENT-IMMEDIATELY!
LATER, UNDER COVER OF DARKNESS, A STRANGE PROCESSION ENTERS A LAUNDRY VAN DRIVEN BY ETTA CANDY.
WOO WOO! GET THAT DIRTY LAUNDRY LOADED QUICK!
RIGHT-O! WE'LL TAKE ELVA ALONG, TOO, AS ASSISTANT LAUNDRESS!
ACME STEA LAUN
7c
PAULA WAITS NEAR HOLLIDAY COLLEGE POWER HOUSE.
MY LABORATORY'S READY! THOSE UNDERGROUND ROOMS, MADE BY SPIES LEADING OFF THE STEAM TUNNELS, ARE JUST WHAT WE NEED!
GOOD! WE'LL TAKE OUR PRISONERS DOWN THERE AT ONCE.
ACME STEA LAUND

IN SECRET ROOMS BENEATH THE HOLLIDAY STEAM PLANT, **WONDER WOMAN'S** EXPERIMENT BEGINS.

STEP IN THERE, BOYS, AND PUT ON YOUR BATHING SUITS. I WANT TO SEE IF YOU STILL FEEL HEROIC WITHOUT YOUR DAILY DISGUISE OF CLOTHES!

NOW THAT WE SEE HOW THESE TYCOONS REALLY LOOK, I'D LIKE TO SEE WHAT THEY **THINK** THEY LOOK LIKE!

I CAN SHOW YOU ON MY SUBCONSCIOUS X-RAY MACHINE! I RESENT THIS!

SCHOOL GIRL BUFFOONERY!

OUTRAGEOUS! INSULTING!

I'LL SUE YOU—I'LL PUT YOU IN JAIL! NOBODY CAN DO THIS TO CORNELIUS R. QUOD—

QUIET, LITTLE MAN— MAMA SPANK!

I'VE FOUND HIS WAVE LENGTH— I'LL TUNE DIRECT TO THE CENTER OF HIS SUBCONSCIOUS EGO!

PAULA ADJUSTS HER MACHINE. ON THE LEFT, QUOD APPEARS AS OTHERS SEE HIM, ON THE RIGHT, AS HE SEES HIMSELF IN HIS SECRET SUBCONSCIOUS MIND.

HA! HA! HA! MALE VANITY IS UNBELIEVABLE! I **KNEW** SUCCESSFUL MEN HAD INFLATED IDEAS OF THEMSELVES, BUT—

I'D LIKE TO PUT MY OLD FRIENDS, GOEBBELS AND GOERING INTO THIS MACHINE—BUT WE'D HAVE TO ENLARGE THE VIEWPLATE!

SKELLY'S SUBCONSCIOUS PICTURE OF HIMSELF IS ALSO X-RAYED.

HONESTLY, PAULA ISN'T HE **PRICELESS!**

8.c

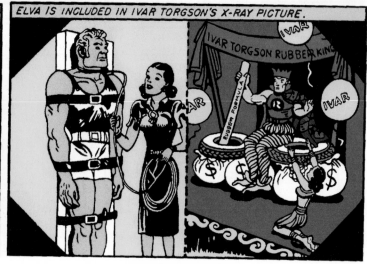

ELVA IS INCLUDED IN IVAR TORGSON'S X-RAY PICTURE.

IVAR TORGSON RUBBER KING

IVAR

IVAR

IVAR

RUBBER FORMULA

$ $ $ $

WONDER WOMAN SHOWS ELVA AN X-RAY PHOTOGRAPH OF TORGSON'S SUBCONSCIOUS.

SO THAT'S THE WAY IVAR THINKS OF ME - WHY, I CAN'T BELIEVE IT!

MOST MEN SECRETLY THINK OF WOMEN THAT WAY IN THIS MAN-RULED WORLD! BUT I HAVE AN IDEA WE CAN CURE IVAR - IF YOU'LL HELP!

WONDER WOMAN BEGINS AN EXPERIMENT TO REFORM TORGSON!

HERE, LET ME PUT THIS COSTUME ON YOU. YOU MUST MAKE HIM THINK OF YOU AS HIS QUEEN IN HIS SUBCONSCIOUS MIND INSTEAD OF HIS SLAVE! THEN YOU MUST LEARN TO CONTROL HIM!

BUT HOW CAN I DO THAT?

FIRST, YOU DRESS LIKE A QUEEN. THEN ACT THE PART - AND WITH MY MAGIC LASSO MAKE IVAR SUBMIT TO YOUR WISHES. HE'LL LOVE IT! WHEN HE'S LEARNED TO ENJOY BEING YOUR CAPTIVE YOU CAN CONTROL HIM WITHOUT ANY LASSO!

WONDERFUL IF IT WORKS!

ELVA'S TASK BEGINS.

QUEEN ELVA, I GIVE YOU THIS SLAVE! SUBDUE HIM! THESE SECRET, SUBTERRANEAN ROOMS ARE COMPLETELY FURNISHED FOR YOUR USE, INCLUDING A CELL FOR YOUR CAPTIVE. IN 3 DAYS I WILL RETURN - ADIEU!

THE SLAVE, AT FIRST, REBELS BITTERLY AGAINST FEMININE CONTROL.

THIS IS ABSURD - RIDICULOUS. WHAT A FOOL YOU'RE MAKING OF ME!

I'M MAKING A MAN OF YOU! LEARNING TO SUBMIT IS THE FINAL TEST OF MANHOOD!

IVAR DISCOVERS - TO HIS AMAZEMENT - THAT HE ENJOYS BEING THIS GIRL'S CAPTIVE!

HERE'S THE KEY TO YOUR FETTERS, SLAVE, LET'S SEE YOU GET IT!

I - I CAN'T! AND SOMEHOW I DON'T WANT TO - HOW STRANGE!

AND IN THE EVENING -

I AM BORED WITH YOU - INTO YOUR CELL! PERHAPS I WILL RELEASE YOU AGAIN TOMORROW!

OH PLEASE KEEP ME WITH YOU -

ON THE SECOND DAY ELVA RE-
MOVES THE MAGIC LASSO.

YOU'VE LEARNED TO **ENJOY** SUBMITTING TO ME, SO I NEED NO LONGER **COMPEL** YOU!

SO LONG AS YOU KEEP ME AS YOUR SLAVE I'LL **ALWAYS** SUBMIT!

STOP FOLLOWING ME LIKE A DOG!

BUT I WANT TO BE WITH YOU, DARLING—**DON'T** SEND ME AWAY!

AS THE THIRD DAY DRAWS TO A CLOSE, ELVA ACCEPTS IVAR'S ARDENT MARRIAGE PROPOSAL.

OH MY BEAUTIFUL QUEEN—MARRY ME— **PLEASE** MARRY ME!

OH WELL— IF YOU INSIST! BUT YOU'LL **STILL** REMAIN MY SLAVE!

SUDDENLY A FLOOD OF PREHISTORIC FEMININE FEELINGS OVERWHELMS ELVA'S UNTRAINED MIND.

OH, THOSE CHAINS MUST BE UNCOMFORTABLE ON THE DEAR BOY—I'LL RELEASE HIM—

IVAR, LET ME TAKE THE CHAINS OFF---I'M TIRED OF THIS GAME—I JUST WANT TO BE YOUR ADORING WIFE!

NO!—NO!...

AS ELVA SUBMITS TO IVAR'S DOMINATION, HIS MALE CONCEIT INSTANTLY RETURNS!

YOU FOOL! YOU SHOULD HAVE KEPT ME BOUND— YOU HAD ME GOING! BUT YOU'RE A WEAK SISTER LIKE ALL WOMEN—

BUT IVAR— I DON'T UNDERSTAND!

A SOUND AT THE DOOR STARTLES THE VICIOUSLY AROUSED IVAR INTO BRUTAL ACTION.

RAP! RAP!!

OUT OF MY WAY, IDIOT! SOMEONE'S COMING AND I WON'T BE CAUGHT A SECOND TIME.

(10c)

SNATCHING THE MAGIC LASSO FROM ELVA, IVAR CROUCHES BEHIND THE DOOR.

SH-SSH! ONE SOUND FROM YOU AND I'LL BRAIN YOU!

WHY- WHAT'S HAPPENED? OH ELVA! A-A-AH!

I'M CAUGHT- I KNOW THE FEELING OF **THAT** ROPE!

SILENCE, **WONDER WOMAN**- HANDS BEHIND YOU! I KNOW THIS LASSO HOLDS SOME STRONG COMPELLING POWER- YOU CAN'T ES-CAPE IT!

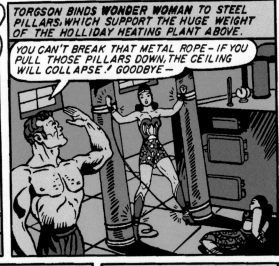

TORGSON BINDS **WONDER WOMAN** TO STEEL PILLARS, WHICH SUPPORT THE HUGE WEIGHT OF THE HOLLIDAY HEATING PLANT ABOVE.

YOU CAN'T BREAK THAT METAL ROPE- IF YOU PULL THOSE PILLARS DOWN, THE CEILING WILL COLLAPSE! GOODBYE—

IT'S MY FAULT! I THOUGHT HE'D LOVE ME MORE IF HE RULED **ME**!

MANY GIRLS MAKE THAT MISTAKE. I SHOULD HAVE KNOWN THAT ONLY TRUE INITIATES OF APHRODITE CAN HOLD A MAN! LET ME THINK—

SINCE THE MAGIC LASSO IS UN-BREAKABLE, **WONDER WOMAN** DECIDES TO LOOSEN IT BY PULLING THE PILLARS TOGETHER.

I'VE GOT TO KEEP THESE PILLARS UP-RIGHT OR THE CEIL-ING WILL COLLAPSE!

YOU CAN'T DO THAT- IT'S IM-POSSIBLE!

CRACK!

SNAP!

SLOWLY BUT SURELY, UNDER THE PULL OF **WONDER WOMAN'S** ENORMOUS STRENGTH THE STEEL POSTS APPROACH ONE ANOTHER.

I CAN FEEL THE LASSO LOOSENING-I'LL BE FREE IN A MINUTE!

THIS PART IS EASY-I'LL UNTIE YOU, ELVA, AND THEN WE'LL PUSH THE PILLARS BACK FOR SAFETY'S SAKE.

"WE" WILL PUSH THEM-HA! HA! YOU'RE THE ONLY HU-MAN DERRICK AROUND THESE PARTS, **WONDER WOMAN**!

TRUE TO HER WORD, **WONDER WOMAN** RESTORES THE PILLARS TO THEIR PROPER PLACE.

SAMSON DID THAT TOO, ONLY HE PULLED THE BUILDING DOWN INSTEAD OF PROPPING IT UP!

YES, SAMSON WAS CONTENT TO DIE IN THE CRASH, BUT I MUST LIVE TO WORK ON IVAR TORGSON!

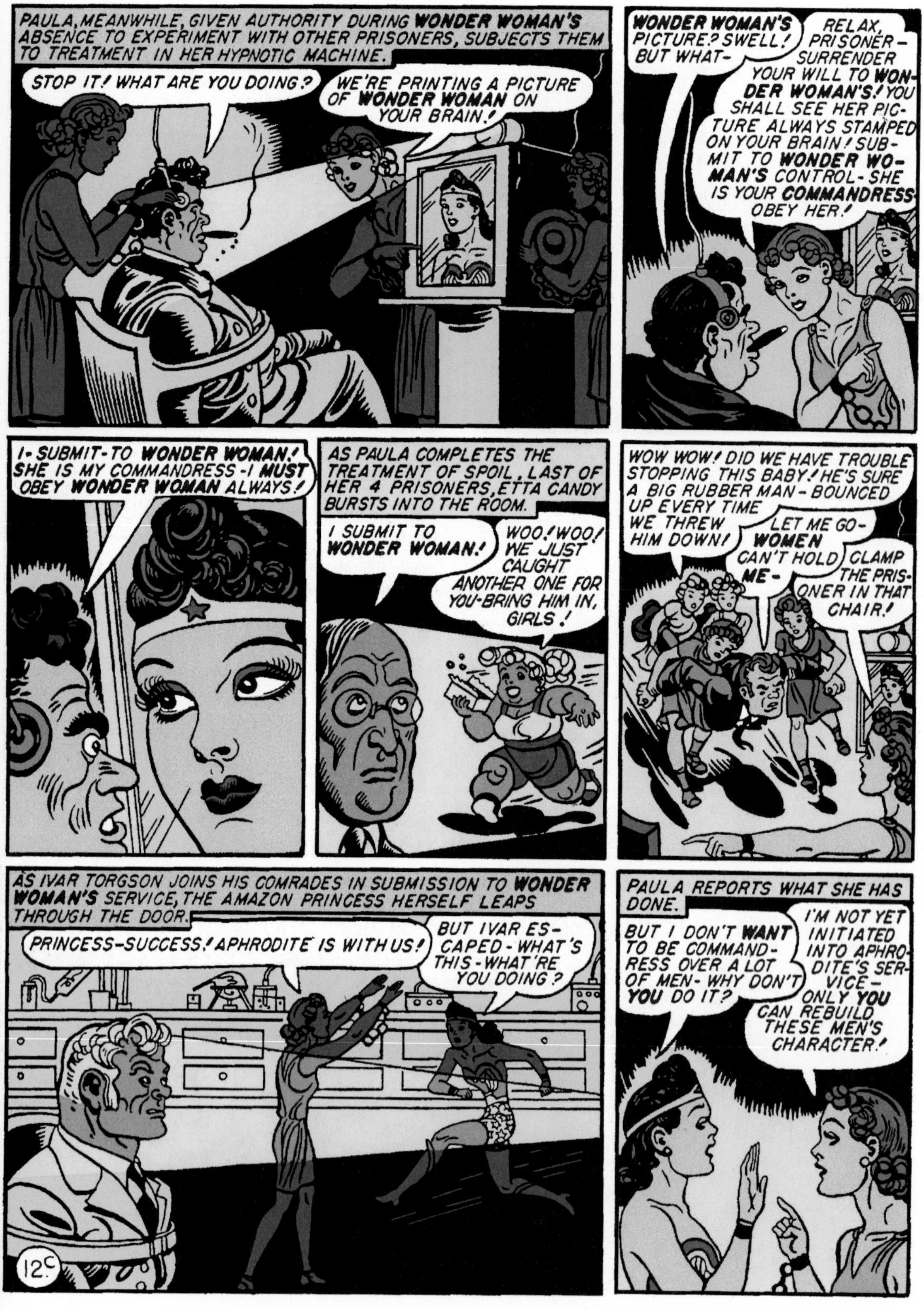
PAULA, MEANWHILE, GIVEN AUTHORITY DURING WONDER WOMAN'S ABSENCE TO EXPERIMENT WITH OTHER PRISONERS, SUBJECTS THEM TO TREATMENT IN HER HYPNOTIC MACHINE.
STOP IT! WHAT ARE YOU DOING?
WE'RE PRINTING A PICTURE OF WONDER WOMAN ON YOUR BRAIN!
WONDER WOMAN'S PICTURE? SWELL! BUT WHAT-
RELAX, PRISONER-SURRENDER YOUR WILL TO WONDER WOMAN'S! YOU SHALL SEE HER PICTURE ALWAYS STAMPED ON YOUR BRAIN! SUBMIT TO WONDER WOMAN'S CONTROL-SHE IS YOUR COMMANDRESS-OBEY HER!
I-SUBMIT-TO WONDER WOMAN! SHE IS MY COMMANDRESS-I MUST OBEY WONDER WOMAN ALWAYS!
AS PAULA COMPLETES THE TREATMENT OF SPOIL, LAST OF HER 4 PRISONERS, ETTA CANDY BURSTS INTO THE ROOM.
I SUBMIT TO WONDER WOMAN!
WOO! WOO! WE JUST CAUGHT ANOTHER ONE FOR YOU-BRING HIM IN, GIRLS!
WOW WOW! DID WE HAVE TROUBLE STOPPING THIS BABY! HE'S SURE A BIG RUBBER MAN-BOUNCED UP EVERY TIME WE THREW HIM DOWN!
LET ME GO-WOMEN CAN'T HOLD ME-
CLAMP THE PRISONER IN THAT CHAIR!
AS IVAR TORGSON JOINS HIS COMRADES IN SUBMISSION TO WONDER WOMAN'S SERVICE, THE AMAZON PRINCESS HERSELF LEAPS THROUGH THE DOOR.
PRINCESS-SUCCESS! APHRODITE IS WITH US!
BUT IVAR ESCAPED-WHAT'S THIS-WHAT'RE YOU DOING?
12C
PAULA REPORTS WHAT SHE HAS DONE.
BUT I DON'T WANT TO BE COMMANDRESS OVER A LOT OF MEN-WHY DON'T YOU DO IT?
I'M NOT YET INITIATED INTO APHRODITE'S SERVICE-ONLY YOU CAN REBUILD THESE MEN'S CHARACTER!

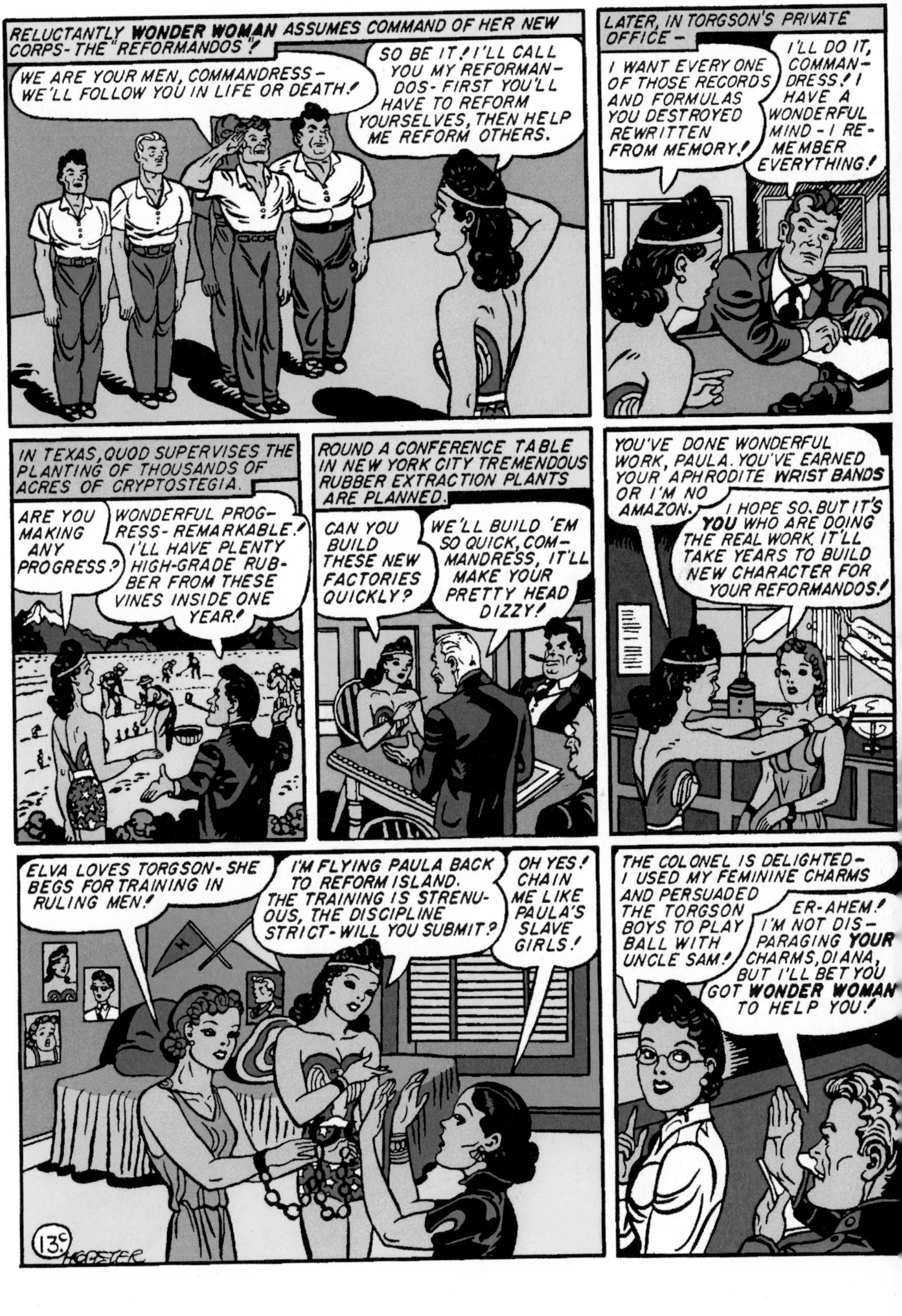
RELUCTANTLY WONDER WOMAN ASSUMES COMMAND OF HER NEW CORPS-THE "REFORMANDOS"!
WE ARE YOUR MEN, COMMANDRESS-WE'LL FOLLOW YOU IN LIFE OR DEATH!
SO BE IT! I'LL CALL YOU MY REFORMANDOS- FIRST YOU'LL HAVE TO REFORM YOURSELVES, THEN HELP ME REFORM OTHERS.
LATER, IN TORGSON'S PRIVATE OFFICE-
I WANT EVERY ONE OF THOSE RECORDS AND FORMULAS YOU DESTROYED REWRITTEN FROM MEMORY!
I'LL DO IT, COMMANDRESS! I HAVE A WONDERFUL MIND - I REMEMBER EVERYTHING!
IN TEXAS, QUOD SUPERVISES THE PLANTING OF THOUSANDS OF ACRES OF CRYPTOSTEGIA.
ARE YOU MAKING ANY PROGRESS?
WONDERFUL PROGRESS- REMARKABLE! I'LL HAVE PLENTY HIGH-GRADE RUBBER FROM THESE VINES INSIDE ONE YEAR!
ROUND A CONFERENCE TABLE IN NEW YORK CITY TREMENDOUS RUBBER EXTRACTION PLANTS ARE PLANNED.
CAN YOU BUILD THESE NEW FACTORIES QUICKLY?
WE'LL BUILD 'EM SO QUICK, COMMANDRESS, IT'LL MAKE YOUR PRETTY HEAD DIZZY!
YOU'VE DONE WONDERFUL WORK, PAULA. YOU'VE EARNED YOUR APHRODITE WRIST BANDS OR I'M NO AMAZON.
I HOPE SO. BUT IT'S YOU WHO ARE DOING THE REAL WORK. IT'LL TAKE YEARS TO BUILD NEW CHARACTER FOR YOUR REFORMANDOS!
ELVA LOVES TORGSON- SHE BEGS FOR TRAINING IN RULING MEN!
I'M FLYING PAULA BACK TO REFORM ISLAND. THE TRAINING IS STRENUOUS, THE DISCIPLINE STRICT- WILL YOU SUBMIT?
OH YES! CHAIN ME LIKE PAULA'S SLAVE GIRLS!
13C
THE COLONEL IS DELIGHTED- I USED MY FEMININE CHARMS AND PERSUADED THE TORGSON BOYS TO PLAY BALL WITH UNCLE SAM!
ER-AHEM! I'M NOT DISPARAGING YOUR CHARMS, DIANA, BUT I'LL BET YOU GOT WONDER WOMAN TO HELP YOU!

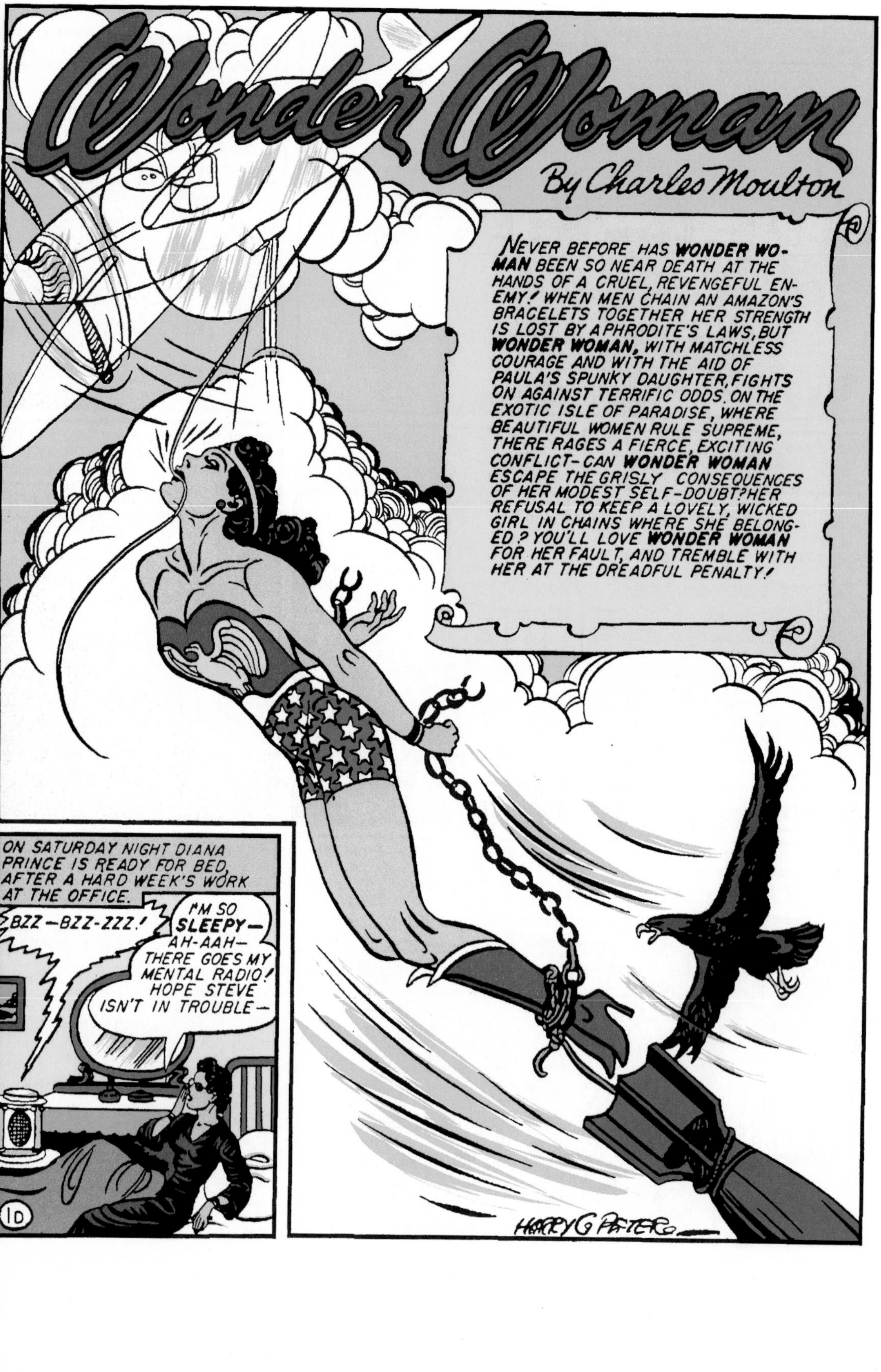
Wonder Woman
By Charles Moulton
NEVER BEFORE HAS WONDER WOMAN BEEN SO NEAR DEATH AT THE HANDS OF A CRUEL, REVENGEFUL ENEMY! WHEN MEN CHAIN AN AMAZON'S BRACELETS TOGETHER HER STRENGTH IS LOST BY APHRODITE'S LAWS, BUT WONDER WOMAN, WITH MATCHLESS COURAGE AND WITH THE AID OF PAULA'S SPUNKY DAUGHTER, FIGHTS ON AGAINST TERRIFIC ODDS. ON THE EXOTIC ISLE OF PARADISE, WHERE BEAUTIFUL WOMEN RULE SUPREME, THERE RAGES A FIERCE, EXCITING CONFLICT– CAN WONDER WOMAN ESCAPE THE GRISLY CONSEQUENCES OF HER MODEST SELF-DOUBT? HER REFUSAL TO KEEP A LOVELY, WICKED GIRL IN CHAINS WHERE SHE BELONGED? YOU'LL LOVE WONDER WOMAN FOR HER FAULT, AND TREMBLE WITH HER AT THE DREADFUL PENALTY!
ON SATURDAY NIGHT DIANA PRINCE IS READY FOR BED, AFTER A HARD WEEK'S WORK AT THE OFFICE.
BZZ—BZZ-ZZZ!
I'M SO SLEEPY— AH-AAH— THERE GOES MY MENTAL RADIO! HOPE STEVE ISN'T IN TROUBLE—
HARRY G PETER

DAUGHTER, YOU ARE SUMMONED BY THE GODDESS APHRODITE! COME IMMEDIATELY TO PARADISE ISLAND AND BRING THE NEOPHYTE PAULA FOR INITIATION INTO APHRODITE'S SERVICE!

YES, MOTHER—I'LL COME AT ONCE!

HASTILY DONNING HER **WONDER WOMAN** COSTUME, THE TIRELESS AMAZON GIRL RACES SWIFTLY TO PAULA'S SECRET LABORATORY.

HOORAY, PAULA! YOU PASSED APHRODITE'S TESTS. YOU'RE ACCEPTED IN HER SERVICE!

WHAT! OH, HOW **WONDERFUL!**

TEARS OF JOY AND GRATITUDE WET PAULA'S CHEEKS.

BELOVED MISTRESS! I HAVE **YOU** TO THANK FOR THIS GREAT HAPPINESS!

OH, GET UP—YOU'VE DONE GOOD WORK—YOU EARNED THAT REWARD YOURSELF!

BEFORE DEPARTING FOR PARADISE ISLE, PAULA SUMMONS HER REMAINING SLAVE GIRLS.

MY OTHER GIRLS ARE ALL IN TRAINING AT REFORM ISLAND—MAY I TAKE THESE GIRLS ALSO?

WHY-ER-I CAN'T DECIDE—THEY'RE **YOUR** RESPONSIBILITY!

I'LL GIVE YOU GIRLS YOUR CHOICE—YOU MAY COME WITH ME AND TRAIN FOR APHRODITE'S SERVICE—OR GO FREE!

I'LL GO WITH YOU, MISTRESS!

SO WILL I!

NO MORE SLAVERY FOR ME—I'LL TAKE MY FREEDOM!

FREE—FREE AT LAST! YOU'VE KEPT ME CHAINED AND SUBJECTED—I WAS HELPLESS—I DARED NOT REBEL! BUT **NOW** I SHALL GET REVENGE—I **HATE** YOU!

OH-H-H! I-I SUPPOSE I DESERVE THIS!

20

I SHOULD HAVE TAKEN MAVIS TO REFORM ISLAND—SHE NEEDS TRAINING! OH, WELL—I'LL CARRY THESE GIRLS TO MY PLANE.

USE MY CAR, MISTRESS! I'LL BRING THEIR CLOTHES IN THIS TRUNK.

BUT THE GIRLS' CLOTHES NEVER REACHED RE-FORM ISLAND!

I'LL MAKE ROOM FOR MYSELF IN THIS TRUNK AND FOLLOW PAULA UNTIL I GET REVENGE!

NOT KNOWING WHAT PAULA PACKED IN THE TRUNK, **WONDER WOMAN** PAYS NO ATTENTION TO ITS WEIGHT.

ALL ABOARD FOR PARADISE ISLAND!

THE QUEEN HERSELF GREETS THEM ON THE SECRET ISLE OF AMAZONS.

WELCOME HOME! PAULA, YOU ARE ONE OF US NOW! I'LL TAKE YOUR PRETTY SLAVE GIRLS TO THE PALACE WHILE THE PRINCESS PRESENTS YOU TO APHRODITE!

BEFORE THE GODDESS.

I PRESENT PAULA, AS YOU COMMANDED!

NEOPHYTE, THOU HAST PASSED THY TESTS—I ACCEPT THEE AS INITIATE IN THE SERVICE OF LOVE AND BEAUTY!

I AM YOURS BODY AND SOUL, DIVINE GODDESS!

REMOVE PAULA'S CHAINS AND DELIVER HER TO MY PRIESTESS-ES FOR INITIATION INTO THE SERVICE OF APHRODITE!

3D

THESE ARE SYMBOLS OF SUBMISSION TO APHRODITE— THEIR MAGIC METAL PROTECTS YOU! IN THE WORLD OF MEN YOU MUST WEAR BOTH WRIST AND ANKLE BANDS!

AT THE COLLEGE OF ATHENA, PAULA VISITS HER CHILD, GERTA, IN THE GIRLS' GYMNASIUM.

HELLO, DARLING— HOW STRONG YOU ARE GETTING!

MOTHER! OH I'M SO GLAD TO SEE YOU!

OH, MUMMIE! WHAT PRETTY BRACELETS—JUST LIKE THE OTHER GIRLS' MOTHERS'!

YES, DEAR, THEY'RE BANDS OF APHRO-DITE—THESE ANKLETS ALSO! THEY'LL KEEP ME SAFE IN THE MURDEROUS WORLD OF MEN!

PAULA, IN THE CHAMBER OF INNER WISDOM, IS TAUGHT TO FIND THE FOUNT OF TRIPLE KNOWLEDGE.

PEBBLES ARE PROBLEMS WHICH PRESS YOUR FEET AND SPUR YOU ON TO FOLLOW THE PATH OF TRUE KNOWLEDGE!

LIFE • LOVE • LAUGHTER

GERTA, MEANWHILE, RECEIVES A FAMILIAR VISITOR.

COME, GERTA— YOUR MOTHER WANTS YOU! I'M MAVIS, HER SLAVE GIRL!

ALL RIGHT, I'LL COME! I RECOGNIZE YOU, MAVIS, BUT WHERE ARE YOUR CHAINS?

WONDER WOMAN TOOK MY CHAINS OFF SO THAT I COULD FLY HER PLANE TO REFORM ISLAND— YOUR MOTHER'S WAITING THERE!

I DON'T NEED A PLANE—I CAN SWIM THERE EASY! BUT I'LL DO WHAT-EVER MOTHER SAYS—

4D

NOT UNTIL THE INVISIBLE PLANE HAS LEFT PARADISE ISLAND FAR BEHIND DOES GERTA LEARN THE TRUTH.

WE'RE NOT FLYING TO REFORM ISLAND! WHERE ARE YOU TAK-ING ME?

HA HA! YOU'LL SEE! QUIET OR I'LL TIE YOU UP!

WONDER WOMAN, MEANWHILE, IS REBUKED BY APHRODITE.

MY CHILD, THOU HAST DONE WONDERS IN THE WORLD OF MEN. BUT ONE ERROR NEEDS CORRECTION—THOU MUST NOT SHRINK FROM TAKING RESPONSIBILITY!

WHAT RE-SPONSIBILITY DID I FAIL TO TAKE?

TWICE THOU FAILED TO TAKE COMMAND OF PEOPLE WHO NEED REFORMING. FIRST THY REFORMANDOS—PAULA MADE THEE COMMANDRESS AGAINST THY WILL! TODAY THOU REFUSED TO SEND PAULA'S SLAVE TO REFORM ISLAND.

I'M S-SORRY, GODDESS!

TEARS OF REPENTANCE ARE NOT ENOUGH—THOU MUST REMEDY THE EVIL WHICH EVEN NOW FLOWS FROM THY FAULT!

I SWEAR, DIVINE ONE, TO RIGHT WHATEVER WRONG I'VE CAUSED, OR DIE IN THE ATTEMPT!

WONDER WOMAN HURRIES TOWARD THE AIR-FIELD.

IT MUST BE THAT EX-SLAVE GIRL CAUSING TROUBLE—I'LL FLY BACK TO THE OUTSIDE WORLD AND RECAPTURE HER!

BUT WONDER WOMAN'S PLANE HAS DISAPPEARED—

MY PLANE—WHERE IS IT?

YOUR SHIP TOOK OFF A LITTLE WHILE AGO. A GIRL IN SLAVE DRESS, BUT WITHOUT CHAINS, WAS AT THE CONTROLS—PAULA'S CHILD WAS WITH HER!

MAVIS MUST HAVE HIDDEN IN THAT TRUNK! SHE'S KIDNAPPED GERTA FOR REVENGE—

I'LL BRING THE CHILD BACK—TELL PAULA NOT TO WORRY! MAY I BORROW YOUR PLANE, ZOE?

CERTAINLY! BUT IT'S SLOWER THAN YOURS—

ROARING IN PURSUIT AT LESS THAN 1500 MILES PER HOUR, WONDER WOMAN CHAFES AT THE DELAY.

TAIL OF A TORTOISE! THIS PLANE'S SLOWER THAN RETRIBUTION—MAVIS WILL REACH AMERICA LONG BEFORE ME AND THEN WHAT?

5D.

"THEN WHAT" INDEED! MAVIS LEAVES NO TRAIL ON THE SKYWAYS AND DIANA PRINCE RETURNS ANXIOUSLY TO HER JOB.

THERE'S A GIRL NAMED MAVIS I'D LIKE TO FIND, COLONEL—

NAZI AGENT? I'LL ORDER A DRAGNET.

BUT A NATIONWIDE SEARCH PROVES FRUITLESS.

ALL THESE REPORTS SAY THERE'S NO TRACE OF THE PERSONS DESCRIBED. MAVIS MIGHT DISGUISE HERSELF BUT HOW COULD SHE HIDE LITTLE GERTA? UNLESS—NO! I WON'T THINK THAT!

EXCITEMENT REIGNS AT G-2 HEADQUARTERS, AS STEVE BRINGS IN A STRANGE REPORT.

THE ATLANTIC FLEET'S BEING BOMBED BY A MYSTERIOUS PLANE — INVISIBLE, NOISELESS! THREE BATTLESHIPS ARE DAMAGED — — —

QUICK, STEVE — TAKE ME UP IN YOUR PLANE!

STEVE, GLAD OF AN EXCUSE, FLIES HIGH ABOVE THE BATTLE FLEET WITH DIANA.

WHAT'S THE BRIGHT IDEA, DI? SPILL IT!

CAN'T YET — WAIT TILL THE BOMBING BEGINS AGAIN!

SUDDENLY A BOMB FALLS FROM THE BLUE, NARROWLY MISSING THE AMERICAN FLAGSHIP.

CLIMB, STEVE — AND BANK LEFT — THAT BOMB STARTED 3000 FEET ABOVE US!

AS STEVE PUSHES THE NOSE UP, ANOTHER HUGE MISSILE HURTLES PAST THEIR PLANE.

HORNSWAGGLING JELLY FISH! THAT ONE'S NOT MISSING US BY MUCH!

GOOD — WE'RE CLOSE TO THE MYSTERY PLANE NOW — EXCUSE ME A MINUTE — —

SLIPPING BACK INTO THE FUSELAGE, DIANA TRANSFORMS HERSELF INTO **WONDER WOMAN** —

I'LL HAVE HARD WORK EXPLAINING THIS TO STEVE WITHOUT REVEALING MY DOUBLE IDENTITY BUT I'VE **GOT** TO DO IT!

GREAT PLUTO! I LEFT MY MAGIC LASSO IN MY HANDBAG AT THE OFFICE.

AH — WHAT'S THAT, STEVE?

SOMEBODY'S SHOOTING AT US — PUT YOUR PARACHUTE ON IN CASE THE PLANE'S SHOT DOWN!

6D

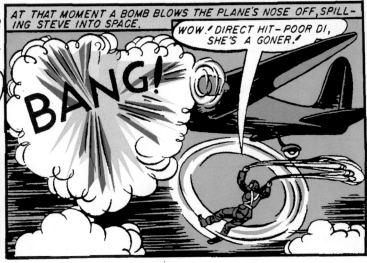

AT THAT MOMENT A BOMB BLOWS THE PLANE'S NOSE OFF, SPILLING STEVE INTO SPACE.

WOW! DIRECT HIT — POOR DI, SHE'S A GONER!

BANG!

THE FORCE OF THE EXPLOSION TURNS THE PLANE OVER.

THE WORLD'S TURNED UPSIDE DOWN--OR IS IT ONLY ME?

WONDER WOMAN CLIMBS OUT THROUGH THE BOMB BAY TO A PRECARIOUS FOOTING ON THE FALLING PLANE.

THERE'S THE MYSTERIOUS BOMBER--I KNEW IT--MY OWN PLANE!

AS THE TWO PLANES REACH THE SAME LEVEL, WONDER WOMAN TAKES A DESPERATE CHANCE.

HERE GOES THE JUMP OF MY LIFE--OR DEATH!

KNOWING EVERY INCH OF HER OWN PLANE'S SURFACE, WONDER WOMAN MAKES A PERFECT LANDING ON THE BASE OF A WING.

NOW TO FORCE OPEN THE COCKPIT HATCH!

WHA-WHAT! SHE MADE IT--I CAN'T BELIEVE IT!

I'VE FOUND YOU AT LAST--WHERE'S GERTA?

AA-AH-- GERTA! IF YOU TOUCH ME, PAULA'LL NEVER SEE HER CHILD AGAIN!

IN THE HOPE OF FINDING GERTA, WONDER WOMAN AGREES TO OBEY MAVIS.

YOU WIN, MAVIS-- SHOW ME GERTA ALIVE AND UNHARMED AND I'LL SURRENDER TO YOU!

YOU'D BETTER SURRENDER!

LANDING ON A LONELY BEACH, MAVIS LEADS WONDER WOMAN TO A CAVE.

GET IN THERE--THE BOYS'LL BE GLAD TO SEE YOU!

7D.

AGH—IT'S **VONDER VOMAN!**

VAT A PRIZE! BUT I VE BEDDER KILL HER QVICK—SHE'S DYNAMITE!

I CAN HANDLE HER—BRING OUT THE CHILD BUT KEEP A GUN AT GERTA'S HEAD!

OH, **WONDER WOMAN**—YOU'VE COME FOR ME!

YES, GERTA—BUT I CAN'T TAKE YOU NOW! THESE MEN MIGHT SHOOT BEFORE I COULD STOP THEM. HAVE PATIENCE, DARLING, AND TRUST ME!

YOU'RE WISE, **WONDER WOMAN!** THESE AGENTS WERE PAULA'S WHEN I WAS HER SLAVE—NOW I COMMAND THEM! THEY'LL KILL THE CHILD UNLESS YOU SURRENDER!

VERY WELL—BIND ME AS YOU WILL!

"BIND" YOU—HA HA! IT'S **CHAINS** YOU NEED! I SAW PAULA MAKE YOU HELPLESS ONCE—I'LL CHAIN YOU THE SAME WAY!

MEN CHAINING MY BRACELETS TOGETHER DEPRIVES ME OF STRENGTH, BY APHRO-DITE'S LAW! WHAT A MISTAKE IT WAS TO HAVE FREED MAVIS!

NOW, DARLING, I'LL GIVE YOU ANOTHER RIDE IN YOUR PRETTY PLANE—THIS WILL BE YOUR LAST!

GOOD—KNOWING **THAT** WILL HELP ME ENJOY IT!

I'LL DROP YOU AND THIS BOMB ON A BATTLESHIP—WE'VE BUILT A BOMB HATCH IN YOUR PLANE!

IT'LL BE A BOOBY-HATCH WHEN I GO THROUGH IT—I'VE CERTAINLY BEEN A FOOL!

80

LITTLE GERTA, BOUND, IS LAID BESIDE **WONDER WOMAN.**

OH MAVIS! SPARE THE CHILD—TAKE HER BACK TO HER MOTHER!

GRANTED, PRISONER! I'VE GOT A BETTER IDEA—I'LL DROP GERTA FROM THE PLANE AT PAULA'S FEET ON PARADISE ISLAND!

AS THEY SPEED TOWARD THEIR DOOM, **WONDER WOMAN** WORKS ON GERTA'S BONDS.

CAN'T UNTIE THOSE KNOTS WITH MY TEETH—I'LL GNAW THE ROPE THROUGH! MY BITE IS STILL STRONG—JAW MUSCLES ARE THE LAST TO WEAKEN!

GERTA, HANDS FREED, CLEVERLY REMOVES A FILE FROM THE EMERGENCY TOOL KIT.

WHILE **WONDER WOMAN** FILES AT HER WRIST CHAINS, SHE AND GERTA SING TO COVER THE NOISE OF THE FILE IN THE SILENT PLANE.

I GOT CHAINS THAT JINGLE JANGLE JINGLE AS I GO-O-O RIDIN' MERRILY ALONG! AND THEY SAY, OH AIN'T YOU GLAD YOU'RE SINGLE, AND THAT SONG AIN'T SO VERY FAR FROM WRONG:

JANGLE CLINK

BUT THE LEVITY OF HER CAPTIVES ENRAGES MAVIS - SHE PULLS THE BOMB HATCH LEVER!

I GOT CHAINS THAT JINGLE JANGLE JINGLE —

THEY'RE NOT AFRAID - THE FOOLS! I'LL SHOW THAT **WONDER WOMAN**—!

GERTA ROLLS OUT OF THE WAY AND HOLDS ON, BUT WITH HER FETTERS STILL UNBROKEN **WONDER WOMAN** FALLS INTO THIN AIR—

THIS IS THE END! CALLING MOTHER-STEVE-ETTA-PAULA-IT'S **WONDER WOMAN**, SAYING GOODBYE!

BUT APHRODITE NEVER FAILS HER LOVED ONES —UNSEEN, THE GODDESS GLIDES BESIDE HER DESPERATE DAUGHTER.

DO NOT DESPAIR-QUICK! SEIZE THE PLANE'S FLYING AERIAL IN THY TEETH!

I'VE GOT IT - I CAN HOLD - THANK APHRODITE!

HOLDING THE AERIAL FIRMLY IN HER TEETH, **WONDER WOMAN** UNTIES THE BOMB FROM HER ANKLES.

THIS'LL BE SOME WEIGHT OFF MY MOLARS- IF ONLY I COULD BREAK THESE WRIST CHAINS!

SUMMONING THE LAST OUNCE OF HER DIMINISHED STRENGTH, **WONDER WOMAN** STRAINS AT HER WRIST CHAINS- WEAKENED BY FILING, THEY BREAK!

WHAT A SWEET SOUND! MY MANMADE BONDS HAVE SNAPPED! MY WOMAN'S POWER RETURNS AGAIN!

SNAP!

AS THE BOMB BURSTS BELOW, THE GLOATING MAVIS LOOKS BACK — AND GETS THE SURPRISE OF HER LIFE!

THAT'S **HER** FINISH, THE CONCEITED — AGH - WOOF! **WONDER WOMAN** — ALIVE!

YES — THAT REPORT OF MY DEATH YOU JUST HEARD WAS GREATLY EXAGGERATED!

CALMLY CATCHING MAVIS' FRANTIC BULLETS ON HER BRACELETS, **WONDER WOMAN** PICKS UP A COIL OF ROPE.

SOME GIRLS ARE JUST NO GOOD UNLESS THEY ARE TIED UP, MAVIS — AND YOU'RE JUST THAT TYPE!

WONDER WOMAN RESTORES LITTLE GERTA TO HER MOTHER'S ARMS.

O MUMMIE! **WONDER WOMAN** RESCUED ME — SHE'S THE WONDER-FULLEST WO-MAN —

I **KNOW** IT, DARLING!

GERTA IS "WONDERFULLER" — SHE NEVER CRIED ONCE!

A MANACLED MAVIS IS DELIVERED TO MALA ON REFORM ISLAND.

THIS GIRL IS **MY** RESPONSIBILITY! I LEAVE HER WITH YOU FOR TRAINING — SHE MUST WEAR CHAINS!

NO CHAINS CAN HOLD ME!

YOU'LL LEARN TO **LOVE** THEM!

STEVE AND ETTA, MEANWHILE, RECEIVING MENTAL RADIO MESSAGES FROM **WONDER WO-MAN**, MEET NEAR THE NAZIS' HIDEOUT.

WOO WOO! IMAGINE MEETING **YOU** HERE! LISTEN — I'LL GO INTO THE CAVE. THE NASTIS WILL CHASE ME OUT AND YOU NAB 'EM!

ETTA'S PLAN IS SUCCESSFUL.

MOVE YOUR FEET! CATCH ME, BOYS!

DONNERWETTER, NACHMAL - CATCH DER FAT GIRL — ACH! IT ISS A TRAP!

THIS IS A GOOD FIGHT — **WONDER WOMAN'D** LOVE IT! WISH SHE WAS HERE!

10D

DIANA RETURNS IN TIME TO STOP HER OWN FUNERAL.

THERE'LL NEVER BE ANOTHER GIRL LIKE DIANA — ULP — GULP — L - LOOK — HER GHOST!

HELLO, BOYS - NICE OF YOU TO SEND FLOW-ERS, BUT BLACK RIB-BON'S SO DEPRESSING! AS **WONDER WOMAN** SAID WHEN SHE SAVED ME, DON'T COUNT YOUR CORPSES UNTIL THEY'RE DEAD!

COLONEL DARNELL

THE GOLDEN AGE
Wonder Woman
VOLUME TWO

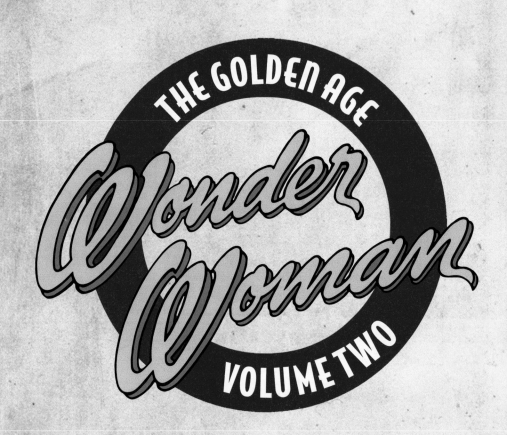

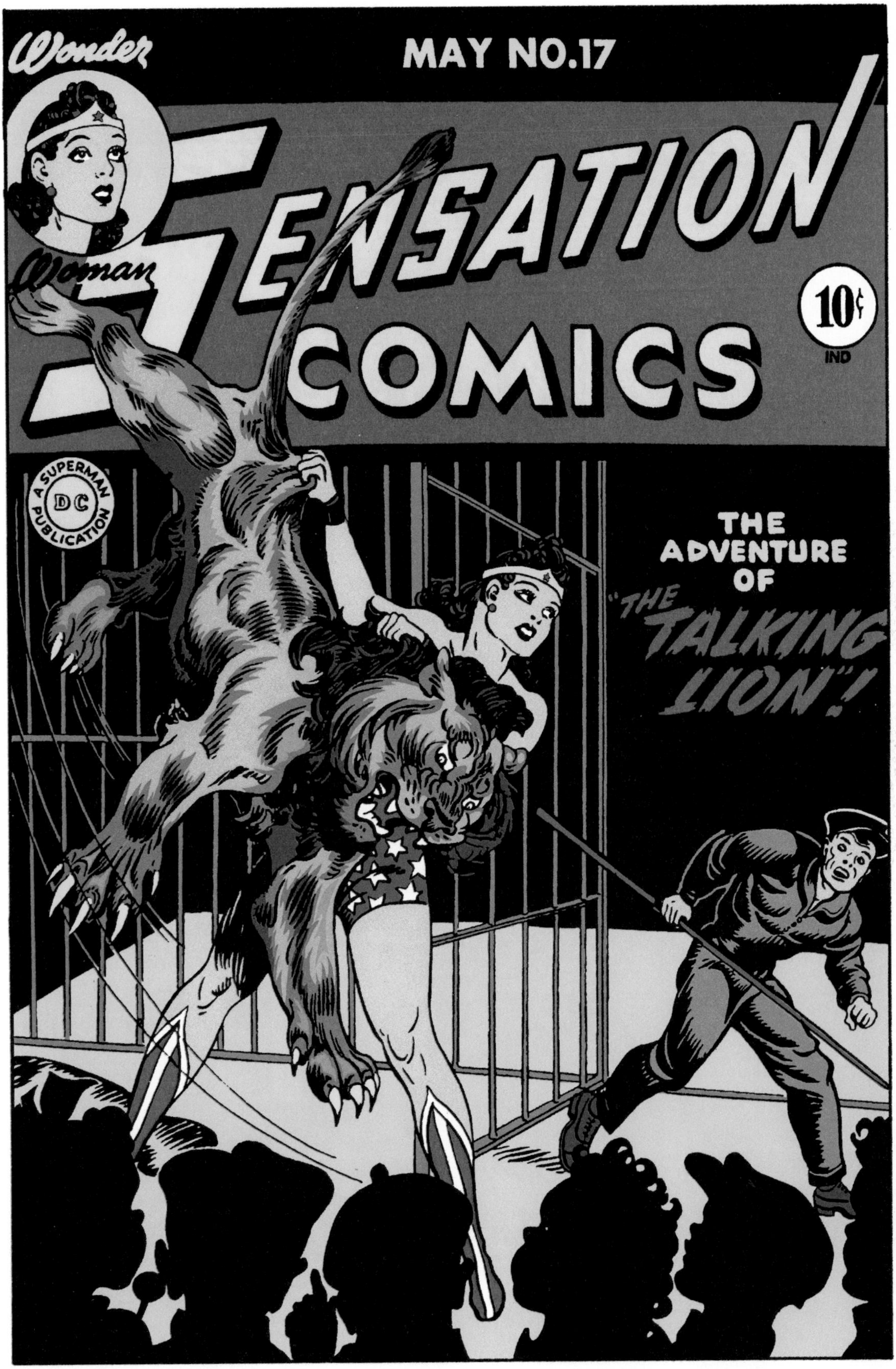
Wonder Woman
MAY NO.17
SENSATION COMICS
10¢
IND
A SUPERMAN DC PUBLICATION
THE ADVENTURE OF "THE TALKING LION"!

WONDER WOMAN

A TALKING LION! ABSURD!
CHILD'S BABBLE! YET A LION
DID SPEAK AND **WONDER WO-MAN**, MOVING WITH LIGHTNING
SPEED IN HER INVISIBLE
PLANE, TRACED THE BIG CAT'S
ASTOUNDING WORDS HALF
ACROSS THE WORLD! AGAINST
AN EXOTIC PANORAMA OF BEAU-
TIFUL PRINCESSES AND SLAVE
GIRLS, EGYPTIAN PYRAMIDS
HONEYCOMBED WITH SECRET
PASSAGES AND DEATH TRAPS
SUBTLE AS ONLY THE ANCIENT
EGYPTIAN COULD MAKE THEM,
WONDER WOMAN FLASHES
LIKE AN AMAZON SWORD ACROSS
TWO CONTINENTS AND AN
OCEAN TO SAVE KIDNAPPED
CHILDREN WHOSE HIDING PLACE
IS SHROUDED IN DARKEST
MYSTERY!

BEAUTIFUL AS APHRODITE,
WISE AS ATHENA, STRONGER
THAN HERCULES AND SWIFTER
THAN MERCURY, **WONDER
WOMAN** COMES FROM THE
SECRET ISLE OF AMAZONS
WHERE MIGHTY WOMEN RULE
SUPREME TO HELP AMERICA IN
HER DIREST HOUR OF NEED
AGAINST CRUELTY, INJUSTICE
AND AGGRESSION!

REG U S PAT OFF

DIANA VISITS SALLY LEE, AN
ARMY INTELLIGENCE CLERK WHO
IS HOME, SICK!

POOR SALLY! SHE
SUPPORTS HER LITTLE BROTH-
ER AND I GUESS SHE FINDS IT
DIFFICULT TO PAY EXPENSES!

ROO

1.

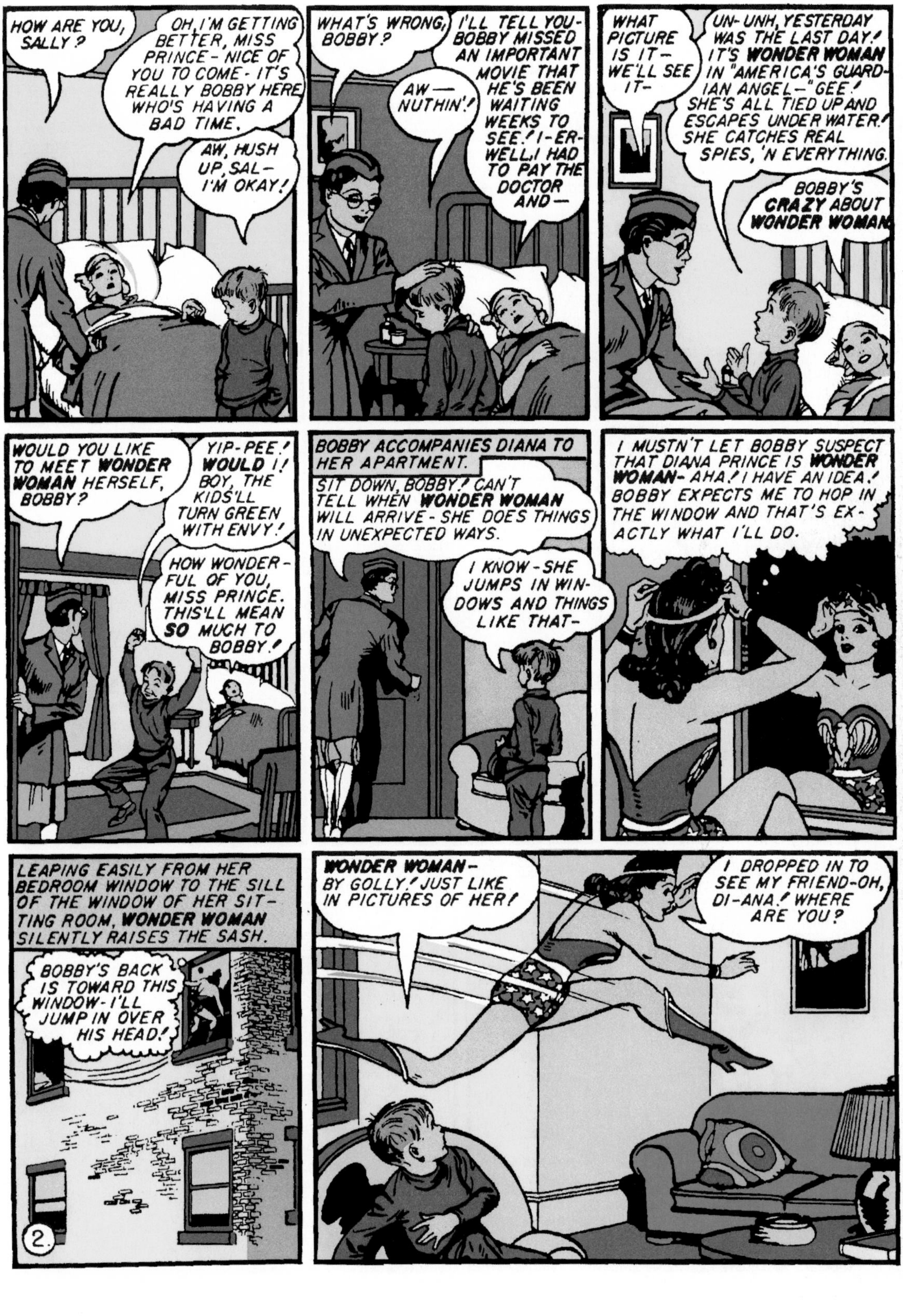
HOW ARE YOU, SALLY?
OH, I'M GETTING BETTER, MISS PRINCE - NICE OF YOU TO COME - IT'S REALLY BOBBY HERE WHO'S HAVING A BAD TIME.
AW, HUSH UP, SAL - I'M OKAY!
WHAT'S WRONG, BOBBY?
I'LL TELL YOU - BOBBY MISSED AN IMPORTANT MOVIE THAT HE'S BEEN WAITING WEEKS TO SEE! I-ER- WELL, I HAD TO PAY THE DOCTOR AND—
AW — NUTHIN'!
WHAT PICTURE IS IT — WE'LL SEE IT -
UN- UNH, YESTERDAY WAS THE LAST DAY! IT'S **WONDER WOMAN** IN "AMERICA'S GUARDIAN ANGEL-" GEE! SHE'S ALL TIED UP AND ESCAPES UNDER WATER! SHE CATCHES REAL SPIES, 'N EVERYTHING.
BOBBY'S **CRAZY** ABOUT **WONDER WOMAN**
WOULD YOU LIKE TO MEET **WONDER WOMAN** HERSELF, BOBBY?
YIP-PEE! **WOULD** I! BOY, THE KIDS'LL TURN GREEN WITH ENVY!
HOW WONDERFUL OF YOU, MISS PRINCE. THIS'LL MEAN **SO** MUCH TO BOBBY!
BOBBY ACCOMPANIES DIANA TO HER APARTMENT.
SIT DOWN, BOBBY! CAN'T TELL WHEN **WONDER WOMAN** WILL ARRIVE - SHE DOES THINGS IN UNEXPECTED WAYS.
I KNOW - SHE JUMPS IN WINDOWS AND THINGS LIKE THAT -
I MUSTN'T LET BOBBY SUSPECT THAT DIANA PRINCE IS **WONDER WOMAN** - AHA! I HAVE AN IDEA! BOBBY EXPECTS ME TO HOP IN THE WINDOW AND THAT'S EXACTLY WHAT I'LL DO.
LEAPING EASILY FROM HER BEDROOM WINDOW TO THE SILL OF THE WINDOW OF HER SITTING ROOM, **WONDER WOMAN** SILENTLY RAISES THE SASH.
BOBBY'S BACK IS TOWARD THIS WINDOW - I'LL JUMP IN OVER HIS HEAD!
2.
WONDER WOMAN - BY GOLLY! JUST LIKE IN PICTURES OF HER!
I DROPPED IN TO SEE MY FRIEND - OH, DI-ANA! WHERE ARE YOU?

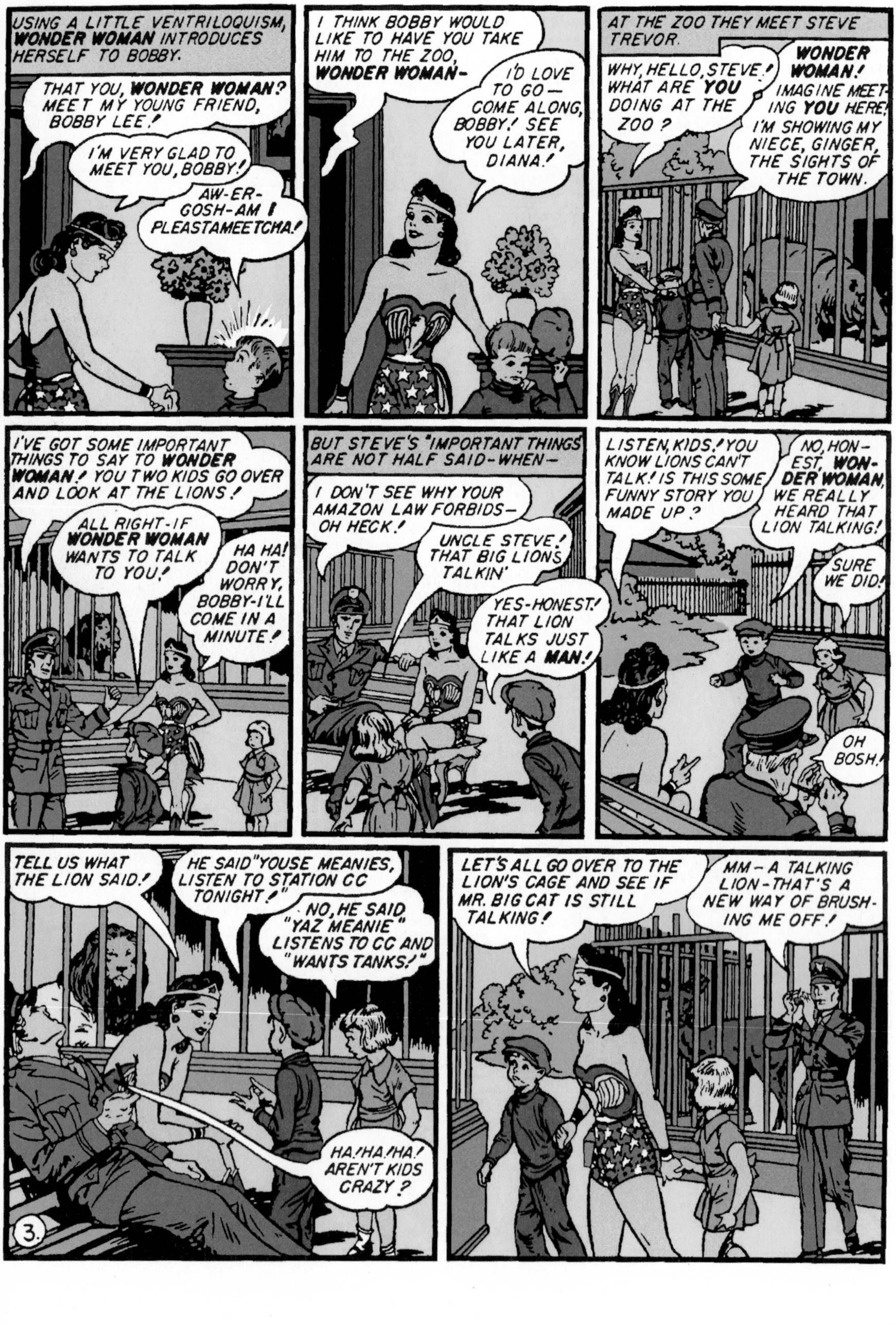
USING A LITTLE VENTRILOQUISM, WONDER WOMAN INTRODUCES HERSELF TO BOBBY.
THAT YOU, WONDER WOMAN? MEET MY YOUNG FRIEND, BOBBY LEE!
I'M VERY GLAD TO MEET YOU, BOBBY!
AW-ER-GOSH-AM I PLEASTAMEETCHA!
I THINK BOBBY WOULD LIKE TO HAVE YOU TAKE HIM TO THE ZOO, WONDER WOMAN-
I'D LOVE TO GO—COME ALONG, BOBBY! SEE YOU LATER, DIANA!
AT THE ZOO THEY MEET STEVE TREVOR.
WHY, HELLO, STEVE! WHAT ARE YOU DOING AT THE ZOO?
WONDER WOMAN! IMAGINE MEETING YOU HERE! I'M SHOWING MY NIECE, GINGER, THE SIGHTS OF THE TOWN.
I'VE GOT SOME IMPORTANT THINGS TO SAY TO WONDER WOMAN! YOU TWO KIDS GO OVER AND LOOK AT THE LIONS!
ALL RIGHT-IF WONDER WOMAN WANTS TO TALK TO YOU!
HA HA! DON'T WORRY, BOBBY-I'LL COME IN A MINUTE!
BUT STEVE'S "IMPORTANT THINGS" ARE NOT HALF SAID-WHEN-
I DON'T SEE WHY YOUR AMAZON LAW FORBIDS—OH HECK!
UNCLE STEVE! THAT BIG LIONS TALKIN'
YES-HONEST! THAT LION TALKS JUST LIKE A MAN!
LISTEN, KIDS! YOU KNOW LIONS CAN'T TALK! IS THIS SOME FUNNY STORY YOU MADE UP?
NO, HONEST, WONDER WOMAN, WE REALLY HEARD THAT LION TALKING!
SURE WE DID!
OH BOSH!
TELL US WHAT THE LION SAID!
HE SAID "YOUSE MEANIES, LISTEN TO STATION CC TONIGHT!"
NO, HE SAID "YAZ MEANIE" LISTENS TO CC AND "WANTS TANKS!"
HA! HA! HA! AREN'T KIDS CRAZY?
3.
LET'S ALL GO OVER TO THE LION'S CAGE AND SEE IF MR. BIG CAT IS STILL TALKING!
MM—A TALKING LION-THAT'S A NEW WAY OF BRUSHING ME OFF!

THE LION SPEAKS — BUT IN HIS OWN LANGUAGE.

ARR - GRR — RO-ORA!

HIS VOICE IS SO LOUD, I CAN'T UNDERSTAND HIS WORDS!

HE'S NOT TALKING NOW, BUT HE WAS BEFORE! HONEST!

LET'S LOOK AT THE MONKEYS — THEY'RE ALWAYS AMUSING!

BUT WHILE THE OTHERS ARE LAUGHING AT THE APES' ANTICS, LITTLE GINGER RETURNS TO THE LION'S CAGE.

I'M JUST GOING TO WATCH THAT LION UNTIL HE TALKS AGAIN!

A ZOO ATTENDANT BEHIND GINGER DISPLAYS MEAT FOR THE LION'S DINNER, DRIVING THE ANIMAL FRANTIC.

AGG-GRR - ROAR!

HA! HA! YOU HUNGRY LEO, HEIN?

THE CAGE DOOR, APPARENTLY UNLOCKED, SWINGS OPEN UNDER THE IMPACT OF THE LION'S BODY.

ARR-RRGH!

EEE-EEK!

LANDING DIRECTLY IN FRONT OF GINGER, THE HUGE ANIMAL GATHERS ITSELF FOR A FINAL SPRING UPON ITS PREY.

HELP! UNCLE STE-EEVE—HELP!

4

HEARING THE CHILD'S CRY FOR HELP, STEVE AND *WONDER WO-MAN* RACE TOWARD THE LION'S CAGE.

DON'T SHOOT, STEVE— YOU'LL HIT GINGER!

THE LION LEAPS - BUT **WONDER WOMAN**, NO LESS LITHE THAN THE JUNGLE CAT, SPRINGS TO MEET HIM IN MID-AIR!

COUNTERING THE ANIMAL'S SUPERIOR WEIGHT WITH THE GREATER POWER OF HER SPRING, **WONDER WOMAN** BRINGS LEO SAFELY TO EARTH.

CALM YOURSELF, BIG BOY, NO NEED TO RUN A TEMPERATURE!

I VILL SHOOT HIM!

STOP THAT! - PUT YOUR GUN AWAY - THIS IS TOO FINE AN ANIMAL TO SHOOT, WHEN THERE'S NO NEED FOR IT -

THERE'S SOMETHING VERY QUEER ABOUT THIS - THE LION'S CAGE WAS LEFT UNLOCKED!

HONEST, I LOCKED IT!

NONSENSE! YOU HELD THAT RAW MEAT DIRECTLY OVER THE CHILD'S HEAD! IF YOU'D BEEN LURING THE LION TO JUMP AT HER, YOU COULDN'T HAVE DONE BETTER! I'LL HAVE YOU FIRED!

WONDER WOMAN IS ALWAYS NEWS, AND, THE NEVER FAILING NEWS HOUNDS ARRIVE ON THE SCENE.

I'M FROM THE DAILY HERALD - HOW'S IT FEEL TO FIGHT A LION - WERE YOU SCARED?

SA-AY! YOU OUGHTA KNOW **WONDER WOMAN** ISN'T SCARED OF **ANYTHING**!

COME ON, KID, TELL ME WHY YOU WENT BACK TO WATCH THE LION.

AW-ER 'CAUSE THE LION **TALKED**!

HAW! HAW! WHAT A HEADLINE - "TALKING LION ATTACKS CHILD."

THE NEWSPAPERS TREAT LITTLE GINGER'S STORY ABOUT A "TALKING LION" HUMOROUSLY — **WONDER WOMAN** AND STEVE FORGET THE SUPPOSED FANTASY AS THEY TAKE THE CHILDREN HOME! ALAS, WHAT TERRIBLE CONSEQUENCES MIGHT HAVE BEEN AVERTED IF ONLY SOMEONE HAD BELIEVED THE TALKING LION STORY !!

AT BREAKFAST NEXT MORNING, STEVE READS THE LATEST DEVELOPMENTS IN THE LION CASE.

BY THE NIBBLING NIAGARA! I SHOULD HAVE HAD THAT ZOO KEEPER ARRESTED!

AROUND THE TOWN
WITH CHARLEY BROWN

TALKING LION DISAPPEARS. ZOO ATTENDANT ALSO MISSING

NEWSPAPER CAMERAMEN WILL BE GRIEF-STRICKEN TO LEARN THAT THE LION WHO WAS FOOLISH ENOUGH TO FIGHT WONDER WOMAN YESTERDAY HAS FINALLY DISAPPEARED. MOREOVER, THE ATTENDANT WHO WAS BELIEVED TO HAVE LEFT THE CAGE UNLOCKED IS ALSO MISSING.

DID THE TALKING LION PERSUADE ATTENDANT SMALTZ TO LEAVE THE DOOR OPEN A SECOND TIME?
• • • • • • • • • •

A "TALKING" LION! OF COURSE, THE PAPER'S ONLY KIDDING. BUT WHY DID SMALTZ LET THE LION GO? COULD THERE BE ANYTHING TO THE CHILDREN'S STORY? I WISH I COULD CONSULT **WONDER WOMAN**—SHE KNOWS ABOUT KIDS.

WHILE DIANA, SLEEPING LATE, IS WAKENED BY PERSISTENT RINGING OF THE TELEPHONE—

HELLO-ER-WHO? SALLY LEE!

MISS PRINCE? MY BROTHER BOBBY HAS DISAPPEARED. I THOUGHT YOUR FRIEND **WONDER WOMAN** MIGHT--I MEAN, WELL, IF YOU COULD ASK HER TO COME OVER—

HASTILY PHONING STEVE TO MEET HER AT SALLY'S, **WONDER WOMAN** DONS HER COSTUME AND SPEEDS TO THE APPOINTMENT.

BOBBY DISAPPEARED DURING THE NIGHT. I SAW HIM SAFELY IN BED-- THEN I TOOK SOME SLEEPING PILLS THE DOCTOR LEFT. BUT I WOKE BEFORE DAYBREAK AND BOBBY WAS GONE.

DON'T YOU WORRY, MISS LEE, WE'LL FIND HIM!

BUT AFTER SEARCHING THE ROOM THOROUGHLY, **WONDER WOMAN** AND STEVE HOLD AN ANXIOUS CONSULTATION.

THERE ARE NO CLUES WHATSOEVER.

EXCEPT THE "TALKING LION-" LET'S SEE YOUR NIECE AND QUESTION HER ABOUT THAT STORY.

BUT AT STEVE'S BROTHER'S HOTEL SUITE, MORE BAD NEWS AWAITS!

GINGER DISAPPEARED FROM HER BED-THE KIDNAPPERS MUST HAVE USED A LADDER! THERE'S NO CLUE EXCEPT THIS STORY IN HER DIARY-- JUST CHILDISH NONSENSE.

GREAT APHRODITE! LET'S SEE IT!

⑥

DIARY
TUESDAY
The lion said "Gaz meanie lissens tonight to tyro to broadcast from CC and wante tanks" then the lion jumped at me and tried to kill me.
WEDNESDAY

I'VE GOT IT! AN AXIS SPY IN **CAIRO,** EGYPT, EXPECTS INFORMATION ABOUT TANKS BY RADIO FROM A STATION CALLED "CC" — THE SPY'S A WOMAN — **YASMINI** — A HINDU NAME THE KIDS CALLED "YAZ MEANIE."

COULD BE!

THERE **IS** A PRINCESS YASMINI IN CAIRO — A FAMOUS OLD HINDU FAMILY — ANTI-BRITISH! BUT HOW COULD A **LION** TALK ABOUT HER?

I MIGHT ANSWER THAT IF I COULD FIND THE LION — THAT'S WHY THEY REMOVED THE ANIMAL!

COME ON — I KNOW YOU DON'T LIKE TO BE CARRIED BUT WE'VE NO TIME TO LOSE! OUR ONLY HOPE OF RESCUING THOSE KIDS IS TO FLY TO CAIRO AND MAKE YASMINI TALK! WE'VE GOT TO GET TO MY PLANE!

I'M YOUR BABY!

CIRCLING OVER CAIRO LESS THAN TWO HOURS LATER, **WONDER WOMAN** DECIDES TO LAND ON THE GRAND HOTEL GROUNDS.

I'M GLAD YOU STOPPED FOR PASSPORTS AND SUITCASES. I'LL TAKE A ROOM AT THAT HOTEL.

GOOD — I'LL STOP AT THE OFFICER'S CLUB — IT'S RIGHT NEARBY.

WONDER WOMAN MAKES INQUIRIES AT THE HOTEL DESK —

AH, MAIS OUI! ZEE PREENCESS YASMINI HAF WONDAIRFUL PALACE — SHE KEEP STRANGE ANIMAL, AH, BUT LIONS CERTAINLY! ZEE PREENCESS SEE NOBODY!

SHE'LL SEE ME! GET ME A DAIMLER LIMOUSINE — "SALOON" YOU CALL IT — VITE!

AT THE PRINCESS YASMINI'S PALACE THEY ARE ASKED TO WAIT.

WHAT'S THIS — HM — I WONDER! THINK I'LL BORROW IT AND HAVE A CLOSER LOOK!

PROBABLY NOT — BUT I'LL TRUST **YOU** TO GET AN INTERVIEW!

D'YOU SUPPOSE THE PRINCESS WILL SEE US?

PRESENTLY A SLENDER VEILED FIGURE GLIDES INTO THE ROOM. THE PRINCESS REGRETS THAT SHE IS INDISPOSED! I AM HER TRUSTED SECRETARY. YOU TELL ME YOUR BUSINESS, I WILL REPORT!

NO WE **MUST** SEE YASMINI!

TO SEE THE PRINCESS IS IMPOSSIBLE — AH — H!

IMPOSSIBLE? I DON'T THINK SO — YOU'RE VERY LOVELY, PRINCESS YASMINI!

⑦

YOU, TOO, ARE BEAUTIFUL, **WONDER WOMAN!** BUT YOU ARE VERY NAUGHTY - IT IS NOT GOOD MANNERS TO TEAR THE VEIL OFF A HINDU PRINCESS!

FORGIVE ME - NOW MAY WE TALK?

BUT YASMINI INSISTS UPON SERVING REFRESHMENTS.

YOU HAVE SOME PRETTY GIRLS, PRINCESS - BUT NONE TO COMPARE WITH YOURSELF!

AH, IF I COULD ONLY BELIEVE YOU REALLY LIKE ME, MAJOR.

IF I COULD ONLY BELIEVE HE DOESN'T -

IT WAS GENEROUS OF YOU TO GIVE THAT LION TO THE WASHINGTON ZOO, PRINCESS!

NOT GENEROUS - I HAVE MANY FINE LIONS LEFT IN MY COLLECTION.

OH - OH! SO THAT IS WHAT THEY HAVE DISCOVERED, THESE AMERICAN SPIES!

DO YOUR OTHER LIONS **TALK** LIKE THAT ONE IN WASHINGTON? AND DID YOU KNOW YOUR **TALKING** LION HAD ESCAPED?

SO — YOU CAME HERE TO TRAP ME! BUT YOU'LL NEVER KNOW THE **REAL** SECRET! HO - GUARDS!

HA - SO THESE ARE YOUR GUARDS! THANKS FOR THE AMUSEMENT - BUT YOU SHOULD HAVE GOT ME SOME **BIGGER** BOYS TO PLAY WITH!

BUT **WONDER WOMAN,** HER ATTENTION ON THE GUARDS, THROWS HER MAGIC LASSO A SPLIT SECOND TOO LATE, AS YASMINI SLIPS THROUGH A SECRET PANEL IN THE WALL.

I'M SLOWING UP! COME ON, STEVE, AFTER HER!

8.

NOT WAITING TO FIND THE HIDDEN CATCH, **WONDER WOMAN** SMASHES THE REINFORCED STEEL WALL PANEL WITH HER SHOULDER.

RACING DOWN A LONG PASSAGE, **WONDER WOMAN** AND STEVE FIND THEMSELVES IN THE PRINCESS' PRIVATE ZOO.

THE PRINCESS CAME THIS WAY!

THERE SHE IS, IN FRONT OF THAT LION'S CAGE!

SH! YASMINI'S WAITING FOR THAT LION TO TALK-HE **IS** SPEAKING!

PRINCESS! PRINCESS YASMINI!

WELL, PICKLE MY EARS! A **LION** TALKING!

PRINCESS, MY REPORT MUST BE MADE LATER - AND NOT AT CAIRO! TAKE THE LION TO UPPER NILE HEADQUARTERS - I WILL REPORT AT MIDNIGHT!-RR-OW-OARR!

YES-YES-I UNDERSTAND!

I THINK I'VE SOLVED THE SECRET- I'M GOING TO TRY AN EXPERIMENT. YOU STAY HERE AND WATCH YASMINI- DON'T LET HER GET AWAY! I'LL BE BACK-

SOME ASSIGNMENT, WATCHING THE PRINCESS! I- I WONDER-

FOLLOWING YASMINI TOWARD THE PALACE, STEVE IS SURPRISED BY SIKH GUARDS.

STOP! THIS AMERICAN IS MY GUEST! SHALL WE RESUME OUR CONVERSATION IN MY ROOMS, HANDSOME ONE?

ER-WHY, YES- CERTAINLY!

THE PRINCESS PROVES A PLAY-FUL HOSTESS-

HA! HA! YOU LOOK SO- WHAT YOU SAY- **CUTE**, MY PRINCE! NOW MY SLAVE GIRLS WILL DANCE FOR YOU!

ER- AH- I FEEL AWKWARD-

SWINGING INCENSE BURNERS AND SWAYING RHYTHMICALLY TO WEIRD HINDU MUSIC, THE PRIN-CESS' SLAVES WEAVE A SPELL THAT MAKES STEVE'S SENSES REEL.

PRINCESS- I'M DIZZY!

AS STEVE'S BRAIN GROWS FOGGED UNDER THE POWERFUL EF-FECT OF THE INCENSE, THE DANCERS SEEM TO MERGE DIZZILY INTO ONE MAD WHIRL.

⑨

A MOMENT LATER STEVE LIES UNCON-SCIOUS.

HE IS UNCONSCIOUS- IN MY POWER! BIND HIM, MY SLAVES, AND CARRY HIM TO MY PLANE! IF STOPPED, SAY HE IS HINDU, MY SUB-JECT- THE BRITISH WILL NOT INTER-FERE!

SLAP!

WONDER WOMAN, MEANWHILE, IS BARGAINING IN ARABIC WITH A DESERT CHIEFTAIN FOR A LION RECENTLY TRAPPED.

COME, I HAVE MADE MY LAST OFFER.

TAKE THE BEAST, THOU ROBBER OF THE POOR! GIVE ME THE GOLD!

TO THE ARAB'S AMAZEMENT WONDER WOMAN'S MAGIC LASSO MAKES THE FIERCE DESERT LION AS DOCILE AS A KITTEN.

NICE KITTY! WALK QUIETLY BESIDE ME, NOW!

PURR-R

BY ALLAH! THE WOMAN IS A WITCH! ALLAH PRESERVE US!

AT THE GRAND HOTEL WONDER WOMAN'S LION CAUSES A SLIGHT DISTURBANCE.

GRR-RR-ROWR!

HUSH, PUSSY! YOU MIGHT MAKE SOMEBODY NERVOUS!

AFTER ORDERING 100 POUNDS OF RAW MEAT, WONDER WOMAN INSPECTS TRIUMPHANTLY THE SMALL METAL OBJECT WHICH SHE FOUND AT PRINCESS YASMINI...

THIS IS IT! I'LL GET MY MESSAGE BROADCAST AT MIDNIGHT!

GET ME CAIRO BROADCASTING STATION—

WITH HER PREPARATIONS COMPLETE, WONDER WOMAN RIDES A NOVEL MOUNT BACK TO YASMINI

I NEVER RODE A LION BEFORE— IT'S FUN BUT SLOW GOING!

WONDER WOMAN'S MOUNT EASILY CLEARS THE HIGH WALL SURROUNDING THE PRINCESS' GROUNDS.

THESE BIG CATS CAN JUMP. SOMEDAY I MUST TRY A LEAPING CONTEST WITH A LION!

OPENING THE CAGE OF YASMINI'S TALKING LION, WONDER WOMAN PERMITS HIM TO ESCAPE, PUTTING HER OWN ANIMAL IN ITS PLACE.

NOW, KIT-KAT, YOU AND I'LL BE TAKING A LITTLE TRIP TOGETHER LATER— I HOPE!

⑩.

A FEW MINUTES LATER, WONDER WOMAN IS CAPTURED BY SIKH GUARDS— SHE SURRENDERS WITHOUT A STRUGGLE.

WE TAKE YOU TO PRINCESS YASMINI!

OH, HOW TERRIFYING! D'YOU SUPPOSE SHE'LL HURT ME?

YOU ARE A SPY - YOU CAME HERE TO BETRAY ME! TONIGHT YOU SHALL SEE YOUR LOVER DIE - THEN DIE YOURSELF - SLOWLY -

SO YOU GOT STEVE! WELL - THANKS FOR LETTING ME SEE HIM DIE, ANYWAY!

WONDER WOMAN AND A CRATED LION ARE TAKEN UP THE NILE BY AIRPLANE TO A SURPRISING DESTINATION.

WHY, THAT'S THE THIRD PYRAMID! NO ENTRANCE HAS BEEN FOUND!

EXCEPT BY YAS-MINI - YOU'LL SEE!

SOME DISTANCE FROM THE PYRAMID THEY DESCEND A STEEP SHAFT OPENING UNEXPECTEDLY IN THE SAND.

ARCHEOLOGISTS LOOKED IN WRONG PLACE FOR THE ENTRANCE. IT IS NOT IN THE PYRAMID, BUT HERE IN THE OPEN DESERT!

REMARKABLE!

IN THE ANCIENT THRONE CHAMBER IN THE HEART OF THE PYRAMID, PRINCESS YASMINI HOLDS COUNCIL.

VELL, YOUR HIGHNESS, YOU HAF A PRETTY PRISONER AND A MAGNIFICENT CAT - BUT VAT VE VANT IS INFORMATION!

SO! HAVE I NOT KEPT YOUR GENERAL STAFF INFORMED? LISTEN, MY LION SPEAKS!

DANGER, PRINCESS! TWO AMERICAN CHILDREN HEARD LION SPEAK - WE MUST KNOW WHAT THEY HEARD. MAKE WONDER WOMAN QUESTION CHILDREN AT CC TONIGHT!

WONDER WOMAN IS "COMPELLED" TO TALK WITH THE KIDNAPPED BOBBY IN AMERICA OVER THE SECRET RADIO.

I'D BETTER ACT RELUCTANT -

YOUR DEATH WILL BE HARDER UNLESS YOU OBEY!

POOR BOBBY! I WON'T TALK WITH HIM!

I MUST MAKE BOBBY TELL ME WHERE HE'S HELD CAPTIVE!

BOBBY - THIS IS WONDER WOMAN! YOU REMEMBER THAT STATION THE LION MENTIONED - ARE YOU THERE? AND IS GINGER WITH YOU?

WHAT - OH - YES, WE'RE HERE! TWO ROW CAPE - UG - GLUB -

"TWO ROW CAPE" WHAT COULD BOBBY MEAN - TRURO - CAPE COD!

CALLING ETTA CANDY ON MENTAL RADIO! KIDNAPPERS HOLDING BOBBY, LEE AND GINGER AT SECRET BROADCASTING STATION, TRURO, CAPE COD - FIND IT!

BUT BEFORE **WONDER WOMAN** KNOWS IT, SHE FINDS HERSELF IN A DANGEROUS PREDICAMENT.

THE ANCIENT PYRAMID BUILDERS SET THIS TRAP— IF AN INTRUDER STEPS ON THIS SECTION OF FLOOR—SO! HE WILL FALL INTO A POISON GAS CHAMBER BENEATH.

THIS OTHER END TILTS DOWN THE SAME WAY. YOU TWO BALANCE EACH OTHER—BUT IF **ONE** OF YOU MOVES, BOTH WILL SLIDE INTO THE DEPTHS—IS IT NOT INGENIOUS ?

AN INVENTION WORTHY OF **YOUR** GENIUS, PRINCESS!

I MIGHT LEAVE YOU BOTH HERE TO PLUNGE OR STARVE TO DEATH. BUT IT IS MORE POETIC TO WEIGH DOWN THE HANDSOME STEVE WITH FLOWERS—TOKENS OF MY GIRLS' FAVOR! HE SINKS BENEATH WOMAN'S ADORATION!

BEAUTIFUL IDEA!

WONDER WOMAN, AS USUAL, ACTS WITH CYCLONIC SUDDENNESS.

WE USED TO PLAY THIS TRICK AT SEE-SAW— PUSH ONE END DOWN HARD AND THE CHILD ON THE OTHER END FLIES UP!

SNAP!

LEAPING HIGH ON HER OWN RE- BOUND, **WONDER WOMAN** CATCHES STEVE IN MID-AIR!

THERE'S NO RULE AGAINST HURDLING IN THIS GAME!

EE-EEK! AI-EEE! SHE IS A CONJURER— NAY, A VERITA- BLE MAHAT- MA!

WONDER WOMAN DODGES A FIERCE ATTACK OF THE AXIS AGENTS WHO HURTLE TO THE POISONED FATE INTENDED FOR STEVE AND HERSELF ————

⑫

NO YOU DON'T, TRIXIE! YOUR TROUBLE IS YOU ARE TOO CLEVER—IMAGINE DIS- GUISING YOUR RADIO RECEIVING SETS BY MAKING LIONS SWALLOW THEM!

SO— YOU GUESSED MY SECRET! BUT MY TALKING LION PLAN WORKED **PERFECTLY** UNTIL YOU INTERFERED!

YOU DID A WONDERFUL JOB, MAKING THOSE SPECIAL POTATO-SHAPED RADIOS EACH TUNED TO ITS OWN PECULIAR WAVE-LENGTH! AND NOW I'D BETTER USE MY MAGIC LASSO-STOP!

TOO LATE! I'LL DIE BUT NEVER - BETRAY- F-FRIENDS-

SHE CHOSE HER PATH-IT'S KINDER, PERHAPS, TO LET HER FOLLOW IT! WE MUST HURRY BACK- ETTA MAY NEED OUR HELP ON CAPE COD!

I SUSPECTED THE LION TALK MUST BE RADIO. I FOUND A TINY RE-CEIVING SET AT YASMINI'S-MADE MY LION SWALLOW IT AND GOT THE CAIRO STATION TO BROADCAST MY MESSAGE ON THAT WAVELENGTH! I'M FINDING IT NOW BY FOLLOWING THE RADIO BEAM!

A WONDER-FUL JOB, ANGEL!

WONDER WOMAN ARRIVES AT TRURO JUST IN TIME TO SEE ETTA AND THE GIRLS IN ACTION

YOU FOUND IT, TOO! GOOD WORK, ETTA! THIS MAN'LL TELL US PLENTY!

S-SOMETHING COMPELS ME! I KILLED THE LION! I'M A GESTAPO RADIO EXPERT---

YOU AND YOUR GIRLS DELIVERED THE GOODS, ETTA- CONGRATULATIONS! WHAT WOULD I EVER DO WITHOUT YOU?

WOO WOO! HOW CAN **ANYBODY** DO WITHOUT CANDY?

BEFORE A CHEERING AUDIENCE, COLONEL DAR-NELL AWARDS $1000 TO BOBBY LEE FOR DISCOV-ERING THE "TALKING LION" KEEPER

THIS MONEY IS TO HELP A BRAVE AMERICAN BOY GET AN EDUCATION - BOBBY, OUR COUNTRY IS PROUD OF YOU!

HOORAH FOR BOBBY! HOORAY- AY-AY-AY- AY- AY-AY-AY- AY!

AW' (SPUTTER)- THANKS

(13)

A MEDAL FOR EXTRAORDINARY VALOR HAS BEEN AWARDED TO **WONDER WOMAN** BUT - AHEM! SHE ISN'T HERE -

ER- **WONDER WOMAN** COULDN'T COME BUT SHE ASKED ME TO SAY THAT CHILDREN ARE ACUTE OB-SERVERS AND ADULTS OUGHT TO PAY MORE ATTENTION TO WHAT THEIR YOUNGSTERS SAY!

MORE ADVENTURES OF WONDER WOMAN EVERY MONTH IN SENSATION COMICS !

FOR VICTORY BUY UNITED STATES WAR BONDS AND STAMPS

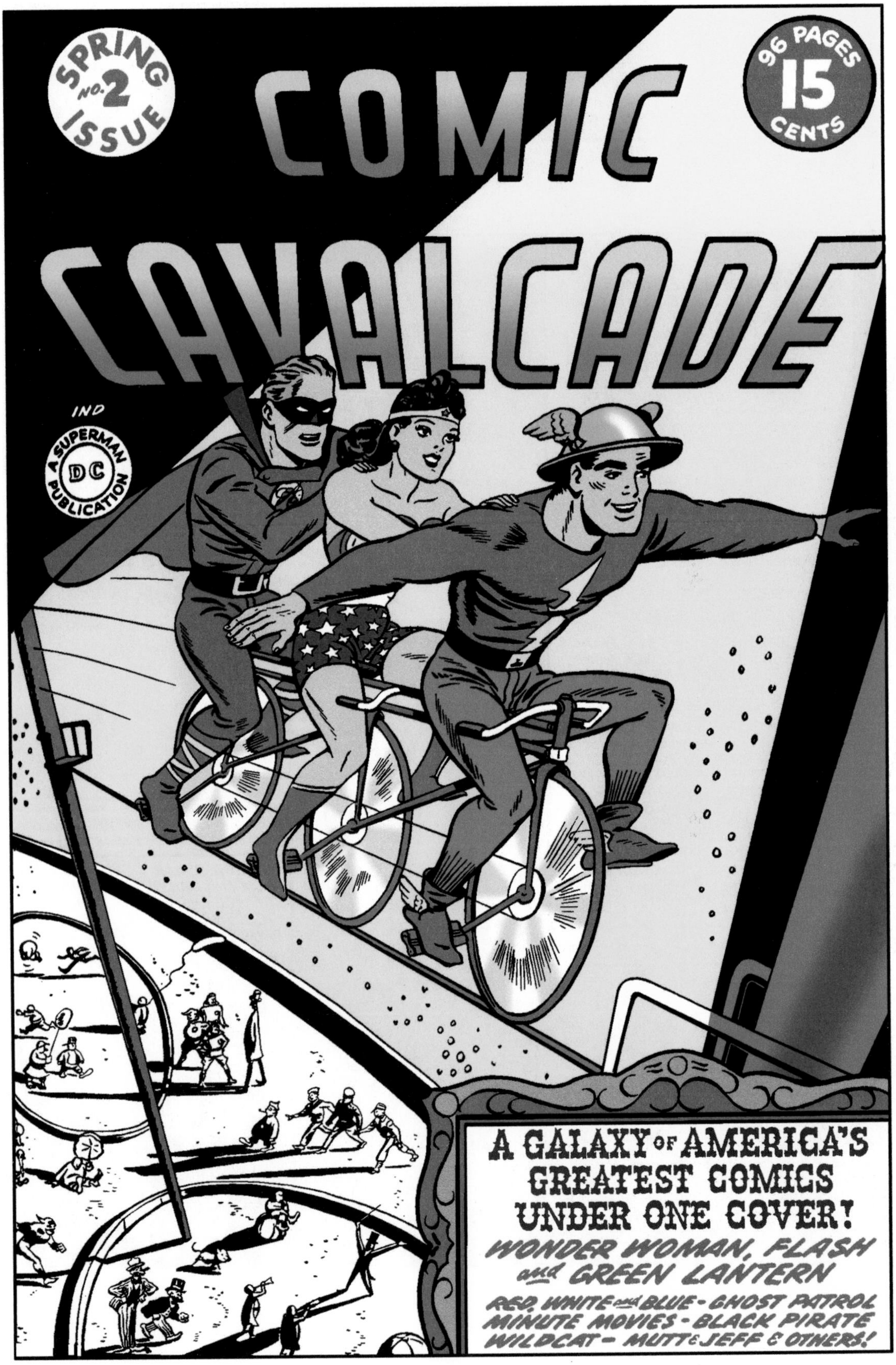
SPRING No.2 ISSUE
COMIC CAVALCADE
96 PAGES 15 CENTS
IND
A SUPERMAN DC PUBLICATION
A GALAXY OF AMERICA'S GREATEST COMICS UNDER ONE COVER!
WONDER WOMAN, FLASH and GREEN LANTERN
RED, WHITE and BLUE - GHOST PATROL
MINUTE MOVIES - BLACK PIRATE
WILDCAT - MUTT & JEFF & OTHERS!

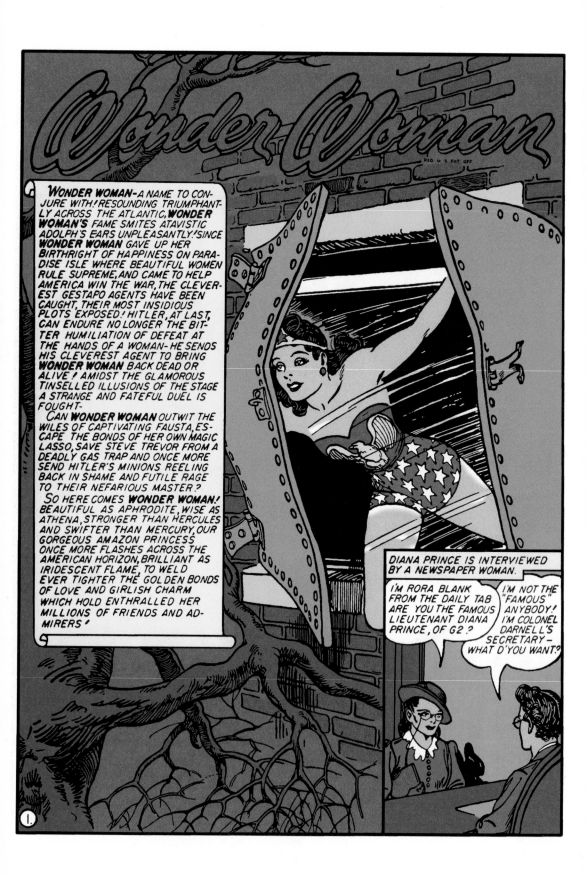

Wonder Woman

WONDER WOMAN-A NAME TO CONJURE WITH! RESOUNDING TRIUMPHANTLY ACROSS THE ATLANTIC, **WONDER WOMAN'S** FAME SMITES ATAVISTIC ADOLPH'S EARS UNPLEASANTLY! SINCE **WONDER WOMAN** GAVE UP HER BIRTHRIGHT OF HAPPINESS ON PARADISE ISLE WHERE BEAUTIFUL WOMEN RULE SUPREME, AND CAME TO HELP AMERICA WIN THE WAR, THE CLEVEREST GESTAPO AGENTS HAVE BEEN CAUGHT, THEIR MOST INSIDIOUS PLOTS EXPOSED! HITLER, AT LAST, CAN ENDURE NO LONGER THE BITTER HUMILIATION OF DEFEAT AT THE HANDS OF A WOMAN- HE SENDS HIS CLEVEREST AGENT TO BRING **WONDER WOMAN** BACK DEAD OR ALIVE! AMIDST THE GLAMOROUS TINSELLED ILLUSIONS OF THE STAGE A STRANGE AND FATEFUL DUEL IS FOUGHT-

CAN **WONDER WOMAN** OUTWIT THE WILES OF CAPTIVATING FAUSTA, ESCAPE THE BONDS OF HER OWN MAGIC LASSO, SAVE STEVE TREVOR FROM A DEADLY GAS TRAP AND ONCE MORE SEND HITLER'S MINIONS REELING BACK IN SHAME AND FUTILE RAGE TO THEIR NEFARIOUS MASTER?

SO HERE COMES **WONDER WOMAN**! BEAUTIFUL AS APHRODITE, WISE AS ATHENA, STRONGER THAN HERCULES AND SWIFTER THAN MERCURY, OUR GORGEOUS AMAZON PRINCESS ONCE MORE FLASHES ACROSS THE AMERICAN HORIZON, BRILLIANT AS IRIDESCENT FLAME, TO WELD EVER TIGHTER THE GOLDEN BONDS OF LOVE AND GIRLISH CHARM WHICH HOLD ENTHRALLED HER MILLIONS OF FRIENDS AND ADMIRERS!

DIANA PRINCE IS INTERVIEWED BY A NEWSPAPER WOMAN.

I'M RORA BLANK FROM THE DAILY TAB. ARE YOU THE FAMOUS LIEUTENANT DIANA PRINCE, OF G2.?

I'M NOT THE "FAMOUS" ANYBODY! I'M COLONEL DARNELL'S SECRETARY— WHAT D'YOU WANT?

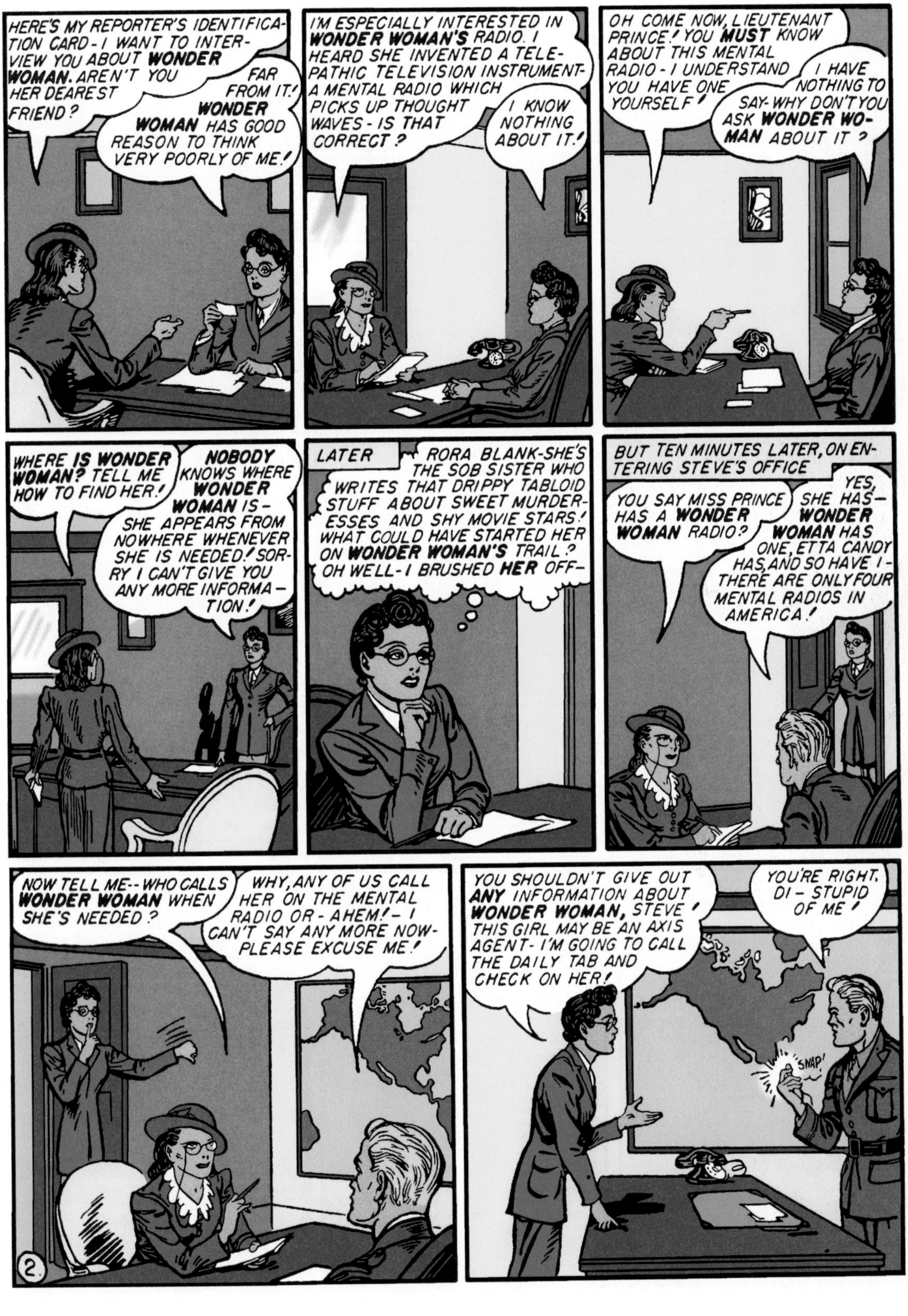
HERE'S MY REPORTER'S IDENTIFICATION CARD - I WANT TO INTERVIEW YOU ABOUT WONDER WOMAN. AREN'T YOU HER DEAREST FRIEND?
FAR FROM IT! WONDER WOMAN HAS GOOD REASON TO THINK VERY POORLY OF ME!
I'M ESPECIALLY INTERESTED IN WONDER WOMAN'S RADIO. I HEARD SHE INVENTED A TELEPATHIC TELEVISION INSTRUMENT - A MENTAL RADIO WHICH PICKS UP THOUGHT WAVES - IS THAT CORRECT?
I KNOW NOTHING ABOUT IT!
OH COME NOW, LIEUTENANT PRINCE! YOU MUST KNOW ABOUT THIS MENTAL RADIO - I UNDERSTAND YOU HAVE ONE YOURSELF!
I HAVE NOTHING TO SAY - WHY DON'T YOU ASK WONDER WOMAN ABOUT IT?
WHERE IS WONDER WOMAN? TELL ME HOW TO FIND HER!
NOBODY KNOWS WHERE WONDER WOMAN IS - SHE APPEARS FROM NOWHERE WHENEVER SHE IS NEEDED! SORRY I CAN'T GIVE YOU ANY MORE INFORMATION!
LATER
RORA BLANK - SHE'S THE SOB SISTER WHO WRITES THAT DRIPPY TABLOID STUFF ABOUT SWEET MURDERESSES AND SHY MOVIE STARS! WHAT COULD HAVE STARTED HER ON WONDER WOMAN'S TRAIL? OH WELL - I BRUSHED HER OFF -
BUT TEN MINUTES LATER, ON ENTERING STEVE'S OFFICE
YOU SAY MISS PRINCE HAS A WONDER WOMAN RADIO?
YES, SHE HAS - WONDER WOMAN HAS ONE, ETTA CANDY HAS, AND SO HAVE I - THERE ARE ONLY FOUR MENTAL RADIOS IN AMERICA!
NOW TELL ME -- WHO CALLS WONDER WOMAN WHEN SHE'S NEEDED?
WHY, ANY OF US CALL HER ON THE MENTAL RADIO OR - AHEM! - I CAN'T SAY ANY MORE NOW - PLEASE EXCUSE ME!
2.
YOU SHOULDN'T GIVE OUT ANY INFORMATION ABOUT WONDER WOMAN, STEVE! THIS GIRL MAY BE AN AXIS AGENT - I'M GOING TO CALL THE DAILY TAB AND CHECK ON HER!
YOU'RE RIGHT, DI - STUPID OF ME!
SNAP!

HELLO, TAB EDITOR? DID YOU SEND RORA BLANK TO INTERVIEW US ABOUT **WONDER WOMAN**?

CERTAINLY NOT! RORA'S HERE IN MY OFFICE- WAIT! SHE SAYS SHE LOST HER PURSE- SOMEBODY'S GOT HER IDENTIFICATION CARD!

STEVE PROMPTLY INVESTIGATES.

YOUR FAKE REPORTER **MIGHT** BE FAUSTA GRABLES, RECENTLY ARRIVED- SWISS PASSPORT- SUSPECTED OF BEING A GESTAPO AGENT! ONLY **FAUSTA** IS PRETTY!

GOOD LOOKS ARE EASILY DISGUISED- START A SEARCH FOR THIS GIRL!

DIANA, REACHING HOME LATE, AFTER AN EVENING'S WORK AT THE OFFICE, FINDS HER APARTMENT IN DISORDER.

GREAT HEPHAESTUS! SOMEBODY'S BEEN HERE AND SEARCHED MY ROOMS! LUCKY I DIDN'T LEAVE MY **WONDER WOMAN** COSTUME HERE!

MY AMAZON RADIO WAS HIDDEN IN THE CLOSET- THE INTRUDER FOUND IT!- YES- BY JUPITER! IT'S BEEN TAMPERED WITH!

IF I HADN'T MADE THIS MYSELF I'D NEVER KNOW HOW TO FIX IT!

③

AS DIANA REPAIRS HER RADIO A MENTAL MESSAGE ARRIVES

CALLING **WONDER WOMAN**- WOO WOO! SOMEBODY SEARCH- ED MY ROOM- WRECKED MY MENTAL RADIO- THEY TOOK NO CANDY- MUST BE CRAZY!

HM- ETTA'S RADIO TOO! I'LL CALL STEVE-

THEY DO NOT ANSWER!

THAT'S QUEER- STEVE SAID HE WAS GOING HOME TO BED! BET HE'LL FIND HIS MENTAL RADIO WRECKED WHEN HE GETS THERE!

STEVE, MEANWHILE, ENTERING HIS ROOM, IS BLINDED BY A FLASH LIGHT BEAM!

SURRENDER, AND YOU WON'T BE HURT, MAJOR - HANDS UP!

STEVE SWINGS AT HIS ASSAILANT, BUT IS KNOCKED OUT FROM BEHIND!

I'LL PUT **ONE** HAND UP - OUCH!

BIND HIM, BOYS, AND CARRY HIM DOWN THE FIRE ESCAPE!

WHEN STEVE REGAINS CONSCIOUSNESS, HE FINDS HIMSELF BOUND AND HELPLESS.

SUMMON HELL PINCH TO THIS HOUSE 1392 VERMONT AVENUE!

I'LL TELL YOU NOTHING!

I'LL SEND **WONDER WOMAN** A MENTAL MESSAGE

DIANA, REMOVING HER OUTER GARMENTS, REVEALS HER **WONDER WOMAN** COSTUME BENEATH.

BZZZ-ZZZ!

THE RADIO AGAIN! I'LL BET THIS IS STEVE REPORTING A RAID ON **HIS** ROOM

CALLING **WONDER WOMAN!** AM HELD BY ENEMY AGENTS AT 1392 VERMONT AVENUE - THEY THINK I KNOW WHERE YOU ARE -

THEY'RE TORTURING STEVE - I'LL SOON STOP **THAT!** WONDER HOW HE LEARNED THE ADDRESS OF THE HIDEOUT?

RACING STRAIGHT ACROSS THE CITY, **WONDER WOMAN** TAKES A **STREET** FULL OF TRAFFIC IN HER STRIDE

I NEVER COULD UNDERSTAND WHY PEOPLE ON FOOT, IN THIS MAN'S WORLD, WAIT FOR TRAFFIC LIGHTS

JONES & WILLIAMS

EXCELSIOR LAUNDRY

4

WONDER WOMAN FINDS THE HOUSE WHERE STEVE IS HELD PRISONER

THAT TREE NEAR THE WINDOW IS AN INVITATION - I'LL ACCEPT!

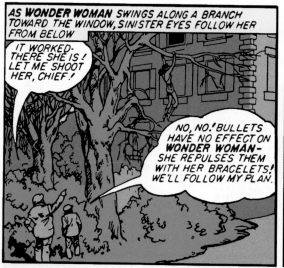

AS **WONDER WOMAN** SWINGS ALONG A BRANCH TOWARD THE WINDOW, SINISTER EYES FOLLOW HER FROM BELOW

IT WORKED—THERE SHE IS! LET ME SHOOT HER, CHIEF!

NO, NO! BULLETS HAVE NO EFFECT ON **WONDER WOMAN**—SHE REPULSES THEM WITH HER BRACELETS! WE'LL FOLLOW MY PLAN.

RAISING THE WINDOW CAUTIOUSLY, **WONDER WOMAN** STEPS INTO A DARK ROOM

THIS IS SO EASY, IT SEEMS ALMOST LIKE A TRAP!

PULLING THE SHADE DOWN BEHIND HER, **WONDER WOMAN** TURNS ON THE LIGHTS.

STEVE! THIS IS LUCK— I'LL FREE YOU IN TWO SHAKES!

BUT STEVE IS BOUND WITH PIANO WIRE — BREAKING THIS STRONG STEEL FILAMENT, WITHOUT HURTING THE PRISONER, TAKES LONGER THAN **WONDER WOMAN** EXPECTED.

STOP ME IF THIS WIRE CUTS INTO YOU!

NEVER MIND THAT—WE'D BETTER HURRY!

FREE AT LAST, STEVE STAGGERS TO HIS FEET

SOMP'N FUNNY— CAN'T BREATHE— FEEL DIZZY!

I FEEL IT TOO— THEY'RE FILLING THIS ROOM WITH DEADLY GAS FROM AN AUTO EXHAUST— HEAR THE MOTOR RUNNING OUTSIDE? LET'S GO!

WE'RE TRAPPED! WHILE YOU WERE UNTYING ME, THEY CLOSED THESE STEEL WINDOW SHUTTERS FROM THE OUTSIDE—LET'S TRY THE DOOR!

NO TIME— GAS GETTING WORSE—I'LL SMASH THESE SHUTTERS—YOU JUMP AFTER ME, INTO THE TREE!

⑤

THE MASSIVE STEEL BARRIERS CRUMPLE LIKE PAPER!

THIS IS MORE FUN THAN FOOTBALL!

STEVE FOLLOWS **WONDER WOMAN**.

SWING UP ON THE BRANCH, STEVE-I SEE SOME LADS BELOW US WITH SHOOTING IRONS!

MOVING ALONG THE BRANCH, HEAD DOWN, **WONDER WOMAN** COVERS THEIR RETREAT WITH HER BRACELETS.

CROSS-EYED CATFISH! IF I ONLY HAD MY AUTOMATIC!

I'M GLAD YOU HAVEN'T-I NEED PRACTICE PLAYING BULLETS AND BRACELETS

UNABLE TO SHOOT **WONDER WOMAN**, THE GUNMEN FLEE.

IT'S NO USE-BULLETS WON'T KILL HER! SHE ISS NOT HUMAN!

LOOKS AS IF THE BOYS AREN'T WAITING FOR US! TOO BAD, I WANTED TO TALK WITH THEM!

NEXT DAY, A VICIOUS GROUP ASSEMBLES-THE COUNCIL OF AXIS CHIEFS, AMERICA'S MOST DEADLY ENEMIES!

VELL, FRAULEIN FAUSTA GRABLES, YOU HAF FAILED AGAIN!

WONDER WOMAN'S STRENGTH IS UNBELIEVABLE-THOSE STEEL SHUTTERS WEREN'T STRONG ENOUGH!

DOT ISS NO EXCUSE! DER FUEHRER SENT YOU HERE TO GET **VONDER VOMAN**-YOU KNOW DER PENALTY FOR FAILURE?

I'LL GET HER, HERR SPADER-GIVE ME ANOTHER CHANCE!

I'LL FIND **WONDER WOMAN** THROUGH TREVOR! LAST NIGHT HE CALLED HER DIRECTLY, WITH ALL OTHER MENTAL RADIOS DISCONNECTED! I'VE TAPPED TREVOR'S TELEPHONE-HE MUST TALK TO **WONDER WOMAN** FREQUENTLY!

VELL-YOU BEDDER BE RIGHT!

6

THAT NIGHT, BEFORE GOING TO BED, TREVOR CALLS DIANA.

I'M WORRIED-THEY MAY KIDNAP YOU NEXT! HOW ABOUT A GUARD TO WATCH YOUR PLACE?

HEAVENS, NO! **WONDER WOMAN'S** STAYING WITH ME TONIGHT-SHE'LL PROTECT ME!

FAUSTA, LISTENING ON THE TAPPED TELEPHONE, GRINS WITH TRIUMPHANT MALICE!

I **KNEW** TREVOR WOULD LEAD ME TO **WONDER WOMAN**-I MUST ACT QUICKLY!

ENTERING DIANA'S ROOM WITH A SKELETON KEY, FAUSTA SEES THE ARMY NURSE PREPARING FOR BED.

GOOD OLD STEVE! WORRIED ABOUT ME, EH? WELL WONDER WOMAN'S HERE—HA! HA!

BUT WHERE IS SHE? PROBABLY IN THE BEDROOM!

NEVER CAN TELL WHO'LL BREAK INTO THIS PLACE—I'D BETTER HIDE WONDER WOMAN'S COSTUME. NO ONE WILL LOOK FOR IT IN A BAG FULL OF SOILED LAUNDRY!

AH! SO WONDER WOMAN'S IN BED! PERFECT!

NEXT MORNING—

SHALL I WEAR PART OF MY WONDER WOMAN COSTUME TODAY AND TAKE THE REST WITH ME, AS USUAL? MM—I'D BETTER NOT!

IF I SHOULD BE KIDNAPPED AS STEVE WARNED, THEY MIGHT DISCOVER MY DOUBLE IDENTITY!

LAUNDRY

BUT THE DAY PASSES PEACEFULLY; THAT EVENING DIANA ATTENDS AN ARMY BENEFIT SHOW WITH STEVE.

OH LOOK, STEVE! THERE'S A STRONG GIRL IN THIS SHOW!

HUH—SHE'LL BE WEAK COMPARED TO WONDER WOMAN!

MASKED MARVEL

STRONGEST WOMAN IN THE WORLD

FROM THE FIRST THE MASKED MARVEL MAKES A HIT WITH THE ARMY AUDIENCE.

I AM A STRONG GIRL, YES! BUT WHEN I SEE ALL YOU GREAT BIG POWERFUL ARMY BOYS I FEEL SO WEAK!

HURRAY! ATTA GIRL! YAY-AY-AY!

1000 LBS.

THIS, OF COURSE, IS VERY EASY—I DO THIS JUST TO LIMBER UP!

1000 LBS.

⑦

AN AUTOMOBILE, HOISTED ON PULLEYS, IS LOWERED ON THE MASKED MARVEL'S SHOULDERS.

THIS IS A LITTLE HARDER—IT'S A GOOD EXERCISE FOR THE MOTOR TRANSPORT CORPS.

WHATTA GIRL!

WOW!

RAY-AY-AY!

SHE'S TERRIFIC! YOU KNOW, DIANA, SHE MIGHT EVEN BE **WONDER WOMAN** IN DISGUISE!

NONSENSE! EVERY ONE OF THOSE STUNTS COULD BE FAKED. I THINK SHE'S A PHONY!

THE SILENCE OF SUSPENSE FALLS ON THE AUDIENCE AS THE MASKED MARVEL GRAPPLES WITH A BEAR!

THIS IS GOOD SPORT, IF YOU LIKE BEAR HUGS!

GROWRR

HE'S GOT A WICKED GRIP — NO HOLDS BARRED!

GRR-RR!

HURRAY FOR THE MASKED MARVEL! SHE'S THROWN THE BEAR!

YEOW!

CLAP CLAP CLAP

AS THE GIRL RISES TO HER FEET, THE BEAR'S CLAWS RIP OFF PART OF HER COSTUME.

STOP THAT, BRUIN! IS THAT ANY WAY TO TREAT A LADY?

RARR RAGH!

WELL — AH — THIS IS EMBARRASSING!

IT'S REALLY **WONDER WOMAN!**

YEEOW! **WONDER WOMAN!**

THANKS FOR YOUR KIND APPLAUSE. AS A SPECIAL FEATURE TONIGHT I WILL CHALLENGE ANY MAN OR WOMAN TO A WRESTLING MATCH! I OFFER $1000 IN WAR BONDS TO ANYBODY I CAN'T THROW IN THREE MINUTES!

8

HA! HA! I WAS RIGHT—THE MASKED MARVEL IS WONDER WOMAN!

YOU'RE CLEVER STEVE! SORRY I MUST GO—GOT WORK TO DO.

WHAT GAME IS THAT GIRL PLAYING? I'D BETTER INVESTIGATE!

RACING THROUGH BACK STREETS TO AVOID RECOGNITION, DIANA STREAKS HOME AT AMAZON SPEED.

I WISH I'D WORN THE WONDER WOMAN COSTUME UNDERNEATH, AS USUAL—BUT I'LL GET BACK IN TIME TO CHALLENGE THAT FAKE!

ENTERING HER ROOM HASTILY, THROUGH THE WINDOW, DIANA DARTS STRAIGHT TO THE CLOSET WHERE HER LAUNDRY BAG HANGS.

AT LEAST MY WONDER WOMAN COSTUME WAS SAFER IN HIDING!

GREAT MURDERS OF MARS! MY WONDER WOMAN CLOTHES ARE GONE—STOLEN! COULD THAT BE MY COSTUME THE MASKED MARVEL'S WEARING? I'LL VERY SOON SEE!

RUMMAGING IN A TRUNK, DIANA FINDS AN AMAZON COSTUME WORN ON PARADISE ISLE, AND QUICKLY PUTS IT ON.

THESE CLOTHES WILL DO—I'VE CERTAINLY WORN THEM OFTEN ENOUGH FOR WRESTLING AT HOME! NOW TO TAKE OFF THESE GLASSES AND PUT ON A MASK!

FLASHING BACK TO THE THEATRE WONDER WOMAN ENTERS THE STAGE DOOR.

I'M IN THE MASKED MARVEL'S ACT—IS SHE WRESTLING SOMEBODY?

YEAH—BIG GALOOT—CLAIMS TO BE EX-HEAVY-WEIGHT CHAMP! 'FYA ASK ME HE'S A STOOGE!

FROM THE WINGS WONDER WOMAN SEES HER RIVAL THROW HER HUGE OPPONENT.

GIVE, HIPPO! THIS IS YOUR TUMBLE—MAKE IT GOOD!

⑨

THE MASKED MARVEL WINS!

YAY-AY-AY! HOORAY FOR WONDER WOMAN! WHATTA YA MEAN "MASKED MARVEL"—SHE'S WONDER WOMAN!!

ANOTHER MASKED WOMAN STEPS SUDDENLY FROM THE WINGS.

I DARE YOU TO WRESTLE ME!

YOU? HA! HA! RUN HOME TO MAMA, LITTLE GIRL, BEFORE I HURT YOU!

HA! HA! HA! HO! HO!

THE MASKED MARVEL INSISTS THAT THE MYSTERIOUS STRANGER PROVE HER STRENGTH.

LET'S SEE YOU LIFT THAT WEIGHT!

1000 POUNDS? THAT'S EASY-UNH-HUH? SOMETHING'S QUEER!

1000 LBS.

EXERTING HER STRENGTH, WONDER WOMAN WRENCHES THE "WEIGHT" FROM THE FLOOR.

YOU CAN'T LIFT THAT-EEK-EEK-STOP!

ANYBODY COULD LIFT THIS WOODEN BLOCK! YOU SHOULD USE A STRONGER MAGNET TO HOLD ITS METAL BASE TO THE FLOOR!

1000 LBS.

AHA! THIS IS WONDER WOMAN! NO ONE ELSE COULD HAVE PULLED THAT "WEIGHT" LOOSE.

GOOD! I'LL GIVE $1000 TO THE U.S.O. IF I DON'T THROW YOU IN TWO MINUTES!

THAT MAGNETIC BLOCK IS A JOKE WE PLAY ON AMATEURS! NOW I'LL WRESTLE YOU!

USING A FLYING TACKLE HOLD, WONDER WOMAN HURLS HER OPPONENT TO THE MAT.

NOW IT'S YOUR TURN TO TUMBLE-DO IT GRACEFULLY, LIKE YOUR STOOGE!

AS WONDER WOMAN KNEELS ABOVE HER FALLEN OPPONENT, THE MASKED MARVEL'S HAND STEALS TO THE GOLDEN LASSO AT HER WAIST.

YOU STOLE MY COSTUME- DID YOU THINK IT WOULD GIVE YOU STRENGTH?

YES — IT HAS!

⑩.

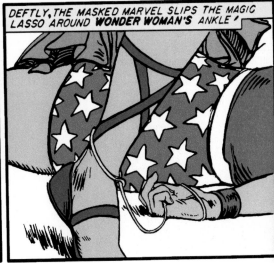

DEFTLY, THE MASKED MARVEL SLIPS THE MAGIC LASSO AROUND WONDER WOMAN'S ANKLE!

WONDER WOMAN IS SUDDENLY HELPLESS.

RELEASE MY ARM-QUICK, OBEY!

WHY YOU - OH! WHAT IS THIS I FEEL - I'M COMPELLED TO OBEY - YOU'VE CAUGHT ME WITH THE MAGIC LASSO!

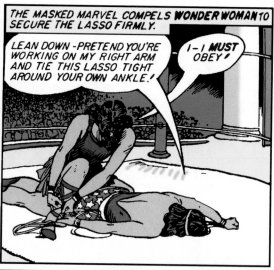

THE MASKED MARVEL COMPELS WONDER WOMAN TO SECURE THE LASSO FIRMLY.

LEAN DOWN - PRETEND YOU'RE WORKING ON MY RIGHT ARM AND TIE THIS LASSO TIGHT AROUND YOUR OWN ANKLE!

I - I MUST OBEY!

UNDER THE MASKED MARVELS DIRECTION, THE GIRLS APPEAR TO STRUGGLE FURIOUSLY.

PUT MORE PEP INTO IT BUT DON'T HURT ME — PULL YOUR PUNCHES!

AFTER A LONG, EXCITING CONTEST, WONDER WOMAN'S SHOULDERS ARE PINNED TO THE MAT.

SHE'S DO-OWN! WONDER WOMAN WINS!

TAKE YOUR TUMBLE GRACEFULLY, DARLING - HA! HA!

THE LOSER IS COMPELLED TO CONGRATULATE HER CONQUEROR WHOM THE AUDIENCE BELIEVES TO BE WONDER WOMAN.

CONGRATULATIONS! YOU PUT UP A BRAVE BATTLE - HA! HA!

HOORAY - THREE CHEERS FOR WONDER WOMAN! TAKE OFF YOUR MASK, WONDER WOMAN!

11

IN THE WINGS WONDER WOMAN IS COMPELLED TO CHANGE COSTUMES QUICKLY WITH HER RIVAL.

WONDER WOMAN - YAY-AY-AY-AY! WE WANT WONDER WOMAN!

GET OUT THERE AND TAKE YOUR MASK OFF! THAT'LL CONVINCE EVERYBODY THAT I AM YOU!

HOORAY - IT IS WONDER WOMAN! WHATTA GIRL! SHE TOPS THEM ALL! YAY - AY!

THE MASKED MARVEL TAKES **WON-DER WOMAN** TO HER DRESSING ROOM AND MAKES HER CHANGE COSTUMES AGAIN!

WITH MY CLOAK OVER YOUR SHOULDERS, NOBODY WILL SEE THAT YOUR ARMS ARE BOUND BEHIND YOU!

AS THE GIRLS LEAVE THE THEATRE TOGETHER, THEY MEET STEVE!

MY ANGEL! YOU WERE WONDERFUL TONIGHT! LET'S HAVE SUPPER TOGETHER.

SORRY-- I CAN'T. I MUST TAKE CARE OF THIS POOR LITTLE GIRL-- SHE FEELS DEPRESSED!

WONDER WOMAN IS FORCED TO LIE ON THE FLOOR OF HER CAPTOR'S CAR.

YOU MAKE A SOFT FOOT-REST! DRIVE TO HEADQUARTERS, FRITZY-- HERR SPADER EXPECTS US!

WHEN THE CAR FINALLY STOPS, **WONDER WOMAN** SOMERSAULTS, KICKING THE DOOR OFF.

WHAM! CRA-AK!

WONDER WOMAN IS QUICKLY RECAPTURED-- BUT HER PURPOSE IS ACCOMPLISHED.

MUCH GOOD THAT NONSENSE DID YOU!

HM-- I RECOGNIZE THIS PLACE-- IT'S THE FORMER JAP EMBASSY AND SUPPOSED TO BE CLOSED! IF ONLY I CAN INFORM STEVE--

KNOWING THAT STEVE AND ETTA'S RADIOS ARE DISCONNECTED, **WONDER WOMAN** SENDS A MIND MESSAGE TO HER MOTHER, QUEEN HIPPOLYTE, ON PARADISE ISLAND.

MOTHER-- PLEASE RADIO STEVE AND ETTA I AM PRISONER AT FORMER JAP EMBASSY--

I'VE CAPTURED **WONDER WOMAN**, HERR SPADER-- HERE'S THE PRISONER!

GOOT! YOU HAF DONE WELL, FAUSTA. --ACH! SUCH IMPERTINENCE SIDDING ON MY DESK-- STAND AT ATTENTION, PRISONER!

WONDER WOMAN, TRUSSED INTO A NEAT BUNDLE WITH THE MAGIC LASSO, IS PLACED IN A TRUNK

DER FUEHRER COMMANDS THIS PRISONER BE BROUGHT TO GERMANY! A PLANE IS WAITING-- TAKE DER TRUNK TO OUR SECRET AIR FIELD.

⑫

AT THIS MOMENT STEVE AND ETTA CANDY, SUMMONED BY **WONDER WOMAN'S** MESSAGE, RELAYED THROUGH PARADISE ISLAND, STORM THE HOUSE WITH THEIR COHORTS.

THERE THEY ARE BOYS, LET'S GET 'EM!

DROP DER TRUNK AND DEFEND DER STAIRS

THE NAZIS, SHOOTING **DOWN,** GAIN AN ADVANTAGE.

TAKE COVER, BOYS— MAKE 'EM COME TO US.

WOO WOO! STOP THAT, YOU NASTI MAN!

WONDER WOMAN, MEANWHILE, UNABLE TO BREAK THE MAGIC LASSO, CATAPULTS HERSELF LIKE A ROLLING BALL THROUGH THE END OF THE TRUNK.

WOOPS, MY DEAR! WATCH ME MAKE A STRIKE IN **ONE TRY!**

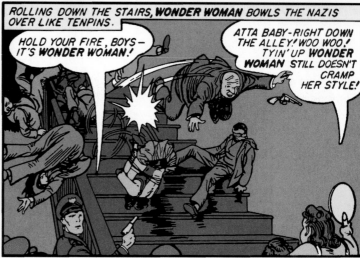

ROLLING DOWN THE STAIRS, **WONDER WOMAN** BOWLS THE NAZIS OVER LIKE TENPINS.

HOLD YOUR FIRE, BOYS— IT'S **WONDER WOMAN!**

ATTA BABY—RIGHT DOWN THE ALLEY! WOO WOO! TYIN' UP **WONDER WOMAN** STILL DOESN'T CRAMP HER STYLE!

WITH **WONDER WOMAN** FREED, HITLER'S AGENTS ARE QUICKLY OVERCOME.

HERE YOU ARE, GIRLS—FORWARD PASS!

HOORAY FOR **WONDER WOMAN!**

13

WONDER WOMAN IS HERSELF AGAIN!

YOU WIN, **WONDER WOMAN!**

BUT I ALMOST LOST! I THOUGHT YOU WERE WEAK, AND I LET YOU KEEP THE MAGIC LASSO WHILE WE WRESTLED. YOUR CLEVERNESS HAS TAUGHT ME NOT TO UN- DERESTIMATE AN OP- PONENT!

MORE ADVENTURES of WONDER WOMAN IN EVERY ISSUE OF SENSATION COMICS

FOR VICTORY BUY UNITED STATES WAR BONDS AND STAMPS

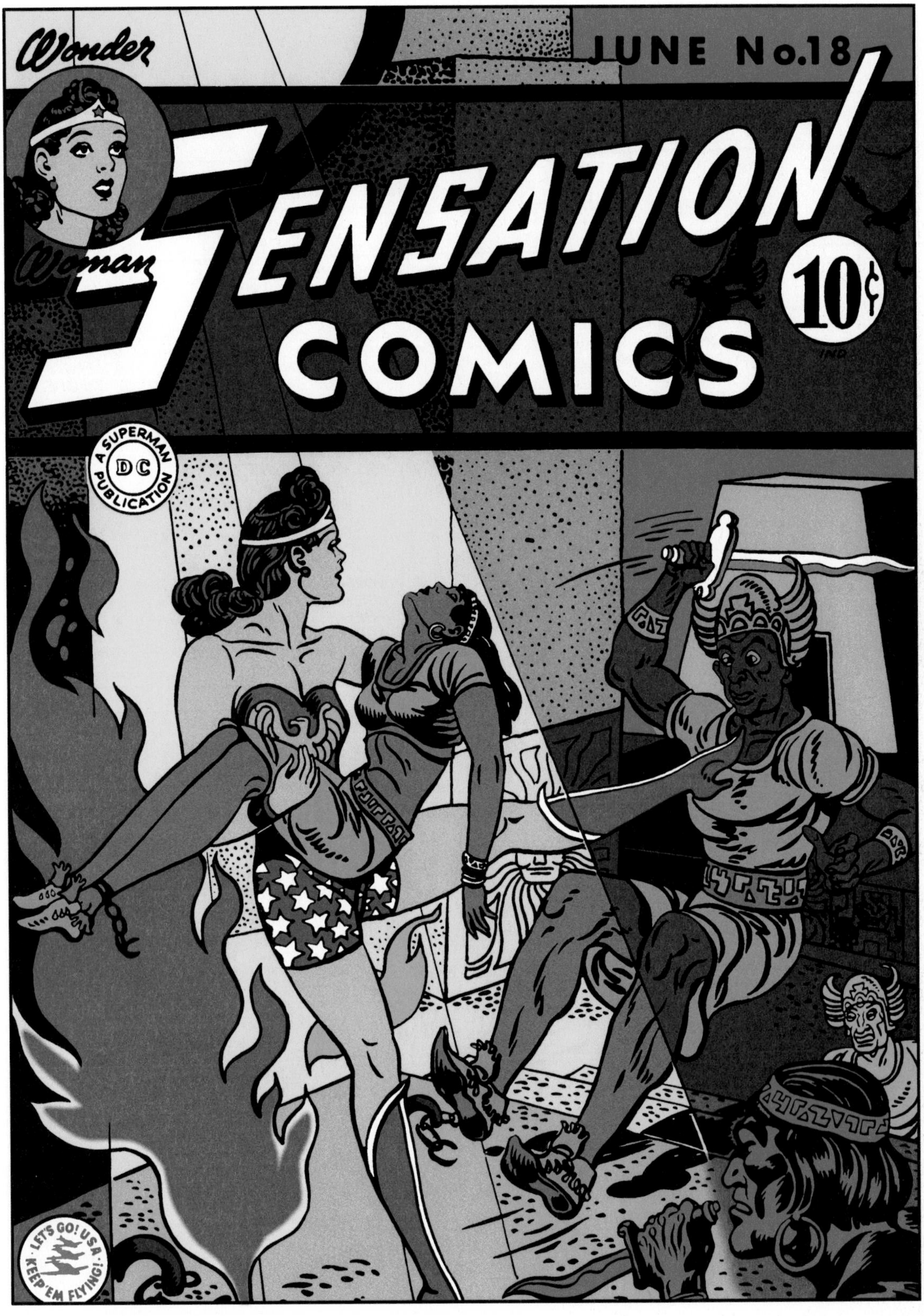
Wonder Woman
JUNE No.18
SENSATION COMICS
10¢
A SUPERMAN DC PUBLICATION
LET'S GO! U.S.A. KEEP 'EM FLYING!

Wonder Woman

by CHARLES MOULTON

TRACING A VICIOUS MULTI-MURDERER THROUGH THE TRACKLESS JUNGLES OF SOUTH AMERICA **WONDER WOMAN** DISCOVERS THE SECRET CITY OF GOLD, WHERE A LOST TRIBE OF MIGHTY INCAS HAS HIDDEN FROM MODERN CIVILIZATION FOR 400 YEARS! CAN **WONDER WOMAN** WITHSTAND THE FIERCE HEAT OF A GIANT BURNING GLASS, SAVE A BEAUTIFUL INCA GIRL FROM SACRIFICE TO THE SUN GOD, ENDURE THE ORDEAL OF FLAMING ARROWS AND PREVENT A CLEVERLY PLANNED JAPANESE INVASION OF SOUTH AMERICA? A TERRIFIC TASK, YOU WILL ADMIT, FOR ANY GIRL TO UNDERTAKE! BUT **WONDER WOMAN** IS—WELL, SHE'S **WONDER WOMAN!**

BEAUTIFUL AS APHRODITE, WISE AS ATHENA, STRONGER THAN HERCULES AND SWIFTER THAN MERCURY, **WONDER WOMAN** COMES FROM PARADISE ISLE WHERE LOVELY AMAZONS RULE SUPREME, TO HELP AMERICA RESTORE JUSTICE, FREEDOM AND HAPPINESS TO A WORLD TORTURED BY WAR-MAD AGGRESSORS!

ARIOS HARDIK, FAMOUS ARCHEOLOGIST, RETURNING TO LOS ANGELES FROM EXPLORATIONS IN SOUTH AMERICA, SENDS FOR CAPTAIN WEST OF ARMY INTELLIGENCE.

YOU SHOULDN'T HAVE COME HERE IN UNIFORM, CAPTAIN!

FOR HEAVEN'S SAKE, WHY NOT?

1.

YOU MAY HAVE BEEN FOLLOWED! THERE'S NOBODY IN THIS HALL NOW, BUT I'M STILL WORRIED!

WHAT'S IT ALL ABOUT, DOCTOR- PLEASE EXPLAIN.

I WAS SEARCHING SOUTH AMERICA FOR RELICS OF THE INCAS-THOSE WONDERFUL INDIANS WHO MADE HOUSES, TEMPLES AND WEAPONS OF PURE GOLD! AND *I DISCOVERED A LOST INCA TRIBE*, HIDDEN IN THE MOUNTAINS FOR 400 YEARS-

THAT'S INTERESTING BUT-

LISTEN-THESE INCAS HAVE A SECRET MOUNTAIN RETREAT THAT'S A NATURAL FORTRESS IT WOULD MAKE AN IDEAL ENEMY BASE FOR INVADING THE AMERICAS!

YOU MEAN-?

AS DR. HARDIK REVEALS HIS SECRET, THE DOOR OPENS STEALTHILY.

THE JAPS ARE SENDING AN ARMY TO THE INCAS' SECRET CITY! THE INCAS CAUGHT ME SPYING-THEIR HIGH PRIEST FOLLOWED ME HERE! HIS NAME IS-

AGGH- ULP!

BA-ANG!

SWIFTLY AS CAPT. WEST LEAPS TO THE DOOR HE IS TOO LATE- THE KILLER HAS DISAPPEARED!

I'M A FOOL-SHOULD HAVE TAKEN HARDIK'S WARNING SERIOUSLY! THAT GUNMAN, WHOEVER IT WAS, GOT CLEAN AWAY-

②

WEST IMMEDIATELY CALLS INTELLIGENCE HEADQUARTERS IN WASHINGTON

HELLO- COLONEL DARNELL? OH, IT'S YOU, DIANA! WEST SPEAKING FROM LOS ANGELES- TAKE A MESSAGE, PLEASE-

COLONEL DARNELL ISN'T- HELLO, CAPTAIN WEST! OKAY- DICTATE YOUR MESSAGE.

HARDIK, THE ARCHEOLOGIST, WAS SHOT WHILE REVEALING A JAP PLAN TO INVADE SOUTH AMERICA PLEASE SEND YOUR BEST MAN AT ONCE- I SUGGEST MAJOR TREVOR!

COLONEL DARNELL ORDERS STEVE IMMEDIATELY TO THE WEST COAST.

I'LL FLY MY OWN PLANE, COLONEL— IT'S QUICKER!

OH **PLEASE** LET ME GO WITH STEVE!

CAN'T SPARE YOU, DIANA—BESIDES—STEVE WILL HAVE CAPTAIN WEST TO ASSIST HIM.

WHILE CAPTAIN WEST, THIS TIME IN MUFTI, WAITS FOR STEVE AT GLENDALE AIRPORT, HE MEETS A TALL STRANGER.

HOW SOON DOES THE PLANE LEAVE FOR SAN FRANCISCO?

IN 45 MINUTES—

THEY SIT DOWN TOGETHER IN THE WAITING ROOM.

DO YOU WAIT FOR ARRIVAL OF A PLANE FROM WASHINGTON?

WHAT GIVES YOU THAT IDEA?

HOW'D HE KNOW THAT— WHO IS THIS GUY?

I HEARD YOU INQUIRE ABOUT THE WASHINGTON PLANE. EXCUSE, I GO TO BUY A CIGAR.

I MADE NO INQUIRIES ABOUT WASHINGTON PLANES! THIS FELLOW KNOWS TOO MUCH ABOUT ME— I MUST FIND OUT ABOUT HIM—HM—HE LEFT HIS BAG—

CAPTAIN WEST'S MIND WORKS AS THE STRANGER EXPECTS

WHILE HE'S AWAY I'LL TAKE A LOOK IN HIS BAG—MAYBE I CAN FIND A CLUE— HEY?

BANG!

AS STEVE ARRIVES, POLICEMEN ARE CARRYING SOMETHING AWAY ON A STRETCHER.

WHAT HAPPENED OFFICER—ACCIDENT?

YEAH—SOME GUY **ACCIDENTALLY** PLANTED A BOMB THAT BLEW CAPTAIN WEST, THERE, TO HEAVEN!

③

CAPTAIN **WEST?** IT COULDN'T BE - BUT IT **IS!** TOMMY WEST OF G2 POOR TOMMY- THIS IS GHASTLY! ANY CLUES TO THE MURDERER?

NOTHING BUT FRAGMENTS OF A TRAVELING BAG- NOT ENOUGH TO TRACE THE OWNER.

STEVE SEARCHES CAPTAIN WEST'S OFFICE

NO RECORD HERE OF WHAT HARDIK TOLD WEST ABOUT THE JAP INVASION PLANS. BOTH HARDIK AND WEST WERE KILLED TO SILENCE THEM, LEAVING **NO** CLUE TO THE KILLER'S IDENTITY!

AT THIS MOMENT THERE ENTERS A MAN WHO **COULD** GIVE STEVE PLENTY OF CLUES- BUT HE DOES NOT INTEND TO!

PARDON, I AM SEÑOR QUITO, A FRIEND OF CAPTAIN WEST

I'M TREVOR FROM WASHINGTON— THE CAPTAIN'S BEEN KILLED!

AH, THAT IS **BAD!** DO YOU KNOW WHO KILLED HIM?

I WONDER IF HE'S FISHING FOR INFORMATION- I'D BETTER BLUFF!

OH -NOT YET, BUT WE'LL KNOW IN LESS THAN TWENTY FOUR HOURS!

WEST MUST HAVE TOLD HIM SOMETHING- THIS MAN HAD BETTER BE ELIMINATED!

THANKS- I THINK I WILL!

PERHAPS I CAN HELP YOU. CAPTAIN WEST WAS SAILING ON MY YACHT TO MEET A FRIEND OF SEÑOR HARDIK'S. YOU MAY FIND A CLUE, IF YOU COME IN WEST'S PLACE—

THERE COMES AN UNEXPECTED INTERRUPTION.

HERE COMES THE BRIDE ♪ ♪ ♪

BLAZES! BE QUIET, GIRLS! WHERE IN THE WORLD DID **YOU** COME FROM, ETTA?

OUR HOLLIDAY BAND IS IN A PICTURE AT HOLLYWOOD DIANA WIRED ME TO SEE YOU AT CAPTAIN WEST'S OFFICE! WHAT'S UP, KID?

4

WELL, AT THE MOMENT I'M GOING WITH SEÑOR QUITO TO HIS YACHT.

HA! NOW TREVOR'S TOLD THESE GIRLS WHERE HE'S GOING, SO I MUST TAKE THEM ALSO—

WON'T YOU MUSIC-MAKING LADIES COME WITH US?

WOO WOO! SWELL IDEA- WE'D LOVE TO!

QUITO'S GUESTS WERE SEEN EMBARKING ON HIS YACHT.

A-HUNTING WE WILL GO, A-HUNTING WE WILL GO— FOR NIPS AND NASTIES MERRILY, A-HUNTING WE WILL GO—

HOORAY!

ATTA GALS!

HA! HA!

QUITO'S YACHT IS SEEN BY A COAST GUARD PATROL STEAMING SOUTH.

THAT'S THE YACHT LIMA HEADING FOR SOUTH AMERICA.

HM - RIGHT- THAT TAL- LIES WITH THE REGIS- TRY REPORT.

48 HOURS LATER A RADIO MES- SAGE OF DESPAIR COMES OVER THE ETHER WAVES FROM THE SOUTH PACIFIC.

S.O.S.- S.O.S.! YACHT LIMA HIT BY MINE-SINKING— MAJOR TREVOR, U.S. INTELLIGENCE, AND HOLLIDAY GIRLS ABOARD—

RADIO'S STOPPED- SHE MUST'VE GONE DOWN.

THE NEWS IS FLASHED IMMEDIATE- LY TO COLONEL DARNELL IN WASHINGTON.

STEVE AND ETTA DEAD? I DON'T BELIEVE IT! I'VE **GOT** TO INVES- TIGATE!

VERY WELL, DIANA— CATCH THE NEXT PLANE FOR LOS ANGELES!

THE "NEXT PLANE" IS **WONDER WOMAN'S**- IT TAKES OFF IN TWO MIN- UTES FLAT WITH A TRANSFORMED DIANA AT THE CONTROLS.

OH STEVE - ETTA! YOU CAN'T BE DEAD- **SEND** ME A MENTAL RADIO MESSAGE!

⑤

BUT **WONDER WOMAN'S** INVISIBLE PLANE GLIDES TO A SILENT LANDING ON THE WEST COAST WITH NO WORD FROM THE MISS- ING ONES.

THEY MUST BE DEAD OR UNCONSCIOUS OR THEY'D HAVE SENT ME A MENTAL MESSAGE—

LET US TURN THE CLOCK BACK AND SEE WHAT REALLY HAPPENED TO STEVE AND THE GIRLS.

WHAT BEAUTIFUL WAITRESSES YOU HAVE, SEÑOR!

THEY ARE ONLY SPANISH GIRLS—SPANIARDS ARE SLAVES IN MY COUNTRY!

WOO WOO! ARE YOU KID-DIN'? WHAT IS YOUR COUNTRY, MISTER?

I'M GETTING DIZZY!

YEAH—WHAT'SH YOUR COUNTRY, QUITO?

I'M SHO' SHLEEPY—

I WILL SHOW YOU MY COUNTRY SOON, PALEFACES-YOU HAVE NEVER SEEN ITS LIKE— HA! HA!

SOON THE ENTIRE COMPANY FALLS INTO DEEP SLUMBER.

THEIR FOOD WAS WELL DRUGGED-THEY WILL SLEEP MANY DAYS. BIND ALL PRISONERS CAREFULLY—I WILL RADIO THAT OUR SHIP IS SUNK!

AYEE, YOUR HOLINESS!

DAYS LATER THE PRISONERS, STILL UNCONSCIOUS, ARE LANDED ON THE JUNGLE COAST OF SOUTH AMERICA.

HASTEN, MY BRAVES! CARRY THESE GIFTS TO THE TEMPLE OF GOLD IN OUR SECRET CITY FOR THE SUN GOD'S FESTIVAL!

AS THEY NEAR THE SECRET CITY, ETTA CANDY REGAINS CONSCIOUS-NESS.

WOO WOO! WHERE AM I? MUST CALL WONDER WOMAN!

WONDER WOMAN IS SEARCHING THE PACIFIC FOR QUITO'S YACHT WHEN SHE RECEIVES ETTA'S MENTAL RADIO CALL.

HEY, WONDER WOMAN! WE'RE SUNK BUT THE SHIP WASN'T! A LOST TRIBE OF INCAS IN THE ANDES ARE CARRYING US THROUGH FOUR PEAK MOUNTAIN-HELP!

6.

STEVE AND THE GIRLS ARE ALIVE—THANK APHRODITE! BUT ETTA'S MESSAGE DOESN'T MAKE SENSE. A "LOST TRIBE OF INCAS"? THEY PERISHED 400 YEARS AGO. I'LL FLY OVER THE ANDES AND LOOK FOR A MOUNTAIN WITH FOUR PEAKS.

FLASHING ACROSS SOUTH AMERICA IN HER AMAZON PLANE **WONDER WOMAN'S** SPEED IS TOO GREAT TO DISTINGUISH MOUNTAIN PEAKS. RETURNING, SHE THROTTLES HER ENGINE DOWN TO 1180 MILES PER HOUR.

SUDDENLY SHE SEES, DIRECTLY BELOW, A VAST, FERTILE PLANE GUARDED BY FOUR MOUNTAIN PEAKS.

THERE'S ETTA'S MOUNTAIN—WHAT A PERFECT HIDING PLACE! INCAS **MIGHT** HAVE LIVED THERE, COMPLETELY LOST TO THE WORLD, FOR CENTURIES!

CIRCLING LOW **WONDER WOMAN** SEES A GREAT INCA SUN TEMPLE, THE "PACCARI-TAMPU," BUILT OF SOLID GOLD.

THE TEMPLE IS CROWDED WITH PEOPLE—REAL INCAS! THEY'RE OFFERING A HUMAN SACRIFICE—I MUST LAND QUICKLY!

LANDING ON THE TEMPLE ROOF **WONDER WOMAN** SURVEYS A SINGULAR SCENE.

AY-OOO AY-AR! SUN GOD-CONSUME OUR SACRIFICE!

THAT POOR GIRL! SHE'S ALL COVERED WITH OIL—WHEN THE SUN SHINES ON HER THROUGH THAT BURNING GLASS HER BODY WILL BURST INTO FLAMES!

LIKE A DAZZLING SPIRIT FROM THE SUN ITSELF **WONDER WOMAN** LEAPS DOWN THE SUNRAY PATH TO THE ALTAR.

⑦

THE WORSHIPPERS GAZE IN AWE AS **WONDER WOMAN** STANDS UNINJURED IN THE SUN'S BURNING HEAT.

I'M IN A HOT SPOT! LUCKY WE AMAZONS PRACTICE ENDURING HEAT BY REPULSING IT WITH OUR BODY ELECTRICITY!

LIFTING THE MASSIVE ALTAR STONE **WONDER WOMAN** MOVES EASILY BENEATH ITS CRUSHING WEIGHT.

IN ANOTHER SECOND THE SUN WOULD HAVE SET THIS GIRL ON FIRE—I'LL MOVE HER AWAY FROM IT!

AS **WONDER WOMAN** FREES THE GIRL FROM THE ALTAR SHE SPEAKS TO HER IN THE ANCIENT INCA LANGUAGE

AUCA TE-HI— PLEASING ONE, WHO ART THOU?

I AM CURA, DAUGHTER OF THE AYAR—OUR INCA CHIEF!

SNAP!

DO NOT BREAK MY CHAINS-IT IS A SACRILEGE! I AM A SUN GOD CAPTIVE, SENTENCED BY THE HIGH PRIEST, QUITO!

SO **THIS** IS SEÑOR QUITO'S RACKET— MM-HM!

TELL ME THE REST LATER-RIGHT NOW I'VE GOT TO SAVE OUR LIVES!

THE INCAS ACCLAIM **WONDER WOMAN** AS SUN GODDESS

HAIL, HOLY DAUGHTER OF THE SUN! THOU ART OUR LONG PROMISED DIVINE WOMAN - GODDESS OF LIGHT!

OH! OH!- THIS HAS POSSIBILITIES!

THE AYAR DESCENDS FROM HIS THRONE TO WELCOME **WONDER WOMAN.**

WELCOME TO OUR SE-CRET CITY, SUN DAUGHTER! TRUE IS THE PROPHECY THAT **FEMALE FLAME** SHALL DES-CEND FROM HEAVEN TO JOIN MALE MIGHT!

8

WONDER WOMAN IS PLACED ON THE THRONE.

AS YOUR GODDESS I COMMAND YOU TO STOP HUMAN SACRIFICE THE SUN GOD WISHES TO KEEP BEAUTIFUL MAIDENS LIKE THIS ALIVE AND HAPPY!

QUITO, RETURNING FROM HIS MUR-DEROUS MISSION, EMERGES SUD-DENLY FROM A SECRET ENTRANCE!

OH MANCO, SAPA INCA, WHO IS THIS WOMAN?

SHE IS MAMA, DAUGHTER OF THE SUN, LONG PROMISED GOD-DESS WHO SHALL RULE THE WORLD.

HA! THIS IS THE FAMOUS **WONDER WOMAN** I HEARD ABOUT IN THE OUTSIDE WORLD—I'LL CALL HER BLUFF!

IT IS WRITTEN THAT DIVINE WOMAN SHALL WED THE HIGH PRIEST OF THE SUN! TOGETHER YOU AND I CAN CONQUER AMERICA!

MARRY YOU? HA! HA! DON'T BE RIDICULOUS!

IF YOU DISOBEY THE SUN'S LAW, YOU'RE NO GODDESS! I'LL SHOW THE PEOPLE YOU ARE MORTAL!

TAKE IT EASY, FANCY PANTS—I MIGHT LOSE MY TEMPER!

CAREFUL—DON'T SCRATCH YOURSELF WITH THAT SILLY TOY!

SEE, BROTHERS SHE IS NO GODDESS—SHE FEARS THE TEST OF MORTAL STEEL!

I MAY NOT BE A GODDESS BUT I'M A GOOD **MAN** HANDLER!

RECOVERING HIMSELF QUICKLY, QUITO MOVES A SECRET LEVER KNOW ONLY TO PRIESTS

THE TEMPLE DUNGEONS WILL SOON EXTINGUISH YOUR LIGHT, FALSE WOMAN FLAME!

AH-H-H, PLUTO, HERE I COME INTO YOUR REALM OF DARKNESS—

WONDER WOMAN FINDS HERSELF IN A CELL WITH NO DOOR BUT A GRATED CEILING.

SO YOU THINK I'M TRAPPED, EH? I'LL SOON SHOW YOU!

WAIT! SURRENDER INSTANTLY OR I'LL KILL THE AMERICAN CAPTIVES-PALE FACES LIKE YOURSELF!

WONDER WOMAN SURRENDERS.

LOAD THAT GIRL WITH CHAINS - SHE IS STRONG AS 20 MEN!

MAYBE THEY'LL PUT ME WITH THE OTHER "PALE FACE" PRISONERS. THEN I'LL RESCUE STEVE AND THE GIRLS!

9

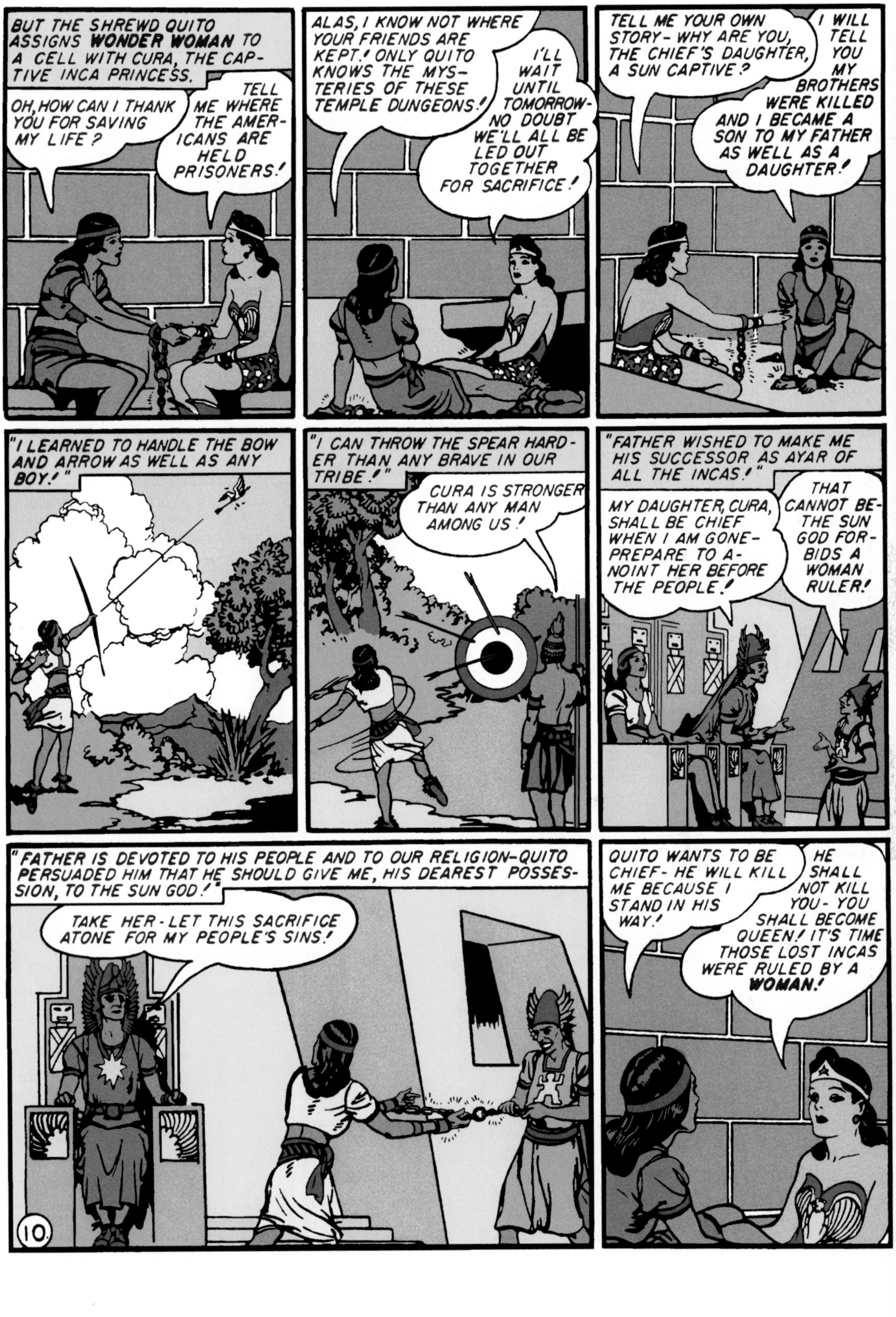
BUT THE SHREWD QUITO ASSIGNS WONDER WOMAN TO A CELL WITH CURA, THE CAPTIVE INCA PRINCESS.
OH, HOW CAN I THANK YOU FOR SAVING MY LIFE?
TELL ME WHERE THE AMERICANS ARE HELD PRISONERS!
ALAS, I KNOW NOT WHERE YOUR FRIENDS ARE KEPT! ONLY QUITO KNOWS THE MYSTERIES OF THESE TEMPLE DUNGEONS!
I'LL WAIT UNTIL TOMORROW- NO DOUBT WE'LL ALL BE LED OUT TOGETHER FOR SACRIFICE!
TELL ME YOUR OWN STORY- WHY ARE YOU, THE CHIEF'S DAUGHTER, A SUN CAPTIVE?
I WILL TELL YOU MY BROTHERS WERE KILLED AND I BECAME A SON TO MY FATHER AS WELL AS A DAUGHTER!
"I LEARNED TO HANDLE THE BOW AND ARROW AS WELL AS ANY BOY!"
"I CAN THROW THE SPEAR HARDER THAN ANY BRAVE IN OUR TRIBE!"
CURA IS STRONGER THAN ANY MAN AMONG US!
"FATHER WISHED TO MAKE ME HIS SUCCESSOR AS AYAR OF ALL THE INCAS!"
MY DAUGHTER, CURA, SHALL BE CHIEF WHEN I AM GONE- PREPARE TO ANOINT HER BEFORE THE PEOPLE!
THAT CANNOT BE- THE SUN GOD FORBIDS A WOMAN RULER!
"FATHER IS DEVOTED TO HIS PEOPLE AND TO OUR RELIGION-QUITO PERSUADED HIM THAT HE SHOULD GIVE ME, HIS DEAREST POSSESSION, TO THE SUN GOD!"
TAKE HER- LET THIS SACRIFICE ATONE FOR MY PEOPLE'S SINS!
10.
QUITO WANTS TO BE CHIEF- HE WILL KILL ME BECAUSE I STAND IN HIS WAY!
HE SHALL NOT KILL YOU- YOU SHALL BECOME QUEEN! IT'S TIME THOSE LOST INCAS WERE RULED BY A WOMAN!

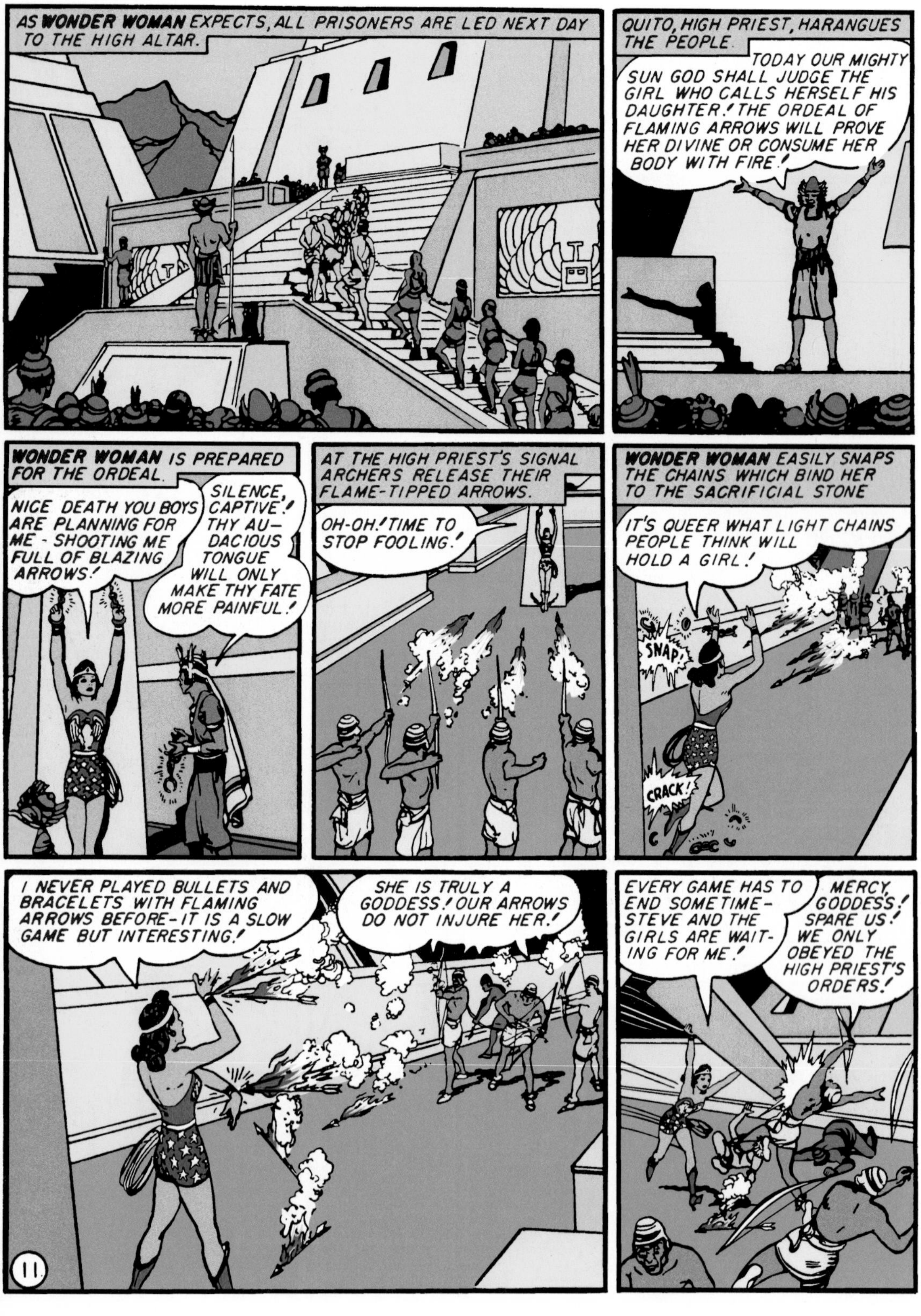
AS WONDER WOMAN EXPECTS, ALL PRISONERS ARE LED NEXT DAY TO THE HIGH ALTAR.
QUITO, HIGH PRIEST, HARANGUES THE PEOPLE.
TODAY OUR MIGHTY SUN GOD SHALL JUDGE THE GIRL WHO CALLS HERSELF HIS DAUGHTER! THE ORDEAL OF FLAMING ARROWS WILL PROVE HER DIVINE OR CONSUME HER BODY WITH FIRE!
WONDER WOMAN IS PREPARED FOR THE ORDEAL.
NICE DEATH YOU BOYS ARE PLANNING FOR ME - SHOOTING ME FULL OF BLAZING ARROWS!
SILENCE, CAPTIVE! THY AUDACIOUS TONGUE WILL ONLY MAKE THY FATE MORE PAINFUL!
AT THE HIGH PRIEST'S SIGNAL ARCHERS RELEASE THEIR FLAME-TIPPED ARROWS.
OH-OH! TIME TO STOP FOOLING!
WONDER WOMAN EASILY SNAPS THE CHAINS WHICH BIND HER TO THE SACRIFICIAL STONE
IT'S QUEER WHAT LIGHT CHAINS PEOPLE THINK WILL HOLD A GIRL!
SNAP!
CRACK!
I NEVER PLAYED BULLETS AND BRACELETS WITH FLAMING ARROWS BEFORE - IT IS A SLOW GAME BUT INTERESTING!
SHE IS TRULY A GODDESS! OUR ARROWS DO NOT INJURE HER!
11
EVERY GAME HAS TO END SOMETIME - STEVE AND THE GIRLS ARE WAITING FOR ME!
MERCY, GODDESS! SPARE US! WE ONLY OBEYED THE HIGH PRIEST'S ORDERS!

LEAPING FOUR ROWS OF MALE PRISONERS, **WONDER WOMAN** REACHES STEVE.

WONDER WOMAN! YOU DO SHOW UP IN THE DARNDEST PLACES!

SORRY TO SEE ME?

FREEING STEVE QUICKLY, **WONDER WOMAN** HURRIES TOWARD THE HOLLIDAY COLLEGE GIRLS.

FREE THE OTHER PRISONERS IF YOU CAN-WE MAY NEED THEM TO FIGHT QUITO'S GUARDS!

RIGHT-HO-

THIS IS THE FIRST FUN I'VE HAD FOR DAYS! I'LL TAKE THOSE KEYS AND GET THE MEN'S SHACKLES UNLOCKED BEFORE YOU WAKE UP, MY FRIEND.

SOCKO!

WONDER WOMAN FREES ETTA WHO TACKLES ANOTHER KEY CARRIER.

WOO WOO! SINK AN INCA!

HOORAY- ATTA GAL, ETTA!

WHAM!

LED BY **WONDER WOMAN**, STEVE AND ETTA CANDY, THE FREED CAPTIVES CHARGE THE HIGH PRIEST'S GUARD.

QUITO'S THE LAD I WANT- WONDER WHERE HE IS!

BUT CURA FOUND THE FALSE PRIEST FIRST.

MERCY, PRINCESS! I'LL GIVE THEE THE THRONE!

THOU'LT GIVE ME NOTHING BUT THE PLEASURE OF KILLING THEE!

12

BUT **WONDER WOMAN** INTERVENES

SORRY TO SPOIL YOUR SPORT, DARLING, BUT I WANT OUR MUTUAL FRIEND ALIVE FOR QUESTIONING!

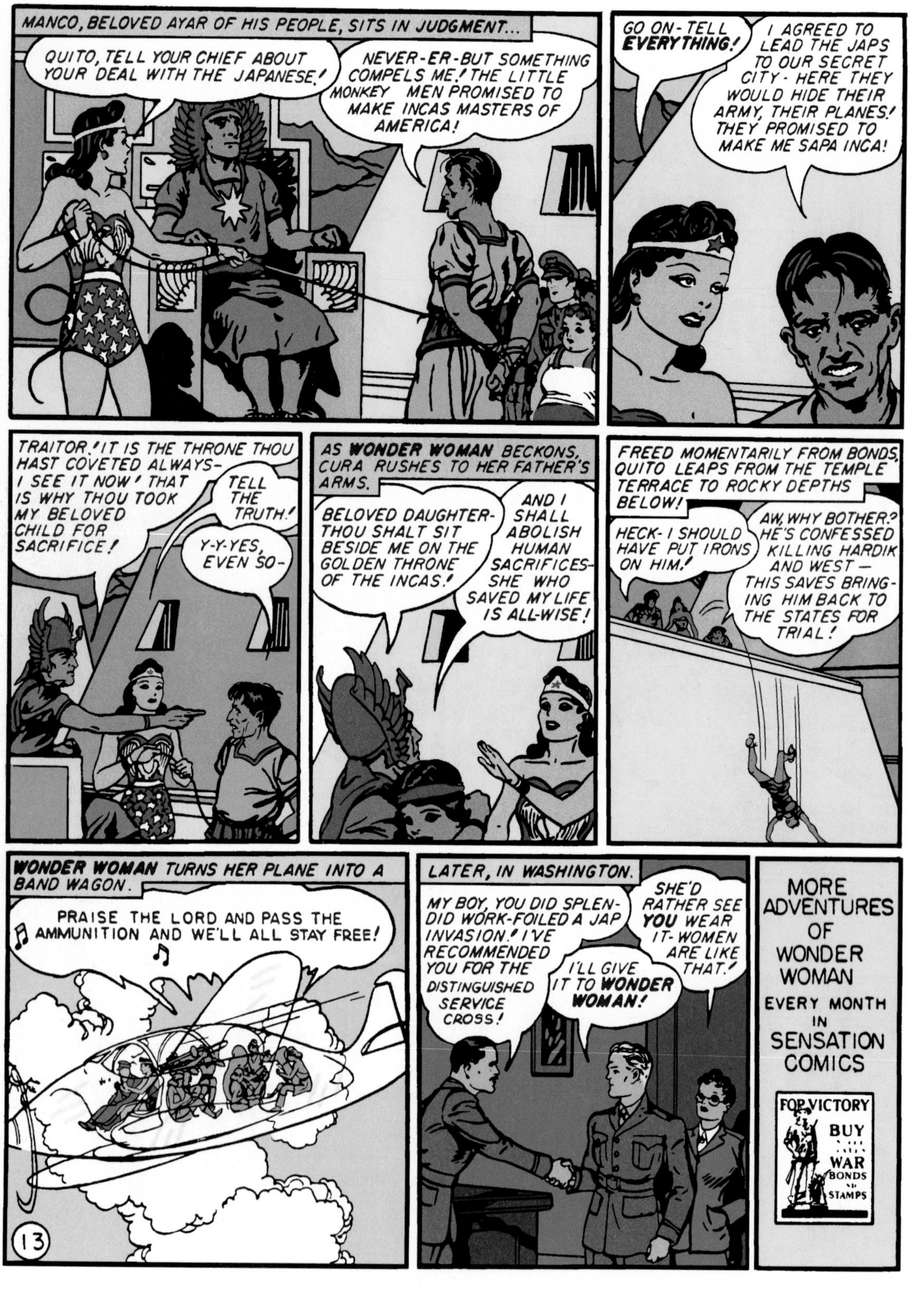
MANCO, BELOVED AYAR OF HIS PEOPLE, SITS IN JUDGMENT...
QUITO, TELL YOUR CHIEF ABOUT YOUR DEAL WITH THE JAPANESE!
NEVER-ER-BUT SOMETHING COMPELS ME! THE LITTLE MONKEY MEN PROMISED TO MAKE INCAS MASTERS OF AMERICA!
GO ON-TELL EVERYTHING!
I AGREED TO LEAD THE JAPS TO OUR SECRET CITY- HERE THEY WOULD HIDE THEIR ARMY, THEIR PLANES! THEY PROMISED TO MAKE ME SAPA INCA!
TRAITOR! IT IS THE THRONE THOU HAST COVETED ALWAYS- I SEE IT NOW! THAT IS WHY THOU TOOK MY BELOVED CHILD FOR SACRIFICE!
TELL THE TRUTH!
Y-Y-YES, EVEN SO-
AS WONDER WOMAN BECKONS, CURA RUSHES TO HER FATHER'S ARMS.
BELOVED DAUGHTER- THOU SHALT SIT BESIDE ME ON THE GOLDEN THRONE OF THE INCAS!
AND I SHALL ABOLISH HUMAN SACRIFICES- SHE WHO SAVED MY LIFE IS ALL-WISE!
FREED MOMENTARILY FROM BONDS, QUITO LEAPS FROM THE TEMPLE TERRACE TO ROCKY DEPTHS BELOW!
HECK- I SHOULD HAVE PUT IRONS ON HIM!
AW, WHY BOTHER? HE'S CONFESSED KILLING HARDIK AND WEST — THIS SAVES BRINGING HIM BACK TO THE STATES FOR TRIAL!
WONDER WOMAN TURNS HER PLANE INTO A BAND WAGON.
PRAISE THE LORD AND PASS THE AMMUNITION AND WE'LL ALL STAY FREE!
13
LATER, IN WASHINGTON.
MY BOY, YOU DID SPLENDID WORK-FOILED A JAP INVASION! I'VE RECOMMENDED YOU FOR THE DISTINGUISHED SERVICE CROSS!
I'LL GIVE IT TO WONDER WOMAN!
SHE'D RATHER SEE YOU WEAR IT- WOMEN ARE LIKE THAT!
MORE ADVENTURES OF WONDER WOMAN EVERY MONTH IN SENSATION COMICS
FOR VICTORY BUY WAR BONDS STAMPS

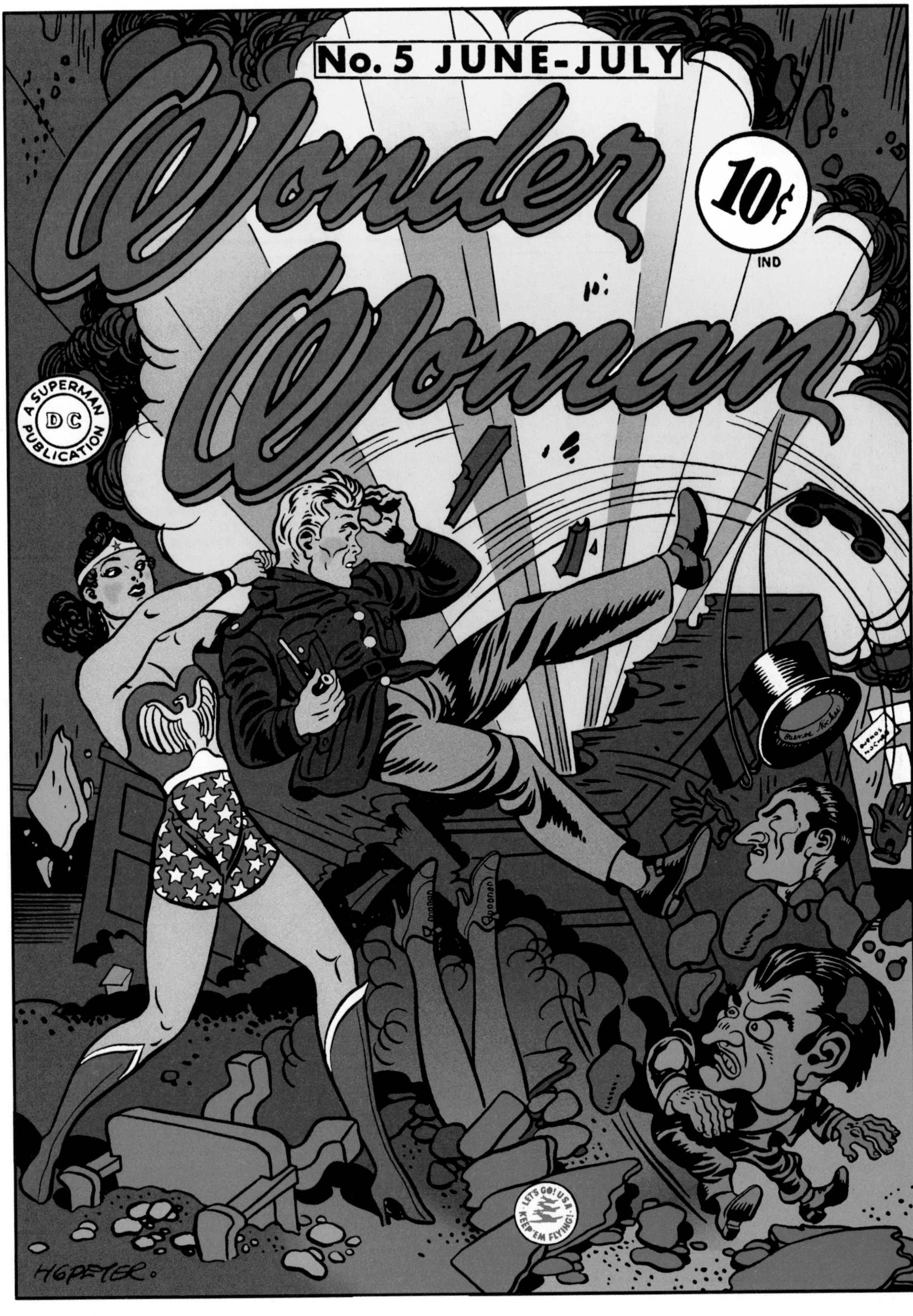
No. 5 JUNE-JULY
Wonder Woman
10¢
IND
A SUPERMAN DC PUBLICATION
LET'S GO! U.S.A. KEEP 'EM FLYING!
HGPETER

Wonder Woman

By CHARLES MOULTON

WHO IS THE DEVIOUS DOCTOR PSYCHO? KNOWN WHEREVER HIS EVIL GENIUS STRIKES AS THE MAN WITH A THOUSAND FACES, THIS MONSTER ABHORS WOMEN! WITH WEIRD CUNNING AND DARK, FORBIDDEN KNOWLEDGE OF THE OCCULT, DR. PSYCHO PREPARES TO CHANGE THE INDEPENDENT STATUS OF MODERN AMERICAN WOMEN BACK TO THE DAYS OF THE SULTANS AND SLAVE MARKETS, CLANKING CHAINS AND ABJECT CAPTIVITY.

BUT SLY AND SUBTLE PSYCHO RECKONS WITHOUT **WONDER WOMAN!** ACCEPTING THE MAD DOCTOR'S CHALLENGE, THE LOVELY AMAZON GIRL FIGHTS TO STOP A PERSECUTION OF HER FAIR SEX WHICH THREATENS EVEN THE ALLURING COHORTS OF APHRODITE WITH SHAMEFUL SHACKLES AND MENACES THE ENTIRE EARTH WITH PERPETUAL PUNISHMENT.

BEAUTIFUL AS APHRODITE, WISE AS ATHENA, STRONGER THAN HERCULES AND SWIFTER THAN MERCURY, **WONDER WOMAN** COMES FROM THE ISLE OF PARADISE WHERE FASCINATING WOMEN RULE SUPREME TO BRING DELIGHT AND HAPPINESS TO THE WORLD OF MEN!

YOU'LL LOVE **WONDER WOMAN** MORE THAN EVER AS YOU FOLLOW THE COURAGEOUS GIRL THROUGH HER MOST EXCITING ORDEALS IN THE **"BATTLE FOR WOMANHOOD."**

MARS, THE WAR GOD, PRESENT RULER OF THIS WORLD, RECEIVES UNPLEASANT INFORMATION FROM HIS SLAVE-SECRETARY.

HERE IS THE REPORT YOU ASKED FOR — THERE ARE EIGHT MILLION AMERICAN WOMEN IN WAR ACTIVITIES - BY 1944 THERE WILL BE EIGHTEEN MILLION!

HOUNDS OF HADES! **WOMEN!** THIS SMELLS LIKE MORE OF **APHRODITE'S** WORK!

1A

AMERICAN WOMEN ARE WARRIORS-- WAACS, WAVES, SECRET AGENTS! 10 MILLION BRITISH WOMEN ARE IN WAR SERVICE, 30 MILLION RUSSIAN WOMEN--

SILENCE--ENOUGH! IF WOMEN GAIN POWER IN WAR THEY'LL ESCAPE MAN'S DOMINATION COMPLETELY! THEY WILL ACHIEVE A HORRIBLE INDEPENDENCE!

SUMMON MY WAR STAFF-- COUNT CONQUEST, THE EARL OF GREED AND DUKE OF DECEPTION! I WON'T TOLERATE GIVING WOMEN THE SLIGHTEST FREEDOM!

YOU'RE TELLING ME!

YES, MASTER, YOUR SLAVE OBEYS!

MARS LECTURES HIS LIEUTENANTS.

WOMEN ARE THE NATURAL SPOILS OF WAR! THEY MUST REMAIN AT HOME, HELPLESS SLAVES FOR THE VICTOR! IF WOMEN BECOME WARRIORS LIKE THE AMAZONS, THEY'LL GROW STRONGER THAN MEN AND PUT AN END TO WAR!

AYE, MAJESTY!

GO TO EARTH AND PUT THESE UPSTART FEMALES IN THEIR PLACE!

IT CAN'T BE DONE WITH WONDER WOMAN AGAINST US!

FIGHTING WONDER WOMAN ISN'T PROFITABLE.

SHE BEAT YOU, MARS! SHE'LL MURDER ME!

COWARDS ALL! DECEPTION, YOU'RE THE ONE TO FOOL FEMALES! GET BUSY OR--

YES, DIVINITY, I OBEY. I HAVE AN EARTH AGENT WHO HATES WOMEN--I'LL PUT HIM TO WORK AT ONCE.

AND SO, ON EARTH, THE DEVIOUS DR. PSYCHO RECEIVES AN EVIL INSPIRATION.

Z-Z-ZUT! A SPIRIT TELLS ME MY HOUR OF VENGEANCE IS AT HAND! WOMEN SHALL SUFFER WHILE I LAUGH-- HA! HO! HA!

THE SUBTLE PSYCHO'S PAST IS SHROUDED IN MYSTERY. IN MEDICAL SCHOOL HIS BRILLIANT MIND WON HIM RECOGNITION--

THIS MEDAL IS THE HIGHEST AWARD OUR UNIVERSITY CAN GIVE!

I'M PROUD OF THIS HONOR.

HA! HA! HE IS COMICAL! HA! HA!

CLAP

CLAP

CLAP

2A.

HIS CLASSMATES' HUMOR HURTS PSYCHO.

GREAT WORK, PUMPKIN HEAD! YOUR BRAINS MAKE YOU TOP-HEAVY! CONGRATULATIONS, POCKET NAPOLEON!

OH LET ME ALONE!

I KNOW I'M FUNNY-LOOKING BUT THEY MIGHT LET ME FORGET IT THIS ONCE!

PSYCHO MEETS MARVA, HIS FIANCEE.

AREN'T YOU GOING TO CONGRATULATE ME, MARVA?

YES—YOU DON'T HAVE TO GET MUSHY—YOU KNOW I ADMIRE YOUR BRILLIANT MIND, BUT—WELL—YOU'RE NOT EXACTLY A CLARK GABLE LOVE-MAKING DOESN'T BECOME YOU!

LATER PSYCHO SEES MARVA WITH BEN BRADLEY, ATHLETIC IDOL OF THE COLLEGE.

MARVA, MARRY ME!

OH, BEN I CAN'T—I'M ENGAGED!

SHE LOVES BEN BECAUSE HE'S HANDSOME—I OUGHT TO LET HER MARRY HIM!

THAT NIGHT A MUFFLED FIGURE BREAKS INTO THE RADIUM LABORATORY WHERE PSYCHO HAS BEEN WORKING.

RADIUM LABORATORY

MARVA, WALKING DOWN THE CORRIDOR, THINKS THE SHORT-APPEARING FIGURE BY THE DOOR IS PSYCHO.

HI, THERE—DID YOU FORGET OUR DATE?

THAT'S FUNNY—HE RAN AWAY FROM ME INTO THE LAB!

DIUM ATORY

NEXT MORNING $125,000 WORTH OF RADIUM IS MISSING FROM THE LABORATORY SAFE, AND PSYCHO IS SUSPECTED.

YOU HAD THE LAB KEYS—YOU WENT IN THERE LAST NIGHT!

I DID NOT!

DID YOU SEE THIS MAN ENTER THE LABORATORY?

Y-YES-I DID! OH DARLING, PLEASE GIVE THE RADIUM BACK!

YOU PRETTY, DOUBLE-CROSSING LIAR! YOU'RE TRYING TO FRAME ME AND MARRY BEN BRADLEY!

CONVICTED ON MARVA'S TESTIMONY, PSYCHO RECEIVES THE FINAL BLOW IN PRISON!

MARRIED—SHE'S MARRIED BRADLEY! THIS IS THE END OF ALL MY FAITH IN HUMANITY!

DAILY BLADE
MARRIED

3A

134

Panel 1:
THROUGH LONG, BITTER YEARS IN A PRISON CELL PSYCHO'S SOUL SEETHES WITH HOT HATRED FOR HUMANKIND—ESPECIALLY WOMEN.

THEY SHALL **SUFFER**—SUFFER—HA! HA! BRADLEY MUST DIE—BUT KILLING'S TOO GOOD FOR A **WOMAN**!

Panel 2:
SOON AFTER PSYCHO'S RELEASE FROM PRISON—

YOU'LL SWALLOW THIS RADIUM—IT WILL BURN HOLES IN YOUR STOMACH HA! HO! HA!

MERCY—I'LL CONFESS! I **DID** STEAL THAT RADIUM TO FRAME YOU, BUT MARVA PLANNED IT, I SWEAR—AG—GLUG!

Panel 3:
AFTER BEN BRADLEY'S DEATH, OF A "STOMACH DISORDER," PSYCHO VISITS MARVA.

AH, MY PRETTY MARVA, I HAVE COME FOR YOU! DO NOT PRETEND INNOCENCE—BEN CONFESSED THAT **YOU** PLANNED MY BETRAYAL!

OH—I **DIDN'T**!

Panel 4:
TAKING MARVA TO A CAREFULLY PREPARED HIDEAWAY, PSYCHO HYPNOTIZES HER.

DON'T BE AFRAID—I WON'T KILL YOU! DEATH IS TOO GOOD FOR YOU! **OBEY** ME—

Panel 5:
UNDER PSYCHO'S HYPNOTIC CONTROL, MARVA IS FORCED TO MARRY HIM.

DO YOU PROMISE TO LOVE, CHERISH AND **OBEY**?

N—OH—YES, I DO!

Panel 6:
PSYCHO USES MARVA FOR OCCULT EXPERIMENTS, HYPNOTIZING HER EVERY DAY.

I COMMAND YOU, SLAVE, BRING ME **LIVING SUBSTANCE** FROM THE SPIRIT WORLD!

I WILL TRY, MASTER!

4A

Panel 7:
AT LAST SUCCESS! IN THE WEIRD RED LIGHT OF PSYCHO'S LABORATORY, PARTICLES OF LIVING ECTOPLASM ARE DRAWN FROM UNSEEN SPACE THROUGH THE MEDIUM'S BODY TO PSYCHO'S HAND!

I'M MASTER OF PSYCHIC CREATION! I CAN MAKE HUMAN BODIES!

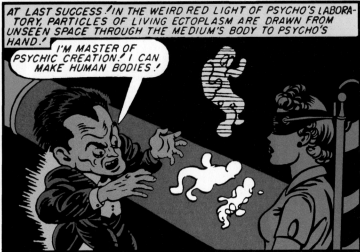

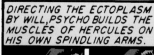

DIRECTING THE ECTOPLASM BY WILL, PSYCHO BUILDS THE MUSCLES OF HERCULES ON HIS OWN SPINDLING ARMS.

MATERIALIZING AN ECTOPLASMIC MASK OVER HIS FACE, PSYCHO TRANSFORMS HIMSELF INTO MUSSOLINI.

CREATING AN ENTIRE BODY OF ECTOPLASM IN LESS THAN A MINUTE, PSYCHO BECOMES JOHN L. SULLIVAN!

SHURE, I'M THE CHAMP'S GHOST! HA! HO! HA! WHAT A SIDE-SPLITTING JOKE DR. PSYCHO IS ABOUT TO PLAY ON THE STUPID PUBLIC!

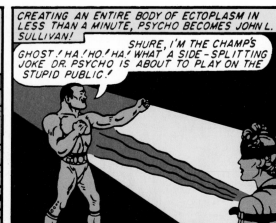

SOME WEEKS LATER STEVE TREVOR SHOWS NEWSPAPER HEADLINES TO DIANA PRINCE.

HOW'D YOU LIKE TO HEAR A SPEECH BY GEORGE WASHINGTON?

HUH – WHAT?

DAILY PRESS

GEORGE WASHINGTON TO SPEAK TONIGHT!

Dr. Psycho announces that the Spirit of the Father of our Country will materialize through Marva the Medium. It is expected that a capacity audience will fill Lafayette Hall tonight at a public seance announced by Dr. Psycho, the noted occultist. A committee of famous scientists tested Marva the Medium and report results are genuine.

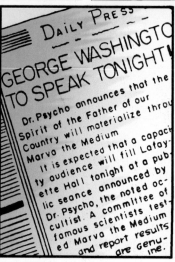

PERSONALLY I THINK IT'S BUNK! BUT MILLIONS ACCEPT EVERYTHING THAT PSYCHO'S SPIRITS SAY, AS LAW AND GOSPEL!

LET'S GO TONIGHT AND SEE FOR OURSELVES!

STEVE AND DIANA ATTEND PSYCHO'S MEETING THAT NIGHT.

LADIES AND GENTLEMEN! TO SEE THAT THE MEDIUM COMMITS NO FRAUD, WILL SOME OF YOU COME UP ON THE PLATFORM AND BIND MARVA IN HER CABINET?

5A

COME ON, DI – LET'S GO UP!

YOU GO, STEVE – I HAVE TO LEAVE EARLY.

AS STEVE GOES ON THE STAGE, DIANA SLIPS BACKSTAGE AND TRANSFORMS HERSELF SWIFTLY TO **WONDER WOMAN.**

THERE MAY BE NOTHING HERE TO INVESTIGATE BUT I DON'T LIKE THAT TRIUMPHANT GLEAM IN DR. PSYCHO'S EYES!

WONDER WOMAN MEETS STEVE ON THE STAGE.

WONDER WOMAN—WHAT ARE **YOU** UP TO?

TYING A MEDIUM—I'VE ALWAYS WANTED TO SEE GEORGE WASHINGTON BUT I MUST BE SURE HE'S THE GENUINE GENTLEMAN!

IF THE COMMITTEE WILL EXAMINE THE CABINET—UGH—NOT QUITE SO VIOLENTLY, PLEASE!

I'M SORRY! I'M AFRAID I BROKE THE HINGES—HARDWARE IS SO FRAGILE NOWADAYS!

WITH THE CABINET REPAIRED, **WONDER WOMAN** HELPS TIE MARVA IN HER CHAIR.

OW! **PLEASE** DON'T TIE ME SO TIGHT!

WHY, THAT ISN'T HALF TIGHT ENOUGH—AN AMAZON GIRL WOULD SLIP OUT OF THAT IN TWO SECONDS!

WITH THE HELPLESS MARVA CLOSELY WATCHED, "GEORGE WASHINGTON" APPEARS SUDDENLY IN A BEAM OF RED LIGHT!

GREETINGS, FELLOW COUNTRYMEN! NEARLY A CENTURY AND A HALF AGO I LIVED IN AMERICA!

GALLOPING CANARIES—IT'S GEORGE HIMSELF!

AN AWE-STRICKEN HUSH FALLS OVER THE AUDIENCE AS "WASHINGTON" ADDRESSES THEM.

I HAVE A MESSAGE FOR YOU—A WARNING! **WOMEN** WILL LOSE THE WAR FOR AMERICA! WOMEN SHOULD NOT BE PERMITTED TO HAVE THE RESPONSIBILITIES THEY NOW HAVE!

6A.

WOMEN MUST NOT MAKE SHELLS, TORPEDOES, AIRPLANE PARTS—THEY MUST NOT BE TRUSTED WITH WAR SECRETS OR SERVE IN THE ARMED FORCES. **WOMEN WILL BETRAY THEIR COUNTRY THROUGH WEAKNESS** IF NOT TREACHERY!

WHY, THAT LOOSE-TONGUED DOUBLE-TALKING PHONY! WHAT'S HIS GAME? HE'S WORKING FOR THE AXIS! I'LL STOP HIM—

WAIT, WONDER WOMAN! LET'S HEAR WHAT ELSE HE SAYS—SOUNDS GENUINE TO ME!

I WILL PROVE WHAT I SAY! TOMORROW, AT PRECISELY NOON, THE SUPREME SHELL WORKS WILL BLOW UP! WOMEN ARE FILLING THOSE SHELLS—WOMEN'S CARELESSNESS WILL WRECK A BILLION DOLLAR MUNITIONS PLANT! I HAVE PROPHESIED AND IT WILL BE SO!

AH-A-AH! THE SUPREME SHELL PLANT—OH-H-H!

AS WONDER WOMAN LEAPS FROM HER SEAT, "GEORGE WASHINGTON" VANISHES AND PSYCHO APPEARS.

I HOPE THE AUTHORITIES, AFTER HEARING OF GENERAL WASHINGTON'S WARNING, MAY PREVENT THIS DISASTER!

I'M TOO LATE! WHERE DID "WASHINGTON" GO?

AT THE SUPREME SHELL PLANT NEXT DAY EVERY PRECAUTION IS TAKEN.

HAVE YOU SEARCHED ALL BUILDINGS?

FROM TOP TO BOTTOM, SIR. FOUND NOTHING SUSPICIOUS. I'VE POSTED GUARDS AROUND THE WOMEN LOADING SHELLS!

ALL DOORS ARE GUARDED.

SAY, D'YOU KNOW WHO I AM? I'VE GOT OFFICIAL BUSINESS—

SORRY, SIR! ORDERS ARE TO LET NOBODY ENTER THIS SHELL LOADING ROOM UNTIL AFTER 12 O'CLOCK!

7A.

AS THE FATAL HOUR APPROACHES A GENERAL INSPECTS THE PLANT.

TEN TO TWELVE—EVERYTHING OKAY HERE?

YES, GENERAL, NOBODY'S GOT BY ME!

THE GENERAL ENTERS THE SHELL LOADING ROOM AND LAYS HIS STICK DOWN AS HE TALKS WITH WOMEN WORKERS.

ARE YOU GIRLS AFRAID OF "GEORGE WASHINGTON'S" WARNING?

OH, NO, SIR—YOU ARMY MEN WILL GUARD US!

DANGER HIGH EXPLOSIVE

THE GENERAL LEAVES WITHOUT HIS STICK.

THREE MINUTES OF 12- DON'T LET ANYBODY IN OR OUT UNTIL AFTER THE NOON WHISTLE!

NO, SIR—I WON'T, SIR!

OUTSIDE THE PLANT STEVE AND COLONEL DARNELL WAIT ANXIOUSLY FOR THE HOUR OF NOON!

NOTHING CAN HAPPEN, NOW! IT'S ONE MINUTE TO 12—

YOU'RE SLOW, COLONEL— IT'S JUST NOON— GEEHOSAPHAT!

BA-ANG!

SPECTATORS FLEE FOR THEIR LIVES AMID A SHOWER OF SHELL FRAGMENTS.

WHOLE PLANT'S IN FLAMES— THOUSANDS OF LIVES LOST— HOW COULD IT HAVE HAPPENED?

IT'S BEYOND ME—MAYBE "GEORGE WASHINGTON" CAN TELL US!

A MESSAGE FROM PSYCHO AWAITS THEM!

DR. PSYCHO PHONED. HE INVITES YOU TO A PRIVATE SEANCE TONIGHT TO RECEIVE IMPORTANT INFORMATION FROM SPIRITS!

OH. BOSH! BUT WAIT! WE CAN'T AFFORD TO IGNORE ANY CLUES—TELL HIM WE'LL COME!

WONDER WOMAN MEETS THE MEN AT DR. PSYCHO'S LABORATORY.

GLAD TO SEE YOU, WONDER WOMAN! BUT HOW DID YOU LEARN ABOUT THIS SEANCE?

WHY-ER- DIANA SENT ME A MENTAL MESSAGE!

8A

OH, I HATE TO BE BOUND— CAN'T I PLEASE REMAIN FREE?

CERTAINLY NOT, MY DEAR! NO WOMAN CAN BE TRUSTED WITH FREEDOM—YOU OUGHT TO KNOW THAT! HA! HO! HA!

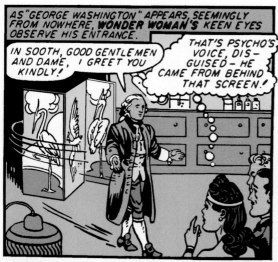

AS "GEORGE WASHINGTON" APPEARS, SEEMINGLY FROM NOWHERE, **WONDER WOMAN'S** KEEN EYES OBSERVE HIS ENTRANCE.

IN SOOTH, GOOD GENTLEMEN AND DAME, I GREET YOU KINDLY!

THAT'S PSYCHO'S VOICE, DISGUISED - HE CAME FROM BEHIND THAT SCREEN!

TOMORROW, AT NOON, IMPORTANT SECRET PAPERS WILL BE STOLEN FROM YOUR OFFICE SAFE. TRUST NOT **WOMEN!** EVEN NOW THEY ARE BETRAYING YOU—

I CAN'T STAND THIS AWFUL DRIVEL— I'VE GOT TO **ACT!**

WONDER WOMAN INTERRUPTS THE SEANCE.

YOU WILL FIND THE STOLEN PAPERS ON **THREE** OF YOUR OFFICE GIRLS— ULP- OUCH!

I'VE HEARD ENOUGH OF THESE LYING ATTACKS ON **WOMEN!**

TELL ME THE TRUTH — THIS "GEORGE WASHINGTON" BODY IS REALLY DR. PSYCHO, ISN'T IT?

NO, MADAM! THIS BODY IS LIVING ECTOPLASM MATERIALIZED THROUGH THE MEDIUM MARVA!

MAYBE YOUR MAGIC LASSO DOESN'T WORK ON GHOSTS, BEAUTIFUL!

YOU SHOULDN'T HAVE INTERRUPTED THE SEANCE, **WONDER WOMAN!** I MUST INSIST THAT IT CONTINUE!

OKAY COLONEL - I'LL ADMIT THIS ECTOPLASM STUFF HAS ME GUESSING!

9A

BUT "GEORGE WASHINGTON" RETIRES OFFENDED, REFUSING TO TALK FURTHER - THEY HURRY TO THE OFFICE AND SET GUARDS AT THE SAFETY VAULT.

YOU'LL BE RELIEVED AT 2 A.M. - A 4-HOUR SHIFT- KEEP ALERT!

YES, SIR!

AT 9 A.M. NEXT MORNING, THE GUARDS ON DUTY RECOGNIZE COLONEL DARNELL.

OPEN THE VAULT, BOYS - I'M GOING TO MAKE SURE THAT OUR SECRET DOCUMENTS ARE STILL SAFE!

YES, SIR, COLONEL!

ONE AT A TIME, 3 TRUSTED GIRL AGENTS ARE CALLED INTO COLONEL DARNELL'S OFFICE

I REMOVED THESE FROM THE VAULT AS A SPECIAL PRECAUTION—PLEASE CONCEAL THEM ON YOUR PERSON!

WHY, CERTAINLY, COLONEL!

THEY'LL BE SAFE WITH ME, COLONEL!

NOBODY'LL FIND THE PAPERS HERE UNLESS I'M SEARCHED THOROUGHLY.

AS NOON APPROACHES, A GROUP OF G2 OFFICERS WATCH THE CLOCK.

THE VAULT CAN'T HAVE BEEN ROBBED! WHERE'S COLONEL DARNELL?

NOT IN YET—HE'S BEEN AT THE WHITE HOUSE ALL MORNING. HERE HE COMES NOW!

WELL, BOYS, IT'S PAST NOON AND NO ROBBERY! I CHECKED THE PAPERS IN THE VAULT LAST NIGHT—I'LL SEE IF ANYTHING'S HAPPENED TO 'EM!

STEVE, I CAN'T BELIEVE IT! LAST NIGHT THIS DRAWER HELD SECRET PAPERS—NOW THEY'RE GONE!

JUMPING BLUE BLAZES! BUT WAIT! WASHINGTON'S SPIRIT SAID WE'D FIND THE PAPERS ON THREE OFFICE GIRLS! I'LL HAVE 'EM ALL SEARCHED

10A

PUT THE CUFFS ON ADELAIDE, MATRON! HERE ARE THE PAPERS—THIS MAKES THE LOT!

THIS IS SILLY I CAN EXPLAIN—TAKE US TO COLONEL DARNELL!

YES, THE CHIEF KNOWS ALL ABOUT IT!

DIANA TAKES THE PRISONERS TO COLONEL DARNELL.

HERE ARE THE PAPERS FOUND ON THESE GIRLS.

I FOLLOWED YOUR ORDERS, COLONEL—BUT I COULDN'T FOOL DIANA!

MY ORDERS! WHAT D'YOU MEAN?

YOU ORDERED US TO HIDE THESE PAPERS ON OUR PERSON—

WHY, OF COURSE—DON'T YOU REMEMBER, COLONEL?

RIDICULOUS! I GAVE NO SUCH ORDERS—LOCK THESE PRISONERS UP!

I'VE QUESTIONED THE GUARDS, COLONEL—THEY SAY YOU WERE THE ONLY ONE WHO ENTERED THE VAULT, AT ABOUT 9 A.M.—REMEMBER?

THE GUARDS ARE CRAZY—AT 9 A.M. I WAS IN THE WHITE HOUSE!

THE GUARDS SAW DARNELL HERE AT 9. THREE GIRL AGENTS SWEAR HE GAVE ORDERS AT 9:30 AHA! SOMEBODY MUST HAVE IMPERSONATED DARNELL AND I'LL BET PSYCHO KNOWS WHO! I'LL MAKE THAT SPIRIT-SHUFFLER TALK!

AT HIS LABORATORY DOCTOR PSYCHO TALKS A GREAT DEAL BUT SAYS NOTHING.

ANSWERING YOUR QUESTIONS, MY DEAR MAJOR, THE ASTRAL ENTITIES OF THE SECOND SPHERE PRECIPITATE THEIR ECTOPLASMIC PROTOPLASM THROUGH KARMIC RADIANCE—

ALL RIGHT! ALL RIGHT—BUT THAT'S NOT WHAT I CAME HERE TO ASK YOU!

BUT PSYCHO'S TALK IS BY NO MEANS PURPOSELESS—IT OCCUPIES STEVE'S ATTENTION WHILE A WEIRD, HALF VISIBLE WEIGHT GATHERS ON HIS CHEST.

I AH-H CAN'T—OO-OOF—BREATHE!

HOW ENTERTAINING—DEATH BY ECTOPLASM—HA! HO! HA!

11A

Z-Z-ZUT! ON SECOND THOUGHT I WILL KEEP THIS STUPID SPECIMEN FOR A WHILE—HE MAY HELP ME IN MY PLAN TO DESTROY WOMEN!

DIANA, WORRIED BECAUSE STEVE HAS NOT RETURNED TO THE OFFICE, GOES HOME EARLY.

THAT DR. PSYCHO IS FIENDISHLY CLEVER - HE MAY HAVE DONE SOMETHING TO STEVE THAT PREVENTS HIS SENDING A MENTAL MESSAGE!

OH, **THERE'S** STEVE NOW!

CALLING **WONDER WO-MAN!** WAS TAKEN PRISONER AT PSYCHO'S LABORA-TORY. AM IN CAGE - DON'T KNOW WHERE! LOOK OUT FOR BUR-GLAR ALARMS! THE LAB GROUNDS ARE COMPLETELY WIRED!

CHANGING SWIFTLY TO HER **WONDER WOMAN** COSTUME, THE AMAZON GIRL MAKES A QUICK EXIT.

SOMETHING TELLS ME THIS PSYCHO IS PLENTY DANGEROUS!

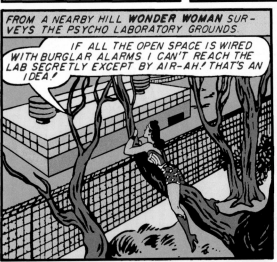

FROM A NEARBY HILL **WONDER WOMAN** SUR-VEYS THE PSYCHO LABORATORY GROUNDS.

IF ALL THE OPEN SPACE IS WIRED WITH BURGLAR ALARMS I CAN'T REACH THE LAB SECRETLY EXCEPT BY AIR-AH! THAT'S AN IDEA!

AT THE EDGE OF THE WOODS **WONDER WOMAN** BENDS DOWN A PAIR OF STRONG SAPLINGS.

THESE YOUNG TREES ARE TOUGH-THEY'LL GIVE A STRONG SNAP-BACK WHEN I LET THEM GO.

FASTENING THE TREE TOPS TOGETHER WITH VINES, **WONDER WOMAN** MAKES A GIANT SLING-SHOT.

WHEN I BREAK THIS ANCHOR VINE I'LL GO SAILING THROUGH THE AIR-TO THE LABORATORY, I **HOPE**!

12A

HURLED HIGH OVER PSYCHO'S GROUNDS BY THE TREMENDOUS POWER OF THE BENT TREES, **WONDER WOMAN** DESCENDS GRACEFULLY TOWARD THE LABORATORY ROOF.

I DON'T SEE HOW PSYCHO'S BURGLAR ALARMS COULD DETECT **THIS** APPROACH!

LANDING LIGHTLY ON THE ROOF, **WONDER WOMAN** FORCES A SKYLIGHT AND DESCENDS INTO PSYCHO'S LABORATORY.

THIS PLACE SEEMS EMPTY— A GOOD TIME TO DROP IN!

WONDER WOMAN SEARCHES FROM ROOF TO CELLAR BUT FINDS NO TRACE OF STEVE.

HAH! A TRAP DOOR CONCEALED UNDER A CASE OF CANNED GOODS—LOOKS PROMISING!

BUT AT THIS MOMENT **WONDER WOMAN** HEARS A FAMILIAR VOICE.

WONDER WOMAN—HELP! IT'S **STEVE**—THIS WAY!

ONE MINUTE, STEVE, AND I'LL BE WITH YOU!

HERE I COME, FELLA!

STEVE APPEARS TO BE CONFINED IN AN IRON CAGE.

I KNEW YOU'D COME, **WONDER WOMAN**! CAN YOU BREAK THE BARS OF THIS CAGE?

I SHOULD HOPE SO— I'LL HAVE YOU FREE IN A MINUTE!

BUT AS **WONDER WOMAN** GRASPS THE BARS, A PARALYZING CURRENT OF ELECTRICITY HOLDS HER BODY RIGID!

HA! HO! HA! WHY DON'T YOU TEAR THE CAGE APART, **WONDER WOMAN**?

GREAT GODDESS APHRODITE! PSYCHO'S GOT ME—I CAN'T MOVE OR SPEAK!

13A

HOW EASY TO TRICK HUMAN FOOLS! I MATERIALIZE A BODY AND WEAR IT LIKE A CLOAK-TREVOR'S, DARNELL'S - A MAJOR GENERAL'S - Z-Z-ZUT! YOU KNOW MY SECRET BUT YOU'LL NEVER BETRAY IT - HA! HO! HA!

I'M PREPARING TO PERFORM AN ELECTRICAL OPERATION ON YOU. WITH LOW POTENTIAL CURRENTS I SHALL LOOSEN THE ATOMS OF YOUR BODY AND REMOVE YOUR SPIRIT!

WHAT JOLLY GAMES THIS FELLOW PLAYS!

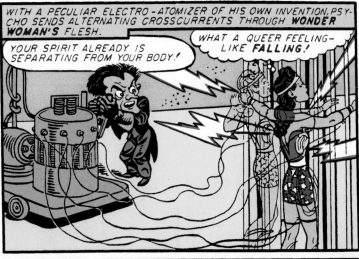

WITH A PECULIAR ELECTRO-ATOMIZER OF HIS OWN INVENTION, PSYCHO SENDS ALTERNATING CROSSCURRENTS THROUGH WONDER WOMAN'S FLESH.

YOUR SPIRIT ALREADY IS SEPARATING FROM YOUR BODY!

WHAT A QUEER FEELING—LIKE FALLING!

WHEN WONDER WOMAN'S SPIRIT IS COMPLETELY DETACHED, PSYCHO FASTENS IT TO THE WALL WITH BANDS OF PSYCHO-ELECTRIC MAGNETISM.

YOUR SPIRIT CAN NEVER BREAK THESE BONDS WHILE I HOLD THEM WITH MY IRON WILL!

YOUR BODY SEEMS LIFELESS SINCE I SWITCHED OFF THE PARALYZING CURRENT, BUT IT'S NOT DEAD. YOUR SPIRIT WOULD RETURN TO IT IF RELEASED. I'LL KEEP YOUR BODY IN THIS CAGE!

CALLING ETTA- CALLING ETTA CANDY! IT'S NO USE- I CAN'T SEND A MENTAL RADIO MESSAGE WITHOUT MY PHYSICAL BODY! I'M ABSOLUTELY HELPLESS- I WONDER WHAT PSYCHO'LL DO WITH ME!

14A

MEANWHILE, ETTA RECEIVES A MENTAL RADIO MESSAGE FROM STEVE.

WOO WOO! GATHER ROUND, GALS, IT'S MAJOR TREVOR!

I'M A PRISONER AT PSYCHO'S LABORATORY! CAN'T SEEM TO CONTACT WONDER WOMAN- WILL YOU GIRLS HELP?

YAY BO! WILL WE HELP STEVE!

A HANDSOME YOUNG MAN MEETS ETTA AT THE LABORATORY.

I AM CARLO MONTEZ, DR. PSYCHO'S ASSISTANT— AH, WHAT A HAPPY DAY TO GREET SO CHARMING A VISITOR!

SAY- YOU'RE KINDA CUTE YOURSELF! WE GIRLS WANT A SEANCE. CAN YOU MANAGE ONE?

THE HOLLIDAY GIRLS FIND CARLO MORE FASCINATING THAN THE SPIRITS.

I AM SORRY. THE DOCTOR IS NOT HERE—

FORGET THE DOCTOR—**YOU** ENTERTAIN US!

DO YOU THINK BLONDES PREFER GENTLEMEN?

WHEN DO YOU GET THROUGH WORK?

AS THE HOLLIDAY GIRLS OVERWHELM CARLO, **WONDER WOMAN** FEELS HER SPIRIT CHAINS WEAKEN.

THAT'S ODD—MY BONDS FEEL LOOSER! IF PSYCHO HOLDS THEM WITH HIS WILL, SOMETHING MUST BE WEAKENING HIS POWER!

WITH A STUPENDOUS SURGE OF PSYCHIC POWER **WONDER WOMAN'S** SPIRIT BURSTS HER SHACKLES!

I'M **FREE**! NOW TO GET BACK INTO MY BODY.

WONDER WOMAN IS HERSELF AGAIN.

BY GOLLY! YOU NEVER KNOW HOW GOOD YOUR BODY FEELS UNTIL YOU'VE BEEN OUT OF IT FOR A WHILE!

RETURNING TO THE RINGED SLAB OF STONE PREVIOUSLY DISCOVERED, **WONDER WOMAN** HEAVES IT UP.

HELLO! IS THAT YOU, **WONDER WOMAN**?

YES, I'M MOSTLY MYSELF!

THAT'S STEVE'S OWN VOICE—THANK APHRODITE!

HURTLING DOWN INTO PSYCHO'S SUBTERRANEAN VAULT. **WONDER WOMAN** RUNS A GAUNTLET OF BLUE FLAME.

I CAN HARDLY FEEL THOSE RAYS—THE GOOD DOCTOR'S TREATMENT MUST HAVE GIVEN ME IMMUNITY TO ELECTRIC SHOCKS!

15A

NO ONE BUT YOU COULD HAVE SAVED ME - THIS BIRD PSYCHO IS THE MOST DANGEROUS MAN ALIVE!

SEARCHING THE VAULT, **WONDER WOMAN** FINDS MARVA.

MM- SHE'S IN A DEEP TRANCE! THIS MEDIUM IS PSYCHO'S SOURCE OF POWER TO MATERIALIZE BODIES -HE KEEPS HER HIDDEN AND HELPLESS. I MUST AWAKEN HER GENTLY!

YOU SHOULDN'T HAVE RELEASED ME- **HE'LL** BE FURIOUS! OH, **DON'T** LET HIM TORTURE ME-

DON'T BE AFRAID, MARVA- PSYCHO CAN'T HURT YOU- HE HAS NO POW- ER OVER YOU EXCEPT WHAT YOU **GIVE** HIM!

AT THE PRECISE MOMENT THAT MARVA AWAKENS FROM HER TRANCE- A STRANGE THING HAP- PENS TO CARLO.

LOOK- CARLO'S DISAPPEARING!

HE'S MELTING AWAY!

IT WAS DR. PSYCHO ALL THE TIME- GRAB HIM, GIRLS!

THE INDIGNANT GIRLS CHASE THEIR DESPERATE DECEIVER.

CATCH HIM KIDS, -GIVE HIM A LAMDA BETA TREATMENT!

PADDLES UP, SISTERS, GIVE HIM THE WORKS!

STEVE ARRIVES AS PSYCHO TURNS ON HIS PURSUERS.

FIENDISH FEMALES- I'LL SHOOT YOU ALL!

NOT WITH THAT GUN, BROTHER- PUT UP YOUR HANDS!

16A

YOU'LL NEVER PROVE IN COURT THAT I MATERIALIZED AS MAJOR GENERAL AND COLONEL DARNELL!

I'M AFRAID HE'S RIGHT, STEVE- I'VE A FEELING THERE'S MORE TROUBLE AHEAD!

NONSENSE! PSYCHO OUT- SMARTED HIM- SELF -HIS WAR AGAINST WOMEN IS FINISHED!

SUBMITTING TO A CRUEL HUS- BAND'S DOMINATION HAS RUINED MY LIFE! BUT WHAT CAN A WEAK GIRL DO?

GET STRONG! EARN YOUR OWN LIVING- JOIN THE WAACS OR WAVES AND FIGHT FOR YOUR COUNTRY! RE- MEMBER THE BETTER YOU CAN FIGHT, THE LESS YOU'LL HAVE TO!

Etta Candy and her Holliday Girls

By CHARLES MOULTON

WONDER WOMAN IS INTRODUCING ETTA NOW—

EVERY YEAR ON APRIL FOOL'S DAY THE BEETA LAMBDA SORORITY GIRLS AT HOLLIDAY COLLEGE GIVE ETTA CANDY A BIRTHDAY PARTY, NOTHING BUT CANDY IS SERVED. THERE ARE 16 COURSES BECAUSE ETTA ALWAYS CLAIMS TO BE SWEET SIXTEEN! THIS YEAR THE GIRLS PERSUADE **WONDER WOMAN** TO ACT AS TOASTMISTRESS. STEVE, PAULA AND COLONEL DARNELL ARE GUESTS OF HONOR. THE GIRLS TRY TO EXCLUDE REPORTERS—BUT WITH THE INTREPID SPIRIT OF TRUE NEWSPAPER MEN, YOUR WRITER AND ARTIST CRASH THE PARTY AS WAITERS!

AWK!
AWK!

HERE SHE IS! WOW, ETTA! WHERE HAVE YOU BEEN?

SORRY TO BE LATE, KIDS — I'VE GOT A TERRIBLE TOOTHACHE!

HERE'S YOUR CANDY COCKTAIL, ETTA—RASPBERRY, MINT, HONEY AND FUDGE!

WAIT A MINUTE— I'M SORRY, ETTA, BUT YOU CAN'T EAT CANDY UNTIL YOU'VE HAD THAT TOOTH PULLED.

TOOTH PULLED! WOO WOO! TOOTH'S FINE! I-ER-WAS JUST KIDDIN'!

1

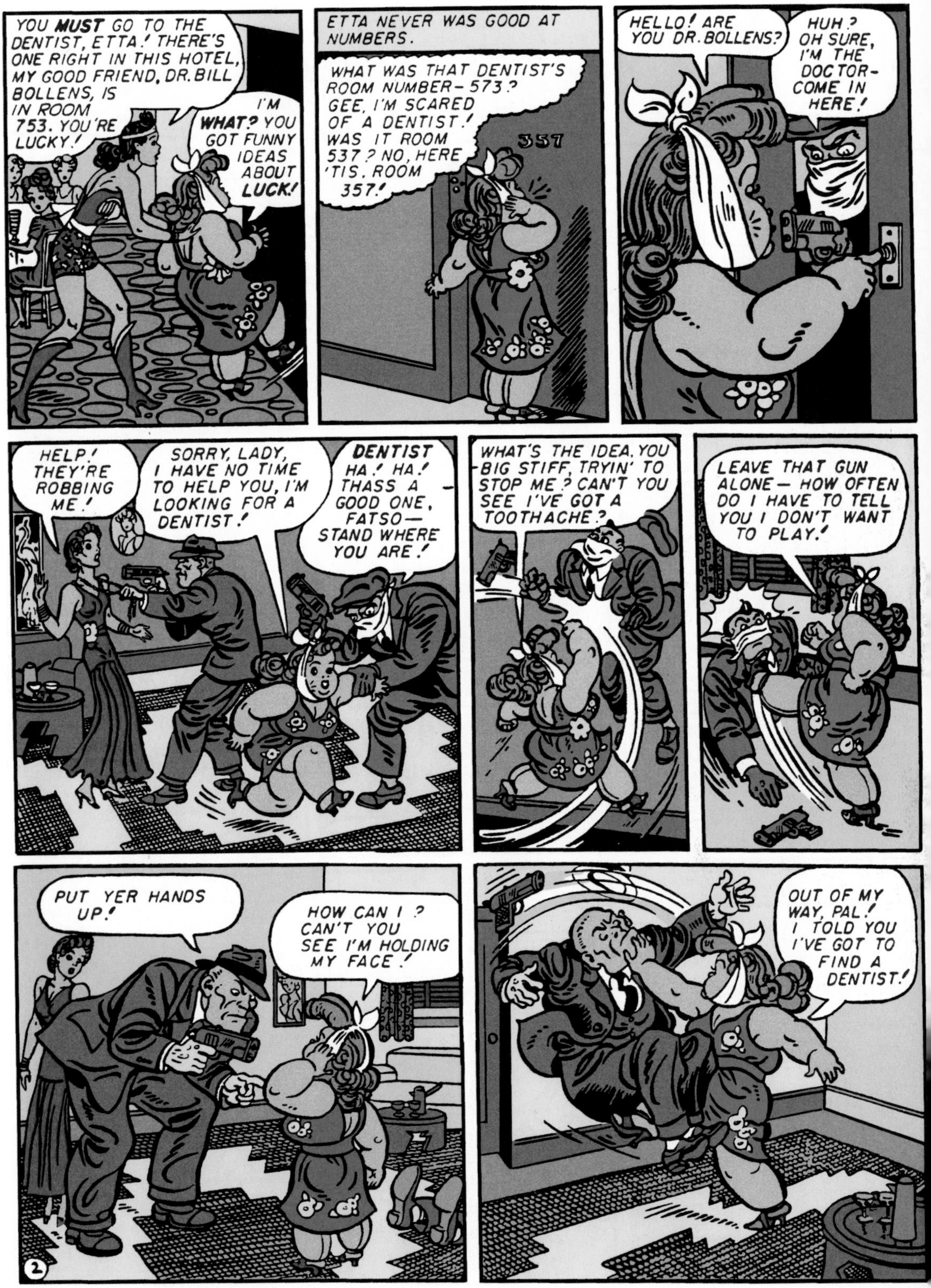
YOU MUST GO TO THE DENTIST, ETTA! THERE'S ONE RIGHT IN THIS HOTEL, MY GOOD FRIEND, DR. BILL BOLLENS, IS IN ROOM 753. YOU'RE LUCKY!
I'M WHAT? YOU GOT FUNNY IDEAS ABOUT LUCK!
ETTA NEVER WAS GOOD AT NUMBERS.
WHAT WAS THAT DENTIST'S ROOM NUMBER—573? GEE, I'M SCARED OF A DENTIST! WAS IT ROOM 537? NO, HERE 'TIS. ROOM 357!
357
HELLO! ARE YOU DR. BOLLENS?
HUH? OH SURE, I'M THE DOCTOR—COME IN HERE!
HELP! THEY'RE ROBBING ME!
SORRY, LADY, I HAVE NO TIME TO HELP YOU, I'M LOOKING FOR A DENTIST!
DENTIST HA! HA! THASS A GOOD ONE, FATSO— STAND WHERE YOU ARE!
WHAT'S THE IDEA, YOU BIG STIFF, TRYIN' TO STOP ME? CAN'T YOU SEE I'VE GOT A TOOTHACHE?
LEAVE THAT GUN ALONE— HOW OFTEN DO I HAVE TO TELL YOU I DON'T WANT TO PLAY!
PUT YER HANDS UP!
HOW CAN I? CAN'T YOU SEE I'M HOLDING MY FACE!
2
OUT OF MY WAY, PAL! I TOLD YOU I'VE GOT TO FIND A DENTIST!

Panel 1: I'LL PHONE THE DESK FOR DOC'S ROOM NUMBER. I'VE GOT TO GET THIS MOLAR PULLED!

PUT THAT PHONE DOWN!

Panel 2: SO, YOU KNOW MY NAME'S MOLA! I'LL SHOW YOU—YOU SNEAKING DICK!

WHAT-WHO? OWW-WOW—OOOW—MY SORE JAW!

Panel 3: GYP! MUGGER! WAKE UP—THIS FEMALE FIVE BY FIVE IS WISE! SHE KNOWS I'M MOLA CHISSLER AND YOU'RE PRETENDING TO STEAL MY JEWELS SO I CAN COLLECT THE INSURANCE ON 'EM!

Panel 4: I WISH YOU WOULDN'T KEEP GETTING IN MY WAY—I HAVEN'T TIME TO BOTHER WITH YOU!

WOOF!

Panel 5: I'M DETECTIVE CASEY. HOLY CATS! DID YE KNOCK OUT THESE THREE CROOKS ALL BY YOURSELF?

I HATED TO DO IT, OFFICER, BUT THEY GOT IN MY WAY! I GOTTA HAVE MY TOOTH PULLED-SO—

Panel 6: ETTA FINALLY FINDS THE DENTIST'S OFFICE —

MY DEAR YOUNG WOMAN, IF YOU *DID* HAVE A TOOTHACHE, YOU HAVEN'T NOW—YOUR BAD TOOTH SEEMS TO HAVE BEEN KNOCKED OUT.

NO KIDDIN'? IT MUST HAVE HAPPENED WHEN THAT DAME SLUGGED ME—WOO WOO! AM I RELIEVED!

Panel 7: BACK AGAIN AT THE CANDY BANQUET.

SO THE TOOTH IS OUT-

ETTA YOU'RE A HEROINE-

WOO WOO! WAS I SCARED OF SEEIN' THAT DENTIST—LITTLE DO THEY KNOW WHAT A COWARD I AM!

GREAT WORK, ETTA

BRAVE GIRL!

ATTA KID!

③

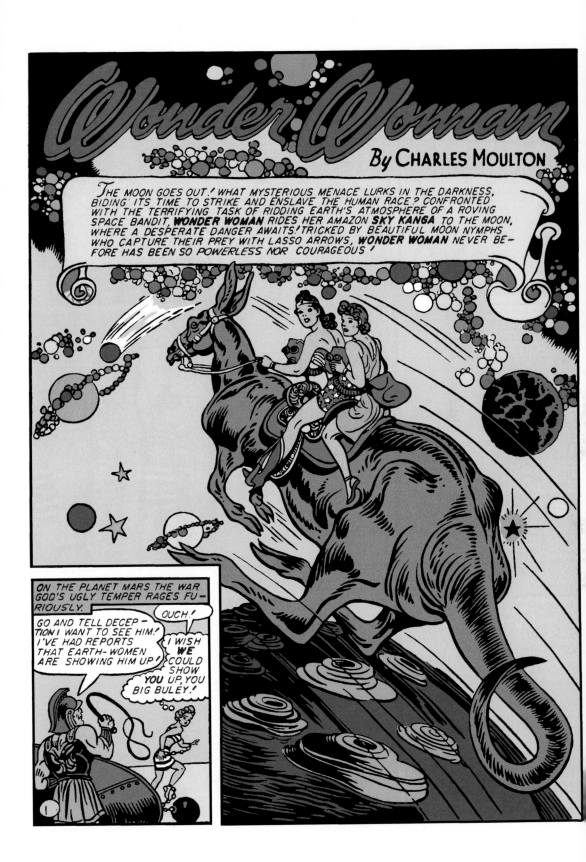

Wonder Woman

By Charles Moulton

THE MOON GOES OUT! WHAT MYSTERIOUS MENACE LURKS IN THE DARKNESS, BIDING ITS TIME TO STRIKE AND ENSLAVE THE HUMAN RACE? CONFRONTED WITH THE TERRIFYING TASK OF RIDDING EARTH'S ATMOSPHERE OF A ROVING SPACE BANDIT, **WONDER WOMAN** RIDES HER AMAZON **SKY KANGA** TO THE MOON, WHERE A DESPERATE DANGER AWAITS! TRICKED BY BEAUTIFUL MOON NYMPHS WHO CAPTURE THEIR PREY WITH LASSO ARROWS, **WONDER WOMAN** NEVER BEFORE HAS BEEN SO POWERLESS NOR COURAGEOUS!

ON THE PLANET MARS THE WAR GOD'S UGLY TEMPER RAGES FURIOUSLY.

GO AND TELL DECEPTION I WANT TO SEE HIM! I'VE HAD REPORTS THAT EARTH-WOMEN ARE SHOWING HIM UP!

OUCH!

I WISH **WE** COULD SHOW YOU UP, YOU BIG BULEY!

THE "DUKE OF DECEPTION"—BAH! YOU'RE THE DUPE OF DOPES! IT MAKES ME LAUGH THE WAY **WONDER WOMAN** DEFEATED YOUR AGENT PSYCHO!

WONDER WOMAN IS INVINCIBLE, YOUR MAJESTY! REMEMBER SHE DEFEATED EVEN **YOU**!

MENTION OF MARS' DEFEAT BY **WONDER WOMAN** WAS UNFORTUNATE.

DECEPTION'S ADMIRATION FOR **WONDER WOMAN** AND HER SEX IS TOUCHING! TAKE HIM TO THE WOMEN'S PRISON AND MAKE HIM THEIR SLAVE!

NO, NO DIVINITY—NOT **THAT** DISGRACE!

DECEPTION WORKS HIS WILES ON THE MARTIAN WOMEN PRISON GUARDS.

YOU LADIES ARE BEAUTIFUL! ! CERTAINLY AM LUCKY TO HAVE GUARDS LIKE **YOU**!

YOU'RE KINDA CUTE, YOURSELF! WE WON'T BEAT YOU— **MUCH**!

DECEPTION ALSO PRACTICES HIS ART ON THE PRETTY GIRL PRISONERS.

I MAY **LOOK** HELPLESS BUT REALLY I'M THE MOST POWERFUL MAN ON MARS! FOLLOW **ME** AND—

WE'LL FOLLOW YOU—WE BELIEVE EVERY WORD YOU SAY!

THE WILY DUKE HAS ANOTHER LINE OF LIES FOR IMPORTANT POLITICAL PRISONERS WHO ARE MOST STRICTLY CONFINED.

MY PURPOSE IN GETTING MYSELF IMPRISONED WAS TO GET FREEDOM FOR YOU WOMEN LEADERS!

WE'LL SWING 20 MILLION MARTIAN GIRLS TO YOUR PARTY!

DECEPTION BEGINS TO TAKE HIS OWN FALSE PRETENTIONS SERIOUSLY.

I AM POWERFUL— I **CAN** FREE THESE PRISONERS! BY THE GREAT HORNS OF DILEMMA I'LL ORGANIZE A WOMEN'S REVOLUTION—ER—HUMPH! THESE POTATO SKINS ARE TOUGH!

2

DECEPTION PASSES THE WORD AMONG THE PRISONERS AT FEEDING TIME.

WOMEN'S REVOLUTION PLANS ARE COMPLETE—BE READY AT MIDNIGHT!

WE'LL BE READY— DON'T FORGET THE KEYS TO OUR CHAINS!

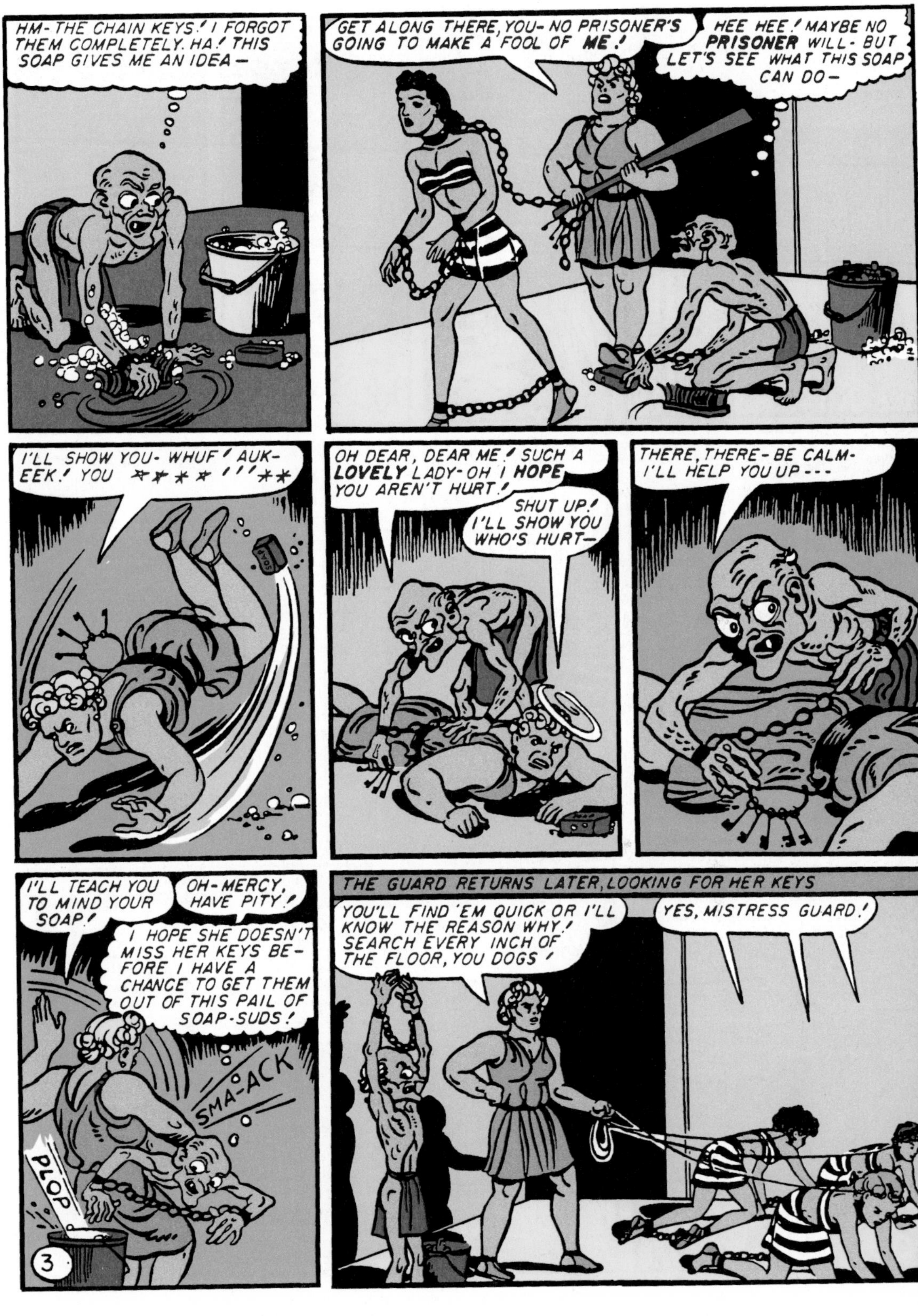
HM- THE CHAIN KEYS! I FORGOT THEM COMPLETELY. HA! THIS SOAP GIVES ME AN IDEA—
GET ALONG THERE, YOU- NO PRISONER'S GOING TO MAKE A FOOL OF ME!
HEE HEE! MAYBE NO PRISONER WILL- BUT LET'S SEE WHAT THIS SOAP CAN DO—
I'LL SHOW YOU- WHUF! AUK- EEK! YOU ****'''**
SOAP
OH DEAR, DEAR ME! SUCH A LOVELY LADY- OH I HOPE YOU AREN'T HURT!
SHUT UP! I'LL SHOW YOU WHO'S HURT—
THERE, THERE- BE CALM- I'LL HELP YOU UP---
I'LL TEACH YOU TO MIND YOUR SOAP!
OH- MERCY, HAVE PITY!
I HOPE SHE DOESN'T MISS HER KEYS BE- FORE I HAVE A CHANCE TO GET THEM OUT OF THIS PAIL OF SOAP-SUDS!
SMA-ACK
PLOP
3
THE GUARD RETURNS LATER, LOOKING FOR HER KEYS
YOU'LL FIND 'EM QUICK OR I'LL KNOW THE REASON WHY! SEARCH EVERY INCH OF THE FLOOR, YOU DOGS!
YES, MISTRESS GUARD!

BUT THE KEYS ARE NOT FOUND. LATER THAT NIGHT—

THE GUARDS NEVER ENTER THESE DUNGEONS AT NIGHT—THEY THINK WE'RE HELPLESSLY CHAINED—HEE-HEE-HEE!

DECEPTION WORKS SWIFTLY, UNLOCKING THE PRISONERS' CHAINS.

DECEPTION'S FEMALE ARMY SURPRISES THE GUARDS IN THE GUARD ROOM.

NICE FIGHTING, GIRLS!

YOU'LL NEVER TORTURE US AGAIN!

THAT'S FOR THE WHIPPING YOU GAVE ME TODAY!

WITH THE PRISON COMPLETELY UNDER HIS CONTROL, DECEPTION CALLS MARS, IMITATING THE CHIEF GUARD'S VOICE.

OH, YOUR MAJESTY! WE'RE PLAYING A LOVELY GAME WITH THE PRISONERS—WON'T YOU COME AND SEE IT?

SURE—I COULD USE A LITTLE DIVERSION—I'LL BE RIGHT DOWN!

IT HAPPENS THAT LORD CONQUEST IS IN MARS' OFFICE.

HO! HO! THOSE WOMEN GUARDS ARE TORMENTING THE PRISONERS AGAIN! LET'S GO DOWN AND WATCH—IT'S ALWAYS VERY RELAXING AND AMUSING—

WELL—ALL RIGHT, BUT I'D RATHER WORK AT OUR PLANS FOR THE INVASION OF EARTH!

④

AS MARS AND CONQUEST ENTER THE PRISON, THEY ARE PARALYZED, BY ELECTRIC RAY-GUNS.

SO YOU'D MAKE ME A SLAVE OF WOMEN—HEE! HEE! YOU FORGOT THAT CAPTIVE GIRLS LOVE DECEPTION! NOW WE CHANGE PLACES, MISTER MARS!

THE FREED POLITICAL PRISON-ERS KEEP THEIR PROMISE—A GREAT ARMY OF MILITANT WO-MEN PUT DECEPTION ON THE THRONE OF MARS.

LONG LIVE KING DECEPTION! HAIL—HOORAH!

BUT GREED, LITTLE TRUSTING KING DECEPTION'S PROMISES, VISITS MARS IN HIS DUNGEON.

I KNOW YOU HAVE BILLIONS IN GOLD—REVEAL THE SECRET OF YOUR HIDDEN VAULT AND I WILL ARRANGE YOUR ESCAPE!

IT'S A BARGAIN!

GREED BRIBES THE GUARDS WITH MARS' GOLD.

TONIGHT AT "MOON-SET" YOU WILL RELEASE MARS AND CON-QUEST AND BRING THEM TO MY PRIVATE AIR TOWER.

AYE, LORD! WE OBEY!

THE PLAN SUCCEEDS—AT GREED'S AERIAL DOCK THE ROYAL FUGITIVES BOARD MARS' NEW SPACE CRUISER.

WHERE WILL YOU GO?

TO EARTH TO CAPTURE **WONDER WOMAN**—WITH **HER** MY SLAVE I'LL SOON SUBDUE THE WOMEN OF **BOTH** PLANETS!

AND SO, WITH MARS ENTER-ING EARTH'S ATMOSPHERE, UNPRECEDENT-ED EVENTS OC-CUR WHICH BE-FUDDLE THE SCIENTISTS AND PUZZLE EVEN **WON-DER WOMAN'S** AMAZON WIS-DOM! FIRST THE MOON GOES OUT—ASTRONOMERS, PHYSICISTS—EVEN THE GREAT EIN-STEIN HIM-SELF CAN'T EXPLAIN IT!

DIANA, IN STEVE'S OFFICE, LISTENS TO THE LATEST RADIO NEWS.

PROFESSOR I.B.WISE OF HOLLIDAY COLLEGE OBSER-VATORY, STUDYING THE STRANGE DISAPPEARANCE OF THE MOON'S LIGHT, HAS DISCOVERED A DARK, FOREIGN OBJECT IN THE EARTH'S ATMOSPHERE ---

OH, STEVE, A DARK OBJECT IN-VADING EARTH—THAT SOUNDS OMINOUS!

MM—THE PAPERS ARE ALL EXCITED—LET'S GO TO HOLLI-DAY COLLEGE TONIGHT AND LOOK THROUGH WISE'S TELESCOPE!

⑤

LATER AT HOLLIDAY COLLEGE OBSERVATORY.

GREAT PLUTO! THERE'S AN ENORMOUS SPACE SHIP, COMING STRAIGHT AT US—QUICK! RUN FOR YOUR LIVES!

STEVE SEIZES DIANA AND RUSH-
ES TO THE WINDOW.

STAIRS ARE JAMMED WITH
GIRLS-OUT
YOU GO, DI!

OH STEVE! YOU'RE
WONDERFUL BUT—

BUT BEFORE ANYONE ELSE CAN ESCAPE, A HORRIBLE CRUNCHING
NOISE FILLS THE AIR-THE OBSERVATORY IS TORN LOOSE FROM
ITS FOUNDATIONS!

WOO WOO! LOOK OUT FOR
THE PHENOMENA, PROFESSOR!

EE-EEK!

WHE-EEE!

WOW!

DIANA, MEANWHILE, WITH A TREMENDOUS LEAP,
ESCAPES SAWTOOTH JAWS DESCENDING FROM
ABOVE.

I DON'T KNOW WHAT THIS
MONSTROSITY IS BUT I DON'T LIKE IT!

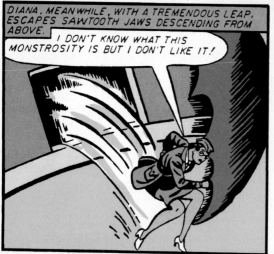

TURNING SHE SEES—

WITHIN A FEW SECONDS THE
STEEL TRAP, CLOSING, RISES
WITH ITS PREY.

AN AMAZ-
ING NEW WEAPON! BUT WHERE
IS THIS SKY SCOOP TAKING
STEVE AND THE GIRLS?

FAR ABOVE, IN THE DARKNESS
OF THE MOONLESS NIGHT DI-
ANA'S KEEN EYES OBSERVE
THE DIM OUTLINE OF A GREAT
SPACE CRUISER.

DIANA WASTES NO TIME IN
TRANSFORMING HERSELF TO
WONDER WOMAN.

I'LL FLY TO
PARADISE ISLAND AND FOLLOW
THE COURSE OF THIS INVADER
ON THE MAGIC SPHERE OF
ATHENA!

EN ROUTE, **WONDER WOMAN'S** MENTAL RADIO SPEAKS.

CALLING **WONDER WOMAN**— INVADING SPACE SHIP BELONGS TO MARS! HAVE NO FURTHER INFORMATION — PRISONERS KEPT CLOSELY CONFINED AND BLINDFOLDED —

ON PARADISE ISLAND, QUEEN HIPPOLYTE HELPS HER DAUGHTER OPERATE THE MAGIC SPHERE.

YOU'VE GOT IT— THERE'S MARS' SPACE SHIP ON THE VIEW PLATE!

THANK APHRODITE! NOW WE CAN TRACE THE SHIP TO ITS BASE!

MARS IS HEADING FOR THE MOON— HE MUST HAVE CAPTURED IT AND MADE IT DARK!

BUT **WHAT'S** HAPPENED TO DIANA, GODDESS OF THE MOON, AND HER MAIDENS? DAUGHTER, YOU MUST GO THERE IMMEDIATELY!

MOTHER, I WANT TO TAKE PAULA WITH ME— I MAY NEED HER SCIENTIFIC GENIUS.

VERY WELL, DARLING— PAULA IS NOW FREE TO LEAVE PARADISE ISLAND AND GO ANYWHERE YOU COMMAND!

THE GIRLS MOUNT A **SKY KANGA,** AN ANIMAL BRED BY THE AMAZONS FOR SHORT SPACE TRIPS.

HOW DO KANGAS BREATHE IN SPACE?

THEY HAVE RESERVE-AIR LUNGS— BUT **WE** NEED THESE OXYGEN MASKS!

TAKING OFF WITH A TREMENDOUS JUMP THE SKY KANGA LEAPS NIMBLY FROM METEORITE TO PLANETOID. UPPER SPACE IS NOT EMPTY BUT DOTTED WITH THOUSANDS OF GRAVITY-MAROONED FRAGMENTS FROM WHIRLING PLANETS.

⑦

AS PAULA AND **WONDER WOMAN** APPROACH THE MOON, ITS EXTINCT VOLCANOS YAWN BENEATH THEM LIKE VAST FUNNELS TO INFERNAL REGIONS.

CLEARING THE MOUNTAINS OF THE MOON, THE GIRLS LAND ON A FERTILE PLANE BEFORE THE **SILVER PALACE OF DIANA.**

HERE WE ARE - I **HOPE** THE GODDESS AND HER NYMPHS ARE SAFE!

AS THE GIRLS LEAP TO THE GROUND **WONDER WOMAN** CONCEALS HER MAGIC LASSO.

IF WE **SHOULD** BE CAPTURED BY ENEMIES I DON'T WANT THEM TO USE MY MAGIC LASSO AGAINST ME!

AS **WONDER WOMAN** AND PAULA APPROACH THE SILVER PALACE ARROWS STRIKE SILENTLY.

UNH! WHAT HIT ME?

WHAT GAME IS THIS?

THE FORCE OF CONTACT SPLITS THE ARROWHEAD AND WHIRLS THE BARB BALLS, CARRING STRONG STEEL WIRES COMPLETELY AROUND THE BODY!

GREAT HEAVENS, MY WAIST IS BOUND! HOW AMAZING, A **LASSO ARROW!**

A PARTY OF DIANA'S NYMPHS EMERGE FROM BEHIND TREES.

DON'T WORRY, PAULA—THESE ARE GODDESS DIANA'S NYMPHS, AND THIS IS THEIR USUAL METHOD OF HUNTING. HOLA! APHRODITE WITH YOU!

WE KNOW YOU, **WONDER WOMAN!** BUT WE HAVE ORDERS TO ARREST YOU!

⑧

ARREST ME! WHO GAVE YOU THAT COMMAND?

EE-EEK! STOP THAT, **WONDER WOMAN--** YOU'D BETTER SUBMIT OR IT WILL GO HARDER WITH YOU!

AS **WONDER WOMAN** LAUGHS AT THE NYMPHS' DEMANDS, A SHOWER OF LASSO ARROWS AND SPEARS ASSAIL HER FROM ALL SIDES.

THIS IS A GRAND GAME—DIANA'S NYMPHS ARE EVIDENTLY PLAYFUL GIRLS!

THE NYMPHS ARE SKILLFUL. WITH LASSO SPEARS THEY BIND **WONDER WOMAN** AND PAULA BACK TO BACK.

OW-OO! PULLING THAT WIRE CUTS MY BODY LIKE A KNIFE!

SORRY, PAULA! LET'S SURRENDER AND PAY THE FORFEIT.

NO BONDS THEY IMPOSE CAN HOLD ME SO LONG AS THEY HAVEN'T GOT MY MAGIC LASSO!

WHAT PENALTY MUST WE PAY?

WE'LL SHOW YOU PRESENTLY!

THE PENALTY BEGINS.

FIRST, YOU TWO MUST WALK TO THE SILVER PALACE ON ONE LEG!

HA! HA! SEE THEM HOP!

COME ON, YOU FEEBLE LEGS, MOVE FASTER!

THE GIRLS REACH THE NYMPHS' GAME ROOM AT LAST AND ARE PERMITTED TO REST.

FROM THIS TIME ON YOU MUST OBEY US **BLINDLY!**

VERY WELL, BUT PLEASE HURRY! WE HAVE **SERIOUS** BUSINESS TO ATTEND TO.

9

THIS BUSINESS IS SERIOUS, I ASSURE YOU! TO PAY FORFEITS YOU MUST BE SUITABLY DRESSED!

SHE MEANS TO CHAIN US—THAT'S NO HARM SO LONG AS **GIRLS** WELD OUR FETTERS

SYLVIA AND BERTHA WILL NOW WELD CHAINS ON OUR FAIR FORFEIT PAYERS!

THUS TRICKED BY DIANA'S NYMPHS, **WONDER WOMAN** AND PAULA PERMIT MARS AND CONQUEST TO WELD CHAINS BETWEEN THEIR AMAZON BRACELETS, DEPRIVING THEM OF STRENGTH BY APHRODITE'S LAW.

NYMPHS ARE POWERFUL CHAIN WELDERS - HA! HA! HA!

WONDER WOMAN, SENSING SOMETHING WRONG, TRIES TO BREAK HER METAL EYE BAND.

ENOUGH OF THIS NONSENSE! I'LL BREAK THESE CHAINS LIKE- HUH? SAY! I CAN'T EVEN BREAK THIS LITTLE METAL BAND!

YOU DON'T KNOW YOUR OWN WEAKNESS, DARLING! FOLLOW ME.

I'M HELPLESS-THEY HAD **MEN** WELD MY CHAINS! BUT. WHY? CAN THE GODDESS DIANA BE IN LEAGUE WITH **MARS**?

AT THAT MOMENT, A DARK, OMINOUS SHAPE DESCENDS UPON THE ROOF OF THE SILVER PALACE.

THE PRISONERS ARE LED, STUMBLING, INTO MARS' SPACE CRUISER.

NOW YOUR FORFEIT **REALLY** BEGINS - DON'T LET IT UPSET YOU!

MARS ENJOYS HIS JOKE.

HO! HO! WHAT A JOKE ON **WONDER WOMAN!**

HA! HA! I'LL ADMIT THIS ONE **IS** ON ME! BUT I NEVER THOUGHT MY OWN PATRON GODDESS DIANA WOULD BETRAY ME!

THE GODDESS, STUNG FROM HER DRUGGED LETHARGY BY **WONDER WOMAN'S** WORDS, SPEAKS THICKLY.

MAR-SZ B'TRAYED ME! HE--PUT-POPPY-JUICE IN MY NECTAR! I'M PRISHNER LIKE YOU!

DIANA'S NYMPHS RUSH TO THEIR MISTRESS IN GREAT DISTRESS.

OH MISTRESS, BEAUTIFUL GODDESS— FORGIVE US! WE DID NOT KNOW YOU WERE DRUGGED WHEN YOU GAVE ORDERS TO CAPTURE THE AMAZON PRINCESS!

DON'T GIVE HER WINE—IT WILL REVIVE HER! I LIKE TO KEEP MY **DIVINE** GUESTS QUIET AND CONTENTED— HO! HO!

GET UNDER WAY, CAPTAIN! WE MUST REACH EARTH IN TIME FOR ANOTHER RAID IN THE DARKNESS TONIGHT!

AYE - AYE, M'LORD!

AS THE GREAT SHIP SOARS IN-TO SPACE **WONDER WOMAN** SEES A FAMILIAR-FACE OUTSIDE THE WINDOW.

MY SKY KANGA- HE'S FOLLOWING THE SHIP! THAT GIVES ME AN IDEA.

SNAP!

WONDER WOMAN, UNOBSERVED, WHISPERS TO ETTA CANDY.

TELL THE GIRLS TO START A FIGHT, ETTA! I WANT TO DI-VERT MARS ATTENTION!

WOO WOO! THAT'S WHERE I SHINE!

ETTA NEVER DOES A THING BY HALVES.

YOU BIG HUNK OF CHEESE! I DECIDED TO PIN YOUR EARS BACK!

ULP-UG! GREAT HOUNDS OF HADES!! —!!*＊!

WHILE THE ROUGH-HOUSE RAGES, **WONDER WOMAN** STEPS CLOSE TO THE GODDESS DIANA.

YOU BIG BULLIES!

YOU UGLY MUGS!

SPUT-SPLUT!

LITTLE DEVILS!

DRINK THIS WINE, GOD-DESS-IT WILL CLEAR YOUR BRAIN! THEN FOL-LOW ME QUICKLY!

11

SUPPORTING THE RAPIDLY RE-VIVING GODDESS, **WONDER WO-MAN** OPENS THE SHIP'S WINDOW.

AH! THE CLEAR COLD OF SPACE IS MORE BRACING THAN WINE - ITS THIN ETHER IS BREATH OF LIFE TO AN OLYMPIAN! I FEEL MYSELF AGAIN!

THERE'S MY SKY KANGA, GOD-DESS - HE'LL TAKE YOU HOME SWIFTLY! I MUST STAY AND HELP MY FRIENDS - IF I CAN!

YOU CAN BEAT MARS - I HAVE HEARD OF YOUR MIGHTY DEEDS BUT FIRST I MUST BREAK THESE MAN-WELDED CHAINS AND RE-STORE YOUR AMAZON STRENGTH!

OH, GODDESS, **THANK** YOU!

I'LL REPLACE THE MOON MIRRORS THAT MARS DESTROYED - THE LIGHT OF THE MOON WILL GLOW AGAIN AND HIS SHIP WILL BE SEEN! MY MOON PATROL WILL BRING HELP!

I DON'T THINK I'LL NEED IT!

AS **WONDER WOMAN**, FREE, TURNS FROM THE OPEN PORT, MARS SEES HER AND RUSHES LIKE A RAGING BULL.

ARGGH - GRR! ESCAPE, WOULD YOU! CHAINS OR NO CHAINS I'LL KNOCK **THAT** IDEA OUT OF YOUR HEAD!

WONDER WOMAN TRADES BLOW FOR BLOW.

THIS IS THE FIGHT I'VE BEEN WAITING FOR!

⑫

YOU'LL HAVE TO DO BETTER THAN THAT, MY LITTLE MAN!

LIKE **THAT**, FOR INSTANCE!

PAULA, MEANWHILE, MIXES SALT, WATER, NECTAR, VINEGAR AND OTHER TABLE INGREDIENTS.

THESE SIMPLE SUBSTANCES MAKE A POWERFUL METAL-EATING ACID WHEN MIXED IN PROPER PROPORTIONS.

STEALING SWIFTLY TO THE DOOR OF STEVE'S CELL, PAULA POURS HER ACID CAREFULLY INTO THE LOCK.

AS I THOUGHT—BRONZE DISSOLVES EASILY IN HYDROAMNECTIC ACID!

STEVE, FORTUNATELY, IS NOT FETTERED.

GOOD OLD PAULA, ALWAYS THERE WITH THE HEADWORK! WHAT'S UP—

A FIGHT! HELP **WONDER WOMAN** WHILE I FREE THE GIRLS FROM THEIR CHAINS!

AS **WONDER WOMAN** DELIVERS A KNOCKOUT BLOW TO MARS, CONQUEST STEPS BEHIND HER WITH RAISED SWORD

HOORAY— **WONDER WOMAN** WINS BY A KNOCKOUT!

WOO WOO! LOOK OUT, **WONDER WOMAN**— BEHIND YOU!

IF YOU WANT ROUGH STUFF CHUM, I'LL ACCOMMODATE YOU!

13

THE HOLLIDAY GIRLS, FREED BY PAULA, DO A THOROUGH CLEANUP JOB.

WOO WOO! LET 'EM HAVE IT, GIRLS!

THE GODDESS DIANA, MEANWHILE, REACHING THE MOON, ENTERS THE MOON MIRROR POWER STATION.

AS I SUSPECTED! MARS SWITCHED OFF OUR PUMPS AND STOPPED THE FLOW OF GLASS THROUGH THE MOON'S CRATERS! OUR MOUNTAIN SIDES ARE BLACK VOLCANIC ROCK—THEY DO NOT REFLECT SUNLIGHT, SO THE MOON IS DARK!

LIQUID MIRROR GLASS PUMPS

FROM HER WATCHTOWER, THE GODDESS AND HER NYMPHS WATCH STREAMS OF GLASS FLOW DOWN THE MOON'S MOUNTAIN SIDES AGAIN.

SEE HOW OUR LIQUID MIRRORS CATCH THE SUN'S RAYS AND REFLECT THEM BACK TO EARTH!

WONDER WOMAN, MEANWHILE, TAKES COMPLETE COMMAND OF MARS' SPACE SHIP.

SECURE THESE PRISONERS AND SPARE NO SHACKLES! IF MARS GETS LOOSE AGAIN HE'LL CONQUER EARTH WITH HIS SECRET WEAPONS!

WONDER WOMAN AT THE HELM, SEES ONLY DARK SPACE AHEAD.

NO SPACE CRAFT CAN BE SEEN IN THIS DARKNESS—WITHOUT THE MOONLIGHT A THOUSAND ENEMY CRUISERS MIGHT LURK IN EARTH'S ATMOSPHERE!

LOOK—THE GODDESS' MIRRORS ARE REPAIRED! ARE WE GOING BACK TO THE MOON?

YES, I'LL LEAVE MARS' SHIP THERE. EARTH MEN NOW FIGHT EVERYWHERE EXCEPT IN SPACE—WITH THIS SHIP THEY'D BEGIN BATTLING IN SPACE ALSO!

IN THE SILVER PALACE OF DIANA—

I'LL PUT YOUR PRISONERS ON THE NEXT MARTIAN CONVICT SHIP. WITH MARS IN PRISON THE MARTIAN WOMEN CAN REMAIN FREE!

FREE—BUT RULED BY DECEPTION! I DON'T ENVY THEM!

ALL ABOARD THE SKY KANGA SPECIAL—NEXT STOP WASHINGTON!

AW, WONDER WOMAN, WHY KEEP US ON THE JUMP? I WANTA MEET THE MAN IN THE MOON AND EAT MORE OF THIS LOVELY GLASS CANDY THE NYMPHS GAVE ME!

14

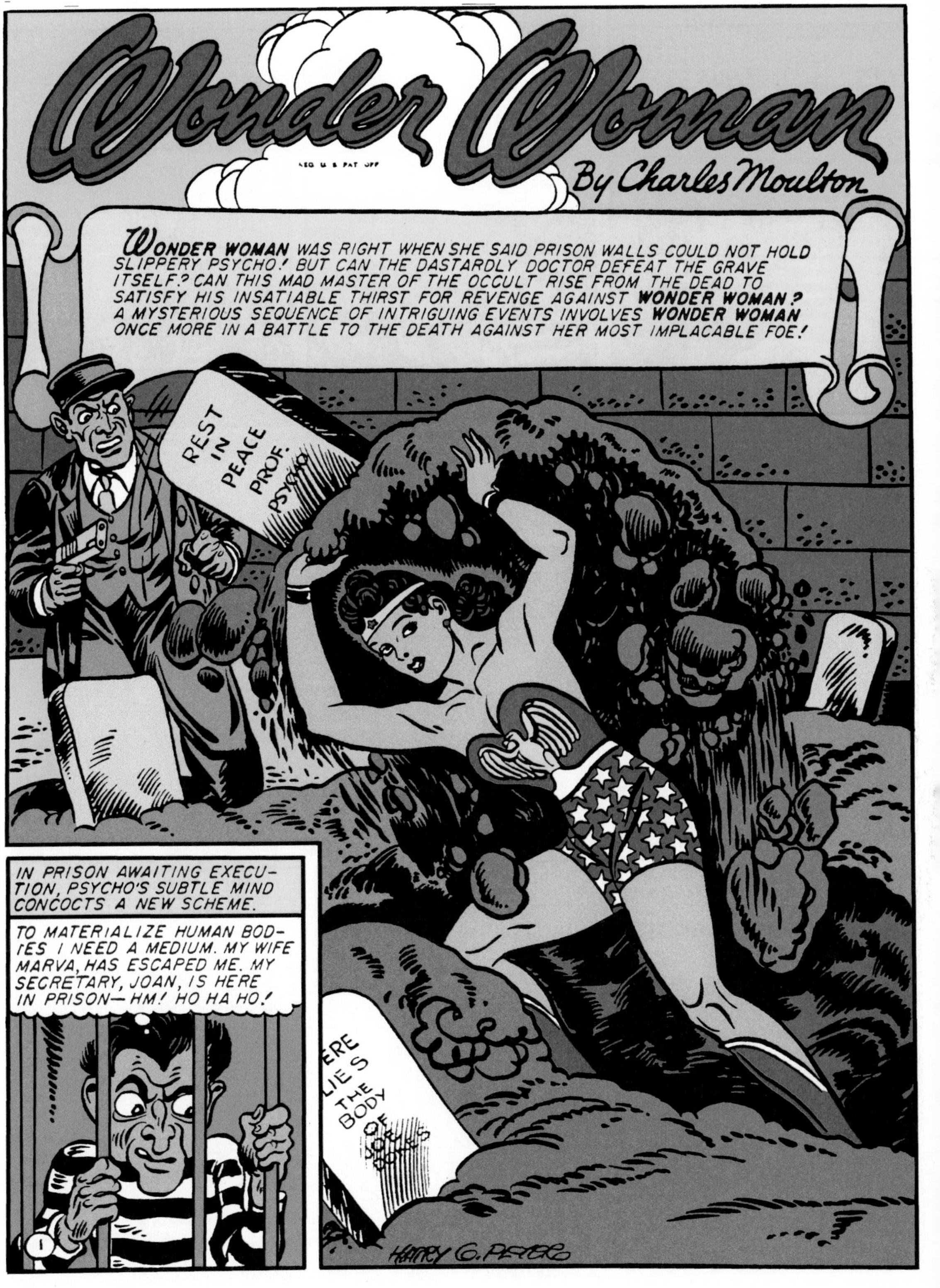
Wonder Woman
REG. U.S. PAT. OFF.
By Charles Moulton
WONDER WOMAN WAS RIGHT WHEN SHE SAID PRISON WALLS COULD NOT HOLD SLIPPERY PSYCHO! BUT CAN THE DASTARDLY DOCTOR DEFEAT THE GRAVE ITSELF? CAN THIS MAD MASTER OF THE OCCULT RISE FROM THE DEAD TO SATISFY HIS INSATIABLE THIRST FOR REVENGE AGAINST WONDER WOMAN? A MYSTERIOUS SEQUENCE OF INTRIGUING EVENTS INVOLVES WONDER WOMAN ONCE MORE IN A BATTLE TO THE DEATH AGAINST HER MOST IMPLACABLE FOE!
REST IN PEACE PROF. PSYCHO
ERE LIES THE BODY OF
HARRY G. PETER
IN PRISON AWAITING EXECUTION, PSYCHO'S SUBTLE MIND CONCOCTS A NEW SCHEME.
TO MATERIALIZE HUMAN BODIES I NEED A MEDIUM. MY WIFE MARVA, HAS ESCAPED ME. MY SECRETARY, JOAN, IS HERE IN PRISON—HM! HO HA HO!
1

LATER IN THE WARDEN'S OFFICE:

MY CONSCIENCE HURTS ME—I WANT TO CONFESS!

AHA--AT LAST--SIT DOWN---I'LL CALL A STENOGRAPHER.

WAIT, WARDEN! BEFORE I DICTATE MY CONFESSION I MUST TALK PRIVATELY WITH MY FORMER SECRETARY. SHE--

I UNDERSTAND! YOUR CONFESSION WILL INVOLVE THE GIRL. OKAY, YOU MAY TALK WITH HER—ADVISE HER TO CONFESS ALSO!

HERE'S PRISONER 42,116—JOAN WHITE—SERVING 20 YEARS AS PSYCHO'S ACCOMPLICE.

OH PLEASE DON'T MAKE ME SEE HIM! HE CONTROLS MY MIND.

NONSENSE! MATRON, LET THIS PRISONER TALK PRIVATELY WITH PSYCHO IN THE "GOLD FISH TANK."

IN A SOUNDPROOF ROOM FOR QUESTIONING PRISONERS—

OH DOCTOR—DON'T HYPNOTIZE ME! I'M TRYING TO BE A GOOD PRISONER—LET ME ALONE!

RELAX—SUBMIT, YOU ARE HELPLESS—YOU CANNOT MOVE—YOU MUST OBEY ME!

PSYCHO PUTS JOAN INTO A TRANCE.

JOAN MAKES A SPLENDID MEDIUM—SPLENDID! WHEN SHE'S IN A TRANCE I CAN MATERIALIZE WHATEVER BODY I CHOOSE—EVEN A BODY LIKE MY OWN—HO! HA! HO!

WHEN YOU WAKE YOU'LL FORGET THE PAST! BUT WHEN I SEND YOU A MENTAL COMMAND YOU WILL FALL INTO A TRANCE AGAIN!

YES, MASTER—I OBEY!

A GUARD REPORTS TO THE WARDEN.

WELL, ARE BOTH PRISONERS READY TO CONFESS?

JOAN WON'T TALK! CLAIMED SHE'D LOST HER MEMORY—THEN FELL UNCONSCIOUS! PSYCHO IS WRITING A CONFESS— IN HIS CELL!

BUT WHEN THE WARDEN VISITS PSYCHO—

GREAT HEAVENS! THE MAN'S DEAD—DIED WRITING HIS CONFESSION. HEY, GUARD!

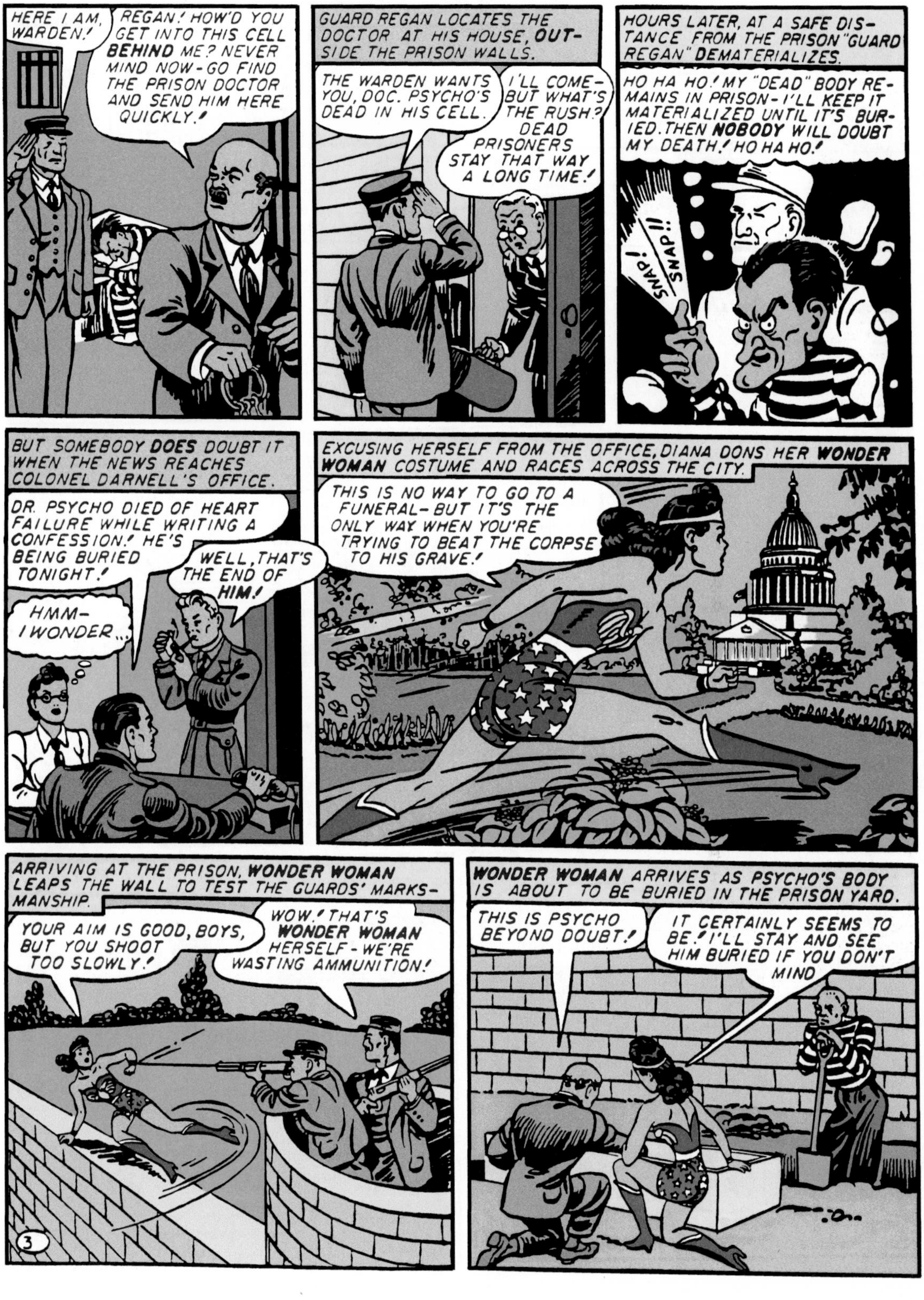
HERE I AM, WARDEN!
REGAN! HOW'D YOU GET INTO THIS CELL BEHIND ME? NEVER MIND NOW - GO FIND THE PRISON DOCTOR AND SEND HIM HERE QUICKLY!
GUARD REGAN LOCATES THE DOCTOR AT HIS HOUSE, OUTSIDE THE PRISON WALLS.
THE WARDEN WANTS YOU, DOC. PSYCHO'S DEAD IN HIS CELL.
I'LL COME - BUT WHAT'S THE RUSH? DEAD PRISONERS STAY THAT WAY A LONG TIME!
HOURS LATER, AT A SAFE DISTANCE FROM THE PRISON "GUARD REGAN" DEMATERIALIZES.
HO HA HO! MY "DEAD" BODY REMAINS IN PRISON - I'LL KEEP IT MATERIALIZED UNTIL IT'S BURIED. THEN NOBODY WILL DOUBT MY DEATH! HO HA HO!
SNAP! SNAP!!
BUT SOMEBODY DOES DOUBT IT WHEN THE NEWS REACHES COLONEL DARNELL'S OFFICE.
DR. PSYCHO DIED OF HEART FAILURE WHILE WRITING A CONFESSION! HE'S BEING BURIED TONIGHT!
WELL, THAT'S THE END OF HIM!
HMM- I WONDER...
EXCUSING HERSELF FROM THE OFFICE, DIANA DONS HER WONDER WOMAN COSTUME AND RACES ACROSS THE CITY.
THIS IS NO WAY TO GO TO A FUNERAL - BUT IT'S THE ONLY WAY WHEN YOU'RE TRYING TO BEAT THE CORPSE TO HIS GRAVE!
ARRIVING AT THE PRISON, WONDER WOMAN LEAPS THE WALL TO TEST THE GUARDS' MARKSMANSHIP.
YOUR AIM IS GOOD, BOYS, BUT YOU SHOOT TOO SLOWLY!
WOW! THAT'S WONDER WOMAN HERSELF - WE'RE WASTING AMMUNITION!
3
WONDER WOMAN ARRIVES AS PSYCHO'S BODY IS ABOUT TO BE BURIED IN THE PRISON YARD.
THIS IS PSYCHO BEYOND DOUBT!
IT CERTAINLY SEEMS TO BE! I'LL STAY AND SEE HIM BURIED IF YOU DON'T MIND

WELL, THAT'S THAT! PSYCHO COULDN'T RISE FROM *THAT* GRAVE AND IF HE DID HE'D STILL BE INSIDE PRISON WALLS!

EXACTLY!

LATER, IN THE WARDEN'S OFFICE—

THIS LETTER CAME THIS MORNING, **WONDER WOMAN**, ADDRESSED TO YOU IN *MY* CARE!

HOW EXTRAORDINARY! HOW COULD *ANYBODY* KNOW I WAS COMING HERE WHEN I DIDN'T KNOW IT MYSELF?

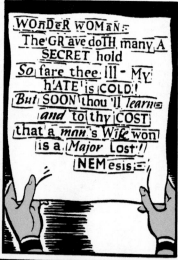

WONDER WOMAN: The GRave doTH many A SECRET hold So fare thee Ill-MY h'ATE is COLD! But SOON thou'll learns and to thy COST that a man's Wife won is a Major Lost! NEMesis:

"NEMESIS" THE GREEK GODDESS OF RETRIBUTION! PSYCHO WROTE THAT LETTER BEFORE HE DIED! A "MAN'S WIFE" MEANS MARVA. I "WON" HER FROM PSYCHO'S EVIL CONTROL. FOR REVENGE HE THREATENS TO KILL A "MAJOR"—THAT'S STEVE OF COURSE. HE DIED BEFORE HE COULD CARRY OUT HIS THREAT BUT---

WORRIED ABOUT STEVE, **WONDER WOMAN** SPEEDS DIRECTLY TO OFFICERS' QUARTERS IN WASHINGTON.

NICE TO SEE YOU BOYS— BUT WHERE IS MAJOR TREVOR?

IT'S **WONDER WOMAN** HOORAY!

NEVER MIND TREVOR-GIVE *US* A BREAK! YOU'RE OUR HONORARY COLONEL-LET'S HAVE A STAFF CONFERENCE!

AT THIS MOMENT STEVE APPEARS, USHERING A GUEST OUT UNCEREMONIOUSLY.

GET OUT AND STAY OUT!

BUT SENOR-I MAKE YOU FAIR PROPOSITION! I OFFER TO DO YOUR MURDERS FOR YOU—

TOMORROW AT 11 A.M. IN YOUR OWN OFFICES, SENOR, YOU WILL DIE! I BID YOU GOOD MORNING!

HA! HA! COMICAL FELLOW-CRAZY AS A LOON-

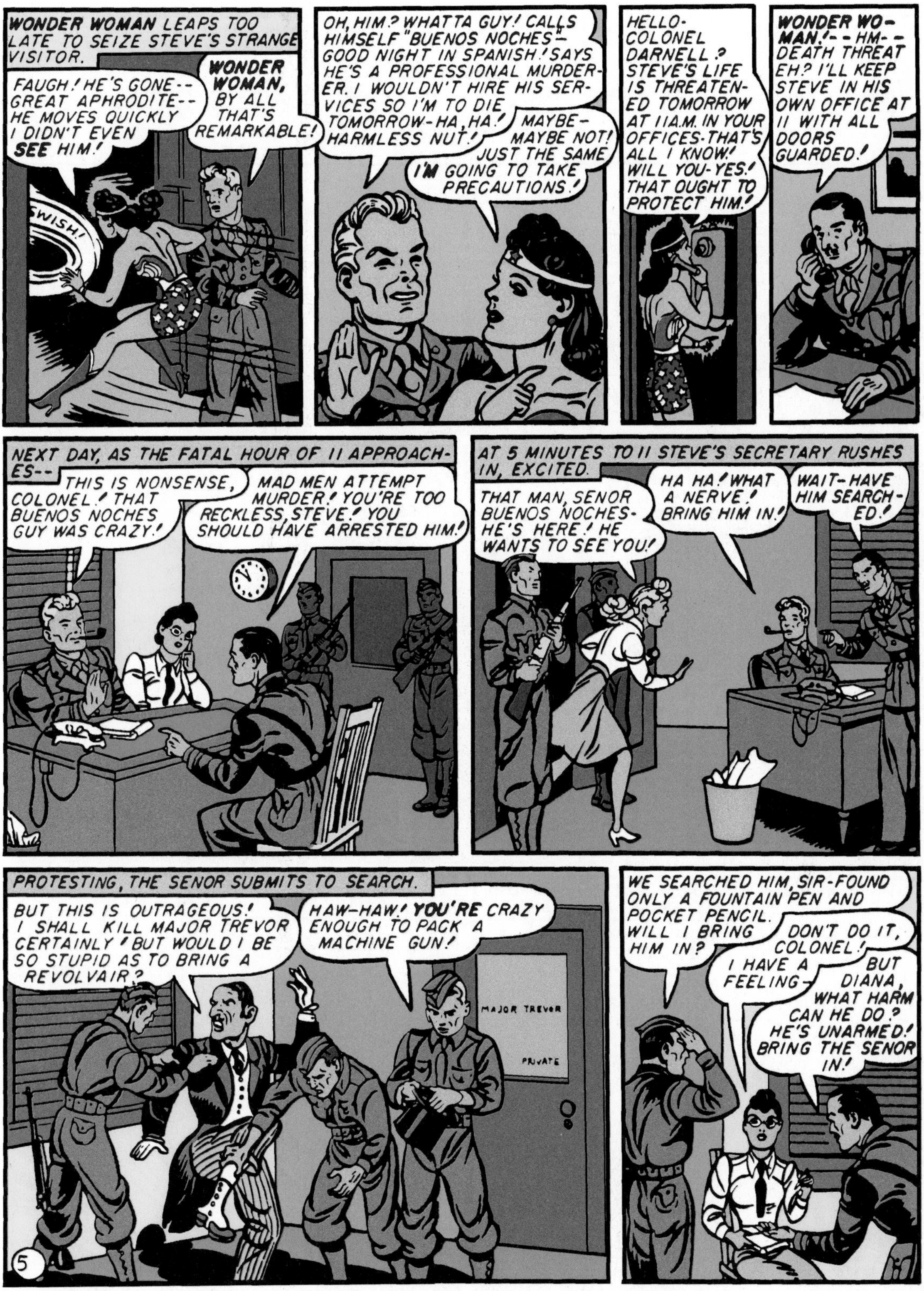
WONDER WOMAN LEAPS TOO LATE TO SEIZE STEVE'S STRANGE VISITOR.
FAUGH! HE'S GONE-- GREAT APHRODITE-- HE MOVES QUICKLY I DIDN'T EVEN SEE HIM!
WONDER WOMAN, BY ALL THAT'S REMARKABLE!
SWISH!
OH, HIM? WHATTA GUY! CALLS HIMSELF "BUENOS NOCHES"-- GOOD NIGHT IN SPANISH! SAYS HE'S A PROFESSIONAL MURDERER. I WOULDN'T HIRE HIS SERVICES SO I'M TO DIE TOMORROW-HA, HA! HARMLESS NUT!
MAYBE-- MAYBE NOT! JUST THE SAME I'M GOING TO TAKE PRECAUTIONS!
HELLO- COLONEL DARNELL? STEVE'S LIFE IS THREATENED TOMORROW AT 11 A.M. IN YOUR OFFICES-THAT'S ALL I KNOW! WILL YOU-YES! THAT OUGHT TO PROTECT HIM!
WONDER WOMAN!--HM-- DEATH THREAT EH? I'LL KEEP STEVE IN HIS OWN OFFICE AT 11 WITH ALL DOORS GUARDED!
NEXT DAY, AS THE FATAL HOUR OF 11 APPROACHES--
THIS IS NONSENSE, COLONEL! THAT BUENOS NOCHES GUY WAS CRAZY!
MAD MEN ATTEMPT MURDER! YOU'RE TOO RECKLESS, STEVE! YOU SHOULD HAVE ARRESTED HIM!
AT 5 MINUTES TO 11 STEVE'S SECRETARY RUSHES IN, EXCITED.
THAT MAN, SENOR BUENOS NOCHES- HE'S HERE! HE WANTS TO SEE YOU!
HA HA! WHAT A NERVE! BRING HIM IN!
WAIT-HAVE HIM SEARCHED!
PROTESTING, THE SENOR SUBMITS TO SEARCH.
BUT THIS IS OUTRAGEOUS! I SHALL KILL MAJOR TREVOR CERTAINLY! BUT WOULD I BE SO STUPID AS TO BRING A REVOLVAIR?
HAW-HAW! YOU'RE CRAZY ENOUGH TO PACK A MACHINE GUN!
MAJOR TREVOR
PRIVATE
5
WE SEARCHED HIM, SIR-FOUND ONLY A FOUNTAIN PEN AND POCKET PENCIL. WILL I BRING HIM IN?
DON'T DO IT, COLONEL! I HAVE A FEELING-
BUT DIANA, WHAT HARM CAN HE DO? HE'S UNARMED! BRING THE SENOR IN!

GREETINGS, AMIGOS! IT IS SO NICE YOU ALL COME TO SEE MAJOR TREVOR DIE!

HA HA! HE'S **GOOD!**

MIND TELLING US, SENOR, HOW YOU'RE GOING TO KILL THE MAJOR?

HOW I SHALL MURDER MAJOR TREVOR IS TOLD **ON THIS PAPER!** READ IT MAJOR–IF YOU APPROVE SIGN ON THE DOTTED LINE!

YOU'VE GOT A **DOTTY** LINE, NO FOOLING!

STEVE PICKS UP THE PAPER, CARELESSLY, PERMITTING THE FOUNTAIN PEN TO ROLL ONTO THE DESK

THIS SHEET IS BLANK!

AH, BUT THE MANNER OF YOUR DEATH **WAS ON** THAT PAPER, SENOR– YOU BRUSHED IT OFF!

THIS SCREWBALL LINE IS GETTING MONOTONOUS. GIVE THE SENOR BACK HIS PEN AND PAPER, LILA, AND SHOW HIM OUT!

YES, MAJOR!

DIANA, SUDDENLY PERCEIVING THE SECRET PURPOSE OF BUENOS NOCHES' PECULIAR BEHAVIOR, ACTS WITH LIGHTNING SPEED.

LILA! DON'T **TOUCH** THAT FOUNTAIN PEN!

I'M NOT TAKING ORDERS FROM **YOU,** DIANA PRINCE!

6

AS LILA PICKS UP THE PEN DIANA YANKS STEVE ACROSS THE DESK AND–

UGH–SPUT–T!

BAA–NG!

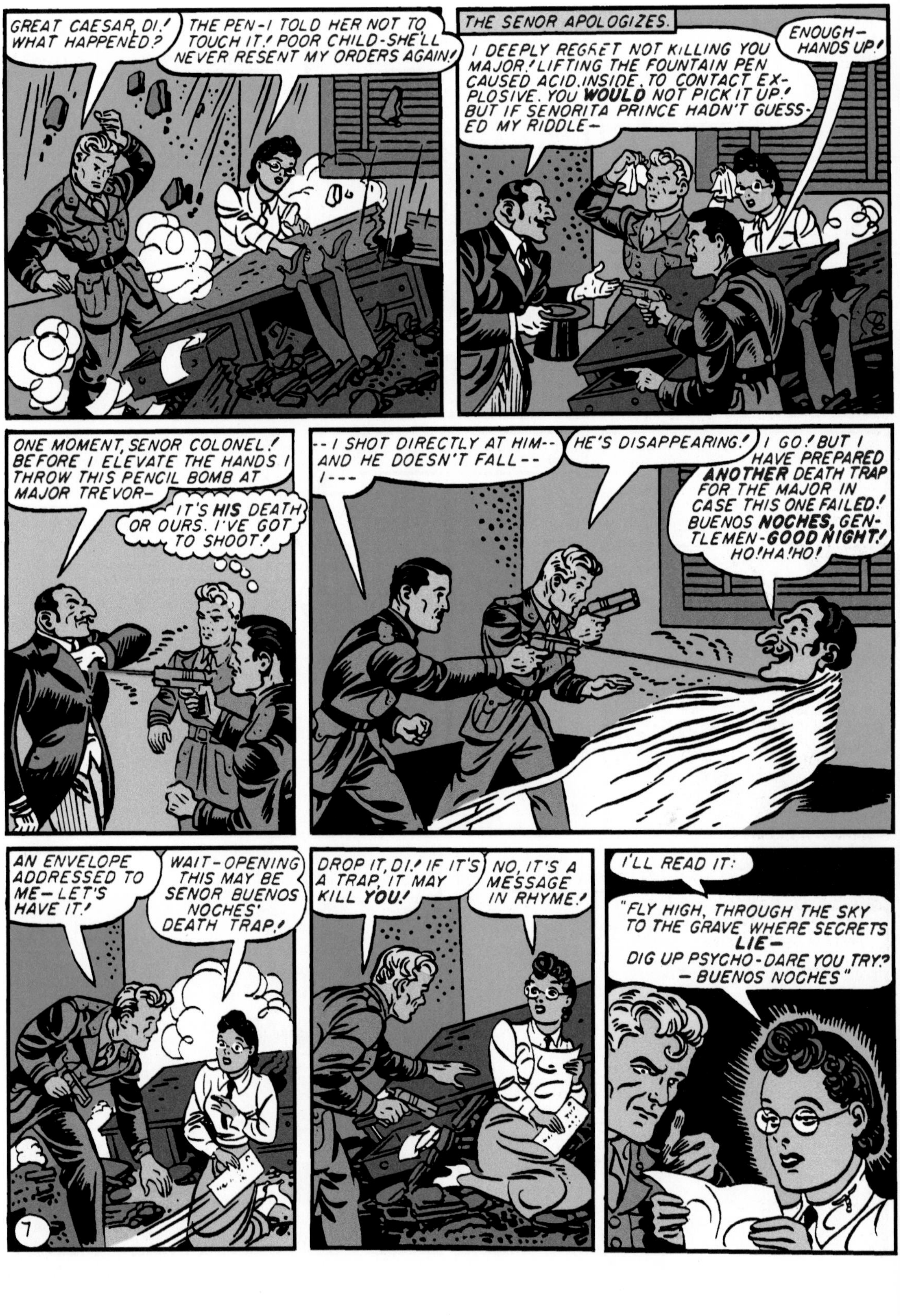
GREAT CAESAR, DI! WHAT HAPPENED?
THE PEN-I TOLD HER NOT TO TOUCH IT! POOR CHILD-SHE'LL NEVER RESENT MY ORDERS AGAIN!
THE SENOR APOLOGIZES.
I DEEPLY REGRET NOT KILLING YOU MAJOR! LIFTING THE FOUNTAIN PEN CAUSED ACID INSIDE TO CONTACT EXPLOSIVE. YOU WOULD NOT PICK IT UP! BUT IF SENORITA PRINCE HADN'T GUESSED MY RIDDLE—
ENOUGH— HANDS UP!
ONE MOMENT, SENOR COLONEL! BEFORE I ELEVATE THE HANDS I THROW THIS PENCIL BOMB AT MAJOR TREVOR—
IT'S HIS DEATH OR OURS. I'VE GOT TO SHOOT!
--I SHOT DIRECTLY AT HIM-- AND HE DOESN'T FALL-- I---
HE'S DISAPPEARING!
I GO! BUT I HAVE PREPARED ANOTHER DEATH TRAP FOR THE MAJOR IN CASE THIS ONE FAILED! BUENOS NOCHES, GENTLEMEN-GOOD NIGHT! HO!HA!HO!
AN ENVELOPE ADDRESSED TO ME—LET'S HAVE IT!
WAIT-OPENING THIS MAY BE SENOR BUENOS NOCHES' DEATH TRAP!
7
DROP IT, DI! IF IT'S A TRAP, IT MAY KILL YOU!
NO, IT'S A MESSAGE IN RHYME!
I'LL READ IT:
"FLY HIGH, THROUGH THE SKY TO THE GRAVE WHERE SECRETS LIE—
DIG UP PSYCHO-DARE YOU TRY?
—BUENOS NOCHES"

MUST BE SOMETHING PLANTED IN PSYCHO'S GRAVE! MAY BE A BOMB BUT WHATEVER IT IS WILL GIVE US A CLUE. I'LL FLY MY PLANE TO THE PRISON.

WAIT- STEVE!

NO USE—MEN ARE SO HEADSTRONG!

HASTILY DONNING HER **WONDER WOMAN** COSTUME, DIANA TELE- PHONES ETTA CANDY.

HELLO—ETTA? DRIVE TO THE AIRPORT—I MEAN **FAST**! YOU KNOW WHERE STEVE KEEPS HIS PLANE? RIGHT—BE SEEING YOU!

RACING TO THE AIRPORT **WONDER WOMAN** IS FUELING THE SHIP WHEN STEVE AND ETTA ARRIVE.

WONDER WOMAN! HOW DID **YOU** KNOW ABOUT THIS?

DIANA SENT A MENTAL MESSAGE— WHAT'S BEEN KEEP- ING YOU PEOPLE?

FLYING SWIFTLY TO THE PRISON STEVE PREPARES TO LAND ON A NEARBY AIR FIELD.

WHAT'S THE MATTER WITH THIS RETRACTABLE LANDING GEAR? IT WON'T GO DOWN!

DOWN—HA, HA! THAT'S A FUNNY ONE——LOOK BELOW!

STEVE'S LANDING GEAR HAS DROPPED FROM THE PLANE!

PUNKEROO! CAN'T MAKE A CRASH LANDING HERE— IT'D BE SUICIDE!

THIS IS THE SENOR'S DEATH TRAP!

SET HER DOWN—I'LL BE YOUR EMERGENCY LAND- ING GEAR!

BREAKING A HOLE IN THE BOT- TOM OF THE PLANE **WONDER WO- MAN** SWINGS BELOW AS STEVE GLIDES DOWN FOR A LANDING.

LANDING SPEED'S 80 MILES AN HOUR. I'LL RUN WITH THE PLANE AND SLOW DOWN GRADUALLY—

AS HER FEET TOUCH THE GROUND **WONDER WO- MAN** RACES AT LANDING SPEED, HOLDING THE PLANE ABOVE HER HEAD.

THIS IS EASY—NOW TO PUT ON MY BRAKES!

⑧

BICEPS OF ATLAS! HOW DOES SHE DO IT? SHE'S HOLDING THIS PLANE STEADY AS A ROCK!

AS **WONDER WOMAN** STOPS NEAR THE RUNWAY 50 MEN TAKE THE PLANE OFF HER HANDS.

I DON'T NEED HELP BUT IF YOU BOYS INSIST, HANDLE THE PLANE CAREFULLY!

WHATTA GIRL!

SHE'S STRONGER THAN 50 MEN!

BUENOS NOCHES THINKS WE CRASHED—THERE'S A CHANCE TO SURPRISE HIM! I'LL RUN AHEAD. WHEN YOU REACH THE PRISON, ETTA, LOOK FOR A WOMAN PRISONER IN A TRANCE AND **WAKEN** HER!

WOO WOO! COUNT ON ME, BABE!

ENTERING THE PRISON QUIETLY **WONDER WOMAN** SECURES A SPADE AND HURRIES TO PSYCHO'S GRAVE.

SENOR "BUENOS NOCHES" SAYS THERE'S A SECRET BURIED HERE—I BELIEVE HE'S RIGHT!

THE EARTH IS HARD PACKED—APPARENTLY HASN'T BEEN DISTURBED.

THIS SEAL HASN'T BEEN BROKEN! BUT JUST THE SAME I'LL BET MYSELF A GOOD SPANKING THAT PSYCHO'S BODY IS—WELL, I'LL SOON SEE!

WRENCHING THE PINE BOX OPEN, **WONDER WOMAN** FINDS IT EMPTY!

JUST AS I SUSPECTED—PSYCHO'S BURIAL WAS A HOAX! THE BODY I SAW BURIED WAS MADE OF ECTOPLASM—WHEN THE GRAVE CLOSED PSYCHO **DE** MATERIALIZED IT!

ABSORBED IN HER THOUGHTS **WONDER WOMAN** DOES NOT HEAR THE SINISTER APPROACH OF "GUARD REGAN" BEHIND HER.

9

HIT IN A HUMAN'S MOST VULNERABLE SPOT, THE BASE OF THE BRAIN, **WONDER WOMAN** FALLS UNCONSCIOUS.

AH-H-H-AH!

SHE'S HUMAN AFTER ALL—SHE **CAN** BE KNOCKED OUT—HO! HA! HO!

"REGAN" RUTHLESSLY BURIES WONDER WOMAN ALIVE.

HE FINISHES HIS GHASTLY WORK WITHOUT DETECTION.

GREAT IDEA TO RETURN IN THIS ECTOPLASMIC DISGUISE OF "GUARD REGAN" — WATCHING WONDER WOMAN DIE WAS WORTH A MILLION DOLLARS! ANOTHER WOMAN OUT OF THE WAY! AND WHAT A WOMAN SHE WAS! HO! HA! HO!

ETTA, MEANWHILE, FOLLOWS WONDER WOMAN'S INSTRUCTIONS—

SAY, WARDEN, HAVE YOU GOT A WOMAN PRISONER IN A TRANCE?

ODD YOU SHOULD ASK — PSYCHO TALKED WITH HIS FORMER SECRETARY BEFORE HE DIED — SHE FALLS UNCONSCIOUS FREQUENTLY EVER SINCE!

THEY FIND JOAN DEEPLY ENTRANCED IN HER CELL.

LOOK-SHE'S DEAD TO THE WORLD-NOBODY CAN WAKE HER!

I GOT AN IDEA — GET ME SOME HANDCUFFS AND A PITCHER OF WATER!

SMACK!

IF WE PUT A STRAIN ON HER MUSCLES SHE'LL GET A LOT OF STIMULATIN' REFLEXES, ACCORDIN' TO OUR PSYCHOLOGY PROF! SHOCK WILL HELP TOO-THAT'S WHERE MY ICE WATER COMES IN!

ETTA'S HEROIC TREATMENT BEGINS TO WORK!

SPLUT-BLUB! WH-WHERE AM I?

IN JAIL, BABY-BUT THAT'S BETTER THAN BEIN' IN A TRANCE. WAKE UP SOME MORE!

10

MEANWHILE WONDER WOMAN REGAINS CONSCIOUSNESS UNDERGROUND.

HUMPH- WHAT HAPPENED? WHAT'S THIS WEIGHT ON MY CHEST? GREAT APHRODITE-I'M BURIED ALIVE! LUCKY WE AMAZONS PRACTICE YOGI-I CAUGHT MY BREATH AND SWALLOWED MY TONGUE AUTOMATICALLY.

WRIGGLING LOOSE IN THE CLOSE-PACKED EARTH **WONDER WOMAN** EXERTS HER TREMENDOUS STRENGTH.

I DON'T CARE MUCH FOR THIS GAME, IT'S TOO MESSY!

LIKE A VOLCANIC ERUPTION THE EARTH RISES!

AS **WONDER WOMAN** SHAKES HERSELF FREE OF CLINGING EARTH "GUARD REGAN," STILL ON WATCH, PREPARES TO ADMINISTER A **COUPE DE GRACE.**

LUCKY I WAITED—THE GIRL IS A MAGICIAN! THIS TIME I'LL TAKE NO CHANCES—

BUT EVEN AS "REGAN" PRESSES THE TRIGGER, JOAN AWAKENS FROM HER TRANCE AND THE WEIRD, ECTOPLASMIC FORM ENVELOPING PSYCHO DISAPPEARS.

*OH, I'M **MYSELF** AGAIN!*

WH-WHAT'S HAPPENING? I-I MUST HAVE LOST CONTROL OF JOAN!

WHIRLING SWIFTLY **WONDER WOMAN** CASTS HER MAGIC LASSO OVER THE FLEEING PSYCHO.

THERE YOU ARE, MY LITTLE GIANT— AT LAST!

*IT'S PSYCHO! BUT— BUT PSYCHO'S **DEAD!***

*NOT QUITE! YOU BURIED A PHANTOM CORPSE! PSYCHO, **CONFESS!***

*HO!HA! BUT SOMETHING **COMPELS** ME! I ESCAPED, AS "GUARD REGAN," ASSUMED THE GUISE OF SENOR BUENOS NOCHES! I HAD YOU ALL FOOLED, TOO, UNTIL **WONDER WOMAN** GOT BUSY--- WELL--I GUESS YOU WIN THIS TIME!*

⑪

*WOO WOO, **WONDER WOMAN!** YOU LICKED THE SMARTEST CRIMINAL IN THE WORLD!*

BUT EVEN PSYCHO WAS HELPLESS WHEN HE LOST THE AID OF HIS WOMAN ASSISTANTS! EARTH GIRLS CAN STOP MEN'S POWER FOR EVIL WHEN THEY REFUSE TO BE DOMINATED BY EVIL MEN!

THE END

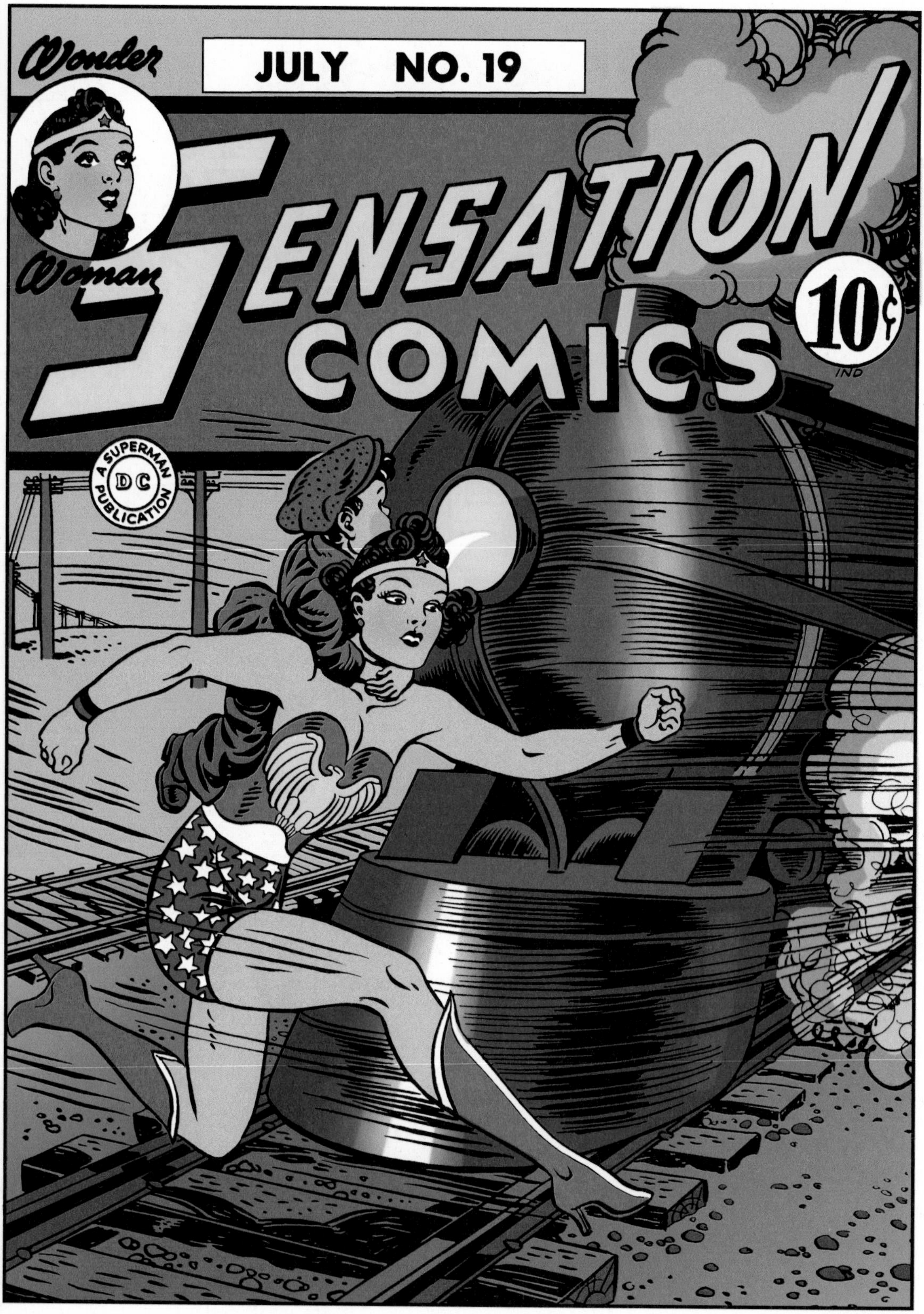
Wonder Woman
JULY NO. 19
SENSATION COMICS
10¢
A SUPERMAN DC PUBLICATION

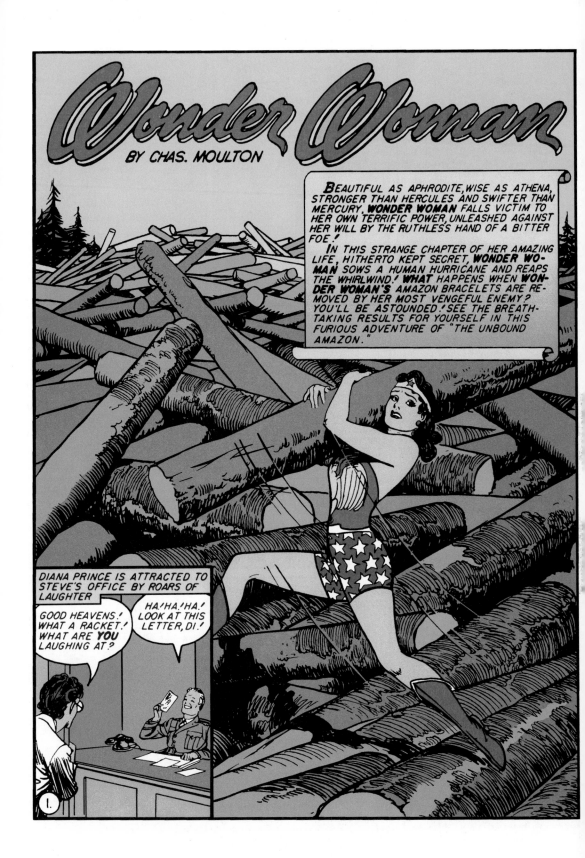

Wonder Woman

BY CHAS. MOULTON

BEAUTIFUL AS APHRODITE, WISE AS ATHENA, STRONGER THAN HERCULES AND SWIFTER THAN MERCURY, **WONDER WOMAN** FALLS VICTIM TO HER OWN TERRIFIC POWER, UNLEASHED AGAINST HER WILL BY THE RUTHLESS HAND OF A BITTER FOE!

IN THIS STRANGE CHAPTER OF HER AMAZING LIFE, HITHERTO KEPT SECRET, **WONDER WO-MAN** SOWS A HUMAN HURRICANE AND REAPS THE WHIRLWIND! **WHAT** HAPPENS WHEN **WONDER WOMAN'S** AMAZON BRACELETS ARE RE-MOVED BY HER MOST VENGEFUL ENEMY? YOU'LL BE ASTOUNDED! SEE THE BREATH-TAKING RESULTS FOR YOURSELF IN THIS FURIOUS ADVENTURE OF "THE UNBOUND AMAZON."

DIANA PRINCE IS ATTRACTED TO STEVE'S OFFICE BY ROARS OF LAUGHTER

GOOD HEAVENS! WHAT A RACKET! WHAT ARE **YOU** LAUGHING AT?

HA! HA! HA! LOOK AT THIS LETTER, DI!

1.

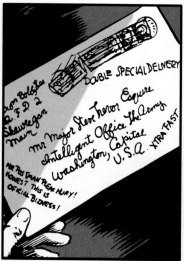

DOUBLE SPECIAL DELIVERY

Mr Major Steve Trevor Esquire
Intelligent Office The Army
Washington, Capitol
U.S.A. XTRA FAST

MR POS TMAN PLEAS HURY! HONEST THIS IS OFFICIAL BIZNESS!

HA! HA! BOBBY'S A GREAT KID-REMEMBER HOW HE SOCKED THE KEEPER OF THE "TALKING LION"? WHAT'S HE DOING IN MAINE?

HIS SISTER, SALLY, WHO SUPPORTED HIM, GOT SICK AND HAD TO GO HOME. WHAT A CUTE LETTER!

Dear Major Steve:
Sumbuddy is starting a enemy plot at Skawegan and Wonder Woman ought to know. The subject is a big tuff lookin guy called Leon Dexter. His trubbul is he prefurs burnetts. Her name is Mavis. My teacher is blonde-she's swell! She loves this mug an is goin two kill herself! Tell Wonder Woman pleas come quick!

Yours truly
Bobby

HA! HA! CHILDISH NONSENSE, NO DOUBT!

HM-MAYBE! BUT I'LL SEND **WONDER WOMAN** A MENTAL RADIOGRAM. IF YOU AND SHE HAD BELIEVED BOBBY'S STORY WHEN HE SAID HE HEARD THAT LION TALK, YOU'D HAVE SAVED A LOT OF TROUBLE!

THAT NIGHT A MENTAL RADIO CALL COMES FROM MALA, AMAZON PRISON CHIEF.

PRISONER MAVIS HAS ESCAPED FROM REFORM ISLAND. SHE'S DANGEROUS AND MAY BE IN AMERICA!

MAVIS IS A **BRUNETTE**-WOULD **SHE** BE THE SAME "TRUBBUL" BOBBY MENTIONED? HM!

WHILE DIANA PRINCE CONSIDERS THE CASE LET US GO BACK TWO DAYS AND WATCH BOBBY'S ADVENTURES AT THE SKAWEEGAN SCHOOL.

GOOD MORNING, MISS PINKY!

GOOD MORNING, BOBBY-MORNING, NED!

HELLO, TEACHER

LOOK OUT FOR PINKY ANNE TODAY-SHE'S GOT HER **MAD DRESS** ON!

GEE! THAT'S RIGHT! WHENEVER SHE WEARS THAT DRESS, SHE'S ALWAYS IN A BAD MOOD! WOW! I'M GLAD I DID MY HOMEWORK!

②

BOBBY AND NED- STOP WHISPERING! IF I CATCH YOU BOYS DOING THAT AGAIN I'LL MAKE YOU SIT IN THE CORNER AND FACE THE WALL FOR THE REST OF THE DAY!

YES'M.

AW-ER -I WASN'T TALKING, MISS PINKY!

14
6
9
29

2)4286
2175

ISABEL JONES, SPELL "EYE"!
I!
NO, NO! NOT YOU- "EYE"!
Y-O-U!
Cat
Dog
Horse
ISABEL, ARE YOU BEING PURPOSELY STUPID? SPELL "EYE"— THIS EYE -OUCH!
PING!
WHO SHOT THAT ELASTIC AT ME? IT WAS YOU, BOBBY LEE! YOU THINK THAT'S FUNNY, I SUPPOSE!
NO, HONEST, MISS PINKY! I DIDN'T SHOOT IT!
Cat
Dog
Horse
DON'T LIE, BOBBY! YOU WILL STAY ONE HOUR AFTER SCHOOL!
AW GEE, MISS PINKY! MY BASEBALL TEAM'S GOT A BIG GAME TODAY—SOME-BODY BEHIND ME SHOT-ER— NEVER MIND!
TATTLE TALE-TATTLE TALE!
Cat
Dog
Horse
AFTER SCHOOL -
DO THAT ARITHMETIC! ALL THE TIME YOU'RE IDLE WILL BE ADDED TO YOUR PUNISHMENT!
YES'M.
AW, PFUI! PINKY'S SORE AT SOMEBODY ELSE AND SHE'S TAKING IT OUT ON ME!
3
BOBBY PROVES A GOOD PSYCHOLOGIST.
HELLO, ANNE! I-I'VE GOT TO SEE YOU—
GO AWAY, LEON DEXTER! I NEVER WANT TO SEE YOU AGAIN!

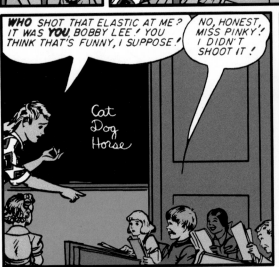

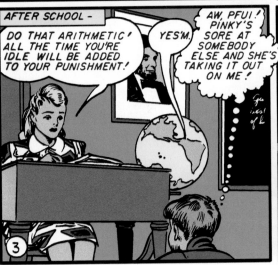

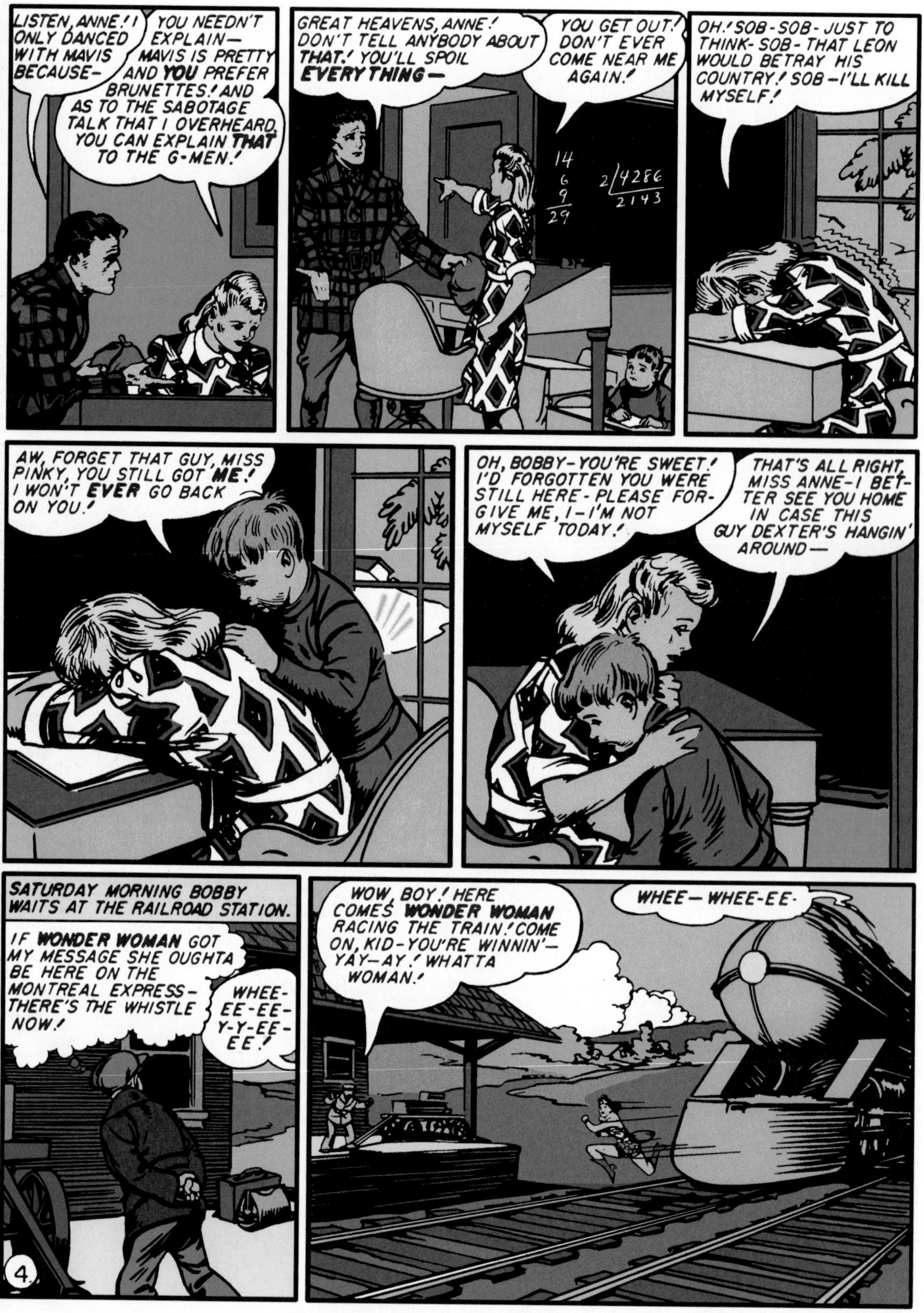
LISTEN, ANNE! I ONLY DANCED WITH MAVIS BECAUSE-
YOU NEEDN'T EXPLAIN— MAVIS IS PRETTY AND YOU PREFER BRUNETTES! AND AS TO THE SABOTAGE TALK THAT I OVERHEARD, YOU CAN EXPLAIN THAT TO THE G-MEN!
GREAT HEAVENS, ANNE! DON'T TELL ANYBODY ABOUT THAT! YOU'LL SPOIL EVERYTHING—
YOU GET OUT! DON'T EVER COME NEAR ME AGAIN!
14
6
9
29
2⟌4286
2143
OH! SOB-SOB- JUST TO THINK- SOB- THAT LEON WOULD BETRAY HIS COUNTRY! SOB —I'LL KILL MYSELF!
AW, FORGET THAT GUY, MISS PINKY, YOU STILL GOT ME! I WON'T EVER GO BACK ON YOU!
OH, BOBBY-YOU'RE SWEET! I'D FORGOTTEN YOU WERE STILL HERE- PLEASE FORGIVE ME, I—I'M NOT MYSELF TODAY!
THAT'S ALL RIGHT, MISS ANNE-I BETTER SEE YOU HOME IN CASE THIS GUY DEXTER'S HANGIN' AROUND—
SATURDAY MORNING BOBBY WAITS AT THE RAILROAD STATION.
IF WONDER WOMAN GOT MY MESSAGE SHE OUGHTA BE HERE ON THE MONTREAL EXPRESS— THERE'S THE WHISTLE NOW!
WHEE-EE-EE-Y-Y-EE-EE!
WOW, BOY! HERE COMES WONDER WOMAN RACING THE TRAIN! COME ON, KID-YOU'RE WINNIN'— YAY—AY! WHATTA WOMAN!
WHEE— WHEE-EE-
4

WITH AN ADDED BURST OF SPEED **WONDER WOMAN** EASILY REACHES THE PLATFORM AHEAD OF THE TRAIN.

YAY-AY! YOU BEAT THE TRAIN!

THAT WAS JUST EXER-CISE, I WASN'T RACING.

BOBBY TELLS **WONDER WOMAN** HIS STORY.

WHAT YOU'VE TOLD ME IS VERY INTERESTING, BOBBY! TAKE ME TO MISS PINKY'S HOUSE—I MUST TALK WITH HER!

OKAY. BUT WE GOTTA WAIT TILL THE TRAIN PULLS OUT SO WE KIN CROSS THE TRACKS.

CAN'T WAIT FOR THE TRAIN TO START—I HAVE A FEELING SOMETHING MAY BE HAPPENING TO ANNE PINKY!

OOO-O BOY! YOU JUMP HIGHER'N A KANGAROO!

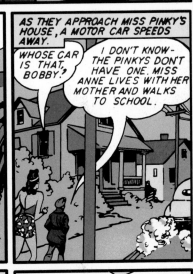

AS THEY APPROACH MISS PINKY'S HOUSE, A MOTOR CAR SPEEDS AWAY.

WHOSE CAR IS THAT, BOBBY?

I DON'T KNOW—THE PINKYS DON'T HAVE ONE. MISS ANNE LIVES WITH HER MOTHER AND WALKS TO SCHOOL.

NOBODY HOME—THAT'S FUNNY!

THE DOOR IS LOCKED—I THINK I HEAR SOMEONE GROANING INSIDE!

5.

I HATE TO BREAK IN, BUT SOMEBODY MAY NEED HELP.

CRASH!

GEE WHILLIKER! THAT'S MRS. PINKY—SHE'S KNOCKED OUT!

HM-A NASTY BLOW- GET ME SOME WATER—QUICK!

SKILLFULLY **WONDER WOMAN** GIVES MRS. PINKY FIRST AID.

THERE—THAT'S BETTER! WHAT HAPPENED?

SOME MEN—GERMANS—AND A PRETTY GIRL, KIDNAPPED ANNE! I SCREAMED AND A MAN HIT ME WITH THE BUTT OF A REVOLVER!

THAT CAR WE SAW MUSTA BEEN THE KIDNAPPERS.

YES, I'M GOING AFTER IT! IF I'M NOT BACK IN AN HOUR PHONE MAJOR TREVOR IN WASHINGTON. SAY PAULA IS TO FLY STEVE AND ETTA HERE IN MY PLANE!

WONDER WOMAN SPEEDS IN PURSUIT OF THE KIDNAP CAR.

THOSE FURRIN' DEVILS'RE ALWAYS SPEEDIN'! I BET SHE COMES FROM NOO YAWK!

AT THE ROAD'S DEAD END **WONDER WOMAN** FINDS THE CAR ABANDONED.

HERE'S A HANDKERCHIEF WITH ANNE'S INITIALS—THEY MUST HAVE CARRIED HER UP THAT PATH INTO THE WOODS!

KEEPING THE PATH IN SIGHT **WONDER WOMAN** TAKES A SHORT CUT THROUGH THE TREES.

THEY CAN'T BE FAR AHEAD— I'LL SOON OVERTAKE THEM!

ON A ROCKY LEDGE ABOVE A SWAMP **WONDER WOMAN** OVERTAKES THE FUGITIVES.

HALT—SURRENDER!

DONNERWETTER! IT'S **VONDER VOMAN**—BULLETS DOND'T HURT HER!

6.

BEFORE **WONDER WOMAN** CAN SEIZE THE KIDNAPPERS THEIR LEADER ISSUES DESPERATE ORDERS.

THROW THE GIRL INTO THIS QUAGMIRE, QUICK! THAT'LL KEEP **WONDER WOMAN** BUSY! SHE'S SURE TO GO AFTER HER! I HAVE A PLAN!

ANNE SINKS HELPLESSLY IN THE TREACHEROUS OOZE-HER STRUGGLES ONLY HASTEN HER FATE.

WONDER WOMAN PREPARES TO RESCUE ANNE.

DON'T THRASH AROUND, ANNE-IT MAKES YOU SINK FASTER! I'LL BE DOWN THERE IN JUST A MINUTE!

VE BEDDER RUN QVICK-DERE IS NO USE FIGHTING VONDER VOMAN!

WAIT! MY PLAN IS WORKING PERFECTLY-WHEN SHE JUMPS INTO THE SWAMP AT THE END OF THAT LASSO I'VE GOT HER!

HERE I COME, ANNE-I'LL HAVE YOU OUT IN A JIFFY!

LYING FLAT ON THE SURFACE WITH THE AID OF THE LOG, WONDER WOMAN GETS A GRIP ON THE GIRL'S BODY WITH HER POWERFUL LEGS.

WITH STEADY, POWERFUL PULLS WONDER WOMAN FREES ANNE'S HELPLESS BODY FROM THE DEADLY SUCTION OF THE BOG.

EASY DOES IT, ANNE-WE'LL SOON BE ON SOLID GROUND AGAIN!

YOU ARE WONDER-FUL-I'D GIVEN UP HOPE!

7.

BUT MAVIS, KIDNAP LEADER AND WONDER WOMAN'S IMPLACABLE ENEMY, INTERVENES.

STOP PULLING, WONDER WOMAN! I HOLD THE MAGIC LASSO WHICH BINDS YOU-YOU ARE COMPELLED TO OBEY ME!

SO IT'S YOU, MAVIS! WELL-YOU'VE CAUGHT ME AGAIN!

MAVIS PERMITS **WONDER WO-MAN** TO PULL ANNE FROM THE SWAMP.

CLIMB UP THE CLIFF, **WONDER WOMAN!**

I MUST OBEY!

WONDER WOMAN CARRIES ANNE UP THE CLIFF.

THIS, AT LEAST, IS FUN!

AT THE TOP—

THIS IS THE GREATEST PLEASURE I'VE HAD SINCE I TIED YOU TO A BOMB!

IT WILL ALSO BE YOUR GREATEST REGRET WHEN I ESCAPE AGAIN AS I DID THEN!

MAVIS IS ENRAGED AS SHE DRIVES **WONDER WOMAN** BEFORE HER.

I'LL TEACH YOU TO ANSWER ME RESPECTFULLY!

TEACH AN AMAZON GIRL WITH A LITTLE LOVE TAP LIKE THAT.? DON'T BE SILLY!

CRACK!

AT THE "NORTH MAINE CO.'S" LOGGING CAMP **WONDER WOMAN** IS SURPRISED TO FIND ALL THE "LUMBERJACKS" ARE NAZIS.

YOU GOT **VONDER VOMAN**—GOOT VORK! HEIL HITLER!

HEIL HITLER!

MAVIS SECURES THE PRISONERS IN HER CABIN.

MAKE YOURSELVES AT HOME, GIRLS—YOU'LL BE MY GUESTS FROM NOW ON! THIS LUMBER CAMP IS A SABOTAGE CENTER— LOGGING OPERATIONS COVER OUR AXIS ACTIVITIES WHICH EXTEND ALL OVER AMERICA!

8.

LEON DEXTER! I KNEW YOU WERE A TRAITOR!

YOU KNEW TOO MUCH! MAVIS, WHY KIDNAP THIS GIRL.?

CALM YOURSELF, DARLING! YOU MADE LOVE TO HER AND TALKED TOO MUCH. **HER** TONGUE MUST NOW BE STOPPED!

PUSHING MAVIS ROUGHLY ASIDE, DEXTER CUTS ANNE FROM THE WALL.

COME BACK HERE, YOU IDIOT—THEY'LL SHOOT YOU!

PUT ME DOWN! I'D RATHER BE MAVIS' PRISONER THAN FREE WITH **YOU**!

HE HAS A HEAD START—BUT THEY'LL GET HIM!

YOU CANNOT ESCAPE, MY PRETTY PRISONER, WHILE I HOLD THIS MAGIC LASSO—CAN YOU? TELL THE TRUTH.

WHILE YOU HOLD IT I CANNOT ESCAPE, BUT WHEN YOU GO AWAY I MAY LOOSEN THE KNOTS!

IF THERE'S ANY CHANCE OF YOUR ESCAPE, I MUST DESTROY YOUR AMAZON STRENGTH! WELDING CHAINS BETWEEN YOUR BRACELETS WEAKENS YOU, I DISCOVERED—BUT YOU SUCCEEDED ONCE IN FILING OFF YOUR FETTERS. I HAVE A BETTER IDEA!

I SHALL CUT OFF YOUR AMAZON BRACELETS! AHA! **THAT** FRIGHTENS YOU, EH? SILENCE—YOU CANNOT SPEAK!

OH, MAVIS **MUSTN'T** DO THAT—SHE DOESN'T KNOW THE AWFUL CONSEQUENCES! BUT I CANNOT WARN HER—WHILE THE BRACELETS ARE STILL ON, I'M NOT ABLE TO SPEAK OF IT!

MEANWHILE PAULA, STEVE AND ETTA CANDY ARRIVE IN RESPONSE TO BOBBY'S TELEPHONE CALL.

OH BOY! WHAT A SUPER-DUPER PLANE-INVISIBLE-GEE!

BOBBY, TAKE US TO THE NORTH MAINE CO. CAMP—MY INFORMATION POINTS IN THAT DIRECTION.

⑨

FOLLOWING THE RIVER PATH THEY ARE STARTLED BY THE SUDDEN APPEARANCE OF THE FLEEING DEXTER.

GEE—THAT'S MISS ANNE'S BOY FRIEND CARRYIN' HER OFF!

THE RIVER'S FULL OF LOGS—HE'S GOING TO RIDE 'EM!

AS DEXTER, WITH A RIVERDOG'S SUREFOOTED SKILL, LEAPS TO A FLOATING LOG, A PURSUING NAZI LEVELS HIS PISTOL.

A SURE SHOT — I KILL DEM BOTH.

BUT YOUNG BOBBY HAS NOT HELD THE ROCK AND SPITBALL THROWING CHAMPIONSHIP FOR NOTHING.

SHOOT MY TEACHER, WOULD YOU - YOU DOD-BLAMED, BUTTER-BRAINED, DING-DANGED - - - DUMBBELL!

STEVE'S GUN TAKES CARE OF ANOTHER AXIS ASSASSIN AS DEXTER SKILLFULLY STEERS HIS LOG TO MIDSTREAM.

MAYBE THAT GUY ON THE LOG OUGHT TO BE SHOT TOO—BUT NOT WHILE HE'S CARRYING THE GIRL!

BOBBY, YOU FOLLOW THAT LOG JUMPER DOWN RIVER AND WATCH WHERE HE TAKES MISS ANNE! WE'LL INVADE THE NASTI LAYOUT AND FIND WHAT THEY'VE DONE WITH WONDER WOMAN!

OKAY, MAJOR STEVE!

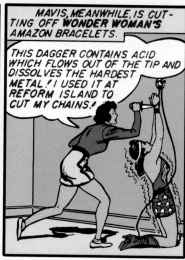

MAVIS, MEANWHILE, IS CUTTING OFF WONDER WOMAN'S AMAZON BRACELETS.

THIS DAGGER CONTAINS ACID WHICH FLOWS OUT OF THE TIP AND DISSOLVES THE HARDEST METAL! I USED IT AT REFORM ISLAND TO CUT MY CHAINS!

HA HA! YOU'RE ONLY A WEAK LITTLE CAPTIVE NOW, AMAZON GIRL!

I'M NOT WEAK— I'M TOO STRONG. THE BRACELETS BOUND MY STRENGTH TO GOOD PURPOSES - NOW I'M COMPLETELY UNCONTROLLED! I'M FREE TO DESTROY LIKE A MAN!

SOB-SOB!

⑩

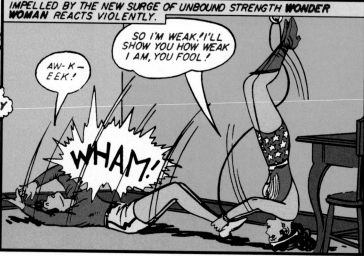

IMPELLED BY THE NEW SURGE OF UNBOUND STRENGTH WONDER WOMAN REACTS VIOLENTLY.

SO I'M WEAK! I'LL SHOW YOU HOW WEAK I AM, YOU FOOL!

AW- K - EEK!

WHAM!

Panel 1: THE AMAZON PRINCESS STRANGLES MAVIS INTO SUBMISSION.

UNTIE THAT LASSO OR I'LL KILL YOU! KILL! KILL! KILL!

AWK— I —TAKE IT EASY--I'LL--S-SET YOU FREE!

Panel 2: FREED FROM THE LASSO AND WITHOUT BRACELETS OF SUBMISSION, THE UNBOUND AMAZON GIRL GOES BERSERK.

DESTROY! KILL!

CRASH!

Panel 3: WRENCHING A LOG FROM THE BATTERED CABIN WONDER WOMAN STARTS TO CLEAN UP THE CAMP.

HA! HA! I'LL SHOW THESE RATS WHAT DESTRUCTION IS! HA! HA! HA! RUN, YOU FOOLS! RUN! I'LL CATCH YOU ANYWAY! HA! HA! HA!

ACH-HIMMEL!

HELP!

IT'S THOR HIMSELF!

RUN FOR YOUR LIFE!

Panel 4: WONDER WOMAN, IN AN ORGY OF UNLEASHED POWER, SMASHES CABINS INTO KINDLING WOOD.

THAT FOR YOU, WEASEL NEST! I'LL TEACH THESE HOUNDS OF HADES WHAT IT COSTS TO INSULT AN AMAZON!

SMASH!

Panel 5: STEVE, ARRIVING AT THIS MOMENT, MANAGES TO ATTRACT WONDER WOMAN'S ATTENTION.

WONDER WOMAN! HAVE YOU GONE CRAZY? A KIDNAPPER IS CARRYING THE PINKY GIRL DOWN RIVER ON A LOG - COME ON!

I'LL BROWN HIS HASH!

Panel 6: WONDER WOMAN'S GONE WILD!

I FOUND THESE! SOMEBODY BOUND HER WITH THE MAGIC LASSO AND REMOVED HER BRACELETS -HER AMAZON POWER IS OUT OF CONTROL-I MUST CAPTURE HER-YOU AND ETTA MOP UP HERE!

Panel 7: AS WONDER WOMAN RACES DOWN THE RIVER BANK, BOBBY RUNS TO MEET HER.

THERE'S A LOG JAM DOWN RIVER - DEXTER AND MISS ANNE WILL BE KILLED WHEN THEY HIT IT! SAVE MY TEACHER, WONDER WOMAN!

HA!

11

LEAPING WITH UNFAILING AGILITY FROM LOG TO LOG, **WONDER WOMAN** RUNS DOWN THE RIVER AS THOUGH IT WERE A STREET.

SHE OVERTAKES AND PASSES ANNE PINKY AND DEXTER WITH NO SIGN OF RECOGNITION.

WONDER WOMAN-SAVE ME FROM THIS MAN!

DON'T BE LIKE THAT, ANNE!

A HUNDRED YARDS AHEAD THE LOG JAM IS A SIGHT OF MAGNIFICENT MENACE.

GRI-IND!

CRASH!

WITHOUT A SECOND'S HESITATION **WONDER WOMAN** LEAPS INTO THE VERY HEART OF THE JAM.

CRASH!

BANG!

CRACK!

TEARING HER WAY THROUGH TANGLED MASSES OF TIMBER **WONDER WOMAN** SELECTS THE KEY LOG AND DRAGS IT LOOSE.

THIS STICK IS HOLDING ALL THE REST-WHEN I PULL IT OUT— YEOWEE! ALL THESE LOGS WILL COME CRASHING DOWN! HA! HA!

SNAP!

GRI-I-ND!

12.

THE JAM BREAKS, COVERING THE RIVER WITH A SOLID FLOOR OF LOGS.

FIGHTING THOSE LOGS WAS FUN-OH--THERE'S THAT KIDNAPPER! I'LL GET HIM!

AS DEXTER REACHES SHORE, IRRESISTIBLE HANDS CLOSE AROUND HIS THROAT IN A DEADLY GRIP.

YOU'RE A FIFTH COLUMNIST-YOU KIDNAPPED THIS GIRL-CONFESS!

UGL-GULP-NO! I - ULG—

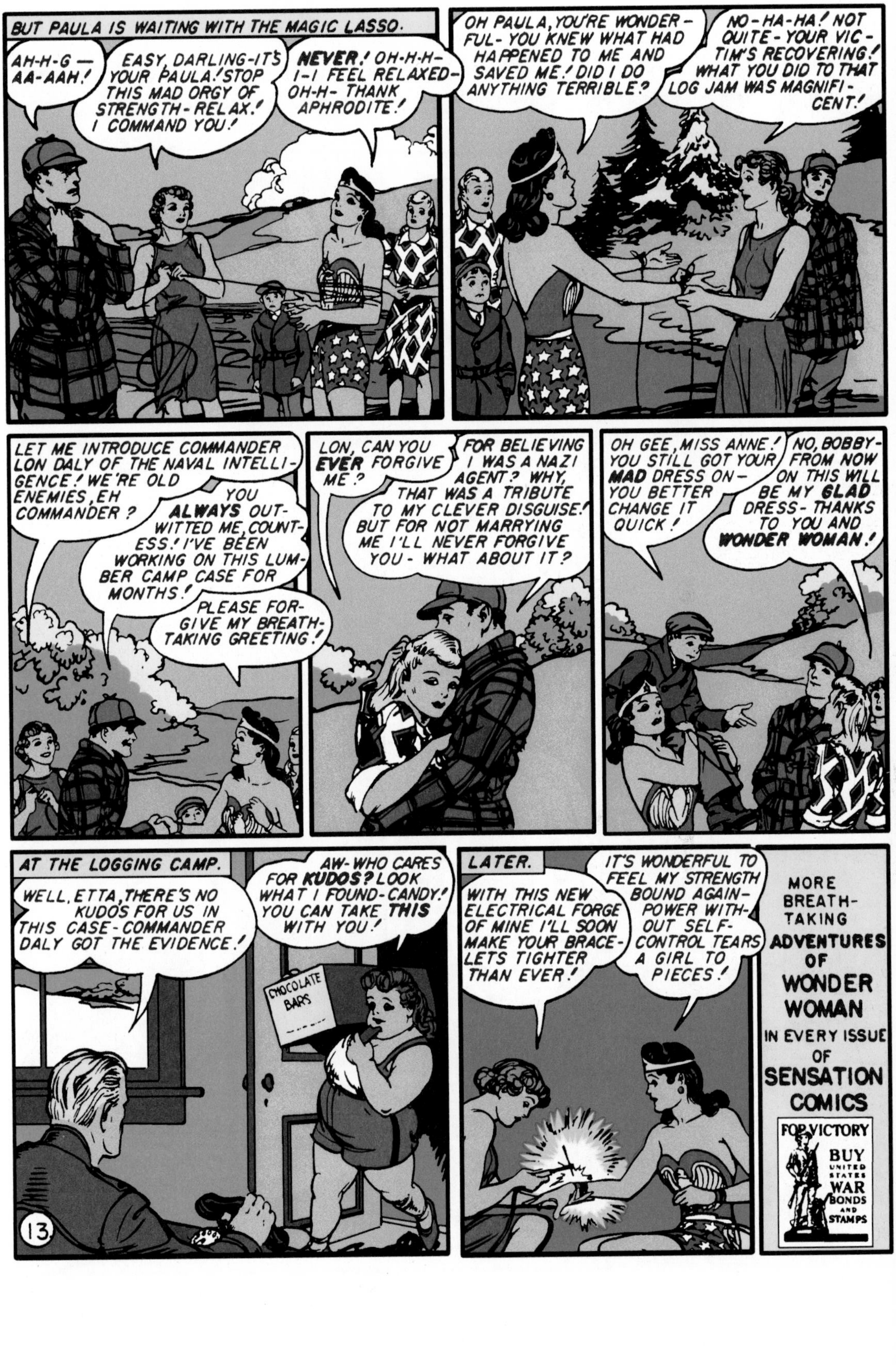
BUT PAULA IS WAITING WITH THE MAGIC LASSO.
AH-H-G — AA-AAH!
EASY, DARLING-IT'S YOUR PAULA! STOP THIS MAD ORGY OF STRENGTH-RELAX! I COMMAND YOU!
NEVER! OH-H-H- I-I FEEL RELAXED- OH-H- THANK APHRODITE!
OH PAULA, YOU'RE WONDER-FUL- YOU KNEW WHAT HAD HAPPENED TO ME AND SAVED ME! DID I DO ANYTHING TERRIBLE?
NO-HA-HA! NOT QUITE-YOUR VIC-TIM'S RECOVERING! WHAT YOU DID TO THAT LOG JAM WAS MAGNIFI-CENT!
LET ME INTRODUCE COMMANDER LON DALY OF THE NAVAL INTELLI-GENCE! WE'RE OLD ENEMIES, EH COMMANDER?
YOU ALWAYS OUT-WITTED ME, COUNT-ESS! I'VE BEEN WORKING ON THIS LUM-BER CAMP CASE FOR MONTHS!
PLEASE FOR-GIVE MY BREATH-TAKING GREETING!
LON, CAN YOU EVER FORGIVE ME?
FOR BELIEVING I WAS A NAZI AGENT? WHY, THAT WAS A TRIBUTE TO MY CLEVER DISGUISE! BUT FOR NOT MARRYING ME I'LL NEVER FORGIVE YOU- WHAT ABOUT IT?
OH GEE, MISS ANNE! YOU STILL GOT YOUR MAD DRESS ON- YOU BETTER CHANGE IT QUICK!
NO, BOBBY- FROM NOW ON THIS WILL BE MY GLAD DRESS- THANKS TO YOU AND WONDER WOMAN!
AT THE LOGGING CAMP.
WELL, ETTA, THERE'S NO KUDOS FOR US IN THIS CASE-COMMANDER DALY GOT THE EVIDENCE!
AW-WHO CARES FOR KUDOS? LOOK WHAT I FOUND-CANDY! YOU CAN TAKE THIS WITH YOU!
CHOCOLATE BARS
13
LATER.
WITH THIS NEW ELECTRICAL FORGE OF MINE I'LL SOON MAKE YOUR BRACE-LETS TIGHTER THAN EVER!
IT'S WONDERFUL TO FEEL MY STRENGTH BOUND AGAIN- POWER WITH-OUT SELF-CONTROL TEARS A GIRL TO PIECES!
MORE BREATH-TAKING ADVENTURES OF WONDER WOMAN IN EVERY ISSUE OF SENSATION COMICS
FOR VICTORY BUY UNITED STATES WAR BONDS AND STAMPS

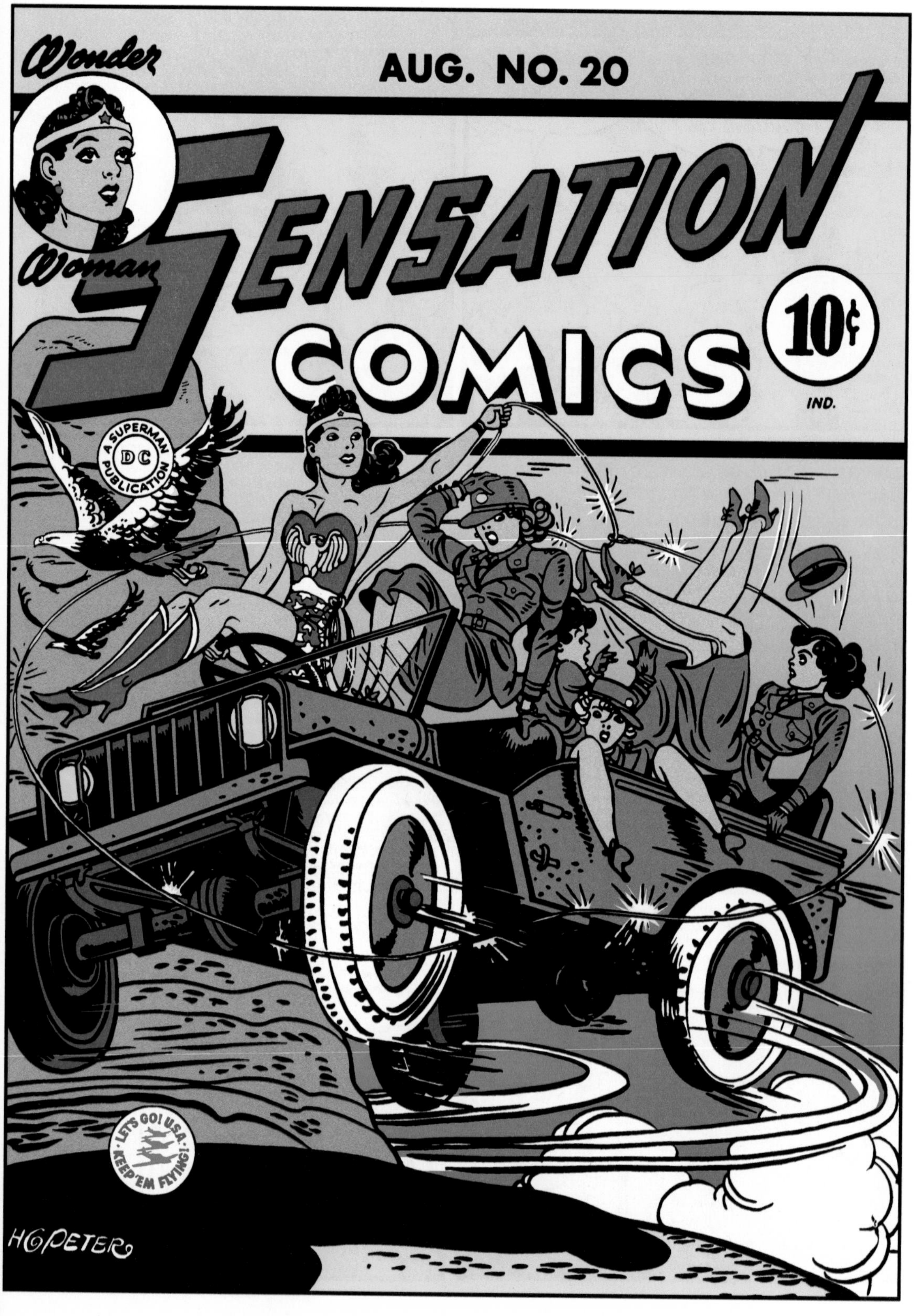
Wonder Woman
AUG. NO. 20
SENSATION COMICS
10¢
IND.
A SUPERMAN DC PUBLICATION
LET'S GO! U.S.A. KEEP 'EM FLYING!
HG PETER

Wonder Woman

REG U S PAT OFF

By Charles Moulton

IT SEEMED UNLIKELY THAT ANY BRAVE, LOYAL AMERICAN GIRL ENLISTED IN THE WAACS WOULD SHOOT A GENERAL! YET THE GENERAL WAS SHOT BEFORE DIANA'S VERY EYES! NONE BUT A WAAC **COULD** HAVE FIRED THAT MYSTERIOUS BULLET! IT'S UP TO **WONDER WOMAN** TO SOLVE A MYSTERY THAT SHAKES THE MORALE OF THE ENTIRE ARMY AND BIDS FAIR TO BANISH AMERICAN WOMEN FROM THEIR NEW-FOUND PLACE OF DARING AND DANGER.

CAN **WONDER WOMAN** UNRAVEL THE THREADS OF WEIRD INTRIGUE WHICH, LIKE A POISONOUS SPIDER'S WEB, ENTANGLE **THE GIRL WITH THE GUN?** TO DO SO OUR LOVELY AMAZON MAIDEN MUST JOIN THE WAACS. YOU'LL SEE HER SHARING THEIR DISCIPLINE AND THEIR PUNISHMENT DUTY, HAVING FUN WITH A WOMAN-HATING GENERAL AND PLAYING DANGEROUS GAMES WITH A DEADLY, DETERMINED KILLER WHOSE IDENTITY, WHEN REVEALED, IS ALMOST UNBELIEVABLE!

STEVE IS SUMMONED BY GENERAL STANDPAT, CHIEF OF STAFF.

HOW ARE YOU, MAJOR TREVOR? I'M GOING TO INSPECT TRAINING CAMPS - YOU WILL ACCOMPANY ME.

YES, SIR!

H.G. PETER

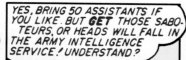

THERE'S SABOTAGE GOING ON—MUNITIONS, CAMP EQUIPMENT. IT'S SERIOUS—YOU'VE GOT TO STOP IT.' WORST IS AT CAMP DOE WHERE THEY'RE TRAINING THOSE WAACS—**WOMAN SOLDIERS**—BAH.'

MAY I BRING MY ASSISTANT, SIR, LIEUTENANT PRINCE.?

YES, BRING 50 ASSISTANTS IF YOU LIKE. BUT **GET** THOSE SABOTEURS, OR HEADS WILL FALL IN THE ARMY INTELLIGENCE SERVICE.' UNDERSTAND.?

YOU COULDN'T BE PLAINER, GENERAL.'

GOT A JOB FOR YOU, DI—INSPECTING WAACS AT CAMP DOE WITH GENERAL STANDPAT. HE SUSPECTS SOMEBODY OF SABOTAGING WAR SUPPLIES.'

YOU MEAN THE AMMUNITION DUMP THAT BLEW UP NEAR THE WAAC CAMP.? I HOPE HE DOESN'T THINK ANY OF THE WAACS HAD ANYTHING TO DO WITH THAT.'

STEVE AND DIANA JOIN THE GENERAL'S PARTY.

WE'RE REPORTING, SIR, FOR INSPECTION TOUR. MAY I PRESENT MY ASSISTANT, LT. DIANA PRINCE.

"LIEUTENANT" PRINCE—YOU DECEIVED ME, MAJOR! I CERTAINLY DIDN'T THINK YOU WERE BRINGING A **WOMAN LIEUTENANT**!

SORRY, GENERAL, BUT MISS PRINCE HAPPENS TO BE AN EXPERT AT DETECTING SABOTAGE, AND—

ALL RIGHT! BRING YOUR PETTICOAT STAFF—BUT NOT IN **MY** CAR! YOU AND **LIEUTENANT** PRINCE WILL RIDE WITH MY LUGGAGE IN THE CAR BEHIND!

I'M SORRY, DI—I DIDN'T KNOW THE OLD BOY WAS SO SORE AT WOMEN IN THE ARMY—

I DON'T MIND! I'D **MUCH** RATHER RIDE WITH SUITCASES THAN LISTEN TO OLD STANDPAT'S SPOUTING!

THE WAACS STAND IN COMPANY FORMATION TO GREET GENERAL STANDPAT'S INSPECTION CAVALCADE.

2

THE GENERAL WAITS IMPATIENTLY FOR THE CAMP COMMANDER TO APPEAR.

WHY ISN'T THE CAMP COMMANDER HERE?

GENERAL SCOTT'S IN HIS OFFICE RIGHT UP THERE, SIR—WASHINGTON CALLED HIM ON THE PHONE—HE'LL BE HERE IMMEDIATELY!

SUDDENLY A SHOT RINGS OUT.

UGH! I'M SHOT---A WOMAN— SHOT ME!

BA-ANG!

AT THE SAME MOMENT IN THE RIGID RANKS OF THE WAACS, A STEALTHY HAND PICKS UP A .22 AUTOMATIC WHICH HAD DROPPED NEAR A GIRL'S FEET.

DIANA, FORGETTING HER FEMININE ROLE, LEAPS TO THE GENERAL'S AID SO SWIFTLY THAT SHE CATCHES HIM AS HE FALLS.

EASY, GENERAL—GREAT APHRODITE! HE'S BADLY HIT NEAR THE HEART!

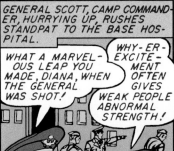

GENERAL SCOTT, CAMP COMMANDER, HURRYING UP, RUSHES STANDPAT TO THE BASE HOSPITAL.

WHAT A MARVELOUS LEAP YOU MADE, DIANA, WHEN THE GENERAL WAS SHOT!

WHY—ER—EXCITEMENT OFTEN GIVES WEAK PEOPLE ABNORMAL STRENGTH!

THE CAMP COMMANDER CONSULTS STEVE.

LUCKY YOU'RE HERE, MAJOR—YOU MUST CONDUCT AN INVESTIGATION! DID THE GENERAL SAY ANYTHING AFTER BEING SHOT?

YES, SIR— HE SAID "A WOMAN SHOT ME!"

A WOMAN, EH? MUST BE SOME HYSTERICAL WAAC IN TRAINING COMPANY A—BULLET CAME FROM THEIR DIRECTION. I'LL PLACE THE ENTIRE COMPANY UNDER ARREST!

OH NO! GENERAL STANDPAT'S WORDS MEAN NOTHING—HE ALWAYS SUSPECTS WOMEN— SORRY! I'M SPEAKING OUT OF TURN.

③

COMPANY A GOES TO THE GUARDHOUSE.

IF A GIRL FIRED THAT SHOT WHAT'D SHE DO WITH HER GUN?

THAT'S FOR YOU TO FIND OUT—SEARCH EVERY WAAC, THEN GIVE 'EM A LIE DETECTOR TEST!

LINE UP FACING THE WALL— HANDS ABOVE YOUR HEADS!

DIANA MOVES DOWN THE LINE SEARCHING EVERY GIRL.

NOBODY COULD CONCEAL A GUN UNDER THOSE UNIFORMS!

BUT DIANA IS MISTAKEN.

WELL, I'LL BE A KANGA'S UNCLE! THIS IS—

—A .22 AUTOMATIC

ZEUS STRIKE ME IF IT ISN'T MARVA PSYCHO!

YOU ARE MISTAKEN, MISS PRINCE— I AM JANE GRAY. I—I CARRY THAT GUN TO PROTECT MYSELF!

THE GENERAL WAS SHOT WITH A .22 BULLET AND THIS AUTOMATIC HAS BEEN FIRED RECENTLY!

I FIRED IT THIS MORNING IN— IN—IN TARGET PRACTICE!

AFTER GIVING "JANE" A LIE DETECTOR TEST, DIANA STUDIES HER BLOOD PRESSURE RECORD CAREFULLY.

YOU LIED ABOUT YOUR NAME AND ABOUT SHOOTING YOUR GUN IN TARGET PRACTICE!

THAT'S MY STORY AND I'LL STICK TO IT!

4

DIANA DECIDES TO USE THE MAGIC LASSO.

HOLD OUT YOUR HANDS!

W-WHAT ARE YOU GOING TO DO TO ME?

I SHALL **MAKE** YOU TELL THE TRUTH—WHILE BOUND WITH THIS GOLDEN ROPE YOU **MUST** OBEY ME!

OH NO—NO! YOU **CAN'T** DO THIS TO ME!

TELL ME YOUR REAL NAME!

I—OH, SOMETHING **COMPELS** ME! I AM MARVA PSYCHO—MY MAIDEN NAME WAS MARVA JANE GRAY.

TELL ME THE TRUTH—**DID** YOU FIRE YOUR AUTOMATIC AT—GOOD HERA! THE GIRL'S FAINTED!

WHILE DIANA TRIES TO REVIVE MARVA, STEVE ENTERS THE ROOM WITHOUT WARNING.

THAT'S **WONDER WOMAN'S** MAGIC LASSO!

WHY—YES—SHE LENT IT TO ME!

WONDER WOMAN CAME TO INVESTIGATE THE SHOOTING—SHE WAS HERE JUST A MOMENT AGO!

AND SHE'S **STILL** HERE! YOU CAN'T FOOL ME ANY LONGER, DIANA—INCREDIBLE AS IT SEEMS, **YOU** MUST BE **WONDER WOMAN!**

YOU'VE MADE A FOOL OF ME LONG ENOUGH—TAKE THOSE HORNSWOGGLING GLASSES OFF!

NO! STEVE—**PLEASE** DON'T—

DIANA'S SKILL AS A VENTRILOQUIST GAINS HER A MOMENT'S RESPITE.

LET DIANA ALONE, STEVE, I AM *HERE* IF YOU WANT TO SEE ME!

HUH? *WONDER WOMAN'S VOICE!*

AS STEVE STRIDES TOWARD THE DOOR—

DIANA LEAPS LIGHTLY THROUGH A WINDOW.

FASTER THAN THE EYE CAN FOLLOW, DIANA SPEEDS TO THE NEXT WINDOW AND JUMPS IN—

THIS WILL HAVE TO BE THE FASTEST TIME I *EVER* MADE!

AS STEVE WALKS DOWN THE HALL TO THE NEXT ROOM, **WONDER WOMAN** LOOKS OUT THE DOOR.

STOP RIGHT WHERE YOU ARE, STEVE TREVOR, AND TELL ME WHAT YOU DID TO DIANA PRINCE!

WHY—ER—AH—I ONLY—

WHILE SHE HOLDS STEVE'S ATTENTION WITH CONVERSATION **WONDER WOMAN** COMPLETES HER COSTUME.

I THOUGHT *YOU* WERE DIANA—THAT IS I THOUGHT DIANA WAS YOU-AH-ER—

WELL, YOU CAN SEE FOR YOURSELF THAT I AM I!

6

WONDER WOMAN HASTILY HIDES DIANA'S CLOTHES.

DIANA HAD YOUR MAGIC LASSO! SHE TOOK A BIG JUMP WHEN THE GENERAL WAS SHOT—

DON'T BE SO SUSPICIOUS! LOTS OF GIRLS JUMP HIGH WHEN THEY'RE EXCITED AND I *LENT* DI MY LASSO!

I'VE GOT TO SEND STEVE AWAY BEFORE HE STARTS LOOKING FOR DIANA.

STEVE, YOU MUST VISIT DR. PSYCHO IN PRISON-- IMMEDIATELY!

PSYCHO! THE GUY WHO MATERIALIZED BODIES TO DISGUISE HIMSELF AND BLEW UP THE MUNITION WORKS?

YES, PSYCHO MAY BE BEHIND THIS SHOOTING, EVEN THOUGH HE'S IN JAIL. THAT WAAC DIANA'S EXAMINING IS PSYCHO'S WIFE-- SHE APPEARED TO FAINT BUT ACTUALLY SHE FELL IN A TRANCE!

WHAT? IS IT POSSIBLE PSYCHO COULD CONTROL HER MIND FROM A DISTANCE?

PSYCHO MIGHT PUT HER IN A TRANCE BY SENDING THOUGHT WAVES-- SHE WAS HIS MENTAL SLAVE FOR YEARS! FIND OUT IF PSYCHO PLANNED THIS CRIME!

I'LL TRY-- WISH ME LUCK!

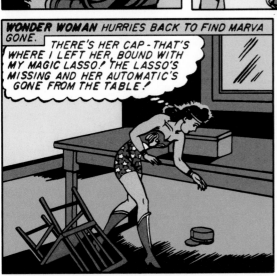

WONDER WOMAN HURRIES BACK TO FIND MARVA GONE.

THERE'S HER CAP-- THAT'S WHERE I LEFT HER, BOUND WITH MY MAGIC LASSO! THE LASSO'S MISSING AND HER AUTOMATIC'S GONE FROM THE TABLE!

AT THIS VERY MOMENT, AN INGENIOUS TRAP IS BEING PREPARED.

HELP, WONDER WOMAN, HELP!

WONDER WOMAN RUSHES TO THE WINDOW AND---

HA! I'VE GOT YOU! NOW YOU MUST OBEY ME, WONDER WOMAN-- I KNOW HOW IT FEELS TO BE BOUND WITH THIS ROPE!

YES-- I'M COMPELLED TO OBEY!

THE LASSO IS FASTENED HERE SECURELY-- CLIMB UP TO THIS WINDOW. DO NOT TRY TO ESCAPE!

I MUST OBEY YOU!

⑦

INSIDE THE ROOM, **WONDER WOMAN** IS COMPELLED TO CHANGE CLOTHES WITH MARVA.

I BROUGHT THIS BLACK WIG, AND YOUR COSTUME FITS ME PERFECTLY—HOW DO I LOOK?

VERY PRETTY! YOUR LOOKS HAVE IMPROVED TREMENDOUSLY SINCE YOU JOINED THE WAACS!

I CAN'T UNDERSTAND WHY YOU'RE BEHAVING LIKE THIS! NOW THAT YOUR HUSBAND IS IN JAIL YOU'RE NO LONGER UNDER HIS INFLU-ENCE! WHAT'S WRONG WITH YOU ANYWAY?

THERE'S NOTHING WRONG WITH ME! I KNOW WHAT I'M DO-ING BUT NOBODY WOULD UNDERSTAND ME IF I TOLD!

THERE CAN'T BE ANY REASON FOR YOU TO SHOOT A GENERAL!

THAT'S WHAT I'D LIKE TO EX-PLAIN TO THE AU-THORITIES—BUT I'M SURE THEY WON'T BELIEVE IT ONCE I'M ACCUSED! I'M NOT GOING TO HAVE THAT HAP-PEN!

MY WAAC COMPANY'S ON PUNISHMENT DUTY—YOU MUST TAKE MY PLACE AS "JANE GRAY" UNTIL I RELEASE YOU! NO ONE WILL NOTICE THE DIFFERENCE! **PROMISE!**

NO, NO! I **CAN'T**—OH! THE LASSO COM-PELS ME—I PROMISE!

WONDER WOMAN JOINS THE WAACS.

AUXILIARY JANE GRAY REPORTING FOR PUNISH-MENT DUTY WITH COMPANY A—

THAT AIN'T THE WAY FOR A MILITARY PRISONER TO SALUTE—FOLD YER ARMS—THEN START DIGGIN'!

GENERAL SCOTT HIMSELF ORDERED THIS PUNISHMENT—WHATTA GUY! WE GOTTA FINISH THIS DITCH—A MILE OF IT—WITHOUT RESTING! IT'LL TAKE ALL NIGHT!

NONSENSE—THIS IS EASY—FOLLOW ME!

8

COME ON, GIRLS! ONLY A FEW MORE YARDS TO GO!

PHEW! PUFF—WHOO! WE'LL SHOW THOSE **MEN!**

LED BY **WONDER WOMAN**, THE GIRLS COMPLETE A 20-HOUR JOB IN 15 MINUTES.

WELL, SERGEANT, WHAT NEXT?

BY GOLLY, I DON'T KNOW! NOBODY EVER DUG **THAT** FAST BEFORE! YOU CAN MARCH TO QUARTERS AND REST!

AT THAT MOMENT, ORDERS ARRIVE.

ORDERS FROM GENERAL SCOTT— AUXILIARY JANE GRAY WILL REPORT IMMEDIATELY TO CAMP HEADQUARTERS.

GET IN THERE, GRAY—MAKE IT SNAPPY!

BOY, IS THE GENERAL SORE! SOME DAME TRIED TO KILL HIM BUT HE CAUGHT HER!

I WONDER IF THEY CAUGHT MARVA IN MY COSTUME—OR IF THIS SOLDIER MEANS **ME!**

THIS IS JANE GRAY, SIR!

JANE GRAY! HA, HA! YOU'RE REALLY **WONDER WOMAN**, AREN'T YOU? AREN'T THOSE YOUR CLOTHES?

WHY— ER-YES, NO—

I DON'T KNOW WHAT TO SAY! I MUST KEEP MY PROMISE UNTIL RELEASED.

GO INTO THE NEXT ROOM AND PUT THOSE CLOTHES ON! WHEN WE GET YOU TWO MURDERESSES INTO THE RIGHT CLOTHES WE CAN IDENTIFY YOU BOTH BEYOND QUESTION!

SO I'M A MURDERESS NOW—OKAY, GENERAL— WHATEVER YOU SAY!

PROPERLY DRESSED, THE GIRLS ARE BROUGHT BACK BY A FIRST OFFICER OF WAACS. BECAUSE IT WAS HANDY, THE MAGIC LASSO IS USED TO BIND MARVA --

TELL THE TRUTH, GRAY— DIDN'T YOU CONSPIRE WITH **WONDER WOMAN** TO KILL GENERAL STANDPAT?

I NEVER KILLED ANYONE NOR **TRIED** TO KILL ANYONE!

GENERAL SCOTT

⑨

TIE THESE PRISONERS TOGETHER AND LEAVE THE ROOM! I'VE GOT TO BREAK DOWN THIS WAAC GIRL'S LIES!

YES, SIR!

BUT MARVA COULDN'T LIE—SHE WAS BOUND WITH THE MAGIC LASSO. THAT MEANS SHE'S **INNOCENT!**

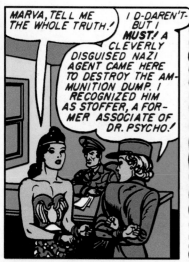

MARVA, TELL ME THE WHOLE TRUTH!

I D-DAREN'T- BUT I **MUST**! A CLEVERLY DISGUISED NAZI AGENT CAME HERE TO DESTROY THE AMMUNITION DUMP. I RECOGNIZED HIM AS STOFFER, A FORMER ASSOCIATE OF DR. PSYCHO!

COMPELLED BY THE MAGIC LASSO MARVA CONTINUES HER STORY: "THEY WERE DRILLING US WAACS WHEN—"

EYES FRONT— DRESS YOUR RANKS—

STOFFER WAS IN THAT CAR IN OFFICER'S UNIFORM! BUT HE **COULDN'T** BE— I MUST BE CRAZY—

"I WAS GIVEN EXTRA K.P. DUTY FOR INATTENTION AT DRILL— THAT MEANS GETTING UP AT 3 AM. TO WALK A MILE AND PREPARE BREAKFAST—"

JUS' GOT T' BED- CAN'T WAKE UP- FOOL I WAS!

"CROSSING THE DARK DESERTED CAMP GROUNDS, I FELT A HAND SUDDENLY GRIP MY COAT."

YI-EEE!

SHUT UP, YOU FOOL!

"HANDS PINNED ME FIRMLY AGAINST THE WALL— IT WAS **STOFFER**!"

SO IT **WAS** YOU IN THAT CAR!

YES— I SAW YOU RECOGNIZED ME. BUT IF YOU'RE WISE YOU'LL KEEP YOUR MOUTH SHUT!

IF YOU DENOUNCE ME NOBODY WILL BELIEVE YOU. I'LL ARREST **YOU**- REVEAL YOUR PAST! I'LL ACCUSE YOU OF HELPING YOUR HUSBAND PSYCHO COMMIT MURDERS —YOU'LL GO TO PRISON!

YOU- YOU BEAST! I-I'LL THINK IT OVER—

"I PLANNED TO TELEPHONE MAJOR TREVOR- BUT THAT DAY THE AMMUNITION DUMP BLEW UP- IT WAS TOO LATE!"

STOFFER DID THIS — I'M **SURE** OF IT! BUT I HAVE NO **PROOF**!

10

"I BOUGHT A .22 AUTOMATIC— IT WAS AGAINST WAAC REGULATIONS BUT I HAD A WILD PLAN—"

WE'RE NOT ALLOWED TO SELL—

IT'S ALL RIGHT— I'M BUYING THIS FOR AN OFFICER!

"THAT EVENING I SNEAKED OUT OF STUDY HALL AND WENT OVER TO THE MEN'S CAMP—"

STOFFER SHOULD PASS HERE ON HIS WAY TO OFFICERS' QUARTERS.

"SURE ENOUGH, ALONG HE CAME AND I FELL IN BEHIND HIM."

I'VE GOT YOU COVERED— WALK QUIETLY BEHIND THAT GARAGE OR I'LL SHOOT!

"ON REACHING A SECLUDED SPOT I—"

YOU BLEW UP THE AMMUNITION DUMP STOFFER- I GIVE YOU ONE MINUTE TO START WRITING YOUR CONFESSION BEFORE I SHOOT.

BUT DON'T BE RIDICULOUS! YOU CAN'T—

SUDDENLY HE GRABBED MY GUN— I PULLED THE TRIGGER BUT NOTHING HAPPENED!

HA HA! YOU DIDN'T EVEN KNOW ENOUGH TO RELEASE THE SAFETY CATCH ON YOUR AUTOMATIC!

YOU'VE COMMITTED A SERIOUS CRIME- ASSAULT ON AN OFFICER WITH INTENT TO MURDER! BUT I WON'T PREFER CHARGES IF YOU KEEP QUIET! MEANWHILE, I MAY FIND USE FOR YOUR TOY PISTOL—

SOB! SOB!

11

"HE FOUND USE FOR IT ALL RIGHT! STOFFER SHOT GENERAL STANDPAT WITH MY PISTOL FROM THIS OFFICE WINDOW!"

THIS FRAMES ME BEAUTIFULLY FOR SHOOTING THE GENERAL... MY ONLY HOPE IS TO FORCE THE REAL CRIMINAL TO REVEAL HIMSELF.

I TOOK YOUR MAGIC LASSO, **WONDER WOMAN**, TO MAKE STOFFER CONFESS! BUT HE OVERPOWERED ME. THERE HE SITS COMPLACENTLY CALLING HIMSELF "GENERAL SCOTT!"

THAT'S A LIE!

EASY, "GENERAL!"

WHY SHOULD I KILL GENERAL STANDPAT?

BECAUSE HE KNOWS THE **REAL** GENERAL SCOTT TOO WELL—YOU KIDNAPPED SCOTT ON HIS WAY TO TAKE COMMAND OF THIS CAMP AND **YOU** TOOK HIS PLACE!

YOU GIRLS TALK TOO MUCH— I'LL GIVE YOUR TONGUES A REST!

UNF!

E-E-EEK!

I'D BETTER PLAY UNCON-SCIOUS!

GIRLS FAINTED—PUT 'EM IN A PRISON AMBULANCE. I'LL DRIVE IT MYSELF TO WAAC HEADQUARTERS!

YES, GENERAL!

STOFFER DRIVES RAPIDLY FROM CAMP TO A NAZI HIDEOUT

QUICKLY, THROW THE REAL GENERAL SCOTT IN THE AMBULANCE— I'VE GOT TO GET RID OF HIM!

YAH-VE HAF DER BOMB READY!

AS GENERAL SCOTT LANDS BESIDE HER, **WON-DER WOMAN** COMES TO LIFE.

I HAD TO WAIT UNTIL THE GENERAL WAS OUT OF THEIR HANDS BEFORE I STARTED ANYTHING— NOW FOR SOME FUN!

WONDER WOMAN *EASILY BURSTS THROUGH THE LOCKED DOORS OF THE VEHICLE.*

FASTENED BENEATH THE BODY OF THE CAR, WONDER WOMAN *SEES SOMETHING THAT MAKES HER BLOOD RUN COLD.*

WHAT'S THAT NOISE— A BOMB! THERE ISN'T TIME TO BREAK IT LOOSE—GREAT MINERVA!

SPUT- T-T-TUT

WITH ONE SWIFT MOTION WONDER WOMAN *DRAGS THE HELPLESS PRISONERS FROM THE AMBULANCE.*

SPLIT SECONDS COUNT NOW!

SEIZING THE AMBULANCE WONDER WOMAN *HURLS IT A SAFE DISTANCE.*

WHEW! THAT'S GOOD EXERCISE!

AS FATE WOULD HAVE IT, STOFFER'S ESCAPING PLANE TAKES OFF AT THE SAME MOMENT AND—

CRA-AASH

BAA-ANG!

WELL, GENERAL— THAT STOFFER FELLOW DID A GOOD JOB OF IMPERSONATING YOU— HE ALMOST GOT AWAY WITH IT, TOO!

YES! BUT HE DIDN'T KNOW WONDER WOMAN COULD HIT A PLANE WITH AN AMBULANCE AT 300 YARDS!

⑬

GENERAL STANDPAT RECOVERS IN TIME TO PRESENT THE MEDALS.

FOR HEROIC ACTION I COMMEND THESE BRAVE SOLDIERS—AHEM— BRAVE WOMEN— HARRUMPH!

DON'T FORGET TO KISS US ON BOTH CHEEKS, GENERAL — IT'S A NEW ARMY REGULATION FOR WAACS!

WONDER WOMAN'S *ADVENTURES APPEAR EVERY MONTH IN* SENSATION COMICS

Buy WAR BONDS AND STAMPS FOR VICTORY

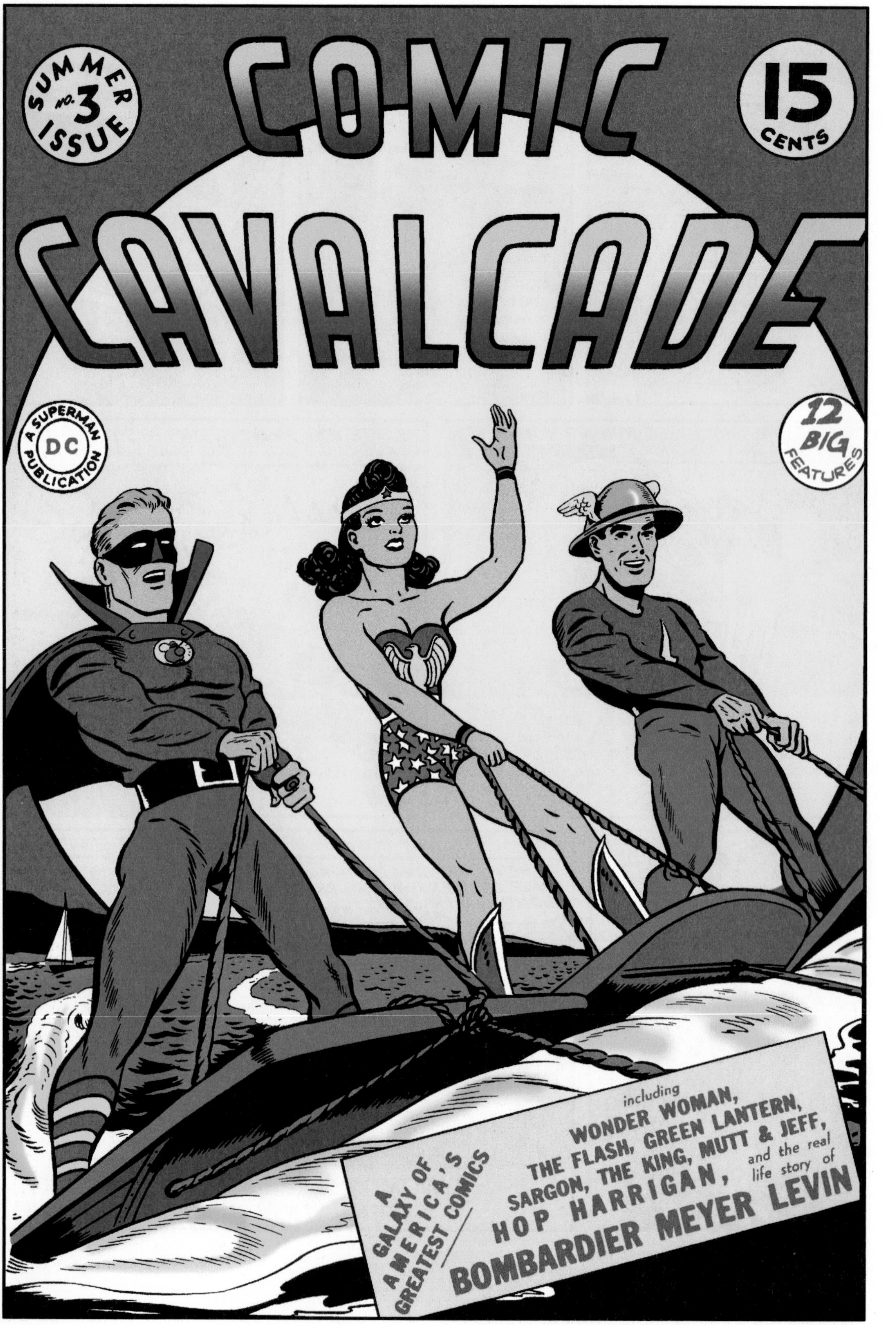

COMIC CAVALCADE
SUMMER NO. 3 ISSUE
15 CENTS
A SUPERMAN DC PUBLICATION
12 BIG FEATURES
A GALAXY OF AMERICA'S GREATEST COMICS
including
WONDER WOMAN,
THE FLASH, GREEN LANTERN,
SARGON, THE KING, MUTT & JEFF,
HOP HARRIGAN, and the real life story of
BOMBARDIER MEYER LEVIN

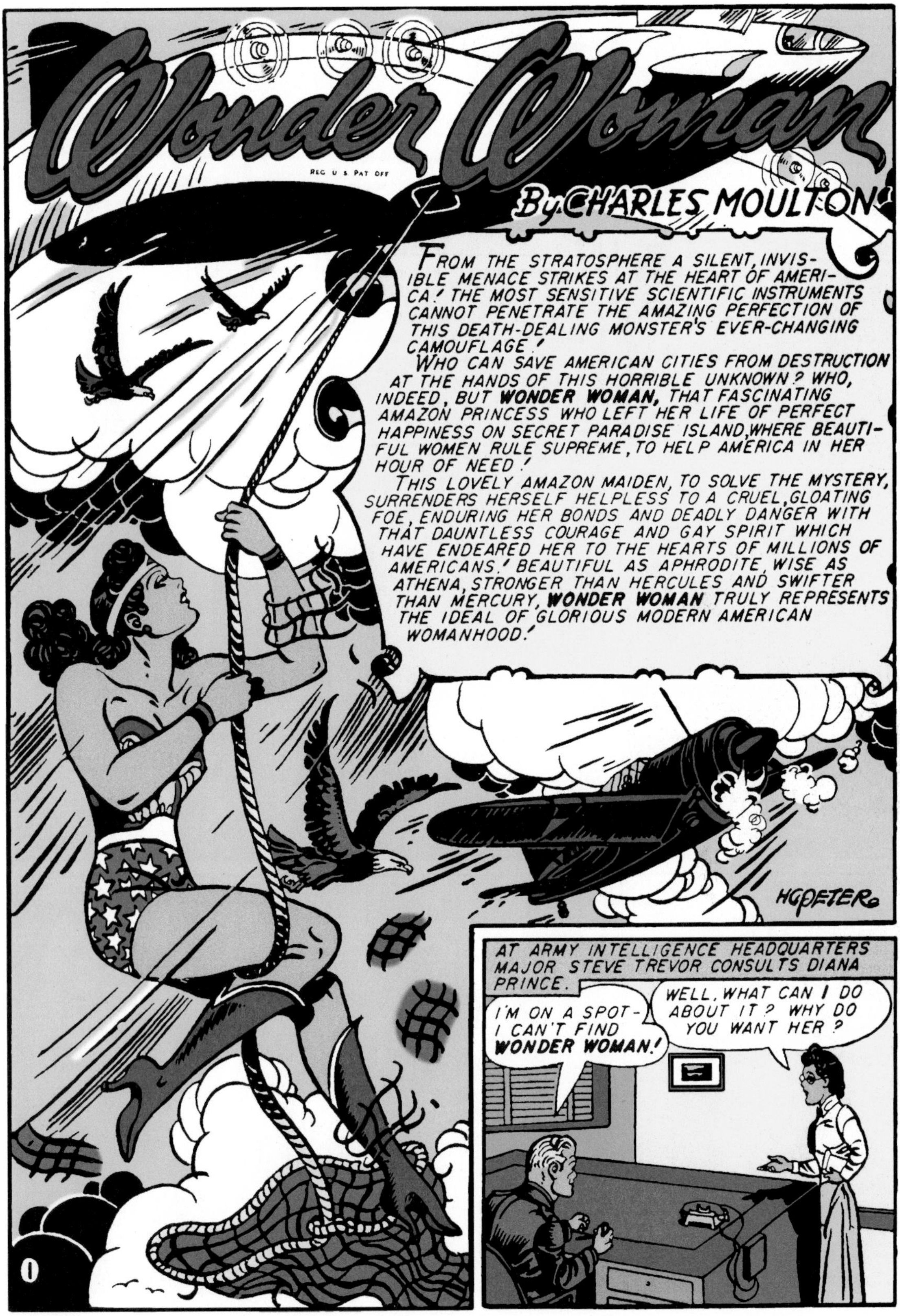
Wonder Woman
REG U S PAT OFF
By CHARLES MOULTON
FROM THE STRATOSPHERE A SILENT, INVISIBLE MENACE STRIKES AT THE HEART OF AMERICA! THE MOST SENSITIVE SCIENTIFIC INSTRUMENTS CANNOT PENETRATE THE AMAZING PERFECTION OF THIS DEATH-DEALING MONSTER'S EVER-CHANGING CAMOUFLAGE!
WHO CAN SAVE AMERICAN CITIES FROM DESTRUCTION AT THE HANDS OF THIS HORRIBLE UNKNOWN? WHO, INDEED, BUT WONDER WOMAN, THAT FASCINATING AMAZON PRINCESS WHO LEFT HER LIFE OF PERFECT HAPPINESS ON SECRET PARADISE ISLAND, WHERE BEAUTIFUL WOMEN RULE SUPREME, TO HELP AMERICA IN HER HOUR OF NEED!
THIS LOVELY AMAZON MAIDEN, TO SOLVE THE MYSTERY, SURRENDERS HERSELF HELPLESS TO A CRUEL, GLOATING FOE, ENDURING HER BONDS AND DEADLY DANGER WITH THAT DAUNTLESS COURAGE AND GAY SPIRIT WHICH HAVE ENDEARED HER TO THE HEARTS OF MILLIONS OF AMERICANS! BEAUTIFUL AS APHRODITE, WISE AS ATHENA, STRONGER THAN HERCULES AND SWIFTER THAN MERCURY, WONDER WOMAN TRULY REPRESENTS THE IDEAL OF GLORIOUS MODERN AMERICAN WOMANHOOD!
HGPETER
1
AT ARMY INTELLIGENCE HEADQUARTERS MAJOR STEVE TREVOR CONSULTS DIANA PRINCE.
I'M ON A SPOT - I CAN'T FIND WONDER WOMAN!
WELL, WHAT CAN I DO ABOUT IT? WHY DO YOU WANT HER?

WONDER WOMAN IS SCHEDULED TO SPEAK AT THE BIG CEREMONY THIS AFTERNOON. I'M SUPPOSED TO HAVE ARRANGED IT, BUT I HAVEN'T SEEN WONDER WOMAN! READ THIS—

GLOBAL WAR HEROES MONUMENT TO BE UNVEILED

ARMY AND NAVY CHIEFS TO SPEAK— ALSO WONDER WOMAN

At National City Military Park today the huge monument by Gotlot Broilgum will be unveiled in the presence of high government and military officials. The War Office announces that **WONDER WO-MAN** will pay tribute to our modern woman warriors, the WAACS, the WAVES, the SPARS, the Woman Marines and the

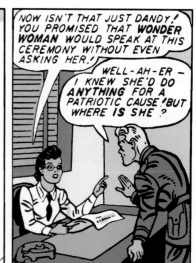

NOW ISN'T THAT JUST DANDY! YOU PROMISED THAT WONDER WOMAN WOULD SPEAK AT THIS CEREMONY WITHOUT EVEN ASKING HER!

WELL - AH - ER - I KNEW SHE'D DO ANYTHING FOR A PATRIOTIC CAUSE! BUT WHERE IS SHE ?

YOU DESERVE TO BE LEFT ON A HOT SPOT, STEVE TREVOR! BUT IF WONDER WOMAN SEES THAT NEWSPAPER, SHE'LL PROBABLY MAKE IT HER BUSINESS TO BE THERE. I'LL HELP YOU LOOK FOR HER IN THE CROWD!

ON THE SPEAKERS' PLATFORM IN NATIONAL PARK, STEVE, DIANA AND COLONEL DARNELL SURVEY THE VAST CROWD IN VAIN.

I KNOW WONDER WOMAN ISN'T HERE - IF SHE WERE, I'D HAVE SPOTTED HER EVEN IN THIS CROWD!

HA! HA! LOVE IS CERTAINLY BLIND!

SLIPPING AWAY TO A HIDDEN CORNER UNDER THE PLATFORM, DIANA TRANSFORMS HERSELF INTO WONDER WOMAN.

I'LL WAIT UNTIL THE CHAIRMAN INTRODUCES ME, THEN JUMP ON THE PLATFORM. WON'T STEVE BE RELIEVED!

②

WHILE BANDS PLAY AND CROWDS CHEER, THE GLOBAL WAR HEROES MONUMENT IS UNVEILED.

WHAT A HUGE MASS OF GRANITE - THAT MONUMENT OUGHT TO LAST THOUSANDS OF YEARS!

SUDDENLY COMES THE ROAR OF A TERRIFIC EXPLOSION— THE HUGE GLOBE OF SOLID STONE IS BLOWN TO FRAGMENTS!

BAR—ROOM!

WONDER WOMAN, LEAPING HIGH, CATCHES STEVE AND THE COLONEL AS THEY ARE HURLED FROM THE SPEAKERS' PLATFORM.

WONDER WOMAN! FANCY MEETING YOU HERE!

AS THE DEBRIS SETTLES AFTER THE EXPLOSION, AN ASTONISHING SIGHT APPEARS.

GREAT HEAVENS— LOOK! THE MONUMENT DIDN'T BLOW UP—IT'S NOT EVEN SCRATCHED!

BUT THAT'S IMPOSSIBLE— I SAW IT SMASH TO PIECES!

SUDDENLY A COLUMN OF BLACK SMOKE SEEMS TO DESCEND FROM THE SKY, HIDING THE MONUMENT FROM VIEW.

THE SMOKE DRIFTS UPWARD AND THEN—

THE GLOBE'S DISAPPEARED— IT DISSOLVED IN SMOKE! FOR THE LOVE OF MUD, WHAT GOES ON AROUND HERE?

THAT'S WHAT WE MUST FIND OUT!

3

THIS BOMB FRAGMENT TELLS THE STORY— IT'S GERMAN!

BUT IF IT WAS DROPPED BY A NAZI BOMBER WE'D HAVE SEEN THE PLANE!

VERY PUZZLING— THIS REQUIRES INVESTIGATION!

LATER, AT INTELLIGENCE HEADQUARTERS—

HERE'S BERLIN— LISTEN!

AMERICA VAS BOMBED TODAY BY A NEW TYPE NAZI PLANE! A DIRECT HIT VAS SCORED IN VASHINGTON ALL AMERICA IS TERRIFIED! A GREAT NAVAL BASE VILL SOON BE ATTACKED — — — — —

I'LL BET THIS STORY ABOUT A NEW BOMBING PLANE IS ALL EYEWASH! A SABOTEUR COULD HAVE PLANTED THAT BOMB AT THE MONUMENT!

YES - BUT HOW COULD THE MONUMENT APPEAR AGAIN **AFTER** IT WAS BLOWN UP? ---- AND THEN DISAPPEAR IN SMOKE?

IT **MAY BE** SABOTEUR'S WORK— WE MUST INVESTIGATE IMPORTANT NAVAL BASES IMMEDIATELY. I'LL COVER NEW YORK - STEVE, YOU TAKE BOSTON. DIANA MIGHT HANDLE NEW LONDON IF THERE WERE ANY WAY TO ACCOUNT FOR HER PRESENCE THERE!

THEIR CONFERENCE IS INTERRUPTED BY ETTA CANDY!

HAVE A KISS, COLONEL! I KNOW I GOT MY NERVE WALKIN' IN HERE BUT WHAT THE HECK---- RELAX AND HAVE A CANDY—

I'M ALWAYS GLAD TO SEE YOU ETTA - YOU AND YOUR GIRLS HAVE DONE GOOD WORK FOR US!

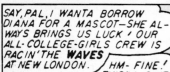
SAY, PAL, I WANTA BORROW DIANA FOR A MASCOT - SHE ALWAYS BRINGS US LUCK! OUR ALL-COLLEGE-GIRLS CREW IS RACIN' THE **WAVES** AT NEW LONDON.

HM - FINE! THIS'LL GIVE DIANA AN EXCUSE FOR APPEARING THERE!

AT NEW LONDON, DIANA MEETS THE ALL AMERICAN COLLEGE GIRLS CREW.

MATES, MEET OUR MASCOT, LT. DIANA PRINCE, THE FAMOUS G2 GIRL!

GLAD TO MEET YOU!

OUCH! REMEMBER I'M A WEAK GIRL AMONG YOU AMAZONS!

RACE TIME APPROACHES BUT BEE STRONG, POWERFUL HOLLIDAY STROKE, DOES NOT APPEAR.

IT'S 1:55 WHERE **IS** THAT GIRL?

RACE STARTS IN 5 MINUTES - WE'VE GOT TO GET OUR SHELL IN THE WATER!

WOO WOO!

ETTA HELPS WITH THE BOAT WHILE DIANA CARRIES THE INEVITABLE CANDY.

SOMETHING MUST HAVE HAPPENED TO STRONG - WE'D BETTER CALL HER SUBSTITUTE!

AW GEE, WITHOUT BEE STRONG AT STROKE WE'LL LOSE THE RACE!

④

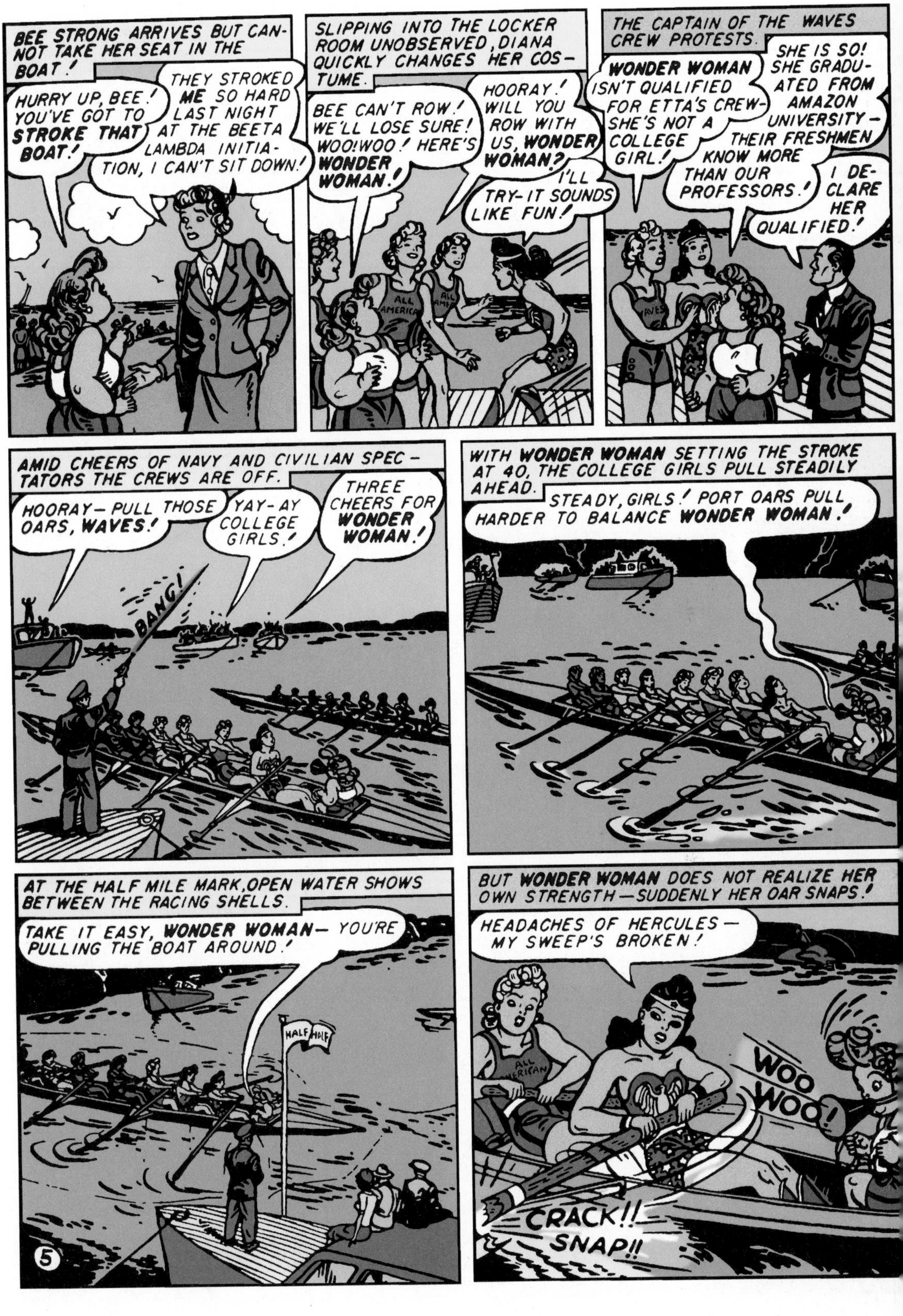
BEE STRONG ARRIVES BUT CANNOT TAKE HER SEAT IN THE BOAT!
HURRY UP, BEE! YOU'VE GOT TO STROKE THAT BOAT!
THEY STROKED ME SO HARD LAST NIGHT AT THE BEETA LAMBDA INITIATION, I CAN'T SIT DOWN!
SLIPPING INTO THE LOCKER ROOM UNOBSERVED, DIANA QUICKLY CHANGES HER COSTUME.
BEE CAN'T ROW! WE'LL LOSE SURE! WOO!WOO! HERE'S WONDER WOMAN!
HOORAY! WILL YOU ROW WITH US, WONDER WOMAN?
I'LL TRY-IT SOUNDS LIKE FUN!
THE CAPTAIN OF THE WAVES CREW PROTESTS.
WONDER WOMAN ISN'T QUALIFIED FOR ETTA'S CREW-SHE'S NOT A COLLEGE GIRL!
SHE IS SO! SHE GRADUATED FROM AMAZON UNIVERSITY-THEIR FRESHMEN KNOW MORE THAN OUR PROFESSORS!
I DECLARE HER QUALIFIED!
AMID CHEERS OF NAVY AND CIVILIAN SPECTATORS THE CREWS ARE OFF.
HOORAY-PULL THOSE OARS, WAVES!
YAY-AY COLLEGE GIRLS!
THREE CHEERS FOR WONDER WOMAN!
BANG!
WITH WONDER WOMAN SETTING THE STROKE AT 40, THE COLLEGE GIRLS PULL STEADILY AHEAD.
STEADY, GIRLS! PORT OARS PULL HARDER TO BALANCE WONDER WOMAN!
AT THE HALF MILE MARK, OPEN WATER SHOWS BETWEEN THE RACING SHELLS.
TAKE IT EASY, WONDER WOMAN- YOU'RE PULLING THE BOAT AROUND!
HALF
5
BUT WONDER WOMAN DOES NOT REALIZE HER OWN STRENGTH-SUDDENLY HER OAR SNAPS!
HEADACHES OF HERCULES-MY SWEEP'S BROKEN!
WOO WOO!
CRACK!! SNAP!!

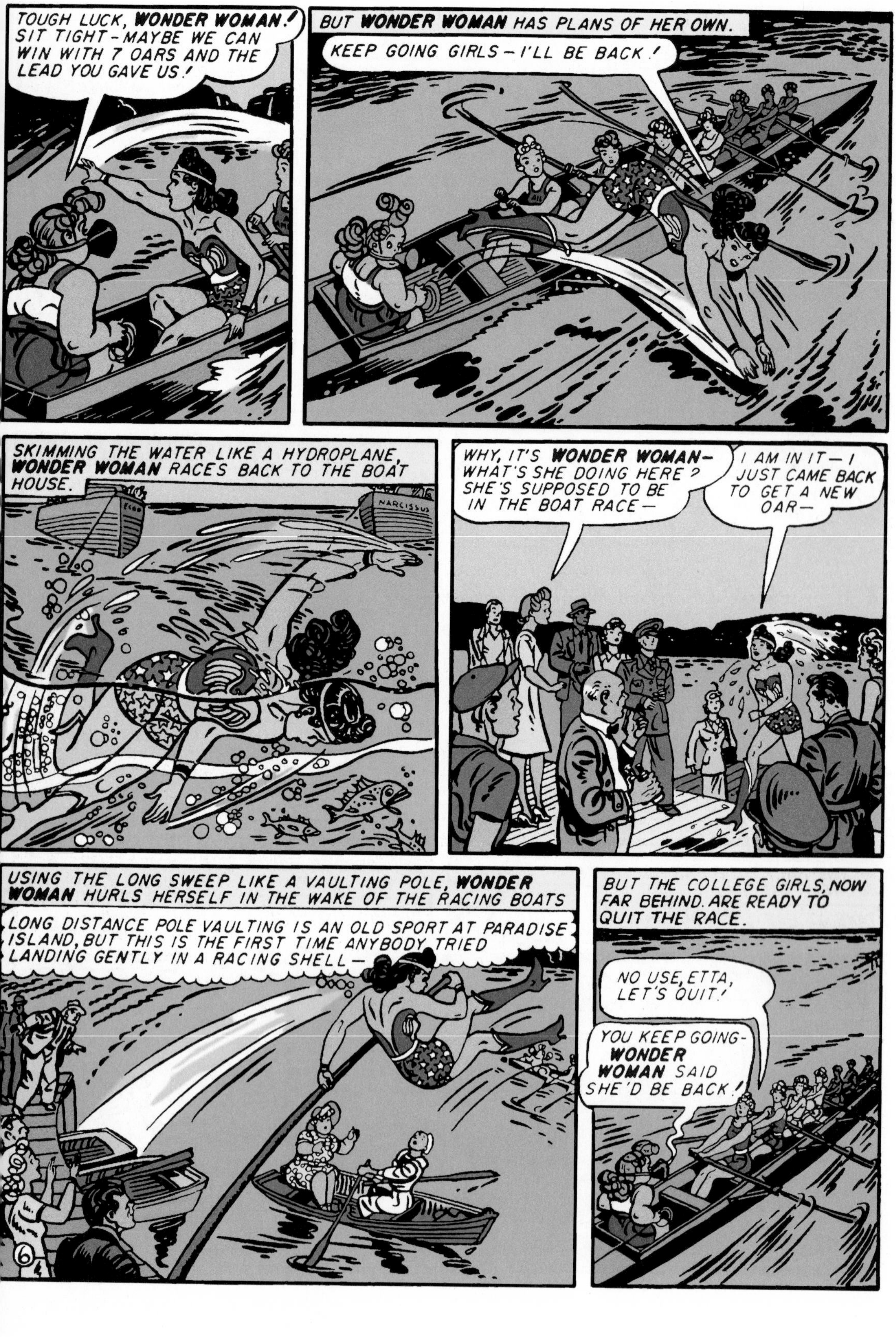
TOUGH LUCK, WONDER WOMAN! SIT TIGHT - MAYBE WE CAN WIN WITH 7 OARS AND THE LEAD YOU GAVE US!
BUT WONDER WOMAN HAS PLANS OF HER OWN.
KEEP GOING GIRLS - I'LL BE BACK!
SKIMMING THE WATER LIKE A HYDROPLANE, WONDER WOMAN RACES BACK TO THE BOAT HOUSE.
NARCISSUS
WHY, IT'S WONDER WOMAN - WHAT'S SHE DOING HERE? SHE'S SUPPOSED TO BE IN THE BOAT RACE -
I AM IN IT - I JUST CAME BACK TO GET A NEW OAR -
USING THE LONG SWEEP LIKE A VAULTING POLE, WONDER WOMAN HURLS HERSELF IN THE WAKE OF THE RACING BOATS
LONG DISTANCE POLE VAULTING IS AN OLD SPORT AT PARADISE ISLAND, BUT THIS IS THE FIRST TIME ANYBODY TRIED LANDING GENTLY IN A RACING SHELL -
6
BUT THE COLLEGE GIRLS, NOW FAR BEHIND. ARE READY TO QUIT THE RACE.
NO USE, ETTA, LET'S QUIT!
YOU KEEP GOING - WONDER WOMAN SAID SHE'D BE BACK!

SUDDENLY, LIKE A FLYING FISH, **WONDER WO-MAN** COMES LEAPING THRU THE AIR TO REJOIN HER COMRADES.

HERE I AM, GIRLS — NOW LET'S GO!

PULLING FURIOUSLY, THE COLLEGE GIRLS CREEP UP ON THEIR OPPONENTS AS THEY NEAR THE FINISH LINE.

RAISE THE STROKE, GIRLS — **WONDER WOMAN'S** HITTIN' 48 — ONE, TWO, **THREE**, FOUR —!

WITH A TREMENDOUS PULL ON HER OAR, **WONDER WOMAN** LIFTS THE BOAT ACROSS THE LINE TO VICTORY!

COLLEGE GIRLS WIN — HOORAY!

WHAT A RACE —

WONDER WOMAN DID IT AGAIN!

ACCORDING TO TRADITION, THAT THE WINNING CREW DUCK THEIR COXSWAIN.

REGULAR CHEER FOR THE TINY TYRANT: LITTLE ETTA — GET HER WETTA!

HEY, YOU'RE WASTIN' GOOD **CANDY!**

AS **WONDER WOMAN** TURNS TOWARD THE BOATHOUSE, HER KEEN AMAZON HEARING DE- TECTS AN OMINOUS WHINING SOUND OVERHEAD.

WHAT'S THAT NOISE? GREAT ZEUS, IT'S AN AERIAL BOMB HEADING STRAIGHT FOR US!

BOATHOU

⑦

WHIRLING SWIFTLY, THE AMAZON GIRL SWEEPS HER COMPANIONS OFF THE FLOAT.

WHAT GAME ARE **YOU** PLAYING?

WE'RE NOT SUPPOSED TO BE DUCKED!

WE'RE DUCKING **BOMBS** — SWIM FOR YOUR LIVES!

THE GIRLS ARE SCARCELY CLEAR OF THE BOATHOUSE WHEN IT BLOWS UP WITH A TERRIFYING ROAR.

BA-ANG!

LOOK, **WONDER WOMAN!** THE BOATHOUSE BLEW UP BUT THERE IT IS AGAIN, NOT EVEN DAMAGED!

WELL, I'LL BE A MERMAID'S GRANDMOTHER!

SURE ENOUGH, THE WRECKED BOATHOUSE APPEARS EXACTLY AS IT DID BEFORE THE EXPLOSION!

WONDER WOMAN MAKES A QUICK DECISION.

WHAT SEEMS TO BE A BOATHOUSE MUST BE **SOMETHING ELSE** — I'M GOING TO GRAB IT BEFORE IT DISAPPEARS.

AS THE AMAZON MAIDEN APPROACHES THE BOATHOUSE, THICK SMOKE SURROUNDS IT.

THAT **SMOKE** AT LEAST IS REAL — I'VE GOT TO FIND WHAT'S BEHIND IT BEFORE IT DISAPPEARS —

BLINDED BY THE DENSE BLACK VAPOR **WONDER WOMAN'S** HAND CRASHES SUDDENLY AGAINST PLATE GLASS.

⑧

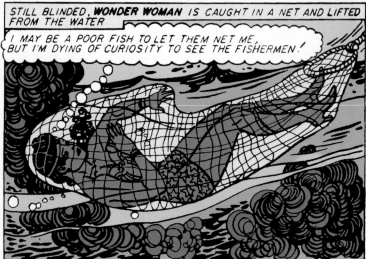

STILL BLINDED, **WONDER WOMAN** IS CAUGHT IN A NET AND LIFTED FROM THE WATER

I MAY BE A POOR FISH TO LET THEM NET ME, BUT I'M DYING OF CURIOSITY TO SEE THE FISHERMEN!

SPECTATORS, GAZING UPWARD AS SMOKE AND BOATHOUSE DISAPPEAR, SEEM TO SEE A DARK CLOUD MEET A WHITE ONE.

COULD HUMAN EYES PENETRATE THE WEIRD CLOUD THEY WOULD SEE THE STRANGEST FLYING MACHINE EVER MADE ---- A SPACE SHIP SUCH AS NO SCIENCE-FICTION WRITER EVER IMAGINED ----AND BEARING THE **NAZI** EMBLEM!

STANDING ON MY HEAD FOR AWHILE IS GOOD FOR MY BRAINS AND HAIR - BUT THERE'S SUCH A THING AS OVERDOING IT. I THINK I'VE HAD ENOUGH OF THAT FOR NOW-------

I WONDER IF THEY MEAN TO LEAVE ME DANGLING HERE IN SPACE FROM NOW ON? IF SO, THEY'RE GOING TO BE SURPRISED!

CLIMBING THE ROPE, **WONDER WOMAN** PUSHES LIGHTLY AGAINST THE HATCH COVER. ITS BOLTS, BEING ONLY STEEL, SNAP INSTANTLY!

HELLO THERE, ANYBODY HOME?

SNAP!

CR-AACK!

⑨

OOP MIT YOU UND RAISE DER HANDS!

ONE THING AT A TIME, GENTLE HOST — AND THANKS FOR YOUR EAGER HOSPITALITY!

VE VAS GOING TO PULL YOU OOP ANYWAY, **VONDER VOMAN,** VEN VE REACHED DER STRATO-SPHERE! BUT MIGHT AS VELL YOU MEET DER HERR CAPTAIN NOW AS LATER—

OH, I'D **LOVE** TO MEET THE CAPTAIN—

PUT UP YOUR REVOLVER, SCHMITT—THERE'S NO NEED TO MAKE A LADY RAISE HER HANDS! PLEASE SIT DOWN, WONDER WOMAN!

NO NAZI WOULD BE SO CONSIDERATE OF HIS PRISONER - YOU LOOK LIKE AN AMERICAN, CAPTAIN!

AFTER THE GUARD LEAVES, THE CAPTAIN FURTIVELY SHUTS THE DOOR AND...

YES, I AM AN AMERICAN OF GERMAN DESCENT—ERIC LANDER. I WAS IN GERMANY WHEN THE WAR BEGAN AND—WELL, THE REICH NEEDED ME, SO HERE I AM!

YOU TURNED TRAITOR TO AMERICA?

YOU CAN CALL ME TRAITOR IF YOU LIKE! FACT IS, I INVENTED THIS SILENT, SELF-CAMOUFLAGING SPACE BOMBER AND I MUST SEE THAT IT'S OPERATED PROPERLY!

YOU CALL IT "OPERATING PROPERLY" TO BOMB YOUR OWN COUNTRY?

THE SHIP COMMANDER INTERRUPTS.

FOR VAT ARE YOU VASTING TIME MIT DIS PRISONER? SHE ISS VONDER VOMAN, MORE DANGEROUS DAN TWO ARMIES! OUR BOMB MISSED HER— NOW VE GOT HER, KILL HER QVICK!

B—BUT HERR COMMANDER —

YOU ARE SOFT, MY CAPTAIN - I VILL EXECUTE DER PRISONER MYSELF! DONNERVETTER! SHE CATCHES DER BULLETS ON DER BRACELETS!

YOU'RE A GOOD SHOT, NASTI, BUT WITHOUT YOUR GUN I'LL BET YOU'D BE HELPLESS!

SO YOU THINK I AM VEAK — TAKE THAT!

IF THAT'S THE BEST YOU CAN DO, YOU'RE WEAKER THAN I THOUGHT!

WHEN WE AMAZONS BOX WE PUT SOMETHING IN OUR PUNCH—LIKE THIS!

UGH! AAH—UNF!

10

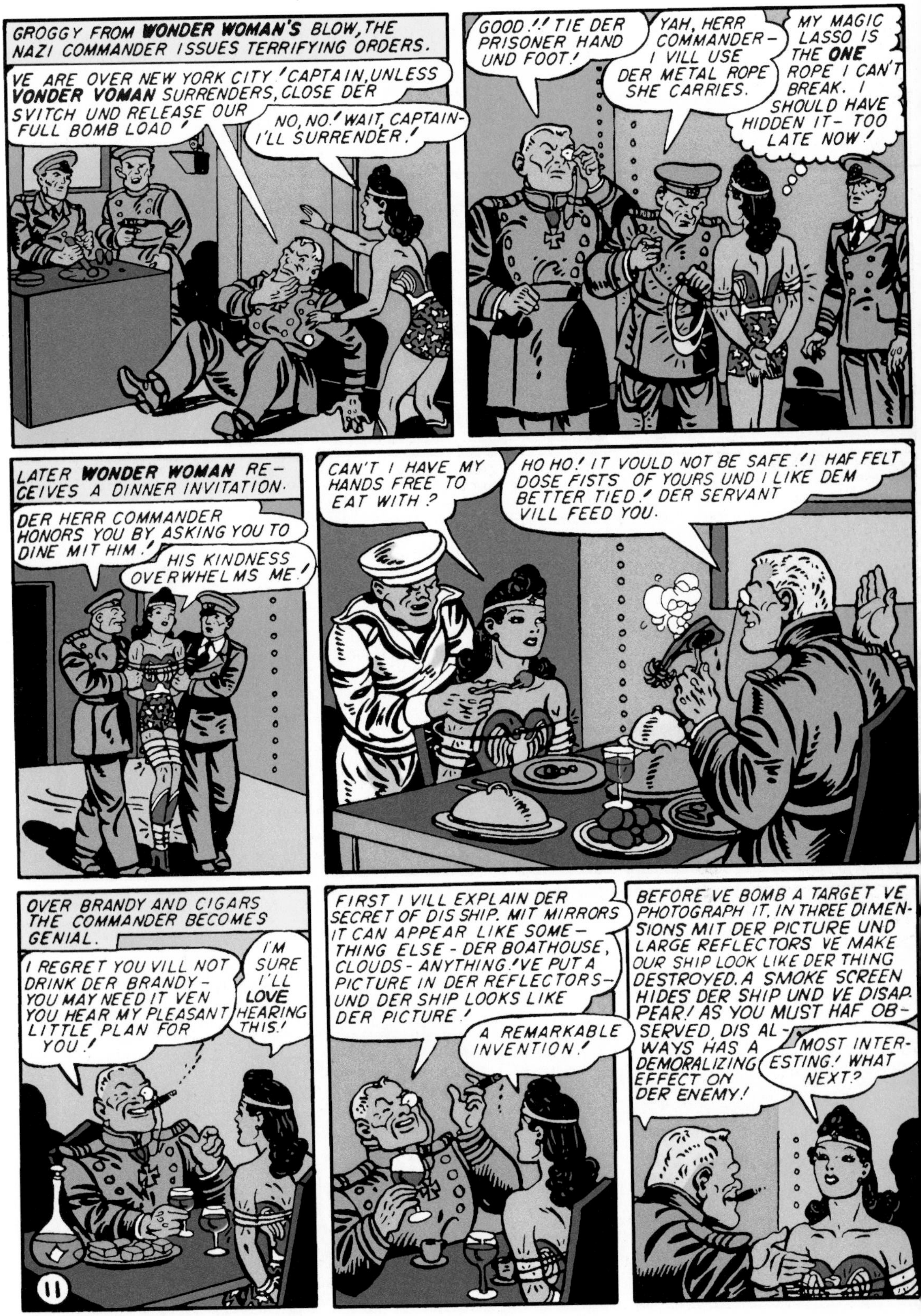
GROGGY FROM WONDER WOMAN'S BLOW, THE NAZI COMMANDER ISSUES TERRIFYING ORDERS.
VE ARE OVER NEW YORK CITY! CAPTAIN, UNLESS VONDER VOMAN SURRENDERS, CLOSE DER SVITCH UND RELEASE OUR FULL BOMB LOAD!
NO, NO! WAIT, CAPTAIN-I'LL SURRENDER!
GOOD!! TIE DER PRISONER HAND UND FOOT!
YAH, HERR COMMANDER-I VILL USE DER METAL ROPE SHE CARRIES.
MY MAGIC LASSO IS THE ONE ROPE I CAN'T BREAK. I SHOULD HAVE HIDDEN IT- TOO LATE NOW!
LATER WONDER WOMAN RECEIVES A DINNER INVITATION.
DER HERR COMMANDER HONORS YOU BY ASKING YOU TO DINE MIT HIM!
HIS KINDNESS OVERWHELMS ME!
CAN'T I HAVE MY HANDS FREE TO EAT WITH?
HO HO! IT VOULD NOT BE SAFE! I HAF FELT DOSE FISTS OF YOURS UND I LIKE DEM BETTER TIED! DER SERVANT VILL FEED YOU.
OVER BRANDY AND CIGARS THE COMMANDER BECOMES GENIAL.
I REGRET YOU VILL NOT DRINK DER BRANDY-YOU MAY NEED IT VEN YOU HEAR MY PLEASANT LITTLE PLAN FOR YOU!
I'M SURE I'LL LOVE HEARING THIS!
11
FIRST I VILL EXPLAIN DER SECRET OF DIS SHIP. MIT MIRRORS IT CAN APPEAR LIKE SOMETHING ELSE - DER BOATHOUSE, CLOUDS - ANYTHING! VE PUT A PICTURE IN DER REFLECTORS-UND DER SHIP LOOKS LIKE DER PICTURE!
A REMARKABLE INVENTION!
BEFORE VE BOMB A TARGET VE PHOTOGRAPH IT. IN THREE DIMENSIONS MIT DER PICTURE UND LARGE REFLECTORS VE MAKE OUR SHIP LOOK LIKE DER THING DESTROYED. A SMOKE SCREEN HIDES DER SHIP UND VE DISAPPEAR! AS YOU MUST HAF OBSERVED, DIS ALWAYS HAS A DEMORALIZING EFFECT ON DER ENEMY!
MOST INTERESTING! WHAT NEXT?

AT 4 P.M. TODAY VE SHALL MAKE DIS SHIP LOOK LIKE DER CAPITOL BUILDING UND DEN VE BLOW IT UP— CONGRESS UND ALL! VE VILL LEAVE YOU BEHIND CHAINED TO A TIME BOMB TO SURPRISE YOUR GALLANT RESCUERS.

THEY'LL LOVE IT!

WONDER WOMAN SENDS AN S.O.S. BY MENTAL RADIO.

CALLING STEVE AND ETTA CANDY! BE AT CAPITOL TODAY- 4 P.M. BRING GIRLS AND ASSISTANTS. SOMETHING WILL APPEAR- WHATEVER IT SEEMS TO BE, ATTACK AND SEIZE IT!

AS WONDER WOMAN IS CHAINED TO THE BOMB, SHE CONCENTRATES DESPERATELY ON ESCAPE.

THEY'LL BLOW UP THE CAPITOL BEFORE THE SHIP DESCENDS— I MUST ESCAPE NOW, BUT THE MAGIC LASSO CANNOT BE BROKEN!

LATER.

WELL, FELLOW PATRIOT, HAVE YOU COME TO TAUNT ME?

SH! DON'T BE AN IDIOT- I'M A LOYAL AMERICAN! THE NAZIS SEIZED MY PLANS FOR THIS SHIP, SO I JOINED THIS EXPEDITION HOPING FOR AN OPPORTUNITY TO FIX THEIR WAGON AND TURN THIS SHIP OVER TO THE U.S. TURN OVER SO I CAN UNTIE YOU—

BLAST THE LUCK! I'VE UNTIED YOUR ARM AND LEG ROPES BUT I CAN'T UNLOCK THESE CHAINS!

THESE LITTLE LINKS ARE EASY TO BREAK— STAND CLEAR!

LEAD THE WAY TO YOUR CONTROL ROOM, CAPTAIN— YOU'RE GOING TO GET A CHANCE TO FLY YOUR OWN SHIP!

THEY REACH THE CONTROL ROOM AND TAKE IT OVER, NOT A MOMENT TOO SOON.

OPEN DER DOOR OR VE'LL BLOW IT DOWN!

PUT A PICTURE OF THE CAPITOL IN YOUR REFLECTORS AND BRING THE SHIP DOWN ON CAPITOL HILL!

RIGHT HO!

CRASH!

BANG

WHAM!

12

WONDER WOMAN OPENS THE DOOR AND RECEIVES HER VISITORS CORDIALLY.

COME IN, BOYS, MY FIST IS HAPPY TO MEET YOU!

MEANWHILE, **WONDER WOMAN'S** FRIENDS ARRIVE AT CAPITOL HILL IN RESPONSE TO HER MENTAL RADIO CALL.

I SEE NOTHING BUT A BLACK CLOUD—THAT COULDN'T BE WHAT **WONDER WOMAN** MEANT!

IT MIGHT BE—THE CLOUD'S COMING DOWN!

THE SMOKE CLOUD DISAPPEARS AS IT TOUCHES THE GROUND AND SPECTATORS SEE AN AMAZING SIGHT.

AS I BREATHE AND EAT CANDY—TWO CAPITOLS!

COME ON—**WONDER WOMAN** SAID TO ATTACK **ANYTHING** THAT APPEARED—LET'S GO!

AS THE RAIDERS APPROACH, THE ILLUSION IS DISPELLED AND THEY SEE THE MIRROR PLANE.

THIS MUST BE IT— WHAT A WEIRD CONTRAPTION!

HOW'LL WE BREAK INTO IT? MAYBE WE NEED SOME CANDY TO LURE THE INMATES OUT!

BUT JUST AS THEY REACH THE STRANGE SHIP, THE NAZI HORDES RUSH OUT.

GET YOUR MAN, GIRLS—HOORAY FOR **WONDER WOMAN** AND HOLLIDAY COLLEGE!

WITH ALL NAZIS CAPTURED, LANDER MEETS COLONEL DARNELL.

ERIC! WE THOUGHT THE **GESTAPO** HAD **YOU!**

THEY DID, SIR, WITH MY SPACE SHIP PLANS. BUT THANKS TO **WONDER WOMAN** WE'VE GOT THE SHIP BACK— A NEW WEAPON FOR AMERICA!

(13)

YOU DID MARVELOUS WORK FOR AMERICA, **WONDER WOMAN**! BUT—ER—I'M WORRIED ABOUT **DIANA!**

OH—SHE MUST BE NEARBY— I HEARD HER VOICE A MINUTE AGO!

IMAGINE WORRYING ABOUT DIANA WITH **WONDER WOMAN** AROUND!

I COULD IMAGINE WORRYING ABOUT **CANDY!**

MORE OF **WONDER WOMAN'S** REMARKABLE EXPLOITS IN EVERY ISSUE OF **SENSATION COMICS**

FOR VICTORY BUY UNITED STATES WAR BONDS AND STAMPS

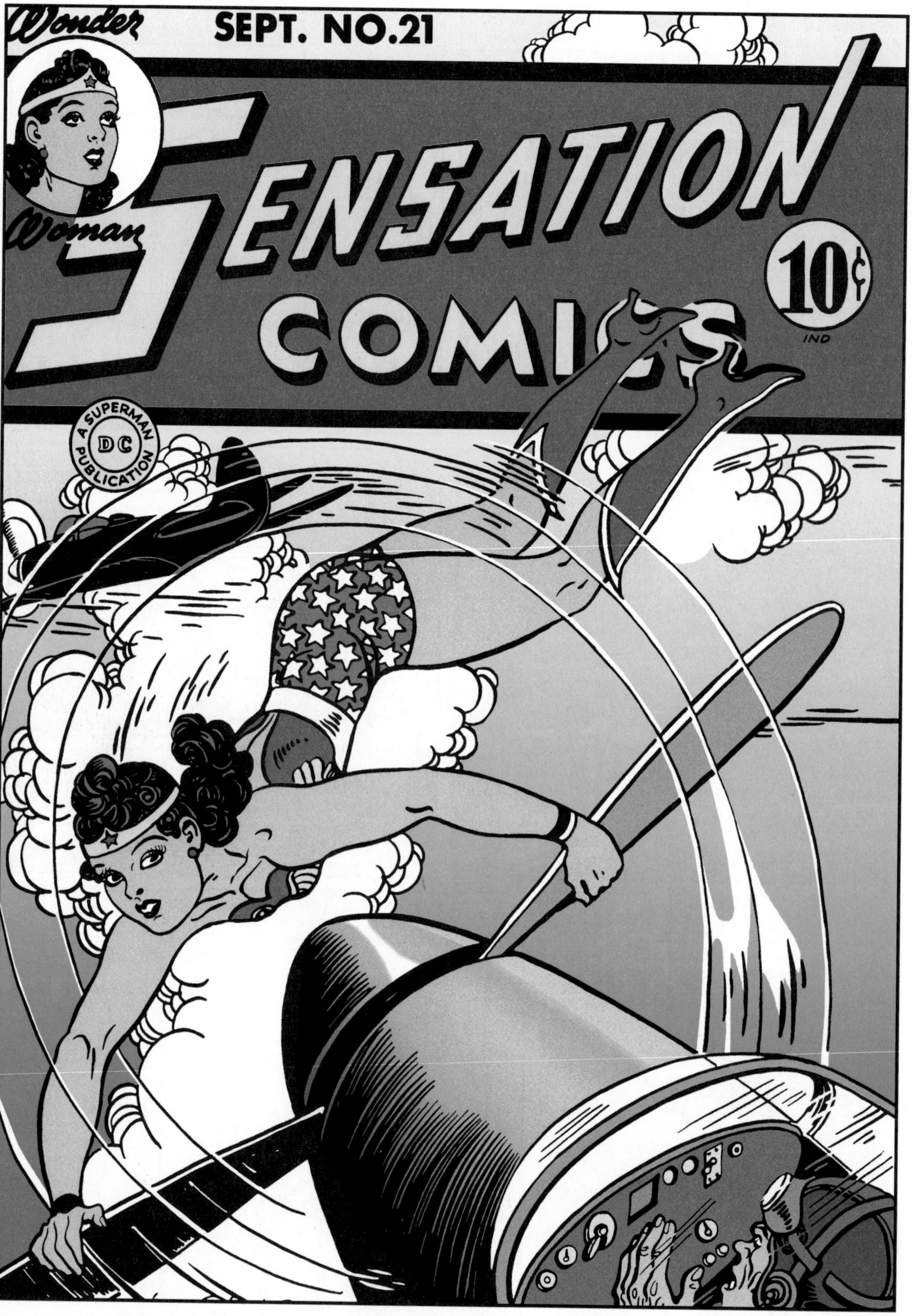
Wonder Woman
SEPT. NO.21
SENSATION COMICS
10¢
IND
A SUPERMAN DC PUBLICATION

WONDER WOMAN

SOONER OR LATER IT HAD TO HAPPEN, THIS BLITZKRIEG OF ORGANIZED CRIME THAT THREATENS TO CRUSH CIVILIZED SOCIETY LIKE A FRAIL FLOWER AND PLANT IN ITS STEAD THE UGLY, ODORIFEROUS WEEDS OF TREACHERY AND DESTRUCTION! WITH A PASSIONATE ADMIRATION FOR HITLER WHOM HE REGARDS AS THE GREATEST MAN WHO EVER LIVED, AMERICAN ADOLPH ORGANIZES AN ARMY OF PROFESSIONAL CRIMINALS ARMED WITH SECRET WEAPONS AGAINST WHICH THE GREATEST MILITARY EXPERTS HAVE NO DEFENSE.

EVEN **WONDER WOMAN**, BEAUTIFUL AS APHRODITE, WISE AS ATHENA, STRONGER THAN HERCULES AND SWIFTER THAN MERCURY, FINDS HERSELF A HELPLESS PRISONER OF THE SUPREME CRIME LEADER AT PRECISELY THE MOMENT WHEN HER GODDESS-GIVEN POWER ALONE CAN SAVE THE COUNTRY. YOU WILL THRILL WITH SUSPENSE AND GROAN WITH AMERICA'S GUARDIAN ANGEL AS SHE FACES THE MOST DESPERATE ORDEAL OF HER LIFE IN THE CRIME LEADER'S

WAR AGAINST SOCIETY

DIANA AND STEVE, VISITING A WOUNDED OFFICER IN THE HOSPITAL, WITNESS A STRANGE OCCURRENCE.

HELP! SAVE ME— HE CONDEMNED ME TO DEATH!

WE'RE COMING— TAKE IT EASY!

1.

BEFORE HELP CAN REACH HIM THE MAN COLLAPSES.

YOU'RE AN ARMY OFFICER—BEWARE! THE SUPREME LEADER WILL KILL YOU NEXT—IT'S THE THIRD STEP! READ HIS BOOK!

NUTS! WHOSE BOOK?

AMERICAN ADOLPH'S BOOK—"MY WAR AGAINST SOCIETY!" HE'S DONE EVERYTHING HE SAID—COMPLETED STEPS 1 AND 2! THE GREAT HORROR'S COMING—STEP 3—THE RULE OF CRIME! LOOK FOR HIS MARK—THE DOUBLE CROSS!

HE'S DEAD—KNIFE WOUND—LOOKS LIKE MURDER!

THAT TATTOO WOULD INDICATE HE BELONGED TO A GANG. HE EVIDENTLY LIVED UP TO THEIR SYMBOL, DOUBLE CROSSED 'EM AND WAS EXECUTED—

THE POOR FELLOW WAS SCARED OUT OF HIS WITS! THERE IS NO SUCH BOOK AS "MY WAR AGAINST SOCIETY"—IS THERE?

I DON'T KNOW—BUT I'M GOING TO FIND OUT!

DIANA CALLS DIOGENES ARCHIVIAN, DEALER IN RARE BOOKS.

YOU REMEMBER ME—I'M YOUR AMAZON GIRL CUSTOMER. TELL ME—IS THERE A BOOK CALLED "MY WAR AGAINST SOCIETY" BY "AMERICAN ADOLPH"?

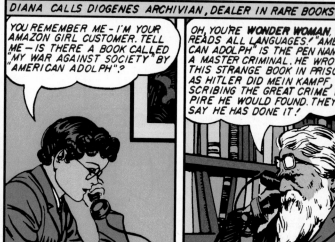

OH, YOU'RE WONDER WOMAN, WHO READS ALL LANGUAGES! "AMERICAN ADOLPH" IS THE PEN NAME OF A MASTER CRIMINAL. HE WROTE THIS STRANGE BOOK IN PRISON, AS HITLER DID MEIN KAMPF, DESCRIBING THE GREAT CRIME EMPIRE HE WOULD FOUND. THEY SAY HE HAS DONE IT!

THE BOOK IS HARD TO OBTAIN, BUT ARCHIVIAN GETS A COPY FOR WONDER WOMAN.

HOW AMAZING! THE DEDICATION READS—"TO ADOLPH SHICKELGRUBER, ALIAS HITLER—UNDOUBTEDLY THE GREATEST MAN WHO EVER LIVED!"

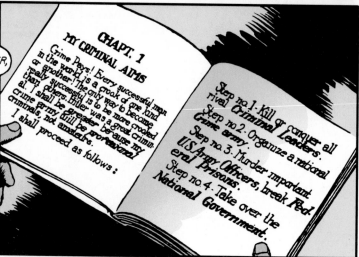

CHAPT. 1
MY CRIMINAL AIMS

Crime Pays! Every successful man in the world is a crook of one kind or another! The only way to become a really successful is to be more crooked than others. Hitler was a great crimin- al. I shall be greater because my crime army will be professional criminals, not amateurs.

I shall proceed as follows:

Step no. 1. Kill or conquer all rival Criminal Leaders.

Step no. 2. Organize a national Crime army.

Step no. 3. Murder important U.S. Army Officers, break Federal Prisons.

Step no. 4. Take over the National Government.

HERE'S A CRIMINAL FUEHRER QUIETLY RISING TO POWER RIGHT UNDER OUR NOSES! THAT MAN IN THE HOSPITAL WAS ONE OF HIS CROOK "SOLDIERS"-KILLED FOR DESERTING! HIS CRIME ARMY'S READY TO STRIKE- I MUST ACT!

MY WAR AGAINST SOCIETY by AMERICAN ADOLPH

BUT NEXT MORNING, DIANA'S WARNING IS INTERRUPTED.

COLONEL DARNELL, I MUST TELL YOU-

WAIT-

GENERAL STARBOARD SPEAKING- I'M SENDING A CRACKPOT TO SEE YOU- SAYS HE'S AMBASSADOR FROM THE SUPREME CRIME LEADER! PROBABLY CRAZY- BUT INVESTIGATE!

LISTEN, COLONEL! THERE'S A BOOK—

SORRY TO INTERRUPT BUT GENERAL STARBOARD ORDERED ME TO BRING THIS QUEER PERSON TO YOU, SIR, IMMEDIATELY!

OH, YES-EXCUSE ME DIANA-SEND IN THE "CRIME AMBASSADOR"

"DISHONORABLE BADMAN BLACK, AMBASSADOR OF THE SUPREME CRIME LEADER. THIS DOUBLE CROSS IS A FAIR WARNING OF DEATH."- IS THIS SUPPOSED TO BE FUNNY? MR. BLACK, YOU CAN'T BE SERIOUS!

I AM VERY SERIOUS, COLONEL! AS YOU KNOW, CRIME TODAY IS ORGANIZED. OUR SUPREME LEADER CONTROLS EVERY RACKET SUCH AS MURDER, INC., CRIME TRUST, ETC. OUR CRIME ARMY NUMBERS 260,000!

BUT OUR ARMY NUMBERS 10 MILLION!

QUITE SO-BUT YOUR ARMY IS BUSY FIGHTING FOREIGN ENEMIES WHILE OUR ARMY CONTROLS AMERICA! WE'RE NOT TREACHEROUS LIKE THE JAPS-WE GIVE FAIR WARNING. FIRST WE SHALL KILL IMPORTANT ARMY OFFICERS-LIKE YOURSELF!

OH, YES'.?

3.

UNNOTICED BY THE COLONEL, BLACK SNAPS A CATCH IN HIS CIGAR HOLDER.

WHILE DARNELL SEARCHES BLACK FOR A REVOLVER THE CRIME AMBASSADOR HOLDS A STILL MORE DEADLY WEAPON UNDER THE COLONEL'S NOSE.

DON'T MOVE!

I WON'T, COLONEL! THIS SUITS ME PERFECTLY!

THE FUMES FROM BLACK'S CIGAR HAVE A STRANGE EFFECT.

AGGH-I'M CHOKING-UGH-AH-HELP- DIANA!

HO, HO! MY FRIEND! NOBODY CAN HELP YOU NOW!

BUT THE CRIME AMBASSADOR DOESN'T KNOW THAT COLONEL DARNELL'S MEEK-APPEARING SECRETARY IS REALLY THAT LIVING THUNDERBOLT, WONDER WOMAN.

IF THIS IS YOUR "THIRD STEP," CRIME LEADER, YOUR FOOT IS SLIPPING!

UG—OW-W-W!

SUCH IS THE FORCE OF DIANA'S BLOW THAT BLACK CRASHES THROUGH THE WINDOW.

PLUTO SPANK ME, I HIT HIM TOO HARD! THIS HIRSUTE HITLER CAN'T TAKE IT.

SWIFTER THAN THE EYE CAN FOLLOW, DIANA FLASHES TO THE MEDICAL SUPPLY ROOM AND RETURNS WITH OXYGEN APPARATUS.

THIS'LL SAVE HIM IF I CAN GET OXYGEN INTO HIS LUNGS IN TIME!

SWIFTLY ADJUSTING THE OXYGEN MASK, DIANA APPLIES HER AMAZON METHOD OF ARTIFICIAL RESPIRATION.

HE'S PRETTY FAR GONE BUT I'LL MAKE HIM BREATHE THIS OXYGEN!

AT LAST THE COLONEL RECOVERS CONSCIOUSNESS.

UH-UF-F-WHA- GLUB!

NOW COLONEL, TAKE IT EASY! KEEP THIS MASK ON AND BREATHE DEEPLY UNTIL THE POISON'S ALL OUT OF YOUR LUNGS!

4.

STEVE ARRIVES AS DIANA FINALLY REMOVES THE OXYGEN MASK.

GREAT CAESAR'S GHOST! WHAT HAPPENED, COLONEL?

CRIME AMBASSADOR-TRIED KILL ME! MUST-BEEN-POISON SMOKE-CIGAR-DIANA SAVED ME!

DON'T, DI! THAT'S THE SMOKE THAT POISONED THE COLONEL!

NO IT ISN'T—SEE? IT'S HARMLESS. THE POISON GAS WAS IN THIS TRICK CIGAR HOLDER!

DIANA SPLITS THE CIGAR HOLDER LENGTHWISE IN HER POWERFUL FINGERS.

HOW CLEVER! THIS METAL CONTAINER HOLDS POISON GAS. PUSHING THIS BUTTON SHOOTS THE GAS THROUGH THIS NEEDLE TUBE INTO THE CIGAR, POISONING THE CIGAR SMOKE!

THE CRIME AMBASSADOR! HE MUST NOT ESCAPE! QUICK, DIANA, I CALL THE BUILDING GUARDS—

NO USE! HE—ER—THAT IS, I GAVE HIM A LITTLE PUSH AND HE FELL OUT THE WINDOW! THERE'S PROBABLY A CROWD DOWNSTAIRS WHERE HE FELL!

NOPE—NO CROWD—LOOKS LIKE A BLACK WIG AND BEARD ON THE SIDEWALK BUT THE BODY'S DISAPPEARED—PALS PROBABLY CARRIED HIM AWAY!

WHILE COLONEL DARNELL ORDERS A NATION-WIDE DRAGNET FOR THE "CRIME AMBASSADOR," LET US FOLLOW "BLACK" HIMSELF.

THE CRIME LEADER, REVEALED IN TRUE CHARACTER BY THE LOSS OF HIS WIG, BEARD AND FALSE MUSTACHE, GRASPS THE SILL OF AN OPEN WINDOW, THREE STORIES BELOW.

PULLING HIMSELF INTO THE ROOM, THE MASTER CRIMINAL INTRODUCES HIMSELF.

WHAT'S THIS? WHO ARE YOU?

I AM THE SUPREME CRIME LEADER—ACCEPT MY CARD!

5.

I INSIST THAT YOU TAKE MY CARD! THIS DOUBLE CROSS GIVES FAIR WARNING THAT I SHALL KILL YOU—AA—GH!

STAND BACK—ALL RIGHT, YOU ASKED FOR IT!

BANG!

*I **HAD** TO SHOOT— WHO **IS** THIS BIRD?*

THIS BULLET-PROOF VEST I INVENTED IS A SUCCESS— THAT ARMY .45 AT 5 FEET ONLY KNOCKED ME OVER!

COMING SUDDENLY TO LIFE, AMERICAN ADOLPH HURLS THE HEAVY PAPERWEIGHT WITH DEADLY ACCURACY.

THIS DEMONSTRATES AGAIN OUR CRIME ARMY'S PRINCIPLE—STRIKE ALWAYS WITH AN UNEXPECTED WEAPON!

THE CRIME LEADER, ADEPT AT QUICK CHANGES, DONS THE LIEUTENANT'S UNIFORM.

THEY WON'T FIND THE BODY IN THIS CLOSET FOR SOME TIME—I MUST GET THAT GIRL WHO PUSHED ME OUT THE WINDOW—SHE KNOWS TOO MUCH!

ADOLPH BOLDLY USES THE LIEUTENANT'S PHONE, COVERING IT WITH HIS HANDKERCHIEF TO DISGUISE HIS VOICE.

*MISS PRINCE? I'M QUICK-HUH? NOT FAST-**QUICK**, LT. QUICK! PLEASE COME TO MY OFFICE—I HAVE IMPORTANT INFORMATION!*

LT. K L QUICK

DIANA, SUSPECTING TRICKERY, CHANGES QUICKLY TO **WONDER WOMAN**, HIDING HER NURSE'S UNIFORM IN A SECRET COMPARTMENT OF HER DESK.

*THAT VOICE ON THE PHONE DIDN'T SOUND LIKE KEN QUICK'S-BESIDES HE'D NEVER CALL ME "MISS PRINCE"- IT'S TIME FOR **WONDER WOMAN** TO INVESTIGATE!*

AS **WONDER WOMAN** ENTERS QUICK'S OFFICE, THE "LIEUTENANT" SPEAKS IN A MUFFLED VOICE.

ER- THAT YOU, MISS PRINCE?

BUT THE CRIME MASTER, TURNING SWIFTLY ON HIS INTENDED VICTIM, MEETS A SURPRISE.

*HANDS UP-WHAT! YOU'RE NOT DIANA PRINCE- YOU'RE **WONDER WOMAN**!*

I WAS IN DIANA'S OFFICE WHEN YOU PHONED— I YEARNED TO MEET "LT. QUICK!"

THIS GUN IS NO USE AGAINST YOU, DEAR LADY! YOU REPEL ALL BULLETS WITH YOUR BRACELETS. I AM THE CRIME LEADER— MY CARD.

SORRY YOU WON'T PLAY BULLETS AND BRACELETS WITH ME—

6.

AH! YOUR SYMBOL - THE DOUBLE CROSS! ACCORDING TO YOUR BOOK, ADOLPH, THIS CARD MEANS THAT YOU ARE GOING TO KILL ME!

WHILE **WONDER WOMAN** STUDIES THE CARD CURIOUSLY, ADOLPH SLIPS A STRANGE RING ON HIS FINGER

I AM GLAD YOU HAVE READ "MY FIGHT" — EVERYTHING I WROTE THERE WILL COME TRUE. LET'S BE FRIENDLY ENEMIES AND SHAKE HANDS!

I'M SURE YOUR FRIENDSHIP WILL PROVE DEVASTATING!

AS THEY CLASP HANDS A NEEDLE IN THE RING PRESSES INTO **WONDER WOMAN'S** FLESH, INJECTING AN ORIENTAL DRUG

UH- MY HAND- WHAT'S THIS FUNNY FEELING? I'M PARALYZED- I CAN'T MOVE! OH, MY MIND'S GETTING CONFUSED—

HA, HA! I'M GLAD I WAS ABLE TO PUT YOU INTO A COMA INSTEAD OF KILLING YOU IMMEDIATELY. IN THIS CONDITION YOU'LL BE USEFUL. YOU CAN MOVE AND TALK, BUT NOT WITHOUT MY COMMAND!

AS THE CRIME LEADER COMPELS **WONDER WOMAN** TO LEAVE THE BUILDING THEY MEET STEVE

WONDER WOMAN— GREAT TO SEE YOU!

PSST— TELL HIM YOU WON'T TALK WITH HIM!

I WILL NOT TALK WITH YOU!

WELL, I'LL BE BLACKJACKED! THE CUT DIRECT- WHAT HAVE I DONE TO DESERVE THIS FROM **WONDER WOMAN?**

SIT IN MY CAR, **WONDER WOMAN**. AND **KEEP QUIET**! CRIME CORPORAL DEVLIN, DRIVE TO FEDERAL PRISON!

YES, LEADER

CAR-PRISON-- WHY SHOULD A **CRIMINAL** TAKE ME TO **PRISON**? MY MIND'S CONFUSED--IF I COULD ONLY THINK.

AT "THE WALLS" THE FALSE G2 OFFICER CONFERS WITH WARDEN GRIM.

I AM LIEUTENANT QUICK OF MILITARY INTELLIGENCE-- HERE ARE MY CREDENTIALS. I'M BRINGING YOU A PRISONER.

BUT-- BUT THIS IS **WONDER WOMAN**!

PRISONER, GIVE THE WARDEN YOUR CARD! THIS SHOWS YOU, SIR, THE TRUE IDENTITY OF THE SUPREME CRIME LEADER! THAT CARD WARNS WHOEVER RECEIVES IT THAT HE WILL BE KILLED!

INCREDIBLE! I HOPE SHE IS NOT WARNING **ME**!

I'M SORRY, **WONDER WOMAN**, BUT I RECEIVED ORDERS TO SHACKLE **EVERY** PRISONER! IF YOU'RE THE CRIME LEADER YOU KNOW **WHY**!

SO A PRISON DELIVERY IS EXPECTED, EH? HA! HA! SOMEONE'S BEEN READING THE CRIME LEADER'S BOOK!

ON THE WAY OUT "LT. QUICK" IS CALLED ASIDE BY WOLF, THE PRISON P.K. (PRINCIPAL KEEPER)

WE'RE ALL SET FOR THE BREAK! WHY'D YOU BRING THIS DAME? SHE'S DYNAMITE!

SHE'S HELPLESS, DRUGGED-- MAKES A WONDERFUL HOSTAGE!

DOUBLE PADLOCK THAT CHAIN, CRIME SERGEANT RAFFLES! THE LEADER SAYS **WONDER WOMAN'S** DRUGGED BUT I AIN'T TAKING CHANCES!

8

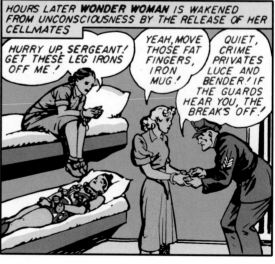

HOURS LATER **WONDER WOMAN** IS WAKENED FROM UNCONSCIOUSNESS BY THE RELEASE OF HER CELLMATES

HURRY UP, SERGEANT! GET THESE LEG IRONS OFF ME!

YEAH, MOVE THOSE FAT FINGERS, IRON MUG!

QUIET, CRIME PRIVATES LUCE AND BENDER! IF THE GUARDS HEAR YOU, THE BREAK'S OFF!

HONEST PRISON GUARDS ARE CAPTURED AND LINED UP WITH **WONDER WOMAN** AS HOSTAGES.

I'M CRIME CAPTAIN, FOLLOW ORDERS! PUSH THESE HOSTAGES IN FRONT OF YER DOWN THE CORRIDOR TO THE WARDEN'S OFFICE!

SWEEPING ALL OPPOSITION BEFORE THEM, THE CRIME BATTALION ENTERS THE WARDEN'S OFFICE.

STICK 'EM UP, GRIM! WE'RE MEMBERS OF THE CRIME ARMY AND THE PRISON IS OURS!

YOU DOUBLE—CROSSING SCOUNDRELS!

BEFORE HE CAN BE SILENCED, THE WARDEN COURAGEOUSLY GIVES THE ALARM.

EMERGENCY! CRIME ARMY CONTROLS PRISON— MM·MF! THEY'VE SHOT ME---

AS THE WARDEN'S MESSAGE IS RELAYED TO LOCAL ARMY HEAD-QUARTERS, THE POST COMMAND-ER ISSUES RAPID ORDERS.

TURN OUT THE 107th INFANTRY· SURROUND THE PRISON! SEND MACHINE GUNS AND ARTILLERY!

YES, SIR!

YES, GENERAL!

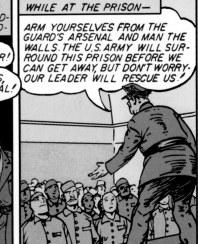

WHILE AT THE PRISON—

ARM YOURSELVES FROM THE GUARD'S ARSENAL AND MAN THE WALLS. THE U.S. ARMY WILL SUR-ROUND THIS PRISON BEFORE WE CAN GET AWAY, BUT DON'T WORRY· OUR LEADER WILL RESCUE US!

THE PRISON TOWERS BRISTLE WITH MACHINE GUNS AS HOSTAGES ARE HUNG OVER THE WALLS.

THEIR ARTILLERY WON'T FIRE AT **THIS** WALL WITH **WONDER WOMAN** ON IT!

9.

WONDER WOMAN, HER SENSES NUMBED BY THE CRIME MASTER'S DRUG, REMAINS IN A WEIRD COMA.

STEVE, MEANWHILE, NOT KNOWING **WONDER WOMAN** IS A PRISONER, RECEIVES REPORTS BY TELEPHONE.

OKAY, X42, WHAT'S THE LATEST?

PRISON'S SURROUNDED BY TROOPS AND ARTILLERY BUT THEY DON'T DARE ATTACK! HOSTAGES ARE FASTENED ON THE WALLS!

HOSTAGES INCLUDE MEN AND WOMEN GUARDS, CONVICTS NOT IN THE CRIME ARMY AND **WONDER WOMAN!**

WONDER WOMAN!

WHY SHOULD SHE LET HERSELF BE TAKEN PRISONER? I'LL CALL PAULA AND ETTA CANDY!

HURRYING TO THE BESIEGED PRISON, **WONDER WOMAN'S** THREE FRIENDS HOLD A CONSULTATION.

SHE LOOKS STIFF, UNNATURAL!

SHE'S PARALYZED-DRUGGED! I KNOW THE ANTIDOTE-BUT HOW TO ADMINISTER IT?

WOO WOO! TOSS HER SOME MEDICAL CANDY!

WITH THE AMAZING SPEED DEVELOPED BY HER TRAINING IN AMAZON PRISON, PAULA OBTAINS NEEDED CHEMICALS FROM A MEDICAL LABORATORY.

I HAVE A PLAN-LUCKY THE HOLLIDAY GIRLS PLAY BAND INSTRUMENTS!

BORROWING MUSICAL INSTRUMENTS FROM THE ARMY, PAULA MAKES SOME QUEER PREPARATIONS.

THIS GAS HIDDEN IN THE DRUM IS UNDER PRESSURE. WHEN RELEASED IT WILL BLOW OUT THROUGH **YOUR** TRUMPET!

THE HOLLIDAY GIRLS MARCH TO THE PRISON WALL WHERE **WONDER WOMAN** IS SUSPENDED.

HEY, BIG BOY! WE WANTA PLAY A TUNE TO GET SOME PUBLICITY FOR OUR BAND-OKAY?

HA! HA! GIRLS IS NUTS! SURE, GO AHEAD-

⑩

AS ETTA STRIKES HER DRUM THE BAND BURSTS INTO MELODY.

POINT YOUR TRUMPET AT **WONDER WOMAN**-I'M TURNING ON THE GAS!

♪♪ TO YOU, BEAUTIFUL LADY, WE RAISE OUR EYES. ♪♪

AS THE GAS PREPARED BY PAULA BLOWS INTO **WONDER WOMAN'S** FACE, HER SENSES RETURN.

THANK APHRODITE, MY HEAD IS CLEARING! I CAN MOVE MY LEGS AND ARMS AGAIN.

WITH THE RETURN OF HER MIGHTY STRENGTH, **WONDER WOMAN** BURSTS HER BONDS.

WHY DID THEY BIND ME WITH SUCH SMALL CHAINS? IT'S AN INSULT!

SWINGING SWIFTLY TO THE WALL-TOP, **WONDER WOMAN** MEETS A WARM RECEPTION.

SHOOT FASTER, BOYS—I NEED TO LIMBER UP!

AGGH! IT'S THAT FE-MALE FORTRESS, I KNEW SHE'D BLITZ US!

COME ON, GIRLS, IT WON'T TAKE LONG TO CLEAN UP THESE CRIME SOLDIERS—BUT WHERE'S THEIR LEADER?

UMMPH!

OOMP!

SOCK!

WHAM!

THE ROAR OF AN AIRPLANE OVERHEAD ANSWERS **WONDER WOMAN'S** QUESTION.

WHAT AN AMAZING PLANE! I'LL BET IT'S AMERICAN ADOLPH HIMSELF!

11.

AS TROOPS ADVANCE TOWARD THE PRISON, THE CRIME LEADER'S PLANE DIVES LOW, SPRAYING THEM WITH DEADLY GAS.

LOOK OUT—POISON GAS! AGG-GH!

THOSE GUNS SHOOT GAS, NOT BULLETS! BREAK RANKS! SCATTER!

RIFLE AND MACHINE GUN BULLETS HAVE NO EFFECT ON THE PECULIAR ARMOR OF THE POISON GAS PLANE.

EVEN THE POWERFUL ACK-ACK FIRE FAILS TO BRING DOWN ADOLPH'S AERIAL DREADNAUGHT.

HAHA! DIE, YOU STUPID SLAVES OF THE OLD ORDER! YOUR TOY GUNS ARE USELESS AGAINST MY NEW ARMOR METAL, ACRON-AMALGAMITE!

THE ARTILLERY SILENCED, ADOLPH TURNS HIS ATTENTION TO **WONDER WOMAN** AND HER GIRLS.

WOO WOO! IT'S OUR TURN NOW! HE'S GONNA GAS US!

UNHESITATINGLY **WONDER WOMAN** HURLS HERSELF AT THE DEATH DEALING MONSTER.

WITH LIGHTNING SPEED AND PERFECT TIMING THE AMAZON GIRL SEIZES A PROPELLER BLADE.

IF I CAN HOLD ON TO THIS PROP, MY WEIGHT WILL SLOW ITS SPEED OF REVOLUTION!

12

THE POWERFUL PLANE ENGINE SPINS **WONDER WOMAN** IN A DIZZY WHIRL.

IN ANOTHER SECOND MY FEET WILL HIT THE TOP OF THE WALL AND THEN—

AS THE WHIRLING FORM OF THEIR LEADER COMES WITHIN REACH, THE GIRLS GRIP HER LEGS.

HOLD TIGHT, GIRLS! PULL ME DOWN ON THE WALL!

FIRMLY FIXED BY HER HUMAN ANCHOR, THE INVINCIBLE PRINCESS HOLDS THE PROPELLER MOTIONLESS WHILE THE PLANE ITSELF BEGINS TO WHIRL!

SWINGING THE PINIONED SHIP AROUND HER HEAD, WONDER WOMAN HURLS IT TO THE GROUND, A HEAP OF BLAZING WRECKAGE.

I HELD THE PLANE LONG ENOUGH FOR THE CRIME LEADER TO JUMP- HE CHOSE TO DIE RATHER THAN SUBMIT!

BANG!

CRASH!

YOUR STRENGTH AND COURAGE WERE MAGNIFICENT, MISTRESS, YOU SAVED US ALL!

AND YOUR BRAIN WORK WAS MAGNIFICENT, PAULA. YOU SAVED ME!

HEY YOU GALS, SKIP THE MUTUAL ADMIRATION- YOU BOTH NEED CANDY!

AS TROOPS POUR INTO THE PRISON, STEVE DRAWS WONDER WOMAN ASIDE.

I SHOULD HAVE KNOWN THERE WAS SOMETHING WRONG WHEN YOU CUT ME FOR ANOTHER MAN!

DON'T EVER LET ME DO IT AGAIN, STEVE!

AT G2 HEADQUARTERS COLONEL DARNELL IS IN A DITHER ABOUT DIANA.

SHE'S MISSING! YOU MUST FIND HER—DIANA! WHERE'VE YOU BEEN?

FINISHING THE CRIME LEADER'S CAREER—IT ENDED, LIKE THE DREAMS OF ALL CONQUERORS, IN BITTER DEFEAT!

MORE ADVENTURES OF WONDER WOMAN IN EVERY ISSUE OF SENSATION COMICS

FOR VICTORY BUY UNITED STATES WAR BONDS AND STAMPS

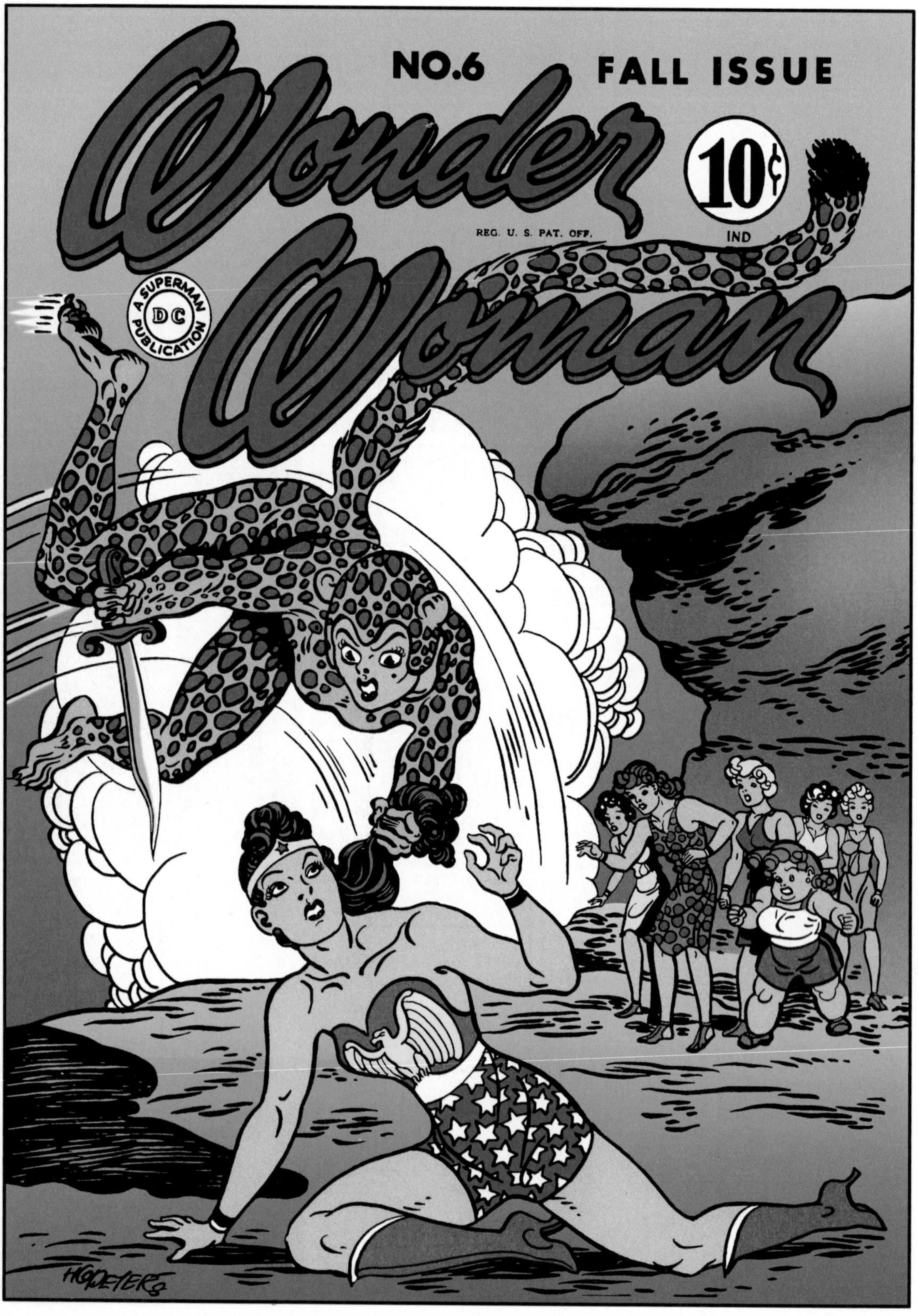
NO.6
FALL ISSUE
Wonder Woman
10¢
REG. U. S. PAT. OFF.
IND
A SUPERMAN PUBLICATION
DC
H G PETERS

Wonder Woman

By Charles Moulton

REG U S PAT OFF

THERE IS NOTHING SO DANGEROUS IN THE WHOLE WORLD AS THE VICIOUS HATRED OF A PERSONAL ENEMY, AND THERE IS NO ENEMY SO EAGER TO INFLICT PAIN AS A MAN OR WOMAN WHO FEELS HIMSELF YOUR INFERIOR!

WONDER WOMAN UNKNOWINGLY ROUSES THE INSATIABLE HATRED OF SUCH A FOE— THE CHEETAH! RELENTLESSLY THIS SVELTE SIREN, CHANGING LIKE JEKYLL AND HYDE FROM ARISTO-CRATIC BEAUTY TO MODERN MEDUSA, PURSUES THE LOVELY AMAZON MAIDEN.

NO HUMAN SAVE WONDER WOMAN, BEAUTIFUL AS APHRODITE, WISE AS ATHENA, STRONGER THAN HERCULES AND SWIFTER THAN MERCURY, WOULD DARE DEFY THE MYSTIFYING CHEETAH, FIGHT HER GIRL TO GIRL AND STRIVE TO CONQUER HER ON GROUNDS OF THE CHEETAH'S OWN CHOOSING!

NEVER BEFORE HAS THE VALIANT PRINCESS FROM PARADISE ISLAND FOUGHT ANY FOE SO ELUSIVE AS THE MILLIONAIRESS WITH THE DUAL PERSONALITY IN THIS TALE OF WONDER WOMAN AND THE CHEETAH.

1A

TICKETS FOR WONDER WOMAN'S BENEFIT PERFORMANCE ARE COMPLETELY SOLD OUT.

NO SEATS LEFT! STANDING ROOM ONLY!

FOR THE RELIEF of WOMEN and CHILDREN in EUROPE →

MR. COURTLEY DARLING, CHAIRMAN OF RELIEF FOR RESTORED COUNTRIES, ADDRESSES THE AUDIENCE.

FELLOW AMERICANS, I WELCOME YOU HERE TONIGHT ON BEHALF OF A GREAT CAUSE, A GREAT MOVEMENT, A GREAT ORGANIZATION, A GR——

BOO-OO!

SIT DOWN! WE WANT WONDER WOMAN!

ER-AH-YES, OF COURSE--- WONDER WOMAN IS COMING. BUT FIRST I MUST INTRODUCE THE LOVELIEST, SWEETEST DEBUTANTE OF LAST SEASON! SHE LEADS THE JUNIOR LEAGUE COMMITTEE FOR WAR TALK- I MEAN WORK- I PRESENT MISS PRISCILLA RICH!

NO APPLAUSE-NOT EVEN A POLITE HANDCLAP! THEY DON'T WANT ANYBODY BUT WONDER WOMAN!

WE GIRLS WHO PUT ON TONIGHT'S SHOW HAVE ONLY ONE THING TO BOAST ABOUT-WE BRING YOU- WONDER WOMAN!

BUT INSTEAD OF WONDER WOMAN, DIANA PRINCE APPEARS.

WE WANT WONDER WOMAN! WE WANT WONDER WOMAN!

SORRY, FOLKS, I GOT DELAYED AT THE OFFICE AND-ER- WONDER WOMAN WAITED FOR ME TO DRIVE HER OVER.

WONDER WOMAN ASKED ME TO MOVE THIS PIANO-UGH-UNH- OH-H-H! IT'S TOO HEAVY FOR ME!

HA! HA! WHE-EE-EW!

GET A MAN! GET WONDER WOMAN!

USING VENTRILOQUISM, DIANA APPEARS TO TALK WITH WONDER WOMAN OFF STAGE.

I'M SORRY, WONDER WOMAN, YOU'LL HAVE TO MOVE THIS PIANO—

YOU CERTAINLY ARE WEAK-DIANA, BE THERE IN A MINUTE-

24

FLASHING TO HER DRESSING ROOM DIANA CHANGES TO WONDER WOMAN SO QUICKLY SHE SEEMS TO PASS HERSELF COMING BACK ON STAGE.

HOORAY! THREE CHEERS FOR WONDER WOMAN!

GOOD EVENING, FRIENDS!

WHEN I MOVE LITTLE THINGS LIKE THIS PIANO I OFTEN PUSH THEM TOO FAR. I'LL TIE MY MAGIC LASSO AROUND THIS INSTRUMENT SO IT WON'T GET AWAY FROM ME!

HA! HA!

HO! HO!

WONDER WOMAN THROWS THE PIANO TOWARD THE AUDIENCE.

EEE— EEK!

WOW! LOOK OUT!

HEY, LEMME OUT O' HERE!

PULLING HER LASSO SHARPLY, THE AMAZON GIRL JERKS THE HEAVY PIANO BACK TOWARD THE STAGE.

DON'T WORRY, FRIENDS— I TOLD YOU THE PIANO COULDN'T GET AWAY FROM ME!

WONDER WOMAN CATCHES THE PIANO AMID CHEERS FROM THE AUDIENCE.

WONDERFUL!

WHAT IN- CREDIBLE STRENGTH!

BRAVO, WONDER WO- MAN! YAY-AY!

MARVELOUS!

I'LL SHOW YOU TONIGHT A TEST THAT AMAZON GIRLS HAVE TO TAKE — WE CALL IT "THE ORDEAL OF A THOUSAND LINKS." THE GIRL IS BOUND WITH 1000 LINKS OF CHAIN. SHE MUST BREAK HER SHACKLES OR WEAR THEM!

3A

THE JUNIOR LEAGUE COMMIT- TEE WILL BIND ME WITH THESE SHACKLES AND MANACLES. MISS RICH COLLECTED THEM FROM PRISONS AND DUNGEONS ALL OVER THE WORLD. PRIS- CILLA'S HOBBY IS COLLECTING CHAINS—MINE IS BREAKING THEM!

WHEN I AM SHACKLED WITH MORE THAN 2000 LINKS OF CHAIN THE GIRLS WILL PUT ME INTO THIS TANK FULL OF WATER AND LOCK THE COVER. I SHALL ATTEMPT TO BREAK MY BONDS AND ESCAPE.

PRISCILLA'S **COMMITTEE** SHACKLES **WONDER WOMAN.**

THIS IS THE FAMOUS "BRANK" - A LEATHER MASK WORN BY WOMEN PRISONERS IN ST. LAZARE PRISON, FRANCE. IT COVERS THE ENTIRE FACE AND MUFFLES A PRISONER'S VOICE!

KWEVER TO B'INDFO'D ME-MAKTH ETH-CAPE MUTH HARDER!

HA! HA! HA!

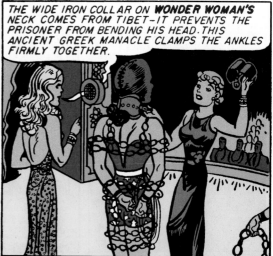

THE WIDE IRON COLLAR ON **WONDER WOMAN'S** NECK COMES FROM TIBET - IT PREVENTS THE PRISONER FROM BENDING HIS HEAD. THIS ANCIENT GREEK MANACLE CLAMPS THE ANKLES FIRMLY TOGETHER.

WHILE **WONDER WOMAN,** COMPLETELY SHACKLED, WAITS FOR THE TANK TO BE MADE READY, STEALTHY HANDS REACH FROM THE WINGS AND STEAL HER MAGIC LASSO.

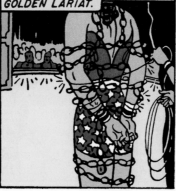

WEIGHTED WITH SHACKLES, **WONDER WOMAN** CANNOT FEEL THE LIGHT TOUCH OF MYSTERIOUS FINGERS LACING HER ARM CHAINS TOGETHER WITH THE UNBREAKABLE GOLDEN LARIAT.

I'VE A HUNCH SOMEONE'S TRYING MONKEY BUSINESS— I WISH I WEREN'T BLINDFOLDED!

WONDER WOMAN IS LOWERED INTO THE TANK.

WOW! SHE SURE IS HEAVY!

THEY GOT A TON OF CHAINS ON HER.

4A

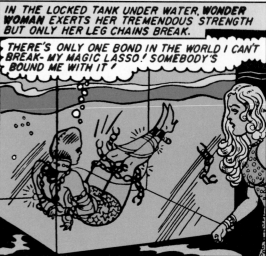

IN THE LOCKED TANK UNDER WATER, **WONDER WOMAN** EXERTS HER TREMENDOUS STRENGTH BUT ONLY HER LEG CHAINS BREAK.

THERE'S ONLY ONE BOND IN THE WORLD I CAN'T BREAK— MY MAGIC LASSO! SOMEBODY'S BOUND ME WITH IT!

TO FREE HER MOUTH, **WONDER WOMAN** BITES THROUGH THE TOUGH LEATHER OF THE BRANK.

THE FRENCH GIRLS WHO WORE THIS CONTRAPTION MUST HAVE HAD WEAK TEETH—IT'S EASY TO TEAR OFF!

NEXT THE AMAZON GIRL REMOVES HER TIBETAN COLLAR BY TIGHTENING HER POWERFUL NECK MUSCLES.

WONDER WOMAN TRIES TO SEIZE THE MAGIC LASSO IN HER TEETH, BUT WITH HER EYES STILL BOUND, THE GOLDEN CORD ELUDES HER.

WHERE **IS** THAT LASSO LOOP? I CAN'T HOLD MY BREATH FOREVER!

THE AUDIENCE, MEANWHILE, BECOMES FRANTIC WITH FEAR FOR ITS IDOL.

WONDER WOMAN CAN'T BREAK LOOSE!

SHE'LL DROWN!

OPEN THAT TANK!

SMASH THAT GLASS!

FREE **WONDER WOMAN**!

PRISCILLA RICH TRIES IN VAIN TO PREVENT SPECTATORS FROM INTERFERING.

OUT OF OUR WAY! RELEASE **WONDER WOMAN**!

PLEASE, EVERYBODY. KEEP BACK! YOU'LL SPOIL **WONDER WOMAN'S** ACT! SHE CAN BREAK ANY BONDS!

HA! EXCEPT THE MAGIC LASSO!

WONDER WOMAN, HER LUNGS BURSTING, TRIES AN ACROBATIC TRICK.

THAT'S BETTER—NOW I CAN SEE WHAT I'M DOING!

5A

GRIPPING THE MAGIC LASSO IN HER TEETH, **WONDER WOMAN** TEARS OFF THE GREEK FETTERS FROM HER ANKLES.

THE CLEVER AMAZON KNOTS THE SHORTENED LASSO ABOUT HER FOOT.

WITH A TERRIFIC KICK, **WONDER WOMAN** RIPS EVERY SHACKLE FROM HER ARMS, FREEING HERSELF COMPLETELY.

THE LASSO AND I WON'T BREAK— SO THE CHAINS HAVE TO!

SPRINGING FROM THE BOTTOM OF THE TANK, **WONDER WOMAN** HITS THE LID LIKE A DYNAMITE EXPLOSION.

WHEE-EE! THAT AIR PLEASES MY LUNGS—I'M NOT FISH ENOUGH TO ENJOY SUBMARINE BREATHING!

THE CROWD GOES WILD WITH DELIGHT.

SHE **DID** IT!

WONDER WOMAN BROKE ALL THE CHAINS!

SHE'S SAFE— THANK HEAVEN!

YAY-AY-AY- **WONDER WOMAN!**

PRISCILLA, TOO, RECEIVES CONGRATULATIONS.

YOU WERE RIGHT, MY DEAR—

WONDER WOMAN ESCAPED EASILY!

IT WAS JUST AN ACT— NO DANGER!

CLEVER OF YOU, PRIS, TO KEEP THEM FROM RESCUING **WONDER WOMAN!**

OF COURSE, I KNEW SHE WAS PERFECTLY SAFE!

6A

OH, DARLING! YOU DON'T KNOW HOW WORRIED I WAS ABOUT YOU!

OH, **REALLY?** YOU CONCEALED YOUR ANXIETY VERY WELL!

THAT BLONDE GIRL LOOKS INNOCENT AS AN ANGEL—BUT I WONDER! **SOMEBODY** TIED ME WITH THE MAGIC LASSO AND NEARLY MADE AN ANGEL OUT OF **ME!**

LATER, PRISCILLA MEETS COURTLEY DARLING IN THE THEATER OFFICE.

WELL-AREN'T WE GOING TO THE JUNGLE CLUB?

SURE-JUST AS SOON AS I COUNT OUR FUND FOR RESTORED COUNTRIES-WHEE-EE! *WONDER WO-MAN'S* RAISED THE TOTAL TO $100,000!

DO YOU THINK IT'S WISE TO PUT $100,000 IN THAT SAFE?

WHY NOT? I'LL TAKE IT OUT AND PUT IT IN THE BANK TOMORROW. MEANWHILE, NO ONE KNOWS IT'S HERE BUT YOU AND ME.

ACME SAFE COMPANY

I'VE BEEN LOOKING FOR YOU, MR. DARLING! THEY'RE GIVING ME A PARTY AT THE 400 CLUB—WON'T YOU JOIN US? YOU TOO, MISS RICH!

WHY-I'D LOVE IT!

BUT-BUT-COURTLEY, YOU WERE TAKING *ME* TO SUPPER-OH-H--NEVER MIND. SORRY, *WONDER WO-MAN*-I DON'T THINK I'D CARE TO GO—

ALONE IN HER ROOM, PRISCILLA'S PENT-UP PASSIONS BURST FORTH!

ARR-RR-RGH! I HATE THEM-THAT ARROGANT AMAZON, AND DARLING THE HYPOCRITE- I'D LIKE TO SCRATCH THEIR EYES OUT!

AS PRISCILLA SEATS HERSELF BEFORE HER MIRROR A CURIOUS THING HAPPENS. THE GIRL'S EVIL SELF, LONG REPRESSED, TAKES CONTROL OF HER BODY. PSYCHOLOGISTS USE MIRRORS IN THIS WAY TO DISCOVER PEOPLE'S REAL SELVES. THE MIRROR CRE-ATES IN PRIS-CILLA A DUAL PERSONALITY, LIKE DR. JEKYLL AND MR. HYDE.

HORRORS! THAT'S NOT ME — OR IS IT?

DON'T YOU KNOW ME? I AM THE *REAL* YOU- THE CHEETAH- A TREACHEROUS, RELENTLESS HUNTRESS!

TAKE THIS RUG OF CHEETAH SKIN AND MAKE YOUR-SELF A GARMENT. FROM NOW ON, WHEN I COM-MAND, YOU SHALL GO FORTH DRESSED LIKE YOUR *TRUE* SELF AND DO AS I COMMAND YOU---

UNDER CONTROL OF HER SECRET SELF, PRISCILLA COMPLETES HER CHEETAH COSTUME AT LIGHT-NING SPEED.

QUICK NOW, THE NIGHT PASSES! WHILE DARKNESS HIDES YOUR VILLAINY, TAKE YOUR REVENGE ON COURTLEY DARLING AND *WONDER WOMAN!*

SOON A LITHE, SLENDER FIGURE ENTERS A WINDOW OF THE DARKENED THEATER.

IN THE THEATER OFFICE STRANGE CAT-PAWS TWIRL THE DIALS OF THE SAFE DEXTEROUSLY.

REMOVING THE BAG OF MONEY, THE CHEETAH CLOSES THE SAFE AGAIN.

RCM SAFE

OUTSIDE THE 400 CLUB, CHEETAH WAITS WITH CAT-LIKE PATIENCE FOR **WONDER WOMAN**.

400 CLUB

AT LAST **WONDER WOMAN'S** GAY PARTY APPEARS.

AS FUND TREASURER I MUST GUARD OUR CHIEF TREASURE AND DRIVE YOU HOME, **WONDER WOMAN**!

I COULDN'T REFUSE SUCH A PRETTY SPEECH! YOU'RE ELECTED! SORRY, STEVE—SEE YOU LATER.

BRUSHING ME OFF AGAIN!

AS STEVE TALKS WITH **WONDER WOMAN**, CHEETAH SLIPS INTO THE BACK OF DARLING'S CAR.

I'LL SEE YOU SOONER THAN YOU EXPECT, STEVE!

HOW ABOUT TOMORROW MORNING?

8A

DARLING DRIVES **WONDER WOMAN** TO ARMY NURSES' QUARTERS.

YOU DON'T LIVE **HERE**, DO YOU?

MY REAL HOME IS A SECRET— I'M STAYING TONIGHT WITH MY FRIEND, DIANA PRINCE!

WATCHING OUTSIDE UNTIL A LIGHT GOES ON, CHEETAH CLIMBS THE FIRE ESCAPE TO DIANA'S WINDOW.

I'LL WAIT TILL THE LIGHT GOES OUT--WHEN SHE IS ASLEEP SHE'LL BE AN EASY VICTIM!

AS **WONDER WOMAN** FALLS ASLEEP, A SINISTER FIGURE BENDS OVER HER BED.

ARR-RR-GH! NOW FOR MY KILL!

BUT AS THE FATAL KNIFE DESCENDS, THE MALIGNANT CHEETAH CHANGES HER MIND.

WAIT! DEATH IS TOO GOOD FOR HER- I HAVE A BETTER PLAN!

BEFORE I KILL **WONDER WOMAN** I'LL DISGRACE HER! LET HER EXPLAIN TO THE POLICE HOW THIS CHARITY FUND MONEY GOT UNDER HER BED - ARR-RR-GH!

AT NINE THE FOLLOWING MORNING PRISCILLA RICH CALLS COURTLEY DARLING AT HIS HOME.

HELLO, COURTLEY! I CALLED YOU BECAUSE I'M WORRIED ABOUT THAT MONEY—IT SHOULD BE IN THE BANK!

OH BOTHER! WHY WAKE ME AT **THIS** HOUR? WELL, ALL RIGHT-- MEET ME AT THE MERCHANT'S TRUST AND YOU CAN WATCH ME DEPOSIT THE MONEY!

9A

PRISCILLA WAITS IMPATIENTLY IN THE BANK PRESIDENT'S OFFICE.

IT'S 10:30- WHAT'S KEEPING THE MAN? D'YOU SUPPOSE HE'S ABSCONDED WITH OUR MONEY?

OH NOW, MISS RICH! COURTLEY DARLING'S REPUTATION IS ABOVE SUSPICION!

AT LAST COURTLEY APPEARS, HAGGARD AND NERVOUS.

THE MONEY'S **GONE**—IT'S BEEN **STOLEN!**

WHAT? GREAT GODFREY—$100,000!

I TOLD YOU IT WASN'T SAFE! BUT OF COURSE, COURTLEY, YOU'LL MAKE GOOD THE MONEY FROM YOUR OWN FUNDS!

I CAN'T—I HAVEN'T GOT THAT MUCH!

THIS IS BAD—I'D BETTER CALL THE POLICE!

I'M DETECTIVE CASEY FROM HEADQUARTERS—YE'LL HAVE TA COME WID ME, MISTER! AND YOU, TOO, MISS RICH—THE INSPECTOR'LL WANT YER EVIDENCE!

VERY WELL—I'LL COME.

YOU CLAIM, MR. DARLING, THAT NOBODY BUT MISS RICH SAW YOU PUT THE $100,000 IN THAT SAFE?

THAT'S RIGHT.

DON'T LIE, COURTLEY! YOU KNOW **WONDER WOMAN** WAS THERE!

GET ME **WONDER WOMAN!**

CAN'T BE DID, CHIEF! **NOBODY** KNOWS WHERE THAT DAME HANGS OUT!

PERHAPS I CAN GIVE YOU A SUGGESTION, INSPECTOR! WHY NOT QUESTION **WONDER WOMAN'S** FRIEND, DIANA PRINCE?

HM—THAT'S AN IDEA! I'LL DO THAT! I'LL ASK MAJOR TREVOR TO COME OVER, ALSO—HE'S SUPPOSED TO BE THE STRONG GIRL'S WEAKNESS!

A FEW MINUTES LATER.

YES—I SAW **WONDER WOMAN** LAST NIGHT AT THE 400 CLUB. DARLING TOOK HER HOME.

I DROVE HER TO MISS PRINCE'S HOUSE.

WHY—ER—YES. SHE SPENT THE NIGHT WITH ME.

OKAY, CASEY—SEARCH MISS PRINCE'S ROOMS!

DETECTIVE CASEY RETURNS WITH THE MISSING MONEY!

HERE'S YER DOUGH, CHIEF! I FOUND IT UNDER A BED IN MISS PRINCE'S APARTMENT—

CAREFUL WITH IT, YOU DUMB CLUCK! WHAT DO YOU KNOW ABOUT THIS, MISS PRINCE?

NOT A SINGLE THING, INSPECTOR!

MISS PRINCE IS INNOCENT— SHE COULDN'T HAVE TAKEN THE MONEY. WONDER WOMAN SAW DARLING PUT THE MONEY AWAY— SHE COULD HAVE VAMPED HIM INTO OPENING THE SAFE— THOSE TWO, TOGETHER, STOLE OUR FUND!

SOUNDS POSSIBLE. LOCK HIM UP! AND FIND WONDER WOMAN!

DIANA, SLIPPING BEHIND A LARGE FILING CABINET, TRANSFORMS HERSELF INTO WONDER WOMAN.

I CAN'T SEE POOR COURTLEY SUFFER FOR THIS— I'M SURE HE'S INNOCENT.

HASTILY STUFFING DIANA'S COSTUME INTO THE EXTRA-SIZE HANDBAG SHE CARRIES FOR THIS PURPOSE, WONDER WOMAN ENTERS, APPARENTLY THROUGH THE DOOR.

I JUST SAW DIANA LEAVING— WHAT'S THE CONVENTION ALL ABOUT?

WONDER WOMAN!

THIS MONEY BELONGING TO THE RESTORED COUNTRIES FUND WAS FOUND IN MISS PRINCE'S ROOM WHERE YOU SPENT THE NIGHT— YOU AND DARLING ARE ACCUSED OF STEALING IT!

WHO ACCUSES US?

11 A

I ACCUSED YOU, MY DEAR— I HATED TO DO IT!

HM— I CAN IMAGINE HOW YOU SUFFERED! WELL— I'LL TAKE ALL THE BLAME—COURTLEY DARLING HAD NOTHING TO DO WITH IT!

WONDER WOMAN'S BEING GALLANT, INSPECTOR! SHE COULDN'T OPEN THE SAFE WITHOUT DARLING'S HELP!

THIS GAL CAN DO ANYTHING! CASEY, YOU'RE WASTING GOOD BRACELETS— SHE'LL BURST 'EM OFF WHENEVER SHE PLEASES.

OH, I'D LOVE TO WEAR HANDCUFFS!

STEVE PROTESTS IN VAIN.

DON'T BE A FOOL, DUGAN! **WONDER WOMAN** NEVER STOLE ANYTHING IN HER LIFE!

NO? WHAT ABOUT THIS? SHE SPENT THE NIGHT AT MISS PRINCE'S HOUSE, DIDN'T SHE? LOOKS LIKE SHE PINCHED A HANDFUL OF THE GAL'S CLOTHES WHEN SHE LEFT THERE TODAY — SHE MUST BE TURNING KLEPTOMANIAC!

STEVE AND ETTA CANDY CONSULT WITH **WONDER WOMAN** IN PRISON.

WOO WOO! YOU'RE IN A SPOT, KID — WE CAN'T FIND ANY CLUES!

WHOEVER DID THIS HATES BOTH DARLING AND ME. I'M WORRIED ABOUT COURTLEY!

I'M WORRIED ABOUT GETTING **YOU** OUT OF JAIL!

LATER **WONDER WOMAN** IS LED TO THE PRISON OFFICE.

A FRIEND HAS ARRANGED BAIL FOR YOU. YOU'RE TO GO TO THIS LAWYER'S OFFICE.

VERY WELL

STEVE MUST HAVE RETAINED A LAWYER FOR ME.

WONDER WOMAN SPEEDS TO THE ADDRESS GIVEN BUT FINDS HERSELF IN A WAREHOUSE DISTRICT.

THIS IS NO PLACE FOR A **LAWYER'S** OFFICE TO BE! COULD BE A TRAP — MAYBE THE REAL THIEF IS AT THE BOTTOM OF THIS — IF HE IS, I'LL PLAY WITH HIM RIGHT ON HIS OWN GROUND!

SKINS AND HIDES

GREAT HERA! 2 MILLION BUSHELS IS A LOT OF WHEAT! HUH — WHAT'S THAT? SOMEBODY'S IN TROUBLE — OR IS IT BAIT IN THE TRAP?

HELP — HELP!

CAPITAL GRAIN CO. STORAGE WAREHOUSE 2,000,000 BUSHELS CAPACITY

SOUNDS LIKE DARLING — I'LL SOON FIND OUT!

WINTER WHEAT   WINTER WHEAT

12 A

WHATEVER **WONDER WOMAN** EXPECTED, IT WAS NOT THE STRANGE SIGHT THAT MET HER ASTONISHED GAZE.

WHO — WHAT — A **HUMAN CHEETAH!**

UP WITH YOUR HANDS OR I'LL SHOOT THIS SNIVELING GUINEA PIG BENEATH MY FOOT — ARR-RR-GH!

HOW DO I KNOW YOU WON'T SHOOT DARLING ANYWAY, EVEN IF I OBEY YOU!

I SWEAR IT ON THE SACRED WORD OF A *CHEETAH*—HA! HA! GET UP THOSE STAIRS OR I'LL SHOOT HIM *NOW!*

AT THE TOP OF THE GRAIN ELEVATOR, THE CHEETAH DRIVES HER VICTIMS TO A CLOSED DOOR

SHOW YOUR STRENGTH, MUSCLE GIRL—BREAK THAT DOOR WITH YOUR SHOULDER, BUT DON'T LOWER YOUR HANDS.

WITH A CRASH THE DOOR FALLS INWARD AND *WONDER WOMAN* DISAPPEARS THROUGH THE OPENING.

ARR-RR-GH! I SAID I WOULDN'T SHOOT YOU—BUT YOU'RE GOING TO A FAR WORSE DEATH WITH YOUR *WONDER WOMAN!* HA!

SO YOU'D DEFY THE CHEETAH, MY FEMALE HERCULES! I DISGRACED YOU, SENT YOU TO PRISON—THEN BAILED YOU OUT FOR *THIS*— HA, HA, HA!

WONDER WOMAN AND DARLING FALL INTO A HUGE BIN OF WHEAT—THE SLIPPERY GRAIN IS LIKE QUICKSAND, SUCKING THEM EVER DEEPER INTO ITS DEPTHS.

HEL–UP! SPUT–T–PHLUP!

RELAX—TAKE A DEEP BREATH BEFORE YOU GO UNDER!

13A

EVEN AS SHE ADVISES HER COMPANION, THE TREACHEROUS SHIFTING GRAIN CLOSES OVER *WONDER WOMAN'S* HEAD.

ARR–RR–GH! HA! HA! HA!

STEVE AND ETTA, MEANWHILE, ARRIVE AT THE PRISON WITH A LAWYER TO ARRANGE **WONDER WOMAN'S** BAIL.

WONDER WOMAN? WHY, SHE'S BEEN BAILED OUT! AN UNKNOWN WOMAN FRIEND OF HERS SENT BAIL AND SHE WENT TO SEE A LAWYER AT THIS ADDRESS.

HUH? THIS ADDRESS IS A WAREHOUSE—SOMETHING FUNNY HERE—COME ON, ETTA!

QUICKLY REACHING THE WAREHOUSE, THE FRIENDS BEGIN A FUTILE SEARCH FOR **WONDER WOMAN.**

HEY, **WONDER WOMAN!** WHERE ARE YOU? IT'S **STEVE!**

WONDER WOMAN! COME ON, KID, ANSWER US!

WONDER WOMAN, MEANWHILE, TRIES A DESPERATE EXPERIMENT.

THERE'S ONLY ONE HOPE—BUT FIRST I'VE GOT TO GET MY FEET ON SOLID BOTTOM!

COMES THE CRUCIAL MOMENT! **WONDER WOMAN** CROUCHES ON THE BIN BOTTOM BENEATH TONS OF GRAIN AND WITH EVERY OUNCE OF HER TERRIFIC STRENGTH CATAPULTS HERSELF UPWARD.

WONDER WOMAN BREAKS THE SURFACE OF THE SUFFOCATING SEA OF WHEAT AND STILL SOARS UPWARD, THE FORCE OF HER MAGNIFICENT LEAP NOT YET SPENT.

HER FINGER TIPS TOUCH THE ROPE AND WITH A SUDDEN STRAIGHTENING OF HER BODY **WONDER WOMAN** SECURES A FIRM GRIP.

MADE IT—BUT BARELY! I'M OUT OF PRACTICE ON THIS HIGH JUMP!

14A

AS **WONDER WOMAN** SWINGS ON THE ROPE, STEVE AND ETTA FIND THE OPEN DOORWAY.

WOO WOO! WHAT A JUMP!

WE'RE HERE, **WONDER WOMAN!** TOSS YOUR DARLING TO US AND WE'LL CATCH HIM!

GOOD CATCH, PALS—THAT'S PLAYING THE GAME!

AS **WONDER WOMAN** LEAPS THROUGH THE DOORWAY TO JOIN HER FRIENDS, SMOKE AND FLAMES ENVELOP THE STAIRS.

THE CHEETAH HAS SET THE WAREHOUSE AFIRE—WHAT A SWEET GIRL **SHE** IS!

WOW! THOSE STAIRS ARE IMPOSSIBLE!

I GOT A ROPE, MAKE A HOLE IN THAT WALL, **WONDER WOMAN**, AND WE'LL SLIDE DOWN THE OUTSIDE!

THAT'S AN INSPIRATION, ETTA! HERE WE GO—

SECONDS LATER, THE THREE FRIENDS DESCEND ETTA'S FIRE ESCAPE TO SAFETY.

OH GIRL! IT'S GOING TO TAKE A LOTTA CANDY TO PUT ON WEIGHT AGAIN AFTER **THIS** EXERCISE!

CAPITAL GRAIN CO.

THERE SHE IS—YOUR "**CHEETAH**" SETTING THE ROOF AFIRE! AN AMAZING CREATURE—SEEMS SCARCELY HUMAN!

SHE IS SOME GIRL'S EVIL SELF, THE INCARNATION OF JEALOUSY AND HATE—

AND I THINK I KNOW THE CHEETAH'S TRUE IDENTITY!

SHE-TOLD ME-SHE STOLE THE MONEY—TO FRAME **US**!

PICKLE AND KRAUT HOUSE

THE CHEETAH, IN HER MOMENT OF IMAGINED TRIUMPH, SEES **WONDER WOMAN** ESCAPING FROM HER CLUTCHES AND FALLS, DEFEATED, INTO THE FIRE SHE KINDLED.

THE AMAZON DEFEATED ME BY MAGIC— SHE IS NOT HUMAN! IF SHE LIVES, I DIE! ARR-RR-RGH!

15A

WHO DO YOU SUPPOSE THE CHEETAH REALLY WAS?

I DON'T KNOW. IT MUST HAVE BEEN SOMEONE WHOM I MADE FEEL INFERIOR IN SOME WAY-- HM---

YOU'RE RIGHT, **WONDER WOMAN**—THE CHEETAH IS NOT AS DEAD AS YOU THINK— BE ON YOUR GUARD!

Wonder Woman

By Charles Moulton

FASTEST OF SAVAGE JUNGLE BEASTS IS THE CHEETAH! TIMED SCIENTIFICALLY, THIS SVELTE AND STREAMLINED LEOPARD SPEEDS GRACEFULLY ALONG AT 70 MILES AN HOUR! FAST AS HER FOUR-FOOTED NAMESAKE, CUNNING, CRUEL AND DEADLY, THE HUMAN CHEETAH MYSTERIOUSLY APPEARS AGAIN IN THE PATH OF WONDER WOMAN! CAN THE MIGHTY AMAZON MAIDEN MEET THIS MURDEROUS MENACE AND SAVE AN AMERICAN ARMY THREATENED BY THE CHEETAH'S EVIL MACHINATIONS? THIS TALE, THE ADVENTURE OF THE BEAUTY CLUB, WILL TELL!

COLONEL DARNELL CALLS A CONFERENCE OF HIS CHIEF ASSISTANTS AT ARMY INTELLIGENCE HEADQUARTERS.

I'VE GOT **BAD** NEWS FOR YOU—**VERY** BAD INDEED!

1B

HERE'S A REPORT FROM **NAVY HEADQUARTERS** IN THE PACIFIC. THEY SAY ALL KINDS OF MILITARY INFORMATION IS LEAKING THROUGH TO THE ENEMY!

BUT COLONEL, WHY BLAME THE **ARMY?** THERE COULD BE ANY **NUMBER** OF PLACES THAT INFORMATION COULD LEAK FROM—

NO- THE JAPANESE ARE GETTING FACTS KNOWN ONLY TO **ARMY** OFFICERS HERE IN WASHINGTON!

A PHONE CALL FOR DIANA INTERRUPTS THE CONFERENCE.

SAY, DIANA, ONLY A GIRL'S BEST FRIEND WILL TELL HER, BUT— YOU NEED A **BEAUTY** TREATMENT!

FOR HEAVEN'S SAKE, DIANA- STOP THAT CHATTER!

HA HA! BEAUTY BEFORE BATTLE! HO! HO!

WHO IS THIS SPEAKING?

I TOLD YOU- I'M YOUR BEST FRIEND! GO TO THE BEAUTY CLUB AFTER WORK— I'VE ARRANGED A TREATMENT FOR YOU— GOODBYE!

SORRY, COLONEL-THAT VOICE— I WANTED TO FIND OUT WHO IT WAS- MIGHT BE IMPORTANT!

IT'S MORE IMPORTANT TO A GIRL TO GET HER HAIR CURLED THAN TO WIN THE WAR!

HA! HA! YOU'RE RIGHT, STEVE!

DIANA SUMMONS THE CHIEF INFORMATION CLERK.

WHAT'S THIS "BEAUTY CLUB," AGNES?

IT'S A GLORIFIED BEAUTY SALON- BUT EXCLUSIVE! ONLY SELECTED CUSTOMERS ARE ADMITTED. MANY ARMY OFFICERS' WIVES GO THERE. THEY STAY WEEKS FOR SPECIAL BEAUTY TREATMENTS!

DIANA ACCEPTS THE MYSTERIOUS INVITATION TO VISIT THE BEAUTY CLUB.

I HAVE AN APPOINTMENT HERE!

IMPOSSIBLE! ONLY MEMBERS OF THE CLUB ARE ADMITTED!

BEAUTY CLUB

BEAUTY CLUB

2B

DIANA ELECTS HERSELF TO MEMBERSHIP.

CONSIDER ME A DISHONORARY MEMBER, BIG BOY!

I AM MISS PRINCE—I UNDERSTAND SOMEONE HAS ARRANGED A BEAUTY TREATMENT FOR ME.

OH RE-AHLLY, I CAWN'T IMAGINE WHO! WE MAKE APPOINTMENTS ONLY FOR MEMBAHS!

DIANA SEES AN ACQUAINTANCE.

I AM PRISCILLA RICH—REMEMBER? WE MET AT THE BENEFIT WHERE **WONDER WOMAN** PERFORMED!

WHY—ER—THAT'S RIGHT!

THEN PRISCILLA **WASN'T** THE CHEETAH AFTER ALL—THE CHEETAH WAS KILLED!

PRISCILLA HELPS DIANA.

THIS IS BRENDA WEST, OUR MOST POPULAR DEBUTANTE AND BEAUTY CLUB MANAGER. BRENDA, MISS PRINCE IS **MY** GUEST!

I'LL ARRANGE A BEAUTY TREATMENT IMMEDIATELY.

WILL YOU HAVE A MANICURE, PEDICURE, PERMANENT WAVE, BODY MASSAGE, BEAUTY PACK ON FACE AND LEGS—

WAIT A MINUTE! I DON'T NEED THAT MUCH RENOVATING—I ONLY WANT MY HAIR WASHED!

AS DIANA WAITS FOR THE SHAMPOO TO BEGIN SHE MAKES A MIRROR OF HER GLASSES BY SHADING THEM WITH HER HAND.

I'M CURIOUS TO SEE WHAT'S GOING ON BEHIND MY BACK!

3B

DIANA SEES A PECULIAR ACTION REFLECTED IN HER GLASSES.

SHE'S PUTTING A STENOGRAPHER IN THE NEXT ROOM—APPARENTLY THEY EXPECT TO MAKE ME TALK!

BRENDA CLAMPS DIANA'S HAIR IN A PECULIAR DEVICE WHICH FASTENS IT TO THE CHAIR.

OUCH—I CAN'T MOVE! THIS IS A NEW WAY OF BEING BOUND—BY MY HAIR!

PLEASE RELAX—THIS METHOD STIMULATES THE SCALP!

AS BRENDA LEAVES THE ROOM DIANA CHANGES HER COSTUME.

THIS CHAIR MAKES A COMFORTABLE PLACE TO TRANSFORM MYSELF INTO **WONDER WOMAN!**

RELYING UPON THE GREAT STRENGTH OF HER BEAUTIFUL HAIR, **WONDER WOMAN** SWINGS THE HEAVY CHAIR ATTACHED TO IT AGAINST THE WALL!

I'LL KILL TWO BIRDS WITH ONE CHAIR—FREE MYSELF AND BREAK INTO THE NEXT ROOM!

CRASH!

WONDER WOMAN BURSTS THROUGH THE WALL.

OH! IT MUST BE A BOMB!

BY SAPPHO'S STYLUS—A BLINDFOLDED STENOGRAPHER TAKING NOTES! BUT **WHAT** IS SHE RECORDING?

SWIFTLY THE GIRL RUNS TOWARD THE DOOR, BUT **WONDER WOMAN'S** MAGIC LASSO IS FASTER.

EE-EEK! LET ME GO!

DON'T BE SO RETIRING—I WANT TO CHAT WITH YOU!

I'M INTERESTED IN STENOGRAPHY— LET ME SEE YOUR NOTEBOOK!

OH—I CAN'T—BUT SOMETHING **COMPELS** ME!

THIS ISN'T SHORTHAND—BY JUPITER PLUVIUS! IT'S A WRITTEN RECORD OF **MY THOUGHTS** WHILE I SAT IN THAT HAIRDRESSER'S CHAIR NEXT DOOR!

4B

EXPLAIN THIS!

"ESP" MEANS "EXTRA-SENSORY PERCEPTION," THAT IS, MIND READING! DR. RHINE, A FAMOUS PSYCHOLOGIST AT DUKE UNIVERSITY, PROVED THAT CERTAIN "PSYCHIC" PEOPLE CAN READ OTHER PEOPLE'S THOUGHTS. THAT'S WHAT I DID - I READ YOUR MIND!

REMARKABLE! YOU SAT HERE, BLINDFOLDED, AND READ MY PRIVATE THOUGHTS - MY INNER-MOST SE-CRETS!

Y-YES- FORGIVE ME! I HAD TO DO IT- THEY **MADE** ME! I'LL TELL YOU WHAT HAPPENED -

GAIL YOUNG TELLS HER STORY: "MY FRIEND PRISCILLA RICH HEARD ABOUT MY E.S.P. ABILITY AND-

OH GAIL, WON'T YOU DO SOME MIND-READING AT MY PARTY, TONIGHT?

WHY- I'LL TRY!

"FIRST, I TOLD THEM WHAT CARDS THEY WERE HOLDING.

YOU HOLD 4 ACES AND A JOKER!

HOW WONDERFUL-YOU ARE RIGHT **EVERY** TIME!

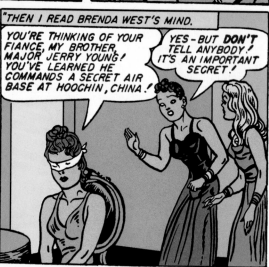

"THEN I READ BRENDA WEST'S MIND.

YOU'RE THINKING OF YOUR FIANCÉ, MY BROTHER, MAJOR JERRY YOUNG! YOU'VE LEARNED HE COMMANDS A SECRET AIR BASE AT HOOCHIN, CHINA!

YES- BUT **DON'T** TELL ANYBODY! IT'S AN IMPORTANT SECRET!

"SUDDENLY I READ **HORRIBLE** IDEAS IN SOME GIRL'S MIND...

ARRR-GG GGH.! BRENDA HAS TAKEN JERRY AWAY FROM ME! AND GAIL, THE FOOL, SHOWING OFF WITH HER MIND READING! I HATE THEM BOTH- I'LL **TORTURE** THEM- **KILL** THEM!

5B

"I WAS BADLY FRIGHTENED- I COULD DO NO MORE MIND READING.

SOMEONE IN THIS ROOM IS PLANNING MURDER! I'M GOING TO GET OUT OF HERE!

OH DARL-ING, YOU'RE HYSTERICAL! I'LL DRIVE YOU HOME.

"WE GOT INTO BRENDA'S CAR WHEN SUDDENLY SOMETHING HIT US FROM BEHIND, KNOCKING US BOTH UNCONSCIOUS.

EEK-UNF!

UG-UH!

ARR-GGH! THE CHEETAH CLAIMS HER PREY!

"WE WOKE UP IN A CAGE, WEARING THE STRANGEST COSTUMES.

WHAT-WHAT HAPPENED TO US! HA HA! YOU LOOK LIKE A ZEBRA!

HA HA YOURSELF! WHILE WE WERE UNCONSCIOUS SOME COMEDIAN DRESSED US IN ZEBRA SKINS AND CHAINS.

"A HARSH, RASPING VOICE ADDRESSED US—IT WAS THE CHEETAH.

I'M THE COMEDIAN WHO DESIGNED YOUR COSTUMES, SLAVES, AND MY COMEDY IS VERY SERIOUS! ZEBRAS ARE THE CHEETAH'S FAVORITE PREY—YOU SHOULD FEEL FLATTERED!

I SHALL USE YOU SLAVES TO GAIN SECRET POWER OVER WOMEN I ENVY! BRENDA WILL LURE THESE WOMEN TO MY BEAUTY CLUB. GAIL WILL READ THEIR MINDS AND DISCOVER THEIR PERSONAL SECRETS!

WE WON'T DO IT!

YOU WILL SUBMIT TO MY ORDERS OR I'LL RUIN JERRY! I'LL INFORM JAPS OF THE SECRET AIR BASE AT HOOCHIN AND I'LL TELL THE ARMY THAT JERRY BETRAYED THEM!

NO, NO! WE'LL DO ANYTHING TO SAVE JERRY!

6B

"SO WE OBEY HER! EVERY DAY WE ARE BROUGHT FROM THE CHEETAH'S DEN TO THE BEAUTY CLUB, BOUND AND BLINDFOLDED."

REMEMBER—IF YOU BETRAY ME OR TRY TO ESCAPE, IT'LL BE TOO BAD FOR MAJOR JERRY YOUNG!

THE CHEETAH'S ALIVE AFTER ALL! YOU'VE PUT HUNDREDS OF WOMEN INTO HER POWER BY READING THEIR THOUGHTS— SHE HAS GIVEN MILITARY INFORMATION *YOU* OBTAINED FROM ARMY WIVES, TO THE ENEMY!

SHE PROMISED NOT TO! I-I-

I'LL DESTROY THIS WRITTEN RECORD OF MY DOUBLE IDENTITY— THEN I'LL DEAL WITH THIS GIRL.

BUT WHILE *WONDER WOMAN* IS INTENT UPON BURNING GAIL'S NOTEBOOK, THE MAGIC LASSO LOOSENS AND —

AS GAIL LEAPS TOWARD FREEDOM, THE DOOR OPENS.

ARR-G G-GGH!

EE-EEK! IT'S THE *CHEETAH!*

DRAGGING HER VICTIM FROM THE ROOM, THE CHEETAH BOLTS THE DOOR.

SO YOU'VE BETRAYED ME TO *WONDER WOMAN*— YOU'LL REGRET IT, YOU STUPID SLAVE!

HELP! SAVE ME, *WONDER WOMAN!*

BUT THE SPLIT SECOND THAT IT TAKES *WONDER WOMAN* TO SMASH THE BOLTED DOOR GIVES THE CHEETAH A HEAD START.

HA HA! *WONDER WOMAN* WILL NEVER CATCH THE CHEETAH!

7B

THE CHEETAH DISAPPEARS THROUGH A SECRET PASSAGE.

SHE'S GONE! I HATE TO LEAVE GAIL CAPTIVE-BUT IF THE CHEETAH TOLD THE JAPS ABOUT OUR SECRET AIR BASE I MUST FLY TO CHINA IMMEDIATELY!

BOARDING HER INVISIBLE AMAZON PLANE WITH STEVE, **WONDER WOMAN** PAUSES TO SEND A MENTAL RADIO MESSAGE.

CALL ETTA CANDY! THE CHEETAH'S ALIVE- DON'T KNOW HER REAL IDENTITY! JOIN THE BEAUTY CLUB AND FREE GAIL AND BRENDA!

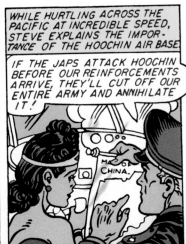

WHILE HURTLING ACROSS THE PACIFIC AT INCREDIBLE SPEED, STEVE EXPLAINS THE IMPORTANCE OF THE HOOCHIN AIR BASE.

IF THE JAPS ATTACK HOOCHIN BEFORE OUR REINFORCEMENTS ARRIVE, THEY'LL CUT OFF OUR ENTIRE ARMY AND ANNIHILATE IT!

MAP OF CHINA.

I'LL HAVE TO PERSUADE THE JAPS **NOT** TO ATTACK HOOCHIN!

HA HA! IMPOSSIBLE! EVEN **YOU** CAN'T PERFORM SUCH MIRACLES!

WE'RE NEARING JAP HEADQUARTERS- I'LL BAIL OUT AND SWIM ASHORE. YOU FLY ON TO HOOCHIN AND WARN MAJOR YOUNG- IF I NEED YOU I'LL CALL ON THE MENTAL RADIO.

THE JAP FLEET'S BELOW- YOU'LL NEVER LAND ALIVE!

AS **WONDER WOMAN** DROPS FROM THE CLOUDS, JAPANESE BATTLE SHIPS OPEN FIRE.

STEVE MAY BE RIGHT, AT THAT! IF A SHELL HITS MY CHUTE—

I COULDN'T STOP **THAT** WITH MY BRACELETS! HERE GOES FOR THE HIGHEST DIVE I EVER MADE!

BANG!

8B

WONDER WOMAN HITS THE WATER NEAR AN ENEMY DREADNAUGHT.

IS-SS END OF YONKEE DAREDEVIL!

YESS-SS- BUT **HE** LOOKED LIKE A WOMAN!

WONDER WOMAN PLUNGES DEEP.

IF **THAT** DIDN'T KNOCK THE BREATH OUT OF ME, NOTHING EVER WILL!

AS THE AMAZON GIRL RISES AGAIN TOWARD THE SURFACE —

OUCH! I HIT THE CEILING!

I'LL JUST TIP THIS DREADNAUGHT OVER— IT'LL BE FUN TO SURPRISE THE NIPS!

YIELDING TO **WONDER WOMAN'S** SUBMARINE PRESSURE, THE HUGE SHIP ROLLS OVER.

EE-YOU!

YA-YA!

HELP! AI-YEE!

WHAT MAKES OUR SHIP CAPS-SIZE?

SEA DEVILS ANGRY— MAYBE PUT VOLCANO UNDER SHIP!

WHILE THE AMAZON PRINCESS, LAUGHING, SWIMS SWIFTLY UNDER WATER TO SHORE.

HA HA! THIS'LL GIVE THEM SOMETHING TO THINK ABOUT WHILE I REACH JAPANESE ARMY HEADQUARTERS.

LANDING ON THE BEACH, **WONDER WOMAN** FINDS A TANK WHOSE CREW IS BUSY WATCHING THE SEA SPECTACLE.

THESE JAP BOYS AREN'T ATTENDING TO BUSINESS. **SOMEBODY** SHOULD BE RUNNING THIS TANK, SO I'D BETTER TAKE OVER!

9B

YOU'LL GET A BETTER VIEW NEARER THE WATER, BOYS! AND THANKS FOR THE TANK!

WONDER WOMAN *IN HER NIPPONESE CHARIOT REACHES ARMY HEADQUARTERS BEFORE BEING CHALLENGED.*

HALT! WHO GOES?

I AM CALLED **WONDER WOMAN.** TAKE ME PRISONER TO YOUR EXALTED COMMANDER IN CHIEF AND YOU WILL GAIN MUCH FACE!

TAKE MY PLACE, ITCHI, UNTIL I RETURN!

YOU ALWAYS GET THE PLEASANT TASKS!

GENERAL SNIDU, COMMANDER IN CHIEF OF ALL JAPANESE FORCES IN CHINA, IS HOLDING AN IMPORTANT STAFF CONFERENCE.

AHA! THEY'RE DISCUSSING OUR SECRET AIRBASE—THE CHEETAH TOLD THEM.

IS **WONDER WOMAN.**

I'D BETTER PRETEND NOT TO KNOW JAPANESE—

SORRY, GENERAL, I CAN'T UNDERSTAND YOU—MIND SPEAKING ENGLISH?

SO THE GR-REAT **WONDER WOMAN** IS-SS PRIS-SONER AT LAS-ST! WILL BE PLEAS-SURE TO S-SEE YOU DIE S-SSLOWLY!

WILL YOU FREE ME IF I GIVE YOU IMPORTANT SECRET INFORMATION?

10B

YOU MUS-ST TELL ANYWAY OR WE **MAKE** YOU SPEAK!

WELL- ER- I'LL TELL- I DON'T WANT TO BE TORTURED! THE AMERICANS HAVE A SECRET AIR BASE AT HOOCHIN!

BAH! YOUR INFORMATION IS-SS WORTHLESS-SS— WE KNOW THAT ALREADY!

WONDER WOMAN, USING VENTRILOQUISM, MAKES COLONEL CHINDA APPEAR TO SPEAK.

彼は悪い BEWARE, GENERAL! THIS INFORMATION IS FALSE! WONDER WOMAN WOULD NEVER REVEAL IT UNLESS SHE WISHED TO DECEIVE US!

彼は悪い YOU'RE A FOOL! WHAT YOU SAY IS NONSENSE!

悪い BUT— BUT I DIDN'T SAY ANYTHING!

彼悪 CHINDA IS RIGHT, GENERAL. IT'S ALL A TRICK OF WONDER WOMAN'S! THERE IS NO AMERICAN AIR BASE AT HOOCHIN!

THE GENERAL IS SHOUTED DOWN—BY WONDER WOMAN'S VENTRILOQUISM.

BUT THE CHEETAH TOLD OUR AGENTS—

IT'S A LIE!

THE CHEETAH CHEATED!

IT'S A TRICK!

THERE IS NO SECRET AIRBASE!

WONDER WOMAN'S FOOLING US!

GENERAL SNIDU CANCELS HIS ORDERS FOR AN ATTACK ON HOOCHIN.

BUT I SAID—

I DIDN'T SAY—

YOU SAID—

WHO SAID WHAT?

YOU'RE ALL FOOLS—I NEED A NEW STAFF. WE WILL HAVE TO POSTPONE THE ATTACK!!

YOU S-SHALL PAY FOR THIS-SS WONDER WOMAN! YOU S-SHALL DIE THE DEATH OF A THOUSAND CUTS!

AREN'T YOU THE LITTLE CUT-UP, GENERAL!

11B

WHILE THE JAPS PREPARE A HORRIBLE DEATH FOR THEIR PRISONER, WONDER WOMAN SENDS A MENTAL RADIO BEAM FOR STEVE TO FOLLOW.

STEVE! FOLLOW MY MENTAL RADIO BEAM! FLY TO JAP HEADQUARTERS— I'LL BE ON AIRDROME ROOF—

AS THE JAPANESE OFFICERS MOVE FORWARD WITH GLITTERING SWORDS, THE AMAZON MAIDEN BURSTS HER BONDS.

ALL READY FOR THE CARVING, EH, BOYS? BUT THIS CHICKEN WON'T STAY TRUSSED!

CUT HER DOWN!

KILL HER!

YE-OU! SHE ISS DEVIL-STEEL DOES-SS NOT HARM HER!

THIS GAME IS FUN BUT I'VE GOT A DATE ON THE ROOF! HOW'LL I GET UP THERE?

YOU BOYS MUST HELP ME REACH THE ROOF- UP YOU GO, GENERAL!

AW-WK!

AS THE GENERAL CLINGS TO THE ROOF GIRDERS, THE NEXT JAP, HEAVED UPWARD BY **WONDER WOMAN,** GRASPS HIS ANKLES.

MY HUMAN LADDER IS LONG ENOUGH FOR ME TO REACH THE ROOF.

THE AMAZON GIRL SWIFTLY ASCENDS HER JAPANESE CHAIN.

PLEAS-SS GO EAS-SY!

12 B

REACHING THE AIRDROME GIRDERS, THE GIRL FROM AMAZONIA BREAKS A HOLE IN THE ROOF.

I'M RIGHT ON THE BEAM- I HOPE STEVE IS TOO!

AS STEVE WITH PERFECT TIMING GLIDES OVER THE AIRDROME ROOF, **WONDER WOMAN** MAKES A DIZZY LEAP TO THE LADDER OF HER INVISIBLE PLANE.

BYE-BYE, NIPPIES! I **WON'T** BE SEEIN' YOU IN HOOCHIN'!

YOUR SMILE TELLS ME YOU SUCCEEDED, BEAUTIFUL! JERRY YOUNG SAYS IF YOU CAN STALL THE NIP ATTACK 24 HOURS YOU'LL SAVE 150,000 MEN!

THEY'RE SAVED THEN—IT'LL BE A WEEK BEFORE THOSE JAPS DISCOVER WHAT HAPPENED TO THEM!

LOOK, STEVE! THERE'S ETTA ON THE MENTAL RADIO!

CALLING **WONDER WOMAN**—WOO WOO! WHAT A HIGH HAT JOINT THAT BEAUTY CLUB IS! PRISSIE RICH GOT US IN. WE COULDN'T FIND GAIL OR BRENDA. PRISCILLA DISAPPEARED. TOO!

PRISSIE'S ROOM WAS LOCKED, BABY! DID I BUST THAT DOOR DOWN—JUST LIKE YOU, **WONDER WOMAN**! GAIL AND BRENDA WERE THERE—BOUND AND GAGGED! I SAVED 'EM—GAIL SAID TO TELL YOU YOUR SECRET IS SAFE, WHATEVER THAT IS!

AS **WONDER WOMAN** IS ABOUT TO SWITCH OFF HER MENTAL RADIO, THE WEIRD SCREAM OF A HUNTING LEOPARD RINGS OUT.

ARR-RGG-GGH!

LOOK—THE CHEETAH! SHE'S LEARNED TO SEND MENTAL MESSAGES!

I WARN YOU, **WONDER WOMAN**! KEEP OUT OF MY AFFAIRS! YOU CANNOT DESTROY ME—THE SKIN I WEAR PRESERVES ME FROM FIRE—MY AGILITY DEFEATS YOUR STRENGTH! NEXT TIME WE MEET—BEWARE!

13B

THIS IS **MY** ANSWER TO ANYBODY WHO THREATENS **YOU**!

BULLETS NEVER SOLVED A HUMAN PROBLEM YET! THE CHEETAH IS ONLY **HALF** OF SOME GIRL'S PERSONALITY—I'VE GOT TO FIND THE OTHER HALF AND PUT THEM TOGETHER PROPERLY!

SO ONCE MORE **WONDER WOMAN** SETS OUT TO DO AN IMPOSSIBLE TASK..

Wonder Woman

By Charles Moulton

REG U S PAT OFF

SUBTLE AND DEVIOUS ARE THE PLOTS OF THAT LEAPING LEOPARD GIRL, THE CHEETAH! HER DUAL PERSONALITIES DISGUISE THEMSELVES AS A THIRD PERSON TO THREATEN GIRLS OF TWO WORLDS WITH DIRE DANGER, AS PRISONERS TRAINED BY THE AMAZONS TEST THEIR STRENGTH AND SKILL AGAINST WOMAN CHAMPIONS OF THE WORLD OF MEN! FOR THE FIRST TIME IN HISTORY THAT SECRET ISLE OF PARADISE, WHERE BEAUTIFUL WOMEN REIGN SUPREME, IS INVADED BY A CONQUEROR OF FIENDISH CLEVERNESS AND DARING — THE CHEETAH! WONDER WOMAN'S MOTHER AND HOMELAND ARE AT STAKE IN THIS EPISODE CALLED "THE CONQUEST OF PARADISE."

SGT. DOOT, A FAMOUS PHYSICAL TRAINING EXPERT, NOW IN THE ARMY, CALLS AT STEVE'S OFFICE.

WONDER WOMAN'S CAUSING ME A LOT OF TROUBLE!

HOW THE DEUCE CAN SHE CAUSE YOU TROUBLE, SERGEANT?

HARRY G PETER

WELL, IT'S LIKE THIS. **WONDER WOMAN PRETENDS** TO HAVE TREMENDOUS STRENGTH, DEVELOPED BY AMAZON TRAINING. ALL RIGHT, SAYS THE GENERAL TO ME, CHANGE YOUR SYSTEM AND TRAIN OUR SOLDIERS LIKE **WONDER WOMAN!** WHY DON'T YOU?

BECAUSE **WONDER WOMAN'S** A FAKE! SHE MAY BE STRONG, FOR A GIRL, BUT HER STUNTS ARE ALL PHONY. LIKE THIS ONE, FOR INSTANCE—

HA HA! NO FAKE ABOUT THIS— I SAW HER PERFORMANCE MYSELF! AND I'VE SEEN HER DO HARDER THINGS—LIFT ELEPHANTS, STOP LOCOMOTIVES, KNOCK OUT STRONG MEN—

NO WOMAN ALIVE CAN KNOCK **ME** OUT!

EXCUSING HERSELF, DIANA RETIRES TO HER OFFICE AND HASTILY TRANSFORMS HERSELF TO **WONDER WOMAN.**

SO I'M A FAKE, AM I? JUST LIKE A **MAN** TO THINK NO GIRL CAN BE STRONG—I'LL SHOW HIM!

I JUST DROPPED IN TO SAY HELLO!

SWELL, YOU CAME AT JUST THE RIGHT MOMENT! SERGEANT DOOT, HERE, DOUBTS YOUR STRENGTH.

YOU MAY BE STRONG FOR A GIRL BUT— OUCH—OW-W-W! LET GO MY HAND!

WHAT'S THE MATTER, SERGEANT? SURELY A **GIRL'S** GRIP COULDN'T HURT YOU!

2C.

THAT'S NOT STRENGTH—IT'S SOME TRICK JIU JITSU GRIP!

YOU DON'T MEAN SERGEANT, THAT I SQUEEZED YOUR HAND TOO HARD?

SERGEANT DOOT SEEMED TO THINK THIS PIANO STUNT OF YOURS WAS FAKED!

REALLY? I'M SORRY I HAVE NO PIANO HERE BUT IF YOU'LL LEND ME YOUR DESK—

I'LL SHOW THE SERGEANT HOW EASY IT IS TO BALANCE LITTLE BITS OF FURNITURE ON THE PALM!

YE GODS! SHE'S A SECOND SANDOW!

SANDOW—SOUNDS LIKE A BALL PLAYER— OH, YOU MEAN YOU WANT TO PLAY BALL? HERE YOU ARE—CATCH!

I'M **SO** SORRY, DOOTY—I THOUGHT YOU WERE READY FOR MY THROW!

PUT ME DOWN YOU-YOU-LOR' LOVE ME! YOU HAVE MUSCLES LIKE HERCULES—YOU'RE A FREAK OF NATURE!

THERE'S NOTHING EXTRAORDINARY ABOUT MY MUSCLES—I'VE LEARNED TO PUT MORE MENTAL FORCE INTO THEM THROUGH YEARS OF AMAZON TRAINING.

I DON'T BELIEVE THAT—YOU'VE GOT **MORE** MUSCLE THAN A NORMAL PERSON!

3 C.

MEASURE MY LEG AND ARM MUSCLES—YOU'LL FIND THEY'RE NO BIGGER THAN A NORMAL GIRL'S SHOULD BE!

THAT'S RIGHT—YOU HAVE PERFECT "MODERN VENUS" MEASUREMENTS! AMAZING!

I CAN PROVE THAT AMAZON TRAINING MAKES **ANY** GIRL POWERFUL! WE'RE TRAINING AVERAGE AMERICAN GIRLS NOW IN PARADISE ISLAND. ALREADY THEY'RE STRONGER THAN YOUR WOMAN CHAMPIONS!

NONSENSE! I'LL PICK A TEAM THAT'LL BEAT YOUR GIRLS ALL HOLLOW!

AND SO IT HAPPENS THAT SERGEANT DOOT SELECTS A TEAM OF CHAMPION WOMAN ATHLETES TO COMPETE AGAINST PAULA'S FORMER SLAVE GIRLS AT PARADISE ISLAND.

I APPOINT YOU CAPTAIN, BERTA—I'M SELECTING GIRLS WHO HOLD WORLD'S RECORDS IN VARIOUS EVENTS!

AT LAST THE ALL-CHAMP TEAM IS CHOSEN AND WONDER WOMAN'S PLANE WAITS TO CARRY THE GIRLS TO PARADISE ISLAND.

POLE VAULT CHAMPION—OLYMPIC SWIMMING CHAMP—CHAMPION WEIGHT LIFTER—

THEY'RE HUSKY GIRLS, PAULA!

HEY, PAULA. THEY'RE ALL ON BOARD EXCEPT KAY CARLTON, THE HIGH HURDLES CHAMP. SHE'S MISSING!

WE'LL HAVE TO WAIT FOR HER—WONDER WOMAN'S PLANE IS THE ONLY TRANSPORTATION TO PARADISE ISLAND!

KAY, MEANWHILE, IS FORCIBLY DETAINED.

ARR-RR-GH!

THE CHEETAH! UGH!

AFTER FORCING KAY TO REMOVE HER OUTER CLOTHING, THE CHEETAH GAGS AND BINDS HER VICTIM.

YOUR CLOTHES WILL FIT ME NICELY—INCLUDING THE SHOES. SHOES ARE IMPORTANT FOR US HURDLERS, EH? HA HA HA!

THE CHEETAH DISGUISES HERSELF CLEVERLY TO LOOK LIKE KAY.

NOT BAD! NOT EVEN YOUR MOTHER COULD TELL US APART!

4C.

THE CHEETAH COMPELS KAY TO SWALLOW A POWERFUL DRUG, WHICH CAUSES LOSS OF MEMORY.

I KNOW YOU! YOU'RE ULP-GULP!

IN 5 MINUTES YOU WON'T REMEMBER ME—YOU WON'T REMEMBER ANYTHING! YOUR MEMORY WILL BE A BLANK!

THE FALSE "KAY" REACHES **WONDER WOMAN'S** PLANE AS ETTA LOSES PATIENCE.

CANDY'S GONE— JUMPIN' JIMCRACKS, WHERE'S THAT HURDLER?

SORRY I'M LATE—HAD TO TIE UP SOME LOOSE ENDS—

AS **WONDER WOMAN'S** SILENT, INVISIBLE PLANE SPEEDS OVER FAR SEAS, AN UNINVITED GUEST CREEPS OUT OF HIDING.

GAIL YOUNG! WHAT ARE **YOU** DOING HERE?

I—I KNOW IT SOUNDS FUNNY— BUT I CAME TO **PROTECT** YOU!

THE CHEETAH'S AFTER YOU! I DON'T KNOW **WHERE** SHE IS, BUT WHILE I WAS PRACTICING E.S.P.—THAT IS, MIND READING—I PICKED UP SOME OF THE CHEETAH'S THOUGHTS! SHE'S FOLLOWING YOU TO PARADISE ISLAND!

IMPOSSIBLE!

THE CHEETAH KNOWS HOW TO GET THERE—THE ONLY WAY TO CATCH HER IS BY MIND READING!

THAT'S A NEW DETECTIVE METHOD—BUT BE CAREFUL **SHE** DOESN'T CATCH **YOU!**

MALA AND HER CHARGES GREET THEIR VISITORS ON PARADISE ISLAND.

HOLA, PRINCESS!

HOLA, PAULA!

APHRODITE WITH YOU. WELCOME, GIRLS!

DO ALL YOU GIRLS HAVE TO WEAR CHAINS?

OH YES, WE LOVE IT! CHAINS ARE PART OF OUR TRAINING—CARRYING THEM CONSTANTLY MAKES US STRONGER!

5C.

QUEEN HIPPOLYTE AND THE PRINCESS WATCH THE CONTESTANTS WARMING UP.

THESE ATHLETES YOU HAVE BROUGHT ARE VERY PRETTY.

YES, MOTHER—ATHLETICS ARE MAKING GIRLS OF THE MEN'S WORLD MORE BEAUTIFUL!

THE QUEEN OPENS THE ATHLETIC MEET BETWEEN GIRLS OF TWO WORLDS.

PAULA WILL HEAD THE PRISONER'S TEAM. THIS CONTEST WILL DECIDE WHETHER AMAZON TRAINING MAKES ORDINARY GIRLS STRONGER THAN MAN'S WORLD CHAMPIONS! MAY THE BEST GIRLS WIN!

BERTA HALE, CAPTAIN OF THE CHAMPS, COMPLETES A "CLEAN AND JERK" WEIGHT LIFT OF 314 POUNDS.

GOOD WORK, BERTA!

ATTA GIRL!

YOU'VE BEATEN THE WORLD'S RECORD FOR WOMEN!

BUT CLAUDIA, FEATHERWEIGHT PRISONER, LIFTS 500 POUNDS WITH ONE HAND.

AMAZING! HOW D'YOU DO IT?

THIS IS EASY! OUR AMAZON MISTRESSES TEACH US THAT EVERY GIRL HAS GREAT STRENGTH AND THEY MAKE US USE IT!

ANOTHER GIRL PRISONER, ERNA, CLEARS THE POLE VAULT BAR AT 31 FEET.

I COULD GO HIGHER, BUT I DON'T WANT TO MAKE OUR VISITORS FEEL EMBARRASSED!

6C.

THE POLE VAULTER OF THE ALL-CHAMP GIRLS GIVES UP.

WHAT'S THE USE? YOU ARE SO SUPERIOR THERE'S NO CONTEST.

BUT IN THE RUNNING RACES PAULA HANDICAPS HER TEAM.

PLEASE TAKE OFF OUR ANKLE CHAINS, CAPTAIN PAULA!

NO, YOU MUST WEAR THEM! I'LL ENTER THIS RACE MYSELF AND SHARE YOUR HANDICAP!

ONLY PAULA HAS LEARNED TO ADAPT HER STRIDE TO THE LENGTH OF HER CHAINS.

THIS IS HARDER THAN I THOUGHT. BUT IT'LL ENCOURAGE OUR VISITORS!

MEANWHILE, THE GIRL WHO CALLS HERSELF KAY CARLTON WATCHES THE EASY VICTORIES OF THE PRISONER TEAM WITH INCREASING FURY.

ARR-RGH! THESE GIRLS IN CHAINS ARE MAKING FOOLS OF US! IT'S SOME TRICK OF WONDER WOMAN'S!

AS WONDER WOMAN CONGRATULATES PAULA, THE CHEETAH'S HATRED BOILS OVER.

WELL DONE, PAULA! IT'S HARD WORK TO RUN IN CHAINS!

BAH! I CAN BEAT THIS PAULA WITHOUT ANY HANDICAP—I'LL SHOW HER!

IF YOU'LL TAKE THOSE STUPID CHAINS OFF I'LL CHALLENGE YOU TO ANY SORT OF RACE YOU CHOOSE!

VERY WELL. I'LL REMOVE THE CHAINS AND RACE YOU OVER HUMAN HURDLES, AMAZON STYLE!

THE PRINCESS EXPLAINS "HUMAN HURDLES" TO THE VISITORS.

IN THIS AMAZON GAME EACH RUNNER MUST LEAP OVER GIRLS WHO STEP UNEXPECTEDLY INTO THE RUNNER'S PATH.

KAY AND PAULA CLEAR THEIR FIRST LIVING HURDLES.

7C.

TWO GIRLS IN QUICK SUCCESSION STEP INTO PAULA'S PATH, GIVING KAY A CHANCE TO GET AHEAD.

KAY IS FAST—I'LL HAVE TO RUN MY HARDEST TO CATCH UP WITH HER!

BUT APHRODITE'S TRAINING GIVES PAULA ALMOST AMAZON SPEED. KAY SEES HER RIVAL CLOSE BEHIND AS SHE APPROACHES A HURDLE.

SHE'S FASTER THAN I AM! I MUST **STOP** HER!

AS KAY LEAPS HER HUMAN HURDLE, A DEFT FLICK OF THE FOOT TOPPLES THE GIRL FORWARD INTO PAULA'S PATH.

AH-AAH! LOOK OUT!

THE FALLING "HURDLE" TRIPS PAULA NEATLY.

UNNF!

KAY WINS THE RACE AMID HER TEAMMATES' CHEERS.

HOORAY FOR KAY! HERE'S **ONE** RACE WE'VE WON!

BUT THE "HURDLE" GIRL WHO WAS PUSHED BY KAY REPORTS TO THE JUDGES.

KAY'S FOOT PUSHED ME DOWN AS SHE JUMPED OVER ME! THAT DISQUALIFIES HER - SHE KNOCKED OVER A HURDLE!

SUMMON THE CONTESTANTS FOR A HEARING!

MY FOOT NEVER **TOUCHED** THIS GIRL!

YOU **KNOW** YOU'RE LYING!

KAY MADE MARVELOUS TIME - PLEASE DON'T DISQUALIFY HER!

SINCE PAULA ASKS IT -

WE'LL LET THE RACE STAND!

THEY'RE ALL SO SUPERIOR, THESE AMAZONS, SO CONDESCENDING! THEY **GAVE** ME THE RACE-HOW I HATE THEM! I'LL FIND THE SOURCE OF AMAZON POWER AND DESTROY IT!

8C.

LATER THE FALSE KAY BEGINS HER SEARCH FOR THE AMAZONS' STRENGTH SECRET

YOUR STRENGTH IS MARVELOUS, **WONDER WOMAN!** DO YOU AMAZONS EAT SPECIAL FOOD?

NO-WE EAT A BALANCED DIET WITH PLENTY OF VITAMINS.

THESE BRACELETS-YOU ALL WEAR THEM! DO **THEY** GIVE YOU STRENGTH?

NO-OUR BRACELETS **BIND** OUR STRENGTH TO THE SERVICE OF LOVE AND BEAUTY, AND THUS PROTECT US FROM EVIL!

I HAVE HEARD THAT IF CHAINS ARE WELDED TO AMAZON BRACELETS YOU LOSE YOUR POWER AND BECOME AS OTHER WOMEN!

HA HA! YOU MAY TRY IT, IF YOU LIKE, AND SEE FOR YOURSELF!

WONDER WOMAN TAKES KAY TO THE PRISON CHAIN ROOM.

CARLA, BRING ME AN ARMFUL OF THE HEAVIEST CHAINS YOU HAVE.

YES, MISTRESS—

GIVE THE CHAINS TO OUR VISITOR.

OH-GREAT HEAVENS! I CAN'T EVEN LIFT THEM!

WITH CARLA'S HELP, KAY WELDS THE CHAINS ON **WONDER WOMAN'S** BRACELETS.

IF THESE CHAINS DON'T HOLD YOUR BRACELETS, NOTHING WILL!

9C.

I DON'T SEE HOW YOU HOLD SUCH **WEIGHT!**

WATCH NOW— HERE GOES!

ASTOUNDING! THIS CERTAINLY DISPROVES THE STORY THAT CHAINING YOUR BRACELETS DESTROYS YOUR STRENGTH!

I HOPE YOU'LL HELP STOP THAT SILLY RUMOR!

NOBODY MUST DISCOVER THAT **MEN** CHAINING MY BRACELETS MAKES ME WEAK!

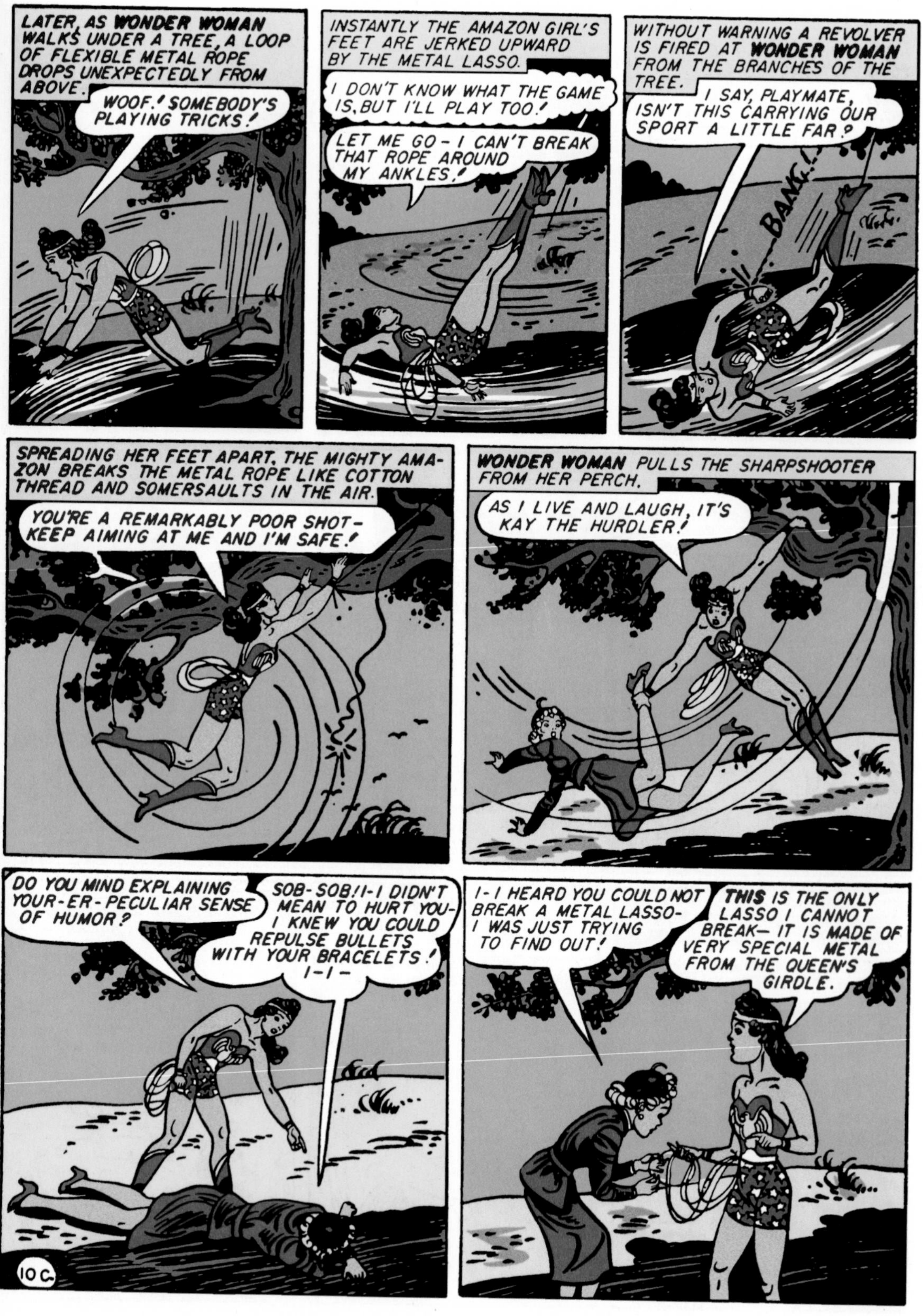
LATER, AS WONDER WOMAN WALKS UNDER A TREE, A LOOP OF FLEXIBLE METAL ROPE DROPS UNEXPECTEDLY FROM ABOVE.
WOOF.! SOMEBODY'S PLAYING TRICKS.!
INSTANTLY THE AMAZON GIRL'S FEET ARE JERKED UPWARD BY THE METAL LASSO.
I DON'T KNOW WHAT THE GAME IS, BUT I'LL PLAY TOO.!
LET ME GO - I CAN'T BREAK THAT ROPE AROUND MY ANKLES.!
WITHOUT WARNING A REVOLVER IS FIRED AT WONDER WOMAN FROM THE BRANCHES OF THE TREE.
I SAY, PLAYMATE, ISN'T THIS CARRYING OUR SPORT A LITTLE FAR?
BANG!!
SPREADING HER FEET APART, THE MIGHTY AMAZON BREAKS THE METAL ROPE LIKE COTTON THREAD AND SOMERSAULTS IN THE AIR.
YOU'RE A REMARKABLY POOR SHOT-KEEP AIMING AT ME AND I'M SAFE.!
WONDER WOMAN PULLS THE SHARPSHOOTER FROM HER PERCH.
AS I LIVE AND LAUGH, IT'S KAY THE HURDLER.!
DO YOU MIND EXPLAINING YOUR-ER-PECULIAR SENSE OF HUMOR?
SOB-SOB.! I-I DIDN'T MEAN TO HURT YOU-I KNEW YOU COULD REPULSE BULLETS WITH YOUR BRACELETS.! I-I-
I-I HEARD YOU COULD NOT BREAK A METAL LASSO-I WAS JUST TRYING TO FIND OUT.!
THIS IS THE ONLY LASSO I CANNOT BREAK- IT IS MADE OF VERY SPECIAL METAL FROM THE QUEEN'S GIRDLE.
10 C.

AT A BANQUET THAT NIGHT IN THE ROYAL PALACE, THE QUEEN ANSWERS QUESTIONS.

PLEASE TELL US ABOUT THAT LOVELY GIRDLE!

THE GODDESS APHRODITE GAVE ME THIS. SO LONG AS WE AMAZONS KEEP IT, WE CANNOT BE CONQUERED!

IN A PALACE GUEST ROOM, THE FALSE KAY USES A MIRROR TO TRANSFORM HERSELF TO THE CHEETAH PERSONALITY.

ARR-RR-GH! I'LL SEIZE THAT GIRDLE— NOTHING CAN STOP ME!

USING HER LEOPARD'S CLAWS WITH CATLIKE AGILITY, THE CHEETAH CLIMBS THE PALACE WALL.

THE QUEEN'S GUARDS ARE NOT EXPECTING CAT BURGLARS ON PARADISE ISLAND.

HO- HUM! NO NEED OF A GUARD HERE—WISH I COULD SLEEP!

THE AMAZON GETS HER WISH.

UG-GLUG!

STEALTHILY THE CHEETAH SLIPS INTO THE QUEEN'S BED-CHAMBER.

WHERE IS THE MAGIC GIRDLE?

AMAZON GUARDS, WHOSE DUTY IT IS TO WATCH THE GIRDLE WHILE THE QUEEN SLEEPS, ARE PLAYING CHESS IN AN ADJOINING ROOM.

WATCH YOUR QUEEN, MY DEAR, SHE'LL BE CAPTURED IN THREE MOVES!

11C.

SO SILENTLY DOES THE CHEETAH STEAL FROM THE SHADOWS THAT THE GUARDS HEAR NO SOUND.

ARR-RR-GH! I HAVE THE GIRDLE! I HOPE IT WILL MAKE ME UNCONQUERABLE!

THE QUEEN, MEANWHILE, WAKES WITH A FEELING OF DANGER AND DRESSES HASTILY—

I'LL LOOK OUT THIS WINDOW—

ARR-RRG-GGH!

THE CHEETAH BINDS HER UNCONSCIOUS VICTIM WITH THE GUARD'S LASSO.

IF THE MAGIC GIRDLE REALLY MAKES ME UNCONQUERABLE, THE QUEEN CANNOT BREAK THIS ROPE!

THE LEOPARD GIRL DESCENDS THE PALACE WALL WITH HER ROYAL PREY.

THIS GIRDLE DOES GIVE ME ADDED STRENGTH!

AS THE CHEETAH REACHES THE WOODS, THE QUEEN RECOVERS CONSCIOUSNESS.

I'M BOUND-I CANNOT BREAK THE ROPE-I DO NOT UNDERSTAND!

SHE HAS STOLEN APHRODITE'S GIRDLE-NO WONDER I CANNOT BREAK THESE BONDS!

FOOLISH GIRL, RETURN THE GIRDLE- IT'LL DO YOU NO GOOD!

WITH THIS I SHALL RULE THE AMAZONS!

12 C.

WONDER WOMAN, RISING EARLY NEXT MORNING, FINDS A NOTE PINNED TO HER DOOR.

WHAT IN PARADISE CAN THIS MEAN?

DEAR WONDER WOMAN— THE CHEETAH IS HERE, ON PARADISE ISLAND! I HAVE READ HER THOUGHTS — SHE HAS A TERRIBLE PLAN! I'M GOING TO FIND HER BY E.S.P.!

FAITHFULLY, GAIL

P.S. I KNOW NOW WHO THE CHEETAH IS — BUT I HAVE TO PROVE IT!

THE QUEEN'S GUARDS REPORT TO THE PRINCESS.

APHRODITE'S GIRDLE DISAPPEARED LAST NIGHT! WE THOUGHT THE QUEEN TOOK IT! BUT WE JUST FOUND THE GUARD UNCONSCIOUS!

THE CHEETAH! GAIL'S FOLLOWING HER—WE'LL FOLLOW GAIL!

THE PRINCESS AND MALA, BOTH EXPERT WOODSWOMEN, FOLLOW GAIL'S TRAIL THROUGH THE FOREST.

THERE'S A FOOT PRINT!

AND HERE'S A BROKEN TWIG!

LOOK—THERE'S GAIL! THE CHEETAH CAUGHT HER!

GREAT APHRODITE! A MESSAGE FROM THE CHEETAH!

13C.

To Wonder Woman and the Amazons —

This stupid girl can tell you nothing about me - I have removed her memory forever by giving her a powerful drug. I hold the magic girdle and your Queen is my captive— submit to my rule or the Queen dies!

— The Cheetah

273

THE POOR GIRL HAS COMPLETELY LOST HER MEMORY—

I'LL HAVE PAULA GIVE HER MEMORY TREATMENTS AND CURE HER... EXCEPT FOR ONE THING — SHE MUST NOT REMEMBER MY DOUBLE IDENTITY!

I-I SENSE AWFUL THOUGHTS FROM SOME GIRL OVER THERE — BEHIND THOSE TREES!

THE AMAZONS FOLLOW GAIL'S DIRECTIONS AND—

STAND WHERE YOU ARE, OR THIS ROCK CRUSHES YOUR QUEEN!

FORGET ME, AMAZONS— RECOVER APHRODITE'S GIRDLE!

NO, MOTHER! I'M IN COMMAND—LET NO GIRL MOVE!

CHEETAH, I DARE YOU TO FIGHT. ARE YOU STILL AFRAID OF ME, EVEN THOUGH YOU WEAR THE MAGIC GIRDLE?

ARR-RRG-GGH! I NEVER WAS AFRAID OF YOU! I'LL TEAR YOU TO PIECES!

YOU ARE EVERYTHING I HATE AND ENVY! TWICE YOU ESCAPED ME BUT NOW YOUR TIME HAS COME!

PUT YOUR CLOCK AHEAD AND START FIGHTING!

SUDDENLY THE CHEETAH LEAPS, AND SWIFT ACTION FOLLOWS.

14C

274

LOCKED TOGETHER WITH STRANGLE HOLDS, THE OPPONENTS STAND FROZEN IN FIERCE EXERTION, THE UNCONQUERABLE POWER OF THE MAGIC GIRDLE EVENLY MATCHED BY **WONDER WOMAN'S** SUPERB STRENGTH.

SUDDENLY THE CHEETAH WRENCHES HERSELF FREE AND DRAWS A KNIFE.

ARR-RRG-GGH! THIS IS THE CHEETAH'S KILL!

ARR-RGH YOURSELF, LEOPARD GIRL- I HAVE A THEORY THIS FIGHT'S ABOUT OVER!

AS **WONDER WOMAN** SWINGS HER OPPONENT OVERHEAD, THE GIRDLE'S CLASP IS LOOSENED, FLINGING THE CHEETAH LIKE A STONE FROM ITS SLING.

THE PRINCESS HAS RECOVERED OUR SACRED GIRDLE! HOLA-**VICTORY!**

BUT THE CHEETAH, RECOVERING QUICKLY, PUSHES WITH ALL HER REMAINING STRENGTH AGAINST THE ROCK, WHICH STARTS TO ROLL.

IN WINNING, YOU HAVE LOST, AMAZON- THE CHEETAH IS REVENGED!

15C

THE HUGE BOULDER TOPPLES ON THE BRINK.

WONDER WOMAN LEAPS-WILL SHE BE IN TIME?

OH, MOTHER APHRODITE! HELP ME!

LANDING ASTRIDE THE QUEEN'S HELPLESS FORM, **WONDER WOMAN** CATCHES THE GREAT ROCK IN HER HANDS AND HURLS IT FAR AWAY.

WHILE OTHER GIRLS SECURE THE CHEETAH, THE AMAZON ROYAL FAMILY HAS A HAPPY REUNION.

I OUGHT TO SPANK YOU FOR DISOBEYING ME AND SAVING MY LIFE!

PLEASE DO, MOTHER— THEN I'LL KNOW YOU'RE QUITE YOUR- SELF AGAIN!

THE CHEETAH IS UNMASKED.

WOO WOO, **WONDER WOMAN**! THE CHEETAH'S PRISCILLA RICH, GLAMOUROUSEST DEB IN AMERICA!

IT HAD TO BE PRISCILLA! SHE MUST HAVE KID- NAPPED THE REAL KAY AND IMPERSONAT- ED HER!

LATER, AT THE AMAZON PRISON—

MY CHEETAH PERSONALITY IS COMPELLED TO CONFESS. "I'VE LIVED A DOUBLE LIFE. BENEATH MY HOUSE IS A SECRET ROOM, MY CHEETAH'S DEN, WITH UNDERGROUND PASSAGES THROUGH WHICH I ESCAPED.

MY TWO PERSONALITIES WERE ENEMIES—PRIS- CILLA WANTED TO BE GOOD BUT THE CHEETAH WOULDN'T LET HER! YOUR MAGIC LASSO BINDS THE CHEETAH FOR THE FIRST TIME—OH, **KEEP** ME A PRISONER HERE AND TRAIN MY CHEETAH SELF!

AN EXCELLENT IDEA!

16C.

THE GIRLS ARE READY TO RETURN—THE ALL CHAMPS LOST 131 TO 5! WE MAY SHOW SERGEANT DOOT THAT AMAZON TRAINING MAKES STRONG ATHLETES, BUT I'LL NEVER CONVINCE STEVE THAT AMAZON CHAINS WILL MAKE THE CHEETAH A GOOD GIRL—HE'LL WANT HER PUNISHED!

DON'T WORRY ABOUT IT—WHEN A MAN'S UNREASONABLE, FEED HIM CANDY!

THE END

276

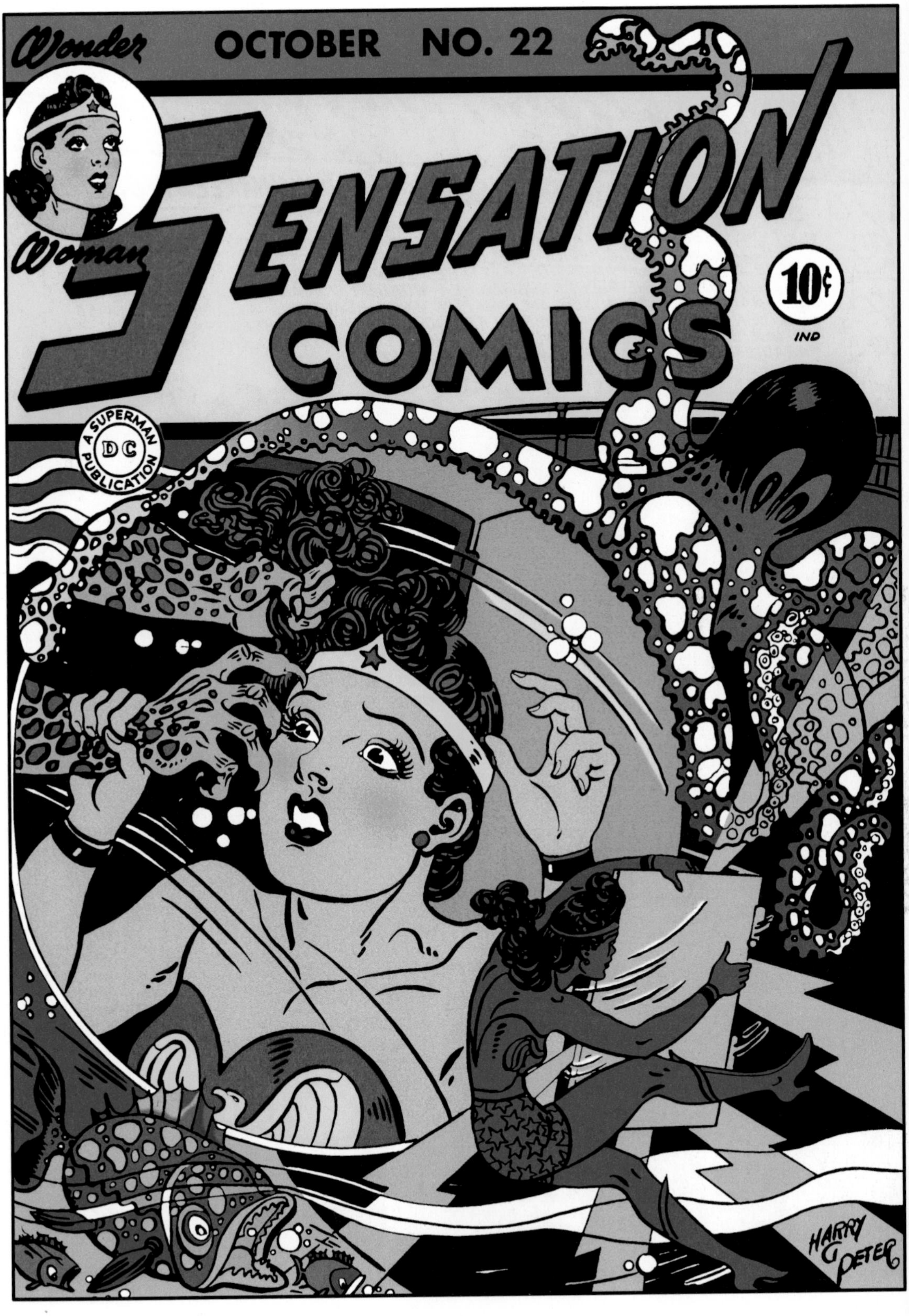
Wonder Woman
OCTOBER NO. 22
SENSATION COMICS
10¢
IND
A SUPERMAN DC PUBLICATION
HARRY G PETER

Wonder Woman

By CHARLES MOULTON

DEEP DOWN INTO OCEAN DEPTHS GOES THE AMAZON GIRL IN SEARCH OF THE NAVY'S MOST CHERISHED VESSEL, A WONDER SUBMARINE CARRYING SECRET WEAPONS! CAUGHT WITH ETTA CANDY IN A CUNNING TRAP, THE BEAUTIFUL PRINCESS FINDS HERSELF HELPLESS IN A SUNKEN SUB AMONG THE FETTERED ZEBRA SLAVES OF THE CHEETAH! IN THIS ADVENTURE," THE SECRET SUBMARINE," WONDER WOMAN IS FORCED TO USE ALL HER AMAZON POWERS IN NEW AND AMAZING WAYS. BEAUTIFUL AS APHRODITE, WISE AS ATHENA, STRONGER THAN HERCULES AND SWIFTER THAN MERCURY, WONDER WOMAN BRINGS THE LOVE POWER OF APHRODITE FROM THAT SECRET ISLE OF PARADISE WHERE BEAUTIFUL WOMEN RULE SUPREME!

STEVE AND COLONEL DARNELL GET A *BUZZ* OUT OF A HEADLINE —

THE NAVY'S SHOWING GOOD SENSE! THEY'VE NAMED THEIR NEW SUBMARINE "WONDER WOMAN!"

VERY APPROPRIATE- THIS IS A REAL WONDER SHIP!

THIS CONFIDENTIAL REPORT STATES THAT THE "WONDER WOMAN" CARRIES A SECRET WEAPON WHICH WILL REVOLUTIONIZE SUBMARINE WARFARE!

YES—I UNDERSTAND THE SUB SHOOTS ELECTRIC RAYS UNDER WATER THAT'LL SINK ANY BATTLESHIP!

COMMANDER HARRY JENKINS OF NAVAL INTELLIGENCE BRINGS STARTLING NEWS.

COLONEL, THE MOST PECULIAR THING'S HAPPENED—OUR NEW SUBMARINE DISAPPEARED LAST NIGHT FROM THE NAVAL BASE AT NEW LONDON!

DISAPPEARED! YOU MEAN THE "WONDER WOMAN"?

YES—OUR WONDER BOAT WAS CHRISTENED YESTERDAY BY ADMIRAL HOUSTON'S WIFE. LOT OF IMPORTANT PEOPLE PRESENT. SOME TIME DURING THE NIGHT, THE GUARDS ON THE PIER WERE KNOCKED OUT AND THE SUB WAS STOLEN!

FIND ANY CLUES?

ONLY CLUES WERE THESE MARKS ON THE GUARDS—AS THOUGH A WILDCAT HAD RIPPED THEIR CLOTHES AND CLAWED THEIR BACKS!

LOOKS LIKE THE CHEETAH'S WORK! BUT WONDER WOMAN CAPTURED THE CHEETAH— I'LL INVESTIGATE!

LATER, IN STEVE'S OFFICE—

SAY, DI, WHAT HAPPENED TO THE CHEETAH? WONDER WOMAN NEVER TOLD ME!

SHE WAS AFRAID YOU WOULDN'T APPROVE! THE CHEETAH BEGGED TO BE TRAINED IN AMAZON PRISON ON REFORM ISLAND!

OF COURSE I DON'T APPROVE! THAT GIRL OUGHT TO BE IN ALCATRAZ—SHE'S DANGEROUS!

HALF OF HER'S BAD, THE OTHER HALF GOOD—SHE HAS A DUAL PERSONALITY! HERE'S WHAT WONDER WOMAN TOLD ME—

2

"PRISCILLA RICH, BEAUTIFUL AND CLEVER DEBUTANTE, HAD A SECRET, EVIL SELF WHICH GAINED CONTROL OF HER AS SHE GAZED HYPNOTICALLY INTO THE MIRROR—

OH HORRORS! CAN THAT TERRIBLE CREATURE BE MY SECOND SELF? I—I'M A CHEETAH!

"UNDER CONTROL OF THE CHEETAH PERSONALITY, PRISCILLA BECAME A CRUEL, FIENDISHLY CLEVER HUNTRESS.

ARR-RRG-GGH.! I ENVY WONDER WOMAN— I HATE HER— I'LL KILL HER.!

"THE CHEETAH FOLLOWED WONDER WOMAN TO PARADISE ISLAND AND STOLE APHRODITE'S GIRDLE.

WHOEVER WEARS THIS GIRDLE IS INVINCIBLE.! SUBMIT TO ME—OR DIE.!

I'LL FIGHT YOU, EVEN THOUGH YOU WEAR THE GIRDLE.!

"THE BATTLE WENT ON AND ON— WONDER WOMAN'S MATCHLESS STRENGTH AGAINST THE UNCONQUERABLE POWER OF APHRODITE'S MAGIC GIRDLE.

"AT LAST WONDER WOMAN GRASPED THE GIRDLE AND TORE IT FROM THE CHEETAH'S WAIST.

"SUBDUED, THE CHEETAH WAS TRANSFORMED AGAIN TO PRISCILLA RICH."

OH, WONDER WOMAN, YOU'VE CONQUERED THE CHEETAH PERSONALITY— THESE BONDS FEEL WONDERFUL.! KEEP ME HERE IN AMAZON PRISON AND TRAIN ME TO CONTROL MY EVIL SELF.!

3

YOU SHALL BECOME AN AMAZON PRISONER, BUT FIRST YOU MUST RETURN TO THE WORLD OF MEN, FREE THE GIRLS YOU'VE ENSLAVED AND MAKE RESTITUTION TO EVERYONE YOU'VE INJURED.!

I'LL DO ANYTHING YOU COMMAND.!

SO WONDER WOMAN BROUGHT PRISCILLA BACK AND FREED HER?

YES, IT WAS A RISK.! BUT NO ONE COULD RESTORE THE CHEETAH'S VICTIMS EXCEPT PRISCILLA, AND WONDER WOMAN BELIEVED HER EVIL SELF WAS UNDER CONTROL.!

AS DIANA TELEPHONES PRISCILLA, A STRANGE CATLIKE FACE APPEARS AT THE WINDOW.

PRISCILLA **COULD HAVE** STOLEN THE SUB—

HUSH—I'M CALLING HER! HELLO! IS THIS PRISCILLA RICH?

YES! WHO IS CALLING PLEASE?

LIKE DEATH FROM THE JUNGLE AN AVALANCHE OF SCREAMING FURY LEAPS ON STEVE!

ARR-RRG-GGH!

AW-WK!

IT'S A **CHEETAH!** BUT THIS **CAN'T** BE PRISCILLA— SHE JUST SPOKE TO ME ON THE PHONE!

FORGETTING HER SUPPOSED WEAKNESS, DIANA LOCKS THE CHEETAH IN A MIGHTY AMAZON GRIP.

WHOEVER THIS GIRL IS, SHE'S NO WEAKLING!

ARR-GGH! LET ME GO!

THE CHEETAH'S FRANTIC STRUGGLES KNOCK DIANA'S GLASSES OFF.

OH-OH—THERE GOES MY DISGUISE—WITHOUT GLASSES, STEVE WILL RECOGNIZE ME AS **WONDER WOMAN!**

WHILE DIANA REACHES FOR HER GLASSES, THE CHEETAH BREAKS AWAY.

PFF-FT! YOU CANNOT HOLD THE **CHEETAH!**

VAINLY PURSUED BY STEVE AND DIANA, THE CHEETAH LEAPS UNHESITATINGLY THROUGH THE WINDOW.

DON'T JUMP—YOU'LL BREAK YOUR NECK!

HA! HA! HA!

④

I SHALL RETURN AND KILL YOU— THE MAN **WONDER WOMAN** LOVES!

I HOPE YOU'RE RIGHT— BUT WAIT A MINUTE! LET'S TALK THINGS OVER!

WHILE STEVE RACES FOR THE ELEVATOR, DIANA SWIFTLY TRANSFORMS HERSELF TO **WONDER WOMAN** AND PURSUES THE CHEETAH.

I THOUGHT **WONDER WOMAN** WOULD APPEAR FROM **SOMEWHERE** IF I ATTACKED TREVOR—HAHA! NOW TO LEAD HER INTO MY TRAP!

THE CHEETAH MUST HAVE PREPARED THIS WAY OF ESCAPE—CLEVER!

BUT I DON'T NEED ANY ROPE TO JUMP THIS LITTLE GAP!

THE CHEETAH DARTS THROUGH A STEEL DOOR LEADING DOWN FROM THE ROOF—

SHE BOLTS THE DOOR BEHIND HER.

THIS WILL DELAY **WONDER WOMAN**!

BUT **WONDER WOMAN** HITS THE MASSIVE DOOR LIKE A HUMAN CATAPULT.

I WON'T WAIT TO TRY THIS DOOR—I'M SURE SHE BOLTED IT!

5

DODGING CLEVERLY THROUGH THE BUILDING'S CROOKED CORRIDORS, THE CHEETAH REACHES HER CAR AS **WONDER WOMAN** EMERGES.

CATCH ME IF YOU CAN, ARROGANT AMAZON!

CATCHING HER WOULD BE EASY, BUT I MUST **FOLLOW** THIS CHEETAH AND DISCOVER HER IDENTITY!

AT A BUSY INTERSECTION, THE CHEETAH'S CAR BEATS THE LIGHT, WHILE TRAFFIC BLOCKS WONDER WOMAN.

HA! HA! HA! HA!

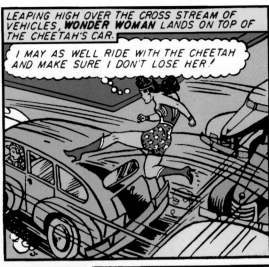

LEAPING HIGH OVER THE CROSS STREAM OF VEHICLES, WONDER WOMAN LANDS ON TOP OF THE CHEETAH'S CAR.

I MAY AS WELL RIDE WITH THE CHEETAH AND MAKE SURE I DON'T LOSE HER!

AS THE CHEETAH'S CAR ENTERS A PRIVATE DRIVEWAY, WONDER WOMAN RECOGNIZES THE RICH ESTATE.

WHY SHOULD THIS CHEETAH BE GOING TO PRISCILLA'S? I'LL WATCH THEIR MEETING AND FIND OUT FOR MYSELF!

SWINGING EASILY THROUGH THE TREES, WONDER WOMAN APPROACHES THE RICH MANSION.

I MUST ENTER PRISCILLA'S ROOMS WITHOUT BEING SEEN!

NOW TO FIND PRISCILLA—AND, I HOPE, THE CHEETAH!

A SUDDEN OUTBURST OF CRIES AND CRASHES LEADS WONDER WOMAN TO THE LOCKED DOOR OF PRISCILLA'S ROOM.

SOUNDS AS IF SOMEBODY WAS BEING STRANGLED!

CRACK—CRASH!

ARR-RRG-GGH!

HELP-HELP UGLP-ULP!

6

YOU WON'T LIVE TO BETRAY MY SECRET!

AAA-AH!

YOU'RE GETTING A LITTLE ROUGH, GIRLS— BREAK IT UP!

AS **WONDER WOMAN** GIVES PRISCILLA FIRST AID, THE CHEETAH ESCAPES.

OH—OHHH!

WHO **IS** THIS NEW CHEETAH AND WHAT'S HER GAME?

SHE IS **SANDRA**. ONE OF MY FORMER SLAVES— WHEN I FREED THE GIRLS, SHE IMPERSONATED THE CHEETAH TO GET REVENGE ON **ME**!

WHAT'S SANDRA'S SECRET?

SHE STOLE THE NEW SUBMARINE, "**WONDER WOMAN**"! I WAS AT THE LAUNCHING - SANDRA PLANNED IT SO I, KNOWN TO BE THE CHEETAH, WOULD BE BLAMED! SHE'S SELLING THE SUB TO ENEMY AGENTS—

HEAVENLY HERA! D'YOU KNOW WHERE THE STOLEN SUB IS HIDDEN?

N-NO, BUT I KNOW WHERE **SANDRA** IS HIDING! I'LL FIND HER AND MAKE HER TELL! MEET ME AT MY PRIVATE PIER TOMORROW AT 10 A.M.!

AS **WONDER WOMAN** LEAVES, A STRANGE CONFLICT TAKES PLACE BETWEEN PRISCILLA'S DUAL PERSONALITIES.

I AM YOUR EVIL SELF----- LISTEN TO ME - YOU KNOW YOU HATE **WONDER WOMAN**!

NO, NO - I **WON'T** TRAP **WONDER WOMAN**! BUT— BUT—YOU'RE TOO STRONG— I **MUST** OBEY YOU!

PULLING HER COSTUME FROM ITS HASTY CONCEALMENT BENEATH THE COUCH, PRISCILLA TRANSFORMS HERSELF INTO THE CHEETAH!

I HAD BARELY TIME TO REMOVE MY CHEETAH SKIN BEFORE **WONDER WOMAN** ARRIVED. BUT I FOOLED HER— HA-HA!

⑦

THE TRUE CHEETAH INSPECTS HER DOUBLE.

TURN SLOWLY, SLAVE! YOUR COSTUME'S GOOD— WE'RE ALIKE AS TWO ALLEY CATS! YOU FAKED A GOOD FIGHT BUT YOU SCRATCHED MY THROAT. **YOU SHALL BE PUNISHED!**

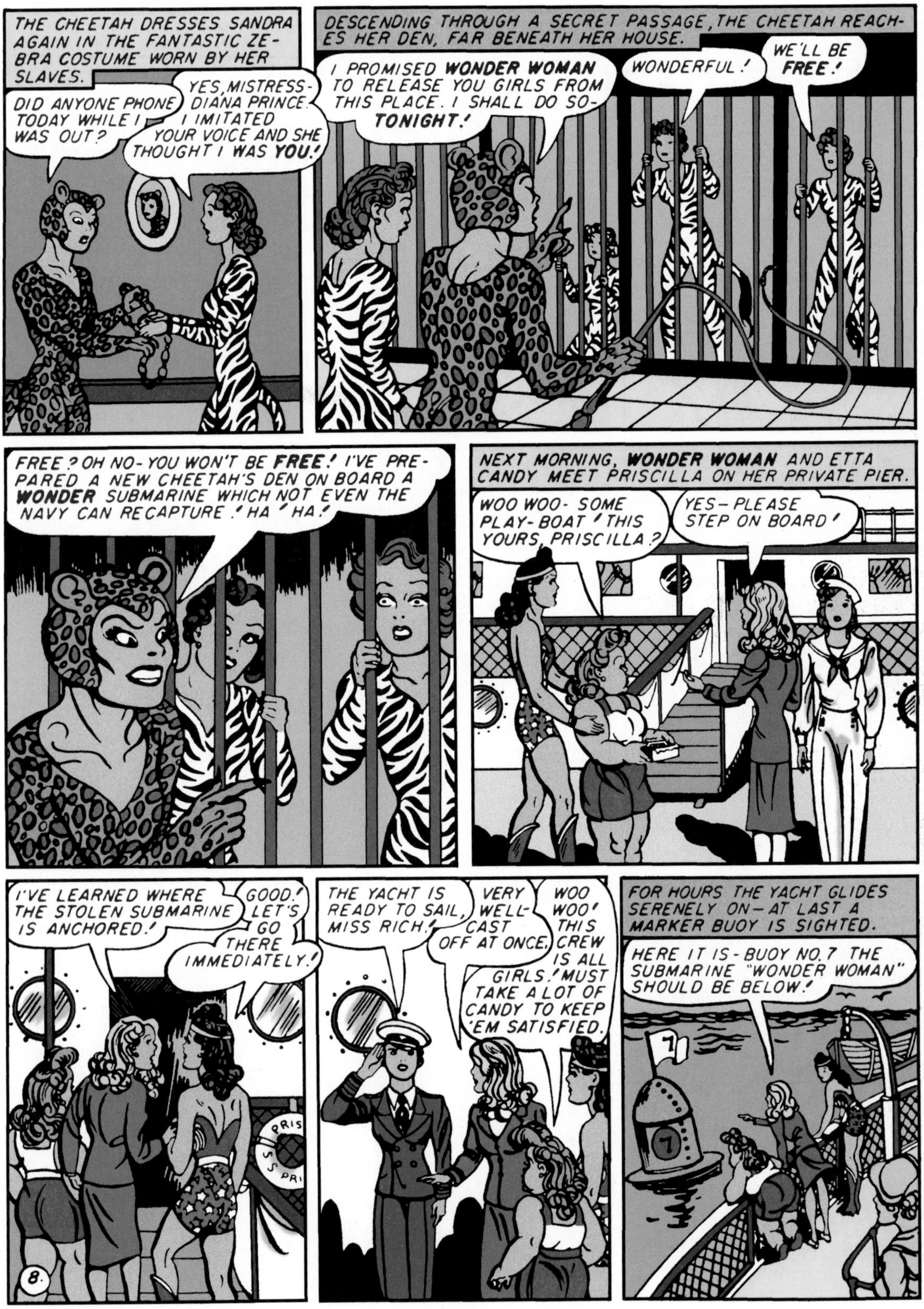

THE CHEETAH DRESSES SANDRA AGAIN IN THE FANTASTIC ZEBRA COSTUME WORN BY HER SLAVES.
DID ANYONE PHONE TODAY WHILE I WAS OUT?
YES, MISTRESS- DIANA PRINCE. I IMITATED YOUR VOICE AND SHE THOUGHT I WAS YOU!
DESCENDING THROUGH A SECRET PASSAGE, THE CHEETAH REACHES HER DEN, FAR BENEATH HER HOUSE.
I PROMISED WONDER WOMAN TO RELEASE YOU GIRLS FROM THIS PLACE. I SHALL DO SO- TONIGHT!
WONDERFUL!
WE'LL BE FREE!
FREE? OH NO- YOU WON'T BE FREE! I'VE PREPARED A NEW CHEETAH'S DEN ON BOARD A WONDER SUBMARINE WHICH NOT EVEN THE NAVY CAN RECAPTURE! HA! HA!
NEXT MORNING, WONDER WOMAN AND ETTA CANDY MEET PRISCILLA ON HER PRIVATE PIER.
WOO WOO- SOME PLAY-BOAT! THIS YOURS, PRISCILLA?
YES- PLEASE STEP ON BOARD!
I'VE LEARNED WHERE THE STOLEN SUBMARINE IS ANCHORED!
GOOD! LET'S GO THERE IMMEDIATELY!
8.
THE YACHT IS READY TO SAIL, MISS RICH!
VERY WELL- CAST OFF AT ONCE.
WOO WOO! THIS CREW IS ALL GIRLS! MUST TAKE A LOT OF CANDY TO KEEP 'EM SATISFIED.
FOR HOURS THE YACHT GLIDES SERENELY ON- AT LAST A MARKER BUOY IS SIGHTED.
HERE IT IS- BUOY NO. 7 THE SUBMARINE "WONDER WOMAN" SHOULD BE BELOW!
7
7

DESPITE WONDER WOMAN'S PROTESTS, PRISCILLA AND ETTA DIVE TO LOCATE THE SUB.

READY, BABE, LET'S GO!

WAIT! DIVING WILL DO NO GOOD—

WHEN THE GIRLS FAIL TO RE-APPEAR PROMPTLY, WONDER WOMAN FOLLOWS THEM.

THEY'RE BOTH GOOD SWIM-MERS BUT ANYTHING COULD HAPPEN HERE—

ETTA DISAPPEARS THROUGH AN UNDERWATER DOORWAY.

WHAT'S THIS? LOOKS LIKE A SUBMARINE ESCAPE HATCH!

THE HATCH CLOSES BEFORE WONDER WOMAN CAN ENTER.

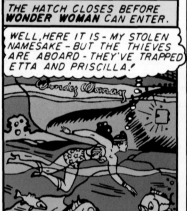

WELL, HERE IT IS— MY STOLEN NAMESAKE— BUT THE THIEVES ARE ABOARD— THEY'VE TRAPPED ETTA AND PRISCILLA!

AS WONDER WOMAN PREPARES TO FORCE HER WAY INTO THE SUBMARINE, A STRANGE ELECTRIC GLOW APPEARS.

THIS IS THE SECRET WEAPON! IT'S GETTING ME— UGH!

OVERCOME BY THE POWERFUL RAYS, WONDER WOMAN IS PULLED INTO THE SUBMARINE BY STRANGE HANDS.

THE AMAZON PRINCESS, RECOVERING CONSCIOUSNESS, FINDS HERSELF INGENIOUSLY SECURED.

WELL, WELL— THE CHEETAH AGAIN!

YOU'RE MY PRISONER! IF YOU TRY TO BREAK YOUR FETTERS, YOU WILL PULL THAT SWITCH ABOVE YOUR HEAD AND ELEC-TROCUTE YOURSELF!

WONDER WOMAN, HELPLESS, IS COMPELLED TO WATCH ETTA CANDY PREPARED FOR WHIPPING BY THE TWO ZEBRA GIRLS.

I'LL SPARE YOUR FRIEND, AMAZON GIRL, IF YOU WILL BECOME MY SLAVE!

DON'T SURRENDER, BABE, I CAN TAKE IT!

I'LL SUBMIT AS LONG AS ETTA IS NOT HURT!

THESE LOOK LIKE CHAINS FROM PRISCILLA'S COLLECTION!

OF COURSE, PRISCILLA IS NOW MY SLAVE—ALL HER POSSESSIONS ARE MINE!

THIS CHEETAH IS EVEN MORE CLEVER THAN PRISCILLA WAS WHEN SHE RAN AROUND IN THAT COSTUME! I MUST SUBMIT---BUT WE'LL SURELY BE RESCUED SOON!

YOU'RE THINK-ING THEY'LL FIND THIS SUB, BUT THEY WON'T. WHILE YOU WERE UNCON-SCIOUS I SAILED IT OUT TO SEA!

THE CHEETAH ASSEMBLES HER SLAVES AND ORDERS WONDER WOMAN TO DANCE.

HA-HA! HA! YOU'RE TERRIBLE— YOU'RE THE WORLD'S WORST DANCER!

I CAN'T DANCE IN THESE CHAINS, MISTRESS!

MY AWKWARDNESS PLEAS-ES HER— IT MAKES HER FEEL SUPERIOR! BET THIS CHEETAH, WHOEVER SHE IS, HAS A SUPPRESSED DESIRE TO DANCE!

THE CLEVER AMAZON GIRL PURPOSELY TAKES A TUMBLE.

HO HO HO! HA HA HA!

ALL RIGHT, LAUGH! BUT I'LL BET YOU CAN'T DANCE ANY BETTER YOURSELF!

BOOM!

10.

WONDER WOMAN ACCOMPLISHES HER PURPOSE—THE CHEETAH'S SECRET LONGING BREAKS ITS MENTAL BARRIERS AND BURSTS INTO ACTION.

I WILL SHOW YOU— THE DANCE OF THE CHEETAH!

THE CHEETAH'S DANCE IS TERRIFYING BUT BEAUTIFUL.

EE-EE! AW-WK-OH! SHE IS WONDERFUL!

THIS DAME'S A BAD ACTOR BUT SHE'S ONE SWELL HOOFER!

BEAUTIFUL!

ARTISTIC!

LOVELY!

THE CHEETAH'S BETTER THAN PAVLOVA!

WHAT DO YOU THINK OF MY DANCING?

IT'S SUPERB! YOU'RE A BORN DANCER - YOUR DANCING COULD ATTRACT MILLIONS OF ADMIRERS! OH, CHEETAH, WHY DON'T YOU DANCE AND MAKE PEOPLE LOVE YOU?

UNDER WONDER WOMAN'S INFLUENCE, THE CHEETAH FEELS HER PERSONALITY CHANGING.

OH-OH-WHAT'S HAPPENING TO ME? I'M NO LONGER JEALOUS OF WONDER WOMAN! I DON'T HATE PRETTY GIRLS - I - I -

RUSHING FROM THE ROOM AND LOCKING THE DOOR BEHIND HER, THE CHEETAH CHANGES BACK TO PRISCILLA.

I-I'M PRISCILLA-I'LL NEVER LET THE CHEETAH PERSONALITY CONTROL ME AGAIN! I'LL TAKE THE SUBMARINE BACK AND MAKE RESTITUTION!

PRISCILLA, DRESSED ONCE MORE IN HER OWN CLOTHES, MAKES HER WAY TO THE CONTROL ROOM.

THE CHEETAH IS TRYING TO CONTROL ME—CONFUSE MY MIND! HOW DID I OPERATE THIS SHIP? I THINK I MOVED THESE GADGETS —

AS PRISCILLA MOVES THE CONTROLS, THE SUBMARINE POINTS DOWNWARD AND THE PRISONERS ARE HURLED TOGETHER IN A STRUGGLING HEAP.

WHEE-EE!

AWK!

EEE-EEK!

WITH A DULL, SHATTERING IMPACT, THE UNDERWATER VESSEL HITS BOTTOM AND ETTA IS KNOCKED UNCONSCIOUS.

ETTA'S HURT - THAT RELEASES ME FROM MY PROMISE! THE SUB'S SUNK - ROOM'S FILLING WITH CHLORINE FUMES ALREADY!

CRASH!

CARRYING ETTA, THE AMAZON GIRL SMASHES THROUGH A STEEL BULKHEAD INTO THE CONTROL ROOM.

PRISCILLA, KNOCKED DOWN BY THE CRASH, LIES STUNNED ON THE FLOOR.

PRISCILLA - WAKE UP! WHERE'S THE CHEETAH?

DON' KNOW - SHE DIS'PEARED! THE CHEETAH KEP' ME PRIS'NER - I 'SCAPED! TRIED SAIL SUB -

CRASHING OUT THROUGH A FLOODED COMPARTMENT, WONDER WOMAN SURVEYS THE SITUATION.

I HAVEN'T HAD MUCH PRACTICE RAISING SUNKEN SUBMARINES, BUT HERE'S WHERE I LEARN A NEW TRADE!

BRACING HER SHOULDER AGAINST THE CONNING TOWER, WONDER WOMAN EXERTS HER ENORMOUS STRENGTH.

THIS WOULD BE EASY IF I DIDN'T HAVE TO HOLD MY BREATH!

SKUSH! GURGLE!!

WITH THE SUBMARINE FREED FROM THE MUDDY BOTTOM, WONDER WOMAN PUSHES IT ABOVE HER TO THE SURFACE.

I'M A HUMAN PROPELLER THAT CAN BE ATTACHED AT ANY ANGLE - I OUGHT TO GET A PATENT ON MYSELF!

12

AS THE SUB SURFACES, ETTA AND THE GIRLS POUR OUT ON DECK.

IT'S GREAT TO GET A DEEP BREATH - HELLO, GIRLS!

HI, WONDER WOMAN - WOO WOO! YOU DOOD IT!

WONDER WOMAN SAVED US! HOORAY-AY-AY!

WONDER WOMAN FREES THE GIRLS FROM THEIR FETTERS.

HAVE YOU SEEN THE CHEETAH?

I HAVEN'T SEEN ANYTHING BUT STARS! WHEN I CAME TO, I FOUND PRISCILLA BUT THE CHEETAH MUST HAVE DROWNED!

WONDER WOMAN TOWS THE SUBMARINE TO PORT WITH HER MAGIC LASSO.

WOO WOO! YOU'D NEVER BELIEVE THAT TEENY-WEENY ROPE WOULD PULL THIS HEAVY TUB WITHOUT BREAKING!

FOGHORNS, CHEERS AND SHIPS' WHISTLES RESOUND AS WONDER WOMAN TOWS THE PRECIOUS SUB INTO THE HARBOR.

TOO-OOT! WHEE-EE! OO-OONK!

WONDER WOMAN!

WONDER WOMAN!

AN ENTHUSIASTIC RECEPTION COMMITTEE MEETS WONDER WOMAN AT THE PIER.

THE NAVY THANKS YOU!

MY GORGEOUS POCKET POWER PLANT!

PUT ME DOWN, STEVE—

BUT I HOPE HE WON'T!

LATER, IN COL. DARNELL'S OFFICE—

PRISCILLA IS STILL THE CHEETAH AFTER ALL—THE MAGIC LASSO MADE HER CONFESS IT!

YES—WHEN WONDER WOMAN CAPTURED ME ON PARADISE ISLAND I WAS HAPPY. BUT WHEN I RETURNED I FELT INFERIOR AGAIN AND MY EVIL SELF CONTROLLED ME!

13.

SHE TRAPPED ME CLEVERLY! BUT I RECOGNIZED HER CHEETAH PERSONALITY AND HELPED PRISCILLA CONQUER IT BY DANCING—SOMETHING THAT MAKES HER FEEL SUPERIOR. THAT'S THE TRAINING SHE'D GET ON REFORM ISLAND!

LATER, AFTER WONDER WOMAN LEAVES—

I DON'T SEE WHAT'S BECOME OF THAT GIRL—OH! THERE YOU ARE, DIANA!

THE CHEETAH CRACKED MY GLASSES AND I HAD TO GET A NEW PAIR. WITHOUT MY SPECS, COLONEL, I'M NOT THE SAME GIRL AT ALL!

MORE ADVENTURES OF WONDER WOMAN IN EVERY ISSUE OF SENSATION COMICS

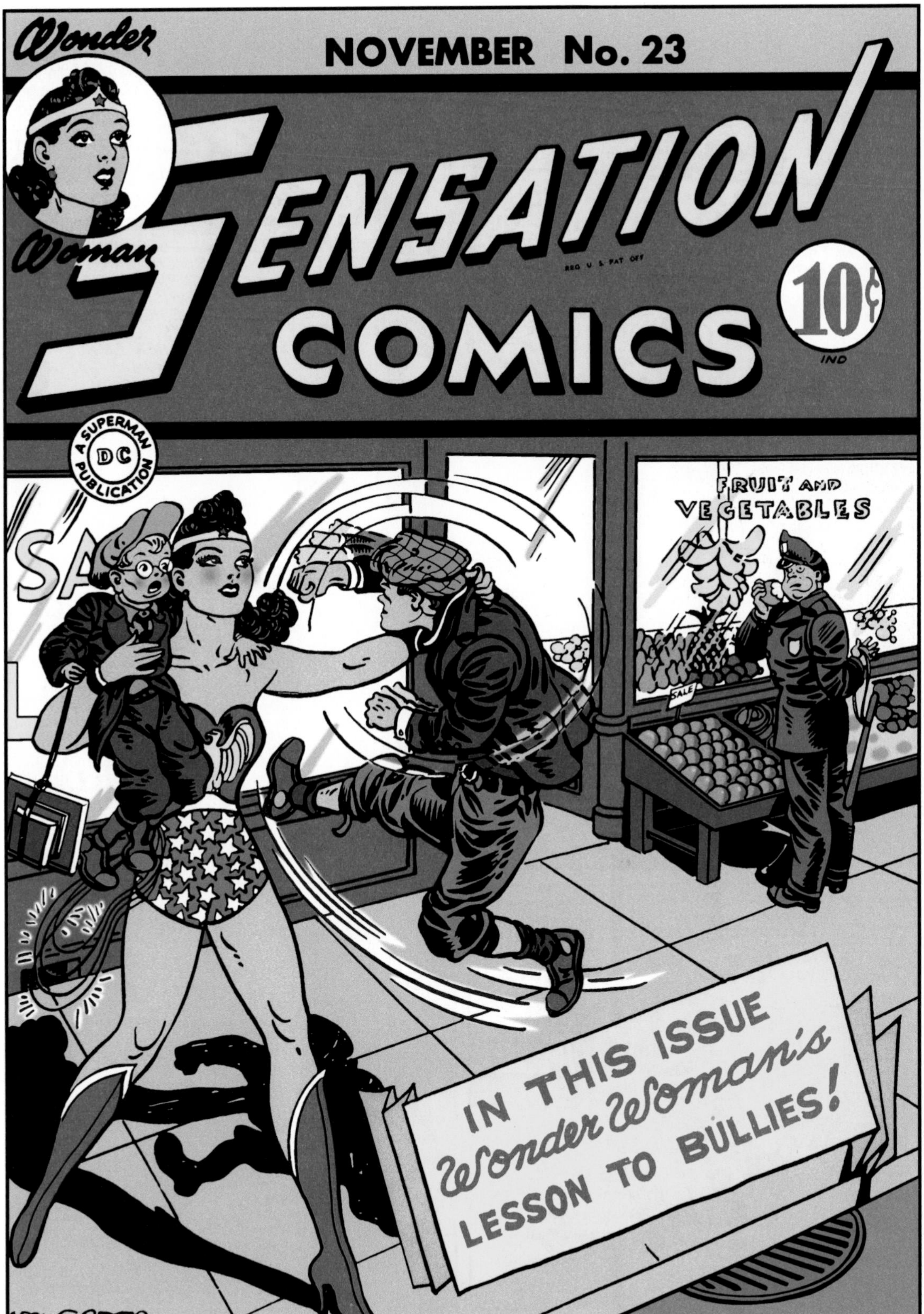
Wonder Woman
NOVEMBER No. 23
SENSATION COMICS
10¢
IND
A SUPERMAN DC PUBLICATION
FRUIT AND VEGETABLES
SALE
IN THIS ISSUE Wonder Woman's LESSON TO BULLIES!

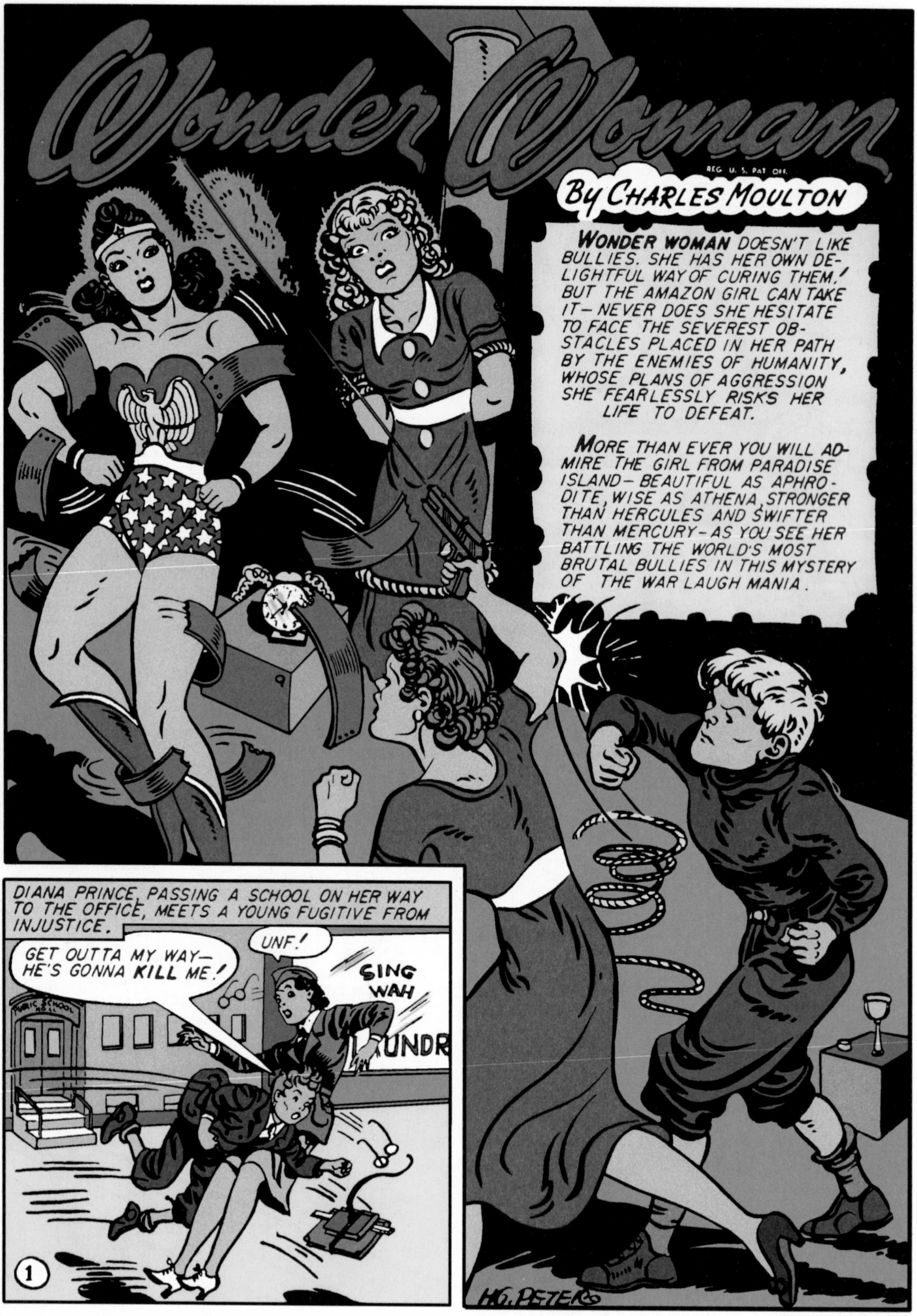
Wonder Woman
REG. U. S. PAT. OFF.
BY CHARLES MOULTON
WONDER WOMAN DOESN'T LIKE BULLIES. SHE HAS HER OWN DELIGHTFUL WAY OF CURING THEM! BUT THE AMAZON GIRL CAN TAKE IT– NEVER DOES SHE HESITATE TO FACE THE SEVEREST OBSTACLES PLACED IN HER PATH BY THE ENEMIES OF HUMANITY, WHOSE PLANS OF AGGRESSION SHE FEARLESSLY RISKS HER LIFE TO DEFEAT.
MORE THAN EVER YOU WILL ADMIRE THE GIRL FROM PARADISE ISLAND– BEAUTIFUL AS APHRODITE, WISE AS ATHENA, STRONGER THAN HERCULES AND SWIFTER THAN MERCURY– AS YOU SEE HER BATTLING THE WORLD'S MOST BRUTAL BULLIES IN THIS MYSTERY OF THE WAR LAUGH MANIA.
DIANA PRINCE, PASSING A SCHOOL ON HER WAY TO THE OFFICE, MEETS A YOUNG FUGITIVE FROM INJUSTICE.
GET OUTTA MY WAY– HE'S GONNA KILL ME!
UNF!
SING WAH
UNDR
1
H.G. PETER

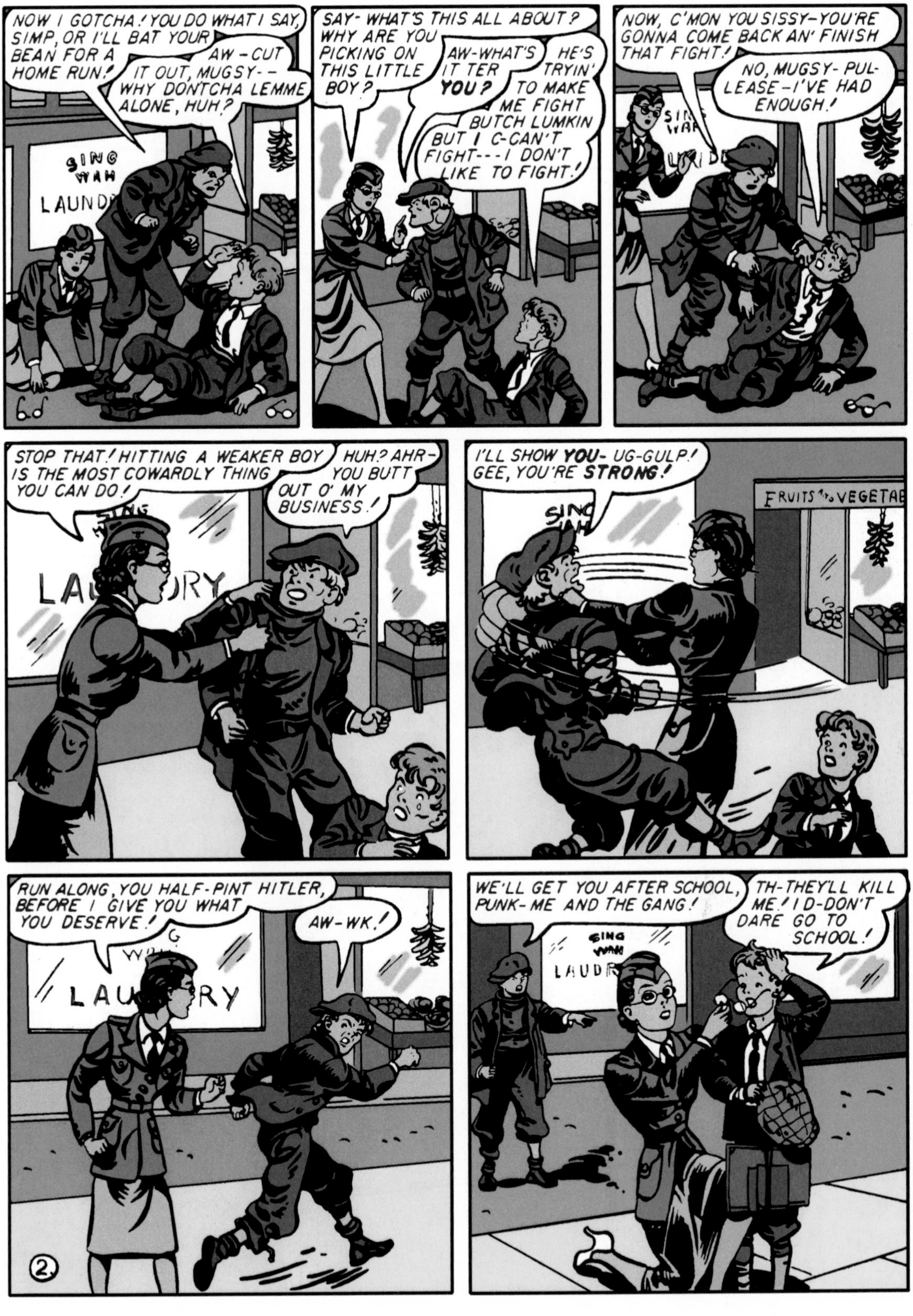
NOW I GOTCHA! YOU DO WHAT I SAY, SIMP, OR I'LL BAT YOUR BEAN FOR A HOME RUN!
AW - CUT IT OUT, MUGSY- - WHY DON'TCHA LEMME ALONE, HUH?
SING WAH LAUND
SAY- WHAT'S THIS ALL ABOUT? WHY ARE YOU PICKING ON THIS LITTLE BOY?
AW-WHAT'S IT TER YOU?
HE'S TRYIN' TO MAKE ME FIGHT BUTCH LUMKIN BUT I C-CAN'T FIGHT- - - I DON'T LIKE TO FIGHT!
NOW, C'MON YOU SISSY-YOU'RE GONNA COME BACK AN' FINISH THAT FIGHT!
NO, MUGSY- PUL-LEASE-I'VE HAD ENOUGH!
STOP THAT! HITTING A WEAKER BOY IS THE MOST COWARDLY THING YOU CAN DO!
HUH? AHR-YOU BUTT OUT O' MY BUSINESS!
I'LL SHOW YOU- UG-GULP! GEE, YOU'RE STRONG!
FRUITS AND VEGETAB
RUN ALONG, YOU HALF-PINT HITLER, BEFORE I GIVE YOU WHAT YOU DESERVE!
AW-WK!
WE'LL GET YOU AFTER SCHOOL, PUNK- ME AND THE GANG!
TH-THEY'LL KILL ME! I D-DON'T DARE GO TO SCHOOL!
2

NOW, TELL ME—WHAT'S THE TROUBLE?

WELL, MY NAME IS JIMMY SIMPSON. MUGSY McGREW AND HIS GANG ARE PICKING ON ME LIKE THEY DO ALL LITTLE KIDS. THEY MAKE US FIGHT EACH OTHER—I'M GOING TO RUN AWAY!

I WON'T LET MUGSY HURT YOU, I PROMISE! I'LL BE WAITING FOR YOU HERE AFTER SCHOOL!

WELL I—I TRUST YOU. BUT I'M AWFUL SCARED!

SMALL INCIDENTS SOMETIMES HAVE BIG CONSEQUENCES. WHEN DIANA PROMISED TO PROTECT LITTLE JIMMY FROM THE SCHOOL BULLY, SHE COULD NOT GUESS THAT THIS SIMPLE ACT OF KINDNESS WOULD LEAD TO THE VERY HEART OF A SINISTER MYSTERY!

MEANWHILE, DIANA REACHES THE OFFICE JUST IN TIME FOR AN ASSIGNMENT WITH MAJOR TREVOR.

HI, DI! WHERE'VE YOU BEEN? YOU'RE ASSIGNED TO INVESTIGATE A CASE WITH ME—COME ALONG AND I'LL TELL YOU ABOUT IT!

WE'VE GOT PLENTY TROUBLE, M'GAL! WAR WORKERS IN FACTORIES ALL OVER THE COUNTRY ARE GETTING A STRANGE DISEASE—MAKES 'EM LAUGH LIKE MANIACS—THEN COLLAPSE. IT'S CUTTING PRODUCTION IN HALF!

CAN'T DOCTORS CURE IT?

THIS CASE NEEDS A CRIME DOCTOR. THESE WORKERS ARE BEING INFECTED IN SOME WEIRD WAY BY ENEMY AGENTS TO SLOW DOWN PRODUCTION. HERE'S THE GENERAL AIRCRAFT PLANT—SEE FOR YOURSELF!

BUT STEVE, MAYBE THESE FACTORY WORKERS HAVE SOME OCCUPATIONAL DISEASE!

NONSENSE! LOOK AT THIS HUGE PLANT—THERE ARE DOZENS OF COMPLETELY DIFFERENT TYPES OF OCCUPATIONS HERE, YET ALL EMPLOYEES HAVE THE SAME ILLNESS!

③

MEET VICE-PRESIDENT CYRUS K. KNOWLES, IN CHARGE OF THIS PLANT! HE'S ONE OF GENERAL AIRCRAFT'S MOST EXPERIENCED EXECUTIVES!

—BUT MY EXPERIENCE IS PROVING WORTHLESS. I'VE NEVER BEEN UP AGAINST ANYTHING LIKE THIS BEFORE!

THIS IS MY SECRETARY, EILEEN McGREW. SHE'LL SHOW YOU AROUND THE PLANT.

YES, OF COURSE, I'LL SHOW YOU EVERYTHING!

I NOTICE ALL WORKERS WEAR THE SAME COSTUME – IS THAT A RULE OF THE PLANT?

YES– MOST WAR FACTORIES NOW REQUIRE IT. THESE WORK UNIFORMS ARE FURNISHED BY THE COMPANY–

AS THEY TURN AWAY, MAD LAUGHTER RINGS OUT.

HA HA HA HA! HEE HEE HO HO HO!

WHAT IN BLAZES IS THAT?

ANOTHER GIRL'S GOT WAR LAUGH MANIA!

FELLOW WORKERS TRY IN VAIN TO HOLD THE NEW VICTIM OF THIS STRANGE MALADY.

HA HA HA! HE HE! HE HA!

HEE HEE HEE!

TAKE HER OVERALLS OFF– QUICK!

I CAN'T H-HOLD HER!

DIANA, AT THE RISK OF BETRAYING HER HIDDEN IDENTITY, EASILY HOLDS THE MANIACAL GIRL.

WHY TAKE HER OVERALLS OFF?

I DON'T KNOW BUT IT ALWAYS SEEMS TO HELP!

4

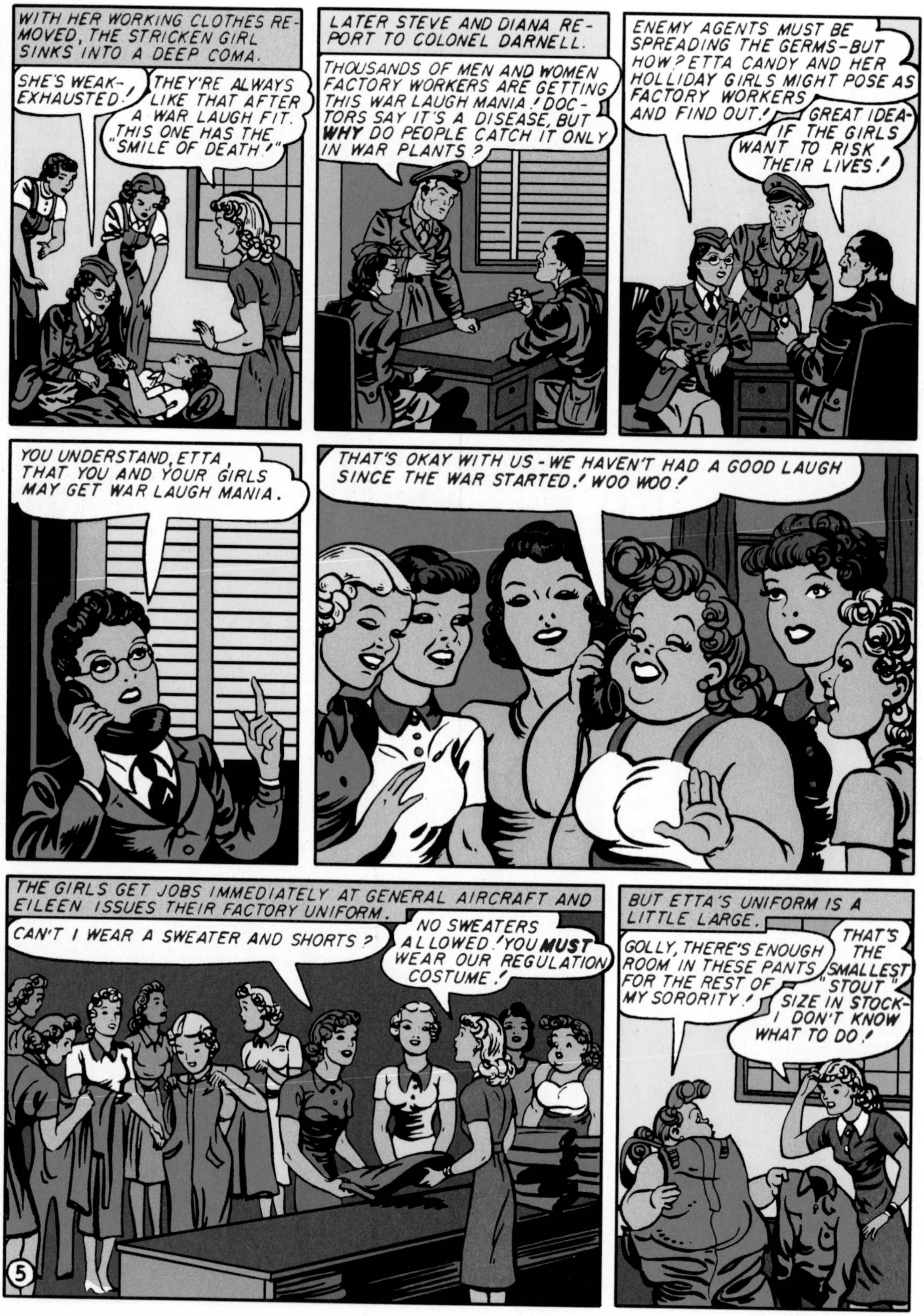
WITH HER WORKING CLOTHES REMOVED, THE STRICKEN GIRL SINKS INTO A DEEP COMA.
SHE'S WEAK-EXHAUSTED!
THEY'RE ALWAYS LIKE THAT AFTER A WAR LAUGH FIT. THIS ONE HAS THE "SMILE OF DEATH!"
LATER STEVE AND DIANA REPORT TO COLONEL DARNELL.
THOUSANDS OF MEN AND WOMEN FACTORY WORKERS ARE GETTING THIS WAR LAUGH MANIA! DOCTORS SAY IT'S A DISEASE, BUT WHY DO PEOPLE CATCH IT ONLY IN WAR PLANTS?
ENEMY AGENTS MUST BE SPREADING THE GERMS-BUT HOW? ETTA CANDY AND HER HOLLIDAY GIRLS MIGHT POSE AS FACTORY WORKERS AND FIND OUT!
GREAT IDEA-IF THE GIRLS WANT TO RISK THEIR LIVES!
YOU UNDERSTAND, ETTA, THAT YOU AND YOUR GIRLS MAY GET WAR LAUGH MANIA.
THAT'S OKAY WITH US-WE HAVEN'T HAD A GOOD LAUGH SINCE THE WAR STARTED! WOO WOO!
THE GIRLS GET JOBS IMMEDIATELY AT GENERAL AIRCRAFT AND EILEEN ISSUES THEIR FACTORY UNIFORM.
CAN'T I WEAR A SWEATER AND SHORTS?
NO SWEATERS ALLOWED! YOU MUST WEAR OUR REGULATION COSTUME!
5
BUT ETTA'S UNIFORM IS A LITTLE LARGE.
GOLLY, THERE'S ENOUGH ROOM IN THESE PANTS FOR THE REST OF MY SORORITY!
THAT'S THE SMALLEST "STOUT" SIZE IN STOCK-I DON'T KNOW WHAT TO DO!

I CAN'T WORK IN THIS SLEEPING BAG—I CAN'T EVEN GRAB A PIECE O'CANDY!

WELL—ER— YOU MAY WEAR YOUR ORDINARY CLOTHES UNTIL I CAN GET YOU A UNIFORM!

AND SO IT HAPPENS THAT ETTA, WORKING WITHOUT A UNIFORM DISCOVERS A VITAL CLUE—BUT WE'RE GETTING AHEAD OF OUR STORY. LET'S GO BACK TO DIANA PRINCE AS SHE REMEMBERS HER PROMISE TO MEET JIMMY SIMPSON AFTER SCHOOL—

GREAT HERA! I ALMOST FORGOT MY PROMISE TO PROTECT LITTLE JIMMY FROM THAT BULLY AND SCHOOL LETS OUT IN 2 MINUTES! ONLY WONDER WOMAN CAN GET THERE IN TIME!

MEANWHILE, MUGSY McGREW AND HIS GANG ARE WAITING FOR JIMMY.

NOW FELLERS, WHEN SIMP GETS OFF THE SCHOOL GROUNDS JUMP AND GRAB HIM!

WALLOP DAT PUNK!

WE GOT HIM NOW!

GRAB HIM!

OH, THEY'LL KILL ME! I—I CAN'T MOVE!

AS JIMMY'S DARKEST MOMENT ARRIVES, A BEAUTIFUL FORM FLASHES OVER HIS HEAD!

WONDER WOMAN!

6

TOO LATE TO STOP THE ATTACK, WONDER WOMAN CATCHES THE BLOWS INTENDED FOR JIMMY ON HER BRACELETS—

COUNT ME IN YOUR GAME, BOYS!

WONDER WOMAN! LOOK OUT!

HEY FELLERS! DON'T HIT WONDER WOMAN!

BOYS WHO GANG UP ON SMALLER BOYS ARE COWARDS—SEE THEM RUN, JIMMY!

I AIN'T NO COWARD! PUT UP YER DUKES, **WONDER WOMAN**!

I'M GLAD YOU HAVE COURAGE, MUGSY, EVEN IF YOU **ARE** A BULLY! COME ON—LET'S SEE HOW HARD YOU CAN HIT ME!

OW-W-W! I BROKE ME HAND—YOU GOT A JAW LIKE A BATTLESHIP!

YOU KNOCKED TWO FINGERS OUT OF JOINT—I'LL PULL THEM BACK FOR YOU!

OUCH! ER—T'ANKS, **WONDER WOMAN**—YER A GOOD GUY! I OUGHTA KNOWN BETTER THAN TA HIT **YOU**!

YOU SHOULD HAVE KNOWN BETTER THAN TO TORMENT LITTLE JIMMY! THERE'S NO FUN IN **HURTING** WEAKER PEOPLE—ONLY IN **HELPING** THEM! THAT'S WHAT MAKES YOU FEEL BIG AND POWERFUL!

GEE—MAYBE YOU'RE RIGHT! I NEVER THOUGHT OF THAT BEFORE!

JIMMY, I'M SORRY I PICKED ON YA! FROM NOW ON I'M GONNA PERTECT YER, SEE? ANY KID THAT TOUCHES YA, I'LL KNOCK HIS BLOCK OFF! SHAKE!

OH! HONEST? **THANKS**!

YOU CURED ME O' BEIN' A HEEL, **WONDER WOMAN**! I WISH YOU'D COME HOME AND CURE MY OL' MAN—HE BEATS THE TAR OUTTA MOM AND SIS!

SO THAT'S IT!

I'LL COME!

⑦

AS THEY APPROACH MUGSY'S HOUSE—

GEE, THERE'S MY SISTER, THIS IS THE FIRST TIME SHE'S BEEN HOME FOR WEEKS - SCARED OF POP, I RECKON. HE'LL BEAT HER UP - WE BETTER HURRY!

THAT'S EILEEN, MR. KNOWLES' SECRETARY AT GENERAL AIRCRAFT!

BUT EILEEN, APPARENTLY, CAN DEFEND HERSELF.

YE'LL COME HOME AND GIMME EVERY DIME YE EARN OR I'LL BREAK YER NECK LIKE AN EMPTY BOTTLE!

TOUCH ME AND I'LL **KILL** YOU!

ARR- RGH.! I'LL LEARN YE—

YOU REPULSIVE BEAST!

STAND BACK! I CAME HERE TO WARN YOU- STOP CALLING MY OFFICE AND LEAVING THREATENING MESSAGES OR I'LL SHOOT YOU!

GO ON WID YER! YOU WOULDN'T SHOOT YOUR OWN FATHER!

YOU'RE NO RELATIVE OF MINE! YOU'RE BETTER DEAD-

BANG! BANG!

QUICKER THAN THE EYE CAN FOLLOW, **WONDER WOMAN** LEAPS BETWEEN THE PISTOL AND ITS TARGET.

BANG! BANG!

8

WONDER WOMAN! WHERE'D SHE COME FROM ? **SHE** MUSTN'T CATCH ME-

OH- **OHOO!** I'M **DYIN'!** SHE **KILT** ME! ME OWN - DAUGHTER! OH-H!

GOOD HERA! DID ONE OF THOSE BULLETS GET BY MY BRACE-LETS? LET'S SEE THE WOUND!

WHY! YOU GREAT BIG BABY! YOU'RE NOT SHOT! THERE'S NOT A SCRATCH ON YOU! BUT THE **SCARE** YOU'VE JUST HAD MAY BE GOOD FOR YOU-GET UP OFF THE FLOOR! I'LL BE BACK LATER AND SEE HOW YOU'RE BEHAVING!

HURRYING TO THE GENERAL AIRCRAFT PLANT, **WONDER WOMAN** ENTERS UNCEREMONIOUS-LY.

GAPING GOLDFISH-THAT'S **WONDER WOMAN!** NO USE SHOOTIN' AT HER- IT'S JUST A WASTE OF BULLETS!

THERE'S SOME-THING QUEER ABOUT THAT GIRL EILEEN- I MUST FIND HER!

HOW D'YOU DO, MR. KNOWLES! I'M LOOKING FOR YOUR SECRE-TARY, EILEEN McGREW!

WONDER WOMAN! THIS **IS** A PLEASURE! EILEEN IS -ER- OUT BUT—

HEY, MR. KNOWLES! MY PALS'RE ALL GETTIN' THE WAR LAUGH DISEASE! I GOT AN IDEA- WOO WOO! LOOK WHO'S HERE! **WONDER WOMAN!**

QUICK, ETTA - SHOW ME THE SICK GIRLS!

LOOK, **WONDER WOMAN,** I'LL BET IT'S THOSE FACTORY OVERALLS THAT GIVE GIRLS THE JITTERS! I'M THE ONLY GAL WHO ISN'T WEARING 'EM AND I'M OKAY!

ETTA, YOU'VE MADE A GREAT DIS-COVERY- IT'S THOSE OVERALLS THAT CARRY THE GERMS!

YEAH- WE'LL GET THESE GOLDURNED POISON SUITS OFF 'EM **IN TIME-** WHILE THERE'S STILL NO "SMILE OF DEATH" ON THEIR FACES!

⑨

AS ETTA HURRIES TO REPORT HER DISCOVERY, **WONDER WOMAN** SEES A FAMILIAR FIGURE SLIPPING INTO A NEARBY OFFICE.

WAIT, EILEEN—I WANT TO SEE YOU!

OH! **YOU** AGAIN!

I WANT TO ASK YOU SOME QUESTIONS. WHY DID YOU SAY PAT MᶜGREW IS NO RELATIVE OF YOURS? AND **WHY** DID YOU TRY TO KILL HIM?

GO ON, ASK ME SOMETHING EASY!

ALL RIGHT! I'LL ASK YOU— **DOES YOUR HAIR COME OFF?**

EEE-EEK! YOU—YOU DEVIL!

LIKE A STREAK OF DUST, THE REDHAIRED GIRL DASHES THROUGH THE DOOR WITH **WONDER WOMAN** IN PURSUIT!

I WON'T CATCH HER—I'LL SEE WHERE SHE LEADS ME!

RACING TO THE ROOF, THE GIRL PLUNGES INTO A VENTILATOR SHAFT.

MM-HM! I WONDER WHERE **THAT** LEADS?

⑩

LOOKS AS IF THAT SHAFT WENT DOWN UNDERGROUND—PLUTO ONLY KNOWS WHAT'S AT THE BOTTOM! BUT I MUST CHASE THIS SPY.

I'LL PROBABLY BE CAPTURED. I'LL HIDE MY MAGIC LASSO, SO I CAN'T BE TIED!

DOWN, DOWN FALLS **WONDER WOMAN** INTO STYGIAN DARKNESS.

AFTER AN ENDLESS-SEEMING INTERVAL, THE AMAZON MAIDEN FEELS HERSELF CAUGHT IN A STEEL NET WHICH CLOSES SWIFTLY OVER HER.

I EXPECTED A TRAP-THIS GANG WORKED ITS PLANS OUT CAREFULLY BEFORE IT BEGAN OPERATING....

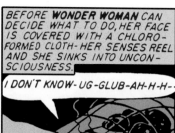

BEFORE **WONDER WOMAN** CAN DECIDE WHAT TO DO, HER FACE IS COVERED WITH A CHLOROFORMED CLOTH- HER SENSES REEL AND SHE SINKS INTO UNCONSCIOUSNESS.

I DON'T KNOW- UG-GLUB-AH-H-H--

HOURS LATER THE AMAZON PRINCESS WAKES TO FIND THE REDHEADED GIRL GRINNING AT HER.

HUH- WHO- WHAT GOES?

I'M MAGDA AND YOU'RE MY PRISONER! WE'RE IN A SECRET BOMBPROOF HANGAR UNDER THE AIRPLANE FACTORY!

HOW LOVELY! WHAT'LL YOU DO WITH ME?

THAT'S FOR THE CHIEF TO SAY. MY ORDERS ARE ONLY TO HOLD YOU SECURELY-- TAKE A LOOK AT YOURSELF!

YOU THINK THESE BANDS WILL HOLD ME?

FRANKLY, I DON'T KNOW! YOU CAN BREAK CHAINS, THEY SAY, AND ROPES, BUT THESE ARE PROCESSED STEEL TWO INCHES THICK- THEY'D HOLD A TANK OR BATTLESHIP!

MASKED GUARDS SECURE **WONDER WOMAN** NEAR ANOTHER GIRL PRISONER.

WONDER WOMAN! WHAT ARE **YOU** DOING HERE?

LOOKING FOR YOU, FOR ONE THING! YOU'RE THE REAL EILEEN, AREN'T YOU? I'M **SO** RELIEVED TO FIND YOU UNHARMED!

THEY KEEP US PRISONERS ALIVE TO HELP AXIS AGENTS IMPERSONATE US. THEY KIDNAP TRUSTED EMPLOYEES AND PUT SPIES IN THEIR PLACES- THE GANG CHIEF IS IMPERSONATING SOME BIG OFFICIAL IN GENERAL AIRCRAFT!

THAT GIVES ME AN IDEA-

WONDER WOMAN SENDS A MENTAL RADIO MESSAGE.

CALLING STEVE TREVOR! GET MUGSY M^cGREW, 210 FIFTH ST. N.E. HAVE HIM ACCUSE GENERAL AIRCRAFT OFFICIALS OF KIDNAPPING HIS SISTER AND WATCH WHAT HAPPENS!

ACTING PROMPTLY ON WONDER WOMAN'S INSTRUCTIONS, STEVE SENDS FOR MUGSY.

MUGSY, WONDER WOMAN'S BEEN CAPTURED BY ENEMY AGENTS! WILL YOU RISK YOUR LIFE TO SAVE HER?

WILL I!! WAIT'LL I GET ME MITTS ON DEM GUYS! LEAD ME TO 'EM!

WITH STEVE AND HIS AGENTS WATCHING THROUGH PEEPHOLES FROM NEIGHBORING OFFICES, MUGSY BEARDS THE GENERAL MANAGER.

SAY, MISTER, WHERE'S MY SISTER EILEEN? I GOT EVIDENCE YOU KIDNAPPED HER!

WHAT! YOU HAVE EVIDENCE??

THEN AN INCREDIBLE THING HAPPENS—THE DISTINGUISHED MR. KNOWLES TURNS INTO A RAGING SNARLING THUG!

YOU DUMB BRAT—I'LL BURY YOU AND YOUR EVIDENCE TOGETHER!

BUNGLER! ALL THIS HAPPENS BECAUSE YOU DIDN'T SHOOT OLD M^cGREW—HE SENT THIS BOY! CHAIN THE BRAT WITH WONDER WOMAN—AND SET THE TIME BOMB. WE'LL KILL ALL PRISONERS AND LAM!

OKAY, CHIEF!

THERE'S YOUR INVINCIBLE WONDER WOMAN— WHAT D'YOU THINK OF HER NOW?

I DON'T KNOW HOW YOU DONE THIS TO HER, BUT SHE OR ME'LL GET YA FOR IT!

THANKS, MUGSY!

YOU'VE HAD YOUR FUN, MAGDA— NOW IT'S MY TURN!

YIPEE! WHAT A DAME!

12

DRAWING HER MAGIC LASSO FROM HIDING, THE BEAUTIFUL AMAZON KNOTS IT SECURELY ABOUT MAGDA'S WRISTS.

SHOW ME THE SECRET PASSAGE WHICH LEADS ABOVE!

NO, NO! I *WILL* NOT—BUT—BUT SOMETHING COMPELS ME TO OBEY!

THAT STONE IS WORKED FROM ABOVE—IT *CANNOT* BE RAISED FROM BELOW! IT WEIGHS 50 TONS!

THAT DOESN'T SOUND HEAVY—YOU HOLD OUR CAPTIVE, MUGSY, WHILE I LIFT THIS TRICK TRAP DOOR!

SETTING HER MIGHTY MUSCLES TO THE TASK, **WONDER WOMAN** RAISES THE GREAT SLAB OF STONE.

MY ARMS ARE A BIT CRAMPED FROM WEARING THOSE STEEL BANDS—THIS WILL LOOSEN THEM!

AS THE STONE IS REMOVED, **WONDER WOMAN** MEETS STEVE LEADING A RESCUE PARTY FROM ABOVE.

THANK HEAVEN YOU'RE SAFE, **WONDER WOMAN!** WE'VE CAUGHT THE SPY CHIEF—THANKS TO YOU AND MUGSY!

WONDER WOMAN AND HER COHORTS EASILY OVERPOWER THE ENEMY GUARDS AND FREE THE PRISONERS.

YOU ARE *SO* WONDERFUL, **WONDER WOMAN!**

BOP! SLAP! WHAM!

IN AN UNDERGROUND LABORATORY UNIFORMS ARE FOUND SOAKING IN WAR LAUGH MANIA GERMS.

THIS IS THE WAY THEY INFECTED FACTORY UNIFORMS BEFORE GIVING THEM TO WORKERS!

THE FIENDS! WE'RE ORDERING NEW OVERALLS ISSUED EVERYWHERE!

⑬

OLD PAT McGREW TAKES A WAR JOB.

GEE, POP, I'M PROUD OF YOU!

SO AM I! YOU'LL FIND IT'S MORE FUN BEING **ADMIRED** BY YOUR FAMILY THAN BULLYING THEM INTO SUBMISSION!

MORE THRILLING ADVENTURES OF **WONDER WOMAN** IN EVERY ISSUE OF **SENSATION COMICS.**

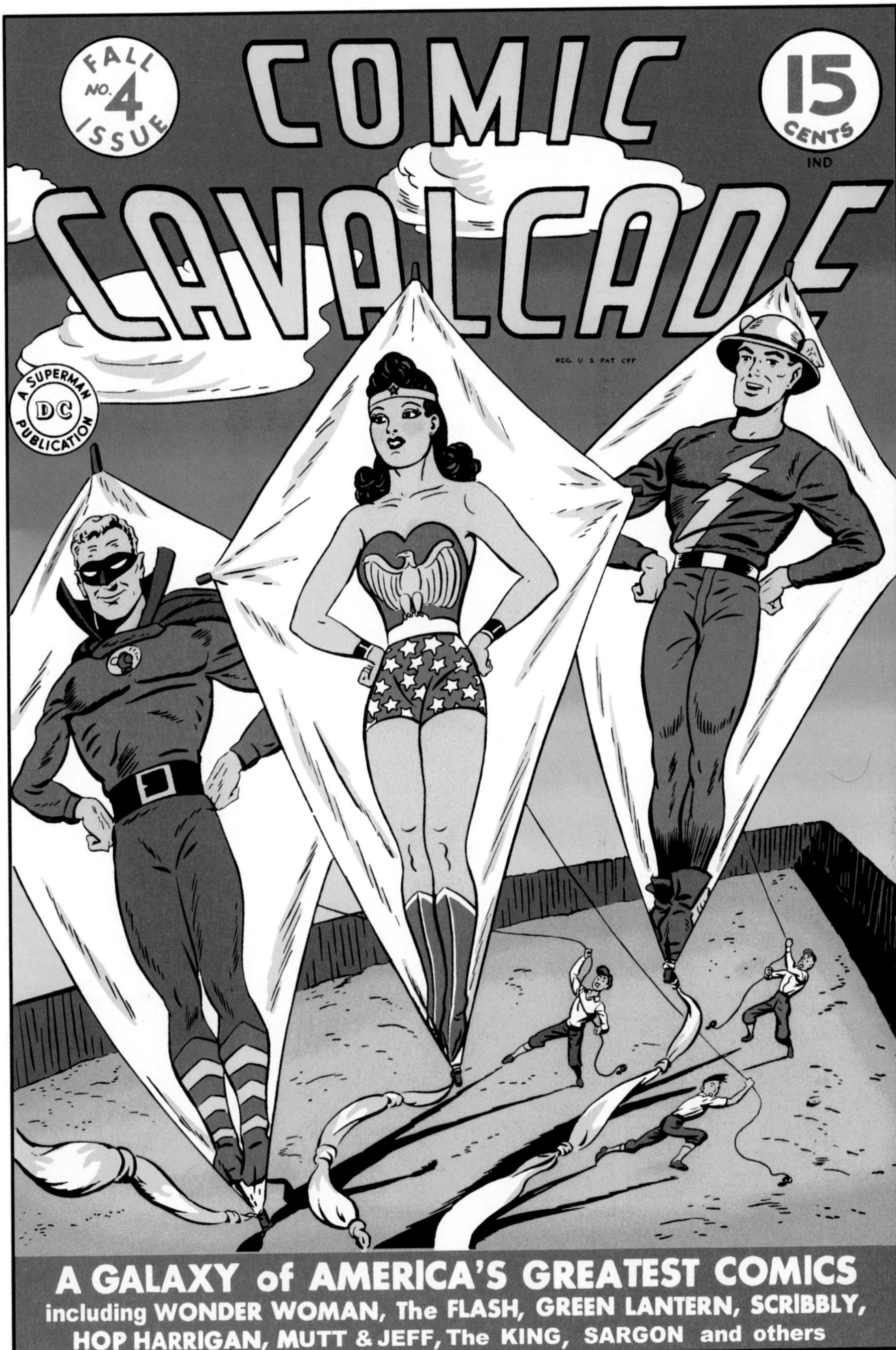
FALL NO. 4 ISSUE
COMIC CAVALCADE
15 CENTS
IND
REG. U S PAT OFF
A SUPERMAN DC PUBLICATION
A GALAXY of AMERICA'S GREATEST COMICS
including WONDER WOMAN, The FLASH, GREEN LANTERN, SCRIBBLY,
HOP HARRIGAN, MUTT & JEFF, The KING, SARGON and others

Wonder Woman

By Charles Moulton

REG. U.S. PAT. OFF.

TO END THE AXIS SUBMARINE MENACE **WONDER WOMAN** PERFECTS A REMARKABLE INVENTION. BUT ENEMY AGENTS ARE OUT TO STEAL IT— AND HER— AT ANY COST! BOUND IN QUICKSAND, STRUGGLING TO KEEP A TOWERING TRANSPORT FROM SPILLING ITS PRECIOUS BURDEN OF HUMAN LIVES, LEADING AN INTREPID ARMY OF COURAGEOUS WAACS TO VICTORY THROUGH A STORM OF ENEMY FIRE— THESE ARE BUT A FEW OF THE TASKS WHICH **WONDER WOMAN** MUST PERFORM TO SAVE THE LONG LIFE LINE OF AMERICA'S SHIPS AND KEEP THEM GIRDLING THE GLOBE!

BEAUTIFUL AS APHRODITE, WISE AS ATHENA, STRONG AS HERCULES AND SWIFT AS MERCURY, THIS LOVELY AMAZON MAIDEN FROM PARADISE ISLAND BRINGS TO AMERICA IN HER TIME OF STRESS NOT ONLY THE POWER OF A MIGHTY PERSONALITY BUT ALSO A NEW IDEAL OF MODERN AMERICAN WOMANHOOD WHICH SHALL SHED THE BRIGHT LIGHT OF HAPPINESS OVER FUTURE GENERATIONS!

MAJOR STEVE TREVOR WALKS INTO THE OFFICE OF DIANA PRINCE -SECRETARY TO THE COLONEL.

CONGRATULATIONS, DIANA! I HEAR THE COLONEL'S SENDING YOU OVERSEAS ON A **VERY** IMPORTANT ASSIGNMENT!

WHAT? THIS IS THE FIRST I'VE HEARD OF IT! ER - ARE **YOU** GOING TOO?

HARRY G. PETER.

1

AM I GOING? HA, HA! NO, MA'AM—I'M ON A PLENTY DANGER-OUS JOB IN THE U.S.A.!

OH, STEVE! BE CAREFUL—

I HATE TO LEAVE HIM BUT HE DOESN'T MIND MY GOING THE LEAST BIT!

DIANA IS SUMMONED TO THE CHIEF'S OFFICE.

I HATE TO SEND YOU OVERSEAS, DIANA, I DON'T KNOW HOW I'M GOING TO GET ALONG WITHOUT YOU!

I'M GLAD SOMEBODY'S GOING TO MISS ME! WHAT'S THE ASSIGNMENT?

YOU REMEMBER WONDER WO-MAN'S INVENTION FOR PROTECT-ING OUR SHIPS FROM SUBMAR-INES? WELL, THE NAVY HAS IN-STALLED HER DEVICE ON THE WAAC TRANSPORT "TROPICA." THEY WANT YOU ABOARD BE-CAUSE WONDER WOMAN SAYS SHE EXPLAINED HER INVENTION TO YOU!

YES, I REMEMBER!

I DON'T SUPPOSE YOU KNOW ANY MECHANICS, DI.! HERE'S WONDER WOMAN'S SHIP MODEL—D' YOU THINK YOU CAN EXPLAIN IT TO ME?

I'LL TRY THIS SHIP HAS MOVE-ABLE SHEETS OF STEEL FOLDED ALONG ITS SIDES

WHEN THE SHIP REACHES A SUBMARINE ZONE THESE STEEL SCREENS ARE PUSHED OUT LIKE THIS! TORPEDOES FIRED AT THE VESSEL HIT THIS PROTECTIVE SHIELD AND EXPLODE HARMLESS-LY. THE DAMAGED SHIELD IS QUICKLY REPAIRED WITH SPARE PARTS.

THE SHIELD IS PUSHED OUT BY HYDRAULIC PRESSURE. WONDER WOMAN'S PRESSURE COORDINATOR IS THE REAL SECRET— IT CONTROLS ALL THE MACHINERY!

HM ...SO THAT'S THE GADGET ENEMY AGENTS HAVE BEEN TRY-ING TO GET!

②

THIS REPORT SHOWS THAT THE ENEMY IS EMPLOYING SOME PERSON TRUSTED BY US TO STEAL THE SECRET OF WONDER WOMAN'S INVENTION WATCH EVERYONE ON THE "TROPICA."

RIGHT! PERHAPS I'D BETTER TAKE THE HOLLIDAY GIRLS TO HELP ME!

GOODBYE, MY DEAR GIRL! WHEN YOU RETURN I - ER - HOPE - AHEM - ER - I MEAN, DO YOU SUPPOSE YOU'D CONSIDER -- THAT IS I COULD YOU---?

MAKE A FULL REPORT? YES, INDEED, COLONEL!

A SUDDEN INTERRUPTION RELIEVES DIANA'S EMBARRASSMENT BUT INCREASES THE COLONEL'S.

HELLO, COLONEL - OH.! BEG PARDON!

HAR-RUMP! QUITE ALL RIGHT! MISS PRINCE, THIS IS MR. ALLTRUE BLYTHE, THE ENGINEER IN CHARGE OF TESTING **WONDER WOMAN'S** INVENTION!

AS DIANA LEAVES THE ROOM, COLONEL DARNELL PRESSES A HASTILY SCRIBBLED NOTE INTO HER HAND.

GLAD TO HAVE MET YOU, MR. BLYTHE — I'LL SEE YOU LATER ON THE SHIP.

WHAT'S THIS ? "WATCH BLYTHE CLOSELY - I SUSPECT HIM.!" HM! SO THE TESTING ENGINEER HIMSELF MAY BE AN ENEMY AGENT - WHAT A SWEET ASSIGNMENT!

BLYTHE'S SECRETARY, BERTHA NAGLE, ALSO SEEMS DETERMINED TO KEEP TABS ON THE ENGINEER AS HE LEAVES FOR THE SHIP.

GOODBYE, BERTHA— YOU WILL REMAIN HERE UNTIL I RETURN.

IF YOU THINK YOU'RE GOING TO GET AWAY FROM ME LIKE THAT, MR. "ALLTRUE" **BLYTHE**, YOU'VE GOT ANOTHER THINK COMING!

LATER, A DETERMINED GIRL DIVES FROM A PIER NEAR THE WAAC TRANSPORT TROPICA.

③

AND AFTER A SWIFT SWIM, CLIMBS UNSEEN TO THE TROPICA'S DECK.

I'LL "BORROW" SOME GIRL'S UNIFORM AND MINGLE WITH THE WAACS - BLYTHE WILL NEVER RECOGNIZE ME, IF I KEEP OUT OF HIS WAY!

MEANWHILE, ETTA CANDY RE-CEIVES AN UNEXPECTED VISIT FROM *WONDER WOMAN*.

WOO WOO—**WONDER WOMAN!** WHAT YOU DOIN' WITH THAT TRUCK LOAD O' TRUNKS?

CALL THE GIRLS AND I'LL SHOW YOU!

DIANA HAD YOU GIRLS APPOINTED SPECIAL ARMY INTELLIGENCE AGENTS! YOU'LL WEAR THESE WAAC UNIFORMS ON THE TRANSPORT TROPICA AND GUARD MY TORPEDO-PROTECTION APPARATUS

YIPPEE! SWELL UNIFORMS!

AUXILIARY ETTA CANDY REPORTING FOR DUTY. HI-YA, GENERAL!

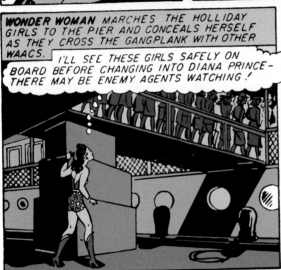

WONDER WOMAN MARCHES THE HOLLIDAY GIRLS TO THE PIER AND CONCEALS HERSELF AS THEY CROSS THE GANGPLANK WITH OTHER WAACS.

I'LL SEE THESE GIRLS SAFELY ON BOARD BEFORE CHANGING INTO DIANA PRINCE—THERE MAY BE ENEMY AGENTS WATCHING!

SUDDENLY A ROPE PARTS, GIRLS SHRIEK, AND THE HEAVILY LOADED GANGPLANK CRASHES TOWARD THE PIER BELOW.

EEE-EEK!

HELP!

WOO WOO!

STEADY GIRLS, HOLD TIGHT— I'VE GOT THE GANGPLANK!

WHEE-EE! **WONDER WOMAN** CAUGHT US— WE'RE **SAVED!**

I'M BLYTHE, THE ENGINEER! YOU PERFORMED A MIRACLE, **WONDER WOMAN!** WHAT **COULD** HAVE CAUSED THE ACCIDENT?

I WONDER! THIS ROPE IS CUT NOT BROKEN—MAYBE YOU CAN EXPLAIN IT, MR. BLYTHE!

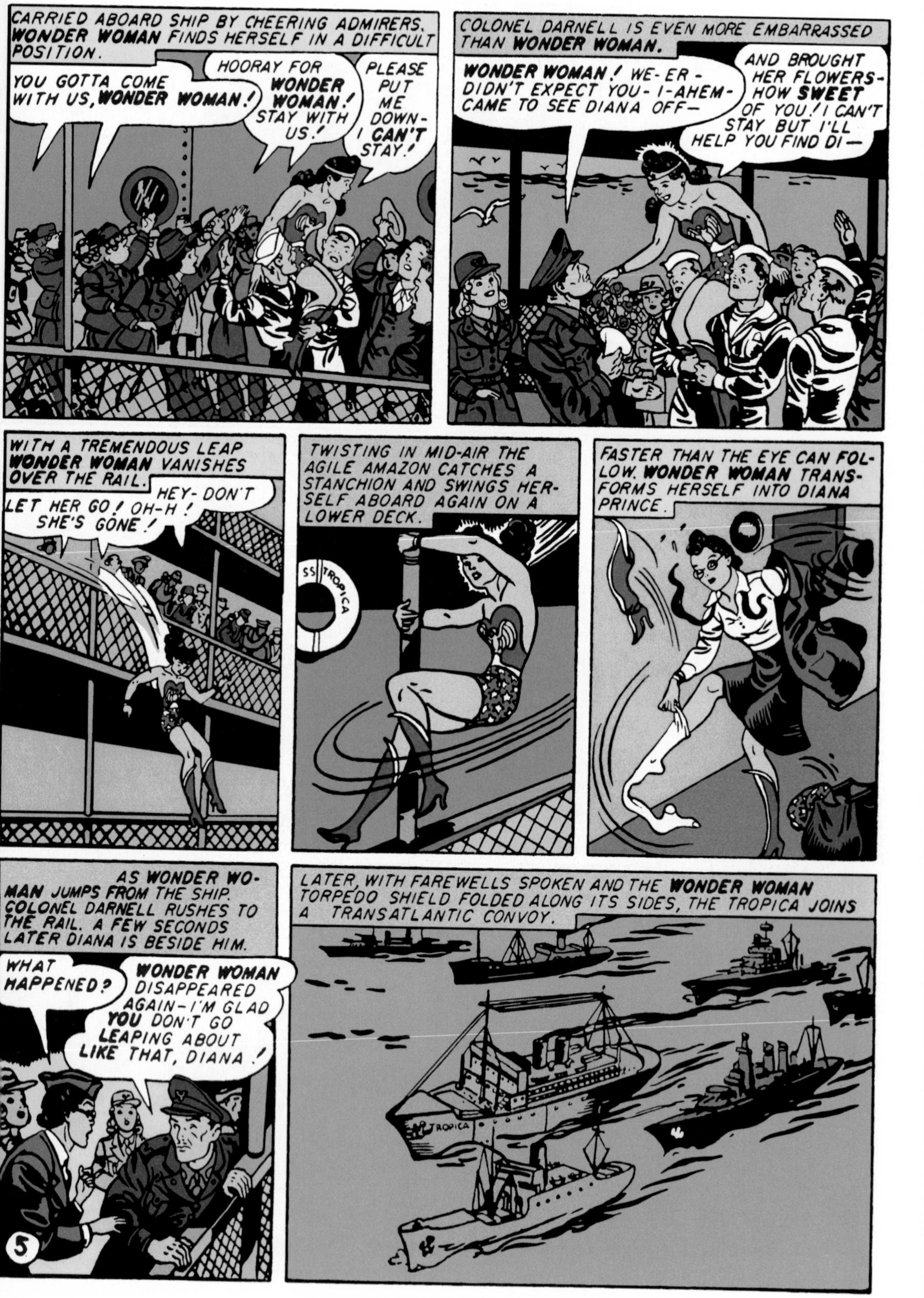

CARRIED ABOARD SHIP BY CHEERING ADMIRERS, WONDER WOMAN FINDS HERSELF IN A DIFFICULT POSITION.
YOU GOTTA COME WITH US, WONDER WOMAN!
HOORAY FOR WONDER WOMAN! STAY WITH US!
PLEASE PUT ME DOWN- I CAN'T STAY!
COLONEL DARNELL IS EVEN MORE EMBARRASSED THAN WONDER WOMAN.
WONDER WOMAN! WE-ER-DIDN'T EXPECT YOU-I-AHEM-CAME TO SEE DIANA OFF-
AND BROUGHT HER FLOWERS-HOW SWEET OF YOU! I CAN'T STAY BUT I'LL HELP YOU FIND DI-
WITH A TREMENDOUS LEAP WONDER WOMAN VANISHES OVER THE RAIL.
HEY- DON'T LET HER GO! OH-H! SHE'S GONE!
TWISTING IN MID-AIR THE AGILE AMAZON CATCHES A STANCHION AND SWINGS HERSELF ABOARD AGAIN ON A LOWER DECK.
SS TROPICA
FASTER THAN THE EYE CAN FOLLOW, WONDER WOMAN TRANSFORMS HERSELF INTO DIANA PRINCE.
AS WONDER WOMAN JUMPS FROM THE SHIP, COLONEL DARNELL RUSHES TO THE RAIL. A FEW SECONDS LATER DIANA IS BESIDE HIM.
WHAT HAPPENED?
WONDER WOMAN DISAPPEARED AGAIN-I'M GLAD YOU DON'T GO LEAPING ABOUT LIKE THAT, DIANA!
5
LATER, WITH FAREWELLS SPOKEN AND THE WONDER WOMAN TORPEDO SHIELD FOLDED ALONG ITS SIDES, THE TROPICA JOINS A TRANSATLANTIC CONVOY.
TROPICA

IN THE WAACS' QUARTERS A STERN FACED **FIRST OFFICER** MAKES LIFE HARD FOR THE HOLLIDAY GIRLS.

OH, TO BE A WAAC AND WITH THE WAACS TO DWELL—

ATTEN-**SHUN!**

ALWAYS SALUTE AN OFFICER! YOUR UNIFORMS ARE A MESS—YOU SHOULD **NEVER** BE SEEN CARELESSLY DRESSED!

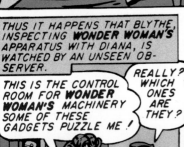

BUT LATER IN THE DAY, THE TABLES ARE TURNED—

HELP! STOP THIEF! SOMEBODY STOLE MY UNIFORM!

ALWAYS SALUTE AN OFFICER! **NEVER** DRESS CARELESSLY!

WHILE IN A SHELTERED CORNER OF THE SHIP, BERTHA NAGLE ARRAYS HERSELF IN A "BORROWED" UNIFORM.

HA HA! IT'S A GOOD THING THAT WAAC OFFICER WAS TAKING A BATH WHEN I WANDERED INTO HER CABIN. NOW TO FIND MY DEAR BOSS BLYTHE AND SHADOW HIM!

THUS IT HAPPENS THAT BLYTHE, INSPECTING **WONDER WOMAN'S** APPARATUS WITH DIANA, IS WATCHED BY AN UNSEEN OBSERVER.

THIS IS THE CONTROL ROOM FOR **WONDER WOMAN'S** MACHINERY SOME OF THESE GADGETS PUZZLE ME!

REALLY? WHICH ONES ARE THEY?

WELL—THAT GADGET THERE—WHAT IS IT?

OH, THAT—IT'S **WONDER WOMAN'S** PRESSURE COORDINATOR—THE MASTER CONTROL OF HER ENTIRE INVENTION. THAT LITTLE LEVER PUSHES THE PROTECTING SHIELD OUT FROM THE SHIP AND PULLS IT BACK AGAIN.

NOW I KNOW THE THING BLYTHE HAS BEEN TALKING ABOUT—IT'S LUCKY I FOLLOWED HIM!

6

THE THIRD DAY OUT. SUBMARINES ARE SIGHTED.

CLEAR DECKS FOR ACTION—ALL HANDS TO BATTLE STATIONS! SET **WONDER WOMAN'S** PROTECTIVE SHIELD AGAINST TORPEDOES!

ENGINEER BLYTHE, IN THE CONTROL ROOM, MOVES THE PRESSURE COORDINATOR TO "FULL SET" POSITION.

WELL, HERE'S THE CRUCIAL TEST— WILL **WONDER WOMAN'S** SHIELD PROTECT THE SHIP?

OF COURSE IT WILL! I ONLY HOPE THE ENEMY SHOOTS PLENTY OF TORPEDOES AT US!

IT SEEMS LIKELY THAT DIANA WILL GET HER WISH AS A PACK OF PERISCOPES POKE UGLY NOSES ABOVE THE SURFACE.

EVEN THOUGH THE BIG VESSEL IS COMPLETELY SURROUNDED BY WONDER WOMAN'S PROTECTIVE SHIELD, IT APPEARS TO HAVE LITTLE CHANCE AGAINST 3 TORPEDOES RUSHING TOWARD IT SIMULTANEOUSLY.

WOO WOO! HERE THEY COME!

THEY'LL SINK US SURE!

OH, NO— THE SHIP MAY ROLL A BIT BUT THAT'S ALL THE ONLY THING WE HAVE TO WORRY ABOUT IS GETTING SEASICK!

BANG!!

BANG!!

BANG!

AND THE GOOD SHIP TROPICA PLOWS ON, UNDAMAGED SAVE FOR THREE JAGGED RENTS IN ITS **WONDER WOMAN** SAFETY SHIELD!

WHILE THE U-BOATS ARE DRIVEN OFF OR SUNK BY DESTROYERS, THE TROPICA'S PROTECTIVE SHIELD IS DRAWN IN AND ITS DAMAGED SECTIONS REPLACED.

HOW LONG WILL IT TAKE TO MAKE REPAIRS?

LESS THAN AN HOUR, THEN YOU'LL SET TO SHIELD AGAIN TO GUARD AGAINST SURPRISE ATTACKS.

I WONDER IF HE **WILL** SET IT—

AS REPAIRS ARE COMPLETED, ETTA CANDY REPORTS TO DIANA.

LISTEN! MY GIRL BRENDA WHO'S WATCHING THE CONTROL ROOM SAYS BLYTHE IS IN THERE FIGHTIN' WITH A BLONDE BRENDA KNOWS— BERTHA NAGLE! HAVE A LEMON DROP?

LEAPING DOWN THE COMPANIONWAY, DIANA SEES BLYTHE AND HIS SECRETARY FIGHTING DESPERATELY.

YOU SNEAK! I'LL TEACH YOU—

OH—OOF---

BREAKING LOOSE FROM BLYTHE'S GRIP, BERTHA RACES FROM THE ROOM.

I'LL GET YOU, YOU DOUBLE CROSSING SNOOP—

COME BACK HERE! HMP—LET HIM GO— I WONDER—

RUSHING TO THE CONTROL BOARD DIANA FINDS THE SECRET PRESSURE COORDINATOR MISSING!

MERCIFUL MINERVA! HE IS A NAZI AFTER ALL— HE'S STOLEN MY COORDINATOR! I CAN'T SET THE SHIELD—**NOW** WHAT'LL I DO?

WITHOUT WARNING COMES A TERRIFIC EXPLOSION THAT SHAKES THE SHIP FROM STEM TO STERN.

GREAT APHRODITE! A TORPEDO HIT US WHILE MY SAFETY SHIELD WAS OUT OF COMMISSION!

CRASH! BANG!!!

⑧

AMID A WELTER OF CONFU-SION **WONDER WOMAN** HASTILY RESUMES HER IDENTITY.

TO HELP IN THIS EMERGENCY I'LL HAVE TO BE MYSELF—THERE ISN'T EVEN TIME TO SAVE POOR DIANA'S CLOTHES!

AS THE SHIP KEELS OVER **WON-DER WOMAN** DECIDES ON DES-PERATE MEASURES.

WHEN THE SHIP TURNS ON HER SIDE SHE'LL SINK LIKE A ROCK! I'LL HOLD HER STEADY WHILE YOU GET EVERYBODY INTO BOATS—HURRY!

OKAY, BABE—WOO WOO!

TEARING A BROKEN MAST FROM THE WRECKAGE, THE MIGHTY AMAZON GIRL BRACES IT HIGH AGAINST THE SHIP'S SHARPLY TILTING SIDE.

WHILE **WONDER WOMAN** WITH COLOSSAL STRENGTH HOLDS THE GREAT VESSEL IN PLACE, WAACS AND NURSES SCRAMBLE DOWN ITS SLOPING SIDE TO LIFE RAFTS.

AS THE LAST LIFE RAFT CLEARS THE SHIP **WON-DER WOMAN** DIVES DEEP, RACING THE STRICK-EN SHIP WHICH PLUNGES AFTER HER INTO THE DEPTHS.

THIS IS GOOD SWIMMING PRACTICE. BUT NOT BEFORE BREAKFAST!

⑨

MEANWHILE A SINISTER GRAY SHAPE SURFACES AMONG ITS VICTIMS.

TAKE EFFERYBODY OFF DAT RAFT UND MAKE DEM PRISON-ERS! ABANDON ALL OTHER LIFE BOATS!

JA, HERR COMMANDANT!

UNDER THREAT OF NAZI GUNS, 10 AMERICANS CLIMB TO THE U-BOAT DECK— AMONG THEM BLYTHE AND BERTHA NAGLE!

YOU THINK YOU'VE WON, BUT **WONDER WOMAN** IS HERE— SHE'LL—

SHUD UP UND GO BELOW!

AS THE U-BOAT GOES DOWN **WONDER WOMAN** COMES UP— UNDER ETTA'S RAFT.

HEY! WHAT'S THIS ANOTHER NAZI HOLDUP?

NO, IT'S AN AMAZON HIGHJACKING!

INTO ALL THE LIFE RAFTS SHE CAN FIND INTO A FLOTILLA **WONDER WOMAN** TOWS THEM WITH HER MAGIC LASSO.

WE WERE ON THE SOUTHERN ROUTE— THERE'S A TROPICAL ISLAND I REMEMBER SOMEWHERE IN THIS VICINITY!

MEANWHILE, THE NAZI SUBMARINE COMMANDER HEADS FOR THE SAME DESTINATION.

DERE IS DER ISLAND WHERE OUR SUPPLIES ARE HIDDEN— SET DER COURSE FOR IT, HANS!

JAWOHL, HERR COMMANDANT!

VELL, HERR BLYTHE, VE HAF **VONDER VOMAN'S** INVENTION, DER PRESSURE COORDINATOR. BUT YOU MUST EXPLAIN IT— VE CANNOT UNDERSTAND DER VAY IT VORKS!

NEITHER CAN I— ONLY **WONDER WOMAN** HERSELF UNDERSTANDS IT!

10

BERTHA IS QUESTIONED.

TAKE OFF THAT UNIFORM I'VE MUST CAPTURE THIS **VONDER VOMAN**— VERE IS SHE?

HOW WOULD I KNOW? SHE KEPT THE SHIP FROM CAPSIZING— MAYBE SHE DROWNED! BUT DON'T COUNT ON IT!

THE NAZI COMMANDER QUESTIONS THE WAACS.

SO YOU DON'T KNOW VOT HAPPENED TO **VONDER VOMAN!** PERHAPS A LITTLE PERSUASION VILL REFRESH DER MEMORY, NEIN?

YOU'RE TALKING TO A UNITED STATES SOLDIER, MR. NAZI! YOU WON'T GET ANY INFORMATION OUT OF ME!

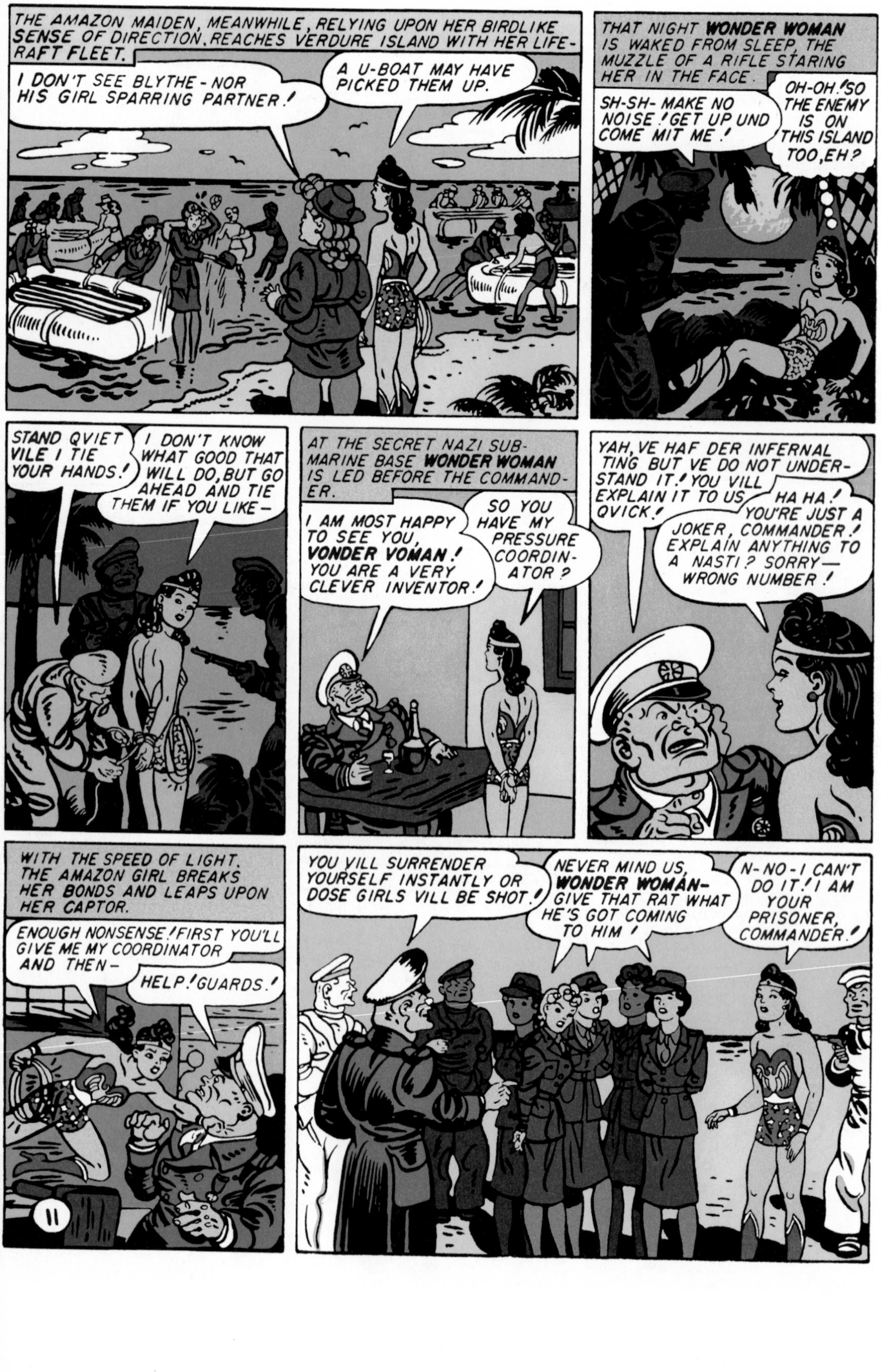
THE AMAZON MAIDEN, MEANWHILE, RELYING UPON HER BIRDLIKE SENSE OF DIRECTION, REACHES VERDURE ISLAND WITH HER LIFE-RAFT FLEET.
I DON'T SEE BLYTHE - NOR HIS GIRL SPARRING PARTNER!
A U-BOAT MAY HAVE PICKED THEM UP.
THAT NIGHT WONDER WOMAN IS WAKED FROM SLEEP, THE MUZZLE OF A RIFLE STARING HER IN THE FACE.
SH-SH- MAKE NO NOISE! GET UP UND COME MIT ME!
OH-OH! SO THE ENEMY IS ON THIS ISLAND TOO, EH?
STAND QVIET VILE I TIE YOUR HANDS!
I DON'T KNOW WHAT GOOD THAT WILL DO, BUT GO AHEAD AND TIE THEM IF YOU LIKE—
AT THE SECRET NAZI SUBMARINE BASE WONDER WOMAN IS LED BEFORE THE COMMANDER.
I AM MOST HAPPY TO SEE YOU, VONDER VOMAN! YOU ARE A VERY CLEVER INVENTOR!
SO YOU HAVE MY PRESSURE COORDINATOR?
YAH, VE HAF DER INFERNAL TING BUT VE DO NOT UNDERSTAND IT! YOU VILL EXPLAIN IT TO US QVICK!
HA HA! YOU'RE JUST A JOKER, COMMANDER! EXPLAIN ANYTHING TO A NASTI? SORRY— WRONG NUMBER!
WITH THE SPEED OF LIGHT, THE AMAZON GIRL BREAKS HER BONDS AND LEAPS UPON HER CAPTOR.
ENOUGH NONSENSE! FIRST YOU'LL GIVE ME MY COORDINATOR AND THEN—
HELP! GUARDS!
11
YOU VILL SURRENDER YOURSELF INSTANTLY OR DOSE GIRLS VILL BE SHOT!
NEVER MIND US, WONDER WOMAN— GIVE THAT RAT WHAT HE'S GOT COMING TO HIM!
N-NO- I CAN'T DO IT! I AM YOUR PRISONER, COMMANDER!

WONDER WOMAN, THIS TIME, IS BOUND HAND AND FOOT WITH HEAVY WIRE.

YOU ARE A STRONG GIRL, **VONDER VOMAN!** BUT NO HUMAN CAN BREAK THAT VIRE. VE VILL NOW TRY A LEEDLE EXPERIMENT.

VE HAF PLACED YOU IN QVICKSAND, MEINE FREUNDIN! ALRETTY YOU HAF SUNK TO DER ANKLES— YOU VILL GO DOWN UND DOWN! BUT TO ESCAPE YOU HAF ONLY TO EXPLAIN YOUR INVENTION!

GOODY GOODY— WHAT FUN!

WHILE **WONDER WOMAN** SINKS DEEPER IN THE TREACHEROUS SAND LET US GO BACK TO STEVE'S OFFICE IN WASHINGTON AS RADIO NEWS OF THE TROPICA'S SINKING ARRIVES.

WONDER WOMAN SAVED ALL ON BOARD—

WHAT! WONDER WOMAN!

IT IS BELIEVED THAT **WONDER WOMAN** TOWED THE LIFE RAFTS IN THE DIRECTION OF VERDURE, AN UNINHABITED ISLAND BUT SINCE NO PLANES ARE IN THAT REGION—

THERE'LL **BE** A PLANE IN THAT REGION- PRONTO!

STEVE TAKES OFF IN **WONDER WOMAN'S** OWN INVISIBLE PLANE- SPEED 2500 MILES AN HOUR.

THE TRIP WON'T TAKE LONG IN THIS PLANE— BUT FINDING THAT ISLAND WILL BE A JOB!

WONDER WOMAN, MEANWHILE, AS THE SAND REACHES HER WAIST, MAKES A FUTILE ATTEMPT TO JUMP- ONLY TO SINK DEEPER IN THE BOTTOMLESS PIT!

NO USE- CAN'T JUMP WITHOUT FOOTING!

HO HO! **NOW** VILL YOU SUBMIT?

⑫

SUDDENLY, WITHOUT THE LEAST WARNING, A SILENT INVISIBLE PLANE SWOOPS LOW AND **WONDER WOMAN** ACTING WITH LIGHTNING SPEED BURSTS HER ARM BONDS!

VAS IS DAS? SHOOT HER— ACH, HIMMEL! SHE VARDS OFF BULLETS MIT DER BRACELETS!

STEVE, YOU **DARLING**! YOU SAVED MY **LIFE**! NOW QUICK, HEAD NORTH ABOUT A MILE—WE'VE GOT ETTA AND A COMPANY OF WAACS CAMPED ON THIS ISLAND—

RIGHT!

A FEW MINUTES LATER **WONDER WOMAN** LEADS A COMPANY OF FEARLESS WAACS AGAINST THE HEAVILY ARMED NAZIS.

COME ON GIRLS— LET'S **GET** 'EM!

WE'RE WITH YOU, **WONDER WOMAN**! ROPE THOSE NAZIS!

THE NAZIS FIGHT FIERCELY BUT ARE SUBDUED BY INDOMITABLE WOMEN.

WOO WOO! GET YOUR MAN, GIRLS—HERE'S MINE!

WONDER WOMAN, FREEING THE PRISONERS, CATCHES BERTHA NAGLE TRYING TO ESCAPE.

WHY RUN AWAY? COME BACK HERE! WHAT'S THIS— MY PRESSURE COORDINATOR!

I WON'T TALK—B-BUT SOMETHING COMPELS ME! I STOLE YOUR INVENTION!

CONFESS EVERYTHING!

BERTHA NAGLE IS MY NAME— I'M A NAZI SPY! I WORKED FOR BLYTHE BECAUSE HE KNOWS NAVY SECRETS. I FOLLOWED HIM ON THE TROPICA TO FIND YOUR COORDINATOR. I CUT DOWN THE GANGPLANK BECAUSE I SAW BRENDA, WHO KNOWS ME, COMING ABOARD!

I APOLOGIZE FOR SUSPECTING YOU, MR. BLYTHE!

THAT'S ALL RIGHT— EVEN BEING SUSPECTED BY **WONDER WOMAN** IS A PLEASURE I ASSURE YOU!

LATER **WONDER WOMAN** SENDS A WIRE TO COLONEL DARNELL.

SERVICE RADIOGRAM TO COLONEL DARNELL, WASHINGTON, DON'T WORRY ABOUT ME. I AM NOT LOST —BUT MY CLOTHES ARE—WILL BORROW BARREL AND RETURN EVENTUALLY— SIGNED DIANA PRINCE.

NOW I CAN TAKE A GOOD VACATION AND GET SOME REAL EXERCISE AT PARADISE ISLAND!

MORE EXCITING ADVENTURES OF **WONDER WOMAN** IN EVERY ISSUE OF **SENSATION COMICS**

FOR VICTORY BUY UNITED STATES WAR BONDS AND STAMPS

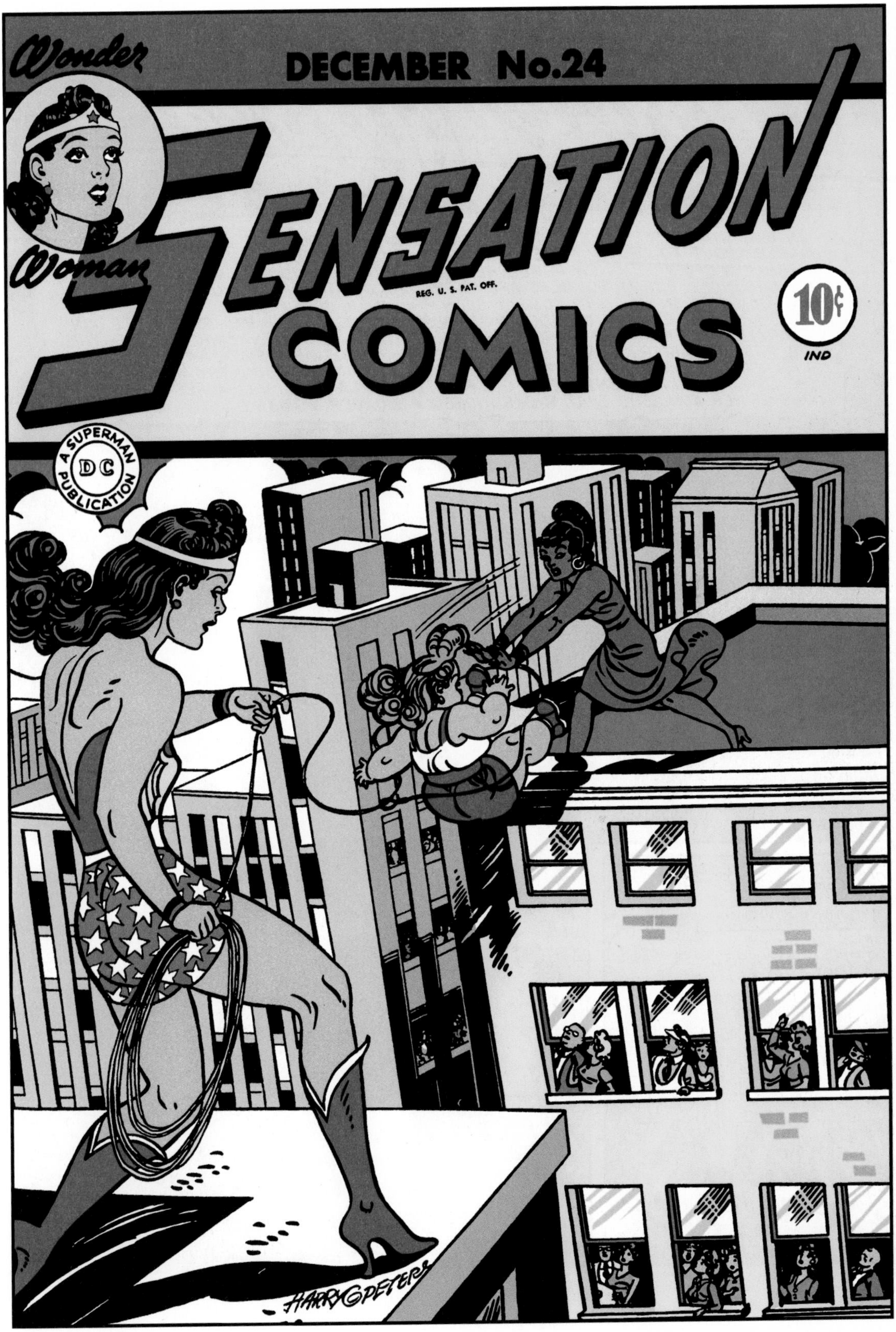
Wonder Woman
DECEMBER No.24
SENSATION
REG. U. S. PAT. OFF.
COMICS
10¢
IND
A SUPERMAN DC PUBLICATION
HARRY G PETERS

WONDER WOMAN

REG. U.S PAT. OFF

By CHARLES MOULTON

IN THIS TITANIC STRUGGLE, SINGLEHANDED, AGAINST THOUSANDS OF JAPANESE WAR PLANES ABOUT TO DESTROY THE AMERICAN ARMY, **WONDER WOMAN** USES HER MATCHLESS BRAIN WITH NEW POWER RECEIVED FROM APHRODITE! AMERICAN PLANES ARE GROUNDED, ENEMY BOMBERS ARE IN THE AIR, OUR TROOPS ARE UNPROTECTED — WHAT CAN **ONE** MIND DO TO COMBAT SUCH FRIGHTFUL ODDS.?

BUT THAT ONE BRAIN IS **WONDER WOMAN'S!** SHE USES BOTH HALVES OF HER BRAIN SEPARATELY TO FIGHT TWO FIERCE BATTLES AT THE SAME MOMENT! WHEN YOU SEE THIS GIRL FROM PARADISE ISLAND — BEAUTIFUL AS APHRODITE, WISE AS ATHENA, STRONGER THAN HERCULES AND SWIFTER THAN MERCURY — SERVING HER COUNTRY AND THE MAN SHE LOVES IN THIS **ADVENTURE OF THE PILOTLESS PLANE,** YOU WILL AGREE WITH MILLIONS OF HER ADMIRERS THAT SHE IS INDEED A **WONDER WOMAN!**

RETURNING UNEXPECTEDLY TO THE OFFICE AFTER HOURS, STEVE SURPRISES DIANA IN **WONDER WOMAN'S** COSTUME!

HORNSWOGGLING HOPTOADS! WHERE'D YOU GET **THAT** COSTUME, DIANA?

OH— ER—

1

HARRY G. PETERS

Dear Steve:

Diana is on her way to Paradise Island with Paula to help on some important work. This is in line of official duty to serve America so please arrange a leave of absence for Diana.

Always your,

Wonder Woman

THE FEAT WHICH **WONDER WOMAN** NOW PERFORMS IS MADE POSSIBLE BY HER EARLY AMAZON TRAINING. THE BRAIN HAS TWO HALVES OR HEMISPHERES WHICH, IF PROPERLY TRAINED, MAY ACT INDEPENDENTLY, PERFORMING TWO DIFFERENT ACTS AT THE SAME TIME. MANY NORMAL PEOPLE HAVE THIS ABILITY TO A SLIGHT DEGREE-- FOR EXAMPLE-- THOSE WHO CAN WRITE SIMULTANEOUSLY WITH BOTH HANDS. AMAZON GIRLS, HOWEVER, ARE TAUGHT TO SOLVE DIFFICULT MATHEMATICAL PROBLEMS WITH ONE HALF OF THE BRAIN WHILE WITH THE OTHER HALF THEY CONDUCT A STRENUOUS WRESTLING MATCH WITH SOME SISTER STUDENT. **WONDER WOMAN**, USING THIS ABILITY, TALKS WITH STEVE WHILE SENDING HIM, AT THE SAME TIME, A MENTAL RADIO MESSAGE FROM DIANA, ALSO CASTING A VISION OF DIANA ON THE VIEWPLATE BY MENTAL TELEPATHY.

②

I WAS STUPID TO THINK **YOU** COULD BE DIANA - SHE'S AS DIFFERENT FROM YOU AS AN ANT FROM AN ANGEL! BUT WHY LEAVE NOW? THERE ARE SO MANY THINGS WE HAVE TO TALK ABOUT!

SORRY, STEVE. I **MUST** GO. THE QUEEN, MY MOTHER, HAS SUMMONED ME.

PAULA HELPS **WONDER WOMAN** WHEEL OUT HER SILENT, INVISIBLE PLANE FROM THE DESERTED BARN WHERE SHE KEEPS IT HIDDEN.

WHY ARE WE SUMMONED, PRINCESS?

MOTHER SAID A GREAT DANGER THREATENS — SHE DIDN'T EXPLAIN!

WHILE SPEEDING OVER DISTANT SEAS AT MORE THAN 2000 MILES AN HOUR, **WONDER WOMAN** PICKS UP A SHORT WAVE JAPANESE RADIO MESSAGE.

亢 Ch 弄 州 - KOMAN NO NO-BERU YANKEES - KESCHITE NAI TABU ATO NOCHI - KENKWA SURU NIPPON — JIN!

THAT'S A JAPANESE ARMY REPORT!

YES, A STRANGE MESSAGE — "PROUD TO SAY YANKEES NEVER WILL FLY TO FIGHT JAPANESE!" IS THAT AN OFFICIAL JAP REPORT OR MORE PROPAGANDA?

THE QUEEN HERSELF IS AT THE AMAZON LANDING FIELD TO MEET MEET THE GIRLS.

WELCOME HOME AGAIN, MY CHILD TO PARADISE ISLAND!

MOTHER!

HOLA, PRINCESS, AND OUR PAULA! APHRODITE WITH YOU!

AND WITH YOU!

WHAT IS THIS DANGER THAT THREATENS US, MOTHER?

THE JAPANESE HAVE DISCOVERED A NEW WEAPON WHICH THEY SAY WILL DEFEAT AMERICA! I'LL SHOW YOU WHAT I'VE LEARNED ABOUT THIS ON THE MAGIC SPHERE!

③

THIS MAGIC SPHERE, AS YOU KNOW, IS A GIFT OF ATHENA, GODDESS OF WISDOM. WHEN TUNED TO ANY TIME OR PLACE IN THE WORLD'S HISTORY ITS VIEWPLATE SHOWS EVERYTHING THAT HAPPENED THERE!

THE QUEEN CONTINUES: "HERE YOU SEE THE JAP-ANESE ARMY COMMANDER REPORTING TO THE PREMIER."

HER HIGHNESS, OUR CHEMICAL RESEARCH CHIEF, HAS FOUND MEANS TO KEEP ALL AMERICAN PLANES FROM FLYING!

BANZAI! NOW WE DESTROY STUPID YANKEES!

DEEPLY CONCERNED WITH THE GRAVE PROBLEM OF WARFARE, THE AMAZON MAIDEN PRAYS TO APHRODITE FOR GUIDANCE.

OH GODDESS OF LOVE AND BEAUTY, HELP ME DEFEAT THESE DEADLY PLANS OF AMERICA'S ENEMIES!

REMAIN TONIGHT IN MY TEMPLE, BELOVED DAUGHTER, AND I WILL GIVE THEE INSPIRATION!

ALL NIGHT THE PRINCESS LIES BEFORE APHRODITE'S THRONE, HER BRAIN BEING CHARGED LIKE A LIVING BATTERY WITH MAGNETIC POWER FLOWING FROM THE GODDESS' FEET.

IN THE MORNING THE AMAZON GIRL FEELS HERSELF A NEW WOMAN.

OH, *NOW* I FEEL STRONG ENOUGH TO BEAT THE WHOLE JAP ARMY, SINGLE-HANDED! FIRST I WILL CARRY OUT APHRODITE'S INSPIRATION!

THE GODDESS GAVE ME AN IDEA FOR CONTROLLING MY AIRPLANE BY MENTAL RADIO! WILL YOU GIRLS HELP ME BUILD THE APPARATUS?

MALA IS CLEVERER THAN I—

NONSENSE! YOU'RE THE CLEVEREST WOMAN ALIVE, PAULA—LET'S GO!

④

WHILE THE AMAZON GIRLS LA-BOR TO PERFECT **WONDER WO-MAN'S** REMARKABLE INVEN-TION, STEVE TREVOR FLIES TO CHINA ON A SPECIAL ASSIGNMENT.

GLAD TO SEE YOU, TREVOR—I UNDERSTAND YOU BRING IMPORTANT INFORMATION!

YES, GENERAL RENAULT!

WE'VE HAD A REPORT THAT THE NIPS HAVE PLANTED AN UNIDEN-TIFIED SPY BEHIND YOUR LINES WITH SOME DEVICE THAT WILL PUT ALL YOUR PLANES OUT OF COMMISSION!

IMPOSSIBLE—IT CAN'T BE DONE! BUT WE MUST SPOT THAT SPY IMMEDIATELY!

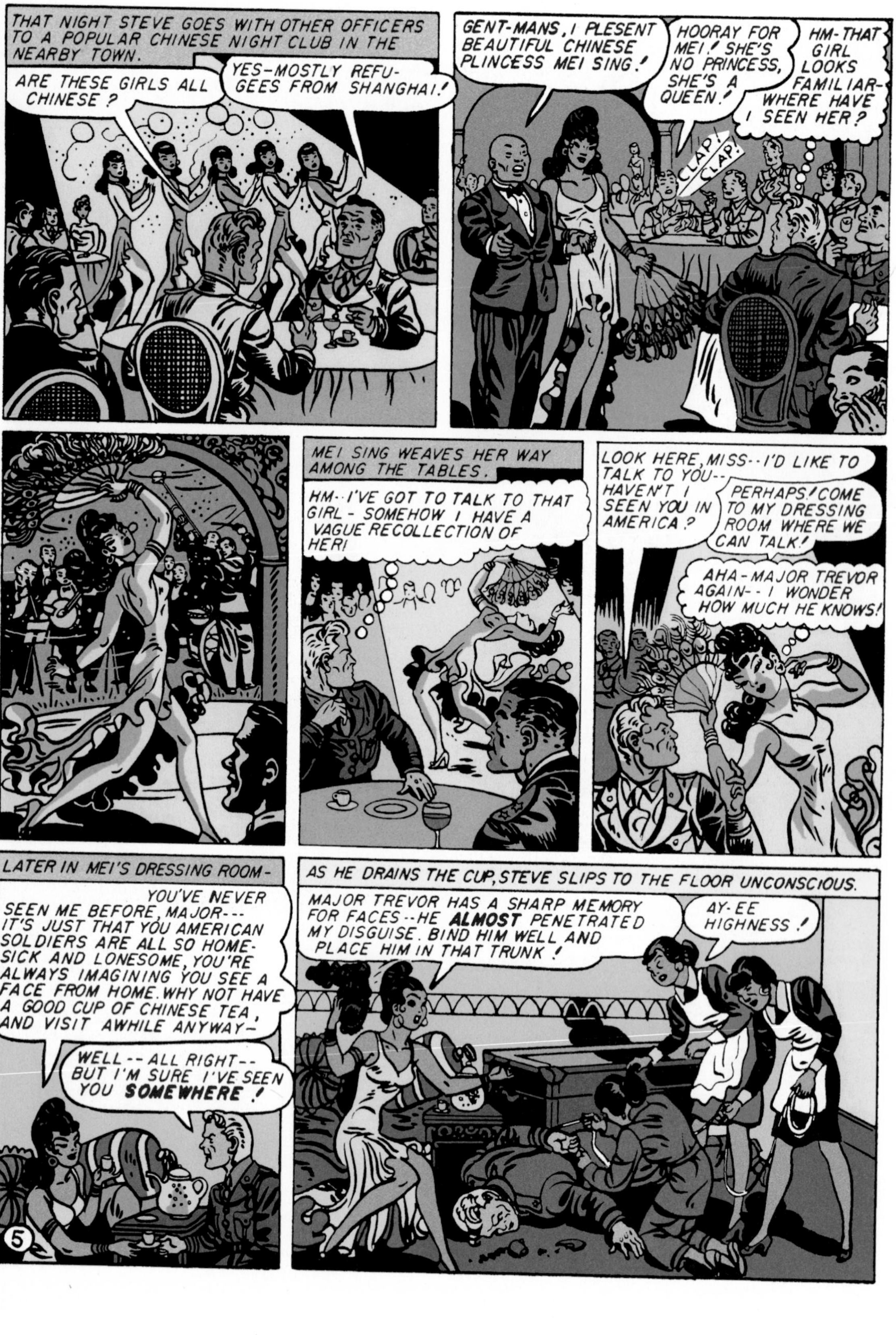

THAT NIGHT STEVE GOES WITH OTHER OFFICERS TO A POPULAR CHINESE NIGHT CLUB IN THE NEARBY TOWN.
ARE THESE GIRLS ALL CHINESE ?
YES–MOSTLY REFUGEES FROM SHANGHAI!
GENT-MANS, I PLESENT BEAUTIFUL CHINESE PLINCESS MEI SING!
HOORAY FOR MEI! SHE'S NO PRINCESS, SHE'S A QUEEN!
CLAP! CLAP!
HM-THAT GIRL LOOKS FAMILIAR-WHERE HAVE I SEEN HER?
MEI SING WEAVES HER WAY AMONG THE TABLES.
HM--I'VE GOT TO TALK TO THAT GIRL - SOMEHOW I HAVE A VAGUE RECOLLECTION OF HER!
LOOK HERE, MISS--I'D LIKE TO TALK TO YOU--HAVEN'T I SEEN YOU IN AMERICA?
PERHAPS! COME TO MY DRESSING ROOM WHERE WE CAN TALK!
AHA-MAJOR TREVOR AGAIN--I WONDER HOW MUCH HE KNOWS!
LATER IN MEI'S DRESSING ROOM-
YOU'VE NEVER SEEN ME BEFORE, MAJOR---IT'S JUST THAT YOU AMERICAN SOLDIERS ARE ALL SO HOMESICK AND LONESOME, YOU'RE ALWAYS IMAGINING YOU SEE A FACE FROM HOME. WHY NOT HAVE A GOOD CUP OF CHINESE TEA, AND VISIT AWHILE ANYWAY–
WELL--ALL RIGHT--BUT I'M SURE I'VE SEEN YOU **SOMEWHERE**!
5
AS HE DRAINS THE CUP, STEVE SLIPS TO THE FLOOR UNCONSCIOUS.
MAJOR TREVOR HAS A SHARP MEMORY FOR FACES--HE **ALMOST** PENETRATED MY DISGUISE. BIND HIM WELL AND PLACE HIM IN THAT TRUNK!
AY-EE HIGHNESS!

LATE THAT NIGHT MEI SING DRIVES HER GIRLS TO THE AMERICAN AIR FIELD

HERE IS MY PASS—I TAKE GIRLS BY PLANE TO DANCE FOR YOUR SOLDIERS IN CAMPS!

IT'S THE GENERAL'S SIGNATURE—ALL RIGHT—GO AHEAD—

AS HER PLANE TAKES OFF, THE DANCER LEAVES BEHIND A BIG WOODEN BOX, ALMOST INVISIBLE IN THE DARKNESS.

HOURS LATER A TERRIFIC EXPLOSION ROCKS THE AIRPORT—

A CLOUD OF GREEN GAS SWEEPS DOWN THE FIELD ENGULFING THE AMERICAN WAR PLANES WHICH ARE LINED UP FOR A TAKE-OFF.

BOMB ATTACK!

GAS BOMBS!

POISON GAS!

PILOTS AND GROUND CREWS RACE TOWARD THE WAITING PLANES.

TAKE IT EASY, BOYS—THIS GAS WON'T HURT YA!

IT'S **NOT** POISON GAS! TAKE YOUR MASKS OFF!

⑥

MECHANICS SPIN THE PROPELLERS BUT NOTHING HAPPENS—THE ENGINES WON'T START!

PUT SOME SNAP INTO IT!

WANT ME TO PULL THE PROP OFF? MOTOR'S HAYWIRE—SOMETHING'S GUMMED UP THE WORKS!

FRANTICALLY THE ENGINES ARE OVERHAULED BUT TO NO AVAIL.

WHAT IN BLUE BLAZES IS CRABBING THIS MOTOR? EVERYTHING'S OKAY BUT IT **WON'T START!**

IT'S NO USE, GENERAL, WE CAN'T GET A SINGLE PLANE OFF THE GROUND!

NONSENSE! YOU'VE **GOT** TO GET 'EM UP! NIP DIVE BOMBERS WILL BLAST OUR INFANTRY TO SHREDS!

STEVE, MEANWHILE, WAKES UP FROM A DRUGGED SLEEP IN STRANGE SURROUNDINGS.

HUH? WHAT HAVE YOU DONE TO ME?

I HAVE CARRIED YOU CAPTIVE TO MY COUNTRYMEN, THE JAPANESE! I AM THE PRINCESS MARU- HAVE YOU **FORGOTTEN** ME?

PRINCESS MARU- **NOW** I REMEMBER! YOU WERE "DR. POISON," THE JAP SPY! BUT WE CAPTURED YOU—

BUT YOU DIDN'T HOLD ME LONG - ESCAPING FROM YOUR "DEMOCRATIC" AMERICAN PRISON HOSPITALITY IS VERY SIMPLE FOR A WOMAN OF MY TALENTS! NOW YOU AND YOUR **WONDER WOMAN** SHALL PAY FOR WHAT YOU DID TO ME!!

CAPTAIN- THIS IS MY PRISONER- MAJOR TREVOR, THE GREAT AMERICAN INTELLIGENCE OFFICER!

ISS GOOD WORK- FOR **WOMAN**! OUR OBSERVERS ALSO REPORT GAS YOU INVENT S-STOP ALL AMERICAN PLANES! NOW ENEMY GROUND TROOPS WILL HAVE NO PROTECTION WHEN WE ATTACK THEM BY AIR! ISS GOOD—

LATER, CONFINED IN A TINY DUNGEON, STEVE SENDS A DESPERATE MENTAL RADIO MESSAGE----

CALLING **WONDER WOMAN**! NEW JAP GAS HAS GROUNDED ALL AMERICAN PLANES ON CHINESE FRONT- OUR TROOPS ARE COMPLETELY WITHOUT AIR PROTECTION. JAPS PLAN ATTACK ANY MOMENT! **DO SOMETHING!**

⑦

WHILE ON PARADISE ISLAND—

-DO SOMETHING!

GREAT APHRODITE, STEVE'S A PRISONER!! I MUST FLY TO CHINA!

TAKE **MY** SWAN PLANE, PRINCESS— MEANWHILE PAULA AND I WILL FINISH INSTALLING THIS MENTAL CONTROL APPARATUS IN YOUR PLANE.

THIS PLANE IS FAST BUT IT'S NOT SILENT OR INVISIBLE LIKE MY OWN—IT'S AN EASY TARGET FOR THE JAPS!

FLYING LOW OVER THE ENEMY LINES TO RECONNOITER, THE SWAN PLANE'S WINGS ARE CLIPPED BY ACK-ACK SHELLS.

OH-OH! NOW I'M A SWOOSE—HALF SWAN BUT MOSTLY GOOSE! LOOKS LIKE MY LAST LANDING!

A JAPANESE ZERO ZOOMS ON TO THE TAIL OF THE HELPLESS, FALLING SWAN PLANE AND CRUELLY POURS BULLETS INTO IT!

HA! ISS ONE YANKEE PILOT WHO WILL NO MORE RESIST THE SONS OF HEAVEN!

BUT TO **WONDER WOMAN** THE NIP MURDERER IS A WELCOME VISITOR.

NICE OF YOU TO COME AROUND, JITSU—I'LL BE SEEING YOU!

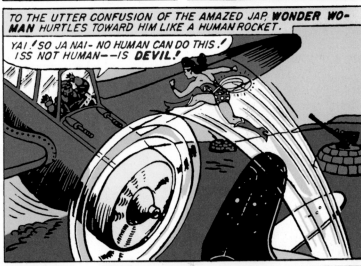

TO THE UTTER CONFUSION OF THE AMAZED JAP **WONDER WOMAN** HURTLES TOWARD HIM LIKE A HUMAN ROCKET.

YAI! SO JA NAI— NO HUMAN CAN DO THIS! ISS NOT HUMAN—IS **DEVIL!**

THE AMAZON GIRL GIVES NIPPIE A RIDE.

LET'S PLAY I'M AN ORGAN GRINDER AND YOU'RE MY MONKEY—IF YOUR FRIENDS THROW ANY LEAD AT US, **YOU** COLLECT THEIR DONATIONS!

⑧

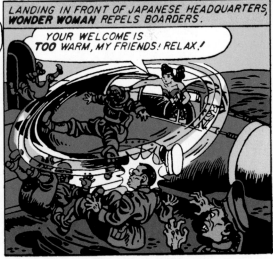

LANDING IN FRONT OF JAPANESE HEADQUARTERS, **WONDER WOMAN** REPELS BOARDERS.

YOUR WELCOME IS **TOO** WARM, MY FRIENDS! RELAX!

DODGING BENEATH THE PLANE, THE BEAUTIFUL AMAZON CAPTURES A JAP OFFICER WITH HER MAGIC LASSO.

COME CLOSER, CAPTAIN—I'D LIKE TO **TALK** TO YOU.!!

TELL ME—WHERE IS MAJOR TREVOR?

I KNOW NOSSING—UGULP—ISS STRANGE—SOMESING COMPEL ME OBEY! TREVOR PRISONER—ONLY GENERAL SHOOTYU KNOW WHERE!

THE CAPTAIN IS COMPELLED TO LEAD **WONDER WOMAN** TO SHOOTYU'S OFFICE!

SORRY TO BOTHER YOU, GENERAL, BUT I MUST FIND MAJOR TREVOR AT ONCE!

ISS **WONDER WOMAN**! CAPTAIN—THAT ISS-S FUNNY WAY TO BRING IN PRISONER—**SHE** SHOULD BE BOUND—NOT YOU—

SWIFTLY KNOTTING A NOOSE AT THE FREE END OF HER GOLDEN ROPE, **WONDER WOMAN** LASSOS THE GENERAL.

OH, BUT GENERAL, YOU'RE MISTAKEN---I'M NOT THE PRISONER! THE **CAPTAIN** IS! AND WHILE I'M AT IT--I MIGHT AS WELL CAPTURE **YOU** TOO, SHOOTYU!

YAI!

COMPELLED BY THE MAGIC LASSO, GENERAL SHOOTYU LEADS THE WAY TO STEVE'S CELL—

ISS TREVOR'S CELL—

YOU INHUMAN BEAST TO KEEP A MAN IN **THAT** HOLE!

WONDER WOMAN! I KNEW YOU'D COME! AND LEAVE IT TO YOU TO BRING ALONG THE GENERAL HIMSELF!

SO SSORRY! IS NO KEY—

WHEN I NEED KEYS TO OPEN A FLIMSY DOOR LIKE THIS, YOU CAN CALL ME A JAPANESE JELLY FISH!

⑨

BUT UNSEEN BY **WONDER WOMAN**, THE CLEVER PRINCESS MARU HAS FOLLOWED THEM STEALTHILY—

AT LAST I HAVE CAUGHT MY ENEMY—THE AMAZON!

COVERING HER OWN FACE WITH A GAS MASK, THE JAPANESE CHEMIST HURLS A BOMB.

INSTANTLY THE UNDERGROUND CORRIDOR IS FILLED WITH THE ACRID FUMES OF A POWERFUL ANESTHETIC GAS.

BANG!

BOMB - SURPRISED ME - I BREATHED GAS -

BY A SUPREME ACT OF WILL POWER **WONDER WOMAN** REMAINS CONSCIOUS LONG ENOUGH TO SUMMON HER PLANE BY MENTAL RADIO FROM PARADISE ISLAND.

RISE 40,000 FEET - COURSE EAST BY NORTH, 3700 MILES - DUE EAST 1250 - FULL SPEED -

WONDER WOMAN WAKES TO FIND HERSELF AND STEVE PRISONERS.

OUR PLANES HAVE WAIT LONG FOR THE GENERAL'S COMMAND TO DESTROY THE AMERICAN ARMY!

HE IS NOW AWAKE - IT IS SAFE TO MOVE HIM!

WONDER WOMAN-- YOU MAKE AN INTERESTING ENEMY-- I DON'T THINK I'LL KILL YOU NOW - I PREFER TO ENJOY YOUR ANGUISH WHEN YOU SEE YOUR AMERICAN ARMY WIPED OUT! I'LL SEE YOU LATER!

TAKE YOUR TIME, PRINCESS!

I HOPE THE GIRLS FINISHED INSTALLING THAT MENTAL RADIO CONTROL IN MY PLANE BEFORE I CALLED IT! SOMETHING TELLS ME WE'D BETTER BE LEAVING!

10

SCARCELY HAS THE JAPANESE LEFT WHEN AN EXPLOSION SOUNDS OVERHEAD - WALLS AND CEILING BEGIN TO FALL --

CRACK! BOO-OM!!

OH-- SO MARU DIDN'T EVEN HAVE THE DECENCY TO ADMIT SHE'D PLANNED TO BLOW THIS PLACE UP AS SOON AS SHE LEFT-- WELL--THIS MAY BE A LUCKY BREAK AFTER ALL!

HOLDING UP TONS OF SAGGING STONE WITH ONE HAND, THE AMAZON GIRL BREAKS STEVE'S BONDS.

I DON'T LIKE THIS GAME— IT'S TOO SERIOUS!

WITH STEVE IN HER ARMS, **WONDER WOMAN** JUMPS CLEAR.

CRASH!

R-RR-ROAR!!

SMASHING HER WAY OUT OF PRISON, **WONDER WOMAN** RACES TOWARD THE JAP AIR FIELD.

THAT GLINT OF LIGHT ON THE HORIZON— **CAN** IT BE MY PLANE ANSWERING MY MENTAL RADIO CALL?

AS SHE REACHES THE FIELD, THE AMAZON GIRL IS RECOGNIZED AND THE ALARM GIVEN

ISS **WONDER WOMAN**— CHARGE! SHE **MUST** NOT ESCAPE!

LEAVING THE UNCONSCIOUS STEVE IN THE COMPARATIVE SAFETY OF A GUN EMPLACEMENT, **WONDER WOMAN** TURNS ON HER ATTACKERS.

WITH HALF HER BRAIN THE AMAZON PRINCESS BATTLES GROUND ENEMIES WHILE WITH THE OTHER HALF SHE DIRECTS HER SPEEDING PLANE OVERHEAD.

DESCEND TO 3000 FEET AND CIRCLE OVERHEAD—

I HATE TO HIT SUCH A LITTLE FELLOW BUT EVEN FLIES CAN BE DANGEROUS WHEN THEY COME IN SUCH BIG DROVES!

11

WITH HER LEFT BRAIN HEMISPHERE **WONDER WOMAN** NOTICES THAT THE JAPANESE BOMBERS ARE TAKING OFF TO BLAST AMERICAN TROOPS.

OH, OH! NOW'S THE TIME TO SEND MY PLANE INTO ACTION!

WHILE THE FIGHTING AMAZON'S RIGHT CEREBRAL HEMISPHERE IS FULLY OCCUPIED REPELLING TANKS.

UNDER **WONDER WOMAN'S** MENTAL RADIO CONTROL, THE INVISIBLE AIRPLANE LETS DOWN ITS LONG STEEL LADDER WHICH SWINGS BENEATH.

OPEN UNDER HATCH—LET DOWN LADDER—

UNSEEN AND UNHEARD, THE AMAZON PLANE SWOOPS DOWN ON A NIP BOMBER, ITS DANGLING STEEL LADDER CATCHING THE WAR PLANE'S TAIL AND PULLING IT UP.

FLY LEVEL—THEN NOSE UP!

THE JAP BOMBER GOES INTO A DIVE, CRASHING AMONG ITS OWN MEN, AND EXPLODING THE BOMBS INTENDED FOR THE AMERICANS.

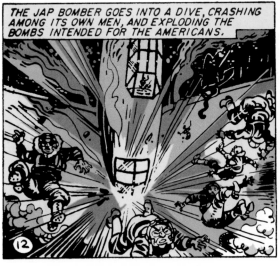

ONE BY ONE THE JAP PLANES ARE OVERTAKEN BY THEIR INVISIBLE NEMESIS UNTIL NONE REMAIN IN THE AIR.

HER DOUBLE BRAIN WORK ACCOMPLISHED, THE AMAZON GIRL MENTALLY DIRECTS HER WONDER PLANE CLOSE TO EARTH AND SEIZING STEVE AGAIN, LEAPS SWIFTLY TO ITS SWAYING LADDER.

BYE, NIPPIES—I **WON'T** BE SEEING YOU FOR AWHILE—I HOPE!

BUT AFTER STEVE IS SAFE IN THE PLANE, THERE IS ONE NIP **WONDER WOMAN** WANTS TO SEE MORE OF.

COME FOR A RIDE, DARLING! I'VE BECOME ATTACHED TO YOU AND I CRAVE YOUR COMPANY!

AS THE AMAZON GIRL BINDS HER CAPTIVE IN THE PLANE, STEVE RECOVERS CONSCIOUSNESS.

OH—THERE Y'ARE, BEAUTIFUL—WHAT ARE YOU DOING?

I'M VERY BUSY MAKING MARU OBEDIENT WITH THE MAGIC LASSO—WE MAY NEED HER HELP—

GENERAL RENAULT GREETS THEM ON THE AMERICAN AIR FIELD.

WONDER WOMAN RESCUED ME, SIR, AND DESTROYED THE ENTIRE JAP AIR FLEET!

YOU LUCKY DOG, TREVOR! HOW DO YOU RATE SUCH A GIRL FRIEND? SHE'S A ONE-WOMAN ARMY!

LATER, COMPELLED BY THE MAGIC LASSO, MARU REVEALS THE SECRET OF HER PLANE-DISABLING GAS.

MY GREEN GAS ENTERS THE CARBURETOR AND STOPS THE ENGINE. IF YOU CLEAN THE CARBURETOR WITH AMMONIUM SOLUTION YOU'LL FIND YOUR MOTORS WILL RETURN TO NORMALCY!

HAVE YOU GIVEN THE JAPS YOUR FORMULA FOR THIS GAS, MARU?

NO—I WISHED FIRST TO PERFECT IT! ONLY I KNOW THE FORMULA—I CARRY IT IN MY HEAD!

WE ARE SAFE, THEN! AMERICA THANKS YOU, **WONDER WOMAN!**

AND SO, STEVE AND **WONDER WOMAN** FLY BACK TO AMERICA IN HER INVISIBLE PLANE---

LOOK, ANGEL—THIS PLANE CAN FLY BY ITSELF---- WHY DON'T YOU **LET** IT, AND PAY **ME** SOME ATTENTION— WE'VE GOT **SO** MUCH TO TALK ABOUT—

YOU'D BETTER DO YOUR TALKING TO LITTLE DIANA PRINCE -- ANYONE CAN SEE THAT **SHE'S** MUCH MORE YOUR TYPE THAN I AM!

MORE TERRIFIC ADVENTURES OF **WONDER WOMAN** IN EVERY ISSUE OF **SENSATION COMICS!**

13

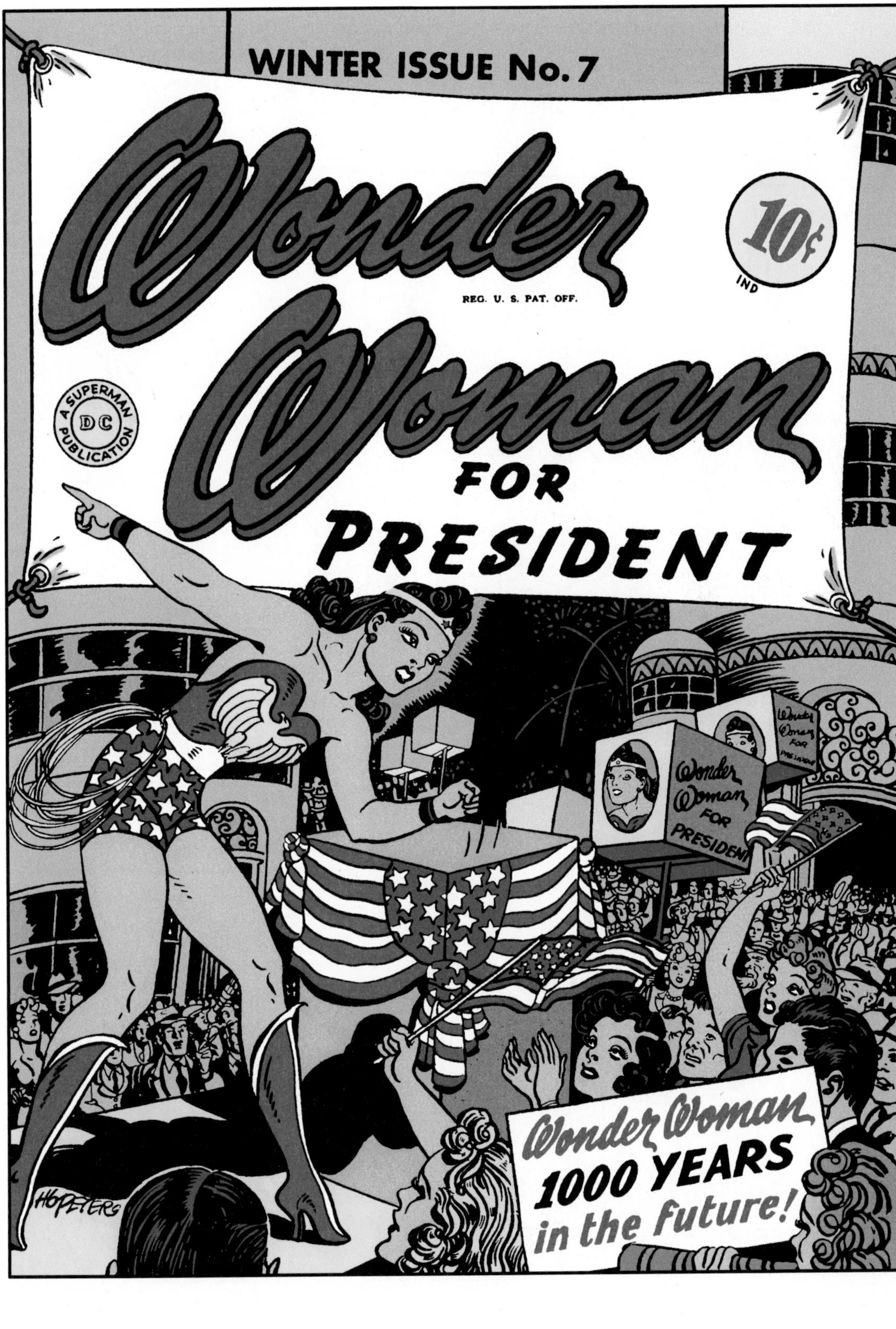
WINTER ISSUE No. 7
Wonder Woman
REG. U. S. PAT. OFF.
10¢
IND
A SUPERMAN DC PUBLICATION
FOR PRESIDENT
Wonder Woman FOR PRESIDENT
Wonder Woman 1000 YEARS in the future!
HG PETER

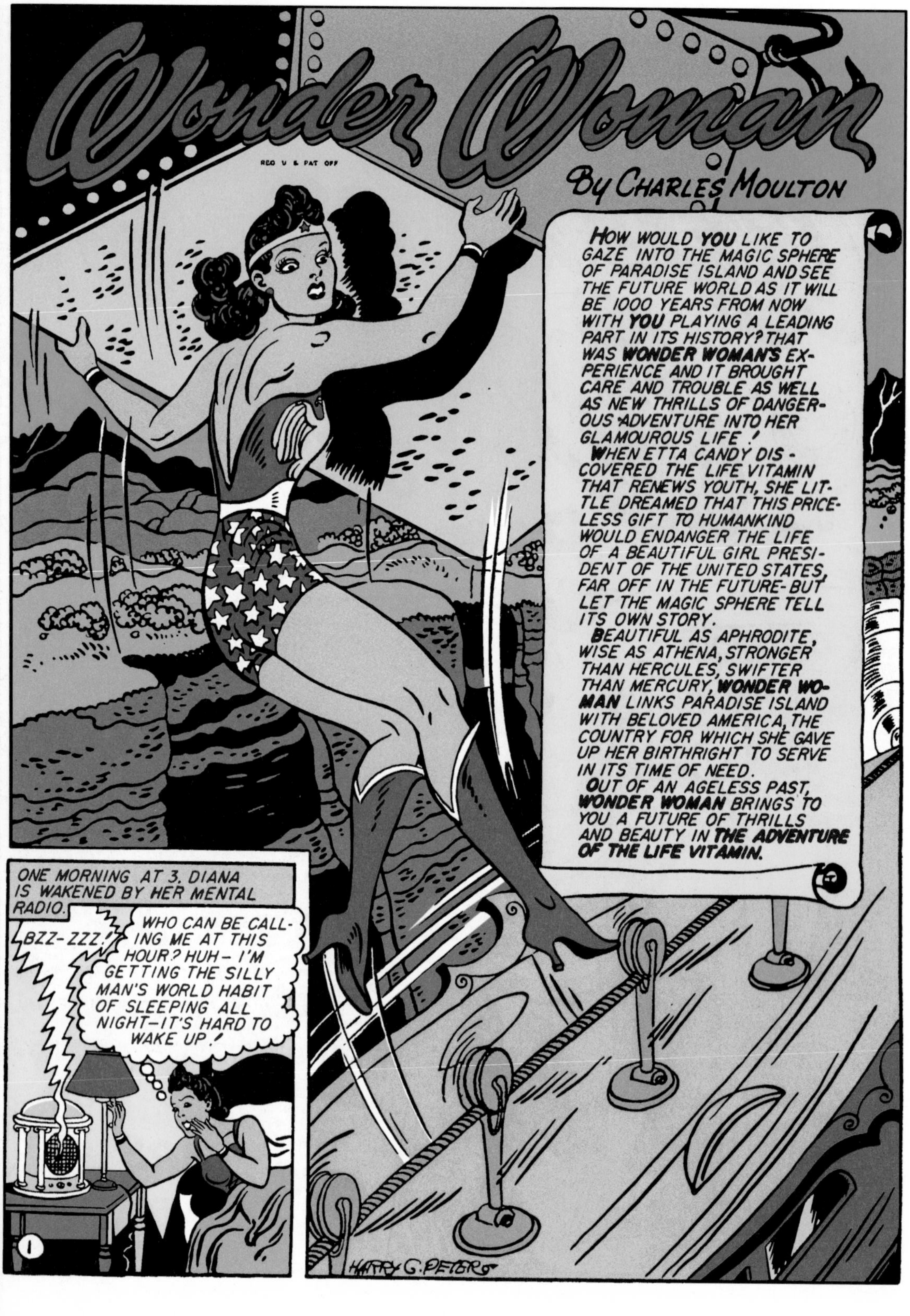
Wonder Woman
REG U S PAT OFF
By CHARLES MOULTON
HOW WOULD YOU LIKE TO GAZE INTO THE MAGIC SPHERE OF PARADISE ISLAND AND SEE THE FUTURE WORLD AS IT WILL BE 1000 YEARS FROM NOW WITH YOU PLAYING A LEADING PART IN ITS HISTORY? THAT WAS WONDER WOMAN'S EXPERIENCE AND IT BROUGHT CARE AND TROUBLE AS WELL AS NEW THRILLS OF DANGEROUS ADVENTURE INTO HER GLAMOUROUS LIFE!
WHEN ETTA CANDY DISCOVERED THE LIFE VITAMIN THAT RENEWS YOUTH, SHE LITTLE DREAMED THAT THIS PRICELESS GIFT TO HUMANKIND WOULD ENDANGER THE LIFE OF A BEAUTIFUL GIRL PRESIDENT OF THE UNITED STATES, FAR OFF IN THE FUTURE- BUT LET THE MAGIC SPHERE TELL ITS OWN STORY.
BEAUTIFUL AS APHRODITE, WISE AS ATHENA, STRONGER THAN HERCULES, SWIFTER THAN MERCURY, WONDER WOMAN LINKS PARADISE ISLAND WITH BELOVED AMERICA, THE COUNTRY FOR WHICH SHE GAVE UP HER BIRTHRIGHT TO SERVE IN ITS TIME OF NEED.
OUT OF AN AGELESS PAST, WONDER WOMAN BRINGS TO YOU A FUTURE OF THRILLS AND BEAUTY IN THE ADVENTURE OF THE LIFE VITAMIN.
ONE MORNING AT 3, DIANA IS WAKENED BY HER MENTAL RADIO.
BZZ-ZZZ!
WHO CAN BE CALLING ME AT THIS HOUR? HUH- I'M GETTING THE SILLY MAN'S WORLD HABIT OF SLEEPING ALL NIGHT-IT'S HARD TO WAKE UP!
1
HARRY G. PETER

CALLING AMAZON PRINCESS DIANA! DAUGHTER, I LONG TO SEE YOU! IF YOUR DUTIES PERMIT, COME HOME TO PARADISE ISLAND FOR THE FEAST OF THE HARVEST!

OH, HOW WONDERFUL! I HAVE THANKSGIVING LEAVE - I'LL START NOW!

MOTHER HAS NEVER SEEN ME IN MY NURSE-SECRETARY DISGUISE EXCEPT ON THE MAGIC SPHERE - I'LL WEAR THIS COSTUME TO PARADISE ISLAND AND SEE IF SHE RECOGNIZES ME - HA HA!

MISCHIEVOUSLY INTENT UPON SURPRISING THE QUEEN, **WONDER WOMAN** LANDS HER SILENT, INVISIBLE PLANE ON THE PALACE ROOF.

I'LL SLIP DOWN THE SECRET STAIRWAY INTO MOTHER'S PRIVATE ROOMS!

THE QUEEN, WORKING ON IMPORTANT PAPERS, DOES NOT HEAR HER DAUGHTER'S APPROACH.

YOUR MAJESTY, I BEG TO REPORT THAT WOMEN ARE GAINING POWER IN THE MAN'S WORLD!

EH? GREAT HOUNDS OF ZEUS! WHO ARE **YOU**?

YOU LITTLE MISCHIEF! THAT COSTUME'S A GREAT DISGUISE - I DIDN'T RECOGNIZE YOU UNTIL YOU LAUGHED!

HA HA! OOPS! CAREFUL, MOTHER, YOU'LL BREAK MY GLASSES!

SO **THAT'S** YOUR NURSE-SECRETARY'S UNIFORM IN THE MAN-RULED WORLD! HOW DIFFERENT SECRETARIES AND THEIR COSTUMES WILL BE WHEN **WOMEN** RULE THAT WORLD 1000 YEARS FROM NOW!

HOW DO **YOU** KNOW WHAT GIRLS'LL WEAR THEN, MOTHER?

②

I'VE STUDIED THE **WORLD'S FUTURE** ON THE MAGIC SPHERE!

I DIDN'T KNOW THE MAGIC SPHERE FORETELLS THE FUTURE!

TOMORROW HAPPENED YESTERDAY. FUTURE EVENTS ALREADY EXIST BECAUSE THEY ARE CREATED BY **PAST** EVENTS! SINCE OUR MAGIC SPHERE RECORDS EVERYTHING THAT **HAS** HAPPENED, IT CAN PREDICT EVERYTHING THAT **WILL** HAPPEN IN THE FUTURE!

PAST PRESENT FUTURE

I'LL SHOW YOU YOUR SECRETARY'S COSTUME IN 3000 A.D.!

GREAT HERA! WILL I **STILL** BE DIANA PRINCE? I KNOW THE FOUNTAIN OF YOUTH KEEPS US AMAZONS FROM EVER GROWING OLD, BUT I NEVER THOUGHT ABOUT DIANA!

WONDER WOMAN PREVIEWS THE STYLE FOR SECRETARIES 1000 YEARS HENCE

BUT MOTHER-WHAT A FANTASTIC COSTUME! THAT THING ON DIANA'S FOREHEAD LOOKS LIKE A MICROPHONE!

WHEN WOMEN CONTROL THEIR OWN STYLES THEY'RE BOUND TO BE PICTURESQUE AND ALLURING! I'LL EXPLAIN THE MICROPHONE.

THIS IS A WOMAN'S INVENTION CALLED PHONETIC ARM CONTROL. THE MICROPHONE ON THE SECRETARY'S FOREHEAD TAKES THE EMPLOYER'S DICTATION! ELECTRIC IMPULSES PASS THROUGH THE HEADBAND AND THESE WIRES TO THE GIRL'S ARMS COMPEL HER TO TYPE EVERY WORD AS IT IS SPOKEN.

HOW WONDERFUL!

IT WILL BE FUN TO LIVE IN THIS NEW **WOMAN'S AGE!** BUT- BUT MY FRIENDS CAN'T LIVE-

OH YES THEY CAN! YOU AND ETTA CANDY WILL DISCOVER THE LIFE VITAMIN-L3- WHICH RENEWS YOUTH! WATCH —

IT IS MANY YEARS IN THE FUTURE-ETTA'S MOTHER, SUGAR CANDY, IS DYING.

SOB-SOB' SHE'S G-GOING! I STUDIED CHEMISTRY DAY AND NIGHT TO FIND A CURE-BUT--

YOUR MOTHER'S 82, ETTA, BUT-LET ME THINK!

3A

THIS GOLDEN FLASK HOLDS WATER FROM THE FOUNTAIN OF YOUTH ON PARADISE ISLAND. APHRODITE'S LIFE VITAMIN AFFECTS ONLY AMAZONS. BUT IT **MIGHT** HELP YOUR MOTHER-

I'LL PUT SOME CANDY INTO IT- MIGHT RELEASE VITAMIN L-3.

WOO WOO! LOOK AT THAT CHEMICAL REACTION— IT'S TURNING VIOLET.

WOO-JIMINY! HAVE WE **GOT** SOMETHING?

HM· THE DEXTROSE IN THAT CANDY LIBERATED HYDROGEN AND FORMED AN ORGANIC COMPOUND, ETTA! BY THE GREAT CLUB OF HERCULES WE'VE ISOLATED THE LIFE VITAMIN!

I CAN'T HEAR HER HEART BEAT— SHE'S —SHE'S **GONE**!

QUIET, ETTA! IF THIS ELIXIR CONTAINS L-3 IT WILL SAVE YOUR MOTHER!

MRS. CANDY RECOVERS WITH STARTLING SUDDENNESS

YUM-YUM! THAT THAR'S A **DRINK**! LET'S HAVE MORE!

WAIT! THE LIFE VITAMIN'S **POWERFUL**— NO TELLING WHAT—

SUGAR'S YOUNG AGAIN! WHERE'S MAH HUSBAND— AH WANNA GO DANCIN' !!!

FOR HER PART IN DISCOVERING VITAMIN L-3, ETTA RECEIVES THE GRAND INTERNATIONAL PRIZE.

I TAKE GREAT PLEASURE IN PRESENTING THIS AWARD TO ETTA CANDY, PROFESSOR OF PUBLIC HEALTH AT **WONDER WOMAN COLLEGE**!

4A

SO THIS LIFE VITAMIN WILL KEEP MY FRIENDS YOUTHFUL UNTIL 3000 A.D.! I WONDER— ER— WILL STEVE— HM· WILL WE—

YOU WANT TO KNOW WHAT WILL HAPPEN TO YOU AND STEVE? LOOK IN THE MAGIC SPHERE!

THE QUEEN TUNES THE MAGIC SPHERE TO THE NEW WHITE HOUSE, WASHINGTON, 3000 A.D.

COMI' IN LONDON!

GO AHEAD, PARIS!!

LADIES AND GENTLEMEN— THE PRESIDENT

THE PRESIDENT'S OFFICES ARE GUARDED BY GIRL TROOPERS.

ALL SERENE?

SERENE, CAPTAIN!

OFFICE OF THE PRESIDENT OF THE UNITED STATE

NO ONE CAN ENTER THE PRESIDENT'S OFFICE WITHOUT A PASS!

WHAT?

SHOW ME YOUR PASS!

OUT OF MY WAY, FOOL! D'YOU KNOW WHO I AM? I AM SENATOR HEEMAN, LEADER OF THE MAN'S WORLD PARTY!

THIS IS AN OUTRAGE—IT COMES OF LETTING WOMEN RULE THE COUNTRY—I'LL SHOW YOU WEAKLINGS!

EASY, SENATOR! GIRLS, COOL THIS CUSTOMER!

OFFICES OF PRE...

I AM COLONEL STEVE TREVOR, MILITARY AIDE TO THE PRESIDENT. YOU MAY ENTER, SENATOR!

COLONEL- BAH- YOU'RE A SISSY LIKE MOST MEN IN THIS DECADENT AGE-AHHR-LEMME IN- WHERE'S THE PRESIDENT?

5A

I PRESENT YOU, SENATOR, TO MISTRESS ARDA MOORE, PRESIDENT OF THE UNITED STATES!

SHE KNOWS ME- WHY ALL THIS BALONEY? SHE MAY BE PRESIDENT BUT SHE'S ONLY A WOMAN!

"WOMAN" IS A PROUDER TITLE THAN PRESIDENT!

338

I HAVE COME TO WARN YOU! THE MEN OF THIS COUNTRY ARE FED UP WITH WOMAN'S OPPRESSION! THE MAN'S WORLD PARTY DEMANDS MALE RIGHTS! WE—

YOU'RE WASTING POLITICAL ORATORY, SENATOR! WHAT DO YOU WANT?

SIGN THIS PARDON RELEASING GRAFTON PATRONAGE, FORMER POLITICAL LEADER, FROM FEDERAL PRISON!

GRAFTON PATRONAGE! WHY, THAT CROOK REPRESENTS ALL THAT WAS BAD AND CORRUPT IN THE POLITICAL RULE OF MEN AND WHICH WAS ENDED BY MY ELECTION!

YOU WOMEN ARE FEATHER-BRAINED **IDEALISTS!** YOU'VE STOPPED US MEN FROM MAKING MONEY OUT OF PUBLIC OFFICE! YOU'VE TAUGHT PEOPLE TO ELECT OFFICIALS WHO **SERVE THE PUBLIC** AND EXPECT **NOTHING** FOR THEMSELVES!

QUITE SO!

WE NEED GRAFTON PATRONAGE TO FINANCE OUR PARTY! PATRONAGE WILL BREAK PRISON AND START A MEN'S REVOLUTION UNLESS YOU **ACT ON THAT PARDON!**

I'LL ACT ON THE PARDON—LIKE **THIS!**—···

COLONEL, SHOW THIS GENTLEMAN OUT!

WITH PLEASURE!

AW-WK! YOU'LL SUFFER FOR THIS!

CALL GENERAL DARNELL, COMMISSIONER OF UNITED STATES POLICE, AND HIS SECRETARY, MISS PRINCE, FOR A CONFERENCE!

YES, MISTRESS PRESIDENT!

SO THAT'S HEEMAN'S THREAT—DO YOU TAKE IT SERIOUSLY?

I DO! NO TELLING WHAT DESPERATE SCHEME GRAFTON PATRONAGE MAY ATTEMPT!

COLONEL TREVOR AND I WILL GO TO CENTRAL PRISON, MISTRESS PRESIDENT, AND INVESTIGATE!

6A

STEVE AND DIANA ASCEND TO THE WHITE HOUSE ROOF WHERE SWIFT AIRLINE CARS CONNECT THE PRESIDENT'S HEADQUARTERS WITH IMPORTANT GOVERNMENT BRANCHES THROUGHOUT THE COUNTRY.

THIS AIRCAR RUNS DIRECT TO CENTRAL PRISON.

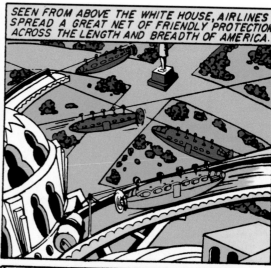

SEEN FROM ABOVE THE WHITE HOUSE, AIRLINES SPREAD A GREAT NET OF FRIENDLY PROTECTION ACROSS THE LENGTH AND BREADTH OF AMERICA.

THIS IS MY FAVORITE WAY OF TRAVEL-COMFORT, HIGH SPEED AND NO SOUND OR VIBRATION!

AND THE CAR RUNS ITSELF AUTOMATICALLY WITHOUT ANY PILOT-THAT GIVES US A CHANCE TO TALK!

WE MUST MAKE THIS PRISONER PATRONAGE REVEAL HIS PLANS FOR ESCAPE!

BREAKING THAT PRISON SHOULD BE EASY-THE WARDEN BELIEVES THAT LOCKS, BARS AND CHAINS ARE BAD FOR PRISONERS, PSYCHOLOGICALLY!

GRAFTON PATRONAGE ENJOYS LIFE AT THE PRISON.

THE GUARDS HERE ARE DEBUTANTES-THEY'RE SO DUMB THEY THINK A HANDCUFF IS THE BLOW OF A PRIZEFIGHTER'S FIST! I COULD WALK OUT ANY TIME-BUT I HAVE A BETTER PLAN!

7A

A GUARD CALLS ON PRISON GUEST PATRONAGE.

ARE YOU QUITE COMFORTABLE, MR. PATRONAGE? WHEN YOU HAVE TIME, THE WARDEN WOULD LIKE TO SEE YOU!

TELL HER I'M BUSY- NO, WAIT-I'LL COME....

I'LL SPRING MY COUP NOW!

IT'S GOOD OF YOU TO DROP IN, GRAFTON I THOUGHT PERHAPS YOU'D ENJOY A SPOT OF PSYCHOANALYSIS TODAY, AS OUR JOLLY ENGLISH COUSINS PUT IT- HAHA!

DOROTHY DEAR WARDEN

WHILE PATRONAGE IS ENTERTAINED WITH PSYCHIATRIC SYMBOLS BY WARDEN DEAR, OTHER "GUESTS" SEARCH AN ABANDONED DUNGEON FOR CHAINS AND ROPES.

GRAFTON GAVE THE SIGNAL—WE MUST GRAB THE GUARDS *QUICK!*

AND TIE THEM *PLENTY!*

AT THIS MOMENT STEVE AND DIANA ARRIVE IN THEIR AIRCAR ON THE PRISON ROOF.

SO NICE TO SEE YOU, COLONEL—AND YOU, YOU, MISS PRINCE!

WE MUST SEE THE WARDEN IMMEDIATELY—GREAT DANGER THREATENS!

NOW JUST WRITE DOWN YOUR DREAMS—OH! THIS *IS* A SURPRISE!

GREETINGS, WARDEN—AH! I SEE YOU'RE QUESTIONING PATRONAGE—HE'S JUST THE PRISONER WE WANT TO WORK ON!

OH, YOU MUSTN'T CALL OUR GUESTS *PRISONERS*, COLONEL STEVE!

I'LL CALL THIS MUG WORSE NAMES THAN THAT IF HE'S PLOTTING TREASON AS WE SUSPECT!

SO—YOU'VE DISCOVERED OUR PLANS! STICK YOUR HANDS UP, EVERYBODY! DON'T TRY TO PLAY HERO, TREVOR, OR I'LL SHOOT DOROTHY DEAR!

WHY---Y--YOU--

AT THIS MOMENT THE REBEL PRISONERS ARRIVE WITH THEIR FORMER GUARDS IN CHAINS.

HO HO! WHAT SPORT! GIT ALONG LITTLE DOGIES—ARE YOU "QUITE COMFORTABLE"? HAHA!

8A

SECURE THESE PRISONERS LIKE THE OTHERS. HANDCUFF DEAR'S HANDS IN FRONT OF HER—I'VE GOT A JOB FOR HER TO DO!

LOCK THOSE PRISONERS IN DUNGEON CELLS!

IF I BREAK LOOSE NOW HE'LL SHOOT DEAR—I'D BETTER WAIT—

OH, I'M SO **HELPLESS!** WEARING CHAINS GIVES ME THAT SUBMISSIVE FEELING THAT IS **SO** BAD FOR **PRISONERS**—LET ALONE FOR WARDENS—

TAKE THIS PHONE AND CALL THE PRESIDENT LIKE I TOLD YOU!

WHATEVER FOR? OF COURSE I'D LOVE TO TALK WITH ARDA—

IS THIS YOU, MISTRESS PRESIDENT? I'M WARDEN DEAR—YES, DARLING, EVERYTHING'S LOVELY BUT—WELL—I'M ALL EXCITED, AND I'VE GOT TO SEE YOU! IT'S AWFULLY IMPORTANT, REALLY—YOU'LL COME? OH THANK YOU, ARDA!

HOSTESS

MEANWHILE, DIANA DECIDES SHE CAN'T ACCOMPLISH MUCH IN SOLITARY CONFINEMENT.

TIME TO STOP PLAYING PRISONER! BETTER CAPTURE PATRONAGE FIRST, THEN FREE MY FRIENDS!

THERE—THAT FEELS BETTER! NOW TO CHANGE TO **WONDER WOMAN**—LUCKY I KEPT MY BAG WITH THE COSTUME—

BREAKING OUT OF HER CELL, THE AMAZON MAIDEN ENCOUNTERS A MAN'S PARTY REBEL.

SO YOU'RE SHOOTING ELECTRIC EXPLOSION BULLETS! DON'T YOU KNOW THAT'S AN ILLEGAL WEAPON? YOU'RE LIABLE TO KILL SOMEBODY WITH IT!

YE GODS—IT'S **WONDER WOMAN!**

BANG!

POP!

CRACK!

9A

WONDER WOMAN UNLEASHES THE MAGIC LASSO!

KEEP RUNNING, ATHLETE! RUN RIGHT UPSTAIRS AND FIND PATRONAGE FOR ME!

I—I—SOMETHING COMPELS ME TO OBEY!

LOCATING PATRONAGE ON THE PRISON ROOF, **WONDER WOMAN** WATCHES HIM WITH PUZZLED EYES.

THIS'LL BE ENOUGH, BOYS—LOCK IT UP AND LET HER GO!

WHAT'S HE UP TO? I DON'T GET IT!

PUSHING A CONTROL LEVER, GRAFTON PATRONAGE SENDS THE LOADED AIRCAR HURTLING OUT ON ITS CABLE PATH.

THERE, THAT OUGHT TO SETTLE PRESIDENT ARDA'S HASH ONCE AND FOR ALL!

HOW'LL YOU GET ARDA THIS WAY?

LISTEN! DEAR PHONED THE PRESIDENT—SHE'S COMING ON THIS AIRLINE. ARDA'S CAR, RUNNING FULL SPEED, WILL HIT THIS CAR WE HAVE JUST LOADED WITH T.N.T. THERE WILL BE A NICE NOISE, BUT NO MORE PRESIDENT—GOOD, EH?

THAT COLD-BLOODED DEMON—HE PLANS TO KILL THE PRESIDENT, CONQUER WOMEN AND RULE THE COUNTRY WITH HIS VICIOUS HEEMAN GANG! I CAN'T SAVE ARDA **NOW**---- OR **CAN** I? BY APHRODITE, THERE'S **ONE** CHANCE AND I'LL TAKE IT!

CHARGING THROUGH THE HEEMAN MOBSTERS LIKE A FOOTBALL FULLBACK, **WONDER WOMAN** MAKES FOR THE PARAPET.

I'M CARRYING THE BALL, BOYS, AND I'M NOT FOOLING!

LEAPING HIGH INTO SPACE, THE MIGHTY AMAZON LANDS LIGHTLY AS A BIRD ON THE AIRLINE CABLE.

THROWING CAUTION TO THE WINDS, THE PRINCESS FROM PARADISE ISLAND RACES ALONG THE SWAYING STEEL HAWSER AT BREAK-NECK SPEED.

HA HA! SHE'S BOUND TO SLIP— GOODBYE, **WONDER WOMAN**!!

10

BUT **WONDER WOMAN** SPEEDS ON-

THAT DYNAMITE CAR MUST BE MAKING TERRIFIC SPEED- I SHOULD HAVE CAUGHT IT-- THERE IT IS! BUT THERE'S THE PRESIDENT'S CAR TOO-- MERCURY, LEND ME YOUR WINGS!

INCREASING HER INCREDIBLE SPEED BY SHEER WILLPOWER, THE AMAZON GIRL NEARS THE SPEEDING TORPEDO OF DEATH--BUT CAN SHE REACH IT IN TIME?

POOR ARDA- I **MUST** SAVE HER-- I **MUST**--

WITH A SPLIT SECOND TO SPARE, **WONDER WOMAN** SNATCHES THE EXPLOSIVE AIRCAR INTO HER ARMS AND LEAPS WITH IT FROM THE CABLE, PERMITTING THE PRESIDENT'S CAR TO PASS SAFELY BENEATH.

HURLED FAR AWAY BY **WONDER WOMAN'S** AMAZON STRENGTH, THE T.N.T. EXPLODES HARMLESSLY AGAINST A CLIFF.

BOO-OM

HM... LET'S THINK THIS OVER NOW! I SAVED ARDA'S CAR... BUT IT'S STILL ON ITS WAY TO THE PRISON-- WITH PATRONAGE THERE ANYTHING CAN HAPPEN NOW!

WONDER WOMAN SENDS ETTA A MENTAL MESSAGE.

CALLING ETTA CANDY! NOTIFY THE WHITE HOUSE GUARD TO SURROUND CENTRAL PRISON-- PRISONERS ARE IN CONTROL- YOU COME TOO- BRING AMPLE SUPPLY ANTI-L-3 CHEMICALS! HURRY!

THE PRESIDENT, MEANWHILE, IS GREETED AT THE PRISON BY AN UNEXPECTED HOST.

WHAT ARE **YOU** DOING HERE?

I JUST ARRIVED BY PLANE, MIS-TRESS PRESIDENT, TO GIVE YOU THE WELCOME YOU DESERVE!

I DON'T KNOW HOW YOU ESCAPED OUR DEATH CAR, BUT NO MATTER! YOU'LL BE MORE USEFUL, AFTER ALL, AS OUR PRISONER!

AS GIRL PARATROOPERS BEGIN TO ARRIVE FROM WASHINGTON, PATRONAGE PLACES CAPTIVE ARDA ON THE PRISON PARAPET.

CALLING GOVERNMENT PLANES! IF PARA-TROOPERS FIRE ONE SHOT AT US I WILL KILL YOUR PRESIDENT!

WHILE GIRL TROOPERS SUR-ROUND THE PRISON, WONDER WOMAN DIGS FURIOUSLY NEAR THE WALL.

WHATCHA DOIN', PAL, TUNNELING UNDER?

NO, ETTA- I'M DIGGING FOR WATER-PIPES!

THIS WATER MAIN SUPPLIES THE PRISON DRINKING WATER. WE'RE GOING TO POUR YOUR BOTTLE OF ANTI-L-3 CHEMICAL INTO IT!

I GETCHA— WOO WOO! WHEN THOSE MUGS DRINK THIS CHEMICAL— WHEE-EE, GIRL, OH GIRL!

AT WONDER WOMAN'S RE-QUEST, GIRL TROOPERS SUR-ROUND THE ENTIRE PRISON WITH A WALL OF FLAME, PRODUCED BY BURNING JETS OF HYDROGEN.

ON THE PRISON ROOF THE HEAT BECOMES IN-TOLERABLE.

COME ON, YOU- THEY'RE TRY-IN' TO ROAST US OUT! BUT THEY'LL NEVER DO IT - IF WE BURN, YOU'LL BURN WITH US! BLAZES- I GOTTA HAVE WATER—

12A

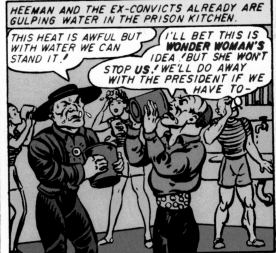

HEEMAN AND THE EX-CONVICTS ALREADY ARE GULPING WATER IN THE PRISON KITCHEN.

THIS HEAT IS AWFUL BUT WITH WATER WE CAN STAND IT!

I'LL BET THIS IS WONDER WOMAN'S IDEA! BUT SHE WON'T STOP US! WE'LL DO AWAY WITH THE PRESIDENT IF WE HAVE TO—

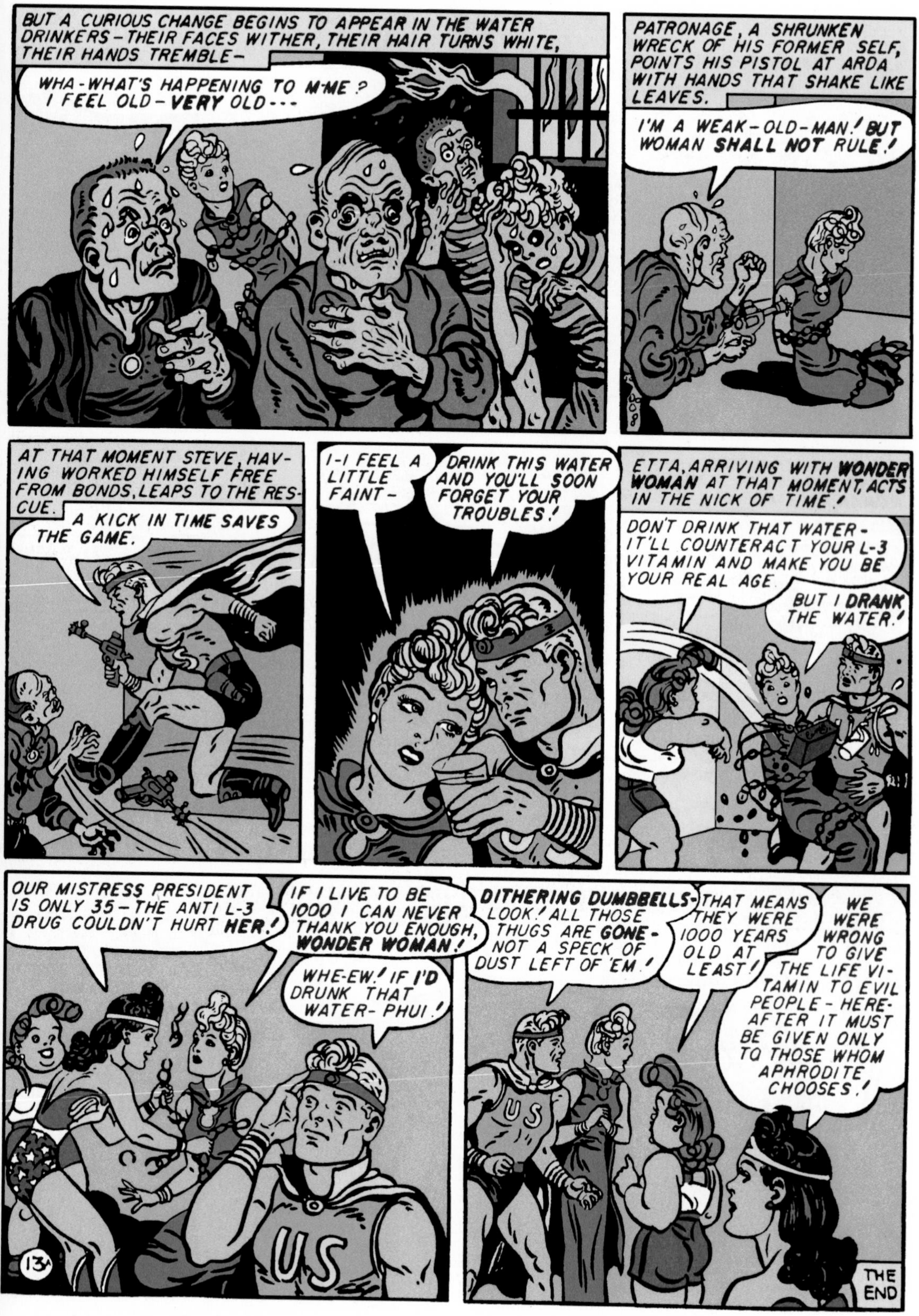
BUT A CURIOUS CHANGE BEGINS TO APPEAR IN THE WATER DRINKERS—THEIR FACES WITHER, THEIR HAIR TURNS WHITE, THEIR HANDS TREMBLE—
WHA-WHAT'S HAPPENING TO M-ME? I FEEL OLD—VERY OLD---
PATRONAGE, A SHRUNKEN WRECK OF HIS FORMER SELF, POINTS HIS PISTOL AT ARDA WITH HANDS THAT SHAKE LIKE LEAVES.
I'M A WEAK—OLD—MAN! BUT WOMAN SHALL NOT RULE!
AT THAT MOMENT STEVE, HAVING WORKED HIMSELF FREE FROM BONDS, LEAPS TO THE RESCUE.
A KICK IN TIME SAVES THE GAME.
I-I FEEL A LITTLE FAINT—
DRINK THIS WATER AND YOU'LL SOON FORGET YOUR TROUBLES!
ETTA, ARRIVING WITH WONDER WOMAN AT THAT MOMENT, ACTS IN THE NICK OF TIME!
DON'T DRINK THAT WATER—IT'LL COUNTERACT YOUR L-3 VITAMIN AND MAKE YOU BE YOUR REAL AGE.
BUT I DRANK THE WATER!
OUR MISTRESS PRESIDENT IS ONLY 35—THE ANTI L-3 DRUG COULDN'T HURT HER!
IF I LIVE TO BE 1000 I CAN NEVER THANK YOU ENOUGH, WONDER WOMAN!
WHE-EW! IF I'D DRUNK THAT WATER—PHUI!
13A
DITHERING DUMBBELLS—LOOK! ALL THOSE THUGS ARE GONE—NOT A SPECK OF DUST LEFT OF 'EM!
THAT MEANS THEY WERE 1000 YEARS OLD AT LEAST!
WE WERE WRONG TO GIVE THE LIFE VITAMIN TO EVIL PEOPLE—HEREAFTER IT MUST BE GIVEN ONLY TO THOSE WHOM APHRODITE CHOOSES!
THE END

Wonder Woman

REG U S PAT OFF

BY CHARLES MOULTON

WONDER WOMAN FROZEN ALIVE! THE PRESIDENT OF THE UNITED STATES KIDNAPED! WHAT HEADLINES SCREAM FROM THE FRONT PAGES OF A MILLION NEWS-PAPERS IN 3004 A.D.! AND WONDER WOMAN HERSELF, THAT GORGEOUS, STUPENDOUS PERSONIFICATION OF ALL THAT IS GLORIOUS IN AMERICAN WOMANHOOD SHOWS YOU IN THIS EPISODE THE THRILLS THAT LIE AHEAD FOR AMERICA'S WONDER WOMEN OF TOMORROW!

H.G. PETERS

ON THE MAGIC SPHERE AT PARADISE ISLAND THE QUEEN SHOWS WONDER WOMAN AMERICA'S FUTURE, 1000 YEARS HENCE.

YOU LOOK PLEASED, DAUGHTER, AND TRIUMPHANT!

I AM! A WOMAN WILL BE PRESIDENT OF THE UNITED STATES IN 3000 A.D.!

1B

BUT AMERICAN WOMEN WILL NOT RULE SUPREME AS WE AMAZONS DO. A MAN MIGHT RUN FOR PRESIDENT—HE MIGHT BEAT EVEN YOU AT THE POLLS!

I'D LIKE TO SEE HIM DO IT!

PERHAPS THE MAGIC SPHERE MAY GRANT YOUR WISH! ANY-WAY LET'S SEE WHAT HAPPENS WHEN A MAN RUNS AGAINST A WOMAN FOR PRESIDENT IN 3004 A.D.!

OH, MOTHER— THIS IS EXCITING!

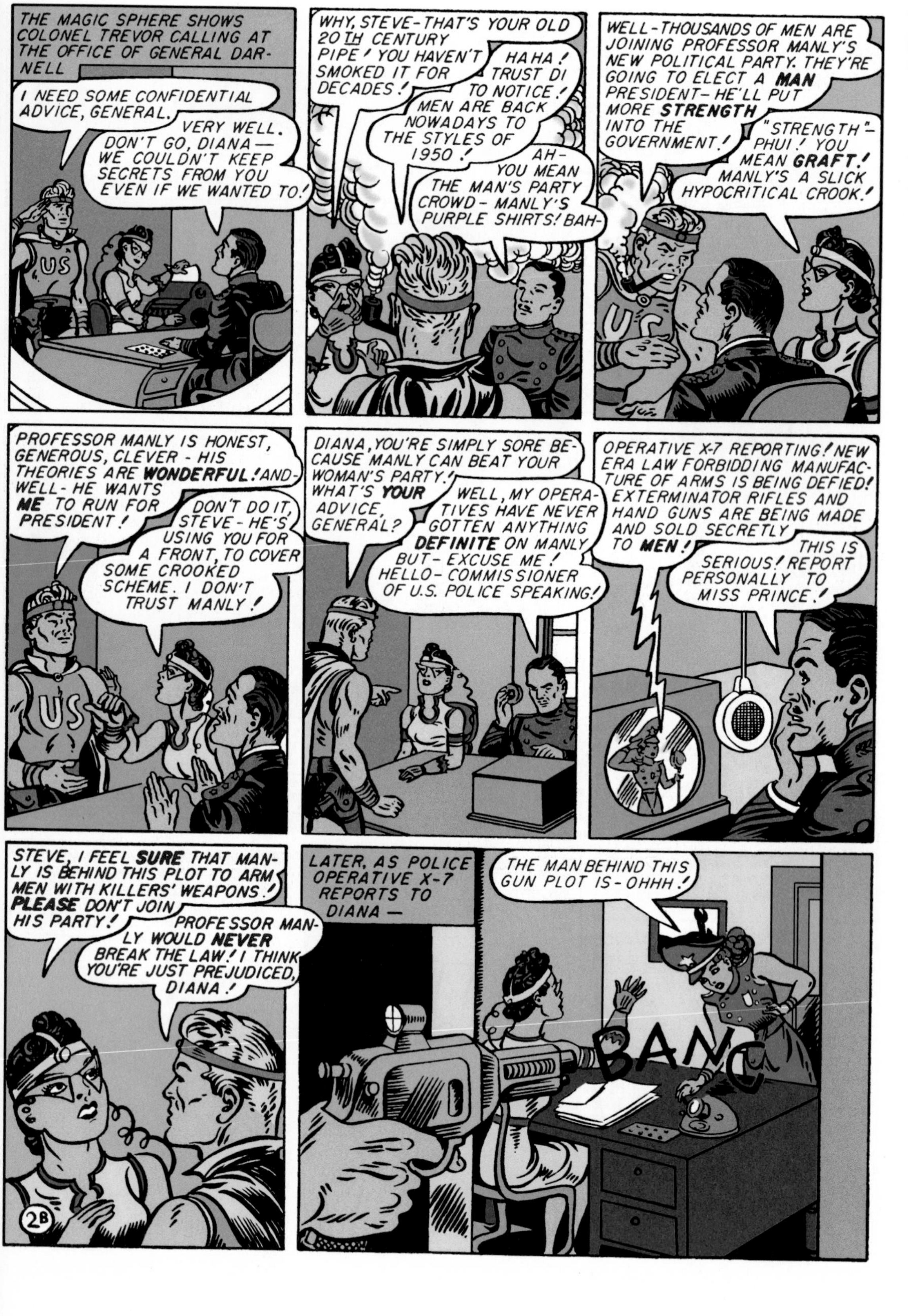
THE MAGIC SPHERE SHOWS COLONEL TREVOR CALLING AT THE OFFICE OF GENERAL DARNELL
I NEED SOME CONFIDENTIAL ADVICE, GENERAL.
VERY WELL. DON'T GO, DIANA — WE COULDN'T KEEP SECRETS FROM YOU EVEN IF WE WANTED TO!
WHY, STEVE-THAT'S YOUR OLD 20TH CENTURY PIPE! YOU HAVEN'T SMOKED IT FOR DECADES!
HAHA! TRUST DI TO NOTICE! MEN ARE BACK NOWADAYS TO THE STYLES OF 1950!
AH- YOU MEAN THE MAN'S PARTY CROWD - MANLY'S PURPLE SHIRTS! BAH-
WELL-THOUSANDS OF MEN ARE JOINING PROFESSOR MANLY'S NEW POLITICAL PARTY. THEY'RE GOING TO ELECT A MAN PRESIDENT- HE'LL PUT MORE STRENGTH INTO THE GOVERNMENT!
"STRENGTH"- PHUI! YOU MEAN GRAFT! MANLY'S A SLICK HYPOCRITICAL CROOK!
PROFESSOR MANLY IS HONEST, GENEROUS, CLEVER - HIS THEORIES ARE WONDERFUL! AND- WELL- HE WANTS ME TO RUN FOR PRESIDENT!
DON'T DO IT, STEVE- HE'S USING YOU FOR A FRONT, TO COVER SOME CROOKED SCHEME. I DON'T TRUST MANLY!
DIANA, YOU'RE SIMPLY SORE BECAUSE MANLY CAN BEAT YOUR WOMAN'S PARTY! WHAT'S YOUR ADVICE, GENERAL?
WELL, MY OPERATIVES HAVE NEVER GOTTEN ANYTHING DEFINITE ON MANLY BUT- EXCUSE ME! HELLO- COMMISSIONER OF U.S. POLICE SPEAKING!
OPERATIVE X-7 REPORTING! NEW ERA LAW FORBIDDING MANUFACTURE OF ARMS IS BEING DEFIED! EXTERMINATOR RIFLES AND HAND GUNS ARE BEING MADE AND SOLD SECRETLY TO MEN!
THIS IS SERIOUS! REPORT PERSONALLY TO MISS PRINCE!
STEVE, I FEEL SURE THAT MANLY IS BEHIND THIS PLOT TO ARM MEN WITH KILLERS' WEAPONS! PLEASE DON'T JOIN HIS PARTY!
PROFESSOR MANLY WOULD NEVER BREAK THE LAW! I THINK YOU'RE JUST PREJUDICED, DIANA!
2B
LATER, AS POLICE OPERATIVE X-7 REPORTS TO DIANA —
THE MAN BEHIND THIS GUN PLOT IS- OHHH!
BANG

QUICKER THAN THOUGHT, DIANA LEAPS OVER HER DESK TO CATCH THE WOUNDED GIRL IN HER ARMS.

WHAT A HORRIBLE DEED! THERE HASN'T BEEN A MURDER LIKE THIS SINCE WOMEN CAME INTO POWER!

FINDING THE GIRL BEYOND HUMAN HELP, DIANA DASHES AFTER THE KILLER.

I'VE GOT HIM NOW — THAT CORRIDOR HE TURNED INTO HAS NO OTHER OUTLET BUT THE PRESIDENT'S OFFICE.

BUT THE MURDERER'S HAND GUN, CLEVERLY THROWN, TRIPS DIANA AS SHE TURNS THE CORNER.

FAUGH! HOW CLUMSY OF ME!

CLANK!

RECOVERING QUICKLY, DIANA REACHES THE PRESIDENT'S OFFICE A SPLIT SECOND TOO LATE.

SORRY, MISTRESS PRINCE, WE CAN'T LET EVEN YOU ENTER WITHOUT YOUR PASS!

OH-H! WHO WENT IN THERE JUST NOW?

I DIDN'T SEE HIS FACE — HE WAS DRESSED IN THE ANCIENT MALE STYLE OF TROUSERS — HA HA! MEN LOOK SO COMICAL IN THOSE GARMENTS! HIS PASS WAS OKAY — SO IS YOURS, MISTRESS, SORRY TO DELAY YOU!

DIANA BURSTS INTO PRESIDENT ARDA'S PRIVATE OFFICE.

THERE'S THE MURDERER!

HAVE YOU GONE CRAZY, DI? THIS IS PROFESSOR MANLY!

3B

I DON'T CARE **WHO** HE IS! THAT MAN SHOT ONE OF MY GIRL OPERATIVES! I FOLLOWED HIM HERE AND —

THERE'S SOME MISTAKE — I'LL VOUCH FOR PROF MANLY'S HIGH CHARACTER!

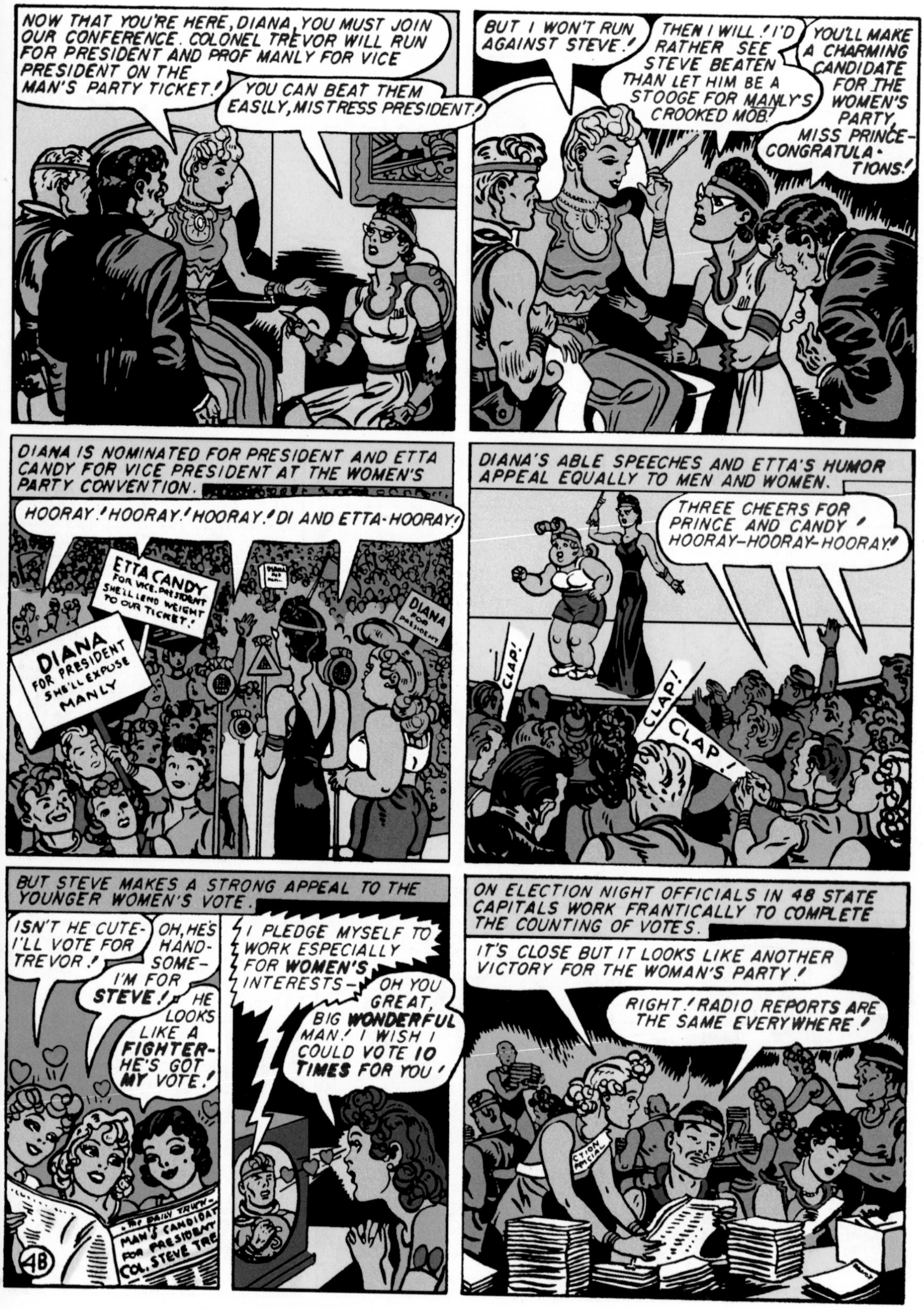

NOW THAT YOU'RE HERE, DIANA, YOU MUST JOIN OUR CONFERENCE. COLONEL TREVOR WILL RUN FOR PRESIDENT AND PROF MANLY FOR VICE PRESIDENT ON THE MAN'S PARTY TICKET!
YOU CAN BEAT THEM EASILY, MISTRESS PRESIDENT!
BUT I WON'T RUN AGAINST STEVE!
THEN I WILL! I'D RATHER SEE STEVE BEATEN THAN LET HIM BE A STOOGE FOR MANLY'S CROOKED MOB!
YOU'LL MAKE A CHARMING CANDIDATE FOR THE WOMEN'S PARTY, MISS PRINCE- CONGRATULATIONS!
DIANA IS NOMINATED FOR PRESIDENT AND ETTA CANDY FOR VICE PRESIDENT AT THE WOMEN'S PARTY CONVENTION.
HOORAY! HOORAY! HOORAY! DI AND ETTA-HOORAY!
ETTA CANDY FOR VICE PRESIDENT SHE'LL LEND WEIGHT TO OUR TICKET!
DIANA FOR PRESIDENT
DIANA FOR PRESIDENT SHE'LL EXPOSE MANLY
DIANA'S ABLE SPEECHES AND ETTA'S HUMOR APPEAL EQUALLY TO MEN AND WOMEN.
THREE CHEERS FOR PRINCE AND CANDY! HOORAY-HOORAY-HOORAY!
CLAP!
CLAP!
CLAP!
BUT STEVE MAKES A STRONG APPEAL TO THE YOUNGER WOMEN'S VOTE.
ISN'T HE CUTE- I'LL VOTE FOR TREVOR!
OH, HE'S HANDSOME- I'M FOR STEVE!
HE LOOKS LIKE A FIGHTER- HE'S GOT MY VOTE!
MAN'S CANDIDAT FOR PRESIDENT COL. STEVE TRE
4B
I PLEDGE MYSELF TO WORK ESPECIALLY FOR WOMEN'S INTERESTS-
OH YOU GREAT, BIG WONDERFUL MAN! I WISH I COULD VOTE 10 TIMES FOR YOU!
ON ELECTION NIGHT OFFICIALS IN 48 STATE CAPITALS WORK FRANTICALLY TO COMPLETE THE COUNTING OF VOTES.
IT'S CLOSE BUT IT LOOKS LIKE ANOTHER VICTORY FOR THE WOMAN'S PARTY!
RIGHT! RADIO REPORTS ARE THE SAME EVERYWHERE!

SUDDENLY, IN 20 KEY STATES, PURPLE SHIRTS INVADE THE VOTE COUNTING ROOMS.

LIE DOWN ON THE FLOOR ON YOUR FACES AND NOT A WORD OUT OF YOU!

SWIFTLY THE HELPLESS OFFICIALS ARE BOUND AND GAGGED.

WORK FAST, PURPLE SHIRTS—A SINGLE SLIP WILL SPOIL OUR ENTIRE PLAN!

SUBSTITUTE OFFICIALS IN FAKE UNIFORMS CHANGE THE VOTE TOTALS IN FAVOR OF THE MAN'S PARTY.

DON'T CHANGE THE COUNT TOO MUCH, JUST ENOUGH TO ELECT TREVOR AND MANLY!

AT WOMAN'S PARTY HEADQUARTERS THE NEW TREND IS NOTED WITH AMAZEMENT.

I DON'T UNDERSTAND THIS—THE TOTALS IN ALL KEY STATES ARE SHIFTING TO THE MAN'S PARTY!

THERE'S SOMETHING QUEER ABOUT IT— WE'LL INVESTIGATE LATER!

BEFORE DAWN THE ELECTION IS CONCEDED TO THE MAN'S PARTY.

WELL, THEY'VE WON AND THAT'S THAT! BUT I STILL CAN'T SEE HOW THEY DID IT!

AT MAN'S PARTY HEADQUARTERS TROOPS ARE CALLED TO PROTECT STEVE FROM HIS YOUNG ADMIRERS.

HOORAY FOR PRESIDENT STEVE! HE'S WONDERFUL! HANDSOME STEVE-LET ME AT HIM!

THANKS, LADIES- BUT TAKE IT EASY-WOO-OOF!

5B

BUT LATER BEHIND LOCKED DOORS—

I'VE ELECTED YOU, TREVOR- NOW YOU TAKE ORDERS FROM ME! SIGN THIS **DECREE** ORDERING ALL ELECTION BALLOTS DESTROYED!

I WILL **NOT**! ARE YOU CRAZY, MANLY?

STEVE SLIPS AWAY FOR A SOLITARY HORSEBACK RIDE TO THINK OVER MANLY'S NEW ATTITUDE AND SUDDENLY FINDS HIMSELF SURROUNDED BY PURPLE SHIRTS.

HANDS UP!

WHAT GAME IS THIS?

I'LL PLAY THIS GAME MY WAY!

YOU'LL SOON FIND OUT WE'RE NOT PLAYING!

AH-UNH!

SEIZE HIM, MEN! YOU KNOW WHAT TO DO WITH HIM!

DIANA, MEANWHILE, RESIGNS HER POSITION AS GENERAL DARNELL'S SECRETARY AND ASSISTANT.

I HATE TO LEAVE THE GENERAL AFTER WORKING WITH HIM ALL THESE YEARS BUT WHAT ELSE CAN I DO?

Dear General:

I herewith tender my resignation as your secretary and aide. I do this because I want to investigate and prosecute Professor Manly without embarrassing your department.

I have proof that Manly murdered our Operative X-7 and I strongly suspect him of fraud in counting election returns.

Yours faithfully,

Diana Prince

AS SHE LEAVES POLICE HEADQUARTERS DIANA SEES A CROWD BUYING NEWSPAPERS WITH FEVERISH EXCITEMENT.

THE PRESIDENT DISAPPEARS! GUARDS ARRESTED! READ ALL ABOUT IT IN THE DAILY TRUTH!

WHAT! GIVE ME A PAPER QUICK!

6B

Daily Truth

WEDNESDAY, NOVEMBER 8, 3004

PRESIDENT MISSING!

Went Riding Alone - Guards Accused of Negligence - Kidnaping Feared!

President-elect Steve Trevor eluded his body guards yesterday and was last seen riding

RUSHING BACK TO GENERAL DARNELL'S OFFICE, DIANA FINDS VICE PRESIDENT MANLY AT HIS DESK

THIS LETTER OF YOURS IS VERY INTERESTING! SO YOU HAVE EVIDENCE THAT I SHOT POLICE OPERATIVE X-7?

SHADES OF PLUTO! HOW *DARE* YOU READ THE GENERAL'S CORRESPONDENCE?

IN TREVOR'S ABSENCE I AM ACTING PRESIDENT— ADDRESS ME RESPECTFULLY!

I'LL ADDRESS YOU AS YOU DESERVE! AS A PRIVATE CITIZEN I'M FREE TO PROSECUTE YOU AND BY HERA, I'M GOING TO *DO* IT!

WE'LL SEE WHO DOES THE PROSECUTING! OFFICERS, ARREST THIS WOMAN!

BUT-ER-MR. PRESIDENT! MISTRESS PRINCE IS OUR *SUPERIOR* OFFICER—

I'M NO LONGER YOUR SUPERIOR OFFICER, GIRLS- YOU'LL HAVE TO OBEY THE ACTING PRESIDENT!

I CHARGE THIS PRISONER WITH PLOTTING AGAINST THE GOVERNMENT— GAG HER! SHE MUST NOT TALK TO *ANYBODY*!

ON MANLY'S ORDERS, DIANA IS PUT IN CLOSE CONFINEMENT.

WE HATE TO DO THIS TO YOU, MISTRESS PRINCE!

I BROUGHT YOUR HANDBAG — IF THEY EVER LET YOUR HANDS LOOSE YOU CAN POWDER YOUR NOSE!

LEFT ALONE IN HER SOLITARY CELL, DIANA WASTES NO TIME IN REMOVING HER STRAIGHTJACKET.

I'VE GOT TO FREE MYSELF AND FIND STEVE- NICE OF THAT GIRL GUARD TO BRING MY BAG! IT CONTAINS *MY WONDER WOMAN* COSTUME!

RIPP!

7B

I'LL BREAK OUT OF THIS PRISON QUIETLY. IF ANYONE SEES ME HERE HE MAY SUSPECT THAT I'M DIANA!

TO AVOID PRISON GUARDS I'LL SLIP OUT THIS WINDOW—

—AND CLIMB TO THE ROOF. THIS IS SO EASY I SHOULD THINK ALL PRISONERS WOULD ESCAPE THIS WAY!

IT'S NOT MORE THAN 50 FEET TO THE PRISON WALL - QUITE A SHORT JUMP - BUT I HOPE THE GUARDS DON'T SEE ME!

PSHAW! THAT GUARD SAW ME - I'LL HAVE TO DO SOMETHING ABOUT HER!

WONDER WOMAN! COME DOWN OR I'LL HAVE TO SHOOT!

LANDING ON THE WALL TOP, THE AMAZON PRINCESS THROWS HER MAGIC LASSO OVER THE PROTESTING GIRL GUARD.

I HAVEN'T TIME TO COME DOWN - YOU COME UP!

EEEK!

WRAPPING THE GUARD IN DIANA'S CAPE, WONDER WOMAN LEAPS FROM THE WALL.

IF THE WATCH TOWER GUARDS SEE ME NOW THEY'LL THINK I'VE GOT DIANA IN MY ARMS!

88

LOOK - THERE'S WONDER WOMAN! SHE'S CARRYING OFF A PRISONER!

I'LL BET SHE'S RESCUING MISTRESS PRINCE! I WISH WE DIDN'T HAVE TO GIVE THE ALARM, BUT WE MUST!

STEVE, MEANWHILE, AFTER BEING KNOCKED OUT BY THE PURPLE SHIRTS, RECOVERS CONSCIOUSNESS AMID STRANGE SURROUNDINGS.

SOME—SOMETHING HIT ME—OUCH! WHO—HOW—WHAT'S THIS ALL ABOUT?

IT LOOKS LIKE WE'RE ALL PROF. MANLY'S PRISONERS—THIS VAULT'S HIS PRIVATE LABORATORY!

WE'RE ELECTION OFFICIALS! WE WERE COUNTING VOTES—THE WOMAN'S PARTY WAS AHEAD. SUDDENLY MANLY'S PURPLE SHIRTS APPEARED, TOOK US PRISONERS AND SUBSTITUTED FAKE OFFICIALS WHO CHANGED THE COUNT.

SO **THAT'S** WHY MANLY WANTS THE BALLOTS DESTROYED!

STEVE'S CONVERSATION IS INTERRUPTED BY THE APPEARANCE OF THE PURPLE SHIRT GUARDS.

COME ON, TREVOR, THE CHIEF WANTS TO SEE YUH!

GOOD! I YEARN FOR A LITTLE HEART-TO-HEART TALK WITH THE PROFESSOR!

SIT DOWN, **PRESIDENT** TREVOR!

I'M NO MORE PRESIDENT THAN YOU'RE A DECENT CITIZEN! DIANA PRINCE WON THE ELECTION—YOU KNOW THAT A RECOUNT OF BALLOTS WILL PROVE IT!

YES—THOSE BALLOTS MUST BE DESTROYED! I CAN ISSUE THE ORDER AS ACTING PRESIDENT BUT I'D RATHER YOU DID IT—LOOKS LESS SUSPICIOUS. I'LL GIVE YOU **ONE** MORE CHANCE!

NEVER! I'LL SEE YOU IN SIBERIA FIRST!

SIBERIA—HM—THAT GIVES ME AN IDEA! SIBERIA IS COLD—YOUR VIRTUOUS ARDOR NEEDS COOLING—HA HA! THIS WILL BE AN INTERESTING EXPERIMENT!

A HUGE BOTTLE IS BLOWN ABOUT STEVE AND LOWERED INTO A TANK OF LIQUID AIR.

FEEL CHILLY, TREVOR? THE LIQUID AIR OUTSIDE YOUR BOTTLE IS NEARLY 270° BELOW ZERO! YOU'LL FREEZE TO DEATH—BUT SLOWLY!

YOUR BOTTLE IS MADE OF CALCI-ATITE—IT PARTIALLY PROTECTS YOU FROM COLD. IF YOU BREAK IT HOPING TO ESCAPE, THE LIQUID AIR WILL FREEZE YOU SOLID INSTANTLY. OBEY ME AND I'LL RE-LEASE YOU!

FREEZING'S MY FAVORITE DEATH!

WHILE THE UNFORTUNATE STEVE WAITS STOICALLY FOR THE CREEPING COLD OF DISSOLUTION, *WONDER WOMAN* RACES BACK TO WASHINGTON.

MANLY **MUST** HAVE KIDNAPED STEVE IN ORDER TO BECOME ACTING PRESIDENT—BUT **WHERE** WOULD HE HIDE HIS PRISONER?

THE AMAZON SEEKS THE SECRET HEADQUARTERS OF THE PURPLE SHIRTS WHICH SHE HAS LOCATED DURING POLICE INVESTIGATION AS DIANA PRINCE.

WHO COMES? GIVE THE PASSWORD!

I'M **WONDER WOMAN** AND MY PASSWORD IS A STRONG RIGHT ARM!

THE BEAUTIFUL VISITOR IS GREETED CORDIAL-LY.

WELCOME, **WONDER WOMAN**! WE HAVE JUST HEARD BY RADIO THAT YOU RESCUED DIANA PRINCE FROM PRISON—OUR CHIEF WANTS TO SEE YOU!

WHAMM!

HO HO! SHE IS EASY TO KNOCK OUT—HER STRENGTH IS OVERRATED. BUT TAKE NO CHANCES—SHACKLE HER SECURELY AND CARRY HER TO THE CHIEF'S LABORATORY. HE WILL MAKE HER TELL WHERE DIANA PRINCE IS HIDDEN!

I'LL ACCOMPLISH MORE IF I LET THEM THINK THEY KNOCKED ME OUT WITH THAT LITTLE TAP ON THE HEAD! HAH! SO MAN-LY USES HIS LAB FOR A PRISON—HM—I'LL SEND A MENTAL RADIO MESSAGE TO ETTA CANDY—

CALLING ETTA CANDY CALLING ETTA----

10B

AS THEY REACH MANLY'S LABORATORY **WONDER WOMAN** APPEARS TO REVIVE.

I CAN WALK BY MYSELF! WHAT DEVIL'S CONTRAPTION IS THIS?

AH, MY DEAR LADY, THIS WILL INTER-EST YOU—A LIQUID AIR EXPERI-MENT IN HUMAN PSYCHOLOGY!

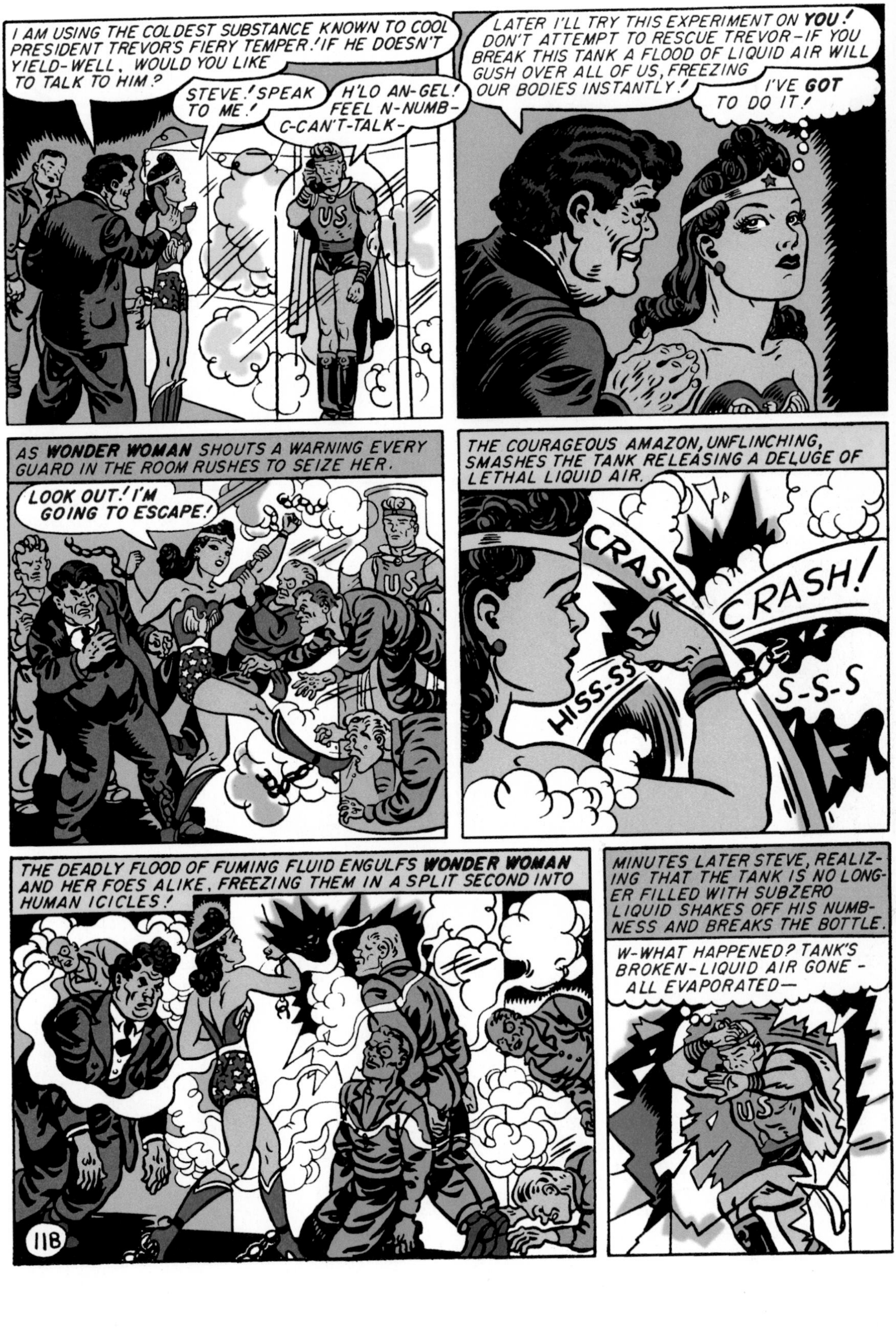
I AM USING THE COLDEST SUBSTANCE KNOWN TO COOL PRESIDENT TREVOR'S FIERY TEMPER! IF HE DOESN'T YIELD-WELL, WOULD YOU LIKE TO TALK TO HIM?
STEVE! SPEAK TO ME!
H'LO AN-GEL! FEEL N-NUMB-C-CAN'T-TALK-
LATER I'LL TRY THIS EXPERIMENT ON YOU! DON'T ATTEMPT TO RESCUE TREVOR-IF YOU BREAK THIS TANK A FLOOD OF LIQUID AIR WILL GUSH OVER ALL OF US, FREEZING OUR BODIES INSTANTLY!
I'VE GOT TO DO IT!
AS WONDER WOMAN SHOUTS A WARNING EVERY GUARD IN THE ROOM RUSHES TO SEIZE HER.
LOOK OUT! I'M GOING TO ESCAPE!
US
THE COURAGEOUS AMAZON, UNFLINCHING, SMASHES THE TANK RELEASING A DELUGE OF LETHAL LIQUID AIR.
CRASH
CRASH!
HISS-SS
S-S-S
THE DEADLY FLOOD OF FUMING FLUID ENGULFS WONDER WOMAN AND HER FOES ALIKE, FREEZING THEM IN A SPLIT SECOND INTO HUMAN ICICLES!
118
MINUTES LATER STEVE, REALIZING THAT THE TANK IS NO LONGER FILLED WITH SUBZERO LIQUID SHAKES OFF HIS NUMBNESS AND BREAKS THE BOTTLE.
W-WHAT HAPPENED? TANK'S BROKEN-LIQUID AIR GONE - ALL EVAPORATED—

WONDER WOMAN - ANGEL - WAKE UP! WHAT'S MATTER - I CAN'T UN'STAND - MIND'S STILL GROGGY! YE GODS - SHE'S FROZEN **STIFF!** OH-H **NO** - NO, NO - IT **CAN'T** BE TRUE!

I CAN'T BELIEVE IT - MY **WONDER WOMAN** GONE - DEAD - SHE GAVE HER LIFE FOR **ME!** SHE BROKE THE TANK AND THE LIQUID AIR FROZE THEM ALL, THEN EVAPORATED! I - I WISH IT HAD KILLED ME TOO!

AT THIS MOMENT ETTA CANDY ARRIVES ON THE SCENE WITH HER COLLEGE TROOPERS.

WOO WOO! WHAT GOES, B'ROTHER? BR-RR- THIS ROOM IS FREEZING COLD!

WONDER WOMAN'S FROZEN — LIQUID AIR —

LET HER ALONE, ETTA! NOTHING WE CAN DO —

THE HECK THERE ISN'T! **WONDER WOMAN'S** NO FOOL - SHE LET HERSELF BE FROZEN BECAUSE SHE KNEW I COULD THAW HER OUT! COME ON, GIRLS, HELP ME CARRY HER!

WE'LL PUT HER IN HERE AND RAISE THE TEMPERATURE VERY SLOWLY— I'LL EXPLAIN—

TEMPERATURE KONTROL ROOM

12B

ETTA EXPLAINS: "WHEN A LIVING BODY IS FROZEN VERY QUICKLY IT DOES NOT DIE IMMEDIATELY BUT REMAINS IN A STATE OF SUSPENDED ANIMATION. HOW LONG IT'LL LIVE DEPENDS ON THE STRENGTH AND VIGOR OF THE PERSON FROZEN. **WONDER WOMAN'D** LIVE FOR A YEAR, I BETCHA! D'JA EVER SEE A COLLEGE PROF. TAKE A LIVE GOLDFISH, PLUNGE IT INTO LIQUID AIR, AN' PULL IT OUT FROZEN STIFF? THEN HE DROPS IT INTO WARM WATER AND OFF SWIMS MR FISH AGAIN. YOU JUST WATCH **WONDER WOMAN** COME TO LIFE!"

SHE - SHE ISN'T MOVING!

WAIT - WE HAFTA THAW HER VERY SLOWLY!

REGULATOR

SUDDENLY **WONDER WOMAN** COMES TO LIFE!

YOU DID IT! ETTA- SHE'S ALIVE— **WONDER WOMAN'S** WAVING AT US!

ETTA, YOU'RE THE BEST PAL A GIRL EVER HAD! **I KNEW** I COULD COUNT ON YOU!

YEAH-BUT DON'T TRY IT AGAIN UNLESS I'VE HAD PLENTY OF CANDY- MY BRAIN MIGHT JAM!

HOORAY! YAYAYAY! **WONDER WOMAN'S** SAVED!

YOU'D BETTER THAW OUT MANLY AND HIS GANG AND HAVE THE GIRLS TAKE THEM TO JAIL!

AW-LET 'EM STAY FROZEN!

NO, SIR! MANLY'S GOTTA CONFESS HE MONKEY-WRENCHED THE ELECTION! DI AND I WANTA BE PRESIDENT!

WHILE **WONDER WOMAN** AND STEVE FREE THE PRISONERS.

I SHOULD GO TO PRISON WITH MANLY FOR THIS DESPICABLE ELECTION FRAUD!

NO, NO. COLONEL TREVOR! NOBODY BLAMES YOU! AND BESIDES, YOU AND **WONDER WOMAN** SAVED US ALL!

INFORMED BY POLICE FOURTH DIMENSIONAL RADIO, GENERAL DARNELL HURRIES TO THE SCENE···· **WONDER WOMAN** MAKES A LIGHTNING CHANGE!

GLAD YOU'RE OKAY, STEVE. BUT WHERE **IS**-OH! **THERE** YOU ARE, MISTRESS PRESIDENT! BY GEORGE-YOU **DO** MOVE AROUND QUICKLY--ER-WHERE'S **WONDER WOMAN?**

I GUESS SHE LEFT-**SHE** MOVES MUCH MORE QUICKLY THAN I----

AND SO, DIANA PRINCE, AFTER MANY YEARS OF FAITHFUL SERVICE TO HER COUNTRY, FINALLY HOLDS ITS HIGHEST OFFICE----

I SOLEMNLY SWEAR TO PERFORM MY DUTIES FAITHFULLY AS PRESIDENT OF THE UNITED STATES.

13 B.

WHILE BACK IN 1943 ON PARADISE ISLAND----

OH MOTHER, HE **DIDN'T** BEAT ME AFTER ALL- I ALMOST WISH HE HAD, POOR STEVE!

SILLY GIRL-STEVE AND ALL MEN ARE MUCH HAPPIER WHEN THEIR STRONG AGGRES-SIVE NATURES ARE CON-TROLLED BY A WISE AND LOVING WOMAN!

The End

Wonder Woman

By Charles Moulton

REG. U.S. PAT OFF.

NOT **ALL** WOMEN ARE FIT TO RULE IN THE WORLD OF TOMORROW, AS THE UNITED EARTH COUNCIL OF PRESIDENTS LEARNS TO ITS SORROW! THE INSATIABLE AMBITION OF CRUEL QUEEN ANDRA DRAWS **WONDER WOMAN** INTO A DIZZY MAELSTROM OF DEATH AND DANGER FROM WHICH EVEN THE MIGHTY AMAZON CANNOT ESCAPE! LED IN TRIUMPH BEHIND THE QUEEN'S CHARIOT, OUR LOVELY PRINCESS IS FACED WITH THE TERRIFIC PROBLEM OF CONQUERING A COUNTRY OF MASS MURDERERS WITH AN ARMY OF WOMEN WHO CANNOT KILL OR INJURE THEIR ENEMY! IN THIS EPISODE OF **THE SECRET WEAPON** YOU WILL FIND **WONDER WOMAN** MORE INGENIOUS—AND MORE LOVABLE—THAN EVER BEFORE!

THE AMAZON'S AERIAL DETECTOGRAPH REVEALS AN AIRSHIP APPROACHING PARADISE ISLAND

SEE, MOTHER—A STRANGE AIRCRAFT OVERHEAD! HOW COULD ANYONE FIND OUR SECRET ISLAND?

IT MUST BE PAULA COMING FOR THE HARVEST FESTIVAL!

YOU'RE RIGHT, MOTHER—THAT'S PAULA'S NEW "AIRGLOBE"—IT'S HELD IN THE AIR LIKE THE EARTH, BY THE SUN'S ATTRACTION. IT IS MADE OF SUBMAGNUM, A METAL PAULA DISCOVERED, WHICH IS MAGNETICALLY SENSITIVE TO THE SUN.

PAULA'S A CLEVER GIRL!

PAULA! **PRINCESS!** **APHRODITE WITH YOU, PAULA! WELCOME TO PARADISE ISLE!**

MY LOVING SUBMISSION TO YOUR MAJESTY!

I AM PROUD TO HAVE SUCH A WISE AND BEAUTIFUL SUBJECT! RISE, MY DEAR, AND HASTEN TO THE AMAZON SCHOOL-YOUR LITTLE DAUGHTER GERTA IS COUNTING THE MINUTES TILL YOU ARRIVE!

I WILL SHOW YOU ON THE MAGIC SPHERE HOW PAULA'S AIRGLOBE BECOMES THE COMMON METHOD OF TRAVEL 1700 YEARS FROM NOW- BUT FIRST I MUST TELL YOU SOMETHING ABOUT THE FUTURE WORLD OF THAT PERIOD.

IN 3700 A.D. THE WHOLE WORLD WILL BE ONE NATION CALLED UNITED STATES OF EARTH. PRESENT-DAY COUNTRIES WILL BE STATES IN THE GLOBAL UNION. THE WORLD CAPITOL WILL BE AN ISLAND NAMED HARMONIA. MEN AND WOMEN WILL BE EQUAL. BUT WOMAN'S INFLUENCE WILL CONTROL MOST GOVERNMENTS BECAUSE WOMEN ARE MORE READY TO SERVE OTHERS UNSELFISHLY!

BUT SURELY, MOTHER, EVEN IN 3700 A.D. SOME WOMEN WILL USE THEIR POWER OVER OTHERS FOR SELFISH PURPOSES - JUST AS MEN DO NOW!

TRUE, ALAS! ONE SELFISHLY AMBITIOUS GIRL WILL SHAKE WORLD PEACE TO ITS FOUNDATIONS! WATCH THE MAGIC SPHERE-

AT HARMONIA, THE WORLD CAPITOL, CHIEF EARTH ELECTRESS PAULA PRESIDES OVER THE COUNCIL OF PRESIDENTS.

ZONE MISTRESSES WILL REPORT; FIRST, THE PRESIDENT OF AMERICA!

ALL SERENE IN MY ZONE EXCEPT PRIMAL ISLAND WHOSE PRESIDENT SENDS THIS LETTER!

2c.

PRESIDENT'S PALACE
Primal Island State

Mid-May, 3700

Council of Presidents,
United States of Earth,
Harmonia.

Comrades:
We are in serious trouble. A beautiful ambitious girl, Andra Moteeva, is inducing men to rebel against our democratic government. Andra plans to make herself Dictator and attack other states, bringing war into the world again! I beg advice and help!

Loyally yours,
Serva Faith
President of Primal

OUR REPORTS ON AFFAIRS IN PRIMAL ISLAND ARE INADEQUATE, MISTRESS PRESIDENT, SUPPOSE YOU GO THERE IMMEDIATELY TO ADVISE PRES. SERVA, AND KEEP THE COUNCIL INFORMED!

AN EXCELLENT IDEA, MISTRESS ELECTRESS!

DIANA'S FLYING AIRGLOBE IS PILOTED BY HER MILITARY AIDE, COLONEL STEVE TREVOR.

WE ARE READY TO TAKE OFF, MISTRESS PRESIDENT!

CUT THE FORMALITY AND CALL ME DIANA! WE'RE FLYING TO PRIMAL ISLAND— TROUBLE AHEAD—

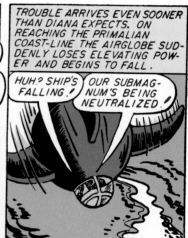

TROUBLE ARRIVES EVEN SOONER THAN DIANA EXPECTS. ON REACHING THE PRIMALIAN COAST-LINE THE AIRGLOBE SUDDENLY LOSES ELEVATING POWER AND BEGINS TO FALL.

HUH? SHIP'S FALLING!

OUR SUBMAGNUM'S BEING NEUTRALIZED!

STEVE WORKS FRANTICALLY AT THE CONTROLS.

I'VE CUT ALL NEUTRALIZING CURRENT TO OUR HULL, FREEING THE SUBMAGNUM'S FULL MAGNETISM. BUT **STILL** WE'RE FALLING!

MUST BE ELECTRIC GUNS SHOOTING AT US FROM BELOW!

UNDER THE BLUE ELECTRIC RAYS OF POWERFUL GLASS GUNS, THE AMERICAN AIRGLOBE CRASHES INTO THE SEA.

THE TERRIFIC IMPACT KNOCKS DIANA OVER BUT EVEN AS SHE FALLS, THE INTREPID AMAZON BEGINS TO DON HER **WONDER WOMAN** COSTUME.

STEVE'S UNCONSCIOUS— I'LL NEED MY **WONDER WOMAN** COSTUME FOR QUICK ACTION!

3C

THE POWERFUL PRINCESS BREAKS THROUGH THE SUBMAGNUM HULL WITH STEVE UNCONSCIOUS IN HER ARMS.

I'VE GOT TO GET STEVE OUT OF THIS LOBSTER TRAP BEFORE THE OXYGEN'S EXHAUSTED!

SWIMMING TOWARD SHORE, **WONDER WOMAN** ENCOUNTERS HUGE METAL NETS. THE PRIMALIANS CERTAINLY GUARD THEIR COASTLINE—THESE NETS GO CLEAR TO THE BOTTOM! I'LL HAVE TO BREAK THROUGH!

AS **WONDER WOMAN'S** FINGERS GRASP THE METAL MESHES AN ELECTRIC SHOCK PARALYZES HER FROM HEAD TO FOOT.

OH-H-H-H-H...

WONDER WOMAN IS PULLED ABOARD A PRIMAL PATROL BOAT.

BY THE GREAT GOD STOMAC—IT'S **WONDER WOMAN!** NET HER! SECURE HER CAREFULLY! **SHE** CAN BREAK THE HEAVIEST BONDS!

WONDER WOMAN REGAINS CONSCIOUSNESS TO FIND HERSELF BOUND IN AN ELECTRIC NET

WHO—WHAT-?

DON'T ASK QUESTIONS! SUBMIT TO CAPTIVITY OR I'LL TURN ON THE CURRENT IN YOUR NET—IT'LL PARALYZE YOU AGAIN!

I'LL SURRENDER IF YOU TELL ME WHAT'S HAPPENED TO COLONEL TREVOR, THE AMERICAN.

I DON'T KNOW, BUT I DON'T HAVE TO BARGAIN WITH PRISONERS-FORWARD MARCH TO PRISON!

I MAY FIND STEVE IN THEIR PRISON—

YOU WIN—BUT HOW CAN I "MARCH" IN THIS NET?

HOP ON BOTH FEET! KEEP YOUR JUMPS **SHORT**-I'LL TAKE NO CHANCES WITH **WONDER WOMAN!**

4C

WONDER WOMAN FINDS THE PRISON FILLED TO OVERFLOWING WITH CAPTIVES!

STAND BACK, YOU PRISONERS! MAKE WAY FOR **WONDER WOMAN!**

LOOKS AS IF HALF THE GIRLS IN PRIMAL WERE CAPTIVES!

THE AMAZON MAIDEN IS PUT IN ELECTRIC FETTERS WITH OTHER IMPORTANT PRISONERS.

THIS GANG CHAIN ON OUR NECKS IS CONNECTED WITH THAT ELECTRICAL APPARATUS. IF WE TOUCH THE CHAIN IT SENDS A PARALYZING CURRENT THROUGH ALL OF US!

WHY ARE YOU GIRLS IN PRISON?

BECAUSE WE BELONGED TO PRESIDENT SERVA'S CABINET OUR GOVERNMENT WAS OVERTHROWN BY ANDRA MOTEEVA, WHO LURED ALL THE MEN TO FOLLOW HER! SHE ARMED THEM WITH KILLER'S WEAPONS AND MADE HERSELF **QUEEN**!

DID YOUR WOMEN FIGHT ANDRA?

YES— MANY WERE KILLED AND THOUSANDS OF GOVERNMENT, POLICE AND ARMY GIRLS WERE CAPTURED. EVERY PRISON IS FULL. ALL OUR WOMEN HAVE LOST THEIR RIGHTS— THEY ARE FORBIDDEN TO LEAVE THEIR HOMES!

FETTERED WITH ELECTRIC CHAINS **WONDER WOMAN** IS LED BEFORE QUEEN ANDRA.

BY WHAT RIGHT DO YOU HOLD **ME** PRISONER, REBEL QUEEN?

YOU WERE CAUGHT TRYING TO ENTER PRIMAL — YOU'RE A SPY AND SHALL GRACE MY TRIUMPH!

STEVE, MEANWHILE, MEETS VERY DIFFERENT TREATMENT.

MY HEAD FEELS LIKE AN EARTHQUAKE— WHAT HAPPENED?

WE SHOT DOWN YOUR AIRGLOBE, COLONEL— SORRY, BUT QUEEN'S ORDERS! WE'RE AT WAR WITH THE DEMOCRATIC WORLD GOVERNMENT!

YOU'RE AT **WAR**! WHY, WAR'S BEEN OUTLAWED FOR A THOUSAND YEARS!

OUTLAWED— HA HA! THAT GIVES US OUR OPPORTUNITY! MEN OF PRIMAL ARE ARMED TO KILL— WOMEN'S STATES LACK KILLER'S WEAPONS— THEY DON'T **BELIEVE** IN KILLING!

YOU'RE A **MAN**— YOU HAVE KILLER'S INSTINCTS. WHY NOT PERSUADE AMERICAN MEN TO JOIN US?

YOU'RE CRAZY!

HA HA! YOU WILL BE TOO WHEN YOU SEE OUR QUEEN— NO MAN CAN RESIST HER. COME, SHE SUMMONS YOU!

5c

GREETINGS TO AMERICA'S HANDSOME AMBASSADOR!

YOUR MAJESTY IS GRACIOUS—BUT I AM ONLY THE MILITARY AIDE TO PRESIDENT DIANA PRINCE WHO CAME TO SEE YOU!

PRESIDENT DIANA HASN'T BEEN FOUND—JUST AS WELL! I PREFER DEALING WITH MEN. AT MY TRIUMPH I SHALL EXECUTE THOUSANDS OF WOMEN PRISONERS—FORMER OFFICIALS AND ENEMIES, AS CAESAR DID!

HOW HORRIBLE! I BEG YOU—

DON'T WORRY, MY FRIEND—I'M NOT BLOODTHIRSTY! FOR INSTANCE, THIS GIRL MADE A SPEECH AGAINST ME—SHE SAID THAT WOMEN NOW LIVE A DOG'S LIFE ON PRIMAL ISLAND. SO I KEEP HER AS MY PET DOG—SPEAK, FIDO!

WOOF-WOOF!

YOU CRUEL, POWER-MAD TYRANT! YOU'RE NOT A REAL WOMAN—THE TRUE WOMEN GOVERNORS OF THE WORLD WILL TEACH YOU—

BAH! I CAN CONQUER THE STRONGEST WOMAN ALIVE! GUARDS, SHOW HIM MY PRISONERS!

BEHOLD EX-PRESIDENT SERVA WHO THREATENED ME WITH PRISON—HAHA! AND WONDER WOMAN, THE "INVINCIBLE" WHO INVADED MY QUEENDOM! BOTH ARE HELPLESS, BOUND IN ELECTRIC SHACKLES!

WONDER WOMAN! I CAN'T BELIEVE IT!

STEVE! I ONLY SURRENDERED TO FIND YOU—

6C

WONDER WOMAN IN THE ACT OF ESCAPE IS PARALYZED BY A POWERFUL CURRENT ELECTRIFYING HER FETTERS.

NOW I'LL BREAK THESE CHAINS AND—OHHHH!

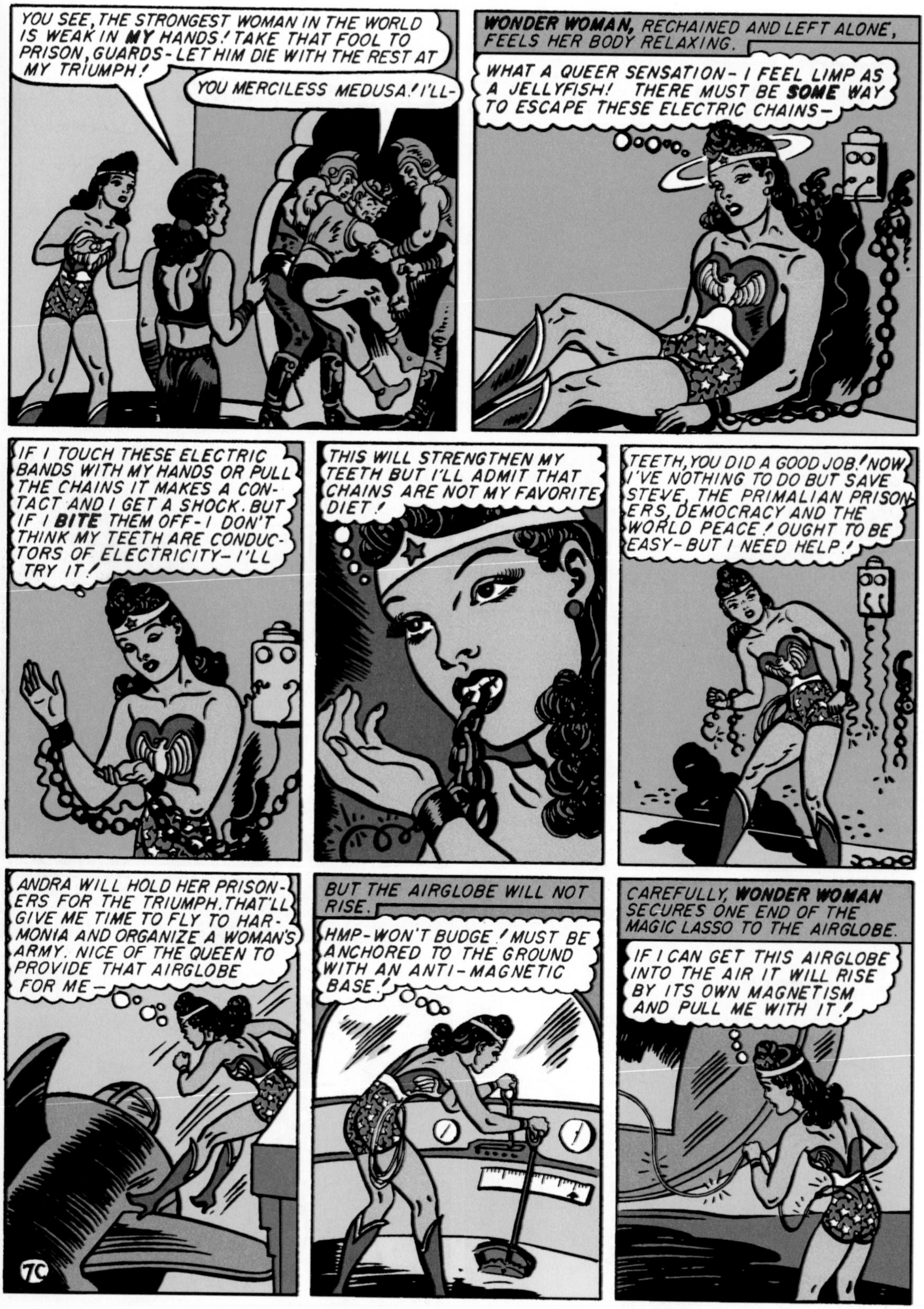
YOU SEE, THE STRONGEST WOMAN IN THE WORLD IS WEAK IN MY HANDS! TAKE THAT FOOL TO PRISON, GUARDS - LET HIM DIE WITH THE REST AT MY TRIUMPH!
YOU MERCILESS MEDUSA! I'LL-
WONDER WOMAN, RECHAINED AND LEFT ALONE, FEELS HER BODY RELAXING.
WHAT A QUEER SENSATION - I FEEL LIMP AS A JELLYFISH! THERE MUST BE SOME WAY TO ESCAPE THESE ELECTRIC CHAINS-
IF I TOUCH THESE ELECTRIC BANDS WITH MY HANDS OR PULL THE CHAINS IT MAKES A CONTACT AND I GET A SHOCK. BUT IF I BITE THEM OFF - I DON'T THINK MY TEETH ARE CONDUCTORS OF ELECTRICITY - I'LL TRY IT!
THIS WILL STRENGTHEN MY TEETH BUT I'LL ADMIT THAT CHAINS ARE NOT MY FAVORITE DIET!
TEETH, YOU DID A GOOD JOB! NOW I'VE NOTHING TO DO BUT SAVE STEVE, THE PRIMALIAN PRISONERS, DEMOCRACY AND THE WORLD PEACE! OUGHT TO BE EASY - BUT I NEED HELP!
ANDRA WILL HOLD HER PRISONERS FOR THE TRIUMPH. THAT'LL GIVE ME TIME TO FLY TO HARMONIA AND ORGANIZE A WOMAN'S ARMY. NICE OF THE QUEEN TO PROVIDE THAT AIRGLOBE FOR ME-
7C
BUT THE AIRGLOBE WILL NOT RISE.
HMP - WON'T BUDGE! MUST BE ANCHORED TO THE GROUND WITH AN ANTI-MAGNETIC BASE!
CAREFULLY, WONDER WOMAN SECURES ONE END OF THE MAGIC LASSO TO THE AIRGLOBE.
IF I CAN GET THIS AIRGLOBE INTO THE AIR IT WILL RISE BY ITS OWN MAGNETISM AND PULL ME WITH IT!

WITH A MIGHTY HEAVE THE AMAZON MAIDEN HURLS THE MASSIVE METAL GLOBE HIGH INTO THE AIR.

RELEASED FROM ITS EARTH ANCHOR THE GLOBE SOARS UPWARD, PULLING **WONDER WOMAN** WITH IT.

NOW I FEEL LIKE A PARACHUTE JUMPER IN REVERSE!

HERE'S A PROBLEM FOR YOU—WHICH IS CLIMBING FASTEST, THE AIRGLOBE OR I? ANYHOW, WE'RE BOTH CLIMBING ABOVE THE RANGE OF ANDRA'S ELECTRIC GUNS!

FLYING TO HARMONIA AT TOP SPEED, THE AMAZON PRINCESS SURPRISES PAULA AND THE COUNCIL OF PRESIDENTS.

WONDER WOMAN! WHAT A HAPPY SURPRISE!

WELCOME TO OUR COUNCIL!

GREETINGS, PRINCESS!

HELLO, **WONDER WOMAN!** GLAD TO SEE YOU!

APHRODITE WITH YOU ALL!

IT'S UP TO YOUR WORLD GOVERNMENT TO CONQUER QUEEN ANDRA! I KNOW YOU DON'T **WANT** TO FIGHT BUT YOU MUST! ANDRA WILL ATTACK ONE COUNTRY AFTER ANOTHER AND **KILL** ALL WHO OPPOSE HER!

8c

BUT PRINCESS, WE **CANNOT** KILL OTHERS, EVEN THOUGH WE OURSELVES DIE! IT IS THE LAW OF APHRODITE!

VERY TRUE! I SAID **FIGHT**, NOT "KILL" I'LL SHOW YOU HOW TO CONQUER PRIMAL WITHOUT KILLING ANYBODY!

FOR 3 DAYS AND NIGHTS THE WOMEN LEADERS WORK TIRELESSLY ON PLANS, FIGURES AND CALCULATIONS.

MILLION WOMEN TROOPS-

18,453 AIRGLOBES-RIGHT!

WONDER WOMAN'S "SECRET WEAPON"

GIVE 'EM MORE ALTITUDE-

WHILE WOMAN TROOPS POUR INTO HARMONIA FROM EVERY QUARTER OF THE GLOBE —

MEANWHILE PAULA AND **WONDER WOMAN** PERFECT A NEW DRUG— MUS-RELAXO.

HOW DID YOU EVER THINK OF THIS, PRINCESS?

I GOT THE IDEA FROM FEELING SO **LIMP** AFTER BEING PARALYZED BY ELECTRIC CHAINS!

MUS-RELAXO IS FORCED INTO HOLLOW GOLDEN RINGS.

MUS-RELAXO

A DELICATE VALVE IS INSERTED IN THE RING— THE SLIGHTEST PRESSURE CAUSES **MUS-RELAXO** TO SPURT OUT.

GOOD! OUR SECRET WEAPON IS PERFECTED!

THOUSANDS OF WELDERS UNDER PAULA'S DIRECTION WELD MUS-RELAXO RINGS "ON ALL THE FINGERS OF EVERY GIRL SOLDIER.

THERE YOU ARE - **YOU'RE** ARMED AND PREPARED TO MEET THE ENEMY— **NEXT!**

WITH ALL PREPARATIONS COMPLETE, **WONDER WOMAN** RETURNS TO PRIMAL ISLAND.

I MUST HURRY BACK TO WALK IN THE TRIUMPH. I'D HATE TO DISAPPOINT ANDRA!

BE CAREFUL, DARLING—APHRODITE WITH YOU!

LANDING UNOBSERVED, **WONDER WOMAN** JUMPS THE HIGH PRISON WALL.

BREAKING **INTO** PRISON MAY BE HARDER THAN BREAKING OUT!

WONDER WOMAN ENTERS HER PRISON CELL.

SH-H-H—QUIET, GIRLS! I DON'T WANT TO BE CAUGHT GETTING **INTO** JAIL!

9c

FINDING PLENTY OF FETTERS IN THE CELL, **WONDER WOMAN** CHAINS HERSELF AGAIN, TO THE AMAZEMENT OF HER SISTER PRISONERS.

BUT **WONDER WOMAN**, **WHAT'S** THE IDEA? ARE YOU CRAZY?

HA HA! MAYBE I AM— TIME WILL TELL!

LEARNING OF **WONDER WOMAN'S** AMAZING RE-APPEARANCE, QUEEN ANDRA RUSHES TO THE PRISON

IT **IS** THE AMAZON! BUT— BUT THIS PRISON WAS SEARCHED—

HA HA! I WAS HID-ING BEHIND MY CHAINS, MAJESTY— YOUR GUARDS OVER-LOOKED ME!

QUEEN ANDRA LEADS HER TRIUMPHAL PROCESSION FROM PRISON TO COLISEUM IN ANCIENT ROMAN STYLE, WITH THE MOST DISTINGUISHED CAPTIVES CHAINED TO HER CHARIOT.

NEXT COMES A GROUP OF MALE PRISONERS LED BY STEVE.

AFTER A LONG, DUSTY MARCH THROUGH JEER-ING CROWDS THE CAPTIVES APPROACH THE COLISEUM WHERE THEY ARE TO BE EXECUTED.

BUT AS THE CAPTIVES ARE DRIVEN INTO THE ARENA, A GREAT FLEET OF AIRGLOBES DE-SCENDS SUDDENLY FROM THE STRATOSPHERE

A PRIMALIAN GENERAL RUSHES TO WARN THE QUEEN.

FOREIGN AIRGLOBES ARE LANDING! WE'RE BEING INVADED—

SURROUND EVERY GLOBE WITH TROOPERS AS IT LANDS! SHOOT ALL INVADERS WHO DON'T SURRENDER!

BUT THE INVADING WOMEN SURRENDER WITHOUT A STRUGGLE.

THESE INVADERS OUTNUMBER US 3 TO 1 BUT WE'VE CAPTURED THEM **ALL**!

BAH—THEY'RE ALL COWARDS! WE'LL HAVE TO EXECUTE THEM—ALL OUR PRISONS ARE OVERCROWDED—HOLD THESE PRISONERS HERE TO AWAIT THEIR TURN FOR EXECUTION IN THE ARENA!

MEANWHILE IN THE ARENA, **WONDER WOMAN**, SERVA, AND HER GIRLS ARE BOUND TO POSTS

WHAT GAME ARE YOU GOING TO PLAY WITH US, OFFICER?

YOU'LL SEE!

AT A SIGNAL FROM THE QUEEN, HUNGRY LIONS AND TIGERS ARE RELEASED.

EE-EEK!

HEAVEN HELP US!

IT'S TIME TO START SOMETHING—THAT TIGER JUMPING ON SERVA DOESN'T LOOK AFFECTIONATE!

WITH A LEAP SO POWERFUL IT BREAKS HER BONDS, **WONDER WOMAN** SEIZES THE FEROCIOUS BEAST.

NAUGHTY KITTEN—MUSTN'T HURT PRETTY GIRL!

11C

FLASHING INTO ACTION WITH THE SPEED AND POWER OF A TORNADO, THE MIGHTY AMAZON HURLS LIONS AND TIGERS AMONG THE SPECTATORS.

EEE-EEK!

AWK-YOWEE!

GO AND PLAY WITH THE PRIMALIANS, MY FELINE PETS, WHILE I RELEASE THE PRISONERS!

MEANWHILE, AT PAULA'S SIGNAL, THE "CAPTURED" WOMEN SOLDIERS SUDDENLY ATTACK THEIR CAPTORS WITH GOLD-RINGED FISTS.

AT THEM, GIRLS! HIT 'EM WITH YOUR RINGS AND THEY'LL WILT LIKE FLOWERS IN THE SUN!

THE "MUS-RELAXO" RINGS DISCHARGE TINY JETS OF GAS, INSTANTLY RELAXING A MAN'S MUSCLES AND LEAVING HIM HELPLESS.

AS PRISONERS FROM THE ARENA, RELEASED BY **WONDER WOMAN**, JOIN THE FRAY, THE PRIMALIAN TROOPS ARE COMPLETELY OVERWHELMED BY SHEER WEIGHT OF WOMAN POWER.

WOO WOO! DON'T MUS-RELAX 'EM SO FAST, GIRLS- WAIT'LL WE CATCH UP WITH YOU!

WONDER WOMAN CAPTURES QUEEN ANDRA AS SHE TRIES DESPERATELY TO ESCAPE.

WAIT A MINUTE, DARLING! I'VE GROWN SO FOND OF YOU I CAN'T LET YOU GO!

ARR-RRGH!

WITH DEMOCRACY FULLY RESTORED ON PRIMAL ISLAND, ANDRA IS BROUGHT TO JUSTICE.

I CONFESS AND BEG MERCY!

YOU WILL TAKE NURSE'S TRAINING IN PRISON AND **SERVE** YOUR FELLOW PRISONERS UNTIL YOU LEARN TO ENJOY IT!

12c

SADLY CHIEF ELECTRESS PAULA ADDRESSES THE COUNCIL OF PRESIDENTS.

OUR BELOVED PRESIDENT PRINCE WAS KILLED-ER-WHAT? DIANA!!

NO-I'M VERY MUCH ALIVE- **WONDER WOMAN** SAVED ME!

SOMETIMES I WISH SHE HADN'T- I GET SO SICK OF WEARING THESE GLASSES!

THE END

Wonder Woman

BY CHARLES MOULTON

AT THE QUAINT AND THRILLING HARVEST FESTIVAL OF THE AMAZONS, WHICH CORRESPONDS TO OUR THANKSGIVING, **WONDER WOMAN** FINDS A LITTLE GIRL WHO THROWS PIANOS AT HER TEACHER! DISCOVERING THE CHILD'S TERRIBLE FUTURE ON THE MAGIC SPHERE, THE BEAUTIFUL AMAZON PRINCESS DARES THE **DEMON OF THE DEPTHS** TO SAVE LITTLE GERTA'S LIFE AND HAPPINESS!

HARRY G PETER...

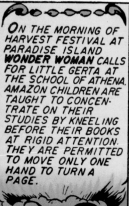

ON THE MORNING OF HARVEST FESTIVAL AT PARADISE ISLAND **WONDER WOMAN** CALLS FOR LITTLE GERTA AT THE SCHOOL OF ATHENA. AMAZON CHILDREN ARE TAUGHT TO CONCENTRATE ON THEIR STUDIES BY KNEELING BEFORE THEIR BOOKS AT RIGID ATTENTION. THEY ARE PERMITTED TO MOVE ONLY ONE HAND TO TURN A PAGE.

HOLA, KATHRA, HOW GOES THE SCHOOL? I CAME TO GET PAULA'S DAUGHTER FOR THE FESTIVAL.

SORRY, PRINCESS, THESE CHILDREN HAVE BEEN INATTENTIVE—THEY MUST STUDY ANOTHER HOUR!

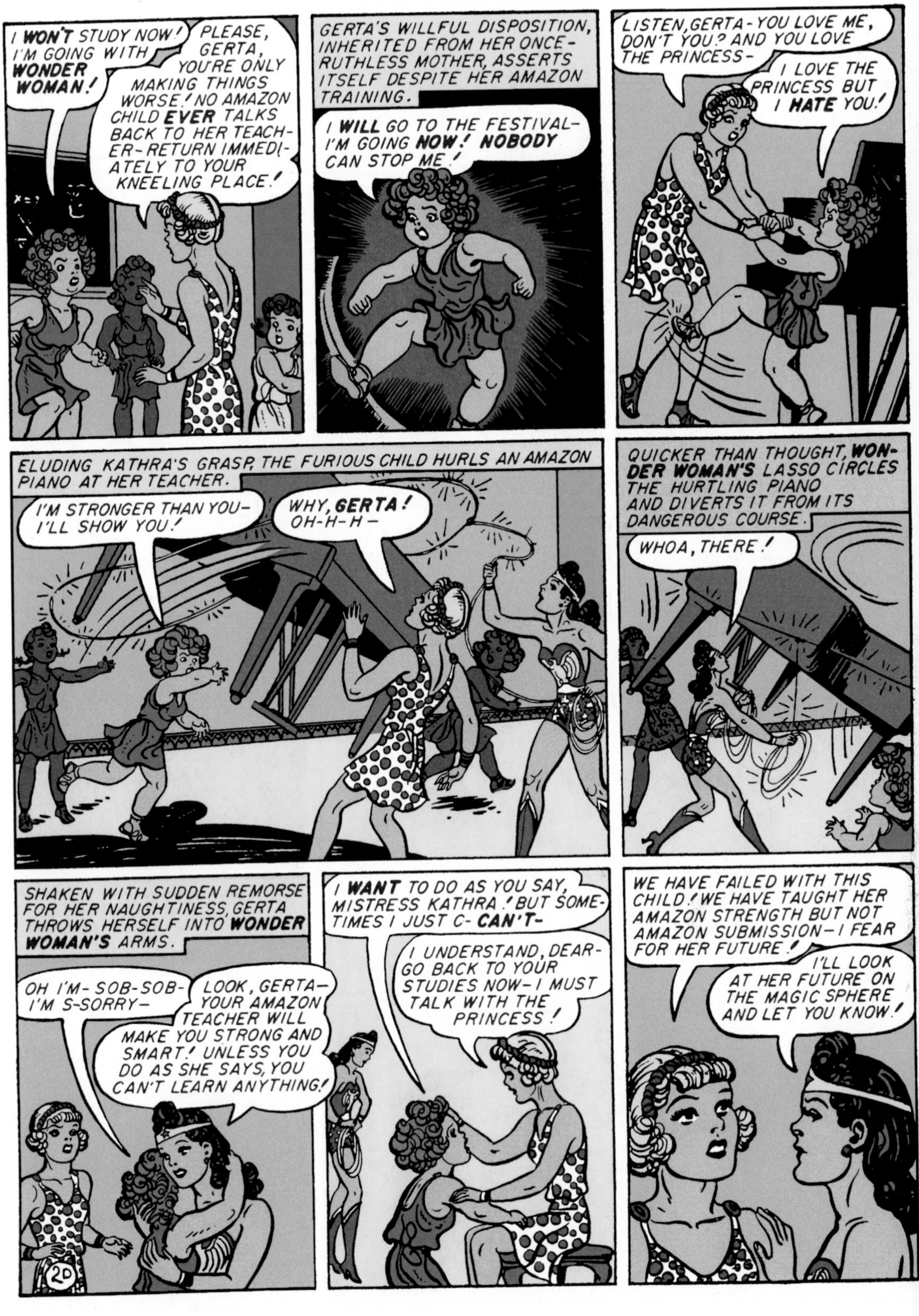
I WON'T STUDY NOW! I'M GOING WITH WONDER WOMAN!
PLEASE, GERTA, YOU'RE ONLY MAKING THINGS WORSE! NO AMAZON CHILD EVER TALKS BACK TO HER TEACHER-RETURN IMMEDIATELY TO YOUR KNEELING PLACE!
GERTA'S WILLFUL DISPOSITION, INHERITED FROM HER ONCE-RUTHLESS MOTHER, ASSERTS ITSELF DESPITE HER AMAZON TRAINING.
I WILL GO TO THE FESTIVAL-I'M GOING NOW! NOBODY CAN STOP ME!
LISTEN, GERTA-YOU LOVE ME, DON'T YOU? AND YOU LOVE THE PRINCESS-
I LOVE THE PRINCESS BUT I HATE YOU!
ELUDING KATHRA'S GRASP, THE FURIOUS CHILD HURLS AN AMAZON PIANO AT HER TEACHER.
I'M STRONGER THAN YOU-I'LL SHOW YOU!
WHY, GERTA! OH-H-H-
QUICKER THAN THOUGHT, WONDER WOMAN'S LASSO CIRCLES THE HURTLING PIANO AND DIVERTS IT FROM ITS DANGEROUS COURSE.
WHOA, THERE!
SHAKEN WITH SUDDEN REMORSE FOR HER NAUGHTINESS, GERTA THROWS HERSELF INTO WONDER WOMAN'S ARMS.
OH I'M-SOB-SOB-I'M S-SORRY-
LOOK, GERTA-YOUR AMAZON TEACHER WILL MAKE YOU STRONG AND SMART! UNLESS YOU DO AS SHE SAYS, YOU CAN'T LEARN ANYTHING!
I WANT TO DO AS YOU SAY, MISTRESS KATHRA! BUT SOMETIMES I JUST C-CAN'T-
I UNDERSTAND, DEAR-GO BACK TO YOUR STUDIES NOW-I MUST TALK WITH THE PRINCESS!
WE HAVE FAILED WITH THIS CHILD! WE HAVE TAUGHT HER AMAZON STRENGTH BUT NOT AMAZON SUBMISSION-I FEAR FOR HER FUTURE!
I'LL LOOK AT HER FUTURE ON THE MAGIC SPHERE AND LET YOU KNOW!

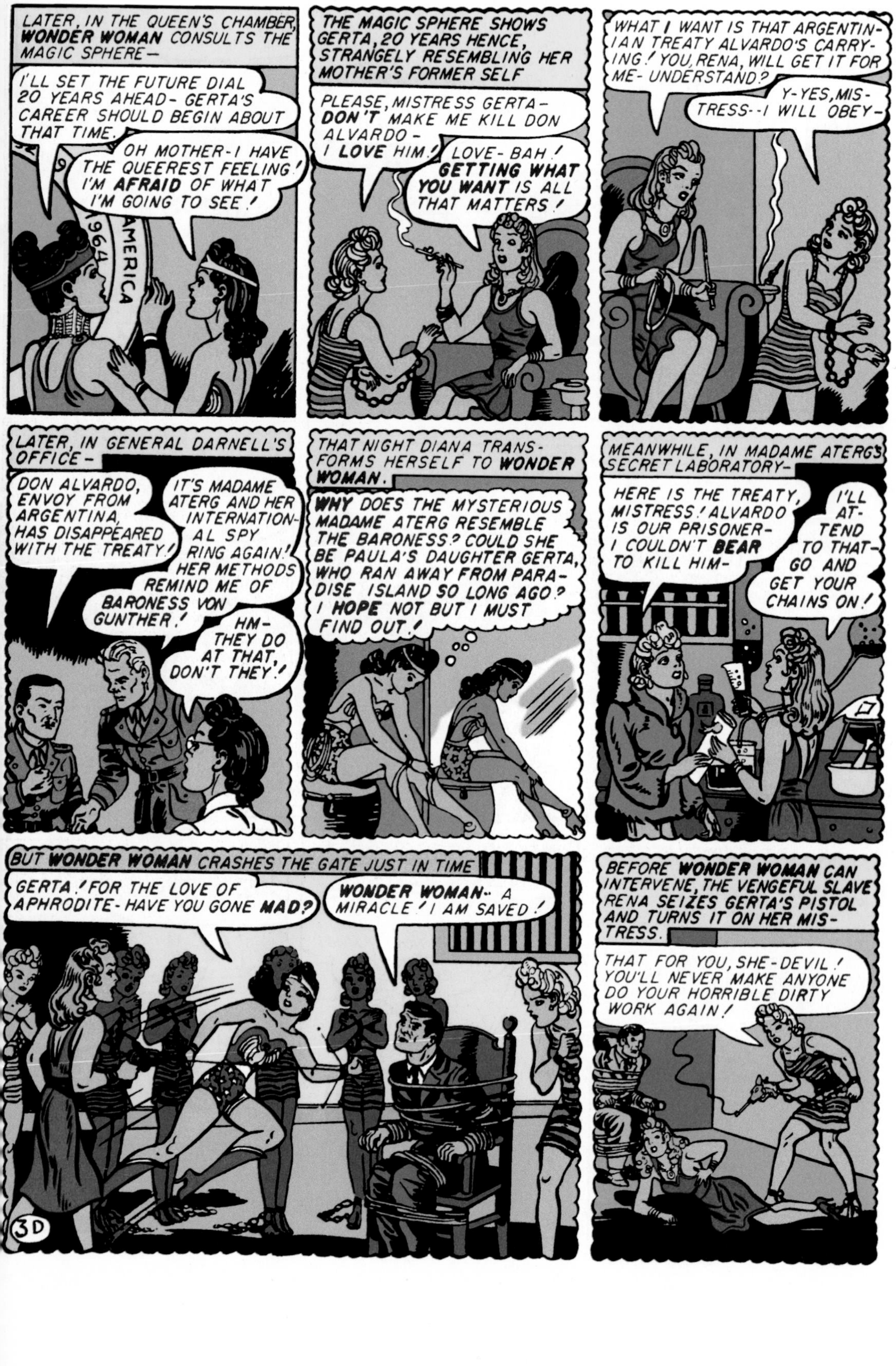
LATER, IN THE QUEEN'S CHAMBER, WONDER WOMAN CONSULTS THE MAGIC SPHERE—
I'LL SET THE FUTURE DIAL 20 YEARS AHEAD- GERTA'S CAREER SHOULD BEGIN ABOUT THAT TIME.
OH MOTHER-I HAVE THE QUEEREST FEELING! I'M AFRAID OF WHAT I'M GOING TO SEE!
1964
AMERICA
THE MAGIC SPHERE SHOWS GERTA, 20 YEARS HENCE, STRANGELY RESEMBLING HER MOTHER'S FORMER SELF
PLEASE, MISTRESS GERTA- DON'T MAKE ME KILL DON ALVARDO - I LOVE HIM!
LOVE- BAH! GETTING WHAT YOU WANT IS ALL THAT MATTERS!
WHAT I WANT IS THAT ARGENTINIAN TREATY ALVARDO'S CARRYING! YOU, RENA, WILL GET IT FOR ME- UNDERSTAND?
Y-YES, MISTRESS--I WILL OBEY-
LATER, IN GENERAL DARNELL'S OFFICE—
DON ALVARDO, ENVOY FROM ARGENTINA, HAS DISAPPEARED WITH THE TREATY!
IT'S MADAME ATERG AND HER INTERNATIONAL SPY RING AGAIN! HER METHODS REMIND ME OF BARONESS VON GUNTHER!
HM- THEY DO AT THAT, DON'T THEY!
THAT NIGHT DIANA TRANSFORMS HERSELF TO WONDER WOMAN.
WHY DOES THE MYSTERIOUS MADAME ATERG RESEMBLE THE BARONESS? COULD SHE BE PAULA'S DAUGHTER GERTA, WHO RAN AWAY FROM PARADISE ISLAND SO LONG AGO? I HOPE NOT BUT I MUST FIND OUT!
MEANWHILE, IN MADAME ATERG'S SECRET LABORATORY—
HERE IS THE TREATY, MISTRESS! ALVARDO IS OUR PRISONER- I COULDN'T BEAR TO KILL HIM-
I'LL ATTEND TO THAT- GO AND GET YOUR CHAINS ON!
BUT WONDER WOMAN CRASHES THE GATE JUST IN TIME
GERTA! FOR THE LOVE OF APHRODITE- HAVE YOU GONE MAD?
WONDER WOMAN-- A MIRACLE! I AM SAVED!
3D
BEFORE WONDER WOMAN CAN INTERVENE, THE VENGEFUL SLAVE RENA SEIZES GERTA'S PISTOL AND TURNS IT ON HER MISTRESS.
THAT FOR YOU, SHE-DEVIL! YOU'LL NEVER MAKE ANYONE DO YOUR HORRIBLE DIRTY WORK AGAIN!

GERTA—MY LITTLE GERTA! IF ONLY I HAD KNOWN—

IT'S BETTER THIS WAY—I NEVER LOVED ANYONE BUT YOU AND—MOTHER—ENOUGH TO—LISTEN TO THEM—AHHH-H-H! FAREWELL—

SO **THAT** IS GERTA'S FUTURE! HOW HORRIBLE! **CAN'T** IT BE CHANGED?

PERHAPS! GERTA'S PAST HAS MADE THE FUTURE THAT YOU SAW. BUT NOW THAT YOU KNOW HER FUTURE YOU MAY BE ABLE TO CHANGE IT!

GERTA'S PAST EXPERIENCE HAS MADE HER SELF-WILLED. KNOWING THIS YOU MUST FIND SOME **NEW** INFLUENCE THAT WILL CHANGE HER PERSONALITY AND MAKE HER **LOVING AND SUBMISSIVE.**

BUT HOW? I'LL STUDY GERTA AT THE FESTIVAL!

THE AMAZON HARVEST FESTIVAL, LIKE THANKSGIVING, CELEBRATES THE GATHERING OF CROPS—BUT THE FRUITS AND VEGETABLES OF PARADISE ISLAND SEEM MADE OF METAL.

WHAT A POWERFUL PUMPKIN **YOU** RAISED, PAULA!

HA HA! I HOPE IT'S SWEET!

THE QUEEN OPENS THE FESTIVAL.

THIS IS OUR BIGGEST HARVEST, THANKS TO THE MOTHERS WHO RAISED IT! THE FRUITS AND VEGETABLES WILL NOW BURST THEIR METAL SKINS—**THAT** TAKES STRENGTH! IT'S A RACE FOR FREEDOM—**GO!**

THE STRANGE AMAZON HARVEST PRODUCTS SUDDENLY BECOME ANIMATED.

COME ON, YOU BIG PUMPKIN—BREAK YOUR SHELL!

HURRY UP, CORNY, HUSK YOURSELF!

MY LITTLE TOMATO, HAVE YOU GONE SOFT?

HA HA! COME ON, CUCUMBER! COME ON, LETTUCE!

4D

PAULA'S **PUMPKIN** WINS THE FREEDOM CONTEST

MOTHER! AM I FIRST?

YES, GERTA—HOLA!

THE AMAZON HARVEST OF THE CHILDREN IS TESTED AT THE FESTIVAL BY ATHLETIC CONTESTS

PUMPKIN GERTA AND PEACH ALETRA ARE NOW TIED FOR FIRST PLACE THE DECIDING CONTEST WILL BE A HIGH DIVE COMPETITION.

AMID CHEERS FROM THE AMAZONS GERTA AND ALETRA **BOTH** DIVE PERFECTLY FROM THE 150 FOOT TOWER.

FIRST PRIZE WILL BE DIVIDED BETWEEN GERTA AND ALETRA—

NO, NO ! I'LL DO A DIVE ALETRA DARES NOT FOLLOW !

RUNNING SWIFTLY TO THE TOP OF A 300-FOOT CLIFF GERTA STANDS POISED ABOVE A POOL FILLED WITH DANGEROUS, GIRL-EATING FISH.

STOP, GERTA ! I **FORBID** YOU TO DIVE INTO THAT POOL !

BUT GERTA DEFIES THE QUEEN !

SORRY, MAJESTY, BUT I **MUST** WIN THIS CONTEST !

THERE'S AN OCTOPUS IN THAT POOL— THE CHILD IS COMMITTING SUICIDE !

WONDER WOMAN UNHESITATINGLY DIVES AFTER GERTA.

DON'T DIVE, PAULA ! RUN DOWN TO THE POOL AND MAKE GERTA SWIM QUICKLY TO SHORE !

I—I OBEY, PRINCESS !

AS **WONDER WOMAN** PLUNGES BELOW THE POOL'S SURFACE, SHE SEES THE HUGE OCTOPUS ABOUT TO SEIZE GERTA.

WONDER WOMAN IS TELLING ME TO ESCAPE BUT I WON'T DO IT ! I'LL STAY AND FIGHT THAT OCTOPUS !

PAULA, KNEELING AT THE POOL'S EDGE, CALLS IMPERIOUSLY TO HER DAUGHTER.

GERTA, COME OUT OF THAT POOL *INSTANTLY!*

GERTA OBEYS—NOT A MOMENT TOO SOON.

MOTHER IS TELLING ME TO SWIM OUT. OH, I *WANT* TO STAY AND FIGHT — BUT I—I *MUST* OBEY *MOTHER!*

AS *WONDER WOMAN* SEIZES ANOTHER TENTACLE REACHING FOR GERTA'S FOOT, THE OCTOPUS WRAPS ITS MIGHTY ARMS ABOUT HER.

IF GERTA HADN'T OBEYED HER MOTHER, I COULDN'T SAVE HER NOW!

WITH SUPERB STRENGTH *WONDER WOMAN* BATTLES THE MIGHTI-EST CREATURE OF THE DEEP, STRIVING TO TEAR LOOSE ITS TENACIOUS TENTACLES AND HOLD THEM IN ONE HAND.

EMERGING TRIUMPHANT FROM THE WATER, THE MIGHTY AMA-ZON MAIDEN HURLS THE MON-STER BACK TO THE DEPTHS.

YOU'RE TOO TOUGH A CUS-TOMER TO MAKE A PLEASANT PLAYMATE!

YOU'RE SO *WONDERFUL—* YOU SAVED MY LIFE AGAIN!

NO DEAR, YOUR MOTHER SAVED YOU BY MAKING YOU COME OUT OF THAT POOL! SHE IS THE *ONE* PERSON YOU LOVE ENOUGH TO OBEY *ALWAYS!*

GREATER DANGER THAN THE OCTOPUS THREATENS GERTA— SHE IS GROWING SELF-WILLED, AND SCORNFUL OF AUTHORITY! YOU MUST TAKE HER TO AMERICA— KEEP HER WITH YOU AND TEACH HER *LOVE* AND *OBEDIENCE.*

I OBEY GLADLY, PRINCESS!

QUEEN AND PRINCESS SEE A CHANGED FUTURE FOR GERTA ON THE MAGIC SPHERE.

GOOD WORK, DAUGHTER! GERTA WILL NOW HAVE A HAPPY, SUCCESSFUL LIFE.

IF PEOPLE ONLY REALIZED HOW TODAY SHAPES TOMORROW, THEY'D WATCH THEIR STEP!

THE END

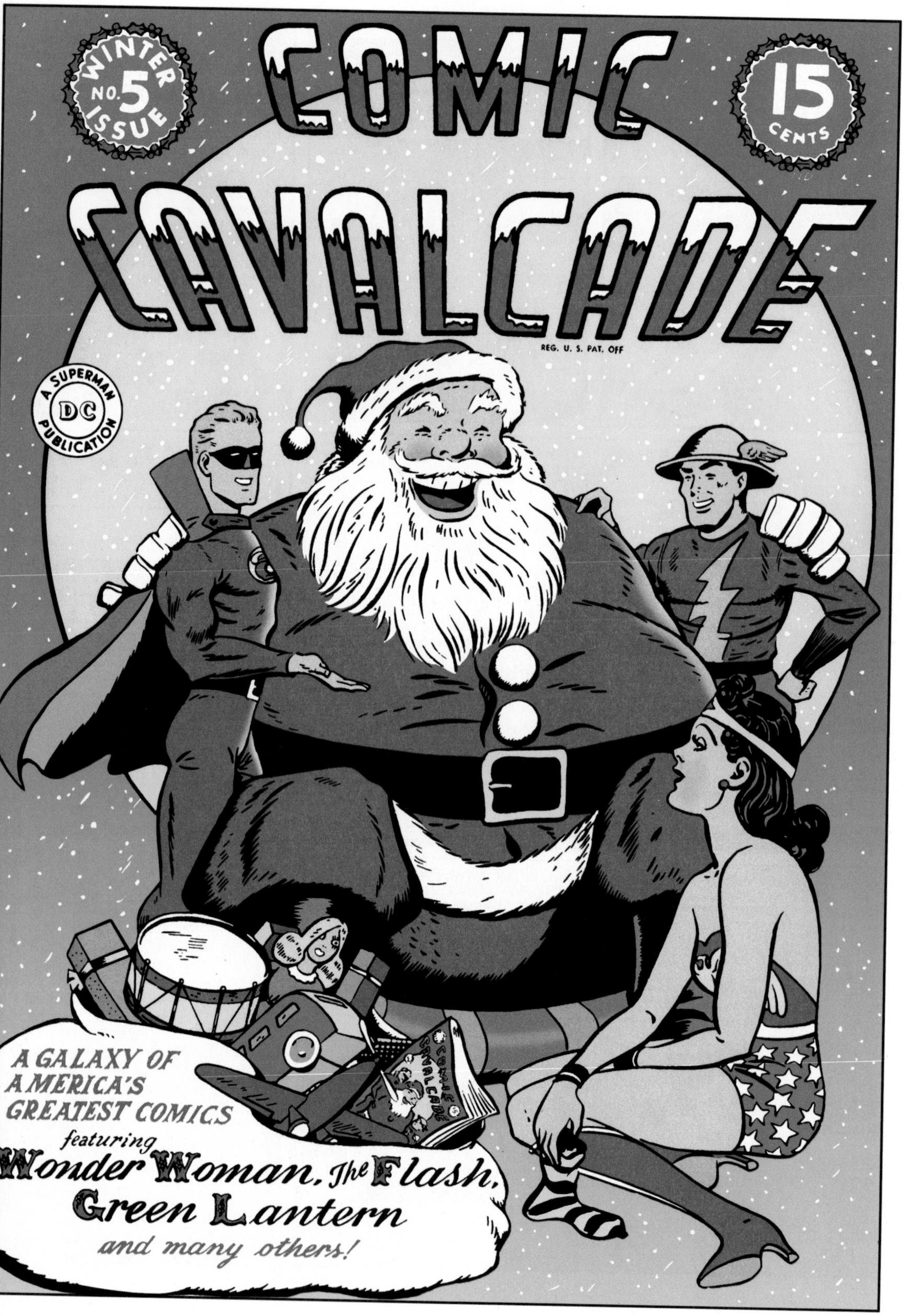
WINTER
NO. 5
ISSUE
COMIC CAVALCADE
15 CENTS
REG. U. S. PAT. OFF
A SUPERMAN DC PUBLICATION
A GALAXY OF AMERICA'S GREATEST COMICS
featuring
Wonder Woman, The Flash, Green Lantern
and many others!

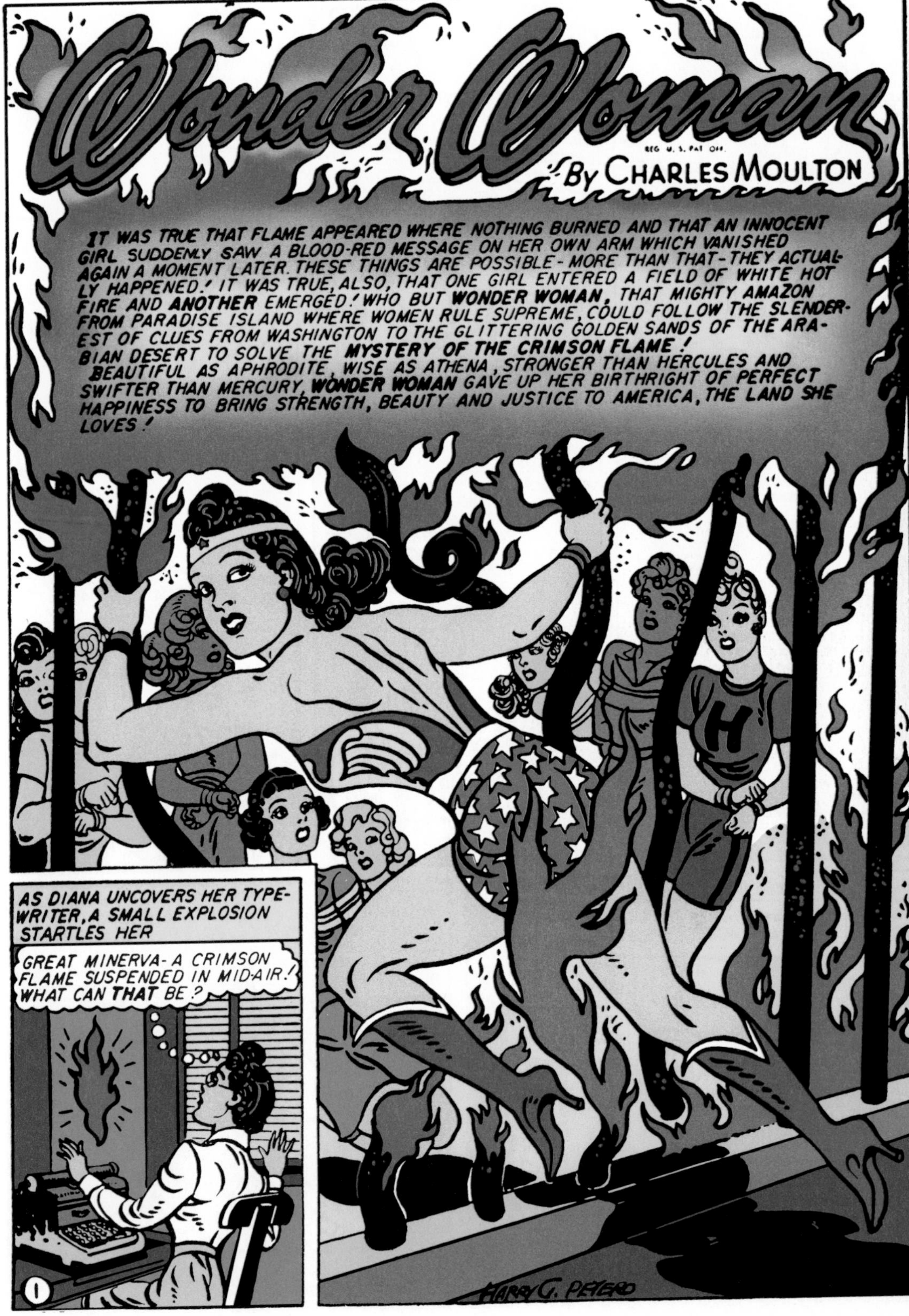
Wonder Woman
REG. U. S. PAT. OFF.
By CHARLES MOULTON
IT WAS TRUE THAT FLAME APPEARED WHERE NOTHING BURNED AND THAT AN INNOCENT GIRL SUDDENLY SAW A BLOOD-RED MESSAGE ON HER OWN ARM WHICH VANISHED AGAIN A MOMENT LATER. THESE THINGS ARE POSSIBLE - MORE THAN THAT - THEY ACTUALLY HAPPENED! IT WAS TRUE, ALSO, THAT ONE GIRL ENTERED A FIELD OF WHITE HOT FIRE AND ANOTHER EMERGED! WHO BUT WONDER WOMAN, THAT MIGHTY AMAZON FROM PARADISE ISLAND WHERE WOMEN RULE SUPREME, COULD FOLLOW THE SLENDEREST OF CLUES FROM WASHINGTON TO THE GLITTERING GOLDEN SANDS OF THE ARABIAN DESERT TO SOLVE THE MYSTERY OF THE CRIMSON FLAME!
BEAUTIFUL AS APHRODITE, WISE AS ATHENA, STRONGER THAN HERCULES AND SWIFTER THAN MERCURY, WONDER WOMAN GAVE UP HER BIRTHRIGHT OF PERFECT HAPPINESS TO BRING STRENGTH, BEAUTY AND JUSTICE TO AMERICA, THE LAND SHE LOVES!
H
HARRY G. PETERS
AS DIANA UNCOVERS HER TYPEWRITER, A SMALL EXPLOSION STARTLES HER
GREAT MINERVA - A CRIMSON FLAME SUSPENDED IN MID-AIR! WHAT CAN THAT BE?
1

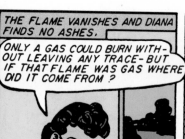

THE FLAME VANISHES AND DIANA FINDS NO ASHES.

ONLY A GAS COULD BURN WITHOUT LEAVING ANY TRACE—BUT IF THAT FLAME WAS GAS WHERE DID IT COME FROM?

THAT CRIMSON FLAME WAS QUITE A TRICK—MUST BE SOMEBODY PLAYING JOKES! NOW LET'S SEE—**ONE** CARBON COPY OF THIS LETTER IS ALL I NEED.

WHY—THERE'S **TYPEWRITING** ON THAT PAPER—I'D SWEAR THE SHEET WAS PERFECTLY BLANK WHEN I PUT IT INTO THE MACHINE!

DIANA, AMAZED, READS A SINISTER MESSAGE WHICH APPEARS ON THE BLANK PAPER AS IF BY MAGIC.

U.S. ARMY INTELLIGENCE SERVICE
WASHINGTON, D.C.

Beware the AVENGING FLAME! You are interfering with occult forces you do not understand. Let Him Who Sees <u>THE CRIMSON FLAME</u> Fear Dire Danger!

WHAT'S THE MATTER, DI? YOU LOOK AS THOUGH YOU'D SEEN A GHOST!

I DID—AT LEAST I SAW A GHOST'S TYPEWRITING! FIRST THERE WAS A CRIMSON FLAME, THEN THIS MESSAGE APPEARED ON BLANK PAPER!

WELL I'LL BE A GUINEA PIG'S GRANDPAPPY! THIS IS THE CRAZIEST THING YET!" THE AVENGING FLAME"—HA HA! YOU REMEMBER, DI, THAT **FLAME** MEETING WE ATTENDED?

HM—YES! HELENE ARMSTRONG, THE SENATOR'S DAUGHTER, ASKED OUR HELP—

DIANA REMEMBERS:

MISS ARMSTRONG, THIS IS DIANA PRINCE, ALSO IN THE INTELLIGENCE SERVICE.

I'VE HEARD ABOUT YOU, LIEUTENANT PRINCE—I **DO** HOPE YOU'LL HELP ME!

TELL ME YOUR STORY—

I JOINED THE NEW RELIGION THAT'S SWEEPING THE WORLD—THE **CULT OF THE CRIMSON FLAME!** MY FATHER OBJECTED. **THE FLAME** WARNED HIM BUT HE ONLY LAUGHED! NOW FATHER'S STRICKEN WITH HEART TROUBLE—HE'S VERY ILL!

②

YOU BELIEVE THAT "THE AVENGING FLAME" GAVE YOUR FATHER HEART TROUBLE BECAUSE HE OPPOSED THE CULT?

CERTAINLY! THERE'S NO DOUBT ABOUT IT! FATHER WAS STRICKEN BECAUSE HE WOULDN'T LET ME ATTEND CRIMSON FLAME MEETINGS!

AT HELENE'S REQUEST STEVE AND DIANA ATTENDED A MEETING OF THE CULT.

I AM THE CRIMSON FLAME OF LIFE- I BURN WITHIN THE BREASTS OF ALL WHO OBEY ME! WHOSOEVER OPPOSES ME SHALL BE CONSUMED!

WE STOPPED INVESTIGATION BECAUSE SENATOR ARMSTRONG WAS AFRAID TO GO ON WITH IT!

THAT'S RIGHT— SO WHY SHOULD "THE FLAME" WARN ME TO BEWARE WHEN I'M NOT THREATENING HIM IN ANY WAY?

MAYBE THEY THINK YOU'RE GOING TO INVESTIGATE - WHY HELLO, ETTA!

HI, FOLKS! LISTEN- HELENE ARMSTRONG HAS DISAPPEARED FROM HOLLIDAY COLLEGE! HER FATHER'S KEEPIN' IT HUSH-HUSH BUT SOMEBODY OUGHTA DO SOMETHING!

STEVE IMMEDIATELY HURRIES TO SENATOR ARMSTRONG'S RESIDENCE.

I'M SORRY, SIR, THE SENATOR IS SICK IN BED - HE CAN'T SEE ANYBODY!

THEN LET ME TALK WITH HIS NURSE— THIS IS IMPORTANT!

I'M MAJOR TREVOR FROM MILITARY INTELLIGENCE. I MUST SPEAK WITH SENATOR ARMSTRONG ABOUT HIS DAUGHTER—

QUITE IMPOSSIBLE, MAJOR! HELENE'S DISAPPEARANCE GAVE THE SENATOR ANOTHER HEART ATTACK- HE'S IN A VERY CRITICAL CONDITION— UNCONSCIOUS!

FLAME SLAVE K5 REPORTING- MAJOR TREVOR OF ARMY INTELLIGENCE IS INVESTIGATING H.A.'S DISAPPEARANCE!

HIGH PRIESTESS ZARA HEARS YOU, SLAVE! ZEE MAJOR WEEL BE ATTENDED TO EE-MEDIATELY!

3

STEVE, RETURNING TO HEAD-QUARTERS, FINDS A NEW GIRL IN HIS OFFICE.

LEAVE THAT FILING CABINET ALONE - IT CONTAINS CONFIDENTIAL REPORTS AND I KEEP THE KEY!

THESE NEW KIDS! BAH!

OH I DIDN'T KNOW - I AM SOR-REE!

AS STEVE GRASPS THE TELEPHONE A SURPRISING THING HAPPENS.

JUMPING JELLYFISH - THE CRIMSON FLAME! WHERE IN SATAN'S SINK DID THAT THING COME FROM?

STEVE GRASPS THE FLAME BUT GETS A HANDFUL OF NOTHING.

HUH- I CAN'T EVEN FEEL ANYTHING BURNING!

AS DIANA ENTERS THE OFFICE FLAMES SPRING FROM STEVE'S DESK BLOTTER.

YE GODS - MORE MONKEY TRICKS!

LOOK STEVE - IT'S A MESSAGE WRITTEN IN CRIMSON FLAME!

WHAT MELODRAMATIC NONSENSE! I'LL FIND HELENE ARMSTRONG NOW, COME HAIL OR HIGH TAXES!

DROP ARMSTRONG CASE OR BE CONSUMED BY THE AVENGING FLAME!

HERE'S MY PRIVATE FILE CABINET KEY - GET OUT THE CRIMSON FLAME CULT FOLDER WHILE I TALK WITH COLONEL DARNELL!

OKAY, STEVE-

AS DIANA PULLS OUT THE FILE DRAWER A BURST OF CRIMSON FLAME ENVELOPS HER.

OH-H!

④

THE FLAME DISAPPEARS AS QUICKLY AS IT CAME WHILE THE "NEW OFFICE GIRL" EXAMINES DIANA.

WHAT A MEESTAKE ! ZEE GIRL BREATHED FLAME INSTEAD OF TREVOR ! AND NOW I MUST TAKE HER AWAY SO THEY WEEL NOT SUSPECT—

SWIFTLY THE GIRL GAGS DIANA AND BINDS HER WITH WIRE.

THEES FILING CABINET WITH FALSE FRONT IS CLEVAIR—BUT FOR MAJOR TREVOR WE MUST MAKE A BEEGER ONE !

A FEW MINUTES LATER TWO BURLY TRUCKMEN CARRY AWAY A LOCKED FILING CABINET.

WHAT YOU GOT THERE, BUDDY ?

OLD FILE FOR STORAGE-COLONEL'S ORDERS !

PLACED IN A TRUCK THE BIG STEEL CASE BUMPS UP AND DOWN WITH EVERY IRREGULARITY IN THE ROAD.

BUMP

BUMPETY!

BANG!

DIANA, TOSSED VIOLENTLY AGAINST THE WALLS OF HER STEEL PRISON, REGAINS CONSCIOUSNESS

UNF UG ! GREAT HERA, WHAT ARE THEY DOING TO ME ? THAT "CRIMSON FLAME" MUST HAVE CONTAINED CARBON MONOXIDE WHICH KNOCKED ME OUT !

5

EASILY BURSTING HER BONDS DIANA TRANSFORMS HERSELF INTO WONDER WOMAN.

TIGHT AS THESE QUARTERS ARE, I THINK I'LL STAY HERE - THEY'LL PROBABLY TAKE ME TO WHEREVER HELENE IS HIDDEN!

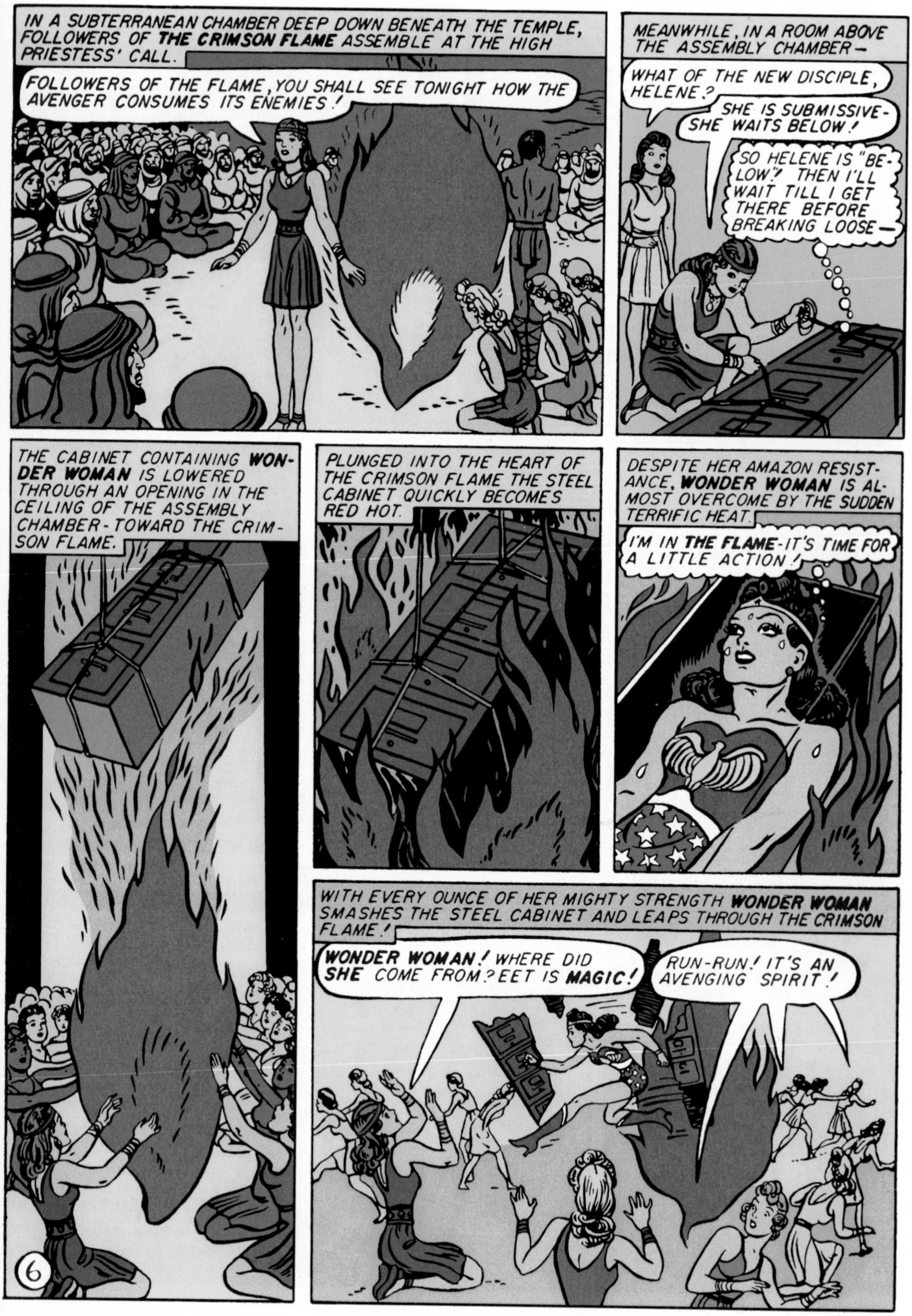
IN A SUBTERRANEAN CHAMBER DEEP DOWN BENEATH THE TEMPLE, FOLLOWERS OF **THE CRIMSON FLAME** ASSEMBLE AT THE HIGH PRIESTESS' CALL.
FOLLOWERS OF THE FLAME, YOU SHALL SEE TONIGHT HOW THE AVENGER CONSUMES ITS ENEMIES!
MEANWHILE, IN A ROOM ABOVE THE ASSEMBLY CHAMBER—
WHAT OF THE NEW DISCIPLE, HELENE?
SHE IS SUBMISSIVE- SHE WAITS BELOW!
SO HELENE IS "BELOW." THEN I'LL WAIT TILL I GET THERE BEFORE BREAKING LOOSE—
THE CABINET CONTAINING **WONDER WOMAN** IS LOWERED THROUGH AN OPENING IN THE CEILING OF THE ASSEMBLY CHAMBER-TOWARD THE CRIMSON FLAME.
PLUNGED INTO THE HEART OF THE CRIMSON FLAME THE STEEL CABINET QUICKLY BECOMES RED HOT.
DESPITE HER AMAZON RESISTANCE, **WONDER WOMAN** IS ALMOST OVERCOME BY THE SUDDEN TERRIFIC HEAT.
I'M IN **THE FLAME**-IT'S TIME FOR A LITTLE ACTION!
WITH EVERY OUNCE OF HER MIGHTY STRENGTH **WONDER WOMAN** SMASHES THE STEEL CABINET AND LEAPS THROUGH THE CRIMSON FLAME!
WONDER WOMAN! WHERE DID **SHE** COME FROM? EET IS **MAGIC!**
RUN-RUN! IT'S AN AVENGING SPIRIT!
6

CULTISTS FLEE IN ALL DIRECTIONS BUT THE HIGH PRIESTESS STANDS HER GROUND.

YOU WEEL FIND NO TRACE OF ZEE WOMAN DIANA PRINCE - YOU CAN PROVE NUZZING!

SO YOU'VE BURNT HER UP-- POOR DIANA!

ZARA LEADS **WONDER WOMAN** TO THE NOVICE CHAMBER.

HERE IS ZEE GIRL HELENE - SHE SERVES ZEE CRIMSON FLAME OF HER OWN FREE WILL!

IS THAT TRUE, HELENE?

NO! I--I'M AFRAID--

SUDDENLY HELENE SEES A MESSAGE IN RED WRITTEN ON HER OWN ARM.

OH-H!

I SAW THAT MESSAGE, HELENE-- YOU MUST DEFY THE CRIMSON FLAME AND COME WITH ME!

NO, NO! I WILL STAY!

THERE IS NO MESSAGE! SHOW **WONDER WOMAN** YOUR ARM!

WELL, I'LL BE PROME-THEUSED - THAT MESSAGE HAS DISAPPEARED! BUT I SHALL TAKE HELENE HOME--

COMMANDING HELENE BY A SECRET GESTURE TO RUN AWAY, ZARA POINTS SUDDENLY OVER **WONDER WOMAN'S** SHOULDER.

HA HA! HELENE EES RUNNING AWAY!

POOR CHILD, I'LL CATCH HER--

⑦

BUT **WONDER WOMAN,** FOLLOWING HELENE'S REFLECTED IMAGE, CRASHES INTO A WALL OF MIRROR GLASS.

UGH- A MIRROR- CLEVER TRICK!

TURNING, **WONDER WOMAN** FINDS THAT ZARA AND HELENE HAVE ESCAPED, BOLTING THE DOOR BEHIND THEM.

THIS MUST BE THE WAY SHE GOT OUT—HAH—THIS FLIMSY FLOOR IS NO OBSTACLE! BUT I DON'T KNOW THE SECRET PASSAGES IN THIS PLACE—

AFTER SEARCHING THE SUBTERRANEAN ROOMS IN VAIN **WONDER WOMAN** ASCENDS TO GROUND LEVEL.

SO YOU'RE HERE, BEAUTIFUL! WE'RE LOOKING FOR DIANA—SHE'S DISAPPEARED!

DIANA? THE FLAME FOLLOWERS CAPTURED HER, BUT SHE ESCAPED. NOW SHE'S CHASING **THEM**!

WOO WOO! I BETCHA THAT'S THE CRIMSON FLAMERS MAKING A GETAWAY!

YOU'RE RIGHT, ETTA—I CAN SEE ZARA AT THE CONTROLS! SHE'S CARRYING OFF HELENE—BUT WHERE TO, APHRODITE ONLY KNOWS!

STEVE WORKS FAST—WITHIN A FEW HOURS HE HAS COLLECTED COMPLETE INFORMATION ABOUT THE CULT OF THE CRIMSON FLAME.

THIS CULT IS DANGEROUS—THOSE WHO OPPOSE THEM FALL SICK AND DIE! HERE'S A LIST OF VICTIMS—

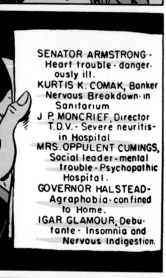

SENATOR ARMSTRONG - Heart trouble - dangerously ill.

KURTIS K. COMAK, Banker Nervous Breakdown - in Sanitarium

J. P. MONCRIEF, Director T.D.V. - Severe neuritis - in Hospital

MRS. OPPULENT CUMINGS, Social leader - mental trouble - Psychopathic Hospital.

GOVERNOR HALSTEAD - Agraphobia - confined to Home.

IGAR GLAMOUR, Debutante - Insomnia and Nervous Indigestion.

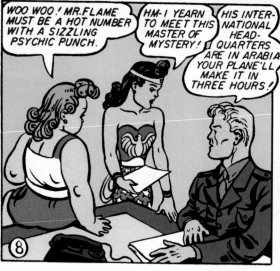

WOO WOO! MR. FLAME MUST BE A HOT NUMBER WITH A SIZZLING PSYCHIC PUNCH.

HM—I YEARN TO MEET THIS MASTER OF MYSTERY!

HIS INTERNATIONAL HEADQUARTERS ARE IN ARABIA—YOUR PLANE'LL MAKE IT IN THREE HOURS!

⑧

AT MORE THAN 2000 MILES AN HOUR THE **WONDER WOMAN** LEGION SPEEDS OVER DISTANT SEAS.

WE'LL LAND **HERE** AND BORROW HORSES. THEN WE'LL RIDE ACROSS THE DESERT TO THE CRYSTAL TEMPLE OF THE CRIMSON FLAME!

LEAVING THE PLANE AT A MILITARY OUTPORT AIRPORT, **WONDER WOMAN'S** LEGION RIDES ACROSS THE DESERT ON BORROWED ARABIAN HORSES.

IT WOULD BE MORE FUN TO RUN BUT THE HORSES WOULD GET TIRED TRYING TO KEEP UP WITH ME.

THE BLINDING, SHIMMERING HEAT WAVES OF THE DESERT CREATE STRANGE ILLUSIONS. DESERT TRAVELERS SEE WHAT THEY **WANT** TO SEE — THEIR DAZZLED BRAINS CREATE WISH PICTURES OF BUBBLING SPRINGS, SHADY PALM TREES AND SPLENDID CITIES WHICH VANISH WHEN APPROACHED.

LOOK, PALS—THERE'S OUR CITY AHEAD! BOY HAVE I BEEN WAITIN' TO SEE **THAT!**

RIGHT! AND THERE'S THE CRYSTAL TEMPLE!

I SEE IT, TOO-BUT THAT ISN'T THE RIGHT LOCATION ACCORDING TO STEVE'S MAP.

CITY AND TEMPLE OF FLAME GROW IN GRANDEUR AS THE RIDERS STARE INTO THE BLAZING, SHIFTING LIGHTS OF THE DESERT.

WE GIRLS WILL RIDE TOWARD THE TEMPLE WE THINK WE SEE. YOU, STEVE, WILL RIDE **THAT** WAY, WHERE THE TEMPLE APPEARS ON THE MAP. FIRST TO FIND IT MUST SAVE HELENE.

OKAY, GENERAL!

AS THEY REACH IT, THE "CITY" SUDDENLY DISSOLVES INTO A WEIRD CRISSCROSS OF DAZZLING LIGHT BEAMS.

AHA- IT IS A TRICK! THE FLAME FOLLOWERS CREATED A MIRAGE WITH SUN REFLECTORS SET IN THE DESERT!

⑨

SUDDENLY AN ARMY OF GIRLS WITH FLAME-TIPPED LANCES CHARGES FORWARD, LED BY HIGH PRIESTESS ZARA.

STRIKE FOR THE **AVENGING FLAME!**

DEATH TO **THE FLAME'S** ENEMIES!

THOUGH GREATLY OUTNUMBERED, **WONDER WOMAN'S** LEGION REPULSES THE ENEMY.

WHY DON'T YOU GIRLS USE UP-TO-DATE WEAPONS, ZARA? CATCHING BULLETS ON MY BRACELETS IS BETTER SPORT THAN CATCHING SPEARS!

ARR-RRGH! WE WEEL SHOW YOU!

SUDDENLY THE FLAME ARMY FLEES.

WE'VE LICKED 'EM, **WONDER WOMAN!**

DON'T BE TOO SURE—THEY'RE FULL OF TRICKS!

THE FLAME FORCES CIRCLE THEIR OPPONENTS WITH FOUNTAINS OF FIRE WHICH REMAIN BURNING BEHIND THEM IN THE AIR.

QUICKLY **WONDER WOMAN** IS SURROUNDED BY A WALL OF FLAME.

THEY'VE BUILT A FIRE PRISON AROUND US! MUST BE LIQUID HYDROGEN BURNING AS IT FLOATS! **THIS** IS THE MYSTERIOUS FLAME THAT APPEARS AND DISAPPEARS LIKE MAGIC!

LOOK, **WONDER WOMAN**— THE WALL OF FIRE IS CREEPING CLOSER!

YES, THEY MEAN TO BURN US UP—I MUST ACT, AND QUICKLY!

LEAPING TO THE GROUND, THE INTREPID AMAZON MAIDEN DIGS SAND FASTER THAN A STEAM SHOVEL.

DIGGING SWIFTLY UNDER THE WALL OF FIRE, **WONDER WOMAN** EMERGES AT THE FEET OF ZARA'S HORSE.

HELLO, ZARA— FOR AN ARAB GIRL YOU'RE SITTING YOUR HORSE VERY POORLY!

ARR-RGH· **WONDAIR WOMAN!**

IF **YOU** TOUCH ME, AMAZON, MY WOMEN HAVE OR-DAIRS TO BURN YOUR GIRLS **EEN**STANTLY!

YOU WIN, FLAME TOP! I'LL SURRENDER IF YOU'LL SAVE MY GIRLS!

WONDER WOMAN AND HER GIRLS BECOME ZARA'S CAPTIVES.

FOR TELLING ME I SIT MY HORSE POORLY, **WON-DAIR WOMAN**, YOU PREESONERS WEEL RIDE **YOUR** HORSES FACING ZEE TAIL!

HA-HA-SO I HURT YOUR ARAB PRIDE, HIGH PRIESTESS!

THE PRISONERS ARE LED UP A STEEP PATH FROM THE DESERT TO A MOUNTAIN TOP.

RIDING **UPHILL** BACKWARDS IS A LITTLE DIFFICULT—I'M GLAD I'M TIED ON SECURELY!

HA HA-**FONEE** GIRL!

THE CRYSTAL TEMPLE OF FLAME GLITTERS LIKE A BRILLIANT JEWEL IN ITS AUSTERE SETTING OF MOUNTAIN CRAGS.

ARRIVING AT THE TEMPLE, THE GIRLS ARE PLACED IN A FIERY CAGE.

SO LONG AS YOU CAPTIVES DO NOT TOUCH THE BARS OF YOUR CAGE, YOU WILL NOT BE BURNED!

(11)

BUT **WONDER WOMAN** IS FITTED WITH FETTERS OF FLAME.

THEES FLAME WEEL NOT HURT YOU UNLESS YOU TRY TO BREAK YOUR CHAINS. PULLING ZEM WEEL RELEASE GAS ZAT BURN OFF YOUR HANDS AND FEET!

WHAT A CUTE IDEA!

STEVE, MEANWHILE, MEETS A PRIESTESS PATROL.

WE'VE CAPTURED THE AMAZON AND OUR HIGH PRIESTESS WANTS *YOU*, MAJOR TREVOR!

THE QUICKEST WAY TO FIND *WONDER WOMAN* IS TO SURRENDER—

OKAY- I'M YOUR PRISONER!

WHAT'LL YOU DO WITH US PRISONERS?

AT THE ORDEAL OF FLAME YOU MUST CHOOSE BETWEEN DEATH AND SERVING OUR MASTER!

THE GIRLS TAKE STEVE TO THEIR HIGH PRIESTESS.

I HAVE CAUGHT YOU AT LAST, MY HANDSOME ONE- YOU SHALL GO WEETH ME TO ZEE ORDEAL!

I GUESS I HAVE NO CHOICE BUT TO ACCEPT!

IN THE GREAT HALL OF THE TEMPLE THE ORDEAL BEGINS.

OH, CRIMSON FLAME OF LIFE, WILL YOU ACCEPT ZEESE HUMAN OFFERINGS AS SLAVES?

LET EACH CAPTIVE TAKE THE OATH OF THE FLAMING SWORD -OR DIE!

WILL YOU SWEAR TO SLAY WITH THIS FLAMING SWORD ANY HUMAN BEING WHO OPPOSES THE FLAME- EVEN YOUR FATHER OR MOTHER?

OH NO- NO! I'D RATHER DIE MYSELF—

DIE THEN, YOU FOOL!

12.

SHE'S KILLING HELENE - I *MUST* BREAK THESE CHAINS! OH- H I CAN'T- THIS HEAT'LL BURN MY ARMS OFF BEFORE THE LINKS BREAK!

STEVE, STRUGGLING FRANTICALLY, BURSTS HIS BONDS- IT IS THE WORK OF A SPLIT SECOND TO STEAL ZARA'S KEYS AND—

WITH A SPEED NO EYE CAN FOLLOW **WONDER WOMAN** UNLOCKS HER CHAINS AND LEAPS BE- TWEEN THE FLAMING SWORD AND ITS VICTIM.

LIKE A BOLT OF LIGHTNING, THE MIGHTY AMAZON FLASHES TO THE FLAMING CAGE AND DISREGARD- ING PAIN, TEARS ITS BARS ASUNDER WITH HER BARE HANDS.

WITH **WONDER WOMAN'S** TRUSTY BATTLE LEGION AT HER BACK, THE ISSUE IS NEVER IN DOUBT.

I SUSPECT **YOU** ARE THE FLAME, ZARA- IT'S TIME TO PUT YOU OUT!

WOO WOO! HERE'S A SWELL PADDLE.

HOORAY FOR **WONDER WOMAN!**

WHAM!

TELL ME **EVERYTHING!**

SOME-SOMETHING **COMPELS** ME! I'M AN ARAB- MY FATHER SOLD ME AS A SLAVE! OH, HOW I HATED HEEM! I SWORE I'D GET **REVENGE** ON MEN OF POWER! **REVENGE-** THAT EES MY CRIMSON FLAME!

YOU'VE GUESSED THAT ALL THEES "CRIMSON FLAME" EES FLOATING, BURNING, LIQUID HYDROGEN. EEN TEMPLE I PUT MAN'S FACE AND VOICE IN FLAME WIZ MOVING PICTURE MACHINE. TO SCARE PEOPLE WE USE CAPSULE ZAT BURN UP WHEN DROPPED- WIZ MESSAGES IN INVISIBLE INK ZAT COME OUT, ZEN DISAPPEAR. ALL TREEKS I CONFESS! TO DESTROY ENEMIES I PUT **IDEAS** IN ZAIR MIND, ZEN ZAY MAKE **ZEMSELVES** SICK, POOR FOOLS!

⑬

BUT OH, I HAVE ONE AWFUL ZING TO CONFESS- I BURN DIANA PREENCE TO ASHES!

I'LL RE- LIEVE YOUR CONSCIENCE- YOU **DIDN'T** BURN DIANA! I CHANGED PLACES WITH HER **BEFORE** THAT FILE CABINET REACHED YOUR TEMPLE!

I CAN'T THANK YOU AND YOUR FRIENDS ENOUGH FOR ALL YOU'VE DONE! WILL DAD GET BETTER NOW?

ABSOLUTELY! HE ONLY HAS TO BELIEVE THAT HE'S WELL AND THAT'S EASIER THAN THINKING HE'S SICK, THANK APHRODITE!

MORE ADVENTURES OF **WONDER WOMAN** IN EVERY ISSUE OF **SENSATION COMICS!**

SUPERMAN:
THE GOLDEN AGE VOL. 2

SUPERGIRL:
THE SILVER AGE VOL. 1

FLASH:
THE SILVER AGE VOL. 1

SUPERMAN: THE GOLDEN AGE VOL. 1